An inveterate traveller, **ALEXANDER STEWART** (above, on the Santa Teresa trek) has walked, trekked and tramped in more than 30 countries around the world. Over the last decade he has written guidebooks for several publishers including for Trailblazer: *New Zealand – The Great Walks*, *The Walker's Haute Route* and *The Peddars Way and Norfolk Coast Path*.

Above all, though, he is drawn back repeatedly to Peru, a country that he first visited more than 15 years ago and which remains something of a first love. As a displacement technique when not working on guidebooks he manages travel websites and, as a freelance travel writer and photographer, contributes articles and photographs to various newspapers and magazines.

Author

The Inca Trail, Cusco & Machu Picchu

First edition: 1999; this fifth edition 2013

Publisher Trailblazer Publications 🖳 www.trailblazer-guides.com
The Old Manse, Tower Rd, Hindhead, Surrey, GU26 6SU, UK

British Library Cataloguing in Publication Data
A catalogue record for this book is available from the British Library

ISBN 978-1-905864-55-3

© **Trailblazer** 2011, 2013: Text and maps (unless otherwise credited)
© **Hugh Thomson**: Text on pp90-102, and pp202-3

Editor: Anna Jacomb-Hood
Cartography: Nick Hill   **Layout**: Anna Jacomb-Hood & Bryn Thomas
Proof-reading: Nicky Slade   **Index**: Anna Jacomb-Hood & Jane Thomas
Photographs (flora): C1: top left and bottom right © Bryn Thomas
C2 top: middle and right © Bryn Thomas; all others © Alexander Stewart
Photographs (other): © Bryn Thomas unless otherwise credited

Acknowledgements

Lots of people have contributed to my time in Peru being a pleasure and have made working on this book over many years and multiple editions such a joy. Thanks go to members of
the INC and SAE who took time to answer my questions, supply information and offer
advice. Elsewhere in Peru, for this edition, special thanks go to Mike Weston, Katia Silva,
Catherine Kina, Justino Onton Vera, Marisol Mosquera, Suzanne van Ommeren, Jan Willem
van Delft and the many street vendors, novoandina chefs, hoteliers, hostal owners, porters,
arrieros and colectivo drivers who enhanced my time away. In Britain thanks go to Hugh
Thomson for sharing his passion for and knowledge of Peru and for contributing the chapter on Inca history, to Alison Roberts for Lima walking tours and Sophie Campbell for work
on the Machu Picchu section. At Trailblazer, thanks as ever to Bryn Thomas for his tireless
patience and perseverance, to Anna Jacomb-Hood for diligent editing and working so hard
to ensure that everything came together, to Nicky Slade for proof-reading, to Nick Hill for
drawing the maps and sketching the archaeological sites and to Jane Thomas for the index.

Finally, thanks to my wonderful wife, who supports my wandering and makes it all
possible whilst ensuring that coming home is still the best bit of every journey.

A request

The author and publisher have tried to ensure that this guide is as accurate and up to date
as possible. Nevertheless, things change. If you notice any changes or omissions that should
be included in the next edition of this book, please write to Trailblazer (address above) or
email us at 🖳 info@trailblazer-guides.com. A free copy of the next edition will be sent to
persons making a significant contribution.

Warning: mountain walking can be dangerous

Please read the notes on when to go (pp10-12), safety (p32 & pp88-9) and on health and
safety in the mountains (pp119-21). Every effort has been made by the author and publisher to ensure that the information contained herein is as accurate and up to date as possible.
However, they are unable to accept responsibility for any inconvenience, loss or injury sustained by anyone as a result of the advice and information given in this guide.

Photos – Front cover and overleaf: Machu Picchu
Opposite: Approaching Dead Woman's Pass (see p224) © Alexander Stewart

Printed on chlorine-free paper by D'Print (☎ +65-6581 3832), Singapore

★ trailblazer

THE
Inca Trail
CUSCO & MACHU PICCHU

ALEXANDER STEWART

With additional material by
HUGH THOMSON
ALISON ROBERTS, HENRY STEDMAN
SOPHIE CAMPBELL & BRYN THOMAS

TRAILBLAZER PUBLICATIONS

Contents

Contents

INTRODUCTION

The mystery of the deep valleys which lie in the quadrant north to north-east of Mount Salcantay have long demanded attention. Separated from Ollantaytambo and Amaybamba by the Grand Canyon of the Urubamba, protected from Cuzco by the gigantic barrier of Salcantay, isolated from Vitcos by deep valleys and inhospitable, high windswept bleak regions called punas, they seem to have been unknown to the Spanish Conquerors and unsuspected by the historians… it appears to have been a terra incognita.

Hiram Bingham, *Lost City of the Incas*

In July 1911 the American explorer Hiram Bingham stumbled across the Inca ruins at Machu Picchu, the archetypal Lost City. The discovery was the realization of many people's dreams and it has since proved to be the inspiration for innumerable adventure tales; none of the world's other great ruins can compare with Machu Picchu's location on a knife-like ridge, amid thick forest, high above a tumultuous river and frequently cloaked in swirling cloud, with the horn of Huayna Picchu punching through the mist and snow-capped mountains glittering on the horizon.

None of the world's other great ruins can compare with Machu Picchu's location

Bingham was directed to the region and along with his Peruvian guides explored the hillside reputed to conceal the ruins. All at once they 'were confronted with an unexpected sight, a great flight of beautifully constructed stone-faced terraces, perhaps a hundred of them, each hundreds of feet long and ten feet high'. Pushing on, 'without any warning', Bingham happened upon a cave carved into a stunningly sculpted structure whose 'flowing lines… symmetrical arrangement of ashlars, and gradual gradation of the courses combined to produce a wonderful effect… It seemed like an unbelievable dream. Dimly, I began to realize that this wall and its adjoining semicircular Temple over the cave were as fine as the finest stonework in the

Impressive Inca stonework on the semicircular Temple at Machu Picchu.

(Opposite): The Intihuatana, the 'hitching post of the sun', stands at the highest point in Machu Picchu (see p359), with superb views of the surrounding peaks and the Urubamba valley far below.

Introduction

Runcu Raccay (see p225) perched above a dizzying drop on the ascent to the Second Pass on the Inca Trail.

Huinay Huayna (see p233), the last ruins on the Inca Trail before you reach Machu Picchu and the most spectacular up to this point.

The imposing peak of **Mt Salkantay** (6264m/ 20,551ft), seen from the Salkantay trek (pp241-51), the first section of the Santa Teresa route. (All photos above © Alexander Stewart).

world. It fairly took my breath away…' Prior to the revelation of Machu Picchu, Bingham had explored and uncovered the ruins at Choquequirao. He was also responsible for discovering two other Inca sites of great importance, Vitcos and Vilcabamba. Countless other expeditions have subsequently explored the region and numerous discoveries have been made, though none as significant as those unearthed by Bingham. In addition to this, a network of Inca roads crisscrossing the mountains and landscapes have been found; these led to the creation of trekking routes for modern-day pilgrims and adventurers to follow. The **Inca Trail** is just one such route, which penetrates the forest and crosses high passes to reach its goal, the ruins at Machu Picchu. Heavily promoted and justifiably popular, the celebrated trek is almost a victim of its own success.

In the wake of stringent regulations imposed to preserve the route, alternative options to reach Machu Picchu have been established and treks to the other Inca sites have developed as genuine alternatives to the crowded classic trek: the **Santa Teresa route** avoids many of the regulations associated with the Inca Trail but still gets you to Machu Picchu following a superb trek through varied landscapes.

The **Choquequirao trek** takes you to these remote ruins perched above the Apurímac valley in a location arguably even more dramatic than that of the better-known site at Machu Picchu.

The **Vilcabamba trek** explores puna, pampa, pasture, cloud forest and rainforest to lead you to Espíritu Pampa, the last refuge of the Incas, the untroubled, unrestored ruins of which are largely still camouflaged and concealed by the forest. However, **check the security situation** before making plans to trek in the Vilcabamba area (see p32).

Epic **trails joining the various sites**, linking the Vilcabamba and Choquequirao routes to the Santa Teresa route, have also been uncovered and now offer the ultimate trekking experience for those with a passion for wilderness and a fascination with the world of the Incas.

Cusco, the Inca capital and a contemporary world-class city, wears its celebrity lightly and remains true to its past. The Incas built temples, palaces, aqueducts and roads worthy of an empire that stretched from Colombia to Chile. The Spanish conquistadors under Pizarro then used the precisely cut stones as the foundations for their opulent churches and monasteries. It's a fascinating place to visit with well-designed museums to fire the imagination, including the new Casa de Concha that houses the artefacts taken from Machu Picchu by Bingham and recently returned from Yale University.

Despite the pressures of mass tourism and the popularity of the better-known sites, it is still possible to explore the Cusco region free from crowds. Just take up the challenge and follow in the footsteps of the pioneers.

Choquequirao (see p308) straddles a ridge surrounded by forest, with terraces clinging to the sheer slopes. (Photo © Alexander Stewart).

On the Vilcabamba trek, the overgrown ruins of **Espíritu Pampa** are still much as Bingham saw them in 1914. (Photo © Hugh Thomson).

Cusco – Plaza des Armas and La Compañía Jesuits' church with its impressive facade.

INTRODUCTION

INTRODUCTION

When to go

The trekking season in Peru typically runs during the dry season from April to October when there is likely to be the most sunshine and least rain on the trails. During this period the trails get particularly busy between June and July and it can

The trekking season runs during the dry season from April to October

be hard to secure permits for some of the most popular treks, such as the classic Inca Trail, without planning a long way in advance. To maximize your enjoyment and escape the worst of the crowds target April-May or September-October for your trip.

At other times of year it is still possible to tackle most of the trails but be aware that in the wet they can become very much trickier propositions than in the dry, and the changeable and occasionally awful weather means that some of the treks are a washout. The Vilcabamba Trail is particularly affected by heavy rain and during continued wet periods you may struggle to find an agency willing to make the trip. If considering trekking independently, you should be an

Below: Sacsayhuaman (see p190) with Cusco in the valley beyond.

experienced trekker before setting off on some of the more arduous, out-of-the-way routes at this time of year. Remember that although Machu Picchu itself is open year-round and can be an enchanting, mysterious place when shrouded in cloud and clear of crowds, the classic Inca Trail is closed completely in February.

A rail service operates between Cusco (Poroy) and Aguas Calientes below Machu Picchu.

FOR HOW LONG?

The popularity of the Cusco region amongst trekkers is entirely understandable. Amongst some exceptionally dramatic scenery are hidden ruins and lost cities to rival anywhere else in the world. The treks described in this book take between two and nine days to complete, with the majority taking four to six days. When calculating how long your trip needs to be, remember to allow a day to travel

For route options see pp27-34 & trekking regulations pp216-7

The popular market held at Pisac (see p196) on Sunday. There are also smaller markets here on Tuesday and Thursday. (Photo © A Stewart).

to and from Cusco and Lima (more if you decide to travel overland rather than fly) and a couple of days in Cusco to aid acclimatization. This last factor is very important and will improve your chances of enjoying and succeeding on your trek and reduce the likelihood of you suffering from altitude sickness and inadvertently endangering your life. Since this is South America you may also want to build in a contingency day in case there are problems with the flights in either direction.

If you haven't pre-booked your trek and are arriving in Cusco hoping to put something together on spec, be prepared to wait a minimum of 4-6 weeks to secure a place on the classic Inca Trail because of the restricted numbers permitted to start the trek each day (see p14). Bear in mind that during the peak season it will take you far longer than this to secure a slot. You should be able to put together a trek on one of the other routes within 2-5 days, though.

LIMA – CLIMATE CHARTS

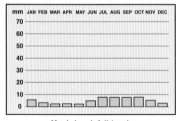

Max/min rainfall (mm)

Max/min temperature (°C)

CUSCO – CLIMATE CHARTS

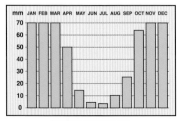

Max/min rainfall (mm)

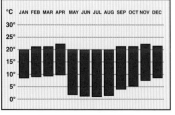

Max/min temperature (°C)

This section is designed to help you plan your trip: to make travel arrangements, calculate how much the trip will cost, and decide both when to go and which trek to take. It also sets out some simple rules to maximize your safety and outlines what to do in an emergency. There is a well-established trekking culture and infrastructure around Cusco. With the use of this book, an internet connection and just a little Spanish it's entirely feasible to organize your entire trip yourself.

Ultimately, though, how you approach your trip is a matter of personal choice and there's no substitute for practical experience when it comes to trekking. That said, the more you plan and prepare, the better equipped you are to deal with events on the ground, allowing you to make the most of the trip.

With a tour group or on your own?

In 2001 the Peruvian authorities outlawed independent trekking in the Machu Picchu Historical Sanctuary and brought in a series of strict regulations as to who could trek the trails to Machu Picchu and how they could tackle them. For a full breakdown of the regulations see box pp216-17 but, essentially, you can now only tackle the classic Inca Trail or any trek that joins it by signing up with a tour company or taking an accredited, licensed guide. When the laws were first introduced, it was still possible to sneak onto the trail without paying. Since then the authorities have tightened up security and clamped down on people not abiding by the rules. Don't attempt the classic Inca Trail without a guide or without paying the proper fees. It's highly unlikely that you'll get away with it and all you're really doing is freeloading. Yes, it is expensive to trek the Inca Trail (see box p14) but the costs of maintaining the route are high and the regulations prevent overcrowding, excessive damage and erosion and help to reduce littering. In actual fact the costs are pretty reasonable for a four-day, supported trek. Besides, almost whatever price you pay, it's still worth it.

For those who don't want to be constrained by the regulations, however, there are plenty of options. If you still want to trek to Machu Picchu take the Santa Teresa trek (see p31) which is as yet largely free from regulations. Alternatively, head to the far less-visited ruins at

Vilcabamba (see p32) or Choquequirao (see p33). For the really adventurous there are also some longer routes that link the various sites (see pp33-5), all of which can be done independently.

HOW TO BOOK

With the advent of tight restrictions on the number of people able to start the Inca Trail each day, your first priority on deciding to tackle the trek is to **book as far in advance as possible**. Long gone are the days of being able to turn up in Cusco with nothing arranged and put together a trek there and then. Around 200 tourists a day are able to begin the walk to Machu Picchu and each of these must have a permit that has been secured and paid for well in advance. Competition for these limited places is fierce and the agencies battling for your business often find they can't offer places for the dates you want if you don't plan ahead.

Ultimately you should try and make a reservation as far in advance as possible once you know your travel dates; during the peak season from July to August you ought to have things in place up to five months ahead of your proposed departure date. Bear in mind that the departure dates aren't flexible though and you are not allowed to change the name or passport details on the

PLANNING YOUR TRIP

❏ Why is it so expensive?

The price of the classic 4-day Inca Trail may seem high but in comparison to other, equivalent treks worldwide it represents good value and has ensured a decent standard of general service, fair treatment of porters and increased revenue for a developing country. The flip side is that trekking on a budget is now nigh on impossible and as a result some less well off individuals, including many Peruvians, are unable to tackle the trek.

The main issue is that there are some **fixed costs** that companies have to absorb whether you are taking a group-service trek or a private-service trek. Over recent years the cost of the classic Inca Trail has risen steeply as the government introduced minimum standards and started to enforce regulations. As a start point, the trek fee has to cover the accompanying crew's wages, food and transport. Then there's the entrance fee to the Inca Trail, which in 2013 was 254 soles/US$99 per person; porters have to pay an entrance fee as well but at a reduced rate. Then there's food and fuel for your meals, the cost of camping kit and first-aid equipment, a bus from Machu Picchu to Aguas Calientes, a train ride from Aguas Calientes to Ollantaytambo and a private bus from Ollantaytambo to Cusco. Plus office costs and bank fees for holding the trek deposit. And, of course, there's the sales tax at 18%. The tax authorities have tightened up this aspect and you can now expect to pay around US$80 per person in sales tax, which is incorporated into the price of the trek. This all needs to be accounted for before the company running the expedition tries to make a profit.

The result is a minimum spend for every company operating an Inca Trail trek, although costs vary considerably from company to company and are dependent on group size. If you choose a company with a smaller group size, expect the operating costs per person to increase to maintain the same level of service. If the company you're researching is offering a trek for a group of 12-14 for much less than US$540 they are having to cut corners somewhere and that's not acceptable.

permit. Also, although Machu Picchu is open year-round, the classic Inca Trail is closed throughout February.

Your second priority ought to be **choosing an agency**. Take time over this as it is an important decision: they are, after all, the ones who will arrange everything, supply the equipment and assign you a guide. Only licensed Peruvian agencies are entitled to sell **permits**, so you will have to make a reservation either directly with one of them, or through a foreign tour company. By booking direct over the internet or by phone you will potentially save yourself money by cutting out the middleman. You will also be dealing directly with the people who will be running and arranging your trip. You can take some satisfaction from the knowledge that whilst the money probably isn't going to the most destitute Peruvians, the money you spend on your trek will at least be going to support the local economy rather than into the pockets of company outside Peru. For a list of the more-established, respected agencies in Cusco with secure online facilities see pp179-86. Alternatively, for the sake of convenience, you may wish to sign up with a foreign tour operator who will make all the arrangements on your behalf, for a fee. However, they will rarely offer you just a trek and nothing else. Airport transfers and accommodation in Cusco will nearly always be included in the package. For a bit extra they'll probably even organize your international flights meaning that you can save yourself a considerable amount of time and hassle. For a selection of those who offer the Inca Trail amongst their activities see pp17-20.

If you fall foul of the regulations and are unable to organize a permit for the dates that you targeted, don't worry, simply check out the alternative route options that are outlined on p30 and covered in detail later in this book. Whatever you do, do not be tempted to purchase tours or treks from sales people working in the airports or bus stations. Reputable companies do not operate like this. Always make a final reservation and conduct all payments in an agency office, making sure to ask for a written receipt and contract.

GROUP SERVICE OR PRIVATE SERVICE TREK

There are two main types of trek: 'group service' and 'private service'. The standard **group service** is the more popular and involves joining a group of trekkers from all over the world, so it can be a very social way of walking. However, you can end up with people of very mixed abilities and interests, meaning you may have to walk slower than you'd usually like. The maximum group size is 16 people, though typically there will be 12-14 on the trail. If the group is larger than eight people, the regulations state that there must be two guides. That said, the trend is for smaller groups as it becomes harder for agencies to secure permits, although the cheaper companies bond together to form large groups. This is the cheapest way of doing the trek. Typically, travelling in a group of 12-14, a trek costs US$540-600; the actual amount depends on the agency and level of service provided. The basic maths ought to prove it's not feasible to run a quality trek for less than US$540; see box opposite. At the other end of the scale, prices can double if you book with a foreign tour operator.

❏ **On the trail with a trekking group**
Typically a day on any of the trails in the company of an agency-guided trek starts with an early wake-up call and cup of tea in your tent. The porters will then bring a bowl of warm water for you to wash in, whilst breakfast is prepared. The first meal of the day usually consists of a hearty combination of fruit, porridge, bread and sometimes eggs. Following this, the day's walk will begin.

During the trek you are only required to carry a day pack containing wet- and warm-weather clothing, adequate water and supplies such as a camera or important documents as the porters or *arrieros* (muleteers/donkey men) will shoulder the bulk of the luggage. In the course of the morning the porters will catch up and overtake you and then will race ahead to prepare lunch at a designated stop. After a brief break in which to eat, the trek continues at a leisurely pace until you arrive at the next evening's campsite, usually well before sunset. This gives you enough time to relax, reflect and unwind before supper and a well-deserved early night.

The other option is to take a **private-service trek**, which is laid on for just you and your friends. Inevitably, if there are only a few of you this is a much more expensive option as the cost of the guide, cook and porters has to be split between just a handful of trekkers. For larger groups, cost is less of an issue. Two people on a private-service trek might expect to pay US$1300 each, whilst four trekkers would pay US$800 and six people expect to cough up US$650 each. Groups of 8-14 people should anticipate spending US$540-620. The maximum group size is still 16, for which each person would pay around US$520. Prices can again vary widely from company to company depending on the sort of service offered. In addition to smaller groups, you will also receive more attention, probably be treated better and enjoy greater comforts than the group-service can offer. By booking a private-service you are also more likely to get the departure dates you want as the agency can close the booking as soon as you sign up; with a group-service they can't confirm the permits until they are ready to book the entire group, so whilst waiting for the last spaces to be filled may occasionally find they've missed the boat and all the permits have been taken. If that's the case, the trek will be cancelled or they will attempt to offer you alternative dates. Ultimately, you get what you pay for.

VISITING MACHU PICCHU WITHOUT DOING A TREK

It is, of course, entirely possible to visit the ruins at Machu Picchu without undertaking any of the treks described here. Most of the companies listed in Cusco and abroad offer basic tours of the ruins and will arrange to shuttle you from Cusco to Aguas Calientes and from there up to the site itself.

It is equally easy, and potentially cheaper, to get to the ruins simply by using public transport. There is a train service from Cusco to Aguas Calientes and a bus service from there to Machu Picchu. For those on a really low budget there is also now a more arduous, more time-consuming but very cheap way of accessing Aguas Calientes by bus followed by a short section of easy walking (see p187).

TOUR OPERATORS AND TREKKING AGENCIES

Booking with an agent in Peru (see box pp179-86) is the cheapest way to organize your trek. Booking with a company from home though can provide additional peace of mind and get you a package that includes flights and transfers, albeit at a price. Many of the operators listed below also operate Lares Valley treks (see box p34), which include a visit to Machu Picchu, but these are not described in this book.

Agencies in the UK and Ireland

● **Amazonas Explorer** (🖥 www.amazonas-explorer.com), based in Peru (Cusco; see p179) but owned by British/Swiss expats, offer the Inca Trail, Choquequirao trek and a 12-day trek to Vilcabamba including Cusco and the Sacred Valley.

● **Andes** (☎ 01556 503929, 🖥 www.andes.org.uk) specialize in climbing expeditions but also tailor-make an Inca Mountain trek that is run on request.

● **Andean Trails** (☎ 0131 467 7086, 🖥 www.andeantrails.co.uk) organize treks for small groups including the Inca Trail, Salkantay and Choquequirao treks, and also offer luxury treks as well as tailor-made itineraries.

● **Audley Travel** (☎ 01993 838620, 🖥 www.audleytravel.com) offer the classic Inca Trail, the Salkantay Trek (staying in lodges; see Mountain Lodges of Peru p183) as well as the Santa Teresa and Choquequirao routes; they can tailor-make a holiday round any of the treks in the region.

● **Charity Challenge** (☎ 020 8346 0500, 🖥 www.charitychallenge.com) offer treks to Machu Picchu, on the Inca Trail from Km104, for a number of charities.

● **Classic Journeys** (☎ 01773 873497, 🖥 www.classicjourneys.co.uk) arrange treks on the classic Inca Trail as well as a selection of extension tours.

● **Discover Adventure** (☎ 01722 718444, 🖥 www.discoveradventure.com) organize ordinary treks on the Inca Trail as well as treks for charity.

● **Exodus** (☎ 0845 863 9616, 🖥 www.exodus.co.uk) arrange a variety of treks and tours which include the Inca Trail.

● **Explore** (☎ 0844 499 0901, 🖥 www.explore.co.uk) is a large company doing Inca Trail, Choquequirao, and Choquequirao to Machu Picchu treks as well as ruins-only tours.

● **Footprint Adventures** (☎ 01522 804929, 🖥 www.footprint-adventures.co .uk) arrange the Inca Trail and Salkantay treks as well as the Santa Teresa route, which they call the Salkantay Nature Trail.

● **G Adventures** (formerly Gap Adventures; ☎ 0844 272 0000, 🖥 www.gadven tures.com) A well-run international organization offering many tours on the Inca Trail and the Salkantay trek.

● **HF Holidays** (☎ 020 8732 1220, 🖥 www.hfholidays.co.uk) offer a tour to Peru which includes Machu Picchu and has the Inca Trail as an option.

● **High Places** (☎ 0114 279 2790 or ☎ 0845 257 7500, 🖥 www.highplaces .co.uk) operate a couple of Peruvian treks including the Inca Trail.

● **Imaginative Traveller** (☎ 01728 862231, 🖥 www.imaginative-traveller .com) offer several trips including the Inca Trail.

● **Intrepid Travel** (☎ 0800 781 1660, 🖥 www.intrepidtravel.com) offer a variety of treks including Machu Picchu.

PLANNING YOUR TRIP

● **Journey Latin America** (☎ 020 8747 8315, ▢ www.journeylatinamerica
.co.uk) are a well-established company for tours to South America; they arrange
Inca Trail, Salkantay and Choquequirao treks and can also tailor-make holidays.
● **KE Adventure Travel** (☎ 017687 73966, ▢ www.keadventure.com) arrange
Inca Trail, Salkantay, and Choquequirao to Machu Picchu treks.
● **Last Frontiers** (☎ 01296 653000, ▢ www.lastfrontiers.com) tailor-make hol-
idays including the Inca Trail, Santa Teresa and Salkantay (the latter on behalf
of Mountain Lodges of Peru; see p183) treks.
● **Llama Travel** (☎ 020 7263 3000, ▢ www.llamatravel.com) specialize in
good-value trekking trips to Peru, including the Inca Trail as well as tours to
Machu Picchu.
● **Mountain Kingdoms** (☎ 01453 844400, ▢ www.mountainkingdoms.com)
offer a variety of treks including the Inca Trail, Salkantay trek with Mountain
Lodges of Peru (see p183) and a trip to Choquequirao.
● **Naturetrek** (☎ 01962 733051, ▢ www.naturetrek.co.uk) organize a Macaws
and Machu Picchu trek, which includes the Inca Trail.
● **Peregrine** (☎ 020 8772 3825, ▢ www.peregrineadventures.com), an
Australian outfit, offer a variety of holidays in the region which include the Inca
Trail and Salkantay treks.
● **Pura Aventura** (☎ 01273 676712, ▢ www.pura-aventura.com) arrange Inca
Trail treks including the Salkantay Mountain Lodges trek (see p183).
● **Rainbow Tours** (☎ 020 7666 1260, ▢ www.rainbowtours.co.uk) tailor-make
tours to Peru and can include the Inca Trail and visits to Machu Picchu; they
also operate the Salkantay Trek staying in Mountain Lodges of Peru lodges (see
p183).
● **Red Spokes** (☎ 020 7502 7252, ▢ www.redspokes.co.uk) organize cycling
trips in Peru as well as the Inca Trail trek, on foot.
● **Spirit of Adventure** (☎ 01822 880277, ▢ www.spirit-of-adventure.com) are
an agent for Amazonas Explorer (see p179) so they can arrange any of the treks
on the Amazonas website.
● **Tucan Travel** (☎ 020 8896 1600, from Eire ☎ 1800 553559, ▢ www.tucan
travel.com) is one of the largest tour operators in the area and organize everything from 7- to 65-day trips to Peru including the Inca Trail. They have an
operations office in Cusco (Av de Sol 616, Office 202).
● **Walks Worldwide** (☎ 0845 301 4737, ▢ www.walksworldwide.com) offer
the Inca Trail and a trek to Espíritu Pampa.
● **World Expeditions** (☎ 020 8545 9030, ▢ worldexpeditions.co.uk) arrange
Inca Trail, Salkantay, and Choquequirao to Machu Picchu treks as well as tours
which include the Inca Trail. They also arrange charity challenges.

Agencies in Continental Europe
● **Austria** El Mundo Reiseburo (☎ 0316 810698, ▢ www.elmundo.at).
● **Belgium** **Allibert Trekking** (☎ 02 526 92 90, ▢ www.allibert-trekking
.com); **Joker** (▢ www.joker.be) Has nine branches in Belgium; **Divantoura**
(☎ 09 223 00 69, ▢ www.divantoura.be) Agents for Explore, see p17.

● **Denmark Inter-Travel** (☎ 33 15 00 77, 🖳 www.inter-travel.dk) Agents for Explore, see p17.
● **France** **Allibert Trekking** (☎ 04 76 45 50 50, 🖳 www.allibert-trekking .com) Has branches in Paris, Chamonix, Chapareillan and Toulouse as well as in Belgium and Switzerland; **Club Aventure** (☎ 08 26 88 20 80, 🖳 www .huwans-clubaventure.fr).
● **Germany Neue Reise Theke** (☎ 03 51 479 3710, 🖳 www.reisetheke.de).
● **Netherlands Adventure World** (☎ 023 5382 954, 🖳 atc@euronet.nl) Agents for Explore, see p17.
● **Switzerland Allibert Trekking** (☎ 022 849 85 51, 🖳 www.allibert-trek king.com).

Agencies in the USA
● **Adventure Life** (☎ 1-800-344-6118, 🖳 www.adventure-life.com) Arrange a variety of tours and treks in the region.
● **Andean Treks** (☎ 1-800-683-8148 or ☎ 617-924-1974, 🖳 www.andean treks.com) have many years of arranging tours and treks throughout Peru.
● **Explore** (☎ 1-800-715-1746, 🖳 www.exploreworldwide.com) See p17.
● **G Adventures** (☎ 1-800-708-7761 or ☎ 1-888-800-4100, 🖳 www.gadven tures.com) G Adventures has agents all over the USA; check the website for one near you. See also p17.
● **Holbrook Travel** (☎ 1-800-541-7111, 🖳 www.holbrooktravel.com) No Inca Trail treks as standard but they offer an Inca Trail service, operating pro- grammes regularly through a non-profit company.
● **Tucan Travel** (New York ☎ 1-855-444-9110, San Francisco ☎ 1-855-444- 9110, 🖳 www.tucantravel.com) See opposite.
● **Wilderness Travel** (☎ 510-558-2488, toll-free ☎ 1-800-368 2794, 🖳 www .wildernesstravel.com) A company with a fine reputation; specializes in cultur- al, wildlife and trekking tours including the Inca Trail, Salkantay Trek and Choquequirao to Machu Picchu route; also offers a trek staying in the Mountain Lodges of Peru, see p183.
● **Wildland Adventures** (☎ 1-800-345-4453, 🖳 www.wildland.com) are a leading eco-tourism operator offering a variety of itineraries including the Inca Trail, Family Adventures, the Amazon rainforest and a Mountain Lodges trek to Machu Picchu, see p183.
● **World Expeditions** (contact World Expeditions in Canada p20; also see opposite).

Agencies in Canada
● **Charity Challenge** (☎ 1-289-239-8239, 🖳 www.charitychallenge.ca) See p17.
● **Explore** (☎ 1-888-216-3401, 🖳 www.exploreworldwide.ca) See p17.
● **G Adventures** (🖳 www.gadventures.com) G Adventures has agents all over Canada; check the website for one near you. See p17.
● **Intrepid Travel** (☎ 1-855-240-4352 or ☎ 1-855-626-6345, 🖳 www.myad venturestore.ca) See p17.

PLANNING YOUR TRIP

● **Tucan Travel** (Toronto ☎ 1-855-566-8660, Vancouver ☎ 1-800-228-8747, 🖥 www.tucantravel.com) See p18.
● **World Expeditions** (🖥 www.worldexpeditions.com/ca) has a branch in Ottawa (toll free ☎ 1-800-567-2216, ☎ 613-241-2700) as well as in Montreal (Expéditions Monde; ☎ 514-844-6364, toll-free ☎ 1-866-606-1721, 🖥 www.expeditionsmonde.com). See p18.

Agencies in Peru
See Cusco, pp179-83.

Agencies in South Africa
● **Exciting Destinations** (☎ 43-735 0983) Agent for Inca Tours, see below.
● **Tucan Travel** (☎ (+27) 0800 983999, 🖥 www.tucantravel.com); see p18.

Agencies in Australia
● **Adventure Associates** (☎ 02-8916 3000, 🖥 www.adventureassociates.com)
● **Adventure World** (☎ 1300 295 049, 🖥 www.adventureworld.com.au) Operate their own tours and are agents for some tours by other agencies.
● **Explore** (☎ 1300 414 151, 🖥 www.exploreworldwide.com.au) See p17.
● **G Adventures** (☎ 1300 796618, 🖥 www.gadventures.com) See p17.
● **Inca Tours** (☎ 02-4351 2133 or toll-free ☎ 1-800 024 955, 🖥 www.incatours.net) Operates a variety of tours and treks.
● **Intrepid Travel** (☎ 1300 018390, 🖥 www.myadventurestore.com) See p17. Intrepid has branches all over Australia, see their website for details.
● **Peregrine** (☎ 03-8601 4444, 🖥 www.peregrineadventures.com) See p18.
● **Tucan Travel** (☎ 02-9326 6633, ☎ 1-300 769249, 🖥 www.tucantravel.com) See p18.
● **World Expeditions** (toll free ☎ 1300 720 000, 🖥 www.worldexpeditions.com.au) has branches in: Sydney (☎ 02-8270 8400, 🖥 enquiries@worldexpeditions.com.au); Melbourne (☎ 03-8631 3300, 🖥 travel@worldexpeditions.com.au); Brisbane (☎ 07-3216 0823, 🖥 adventure@worldexpeditions.com.au); and Perth (☎ 08-9486 9899, 🖥 holiday@worldexpeditions.com.au); see p18.

Agencies in New Zealand
● **Adventure World** (toll-free ☎ 0800 238368, 🖥 www.adventureworld.co.nz).
● **Discover Adventure** (☎ 02 144 5871, 🖥 www.discoveradventure.co.nz) See p17.
● **Explore** (☎ 09 520 1490, 🖥 www.exploreworldwide.co.nz) See p17.
● **G Adventures** (☎ 0800 333307, 🖥 www.gadventures.com) See p17.
● **High Places** (☎ 03 540 3208, 🖥 www.highplaces.co.nz) See p17.
● **Intrepid Travel** (Wellington ☎ 04 473 1907, or Auckland ☎ 09 520 0972, 🖥 www.intrepidtravel.com) See p17.
● **Tucan Travel** (☎ 0800 444 352, 🖥 www.tucantravel.com) has an office in Auckland and is a major operator in the region; see p18.
● **World Expeditions** (☎ 09 368 4161, ☎ 0800-350354, 🖥 www.worldexpeditions.co.nz) See p18.

PORTERS, ARRIEROS AND GUIDES

In most instances you are likely to tackle the treks described here with an agency or tour company from Cusco, indeed in some cases this is the only way of undertaking the treks. The agency will supply you with guides, porters or mules. However, at the time of writing, there were still a number of treks that you could set out on independently, or with *arrieros* (muleteers) and mules that you have hired yourself. These include the Santa Teresa, Vilcabamba and Choquequirao treks as well as those routes linking Vilcabamba with Choquequirao, and Choquequirao with Machu Picchu.

Hiring arrieros and porters

Arrieros can be hired in Cusco. However, the best deal, and the best way of supporting the local economy, is to hire your team of muleteers from the start of the trek or town closest to the trailhead. For the Salkantay and Santa Teresa treks look for arrieros in Mollepata (see box p242); for either the Vilcabamba trek or the Huancacalle to Cachora via Choquequirao trek try Huancacalle (see p273); for the Choquequirao trek, or the Choquequirao to Machu Picchu trek recruit your arrieros in Cachora (see pp301-2).

At the time of hiring, negotiate a fair price for a fair service. Don't exploit the local populace and don't haggle ridiculously hard for the sake of a few *soles* (see p117). The arriero may insist on taking a second mule. This is not a con trick to get you to part with more money, it is an insurance factor should one mule go lame or get injured, or should you need to ride at any point due to exhaustion. At the time make sure you agree exactly what is expected of the arriero. Also agree where he will sleep and who will feed him; you may be required to provide shelter and meals for the duration of the trek. Bear in mind that you will need to factor in a sum for the time it takes the arrieros to return home after the trek, and you should allow for a tip too if they provide particularly good service.

For an arriero, or porter, the rate is around s/42 per day, equivalent to US$15/£10. A tip in the order of 5-10% of the total fee is reasonable, but consider how hard the guy worked on your behalf and give generously.

PLANNING YOUR TRIP

❏ **The life of a porter**
The film *Mi Chacra* (🖥 www.michacrafilm.com), meaning 'My Land', is an award-winning documentary by Jason Burlage that chronicles the life of a porter. Framed by the seasons, the film follows a Peruvian farmer and his family from planting to harvest and through a season as a porter on the Inca Trail. The film was shot on the Inca Trail and in the family's village of Mullacas, in the mountains above the Sacred Valley. It showcases the natural beauty of the Sacred Valley but also provides a window into the lives of the Andean people, whilst painting a vivid portrait of the complexities of rural life and the reality of the conditions for porters working the trek to Machu Picchu.

❑ PORTER WELFARE

Roughly 7000 porters now service the needs of the tens of thousands of tourists who walk the Inca Trail each year. These people have often been exploited in the past and frequently worked with inadequate, inappropriate clothing and gear for derisory wages. While this situation has changed there are still improvements to be made and unscrupulous agencies to be weeded out. There are now several organizations dedicated to the issue of porter welfare who are campaigning for better working conditions and reasonable rates of pay.

As an individual trekking to Machu Picchu, or any of the other sites in the area, there are several things you can do to improve the plight of those making your trek possible. **Let the agency in charge of your trek know that the welfare of porters is important to you.** Make sure they understand that you consider it an important factor when it comes to selecting an agency to run your trek. Porters need fair wages, decent meals and warm, dry overnight accommodation. There is still room for improvement with all of the agencies, but some are markedly better than others. Those offering the classic Inca Trail trek for less than US$540 won't have the porters' best interests at heart or be paying them adequately (see box p14).

Ask how much the porters are paid – the Porters' Law passed in 2002 states **a wage of s/42 per day** for the four-day classic Inca Trail. Unfortunately, the law has been described as 'unimplementable' and sadly most agencies are ignoring this rule and typically paying around s/25-30 per day. This should include food rations and transport to the trailhead although some agencies expect porters to pay for anything more than basic rations and for their own transport to the trailhead or the journey home, a cost that can reduce their income considerably.

The law also states that **porters should not carry in excess of 25kg**, a figure that includes a 5kg personal allowance for items such as blankets and clothes. Although strictly enforced, some companies make great efforts to get round this particular regulation. Don't stand for such sharp practice and say something if you see an abuse being perpetrated. Also enquire about the standard of equipment used by the porters; do they have waterproof clothing? Do they all sleep in tents with integral floors and have access to sleeping bags and mats? Showing you care about such things will encourage all operators and agencies to treat their porters fairly.

On the trek, **try to interact with your porters**. Take time to talk to them and learn something about their lives. Many have low self esteem so be bold and initiate the process, share some coca leaves (see box p84) and pick up a few words of Quechua (*Allillanchu?* means 'How are you?' whilst *Añáy* means 'Thank you'); see also pp363-6. The porters often have colourful stories to tell and can offer you a real insight into Andean traditions and culture.

At the end of the trek **make sure you tip your porters** and that they get the money that is intended for them. Tipping directly to each individual member of the team ensures they receive a fair share. Show them you appreciate the work they have done on your behalf by thanking them verbally and individually.

Report unscrupulous trekking agencies

If you witness porter abuse or neglect, or encounter unscrupulous agencies taking advantage of their porters, bring it to the attention of the guide. Upon your return to Cusco, make an official complaint at the agency office, ideally in front of other potential clients, and if sufficiently bad, submit a report to South American Explorers (see box p137), the International Porter Protection Group, or Andean Travel Web (see opposite). Equally, do let us know if you've had either a particularly good or poor experience on your trek. Your observations will mean that agencies are forced to face the fact that the issue is important and that in order to continue to do business they must respect those porters working for them and look after them properly.

Of course, if you are trekking independently and hiring guides, arrieros or porters directly, you personally need to take responsibility for the welfare of the team you hire, and again abide by the basic guidelines set out above.

International Porter Protection Group (IPPG)

Although not based in Peru the IPPG (⌨ ippg.net) is a volunteer organization that is dedicated to improving the conditions of mountain porters in the tourism industry worldwide. The comprehensive website outlines a number of measures that you can take to ensure you have a positive effect on your porters and their welfare. In addition, on their website, the IPPG recommend you ask the following when booking the Inca Trail:

● Does the company follow the **IPPG's five guidelines on porter safety**? These are:

1. Adequate clothing for protection from bad weather and high altitude should be provided to porters. This may mean windproof jackets and trousers, suitable footwear, socks, hats and gloves.

2. Porters should have access to shelter, either in a room, lodge or tent (the trekkers' dining tent is not acceptable as it rarely has an integral floor and is not usually available until late evening, meaning that the porters potentially have to wait in inclement weather without shelter), sleeping bags and mats as well as cooking equipment.

3. Porters should have the same access to medical care as tourists and also be covered by some form of insurance.

4. Adequate procedures should be in place for the medical evacuation of porters.

5. Porters should carry no more than 25kg according to Peruvian law. Weight limits might need to be adjusted taking into consideration altitude, weather conditions and the state of the path. Child porters should never be employed.

● What is the company's policy on equipment and health care for porters?

● What does the company do to ensure its staff are properly trained to look after porters' welfare?

● Does the company ask about the treatment of porters in its post-trek questionnaire?

● If booking the trek from outside Peru, or through a middleman or agent who hires another agency to run the trek itself, you should also ask about the company's policy on training and monitoring porter care by its ground operator in Peru.

Unfortunately the excellent Inka Porter Project (Porteadores Inka Ñan) which was dedicated to improving conditions for porters and arrieros in the Andes is no longer operational.

Andean Travel Web

⌨ **www.andeantravelweb.com/peru** is a great source of information about Cusco and the attractions in the area including all the trekking opportunities. The non profit-making organization also runs community projects and is dedicated to raising awareness of the issue of porter welfare.

In Cusco you can donate clothing or school equipment at their office (La Casa Cultural, Avenida Pardo 540). The office's overheads are covered by a tour agency, Peru Treks & Adventure (see pp183-4), which means that all the proceeds from your donations reach the communities.

PLANNING YOUR TRIP

Getting to Peru

BY AIR

Getting to Peru by air is relatively straightforward and by far the most common means of accessing the country. All international flights from Europe and North America use Lima's Jorge Chávez International Airport (🖳 www.lap.com.pe), a smart, modern airport voted the Best in South America in 2012.

Airlines with routes to and from Peru (Lima) include Aerolineas Argentina, AeroMéxico, Air Canada, Air France, Alitalia, American Airlines, Avianca, British Airways, Copa Airlines, Delta Airlines, Iberia, KLM, LAN Airlines, Lufthansa, TACA, United Airlines and Varig. Fares vary according to the airline, the time of year and the route you take but are generally quite costly. The two high seasons and thus the most expensive fares are from mid-December to mid-January and July to mid-August.

The majority of the agencies listed on pp17-20 will be able to organize tickets on your behalf; otherwise check out their respective websites to see if you can secure a discount by booking online. For a full online guide to flights in and out of Peru visit 🖳 www.traficoperu.com. International air fares are expensive in Peru as a result of high taxes so you are better off buying an open return if you don't know when you'll be coming back rather than trying to purchase a one-way ticket home once in Peru.

From Europe

Currently, there are no direct flights from the UK or Ireland to Peru (Lima). Flights generally connect with others operating out of gateway cities such as Madrid and Amsterdam. Alternatively they fly via cities in the USA or possibly via other Latin American countries. Flight times are between 16-22 hours depending on the route. Fares from the UK start at around £600 but rise very quickly.

For the best deals look at websites such as: 🖳 www.opodo.com, 🖳 www.ebookers.com, 🖳 www.expedia.co.uk or 🖳 www.cheapflights.com.

UK-based travel agents to consider include: Flight Centre (☎ 0844 800 8660, 🖳 www.flightcentre.co.uk); North South Travel (☎ 01245 608291, 🖳 northsouthtravel.co.uk; STA Travel (☎ 0871 230 0040, 🖳 www.statravel.co.uk) which specializes in fares for students; Trailfinders (☎ 020 7368 1200, 🖳 www.trailfinders.com); Travel Bag (☎ 0871 703 4698, 🖳 www.travelbag.co.uk).

From the USA and Canada

Direct flights to Lima operate out of Atlanta, Dallas, Houston and Los Angeles although the major gateways are Miami and New York. Return fares are US$1200-1600. Air Canada can book you all the way through from Toronto, and operate connecting flights from Montreal, Vancouver and Calgary to Toronto. Fares start from CAN$1400-2000.

For good deals try: Exito Travel (USA ☎ 1 800 655 4053, Canada ☎ 800-670-2605, 🖳 www.exitotravel.com), who specialize in flights to South America; Cheap Flights (🖳 www.cheapflights.ca); STA Travel (☎ 1 800 781 4040, 🖳 www.statravel.com); Travel CUTS/Voyages Campus (☎ 1-800-667-2887, 🖳 www.travelcuts.com).

From Australia and New Zealand
There are no direct flights from either Australia or New Zealand to Peru. Flights are generally via the USA or an alternative South American gateway. Tickets from Australia cost A$1900-2600 whilst fares from New Zealand begin at NZ$2400. For good deals visit 🖳 www.cheapflights.com.au or 🖳 www.cheap flights.co.nz; alternatively, both Flight Centre (🖳 www.flightcentre.com.au or 🖳 www.flightcentre.co.nz) and STA Travel (🖳 www.statravel.com.au or 🖳 www.statravel.co.nz) have offices throughout Australia and New Zealand.

OVERLAND
The Darien Gap separating Panama and Colombia is uncrossed by either roads or railways. This missing chunk of the Pan American Highway effectively prevents all but the most adventurous from travelling overland to Peru. There are routes to Peru from neighbouring South American countries though. Although this isn't quite as straightforward as it might appear, it is possible to access Peru from Bolivia, Brazil, Chile, Colombia and Ecuador.

From **Bolivia** buses from La Paz cross overland into Southern Peru. It is also possible to cross the border on Lake Titicaca and then access Cusco from Puno. Overland travel from **Brazil** to Peru is possible via Iñapari or through the jungle to Puerto Maldonado, which is a short flight or a long bus ride from Cusco. Alternatively, catch a ferry from Manaus to Iquitos, a thrilling journey that takes around 10 days and from where you can fly to Cusco.

The Pan American Highway crosses from **Chile** to Peru between Arica and Tacna on Peru's south coast. Buses from Tacna then go to Arequipa or Puno from where you can connect with others going on to Cusco.

The route into Peru from **Colombia** is hardly ever used but is feasible, crossing from one country to the other at Leticia and then pushing upriver to Iquitos. The Pan American Highway pushes south from **Ecuador** into Peru via Tumbes, from where there are flights and onward bus services to Lima.

Budgeting

The major expense on a trekking trip to Peru, unless you opt for a couple of nights in Cusco's Hotel Monasterio (top suites US$2100 per night; see p170) at the end, is the trek itself. Although for a budget, independent trek on one of the less-popular routes you can get away with saving a little and cutting costs, for an outing on the classic four-day Inca Trail set aside at least US$540 for a basic

PLANNING YOUR TRIP

trek, more if you use a better agency with a well-established reputation or want to trek without any other walkers. Once on the Inca Trail though you won't have to pay for anything other than the occasional soft drink or snack from one of the locals' stands along the way.

Away from the trails and the mountains, Cusco can cost virtually as little or as much as you like. In the main, transport, food and accommodation, the biggest three expenses in most people's travels, are reasonable and good value. You can of course treat yourself to a first-class train ride, a Michelin-starred meal and de luxe accommodation, all of which are readily available in both Lima and Cusco.

As a guide, budget travellers can probably get by on less than US$40 per day, whilst up to US$75 buys you a better meal and the odd taxi ride as well as a private hot shower in a more salubrious place to stay. More than US$100 should mean that you enjoy a comfortable stay and eat very well. A fully guided tour run by an international agency will almost certainly cost you far more though.

ACCOMMODATION

As with most things, you get what you pay for, and cheap, non-tourist accommodation is often available in rather grubby, sleazy parts of town. Basic tourist accommodation starts at around US$5-15 per night for a dorm, and a comfortable double room in a budget hotel should cost you US$25-50. A mid-range hotel might set you back US$50-100 per night. At the other end of the spectrum, rooms in five-star international chain hotels can easily set you back US$300 whilst for luxury accommodation the sky's the limit. The seasons impact heavily on prices, and in Cusco during the height of the season (June to August), you may find prices increase by up to 25%. The same thing happens around a major celebration or fiesta (see pp86-7).

Accommodation on the trek is almost always camping unless you use the eco-lodges of Mountain Lodges of Peru (see p183) on the Santa Teresa Trek, when costs increase, but so does the quality of your overnight stay.

FOOD

By roughing it in the countryside, eating locally sourced produce bought at market or from villagers, you can get by on very little. Even in major towns food can be dirt cheap if you stick to the street vendors who ply their wares at all hours of day and night or take advantage of the good set menu deals available in local restaurants, although hygiene standards are not always of the highest. You ought to be able to find a good meal in a decent, clean restaurant for less than US$10. Top-end venues with superb reputations and food to match, of which there are plenty in Peru, will naturally set you back rather more.

TRANSPORT

Public transport costs are usually very reasonable in Peru, even for long-distance journeys. You are, of course, at the mercy of cramped, dilapidated buses and dozy drivers, but this is the reality of public transport here. Then again, rates are so reasonable it seems churlish to complain. Additional comfort and safety comes at only a slightly higher price if you opt to travel by private, luxury bus.

The exception to the good-value rule is the train from Cusco to Aguas Calientes (see pp370-1), which has far higher rates than you might expect, as it is a monopoly and caters to a captive audience of eager tourists.

Route options

[**See Route Options map pp28-9**]. The treks described in this book offer a selection of routes to Machu Picchu which take various lengths of time and cater for people of varying abilities and interest levels.

The legendary Inca Trail has become a 'must do' for many travellers. However, the popularity of the trek has meant that the trail and the ruins along it have had to deal with an increasing number of visitors. To counter the detrimental effects of this influx, the Peruvian government has imposed a strict limit on the number of people able to start the trek at any one time. The result has been that many people have fallen foul of the regulations and been unable to tackle the trek.

The good news, though, is that there are several alternative treks in the Cusco region, many of them on original Inca trails to less well-known but similarly stunning sites such as Choquequirao and Vilcabamba; routes and ruins that may be more appealing in some respects as you don't have to share them with 500 other people. There are also two much longer, more difficult expeditions that actually link several of the key Inca sites and provide you with a wonderful, broad experience of the region, its history and its archaeological remains.

THE CLASSIC INCA TRAIL   [3-4 days, see pp218-34]

This is the trek that most people think of when picturing Peru: it has become synonymous with the country. Beginning at Km88 on the railway line to Aguas Calientes, the trek follows an original Inca path uncovered in 1911 by Hiram Bingham and developed in 1944 by Dr Paul Fejos, past the restored ruins at Patallacta, Runcu Racay, Sayacmarca, Phuyu Pata Marca, Intipata and Huinay Huayna to arrive eventually at Machu Picchu.

The **43km (26½-mile) trek** is reasonably gruelling; although some of the trek is through exquisite cloud forest and rich subtropical jungle, other stages are through exposed mountain scenery and the path also crosses two steep-sided passes at 4200m/13,750ft.

This trail is subject to the Inca Trail regulations and permits must be secured well in advance of departure. It is closed completely during February.

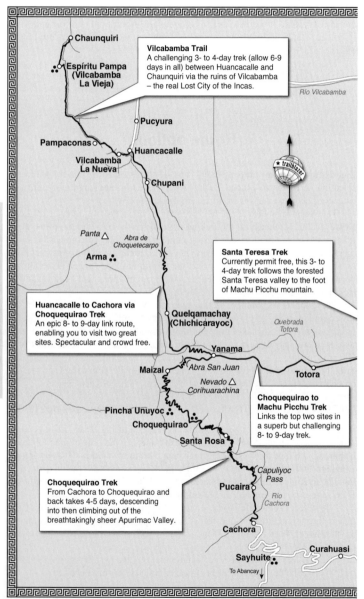

Vilcabamba Trail
A challenging 3- to 4-day trek (allow 6-9 days in all) between Huancacalle and Chaunquiri via the ruins of Vilcabamba – the real Lost City of the Incas.

Santa Teresa Trek
Currently permit free, this 3- to 4-day trek follows the forested Santa Teresa valley to the foot of Machu Picchu mountain.

Huancacalle to Cachora via Choquequirao Trek
An epic 8- to 9-day link route, enabling you to visit two great sites. Spectacular and crowd free.

Choquequirao to Machu Picchu Trek
Links the top two sites in a superb but challenging 8- to 9-day trek.

Choquequirao Trek
From Cachora to Choquequirao and back takes 4-5 days, descending into then climbing out of the breathtakingly sheer Apurímac Valley.

Chaunquiri

Espíritu Pampa (Vilcabamba La Vieja)

Río Vilcabamba

Pucyura

Pampaconas

Huancacalle

Vilcabamba La Nueva

Chupani

Panta △   Abra de Choquetecarpo

Arma

Quelqamachay (Chichicarayoc)

Quebrada Totora

Yanama

Maizal   Abra San Juan

Nevado △ Corihuarachina

Totora

Pincha Unuyoc

Choquequirao

Santa Rosa

Capuliyoc Pass

Pucaira   Río Cachora

Cachora

Curahuasi

Sayhuite

To Abancay

PLANNING YOUR TRIP

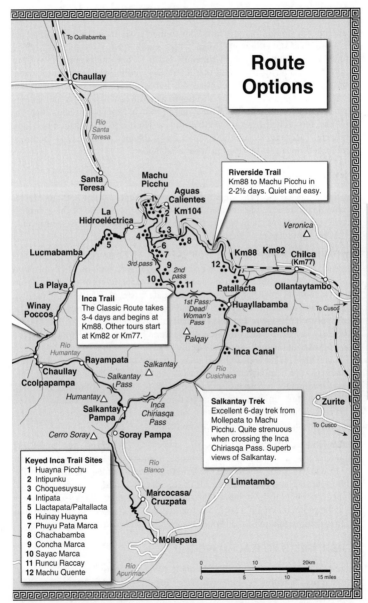

Route Options

To Quillabamba

Chaullay

Rio Santa Teresa

Santa Teresa

Machu Picchu

Aguas Calientes

Riverside Trail
Km88 to Machu Picchu in 2-2½ days. Quiet and easy.

La Hidroeléctrica

Km104

Veronica △

Lucmabamba

Km88 Km82 Chilca (Km77)

3rd pass

2nd pass

La Playa

Km82

Inca Trail
The Classic Route takes 3-4 days and begins at Km88. Other tours start at Km82 or Km77.

Patallacta

Ollantaytambo

Winay Poccos

Huayllabamba

To Cusco

1st Pass: Dead Woman's Pass

Rio Humantay

Rayampata

Salkantay △

Paucarcancha

Chaullay Ccolpapampa

Salkantay Pass

Palqay △

Inca Canal

Rio Cusichaca

Zurite

Humantay △

Inca Chiriasqa Pass

Salkantay Trek
Excellent 6-day trek from Mollepata to Machu Picchu. Quite strenuous when crossing the Inca Chiriasqa Pass. Superb views of Salkantay.

Salkantay Pampa

Cerro Soray △

Soray Pampa

To Cusco

Rio Blanco

Limatambo

Marcocasa/ Cruzpata

Keyed Inca Trail Sites
1 Huayna Picchu
2 Intipunku
3 Choquesuysuy
4 Intipata
5 Llactapata/Paltallacta
6 Huinay Huayna
7 Phuyu Pata Marca
8 Chachabamba
9 Concha Marca
10 Sayac Marca
11 Runcu Raccay
12 Machu Quente

Mollepata

Rio Apurimac

0 10 20km
0 5 10 15 miles

VARIATIONS ON THE CLASSIC TRAIL

There are two straightforward variations to the classic Inca Trail. The first (see p234) **begins at the village of Chilca**, which stands at Km77 on the railway line before tracking alongside the Urubamba River to join the original trail from Km88. Dry and dusty, it isn't all that interesting and not really worth the additional day's hike unless your tour happens to begin from here.

The other option (see p236) is to **begin at Km82**, which offers half a day's more riverside stroll than the Km88 option, but is less monotonous than the Km77 stretch. You also get to visit the ruins at Huillca Raccay, which overlook Patallacta. Trekkers on both these routes are at the mercy of the Inca Trail regulations and must secure a permit well in advance.

SHORTER TRAILS

For those pushed for time or not inclined to mount a 4-day trek to Machu Picchu, there are several options that allow you to get a sense of the approach route to the ruins and then explore the site itself without having to resort to the shuttle bus from Aguas Calientes.

Km104 and the Purification Trail   [2 days, see pp239-40]

There are two route options from Km104 on the railway, both of which take two days to complete, although only one of these is actually spent trekking. From the Inca ruins at Chachabamba you can scale a steep hillside on a narrow, exposed path to reach Huinay Huayna and then join the classic Inca Trail for the final approach to Machu Picchu. Alternatively you can head down the river to Choquesuysuy before tackling an arduous three-hour climb to Huinay Huayna along a route nicknamed the 'Purification Trail'.

Since the Trekker's Hostel at Huinay Huayna has long since closed there is nowhere to stay. Consequently you must descend through Machu Picchu to stay in Aguas Calientes before returning to explore the site the following morning. Both options are subject to the Inca Trail regulations and trek permits must be reserved well in advance. The route is open during February though, when the main, classic approach to Machu Picchu is shut.

Km88 Riverside Trail   [2-3 days, see pp240-1]

From Km88 on the railway line it is possible to follow the Río Urubamba all the way to Km104, from where you are able to ascend to Huinay Huayna via one of two routes. The scenic stroll avoids the tough climbs associated with the classic Inca Trail but it also avoids all the ruins that you would otherwise encounter along the route, making it a far less-attractive option. This trek is also subject to the Inca Trail regulations and should be arranged well in advance.

OTHER TREKS TO MACHU PICCHU

There are two other methods of trekking to Machu Picchu. One is an extended hike that begins with a genuine wilderness experience and a chance to explore the slopes of Mt Salkantay, the sacred mountain of the Incas, before joining the classic Inca Trail for its final three days; the other is an excellent, charming alternative to the classic trail that is currently unregulated and therefore is very popular with those who have fallen foul of the strict Inca Trail regulations.

The Salkantay/Mollepata Trek   [6-7 days, see pp241-51]

The name Salkantay derives from the Quecha word 'Salka', meaning wild, savage or invincible. It is an apt name for the mountain under which this trek, a dramatic extension of the classic Inca Trail, begins. It includes a stretch of wilderness walking largely free from crowds followed by the rather more popular and crowded classic pilgrimage.

Also known as the **Mollepata Trek** by some agencies, trek providers and writers, this trail ascends from the village of Mollepata into the mountains where it climbs over a 4950m/16,235ft knife-like pass on the eastern shoulder of Mt Salkantay. From here it descends into the valley of the Urubamba and joins the classic Inca Trail at Huayllabamba before continuing along the traditional route to reach Machu Picchu. Because it joins the Inca Trail, the Salkantay trek is also subject to the Inca Trail regulations and requires you to have a permit, secured well in advance.

The Santa Teresa Trek   [3-4 days, see pp252-68]

This route to Machu Picchu, via the 'backdoor', has become increasingly popular with those who have failed to book far enough in advance to secure a trek permit for the classic Inca Trail. It is also usually quieter and less heavily used than the traditional route although as more and more people discover it so the amount of traffic on the trail increases. Most agencies offer this trek though they may confusingly refer to it as the Salkantay trek. It's also the only route where some agents offer the option to stay in lodges (see Mountain Lodges of Peru, p183) rather than simply camp.

The 3- to 4-day trek begins from Mollepata and climbs over a pass (4700m/15,420ft) on the western shoulder of Mt Salkantay before descending into the very attractive, forested Santa Teresa Valley. From here it clambers over a ridge into the Aobamba Valley and then joins the Urubamba Valley, finishing at the foot of Machu Picchu Mountain. Although there are hardly any Inca ruins along the trek, it is a very scenic walk through some of the region's most picturesque landscapes. The sprawling, partially uncovered yet highly significant site at Llactapata and the fact that the trek finishes on the doorstep of one of the finest archaeological sites in the Americas are some compensation though.

At present, and despite rumblings to the contrary, this route remains free from the Inca Trail regulations and you are able to trek it independently and arrange your own guide and porters. You do need to pay s/129 (approximately US$50) for an INC permit (see box p217) at Soraypampa if your agency has not incorporated the cost into the total fee; this is in addition to the entrance fee for Machu Picchu. Some agencies might try to avoid the checkpoint so as not to pay the fee but this is not to be condoned.

PLANNING YOUR TRIP

> ❏ **Warning – Vilcabamba Trail**
> At the time of writing, reports from Peru highlighted an increase in activity by narco-traffickers in the Vilcabamba region. In response, the police and military deployed units in the area for security and to curb this activity. The danger is that, as tension heightens, third parties such as locals and tourists will become caught up in the conflict. Consequently, those interested in exploring the area or visiting Vilcabamba are advised to check on the current situation before finalizing their travel plans; talk to South American Explorers (see box p137) or established, responsible agencies with experience of trekking in this region before travelling, as the situation is subject to change. Although theoretically possible, with things the way they are, you should not attempt to trek to Espíritu Pampa independently.

THE VILCABAMBA TRAIL
[6- to 9-day trip with 4 days of walking, see pp268-95]

Note the current security alert (box above). This remote, rarely tackled trek follows the low-level route the Incas took as they fled from the conquistadors deep into the jungle, where they built the last capital of Vilcabamba. The trek itself takes roughly four days but because the path is rarely used it's sometimes overgrown, often muddy in places and prone to damage by landslips so it's worth factoring in additional time. You will also need to take into account the time it takes to get to the out-of-the-way trailheads at Huancacalle and Chaunquiri too, and might want to include additional days in Quillabamba or Huancacalle. It's best to set aside 6-9 days for the entire expedition.

The ruins at Espíritu Pampa, thought to be the site of Vilcabamba, are less immediately spectacular than those at Machu Picchu or Choquequirao, because they lie buried in the thick jungle and haven't been particularly cleared or restored. Instead they have a different type of appeal; much of the magic and reward comes from the jungle that you pass through and the varied flora you are able to see. Since the route isn't subject to any regulations you may trek it independently or arrange your own guides and arrieros to help shoulder the burden.

THE CHOQUEQUIRAO TREK   [4-5 days, see pp296-312]

This trek travels from Cachora to the ruins at Choquequirao, the first major Inca site uncovered outside Cusco and one that is still to be fully explored. Having reached the ruins at the end of the second day you then retrace your steps and walk out along the same trail. With a day at the ruins to explore this extensive site you should reasonably expect the trek to take 4-5 days.

The trek is quite demanding physically as it requires you to descend 1500m/4920ft into the sheer Apurimac Valley in order to cross the Apurimac River (see box opposite), then to climb 1800m/5900ft up the similarly steep opposite cliff to access the ruins perched on a ridge far above. It's hot and dry, and there are few points at which to collect water along the route so you must be prepared to carry additional supplies for much of the trek. However, the vertiginous valley is spectacular and the ruins themselves, which resemble Machu

PLANNING YOUR TRIP

❏ **Choquequirao trek – temporary river crossing**
In 2012 the Choquequirao route was dramatically shut when a series of massive land-slides destroyed the substantial concrete bridge that acted as the only crossing point over the Apurimac River, connecting Playa Rosalina with the start of the uphill climb to Santa Rosa and Marampata. The authorities initially closed the route entirely but enterprising locals and tour operators subsequently set up a traditional oroya (cable car) crossing (see box p298). As the book went to press the authorities made a com-mitment to repair the bridge at a cost of 1.5 million soles and to reopen the route in its original form. However, there was no indication of the timescale for this. Check the situation with agencies or South American Explorers (see box p137) before decid-ing whether to undertake the trek. If the bridge hasn't been completed but you do decide to go ahead, make sure the operator you sign up with is clear on how they will tackle the additional logistical challenge of the crossing.

The damage to the bridge also has implications for the Choquequirao to Machu Picchu traverse and the Choquequirao to Huancacalle and Vilcabamba trek, as both have to use the crossing in the course of the routes. At the time of writing the trekking routes described in this book, both before and after the bridge, remain the same.

Picchu in many respects, are fascinating, meaning that the trek is set to replace the classic trail as the serious hikers' alternative. It isn't currently covered by any regulations, although this may well change as its popularity grows.

COMBINING ROUTES

Many of these routes can be combined but two of the finest combinations are the longer, more adventurous paths that connect Huancacalle to Choquequirao, and Choquequirao to Machu Picchu. Neither is regulated at present and both can be trekked independently with a team you have hired yourself. There are also numerous treks in the mountains and valleys around Cusco (see pp188-214).

Choquequirao to Machu Picchu Trek   [8-9 days, see pp313-25]
This is potentially the finest outing described here. The 8- to 9-day trek links two of the most spectacular Inca ruins by way of a stretch of stunning country-side. From Cachora the path follows the Choquequirao route to the ruins perched precariously high above the Apurímac valley. Descending past the ruins at Pinchu Unyuoc the trail tumbles down one hillside only to clamber steeply up another, before crossing the Abra San Juan and going down to Yanama. From here it cuts away east and climbs through a section of pretty puna to cross another pass in the lee of several giant glaciated peaks before dropping into the jungle to join the Santa Teresa Trek at Ccolpapampa and approaching Machu Picchu via the 'back door'.

Not for the faint-hearted, the route represents quite an undertaking but it does provide you with two exceptional archaeological sites and leads you though a wide range of Peru's vegetation zones so that you'll experience a huge variety of native flora. Note that since the route starts by following the Choquequirao path, it is also affected by the changes to the Apurimac River crossing (see box above).

PLANNING YOUR TRIP

❏ **Lares Valley treks**
A popular alternative to the Inca Trail and its associated routes is the Lares Valley, which lies to the north of Urubamba and is renowned for its traditional Quechua communities and strong weaving culture. There are several variations on trekking routes in this area but all are quiet and scenic, pausing at traditional villages along the way, allowing you to experience something of rural life whilst revelling in the dramatic landscapes of this mountainous territory. As permits are not currently required to tackle these treks, they can also be arranged more easily, although given that train tickets between Ollantaytambo and Aguas Calientes have to be booked it's worth arranging the trip several weeks ahead of your desired departure date. Conversely it also means that agencies operating treks here aren't regulated so the level of service can vary enormously; make sure you book with a reputable agency in order to ensure a degree of quality and to avoid the exploitation of the supporting trekking team. Expect to pay upwards of US$600 per person for a group trek that includes a train trip to Aguas Calientes and access to Machu Picchu.

The most popular route through the Lares Valley is a four-day outing over 33km/20½ miles known as the Weaver's Way. Beginning at the thermal springs just outside Lares, the trek meanders through the traditional textile communities of Huacahuasi and Patacancha on a moderately difficult trail, peaking at the Ipsayccasa Pass at 4500m. A bus then takes you to Ollantaytambo, where a train will take you to Aguas Calientes for a chance to visit Machu Picchu.

Variations include a route from the hamlet of Quishuarani, to the south of Lares, which crosses Huillquijasa Pass (4200m) and visits a series of scenic lakes before joining the Weaver's Way just after Huacahuasi; the first day is slightly harder than the Weaver's Way but the beautiful landscapes are reward enough. Tougher treks include a trip from Quishuarani that follows the route described above but which branches south from the Weaver's Way before Ipsayjasa Pass to instead scale Huacahuasijasa Pass (4500m) and descend to Yanahuara. This trail in turn can be extended by starting in Huarán, a village in the Sacred Valley on the road between Calca and Urubamba, and trekking north via Pachacutec Pass (4200m) for a day to reach Quishuarani.

Huancacalle to Cachora via Choquequirao Trek
[8-9 days, see pp326-38]

This epic trek, which takes 8-9 days and can be done in either direction, sets off from Huancacalle, via the archeological sites at Vitcos and Ñusta España to cross the high pass at Choquetecarpo and descend into the valley beyond, where it passes through the remote, traditional hamlet of Yanama. Beyond here it climbs and descends steeply to cross the Abra San Juan and breach the valley of the Río Blanco before arriving at the partially reconstructed ruins at Pinchu Unuyoc. A further steep ascent leads to Choquequirao, perched high above the plunging Apurímac valley.

After a day exploring the site join the Choquequirao Trek trail as it plunges into and then rears out of the deep canyon to arrive eventually at Cachora. Tough and occasionally tricky to follow, this route is a real challenge. The rewards, though, are spectacular and you will spend much of the walk free from crowds. If tackled in reverse, finishing at Huancacalle, there is the opportunity to then push on to Espíritu Pampa following the route outlined in the

❑ **Other activities**
The Cusco region offers far more than simply trekking. Unless your schedule is tight, you should consider some of the other world-class activities, such as mountain-biking, white-water rafting, ballooning, sky-diving and trips to the rainforest, available on the city's doorstep. For more details see pp184-5.

Vilcabamba Trail description to complete a spectacular traverse that would probably take more than two weeks to complete. However, see box p32.

What to take

Walking in the Andes should not be taken lightly regardless of which trek you choose. An ill-fitting boot or a rucksack that won't adjust properly can cause discomfort and potentially spoil your trip. Try to travel light but strike a compromise between weight and what is really essential, making sure that you have sufficient appropriate clothing to be safe and comfortable. A lot of people make the mistake of overpacking. Given the quality and advances in modern gear, there's no reason to take enormous amounts of equipment or clothing with you. Don't forget that you can always pick up additional things in Peru.

Weight is a vital consideration on treks where you are responsible for carrying your own bags. On those trips where either porters or mules will be carrying most of your luggage, don't use this as an excuse to take unnecessary things just because someone else will be shouldering the load.

FOOTWEAR

Your top priority whilst trekking ought to be the condition of your feet. This will have the single biggest impact on your enjoyment of the trek and your ability to tackle some of the longer, more arduous stages.

Some people manage in a pair of stout trainers but these will not protect your ankles, are not waterproof and could result in you having bruised and sore feet after some of the more gruelling days spent crossing rocky or uneven terrain. Sections of the treks are rough and bumpy and you will definitely have to negotiate stretches of scree, scramble over loose boulders, cross wet, smooth rocks, wade through small streams and possibly trudge through patches of snow. Therefore you will need footwear that is supportive without being too restrictive or rigid, is waterproof, has sewn in tongues, and soles that can grip even in wet conditions. Ideally you should have a pair of sturdy **boots**. Get a pair that has a little room at the toe end to assist circulation and prevent your toes getting crushed or bruised in the course of prolonged periods of descent. Whatever you buy, make sure that your shoes are properly broken in well ahead of the start of your trek; otherwise you may end up with blisters.

Sandals or **flip flops** are a good idea to give your feet a bit of respite at the end of the day. They might also come in useful when crossing small streams.

Some people choose to wear **gaiters** on some of the tougher sections of track to help keep water, mud and other debris out of their boots. They will also stop your shins from getting scratched by the undergrowth.

Telescopic **walking poles** (particularly those containing shock-absorbing springs) are also a good idea, particularly for steep downhill sections, as they can give much-needed support to your knees; however, see p40. Whether you use one or two poles is down to personal preference.

CLOTHES

Since the treks described in this book take you across a range of landscapes and altitudes you will need to carry clothes that are appropriate for a range of temperatures and conditions. Adopt the simple but effective technique of **layering**. The base layer should keep the skin comfortable and dry. The second, insulation layer should trap and retain body heat in order to provide extra warmth, whilst the outer layer must protect you against the wind, rain, snow and even sun.

It is vital that the **base layer** dries easily and helps to conduct sweat away from the body. T-shirts made of synthetic materials do the best job of 'wicking' moisture away from the skin. Wool, silk or cotton are less useful for this layer.

Fleece is the most desirable material for the **insulation layer** since it is light, wind-resistant and quick drying. Wool is also a good insulator but dries very slowly and can become very heavy when wet. Try to ensure that, since you'll be bending and stretching as you work your way across uneven terrain, your lower back is adequately covered.

Your legs need to have as much freedom of movement as possible. Shorts offer the most flexibility. Lightweight, tough trousers are also essential and ideally should be made of rip-stop fabric. In general avoid thick, heavy trousers, especially denim jeans as they restrict movement and can be very difficult to get dry.

The Andes get a lot of rainfall so good **waterproofs** are essential, even in summer. The weather can be highly unpredictable in the mountains and rain can occur pretty much year-round. Modern raincoats made from lightweight, waterproof, highly breathable fabric allow water vapour to pass through the jacket from the inside to the outside but stop water from leaking in. In this way condensation is prevented from forming on the inside of the coat, which would quickly drain away body heat. The arms of the jacket should be long enough to fit over warm under-layers and the coat should have a long-enough tail that your lower back

---

❏ **Old clothes required**
If you have a little spare room in your luggage and can squeeze in some old or unwanted clothes, there are various agencies in Cusco that will accept donations and distribute the clothes to porters or local villages. A good place to start is the office of Andean Travel Web (see box p23), which makes collections and regularly hands out clothes, school equipment and Christmas presents to small communities in the region.

isn't exposed when bending or stretching forward. The coat also ought to have a roomy hood that can be drawn tight but that still provides you with peripheral vision. A variety of pockets in which to store maps, snacks, etc is also useful.

A **hat** provides vital protection against the elements. A wide-brimmed version is a good idea to shield your eyes from the harsh mountain sun. A woolly hat can be useful for keeping your head warm in the evenings or when the temperature drops. Take a pair of **gloves** to keep your hands warm and your fingers flexible at higher altitudes or in less-than-perfect conditions.

EQUIPMENT

Rucksack

If you'll be carrying your own rucksack make sure it fits comfortably; this is vital when choosing a rucksack for a multi-day trek. Get an experienced shop-assistant to fit you with the right-sized pack before buying one. The **hip belt** ought to support about a third of the weight of the pack, with the rest being carried on your shoulders. Make sure that the **straps** are adjustable so that you can alter them to suit the terrain: when climbing it is better to take the weight on your shoulders, whilst when descending it is often more comfortable to release the shoulder straps slightly and tighten the hip belt.

Try not to buy a pack that is too large, otherwise the temptation is to try and fill it. The pack should have easily accessible **compartments** for the items you want most often, such as water bottles, guidebook, maps and snacks. Straps and buckles on the outside of the pack can also be useful for securing trekking poles or other bits of temporarily unnecessary kit. All materials should be robust and long lasting. Stitching on the pack must be high quality and any zips should be resilient and smooth running.

In very heavy rain even the most waterproof of packs can leak. As a precaution you should use a **heavy-duty waterproof inner liner** to protect your gear and a pack cover to sluice off the majority of the rain. For further protection put your things into plastic shopping bags or waterproof 'stuff sacks', which ought to guarantee that everything stays dry.

Sleeping bags and mats

A **sleeping bag** is essential since you will be camping on the trek. Some agencies will hire out or provide sleeping bags as part of the package that they offer. However, if you prefer to use your own bag, a lightweight, compact sleeping bag offering three-season comfort in temperatures of -5°C ought to be sufficient unless you are particularly susceptible to the cold in which case a four-season bag may be more appropriate.

Equally useful and certainly worth taking is a **sheet sleeping-bag** – essentially a sheet folded and sewn along two sides – to use as an inner liner for your main bag, since they offer an extra layer of warmth, are easy to wash and keep the inside of the main sleeping bag cleaner. **Sleeping mats** are also a good idea and can immeasurably improve sleep quality by cushioning you and insulating you from the cold ground. Old-fashioned foam mats are OK but you are better off with a modern, self-inflating Therm-a-rest. These can puncture so take a repair kit with you, too.

Tent

All agencies are obliged to provide tents for the treks you undertake with them. These ought to be of serviceable quality and completely sufficient for your trip. If you are considering trekking independently, make sure you have a light-weight, robust tent that packs up compactly. You need to seal the seams to stop rain getting in. If you decide to travel independently once in Peru, it is possible to hire tents from a number of agencies and equipment stores in Cusco.

Stoves, pans and crockery

On an organized trek the agency is also obliged to provide all the **cooking equipment** and enough crockery and cutlery for the entire group. However, should you want to trek independently, you will need to take your own. Butane **gas stoves** such as the Campingaz ones with the small blue cylinders are per-fectly adequate although you may want to buy cylinders containing a butane-propane mix that will work more effectively at altitude. These are readily available in Cusco. Take light aluminium **pans** that can be stored one inside the other. Plates aren't necessary as long as you don't mind eating from the pan. Do take **cups** and **cutlery** though, as well as some sort of **wire scrubber** to clean the dirty dishes. All of this can be bought or hired in Cusco.

FOOD

Dehydrated or vacuum-packed food is a useful quick energy source or a treat along the trail. There's no need to bring much from home as there are lots of opportunities to buy food in Cusco. Agencies will provide all the main meals for organized treks and probably produce fruit and sweets at opportune moments as well. If you are setting out alone, take food that doesn't weigh too much but which delivers large amounts of carbohydrate. Potato, *quinoa* (an Andean grain) and polenta are all good sources, as are pasta and dried noodles. Dried sausage or tinned meat is also useful. Herbs and spices as well as salt and pepper can help add flavour to otherwise uninspiring suppers. Soups or porridge are great for getting additional hot food and liquid into your body whilst nuts, chocolate and boiled sweets are a good way of raising your spirits, getting a quick boost or winning friends.

TOILETRIES

Take only those toiletries you think you'll actually need. You should aim to be well equipped but take the smallest bottles possible. That said, before you set out on the trek make sure you get everything you might need. Whilst Cusco has several chemists, you are unlikely to find one in the smaller towns at the trail-heads for each trek; certainly won't come across any once the trek has begun.

A checklist should include: **a bar of soap** (keep it in a bag or container; liq-uid soap for washing clothes); **towel** (most outdoor shops now sell low-bulk, highly absorbent microfibre towels); **toothbrush** and **toothpaste** (take only as much toothpaste as you'll need – buy a small tube or take a part-used one to save space and weight); **toilet paper**; **pre-moistened tissues** (for example 'Wet-Wipes'; useful in a number of situations); **earplugs** (may help if sharing a campsite with a crowd of snorers); **lip balm** (essential on higher sections of the trek where the track is exposed to full sun); **tampons**; **contraceptives**.

MEDICAL KIT

Your medical kit should cover most eventualities though hopefully you won't have to use any of it. However, most people find they need to dip into their supplies sooner or later to sort out everyday ailments, such as blisters, caused by trekking. Perhaps most importantly, do not forget to take an adequate supply of any **prescription drugs** that you might need.

A basic medical kit should comprise **hydrocolloid blister pads** and **zinc oxide tape** with a strong adhesive for securing dressings or bandages. **Plasters** are good for covering and protecting minor cuts and injuries. **Sterilized gauze** is useful should you need to soak up blood or pus from a cut or graze. It is also useful in keeping a cut clean and free from infection. **Antiseptic cream** or spray will prevent minor infections from developing.

Anti-inflammatory painkillers such as Paracetamol are helpful in easing the discomfort of bruises or sprains. **Hydrocortisone cream** is a good aid if you suffer from heat rash. **Deep heat spray** will ease minor sprains and help to loosen or warm-up sore muscles. **Hypodermic needles** are essential tools for piercing blisters; use a sterilized needle to dig out a splinter that doesn't have a head/end proud of the skin for a tweezer to grip; **tweezers**, though, can be helpful for less-delicate work. A pair of small, sharp **scissors** is also a good idea. **Bandages** may be needed to cover more substantial wounds or to support damaged joints. An **elasticated knee support** is helpful for weak knees and useful on the long pounding descents.

High-factor **sun-cream** is vital, as the sun at altitude can be very harmful. **Aloe vera** is also useful in the wake of sunburn and to ease the discomfort of windburn, rashes or grazes. Although not strictly necessary, you may wish to take **multivitamin tablets** to supplement your diet in the course of the trek.

MISCELLANEOUS ITEMS

As well as the essential items you may also want to bring a few other bits and pieces. A **watch** is very useful for gauging how far and fast you have travelled as well as keeping track of time. **Sunglasses** help to cut out the sun's glare and will protect you from reflected light.

A **penknife** with all its various blades and tools is invaluable as is a **water bottle/pouch**, preferably with two-litre capacity. The modern Platypus or Camelbak system, whereby a pouch is connected to a tube so you can drink while you walk, is a good idea as it encourages you to drink more. **Water-purifying tablets** or iodine drops are useful if you haven't time to boil the water before drinking it.

PLANNING YOUR TRIP

A reliable, compact waterproof **torch/flashlight** is a good idea, as are extra **batteries** for it. A **head torch** is even better as it means that your hands are still free. **Matches** and/or a **lighter** are necessary to ignite cooking gear. A **whistle** may prove to be a vital survival aid should you get lost or injured and need to attract attention. **String** has several uses – to fasten things to the outside of your pack, for example, or to act as an impromptu washing line.

A **compass** or **GPS unit** (see pp216-17) may be useful if you're trekking independently and could become essential in bad weather as the tracks are poorly defined in places. Note that **walking poles** (see also p36) are acceptable only if the tip is covered by a rubber bung so that the environment isn't damaged.

Finally, you must remember to take degradable **rubbish bags** since it is important that you pack any rubbish out of the mountains and get rid of it responsibly in a town.

PHOTOGRAPHIC EQUIPMENT

Mountains and landscapes are notoriously difficult to photograph well. The results often don't capture the scale or grandeur of the Andes and the powerful sweep and subtle colours of the hillsides quite often don't translate well to prints.

Good-quality, **compact digital cameras** are light, tough and take adequate photographs. **SLR** or **digital SLR** cameras and a couple of lenses offer more scope for creativity and increase your chance of capturing the delicate light and effects found in the mountains. Don't forget your **battery charger** but also **spare batteries**. A **zoom lens** will afford you a greater degree of compositional flexibility without adding too much weight to your bag. A **lens hood** will reduce the glare from the sun, whilst a **UV filter** will cut through the high-altitude haze. A **polarizer** will also cut through the haze and deepen the blue of the sky as well as adding colour and depth to lakes and coasts. For self-timer or longer exposure shots a small, lightweight, sturdy **tripod** is a good idea and a remote **shutter-release cable** is a good investment too.

A **carrying case** that can be attached to your belt or waist strap is useful since it means that your equipment will be readily accessible yet still be well protected. If you have to stop, drop your pack and rummage about for your camera you may be less inclined to use it. Make sure your camera bag is waterproof since there is quite a high likelihood that you'll get rained on.

MAPS

Good-quality, trekking-scale maps of Peru are not all that easy to come by. The **IGN (Instituto Geográfico Nacional)** in Lima produces a series of 1:100,000 scale topographic maps of the country that have contours at 50m intervals as well as spot heights. The legend includes all standard information such as settlements and roads plus a great deal of terrain and vegetation detail. These are also available from South American Explorers (see box p137), which also produces a 1:25,000 scale map of the Inca Trail showing contours, spot heights and places of particular interest along the route. Some specialized map shops outside Peru also sell both IGN and South American Explorer maps.

Stanfords in the UK sells both through its shops (12-14 Long Acre, London WC2E, and 29 Corn St, Bristol BS1) and online at 🖳 www.stanfords.co.uk.

The IGN maps you need for the classic Inca Trail are 2444 (27-r) and 2344 (27-q). For the Vilcabamba Trail you will also need the north-western section of 2344 (27-q) as well as 2244 (27-p) and 2245 (26-p). For the trek to and from Choquequirao search out maps 2343 (28-q) and 2344 (27-q). Be aware that old editions of 27-q do not show Mollepata, the start point for both the Salkantay and Santa Teresa treks; the hamlet is featured on the newer version of the map.

For the longer treks linking several sites, you will need to track down additional maps. For the route from Cachora to Machu Picchu via Choquequirao you'll need maps 2343 (28-q) and 2344 (27-q), whilst to get from Cachora to Espíritu Pampa via Choquequirao or in reverse from Vilcabamba to Choquequirao and then on to Cachora, you will need Nos 2343 (28-q), 2344 (27-q), 2244 (27-p) and 2245 (26-p). There is also a more general 1:200,000 scale map available of the region to the north of Cusco. Although this scale is inadequate for trekking, it does help to put the area into context.

ITMB Publishing (🖳 www.itmb.ca) also produces a detailed road map of *Cusco and South Peru*, updated in 2009. As well as the main map featuring neighbouring towns such as Pisac, Calca and Urubamba, there is a detailed town plan of Cusco at 1:11,000 scale and an inset of the Inca Trail at 1:50,000 scale, in addition to an annotated plan of the ruins at Machu Picchu.

Cusco **town plans** are also available from Editorial Lima 2000, whilst ITMB produces a decent street map of Lima.

RECOMMENDED READING

For a good introduction to Peru's history and culture, see *The Peru Reader: History, Culture, Politics* (Duke University Press). It's a fascinating anthology covering a wide range of subjects.

Guidebooks

Each of the major travel publishers has a guidebook to Peru. The best of these are the *Footprint Guide to Peru* and the *Rough Guide to Peru*. Lonely Planet also produce a very comprehensive *Peru* guide and a briefer guide, *Discover Peru*, which details the highlights in the country for people travelling on an organized tour or who have less time available. Their *Trekking in the Central Andes* highlights selected treks in Peru, Bolivia and Ecuador. Bradt Travel Guides also produce a comprehensive overview of the country, *Peru Highlights*, which contains itinerary suggestions along with all the country's essential must-see sites. Charles Brod's *Apus and Incas* (Inca Expeditions) guide to trekking in the Cusco region is available in Cusco, where you can also find Peter Frost's *Exploring Cusco*.

For a phrasebook Lonely Planet's *Quechua Phrasebook* is recommended.

Expedition reports and travelogues

Lost City of the Incas by Hiram Bingham (Phoenix) is a reprint of the classic account of the rediscovery of Machu Picchu. It's a rip-roaring adventure story, although bear in mind that many of his theories about the site have not stood the test of time (see p343).

For more on Hiram Bingham, his rediscovery of the site and the controversy surrounding the artefacts shipped home, see Chris Heaney's *Cradle of Gold: The Story of Hiram Bingham, A Real Life Indiana Jones, and his Search for Machu Picchu* (Palgrave MacMillan).

Earlier trip reports and accounts of expeditions include *Peregrinations of a Pariah* by Flora Tristan and *Peru, Travel and Exploration in the Land of the Incas* by E George Squier (Macmillan).

Hugh Thomson's *The White Rock: An Exploration of the Inca Heartland* is a fascinating account of a modern explorer and archaeologist at work as the author and colleague Gary Ziegler search for and rediscover the Inca site at Coca Cota in the Vilcabamba region. There's good information on the Incas in general and on past explorers, whilst his book *Cochineal Red* (both published by Phoenix) is a thorough investigation of earlier civilizations, in which Thomson investigates the Moche, Chavin, Nasca and other ancient civilizations of Peru and contains an interesting description of the recent archaeological work at the Inca site of Llactapata, near Machu Picchu. This book is also available as *A Sacred Landscape: The Search for Ancient Peru* (Overlook).

Classic travelogues include those by Ronald Wright, *Cut Stones and Crossroads* (currently out of print), Christopher Isherwood, *The Condor and the Cows* (Vintage Classics) and Matthew Parris, *Inca Kola* (Weidenfeld and Nicholson).

Three Letters from the Andes by Patrick Leigh Fermor (John Murray) is an enthralling, typically lyrical account of the author's trip to Machu Picchu that perfectly captures the landscape and people he encounters.

Eight Feet in the Andes: Travels with a Mule in Unknown Peru (John Murray), describing a journey made in 1983, is Dervla Murphy at her best.

The Incas

There are countless books on the Incas, with titles aimed at everyone from children to academics.

The definitive text is John Hemming's *The Conquest of the Incas* (Macmillan), which ranks as one of the great pieces of historical writing. Hemming's book *Monuments of the Incas*, featuring stunning black and white photography by Edward Ranney, was updated in 2010 and reissued by Thames and Hudson.

The Last Days of the Incas (Simon & Schuster), by filmmaker and journalist Kim MacQuarrie, reads like a riveting novel and covers not only the Conquest but also the exploits of more modern adventurers rediscovering Machu Picchu and Vilcabamba.

Although the Incas had no form of writing there are some fascinating near-contemporary Spanish accounts. The most thorough is by Pedro de Cieza de Léon, a soldier who arrived in Peru in 1548 and recorded the Conquest in *The Discovery and Conquest of Peru* (Duke University Press). Garcilaso Inca de la Vega, the son of an Inca princess and a Spanish conquistador, wrote *The Royal*

Commentaries of the Inca (Andean World), originally published in 1609. It's most interesting for its description of Inca customs and culture, and of Peruvian flora and fauna. The version readily available in Peru is illustrated with some of the naïve drawings by Felipe Huamán Poma de Ayala originally published in his *Nueve Crónica y Buen Gobierno*.

Michael Moseley's illustrated archaeological survey, *The Incas and their Ancestors* (Thames and Hudson) is excellent.

Maria Rostworowski de Diez Canseco's *History of the Inca Realm* provides a Peruvian perspective on the Incas that is scholarly yet accessible.

Art in the Andes, from Chavin to Inca (Thames and Hudson) by Rebecca Stone-Miller is authoritative and well illustrated.

Machu Picchu and other Inca sites

Machu Picchu by John Hemming (Readers' Digest Wonders of Man Series) is a fine book on **Machu Picchu** and its position in Peru's history.

The Machu Picchu Guidebook by Ruth Wright and Alfredo Zegarra (Johnson Books) is a good contemporary guide to the site and its features.

Machu Picchu, Unveiling the Mystery of the Incas (Yale), edited by Yale archaeologists Richard Burger and Lucy Salazar, was published to coincide

PLANNING YOUR TRIP

❑ SOURCES OF FURTHER INFORMATION

Peru

A great place to start is perusing the comprehensive visitor information listed on **Andean Travel Web** (🖳 www.andeantravelweb.com/peru), which focuses on Cusco but also provides good-quality information on Lima, Arequipa, Hauraz, Trujillo, Lake Titicaca, Paracas and the Amazon.

Otherwise, **for general information**, try: 🖳 www.peru.info, the website of the official government tourism agency; or 🖳 www.perulinks.com which has thousands of links on a multitude of topics; 🖳 www.travel-library.com/south_america/peru has exhaustive listings and links for Peru; 🖳 www.yourperuguide.com is also worth looking at, as are 🖳 www.peru.travel/en/ and 🖳 visitperu.com.

Do bear in mind that many 'official' sites are nothing of the sort, just agencies looking to advertise treks and tours.
● 🖳 **www.traficoperu.com** Detailed information on topics as diverse as flights, accommodation, places to eat and car hire
● 🖳 **www.saexplorers.org** South American Explorers' website (see box p137)
● 🖳 **www.livinginperu.com** Expat guide to local news and events.

Cusco

🖳 www.cuscoperu.com is a listings site for Cusco with recommendations and links in English; 🖳 www.cuscoonline.com is also worth a look.

Machu Picchu and the Inca Trail

For information on Machu Picchu and the Inca Trail try the Andean Travel Web site (see above); South American Explorers' website (see box p137); 🖳 projects.exeter .ac.uk/RDavies/inca/ also has details and many links. Otherwise the personal sites of Hugh Thomson (🖳 www.thewhiterock.co.uk) and Gene Savoy (🖳 www.genesavoy .org) are worth a look.

with the Machu Picchu exhibition at the Museum of Natural History at Yale University. Apart from the excellent photographs and the catalogue of 120 objects from the site, the book is also interesting in that it includes Hiram Bingham's original 1913 report of the rediscovery and a scholarly modern overview of Machu Picchu and its significance.

Johan Reinhard refines the theory of Machu Picchu as a cosmological, hydrological and sacred geographical centre in the fourth edition of *Machu Picchu, Exploring an Ancient Sacred Center* (Nuevas Imágenas).

The Machu Picchu Historical Sanctuary by Jim Bartle and Peter Frost (Nuevas Imágenas) is an attractive illustrated look at the region.

Realm of the Incas by Max Milligan (Idlewild) includes a more sumptuous selection of photographs covering far more than just Machu Picchu.

Stone Offerings, Machu Picchu's Terraces of Enlightenment (Lightpoint Press) is an award-winning photographic book by architectural photographer Mike Torrey. The beautiful photos were taken over a few days during the summer and winter solstices. Though quite expensive it would make a perfect souvenir.

In comparison with Machu Picchu, however, there is precious little written about **Vilcabamba**. Vincent Lee's *Forgotten Vilcabamba – Final Stronghold of the Incas* (Sixpac Manco Publications) is by far the most comprehensive book on the site and its history and also contains a number of detailed diagrams of the ruins. Lee also produced an earlier guide, *Sixpac Manco – Travels amongst the Incas*, which contains some of the same information. Gene Savoy described his explorations of the region in *Antisuyu* (Simon and Schuster). John Hemming dedicated a number of chapters in *The Conquest of the Incas* to Vilcabamba and Hugh Thomson also provides good historical information and descriptions of the ruins in *The White Rock*.

Field guides

There aren't many readily available, good-quality, compact field guides for Peru's flora or fauna.

If you don't mind carrying fairly bulky books, John Dunning's *South American Birds*, the comprehensive *Birds of the High Andes* by Jon Fjeldsa and Niels Krabbe, or the *Field Guide to the Birds of Peru* by James Clements and Noam Shany are worth tracking down.

Most useful, though, is the *Field Guide to the Birds of Machu Picchu* by the ornithologist and Cusco resident Barry Walker. Although it's tricky to come by, you should be able to find a copy at the airports in Lima or Cusco, or in bookshops in Cusco.

If you're after more than just birds, *The Travellers' Wildlife Guide to Peru* by David Pearson and Les Beletsky contains superb illustrations of more than 500 of Peru's most common insects, amphibians, reptiles, birds and mammals.

The *Bradt Guide to Peruvian Wildlife*, by Gerard Cheshire, Barry Walker and Huw Lloyd, covers fauna found in the High Andes and focuses on Cusco and the Sacred Valley. There's also a good section on orchids and birds in Peter Frost's and Jim Bartle's *Machu Picchu Historical Sanctuary*, to which Barry Walker has also contributed.

Other books
The Heights of Machu Picchu is Chilean poet Pablo Neruda's epic, inspired by the ruins. It's been called the single most-important piece of South American poetry, with comparisons to TS Eliot's *The Waste Land*.

The Royal Hunt of the Sun is Peter Shaffer's gripping play about the fall of the last Inca, Atahualpa. *To the Last City* (Chatto and Windus) by Colin Thubron is a fictional account of a journey to Vilcabamba that perfectly captures the atmosphere of the place and the trek.

For children, try *The Angry Aztecs and the Incredible Incas* by Terry Deary, in the Horrible Histories series, which has history mixed in with thrilling tales.

Health precautions, inoculations and insurance

Any form of outdoor physical activity carries with it the possibility of accidents and trekking in the Andes is no exception. However, there are certain golden rules to follow on the trail that will help to minimize the risk of accidents or getting lost. To avoid unpleasant or unwanted surprises, always plan each day's walk carefully, study a map and familiarize yourself with the route, the type of terrain to be covered and the length of time you expect to be trekking. There are also a few pre-trek preparations that you can take to further ensure that your walk is trouble-free, as described below.

FITNESS

Whilst a reasonable level of fitness is a good idea, there's no need to go overboard on training for trekking the Inca Trail. You will, however, enjoy the treks a lot more if you are fitter.

Pre-departure fitness preparation
If you lead a largely sedentary existence it is wise to do some pre-departure exercise before trekking. Any type of exercise is better than none at all just to confirm that you can walk for more than a couple of hours at a time, and for more than one day.

The most efficient way to get fit for the trek is to walk up and down hills, preferably carrying at least a partially loaded pack. Climbing a staircase repeatedly will have a similar effect. Jogging helps to build up stamina and endurance. By at least walking regularly your body is becoming attuned to the rhythms and rigours of life on the trail.

The longer treks, from Vilcabamba to Choquequirao, or Choquequirao to Machu Picchu, also require a certain mental resilience as well as physical fitness. Embarking on a trek lasting eight or nine days is a very different proposition to one lasting four or five days. If you have significant doubts about your ability to complete the trek think carefully before committing to it, since there are no opportunities to bail out along the route once you have begun.

HEALTH

Hopefully the worst complaint you'll have to endure is **sunburn**. The high Andean slopes are exposed and, as a result of the thin atmosphere and the reflection of sun off snow, ice or water, you will find that you burn very easily, even on an apparently overcast day. Wear a hat and use high-factor sun-cream to avoid getting burnt. Sun can do just as much damage to your eyes so protect them by wearing sunglasses.

The cold can be just as hazardous when trekking. The weather in the mountains is highly changeable and you should be prepared for sudden drops in temperature. Cold, wet and windy conditions can sometimes be the cause of **hypothermia**. General awareness, being properly equipped and the ability to react to the symptoms promptly should prevent a serious incident.

Blisters are the bane of trekkers and their most common complaint. Friction between the boot and the foot causes a protective layer of liquid to develop beneath the skin. This can take four or five days to heal properly. As with so many things, prevention is far better than cure.

By taking the necessary precautions in advance you ought to be able to avoid blisters altogether. Firstly, make sure that you break in all footwear well in advance of the trek. Wear proper walking socks. Never trek with wet feet as this is a sure-fire way of getting blisters. If your boots get soaked wear plastic bags over dry socks in order to prevent them from becoming wet too. Change into dry socks when you take a break on the trail. Most importantly, never ignore the feeling that your boots may be rubbing; cover the sore area with zinc-oxide tape, a plaster or a specialized blister pad. This will act as an additional layer of skin and should stop the chafing. Vaseline, or at a push lip salve, when rubbed onto a sore toe or heel, can also stop abrasion and delay the onset of a blister.

There are minor adjustments that you can make to your boots depending on the terrain that will help to stave off blisters. Whilst going uphill tighten the upper section of your boot and loosen the laces slightly across the foot. Conversely, when descending, loosen the upper part a little and tighten the laces across the foot.

Should you develop blisters use a clean hypodermic needle to burst them. Allow the blister to dry out and then apply antiseptic cream and a dressing to keep it covered and free from infection.

Inoculations

Before travelling to Peru make sure you have had the following inoculations: **tetanus**, **polio**, **diphtheria**, **tuberculosis**, **hepatitis A** and **typhoid**. If it was a while since your original shot check whether you require a booster. If you are going to the jungle (below 2000m) or intend to tackle either the Vilcabamba, Choquequirao or one of the routes linking either Choquequirao to Vilcabamba or Machu Picchu you should also take a course of anti-**malaria** tablets and consider having a **yellow fever** jab. Some doctors will also suggest you have a **rabies** inoculation if you are intending to tackle one of the longer treks as you may be several days' walk from the nearest transport or the closest hospital.

However, the inoculation won't actually stop you getting the disease, it'll simply buy you more time to get to a hospital.

For a full list of the requirements or recommended jabs look at the US Center for Disease Control and Prevention website (⌨ www.cdc.gov), ask a doctor or visit a travel clinic.

In the UK you can get the latest advice and vaccinations from: Nomad Travellers Store & Medical Centre (clinics in London, Bristol, Manchester, Southampton, Loughton and Bishops Stortford; see ⌨ www.nomadtravel.co.uk for address details) or from Trailfinders (⌨ www.trailfinders.com/services, 194 Kensington High St, London) and Masta (⌨ www.masta-travel-health.com), which has clinics in some Boots stores as well as other places around the country. Travel clinics will, of course, charge for any inoculations they give.

HIGH-ALTITUDE TRAVEL

One of the most common complaints on the various treks described here is **Altitude Sickness** (AMS). Cusco stands at 3360m/11,000ft above sea level and the highest pass described on one of the routes is 5000m/16,400ft. At these altitudes the air pressure is substantially lower than at sea level, having dropped by about one tenth for every 1000m/3300ft of altitude gained. Altitude sickness is caused by the body's inability to get enough oxygen at higher elevations. Since all your vital organs need oxygen to function, this can be a serious condition and, if ignored or left untreated, it can be fatal. However, it is also very common (some of the top hotels in Cusco even have supplementary oxygen in the rooms) and entirely preventable. For a full rundown on the causes, symptoms and treatments of altitude sickness read the section on p120 carefully.

Before you go, if you suffer from heart or lung problems, high blood pressure or are pregnant, you must visit your doctor to get advice on the wisdom of trekking through the Andes.

Acclimatization
The safest way to avoid any problems with altitude is to acclimatize properly (see p120). The worst thing that you can do is fly in from Lima, which is at sea level, try to start a trek the following day and expect your body to be able to cope with the change in altitude. At the very least take a couple of days out to relax in Cusco and allow your body to adjust to the higher elevation. Within a couple of days you'll find moving about much easier and after two weeks you'll barely notice the altitude at this level at all.

INSURANCE

Before setting off make sure you have travel insurance, or are covered by your domestic policies. When choosing travel insurance make sure the policy covers you for trekking the trails described in this book. Most policies will but some might not, so read the small print carefully. For complete peace of mind, take out insurance tailored for trekkers or mountaineers. The British Mountaineering Council (☎ 0161 445 6111, ⌨ www.thebmc.co.uk) offers this for its members.

2

PERU

Facts about the country

Peru! There it was: vast, mysterious, grey-green, dirt poor, infinite, wealthy, ancient, reticent.   **Mario Vargas Llosa**

There are few countries on earth that can rival Peru for diversity. The stories and legends associated with it have fired people's imaginations for centuries, luring visitors to its shores since the Spanish came looking for treasure in the 16th century. Frequently portrayed as the land of unimaginable riches, the bloodiest conquest, the most heart-wrenching ballads and the most merciless revolutionaries, this country of superlatives also boasts the second-highest mountain range in the world, some of the driest deserts, part of the world's largest jungle and endless empty beaches within its borders. Despite these rugged, inhospitable extremes, Peru also ranks as one of the great centres of ancient civilization; the Incas are just one in a long line of highly developed cultures to have evolved and thrived here.

The country has had a chequered recent past coloured by a brutal ruling regime and terrorism. However, it has emerged from these troubled times and is now battling to entrench democracy and to achieve economic progress and growth. The signs are currently positive and although the country is still finding its feet as a modern nation (unemployment remains rife and the lack of real opportunities is a major concern), as confidence in the country grows, so the likelihood of stability becomes more real.

Despite apparent advances and a willingness to embrace the influences of a wider world, the country remains firmly rooted in its indigenous traditions and celebrates its ethnic origins and sense of self. Peruvians are rightly proud of their heritage and the cultural riches their country has to offer.

GEOGRAPHICAL BACKGROUND

Peru is the third-largest country in South America. Covering an area of 1,285,000 square kilometres, it is approximately eight times smaller than the USA but five times the size of the UK.

Geographical regions

Uniquely in South America, there are three distinct geographical regions: *costa* (coast), *sierra* (highlands) and *selva* (jungle).

South America started life conjoined with other continents before splitting away. Mountains were forced up by the collision of two tectonic plates, with the fault line where the two plates pushed together lying offshore and running parallel with the coast. This fault line is the cause of Peru's frequent earthquakes. The formation of the Andes, the longest continuous mountain chain in the world, produced a temperate climate at higher altitudes, whilst the lowlands became dominated by tropical and semi-tropical conditions. The mountains are studded with volcanoes, many of which are extinct but a few occasionally still grumble to themselves.

In cross section, from east to west, the southern Andes have a distinctive profile. In effect, following the coastal desert there are two parallel mountain ranges separated by a high-altitude plain or steppe, which give way to the jungle.

Coast Peru's coast, all 1500 miles of it, is dry, barren and at the mercy of the **Humboldt (or Peru) Current** and the unique conditions that creates. This current is an ocean stream that flows in the direction of the Equator and can extend up to 1000 kilometres offshore. The nutrient-rich water supports an extraordinary abundance of marine life, even though it is very cold. In fact, the water is sufficiently cold to generate a mass of chill air above it. This cold coastal air blocks the warm moist winds blowing in from the Pacific, ensuring that hardly any rain falls on the coast, although clouds and fog are produced. This gloomy **mist,** which lies heavily over Lima for some of the year, is known as *garúa*. The current is largely responsible for the aridity that prevails along Peru's coast and for creating a long thin strip of desert, the Atacama, behind the barrier, which now stretches from Peru into Chile and extends 12-60 miles (20-100km) inland.

Highlands The *sierra*, Peru's central highland regions, which are synonymous with the country, are dominated by the **Cordillera de los Andes**. The Andes, which are the backbone of Peru, form a region called La Sierra. The word comes from the Latin *serra* and literally means 'saw'. There are several branches of the Andes in Peru, including the **Cordillera Blanca** (White Range) that fronts the Amazon, the **Cordillera Negra** (Black Range) that fronts the coast and the smaller but no less dramatic **Cordillera Huayhuash**. Some of the world's highest peaks, including Huascarán (6768m/22,199ft) and Yerupája (6634m/21,760ft) can be found amongst these ranges. The mountain slopes to the east have been heavily eroded by water, which has left them jagged and precipitous with sharp ridges rising between steep valleys. The slopes to the west have suffered comparatively little owing to the scarcity of water so are more even and rolling. Further south the ranges extend into the ridges of Vilcabamba and Vilcanota, which include Mt Salkantay (6271m/20,569ft).

Characteristics of this rugged region include steep, deep valleys and high plateaus known as the *altiplano steppe*, or **alpine zone**. These enormous enclosed plains, trapped by the ranges to either side of them, are in turn distinguished by barren **grasslands**, *puna*, where coarse grasses clump together for survival in the cold air and poor soil. Almost half of Peru's population lives scattered across the sierra despite the brutally inhospitable terrain and thin, freezing air.

PERU

❏ El Niño

Peru is at the mercy of a weather condition known as El Niño. This is an important temperature fluctuation in the surface temperature of the Eastern Pacific Ocean, which can have profound effects on the west coast of South America. The name *El Niño*, from the Spanish for 'little boy', refers to Jesus because the phenomenon is usually noticed around Christmas. There is an opposite effect, called *La Niña*, meaning 'little girl'. The condition is very difficult to predict but historically has occurred at irregular intervals of two to seven years and has usually lasted one or two years.

Essentially, El Niño is a change in the weather that is caused by an alteration in the currents of the Pacific Ocean. A rise in air pressure over the Indian Ocean coupled with a fall in air pressure over the Eastern Pacific means that trade winds in the south Pacific head east. Warm air rises near Peru and warm water spreads from the west Pacific to the East Pacific taking rain with it. The cold Humboldt Current is replaced by El Niño's warm tropical waters, meaning that the damp sea winds are able to roll over the desert, causing torrential rain. An El Niño is most often associated with very wet summers (December to February) when heavy downpours result in serious flooding and can cause enormous devastation. Usually many people die or are made homeless as a result. Other parts of the world are also affected, with drier than usual conditions experienced in South-East Asia and northern Australia increasing bush fires, worsening haze and dramatically reducing air quality.

In addition to the climatic effects, El Niño reduces the upwelling of cold nutrient-rich ocean waters and diverts the Humboldt Current that supports so much of Peru's marine life. At this point, all the fish swim south to colder waters. The local fishing industry can therefore suffer terribly during a prolonged El Niño event.

Although the mechanics of the phenomenon are understood, no-one knows what triggers it, so it is very difficult to predict. Without any means of preparing for it, there is no way to counter the effects. During the last major event, 900 people died and an estimated US$90 billion damage was caused across the world. Worse has happened though and it has been suggested that a strong El Niño led to the demise of the great Moche and Tiahuanaco civilizations, and that the destruction of the fertile farm lands of the Chimú in a similar event led to them having to expand and conquer their neighbours.

Jungle *La selva* is the isolated rainforest region in the eastern part of Peru between the foothills of the Andes and the Amazon basin. Largely unexplored, it contains some of the finest, untouched **rainforest** in the world, including the Manu National Park, considered to be the world's most bio-diverse rainforest. The region where the forest begins on the foothills of the mountains is poetically described by locals as *Las cejas de la selva* or 'eyebrows of the jungle'. This subtropical region is where much of Peru's coffee is grown.

Climate

Temperatures on the **coast** fluctuate but it is almost always dry. During the summer months, from December to April, temperatures reach 25°C to 30°C. Winter is from May to November when typically the cooler temperatures reach 10°C. Winter is characterized by cloud, fog and what little rain that does ever fall, does so at this time. Temperatures in the **central highlands** are more consistent, rising to 20°C during the day and falling to below freezing during the night.

However, the quantity of rainfall varies, with most falling during the wet season from November to March. During these months the evenings tend to be warmer as a result of the cloud cover. June to September tends to be relatively dry. The **jungle** has similar wet and dry seasons to the sierra, being driest from April to October and wettest from November to March. It's hot and humid almost all year though. (For information on when to go see pp10-12).

HISTORICAL OUTLINE

With the Incas taking centre stage it's easy to forget that their time in Peru's long and complex history was relatively short. Their empire, the pinnacle of a series of other notable Pre-Colombian civilizations in South America, was little more than a century old before it was spectacularly brought down in the incredible clash of cultures with the Spanish *conquistadors* in 1532.

Peru – beginnings and the first cities in the Americas

Man first crossed the Bering Strait from Asia over 15,000 years ago and gradually moved south through the Americas. The first traces of human existence in Peru can be dated back to at least 9000BC and the first cultures emerged along the coast where food was abundant in the form of fish. Notable amongst these coastal peoples are the **Chinchorro** who appear to have been the first people in the world to practice mummification. Unlike for the Incas, Chinchorro mummification was for the masses; many have been found, with the earliest mummy radiocarbon-dated back to 5500BC.

These coastal groups gradually developed a farming culture, growing corn and cotton in the pastures of the valleys near the coast and domesticating the llama, alpaca and guinea pig. The settlements grew, in particular along the Supe River north of Lima, and by 3000BC a civilization known as the **Norte Chico** had emerged that was contemporary with the civilizations developing in Egypt and Mesopotamia. The earliest cities in the Americas were in Peru, including **Caral**, which was the capital of a group of 18 city-states. The ruins of Caral near Barranca can be visited and include six stepped pyramids, raised ceremonial platforms and amphitheatres, dated to around 2500BC. Evidence of cassava (yuca) and sweet potatoes show that there were links with the Amazon and that some kind of trade must have been going on from around this time.

One of the striking things about these early South American civilizations is how sophisticated they became without discovering things like pottery making. Currently the oldest ceramic sample was found in the valley of Viru, near Trujillo, and dated back to 1800BC.

The Chavín – Early Horizon period (1000-200BC)

Until the dating of the city of Caral (see above) to around 2500BC, archaeologists believed the site at **Chavín de Huantar**, in the Cordillera Blanca highlands northeast of Caral, to be the earliest example of an urban culture. Chavín culture arose here around 900BC and thrived for about 700 years. This was during what is known as the Early Horizon period, 'horizon' because it's the time when a number of artistic, architectural and religious styles from several different cultures appear to have come together. Shared artistic styles also suggest common belief systems. Metallurgy developed during this period: gold, silver and copper ornaments found near Chiclayo show Chavín-style motifs.

It's been suggested that there may have been some cultural contact between the Olmecs of Central America and the Chavín as both worshipped a fearsome fanged jaguar-man god – a stylized symbol that is a feature of Chavín art. The Chavín religious cult was widespread in Peru, eventually stretching two-thirds of the way along the coast and inland to the central highlands. The religion appears to have involved the use of psychotropic drugs, probably made from the San Pedro cactus, which is often shown in carvings. A shaman would take the drug to aid his transformation from human to animal.

The Chavín dominated Peruvian culture in this Early Horizon period yet since there do not appear to have been wars involving them it seems that this was achieved without force on their part. However, it's been suggested that the powerful **Sechín**, a contemporaneous culture centred on Casma, 380km north of Lima, may have ensured the spread of the cult having adopted it themselves.

Nazca and Moche – Early Intermediate period (200BC-600AD)
As the influence of the Chavín waned, in what is known as the Early Intermediate period (100-600AD) regional cultures began to dominate: in the north, the Moche, and in the south, the Nazca.

Paracas-Necropolis, named after the cemetery 260km south of Lima, was the first phase of Nazca culture and lasted from 300BC to 200AD. It's characterized by exquisite textiles of wool and cotton embroidered with hundreds of detailed figures, wrappings for some of the mummies found in this cemetery. The **Nazcas** are famous today for the Nazca Lines, giant patterns and pictures etched into the desert plain that can best be appreciated from the air. This has led to some far-fetched theories about their creation. Eric von Daniken in *Chariots of the Gods* suggested that they were laid out by alien visitors, as runways for their spacecraft. Maria Reiche, who made a life's work of their study, believed that this was an enormous observatory. More recent studies suggest that they may have been processional routes linking shrines and water sources. Nazca pottery, colourful and striking in design, is also significant.

In the north of Peru, the warlike **Moche** rose to power, creating an empire that extended along the coast from Piura to Casma and lasted from 100AD to 800AD. It's unlikely, however, that this 'empire' was anything more than a large group of autonomous states linked by a shared culture but you can clearly see how it paved the way for the Incas. Organizational skills involved in building monumental structures were honed in the creation of the massive Temple of the Sun at their capital near Trujillo.

Again, as with the late development of pottery in South America, it seems incredible that a culture could develop to this level without the invention of writing. For record keeping, though, it's likely that the Moche used *quipus* (see box p73): strings of coloured threads each with a number of knots as counters, as did the Incas. Moche culture was sophisticated and their fine colourful pottery features scenes from daily life: religious ceremonies, battles, hunting and fishing. There are pots with amazingly lifelike human faces as well as the wide range of the pornographic ceramics for which they've become known.

The demise of the Moche may have been the result of a prolonged drought and then flooding caused by an El Niño in the 6th century AD.

Huari-Tiahuanaco (600-1000AD)

As in the Early Horizon period with the association between the Chavín and their religious cult and the militaristic Sechín who helped spread it, there appears to have been a similar interaction between the cult practised at Tiahuanaco and the Huari (Wari) from around 600AD. However, the people of Tiahuanaco also sought to actively expand their empire so that by the end of the first millennium a large part of Peru was under the control of two cultures – the Huari and the Tiahuanaco.

The site at **Tiahuanaco**, by Lake Titicaca and now in Bolivia, was the capital of that civilization and amongst the impressive ruins you can still see the Gateway of the Sun, the monumental doorway carved with the Gateway God, Viracocha. Although this area had been inhabited since 1500BC it was not until after it had developed as a cultural and religious centre (300BC to 300AD) that it began to expand, creating an empire that eventually encompassed the northern third of Chile, part of western Bolivia and an area of Peru that included Arequipa.

The **Huari** (Wari) were originally based in the central highlands, with their capital near Ayacucho. They were powerful empire builders, dominating the coast and central highlands of Peru from south of Nazca and Cusco almost to the border with modern Ecuador. Their legacy for the Incas was in their urban and agricultural infrastructure: terraces for the efficient cultivation of mountain slopes, drains and canals to control water, and roads to link all parts of their empire. See also box p288.

Chimú and other regional cultures (1000-1450AD)

The repressive Huari were not popular and the unity imposed on much of the country by them began to disintegrate at the start of the second millennium. Regional states, including that of the **Chachapoyas** at Kuélap in the northern highlands), the **Chanca** north of Lima and the **Chimú** near Trujillo, began to replace them. The Chimú built Chan Chan; covering more than 20 sq km this is the world's largest adobe city and was the largest pre-Hispanic city in the Americas. The Chimú were conquered in 1450

Incas (1200-1542AD)   [see Inca History, pp90-102]

The **first eight Incas** (strictly speaking the term refers to the ruler though it has come to mean the people) cover the period from about 1200 to the early 15th century, a time when their power and influence was limited to the Cusco area. It was not until 1438 under **Pachacutec** (see p94) that the drive began to create an empire that was soon to become the largest in pre-Columbian America, stretching north as far as Colombia, south into Chile and Argentina and east into Bolivia.

PERU

The Spanish and the conquest of the Incas [also see pp99-101]

It's likely that the Spanish unknowingly unleashed an advance attack on the peoples of South America in the form of smallpox, which swept south across the continent from Colombia. Some, however, believe it may have been a local sand-fly disease. Whichever it was, it claimed the Inca emperor **Huayna Capac** in 1527 and it's estimated that by 1550 it had decimated between 50% and 75%

Pizarro and Almagro set sail.

FELIPE HUAMÁN POMA DE AYALA, FROM HIS *NUEVE CRÓNICA Y BUEN GOBIERNO* (c1600)

of the population. On his deathbed Huayna Capac further weakened his empire by dividing it between his sons, **Atahualpa** and **Huascar**, pitting them against each other in a civil war.

The Spanish advance on the Americas was rapid after the voyages of Columbus between 1492 and 1503 to the Bahamas, the Caribbean islands, Central America and Colombia. In 1502, **Francisco Pizarro** sailed from Spain with 2500 other colonists in 30 ships. By 1519 he had risen to become mayor and magistrate of Panama City. No doubt inspired by the rumours of gold and silver in the lands to the south he organized his own expedition with Diego de Almagro. He made some preliminary voyages between 1524 and 1528 before returning to Spain to organize funds for a full-scale expedition and to crave the indulgence of the Spanish crown.

Granted the title of Governor of Peru, Pizarro landed near Tumbes in northern Peru in 1532 and marched south with a force of 106 foot-soldiers and 62 horsemen. Having defeated his brother Huascar, Atahualpa was also in the north, at Cajamarca with his army of 80,000 men. That meeting which sealed the fate of the continent is described on p90. In the resulting **Battle of Cajamarca**, on 16 November 1532, Pizarro famously trapped Atahualpa and greedily held him ransom for enough gold and silver to fill three rooms. Even though the ransom was fulfilled Pizarro realized that he could not keep the Inca emperor alive and, after a mock trial, convicted him of treason and of killing his brother. He had him executed in July 1533. Peter Shaffer's play, *The Royal Hunt of the Sun*, is a moving recreation of these final events.

Pizarro nominated a puppet ruler, **Túpac Huallpa**, brother of Atahualpa and Huascar, and marched south to take Cusco. Túpac died on the march so Pizarro replaced him with another brother, **Manco Inca Yupanqui**, who had come from the capital to meet them. Cusco fell in 1534 and the following year Pizarro founded Lima. Manco Inca attempted to retake Cusco, laying siege to the city in 1536 before retreating into the jungle around Vilcabamba. (It was not until 1573 that the Incas were finally subdued).

Viceroyalty of Peru (1542-1826)

With Peru conquered and a handful of seditious conquistadors crushed in 1542, Spain sought to consolidate its hold on the country. In due course the

PERU

Viceroyalty of Peru, as the colony was known, became the most prized asset in Spain's South American empire. Lima, which had been founded in 1535, became increasingly important, with traders all along the coast using its port to send goods out of the country. Over the next 200 years the capital developed into the main political, social and commercial centre for all of the surrounding countries. By contrast, Cusco became a relative backwater.

The *encomienda* system of rule   The rulers of the new colony were the Spanish-born viceroys appointed by the Spanish crown. Immigrants from Spain were given most of the prestigious positions and power was contained by these individuals, who installed a feudal system of rule.

A theoretically fair system of rule, the *encomienda* system, was authorized by the Spanish crown. The premise was that the crown governed and owned everything. This meant that the conquistadors could extract tribute for the crown and personal services for themselves in exchange for converting indigenous people to Christianity. In return for the salvation of their souls, the Indians were forced to give up their bodies and work for the Spanish. In theory, the Spaniards could benefit from the labours of the Indians who lived on the land that they oversaw for the Spanish crown, but neither they nor the Indians could own the land, and the Indians were not to be treated as slaves. Nor could the Spaniards live on this land or pass it on to family or next of kin. Crown agents, *corregidors*, were appointed to supervise and enforce these rules.

Of course, in practice the system failed. The royal administrators found themselves in constant conflict with the *encomenderos*, who had no intention of fully emancipating the Indians or of treating them as equals. Fundamentally the colony was too far from the crown to be properly supervised. Greed inevitably surfaced and those Spaniards holding land were set on making as much money as they could, regardless of the conditions their labour force endured. As governor of Peru, Pizarro gave large groups of Indians to his allies and friends, effectively creating the basic colonial land tenure structure that the crown had set out to avoid. Much of Imperial Spain's wealth was subsequently built from the maltreatment of the descendants of the Incas.

Some of the stories which became known as *La Leyenda Negra* (the **Black Legend**) telling of the violence and brutality, meted out by the Conquistadors on their new colony and its inhabitants, were no doubt true but they do not tell the whole story. The Incas are often portrayed as a harmonious people who endured countless atrocities and abuse at the hands of the Spanish, but they were a warlike, vicious society themselves: if the shoe had been on the other foot, Atahualpa acknowledged that he would have had no qualms about brutally incarcerating the Spanish if he had captured them. Nonetheless, the atrocities endured after the Conquest need to be recounted and recorded as this period was full of terrible violence.

The most horrific incidents related to the giant silver mines at Potosí (now a bleak town in Bolivia), which were discovered in 1545. Forced off their land and conscripted into working in the mines, convoys of pressed Indian labour were driven from their homes to work themselves to death. Hundreds of thousands of

Indians died as a result whilst Spanish coffers were filled with the necessary cash to finance wars across Europe.

Spain loses control The Spanish empire struggled to fully assert itself over its colonies and the crown's laws were frequently flouted. Coupled with this, locally born Spaniards (*Creoles*) became resentful of the fact that they were not entitled to any of the perks or positions of power that the immigrant Spanish enjoyed in Peru. It wasn't until the transition from the Hapsburgs to the Bourbon kings at the start of the 18th century that the empire was able to re-establish control.

Dramatic changes were made to the way that Peru was governed. Control was centralized, laws preventing Creoles from taking up positions of power were tightened and the Jesuits were driven out entirely. Spain's South American territories were also divided up. The creation of Viceroyalties to the north, east and south of Peru meant that the area to be governed by the Viceroy of Peru was decreased so became more manageable. Trade regulations were also revamped and Lima lost its protected status as the country's main docks. Existing taxes were increased and additional levies implemented.

Uprisings in the 18th century These changes and the tightening of control inevitably resulted in resentment. Over the next hundred years a series of protests and rebellions on various scales broke out. In 1740 **Juan Santos Atahualpa** roused a group of forest Indians to revolt and successfully repelled attacks on his stronghold in the high jungle. He never succeeded in extending his power or gaining additional control though and died in 1756. A more important insurgence, drawing on the existing unrest, broke out in 1780. The *mestizo* José Gabriel Condorcanquí symbolically adopted the nickname **Túpac Amaru II**, and whipped up anti-Spanish feeling. Initially just a demonstration against the high charges and duties demanded as well as the harsh employment laws, his rebellion took on a more significant note when he imprisoned a corregidor, massacred a group of 600 Royalist soldiers and attempted to instigate Inca rule. The empire's response was rapid and brutal, with troops from Lima despatched to quell the uprising. Within a year, following a decisive battle at Checacupe, Túpac Amaru was taken into prison, tortured and put to death, although the uprising he inspired staggered on until 1783.

Although ultimately unsuccessful, Túpac Amaru II had demonstrated that there were deficiencies in Spanish rule and that a high level of popular unrest existed. Historians now consider his rebellion an important precursor to Peruvian independence.

Towards independence The late 18th century saw profound changes across the world. The North American colonies gained independence from Britain and France suffered a revolution. Liberal ideas spread across the globe; South America took notice, recognizing that the potential to throw off the shackles of colonialism now existed. Inflammatory articles and newspapers began to appear in Lima; discontent became rife. Peruvian nationalism gained momentum and began to take shape as the philosophy of the Enlightenment pervaded the whole of the country.

The Peninsula War for control of Europe's Iberian Peninsula saw Napoleon cross Spain to attack Portugal before turning on his erstwhile Spanish allies in 1808. The beleaguered Spanish crown called for assistance from its colonies. In return for aid, the colonies demanded a relaxation in the regulations preventing Creoles from holding responsible positions of power and an increased recognition of their general rights, a step that meant that Peru tasted the early stages of independence. By the time that Ferdinand returned to the Spanish throne in 1814 much of South America was in upheaval and Royalist troops were struggling to maintain control. **San Martín** first liberated Argentina then, in 1817, Chile. At the same time **Simon Bolívar** had ejected the Spanish from Venezuela and Colombia. By this stage it was just a matter of time before one of these great liberators reached Peru.

Independent Peru

San Martín, anxious to protect his territories and deprive the Spanish of the prized silver mines at Potosí, arrived first from the south, in 1818. Having persuaded an English naval officer, Lord Cochrane, to attack Lima, San Martín landed in Pisco and marched on the capital. Battling north he reached Lima in time to witness the Viceroy escape with the few Royalist troops he still had. Entering the city without a struggle, he proclaimed independence on 28 July 1821.

San Martín assumed political control as 'Protector of Peru' and initiated some immediate changes, declaring freedom for slaves' children, abolishing Indian service and actually outlawing the term Indian. However, with the Royalists still controlling chunks of the north of the country his changes were largely superficial.

Travelling north, San Martín tried to enlist the aid of Bolívar in routing the remnants of the occupiers. Bolívar, a man predisposed to megalomania, turned down the advance, intent on securing his own fame by achieving victory alone. Relenting, San Martín handed the initiative to his opposite number, who mopped up the last patches of resistance to independence in 1824.

Bolívar absorbed Peru into his vast Andean Confederation, which included Colombia, Venezuela, Ecuador and Bolivia. However, a year after his withdrawal from the country to return to Colombia, the Peruvians abandoned his constitution and in 1826 installed **General La Mar** as president. There quickly followed a series of *caudillos* (military leaders) who assumed power in the absence of any civilians. Plots, counterplots and coups ensued, with **General Gamarra** seizing power in 1829, a move that set the tone for the rest of the country's history. Voted out of office four years later, Gamarra staged another coup in a bid to regain power, but was overwhelmed and exiled. Nonetheless, the military seized control.

In 1835-36 **Santa Cruz** invaded Peru from Bolivia and installed himself as Protector with the ambition of uniting the two countries. Chile and Argentina, in alliance with Gamarra, intervened and at the battle of Yungay in 1839 reinstated Peru's independence. Gamarra was installed as president once again and promptly attacked Bolivia. In 1841 he was slain at the Battle of Yngavi. Peru went on to have six presidents in the course of the next four years.

PERU

Finally, in 1845, **Ramón Castilla** came to office. Riding a wave of enthusiasm and prosperity heralded by the export of *guano* (bird excrement) fertilizer, Castilla oversaw a period of prosperity and real growth. By the early 1860s more than three-quarters of the Peruvian government's revenues were derived from the export of guano. Money was invested in the rail network and a programme of schooling and teaching the indigenous people went a long way to emancipating the slaves. A second term in office saw him develop sugar and cotton as export commodities as the rich guano reserves ran out and cheaper alternatives were discovered. Sadly his successor, **Balta**, couldn't sustain the growth and enormous, ill-conceived expenditure on railways and other engineering works left Peru on the brink of economic collapse. On the back of the 1872 elections the military staged another coup, which was overthrown by a civilian mob and led to the country's first civilian president, **Manuel Pardo**, coming to power.

Despite the proclamation of independence, Spain refused to officially relinquish control of Peru. In 1864 a company of soldiers captured the Chincha Islands, which were responsible for much of the guano that fuelled Peru's early wealth. In alliance with Chile, Ecuador and Bolivia, Pardo went to **war with Spain**. Although the Spanish shelled Lima they never made land and eventually retreated. In 1871 a ceasefire was agreed, but it wasn't until 1879 that the country formally recognized its former colony's status as an independent country.

The War of the Pacific

Peace and stability didn't last long. As Peru's economy collapsed under the weight of foreign debt, deteriorating relations with Chile and a squabble over nitrate-rich deposits located in Bolivia exacerbated the country's problems. When hostilities between Bolivia and Chile boiled over into war in 1879, Peru offered to act as a go-between, having made a secret pact with Bolivia to support each other. In retaliation, Chile declared war on Peru. Early Peruvian victories at Iquique and the sinking of the Chilean corvette *Esmeralda* were offset by the loss of the ironclad frigate *Independencia*, followed by the loss of Tacna and Arica. Further victories on land and at sea saw Chilean forces occupy Lima at the start of 1881. The treaty of Ancón in 1883 ended the dispute but saw Peru cede control of its southern provinces to Chile for 10 years. However, it wasn't until 1929 that an agreement was reached under the terms of which Tacna was returned to Peru, while Chile kept control of Arica and the rich nitrate deposits found there.

British bailout

Following the War of the Pacific, Peru was virtually bankrupt. With the loss of the nitrate rich territories the country's coffers soon ran dry and by 1890 Peru was unable to pay its foreign debts. An international plan to bail out Peru saw the creation of the Peruvian Corporation in London, which assumed the enormous debt in return for control of the economy. Foreign companies assumed control of the rail network and valuable guano production, and were given free access to the country's main ports. Despite the indignity of being bailed out, Peru did stabilize and a semblance of peace returned. The development of copper production buoyed the economy and reforms including direct suffrage, public education and municipal elections helped to ease the plight of the ordinary peasant.

In 1908 one of the big businessmen, **Augusto Leguía**, was elected president. During his tenure foreign investment increased and the capital was modernized, yet he made few concessions to support the poor and resentment swelled. Minor rebellions followed and in 1931, a year into his fourth term, he was ousted by a military coup.

APRA and the army

During the years Leguía had been in power, the Labour movement had steadily been growing in strength. The worldwide Depression in the early 1930s hit Peru hard as demand for its main exports declined drastically. At this time an originally Marxist movement, the **APRA** (Alianza Popular Revolucionaria Americana), stepped up its activity and resistance to what it saw as the financial hegemony of the United States. The group's founder, **Víctor Raúl Haya de la Torre**, stood for election in 1931 calling for state control of the economy and nationalization of key industries, but was defeated. APRA, convinced that the group had been robbed, instigated disturbances in Trujillo targeting the sugar barons there. Fifty military prisoners, including ten officers, were killed in the violent uprising and the brutal retaliation by the army saw almost 5000 people massacred in the desert. In revenge, APRA assassinated the president in 1933.

The organization was promptly banned, but went underground, operating secretly and becoming one of the largest and best-organized political parties in Peru. Legalized again in time for the 1945 election, APRA nominated **José Bustamente** who was a more neutral candidate than the contentious Haya de la Torre. Bustamente went on to win a majority in both the Senate and the Chamber of Deputies. No sooner was he in office than he announced his independence from APRA but, unable to control inflation, he increasingly relied on the army to consolidate his position until inevitably a military coup removed him from office. APRA was banned once more and its members clamped down on so they couldn't continue to work, even clandestinely.

Agrarian reform and military rule

By the time of the 1956 elections a new political threat had emerged. The **National Youth Front** demanded radical reform. Only with the support of an unholy marriage of convenience between a weakened APRA and their traditional enemy, the army, was the then president **Manuel Prado** able to defeat the group's leader **Fernando Belaúnde Terry**. Strikes and disturbances persisted, particularly in the remoter parts of the country, and a bloody revolt led by **Hugo Blanco** broke out in the Cusco region. Peasants seized control of land and began to work their own plots. Landowners were forced to bribe the peasants to come back to work or risk going bankrupt. Although arrested in 1963, Blanco had laid the foundations for agrarian reform.

Following the deadlocked 1962 elections where Haya de la Torre, Belaúnde and General Odría all polled approximately a third of the votes, the army predictably took control. Fresh elections were called in 1963, by which time neither APRA nor the National Youth Front posed a serious threat to society, and Belaúnde swept to power. In order to appease the increasingly agitated campesinos he set about a series of radical agrarian reforms and distributed

500,000 acres of land to the people who were finally entitled to work it for themselves rather than for an absent landlord.

In 1968 the military once again intervened and seized control. Belaúnde was deported and a military regime installed. Relationships with the then Soviet Union and Eastern European countries were developed and various land reform initiatives were launched. The regime took control of industry and handed more land out to the campesinos. Large estates were taken over and reorganized as cooperatives. In 1973 the educational system was overhauled, rural schools were built and the equality of women was recognized. However, the fishing crisis of the 1970s, when stocks dwindled, coupled with the decline in the world price of copper and sugar resulted in increased national debt. Ultimately the army handed back control voluntarily by calling a democratic election in 1978.

Rise of terrorist groups

A new constitution was sketched out and Haya de la Torre eventually became president. His tenure was short lived though and he was replaced in 1980 by Belaúnde, who set about reorganizing the economy along free-market lines. However, his policy to further develop the Amazon and exploit the wealth there failed to stem the rise in inflation, which reached 100% in 1983-84. At the same time, two terrorist groups, the Maoist-inspired **Sendero Luminoso** and the Marxist **MRTA**, began to make their presence felt (see box below). Inflation ran riot as the value of the sol collapsed.

❑ Terrorism – the Shining Path and the MRTA

Over the years, Peru has been menaced by two main terrorist movements: the **Sendero Luminoso** (Shining Path, also known as the Partido Comunista de Perú, Communist Party of Peru) and the MRTA (Movimiento Revolucionario Túpac Amaru, Túpac Amaru Revolutionary Movement). Founded in 1970 along the lines of the Chinese Gang of Four by Abimael Guzmán (aka Comrade or Presidente Gonzalo), Sendero Luminoso are Maoists opposed to global capitalism who have abandoned the possibility of democratic change. In 1976 the group adopted armed struggle as the only means of achieving its ends and bringing about revolution in Peru. Support for the group comes from the large number of disaffected campesinos in the country, especially farmers and families scratching a living in the group's traditional heartland, the highlands around Ayacucho.

Ruthless and savage, the Sendero actively persecuted anyone not allied with them or who didn't actively agree with their philosophy. The revolution was proclaimed through 'teachings' and by terrorizing rural communities into acquiescing, whilst funding came from the cocaine trade and protection rackets. At their height during the 1980s and '90s, members numbered in their thousands and carried out attacks on business interests, local officials, police stations and anything deemed to be interfering with or oppressing the peasantry. Members met secretly and would simply melt back into the obscurity of their villages when put under pressure. Guzmán himself lived mainly underground, rarely seen even by members of his own organization. Nowadays their numbers are vastly reduced, although there is still some limited support for the group abroad and an old website 🖳 www.blythe.org/peru-pcp that is maintained online as an archive for historical and political research.

In 1985 APRA swept to power and **Alan García** was elected president. An ambitious economic programme to cut taxes, reduce interest rates, freeze prices and devalue the currency was intended to solve many of Peru's deep-rooted economic and social problems. The short-term boom this produced led to far worse problems in the long-term and García's resolution to pay off only a tenth of Peru's foreign debt simply led to international banks suspending future loans. The situation rapidly deteriorated, with terrorists and the military, including a right-wing death squad comprising disaffected army personnel and police officers and known as the *Rodrigo Franco Commando*, engaged in a bloody, violent battle that inevitably harmed the campesinos caught in the crossfire more than it did either group actually involved in the struggle. García's abortive attempt to nationalize the banks simply plunged Peru further into disarray and ensured that by the time he eventually went into exile, hounded by allegations of corruption, the country was bankrupt.

1990s – the reign of Fujimori

The 1990 election became one of Peru's most pivotal. In the run-up there were four main candidates: the popular and internationally renowned author **Mario Vargas Llosa** with his right-wing coalition; **Luís Alvacastro**, general secretary of APRA; **Alfonso Barrantes** in charge of a left-wing group; and **Henry Peace** of the United Left. The left were severely split and after five disastrous years in power APRA stood little chance of regaining the presidency, leaving Vargas

The **Committee to Support the Revolution in Peru** (CSRP) also has a website (💻 www.csrp.org), which distributes the writings of the Communist Party of Peru.

Guzmán was captured in 1992 and still languishes in jail; 2012 was the 20th anniversary of his incarceration. The events leading up to his capture in his Lima hideout were made into a book, *The Dancer Upstairs* by Nicholas Shakespeare, which subsequently became a film staring Javier Bardem. In 2003 a ruling that the anonymous trial by military personnel that convicted Guzmán was unconstitutional led to him being retried and again convicted to life in prison. Other rulings delivered by military panels during the Fujimori years have been overturned or annulled though.

The urban-based, Marxist **MRTA** first found support in the shanty towns around Lima. Although more moderate than the Sendero, they have never been as well supported and indeed their capacity and confidence was rocked by an army ambush in 1988 that saw 62 militants killed. They first came to the world's attention on 17 December 1996 when they successfully infiltrated the Japanese ambassador's residence disguised as waiters. They held the building under siege for 126 days, with over 300 hostages including Fujimori's brother and a number of Peru's highest-ranked officials, whilst calling for the release of hundreds of jailed comrades. Four months into the siege, Fujimori authorized Peruvian forces to storm the building. All but one of the hostages were rescued alive, whilst all the terrorists were killed. Later, in 2003, the soldiers involved in the resolution of the stand-off were tried for massacring the terrorists in cold blood, but were acquitted on the basis that they had been involved in a military confrontation. Regardless, the MRTA remains a broken entity today.

P E R U

Llosa the clear favourite. In the event, a brand new, unknown political party, Cambio 90 (Change 90), led by a young college professor of Japanese descent, **Alberto Fujimori**, proved the stiffest challenge. In a notable upset, the unfancied Fujimori defeated the favourite Vargas Llosa.

Once in power, Fujimori reneged on his promises, assumed complete control and rewrote the Peruvian constitution, declaring that he needed a freer hand to introduce market reforms and combat terrorism. He also adopted most of Vargas Llosa's policies. Ever since it has been known as the **President's Coup**, since that is essentially what it amounted to: a bloodless coup d'état.

Fujimori's successes Fujimori embarked on a series of economic reforms designed to turn the country around. Although the prices of many staples such as flour and fuel trebled, he did manage to get hold of the economy and restore international faith in Peru. His greatest success, and the turning point that enabled him to stand for a second term, was the capture of Sendero Luminoso leader Abimael Guzmán in September 1992. Even though Fujimori was unaware of the operation by the secret anti-terrorist police to grab Guzmán at his Lima hideout, he milked the success, publicly displaying the captured terrorist in a giant cage, dressed in a cartoonish prison outfit, and successfully convincing the international media that Peru was no longer a country where terrorists were set to take over.

The Peruvian people responded to his successes and Fujimori secured almost two-thirds of the votes in the 1995 election, when he defeated the former head of the United Nations **Javier Pérez de Cuellar**. Continued economic success, inflation dipped from a record rate of 2777% in 1989 to 10% in 1996, and a peace treaty with Ecuador after skirmishes in 1995, 1997 and 1998 over ownership of oilfields on what the Peruvians claim is their side of the border followed, but at considerable cost to human rights. Despite international aid agencies confirming widespread poverty and unemployment in Peru and the devastating effects of El Niño in 1998, the economy remained buoyant in the run-up to the 2000 elections.

Fujimori loses control Here Fujimori pushed his luck by once more rewriting the constitution in order to permit himself an unprecedented third term in office. Despite a stranglehold on the media Fujimori encountered strong opposition from **Alejandro Toledo**, who represented the interests of Andean communities and cities. Following a hotly contested election full of untruths and deceit, in which a smear campaign accusing Toledo of abandoning an illegitimate daughter and being financially unreliable surfaced amidst allegations of vote rigging and fraud, Fujimori claimed 49.87% of the vote, missing outright victory by 14,000 votes. Toledo withdrew from the contest in protest and Fujimori embarked on an historic third term.

No sooner had he settled back into office than he was forced to resign. Video tapes were leaked to the press of Fujimori's sinister chief assistant, **Vladimiro Montesinos** head of the state intelligence agency SIN (**Servicio de Inteligencia Nacional**), bribing congressmen. In total around 2700 so-called 'Vladivideos' came to light, revealing the extent to which Montesinos had exerted control over the army, the intelligence service and the cocaine mafia through bribes, extortion, intimidation and threats of violence. Montesinos fled to Panama just as it was revealed that he had squirreled away more than US$50 million of what is thought to be drug money in foreign bank accounts. He successfully evaded capture until 2001 when he was held in Venezuela and returned to Peru to stand trial (see box below).

Fujimori clung to power for a further two months. On a routine tour he stopped in Japan and in November 2000 sent his resignation as President of Peru to Congress. He then revealed that he had been a Japanese national throughout his time as president, a disclosure that meant he had illegally spent 10 years at the top since by law the Peruvian president must be a Peruvian national.

❏ Truth and reconciliation

In 2003 Peru formally petitioned Japan for Fujimori's extradition to face multiple counts of bribery, corruption and being an illegal president. The same year, the Truth and Reconciliation Committee reported into the civil war of the 1980s to '90s stating that almost 70,000 Peruvians had been killed. There were also accusations Fujimori had made a US$15 million pay-off to Montesinos when he lost his job; established a programme of forced sterilization of campesino women; and was linked to the Grupo Colina death-squad, who were responsible for a number of assassinations and kidnappings in the early 1990s. Since Peru has no formal extradition treaty with Japan there was no way of removing Fujimori, a Japanese national, and bringing him to trial to face charges. That is until he voluntarily left the country to mount a campaign to be elected president of Peru in 2006, claiming that he would be fully exonerated.

Upon entering Chile he was arrested on an extradition warrant and returned to Peru, the first time a court anywhere in the world had ordered the extradition of a former leader to be tried in his home country for human rights' violations. Following trial in 2007 Fujimori was sentenced to six years in jail for abuse of authority stemming from an illegal search of an apartment belonging to Montesinos' wife, which he ordered without a warrant. He was also fined the equivalent of US$135,000. In a separate trial for human rights' abuses, the charge being that he ordered the murder of 25 people at the hands of military death-squads, he was found guilty and sentenced to 25 years. In 2009 Fujimori was convicted of embezzling and sentenced to a further 7½ years in prison, having admitted to paying Montesinos US$15 million (£9 million) in government funds illegally. It is thought that he admitted the charge to avoid a protracted trial that might have harmed his daughter's candidacy for the 2011 presidential elections (see p65). Although she lost in a close-fought run-off, Keiko Fujimori went on to request a pardon for her father in October 2012 on humanitarian grounds, based on her father's deteriorating health and multiple (surgical) operations for oral cancer.

Montesinos fared little better. Having been traced to Venezuela, captured there and returned to Peru in 2001, he was convicted in 2003 of embezzlement (on relatively minor counts) and sentenced to nine years' imprisonment; he has since received a further tariff of five and eight years on additional counts of bribery and abuse of power, as well as a further 15 years for corruption and conspiracy. Further trials convicted him of involvement in the Death Squad killings and awarded him a 20-year prison term for direct involvement in an arms deal to provide thousands of assault weapons to the Colombian rebel group, the Farc.

PERU

Peru in the 21st century

Fresh elections were called in 2001, with the centrist **Toledo** narrowly defeating Alan García, the man who had so badly damaged Peru's economy in the late 1980s. Toledo stood on a manifesto promising the creation of a million new jobs and a strong, stable economy. Carefully exploiting his Andean ancestry he adopted the nickname Pachacutec after the great Inca emperor. Sadly he was unable live up to his namesake. Having inherited a sceptical, pessimistic populace, a damaged domestic set-up with slow growth and worsening social conditions, Toledo found his popularity rapidly falling. His pledge to create a million jobs remained unfulfilled, unemployment remained a serious problem, taxes increased, pledges to increase salaries fell through and the benefits of what little economic changes he did make failed to filter down to the populace at large.

Crippling strikes, violent street demonstrations and a series of major confrontations in 2002 and 2003 prompted him to call a state of emergency, whilst a series of scandals forced him to reshuffle his cabinet and relaunch his administration. Toledo's approval rating slumped to less than 10%, the lowest of any South American leader and lower even than the disgraced Fujimori (31%), who continued to broadcast a radio show on Radio Miraflores from his home in Japan, despite an international arrest warrant for his involvement with the death squad Grupo Colina.

Return of García in 2006 elections

Sensing an opportunity, **Fujimori** returned from Japan in 2005 to stand for President in the 2006 elections. He was arrested in Chile (see box p63) but was extradited back to Peru where he is now serving a 25-year jail sentence in Lima.

With Fujimori constitutionally banned from appearing on the ballot, the 2006 election became a stand off between the populist **Ollanta Humala**, an indigenous Andean ex-army officer who had served under Fujimori and was backed by the then Venezuelan President, Hugo Chávez, and the ex-president **Alan García** who pledged to rein in public spending and not fritter away the benefits of a positively expanding economy.

Voters, suspicious of Chavez's influence, clearly forgave García for putting Peru on the road to ruin in the 1980s and elected him back into office, much to the chagrin of Chávez who had championed Humala as part of his vision for South American socialist solidarity. Relations between Peru and Venezuela further soured after the election result, when Chávez refused ties with the García administration and accused him of being an American lapdog. In contrast, foreign investors and external observers reacted positively to the result. García's cabinet included APRA members and independents as well as six women. García, styling himself as a mature pragmatist, delivered a degree of stability and prosperity and on the back of economic growth, low inflation and a sensible spending policy, business leaders predicted an Andean renaissance.

However, he made little impact on the crippling poverty affecting so many Peruvians. Inevitably the huge numbers of people living on less than a dollar a day began to lose patience with empty promises and the president's approval rating fell. Demonstrations, strikes and street protests in the run up to the first anniversary of García's return to power soured what had appeared to be one of South America's great political comebacks.

The forced resignation of his entire cabinet in 2008 on the back of allegations of bribery and corruption further tarnished his reputation. An ill-advised law to allow foreign companies to exploit natural resources in the Amazon, passed in 2008, was revoked in 2009 following protests, roadblocks and confrontations between police and Amazon tribes, one of which left more than 30 people dead and 150 hurt near the town of Bagua. García accused the tribes of impeding progress; the tribes claimed they were seeing little benefit from the push to develop Peru's rich natural reserves. Subsequently García also rejected a law that would give indigenous people more power to stop oil and mining projects on their lands. The law was passed by Congress but sent back by García, saying it went too far and that he couldn't let indigenous communities stop development that would benefit all Peruvians. The controversy and outcry continues, causing social friction and endangering the country's stability and prosperity.

García was unable to contest the 2011 election, which began as a fight between two right-wing political parties: Solidaridad Nacional led by a former mayor of Lima, Luis Castaneda Lossio, and Fuerza 2011, led by Keiko Fujimori, daughter of ex-president Alberto Fujimori. Later in the campaign, APRA and Peru Possible, under the leadership of former president Alejandro Toledo, entered the race, along with Ollanta Humala, supported by Alianza Gana Perú (including the Nationalist, Socialist and Communist parties). Fujimori and Humala soon established themselves as front-runners. Fujimori ran on support of the status quo free-market policies but was seen as hindered by her relationship to her disgraced father, whom people feared she might pardon; Humala softened his anti-capitalist stance to look more moderate and talked extensively about making concessions to unite Peru. In one of the tightest and most bitter election races of recent years, neither of the top two candidates achieved the requisite 50% of votes after the first round. A second round run-off saw Humala triumph with just over 51% of the vote.

Other countries, business communities and the world financial markets responded favourably when he announced a moderate cabinet of experienced politicians, allaying fears of radical change. At his inauguration, Humala also promised social inclusion, an increase in the minimum monthly wage and a pension for those over 65. However, his first year in charge was marred by disputes and conflict, particularly in relation to key mining projects, particularly for gold, and his approval rating fell from a high of more than 70% to just over 40%. In response to simmering environmental and social conflicts, Humala shuffled his cabinet.

Humala's challenge will be to deliver on election promises whilst maintaining Peru's impressive economic boom. Simultaneously, he must find alternatives to the current economic model, which has failed to lift millions of Peruvians out of poverty, the same people who voted for him at the election in the hope of being rewarded with a greater slice of Peru's prosperity.

PERU

THE PEOPLE

The vast majority (almost three-quarters) of Peru's 29.5 million inhabitants live in cosmopolitan modern cities. Nonetheless, the society is deeply rooted in the past and just under half the population is **Quechua**. The Quechua living in rural areas prefer to be known as *campesinos* (rural labourers) rather than *indios* (Indians), a term that is considered derogatory. Around a third of the population are *mestizo*, with mixed Spanish and Amerindian heritage and parentage.

Other groups include the **Aymara** living around Lake Titicaca and the **indigenous** tribes living in the Amazon, who number around 250,000.

There is also a small black **Afro-Peruvian** population, mostly living on the coast south of Lima and descended from those unfortunate enough to be brought to Peru as slaves, and a small **Asian** community made up of Chinese and Japanese immigrants. Descendants of the first Spanish families and other European immigrants constitute a small **Caucasian** population.

Life expectancy is 71 years for men and 75 for women.

Education and literacy

About 20% of adult Peruvians living in the countryside are illiterate compared with 4% of urban dwellers. Education is now free and compulsory for both sexes up to the age of 16 – a boon for the 30% or so of Peru's population under the age of 14. This is understandably difficult to enforce in remote rural areas. Nonetheless, the government estimates that most of the country's children have access to primary education, two-thirds go to secondary school and around 25% go on to tertiary education. Publicly funded schools don't have a great reputation and resources are very scarce, so those who can afford it tend to send their children to private schools.

Language

Spanish is the official language of Peru and spoken in all but the most remote areas (for a list of useful words and phrases see pp363-6). However, for a large percentage of the population this is a second language, and **Quechua** (or *Runasimi*, 'the people's mouth'), the official language of the Incas, whom it actually predates, is the indigenous first language. Most of the people who still speak Quechua are concentrated around Cusco and elsewhere in southern Peru. In and around Lima or the other major tourist destinations such as Arequipa and Cusco, English is also understood by some people. In the countryside surrounding Lake Titicaca a handful of people still speak Aymara, an ancient language dating to before the Incas.

There was no written version of Quechua until the 16th century so no standard way of transcribing it exists. Even now it is only fitfully being introduced into schools. As a result you will see the same words written differently. For instance, Inca can be spelt Inka, Cusco is sometimes written as Cuzco or Q'osqo and Sacsayhuaman sometimes shown as Saq'saywaman. The spellings in this book are consistent, if not the only versions of these names.

Religion

From the 16th century onwards the Inca religion was displaced by Roman Catholicism as the conquistadors steadily converted the local population. Nowadays, around 82% of Peru considers itself **Roman Catholic**. The Peruvian church is also the cradle of 'Liberation Theory', a Socialist interpretation of Christianity designed to support the poor.

Although the vast majority of the population ostensibly claim to be Catholic, the reality is that few attend regular church services and a large proportion of this figure practise a form of **Pagan Catholicism**, whereby Catholicism is fused with a series of indigenous, animist beliefs such as the worship of deities from the natural world, including mountains, animals and plants. Viracocha (the creator) is often thought of as the Christian God whilst Pachamama (the earth mother) is represented by the Virgin Mary and seemingly Catholic services generally have many layers of meaning.

An increasing number of the population now state that they are **Protestant** and the greatest threat to Catholicism in Peru comes from the predatory evangelical Protestant groups throughout the country; around 12% of the population now consider themselves affiliated to these churches, some of which are American imports whilst others are homegrown organizations, such as the IEP (Evangelical Church of Peru), which have been active for more than a hundred years.

POLITICS AND ECONOMICS

Politics

Every five years presidential elections are held and at the same time the 120 Congressmen are selected. The president is then responsible for choosing his ministers. Peru is split into 25 departments, each governed by prefects that are also chosen by the president. Departments are further subdivided into provinces, which are further broken up into districts that are in turn run by mayors elected every five years.

Current politics Ollanta Humala, head of the left-wing Gana Perú party, was elected to power in 2011, winning just 51% of the votes in a second-round runoff against Keiko Fujimori. Humala, a former military man, whose human rights credentials have been questioned after his role in subduing the Shining Path terrorists was investigated, had previously led a failed coup against his opponent's father, Alberto Fujimori, in 2000 and had been defeated by outgoing president Alan García in 2006. Humala softened his radical image in the wake of this defeat and distanced himself from Venezuela's then socialist president, Hugo Chávez, a relationship that contributed to his loss of votes locally. Instead, he pledged to follow Brazil's market-friendly model for elevating the poor. Consequently, large percentages of the rural population, particularly in the south, voted for him and his promises to ensure that Peru's economic wealth was more widely distributed. Mario Vargas Llosa celebrated Humala's win saying that it had, 'saved democracy.' Suggesting that Keiko Fujimori was little more than a proxy for her disgraced father, he noted that, 'What's important is that we have been freed from the return to power of a dictatorship that was terribly corrupt and bloody.'

The next elections will be in 2016. Crises facing Humala, particularly over the controversial mining projects in Cajamarca (see pp71-2) have led to the rise of left-wing candidates such as Alberto Moreno, the head of the Peruvian communist party, known as 'Patria Roja'. Adding to the national unease is the fact that by the next election many of the leaders of the Shining Path terrorist group, imprisoned more than 20 years ago, will be out and have sought to set up a political party, Movadef. In general though, there remains widespread cynicism connected with traditional political parties in Peru.

Human rights During the hostilities between Sendero Luminoso and the army, countless campesinos were caught up in the ensuing violence. On the one hand the terrorists used force to cajole and bully the inhabitants of villages to comply with their message and on the other the military massacred anyone suspected of collaborating with the enemy. At the height of the conflict, there are thought to have been 10,000-15,000 secret Sendero members, against whom were ranged more than 6000 troops and anti-terrorist police. During the struggle, thousands of innocent people 'vanished' or were murdered. In 2002 the Truth and Reconciliation Commission, which was set up by the then president Toledo to examine atrocities committed in the 1980s and 1990s by the Sendero Luminoso, MRTA and the Peruvian army, began reporting on the horrific incidents. At the inauguration of the Commission a spokesman summed up the task ahead saying, 'What is absolute, what is definitive is that people were unjustly killed and human rights were violated. We are not trying to open Pandora's Box, we are trying to air things that have been forgotten and stink.'

In 2003 the commission reported back, its chairman remarking that, 'The report we hand in contains a double outrage: that of massive murder, disappearance and torture; and that of indolence, incompetence and indifference of those who could have stopped this human catastrophe but didn't.' In all, 69,280 Peruvians had been killed or had disappeared during the conflict, more than doubling the number used in the past to catalogue the violence and making it one of Latin America's most brutal wars. Ayacucho, the Sendero heartland, bore the brunt of the losses, with campesinos accounting for three-quarters of the victims. Both the terrorists and the army were blamed for the loss of life. For more on this look out for *State of Fear*, a powerful documentary based on the findings of the Commission that tells the story of Peru's war on terror.

An ongoing lawsuit against the government concerns the issue of forced sterilization. As part of a family planning policy during the civil war up to 300,000 sterilizations were performed without the consent of the women. The case was shelved but in 2010 some of the victims from the province of Anta refiled their case.

The economy
Peru's economy reflects its varied geography. The country has bountiful mineral deposits and a range of climates that allows the production of a wide range

of produce. Poor economic guidance, political instability and crippling inflation have in the past brought the country virtually to its knees, though. Currently things are much healthier and the economy is thriving. Nonetheless, the gulf between those who have and those have not is still vast, and there are still a lot of desperately poor Peruvians with few or no prospects.

Fujimori privatized large chunks of state-owned industry and overhauled the tax system. Toledo also followed a pro-market policy. Following the early reforms and a shift to a free market economy the growth rate for real GDP soared to 13% before stabilizing around 7% by 1997. The worst El Niño of the 20th century and the Asian economic crisis in 1998 halved this figure but since 2001 Peru's economy has been one of the fastest growing in South America. Aided by market-orientated economic reforms and a series of privatizations along with higher world prices for minerals, GDP grew from 4.8% in 2004 to 9.8% in 2008 before a dramatic fall in 2009 to 0.9%. Since then the Peruvian economy has continued to grow at an average of 6-9% per year, with a stable exchange rate and low inflation, due partly to a leap in private investment.

Recent economic expansion has been driven by construction, mining, export growth, investment and a swell in domestic demand. The country's chief exports are minerals and metals; Peru is the world's second-largest producer of silver and also mines a significant amount of gold, copper, zinc and lead. Mineral exports have consistently accounted for 50% of the country's export revenue, peaking at 62% of total earnings in 2006. The overdependence on minerals and metals inevitably exposes Peru to global price fluctuations. Other important exports include fishmeal, petroleum, textiles and coffee.

Peru's major trading partners are the US, with whom they signed a free trade agreement in 2006, China, the EU and Japan. Under the Humala administration Peru also concluded negotiations with the European Free Trade Association and signed trade pacts with Chile, Colombia and Mexico as well as South Korea.

On the home front, services make up the largest percentage of GDP (58%), followed by manufacturing (14%), agriculture (7.8%), mining (5.7%) and construction (6%). Annual inflation is around 3%.

Continuing economic problems   Despite the apparently rosy outlook, there are still deep-rooted problems in Peru. The country's wealth is concentrated in the hands of a few and the vast majority of people still have very little. Underemployment continues to be a serious issue and has remained stubbornly high: in 2009 the rate was almost 50%. Unemployment is consistently just over 7% and almost a third of the population lives below the poverty line; 20% earn less than US$2 per day. In contrast, the richest 10% of the population hold more than a third of the country's wealth.

THE ENVIRONMENT

Just like anywhere else, Peru is struggling to reconcile the need to embrace a developing economy and the need to conserve ecologically sensitive parts of the

PERU

❏ Coca and cocaine

Coca leaf (*Erythroxylon coca*) has been part of Andean life for thousands of years and is deeply intertwined into the practical and spiritual fabric of Peruvian society. Illustrations of people using coca can be found on the portrait pots of the Nazca and tools associated with its use date from the Moche culture. In Inca times it was so prized that only the nobility were allowed to use it, but since the arrival of the Spanish, who first tried to ban the practice then realized the value of allowing the indigenous population to chew coca, it has filtered down into common usage.

When a quid of leaves is chewed with a mixture of lime or quinoa and potash called *llipta*, it acts as a stimulant to help suppress hunger, thirst and fatigue. It also eases the effects of altitude, helps to calm nausea and fortify the body. What's more, it provides the recommended daily dose of iron, calcium, vitamin A and phosphorus so it's hardly surprising that local people still believe that it's a universal panacea.

Coca farming Until 1996 Peru was the world's largest coca-leaf producer. Overtaken and now a distant second to Colombia, the country still cultivates 34,000 hectares of coca per year. Easily purchased in Andean markets, it is used by people in all walks of life for many different purposes. The leaves contain 14 alkaloids, one of which is the narcotic cocaine. It has been said though that coca leaf has as much to do with cocaine as an elephant does to ivory – it is the base ingredient from which the final product comes, nothing more.

The leaf in its original, unprocessed form is perfectly legal in Peru and widely used by farmers and labourers involved in back-breaking work, as treatment for everything from toothache to childbirth, in religious ceremonies and as offerings to the *Apus* and as innocuously as in a cup of tea (Mate de coca, see box p84). This is not true of the cocaine that can be derived from it.

Discovery of cocaine First isolated in the 19th century by a scientist called Gaedake, the cocaine alkaloid was initially received as a great scientific discovery and heralded as a pain-killing drug of great potency. Coca wine and other coca-containing preparations were widely sold as medicines and tonics, with claims of a wide range of health benefits. The original version of Coca-Cola was among these.

Cocaine trafficking After the addictive nature of the drug was realized these products became illegal. Unfortunately its abuse and restriction has created a monster. The main problem in Peru is the enormous wealth that production of the drug can bring. Production is generally run by organized, largely Colombian, gangs of narco-terrorists, whose lawless, brutal practices hold sway over some of the remoter sections of Peru. Much of the cocaine base is shipped to neighbouring Colombia for processing into cocaine, while finished cocaine is shipped out from Pacific ports to the international drug market. Increasing amounts are also making their way across the border into Brazil and Bolivia for distribution in Europe.

Since the 1980s the USA's Drug Enforcement Agency (DEA) has put political and economic pressure on Andean countries in a bid to eradicate the problem of cocaine trafficking and abuse by wiping out coca production in the Andes. This broad strategy overlooks the traditional value of the coca leaf to the Andean communities and ignores the poverty that drives campesinos without a viable alternative source of income to try growing it: coca is five or six times more valuable per kilo than coffee.

The internal perception in Peru is that cocaine is a problem of the urban Western world, where the demand is generated. The suspicion is that the war on drugs is cynically fought in the highlands of the Andes, largely out of sight and unreported, rather than in the West itself, because there are no voters or people to upset.

PERU

country. The major issue confronting the country is the **ongoing oil programme** that is devastating chunks of the Peruvian rainforest. Sections of the rainforest have been cut down since the time of the Incas, but never at this rate or over such a large area, and never at such cost. Conservationists and eco-tourism operators are battling to prevent the programmes and the associated problems of **deforestation** and environmental degradation, but they are up against substantial adversaries.

In 2003 the government granted oil companies greater access to indigenous lands throughout much of the Andes. Since then, the rainforest and jungle has come under intense pressure, particularly the area to the north of Quillabamba. There are 11 trillion cubic feet of oil and gas buried beneath the jungle, but it is an area rich in bio-diversity and inhabited by native tribes, many of which have had little or no contact with the rest of the world. International pressure and outcry scared off a number of investors, including Shell, but a gas-production consortium took over what became known as the Camisea Project. Two 800km gas pipes opened up the forest to migrants, loggers and developers; pipelines from the Camisea fields known as Block 88 in the lower Urubamba region cut through the Vilcabamba range and carry oil and gas to an export terminal on the coast, at Paracas. Planned for many years, the project finally got the green light from ex-president Alejandro Toledo in the belief that it would bring great economic benefits to Peru. Since then the government has quietly issued a decree entitling the project to commence oil and gas development in previously protected reserves. Allegedly tribes in these areas have been forcibly removed from ancestral lands, and the common problems associated with deforestation have become apparent, with landslips and increased erosion threatening the hillsides. Communities and farmers in the area have also been hit by infectious diseases and outbreaks. Nonetheless, there is extensive pressure from the gas companies to open up adjacent areas such as the neighbouring Block 56, located on the tribal lands of the Machiguenga indigenous communities, for a project labelled Camisea 2. Local groups and indigenous tribes are up in arms at the prospect, and cite liquid gas and diesel spills as reasons to stop the project. According to a report in 2006 the pipeline was poorly constructed by unskilled labourers, using old, corroded pipes, which meant that in the first 18 months after it became operational, the pipeline ruptured four times. Campaigners also report a decline in the number of fish and animal populations in the region since the start of the project. In 2008 García opened the Amazon to foreign prospectors, a move that caused more than two months' of protests and road blocks that culminated in casualties on both indigenous and police sides of the stand-off, before the ill-advised law was revoked. However, in 2012, Peru's Ministry of Energy approved more gas exploration inside Block 88, which means more seismic testing, wells and disturbances. What's more, the government has taken over an adjoining block of land to the east of Block 88, although the plans for drilling here are still shrouded in secrecy.

Issues have also arisen over **gold mining**, especially in the rich mineral deposits around Cajamarca. American outfit Newmont Mining planned to open

PERU

the country's largest open-pit gold and copper mine, investing US$5bn in the process. The controversial Conga mine has caused conflict though as locals argue that it will harm the local water supply, as water must be moved from four lakes into reservoirs the company will build. Opponents say the reservoirs do not adequately replace the lakes, which also provide groundwater for agriculture and irrigate pasture for livestock, claims the company deny. Bloody riots in and around Cajamarca in July 2012 ended with more than a dozen fatalities. The result has been a stand-off between the mining company and the protestors; President Humala needs the investment, but one of his election pledges was to stop the Conga mine if it threatened the region and surrounding mountain communities. Following the election he announced it was possible to have both 'water and gold' but maintained that reservoirs must provide year-round clean water supplies before the mining company can remove anything from the ground. With polls showing that three-quarters of the local residents opposed the mine, the Conga project has been put on the backburner, although Humala is mindful that the billions of dollars of mining investment is crucial to sustaining Peru's economic growth.

Other problems include the melting of Peru's numerous tropical glaciers. **Global warming** is likely to be the main reason why the glaciers are shrinking since they are melting faster in the dry season than they are being replenished in the wet. The glaciers feed many of Peru's major waterways. If the glaciers disappear there is a very real danger that the rivers will dry up and the land and people dependent on them will suffer. Desertification is a serious threat and the consequences are dire.

CULTURE

Literature

Although Peru has a powerful literary tradition, very few Peruvian writers ever make it into English. To track down some of the harder-to-find titles you may have to look in bookshops in Lima (see p137) or Cusco (see pp165-6).

Many of the classic records of the Conquest are written by the conquistadors, but there are also Peruvian accounts offering a different perspective. **Garcilaso Inca de la Vega** and **Felipe Huamán Poma de Ayala** (see pp42-3) are the two best examples.

The best-known contemporary Peruvian writer is **Mario Vargas Llosa**, whose novels and commentaries stand comparison with those of other great South American literary figures. Essentially a novelist, Vargas Llosa has also written about Peruvian society and culture. The best examples of his complex, meandering narratives are the rather disturbing *Death in the Andes* (Faber and Faber) which deals with the Sendero Luminoso and Peruvian politics, *Aunt Julia and the Scriptwriter* (Picador), a comic novel about a Bolivian scriptwriter who arrives in Lima to write radio plays, which is full of insights into Miraflores society, and *A Fish in the Water* (Farrar, Straus and Giroux) which describes Vargas Llosa's unsuccessful attempt to run for presidency. Vargas Llosa was awarded the Nobel Prize for literature in 2010 in recognition of his writing.

❑ Quipus

The Incas never created a written version of their language. Nonetheless, they were able to communicate complex ideas and record enormous amounts of information by using quipus.

Quipus, which were used by early Andean societies and adopted by the Incas, are essentially a series of different coloured strings with knots tied in them. The colour, position and number of knots in the string could then be read by trained, skilled interpreters. Quipus may have just a few strands, but some have as many as 2000. A group known as Quipucamayocs, the accountants of the Inca society, created and deciphered the knots. They were capable of simple mathematics as well as recording information such as keeping track of *mit'a*, a form of taxation. The system was also used to record the census and to keep track of the calendar.

Record keeper with his quipu.

FELIPE HUAMÁN POMA DE AYALA, FROM HIS *NUEVE CRÓNICA Y BUEN GOBIERNO* (c1600)

Today there aren't all that many quipus left in existence, as the Spanish suppressed the use of them and destroyed a large number. Historians are still attempting to decipher the knots and their messages. Most people maintain that the quipus only recorded numbers, but there is some evidence to support the theory that actually they contain far more information and were effectively written records or books.

Daniel Alarcón is a Peruvian-American author whose work has been featured in the New Yorker magazine. His collection of short stories, *War by Candle Light* (Harper Perennial), touch on a number of aspects of life in Lima, whilst his novel *Lost City Radio* (Fourth Estate) is a thinly veiled look at the disappearances and turmoil associated with the Sendero Luminoso.

José Maria Arguedas is an indigenous author who writes about native Andean people in his novels *Los Ríos Profundos* (*Deep Rivers* – Pergamon Press) and *Yawar Fiesta* (Quartet Books). **Ciro Alegría** also carefully depicts Andean communities in *El Mundo es Ancho y Ajeno* (*Broad and Alien is the World* – Merlin Press). **César Vallejo** is one of South America's great poets and one of the most innovative Spanish-language poets in the world. His romantic imagery and unusual use of language make his poems both beautiful and powerful.

Visual arts

During the late 16th, 17th and 18th centuries a form of painting known as the **Cusco School** flourished in Peru. Formal European subjects and themes such as religion were reinterpreted by indigenous artists who had been taught by Spanish masters such as Juan Iñigo de Loyola, who arrived in 1545. These largely anonymous local artists drew on Spanish Mannerism to create paintings

PERU

of unique and extraordinary beauty that mixed religious and native Andean imagery. The best examples include sumptuously dressed holy figures and archangels armed as soldiers of heaven. The hallmark of Cusco painting is the lack of perspective in the dramatic images, the predominance of red, yellow and earth colours and the application of gold to imitate the appearance of embroidered designs. The best examples can be seen in Cusco Cathedral. In the San Blas district of Cusco you can buy paintings in this style.

Martín Chambi is the best-known Peruvian photographer. His images of Cusco, surrounding villages and communities and the first iconic photographs of Machu Picchu taken in 1920 are internationally renowned. Described by Mario Vargas Llosa as 'a true inventor, a veritable force of invention, a recreator of life', Chambi was a prolific portrait photographer but also captured landscapes exquisitely. These he sold mainly in the form of postcards, a format he pioneered in Peru. In 1990 the Smithsonian Institution published a collection of his pictures, *Martín Chambi – Photographs 1920-1950*. Phaidon also published a collection of his photographs in 2002.

Peruvian cinema suffered as a result of a decision by the then prime minister Fujimori to overturn a law promoting domestic films. Ever since then the industry has remained under funded.

Music and dance
Music and dance are big parts of Peruvian life. Traditional music is a fusion of intercontinental styles using a mix of instruments to produce a generally soulful sound. Key instruments include the *queña*, bamboo flutes of varying lengths; *zampoñas*, double-rowed pan pipes; *charangos*, ten-stringed mandolins with a box made of armadillo shell, as well as drums, guitars, harps and brass instruments.

In the Andes, *huayno* is the staple musical form. This traditional, infectious rhythm relies on wind instruments and lyrics that fuse joy and sorrow. A Spanish version of huayno known as *musica folklórica* also uses string instruments such as mandolins and harps. The traditional huayno tune *El Condor Pasa*, originally written in the 18th century to mark the death of the rebel Túpac Amaru II, achieved international fame when covered by Simon and Garfunkel and still endures today. However, the style has also fused with other sounds such as rock and Colombian *cumbia* to evolve into *chicha*, a form popular in the working-class districts of cities or in the shanty towns and Andean villages. Lyrics focus on love in all its forms but also the harshness of Andean life, drawing on themes such as displacement, exploitation and hardship for its power. The best-known chicha bands include Belem and Los Shapias.

From the coast rises up the sound of *criolla*, which has its roots in both Spain and Africa. The most famous criolla style is the *vals peruano* (the Peruvian Waltz), which is faster than its European equivalent and full of complex guitar melodies, making it ideal for dancing. The best exponents of this form are Chabuca Granda, Susana Baca, Eva Ayllón and the band Peru Negro. Both Baca and Ayllón are also excellent exponents of *landó*, a bluesier style of criolla. Ideally both these styles should be heard live in order to capture the full energy and passion within the music. The bars, clubs and *peñas* in Lima are the best places to catch a performance.

The national dance is the *marinera*. Performed to criolla it is a flirtatious courtship between a man and a woman who circle each other. Other routines include the closely related *zamacueca* and the rather simpler *zapateo*, which translates literally as foot-stomping.

Media

The most-established daily **newspapers** are *El Comercio* (💻 elcomercio.pe), *Expreso* and *La República* (💻 www.larepublica.pe) but they are only published in Spanish. There are also a multitude of tabloid-style papers whose staple material is sex and sport with gruesome accidents or horrific murders thrown in for good measure. Slightly out-of-date US and English newspapers can also be found in Lima. For travel journalism pick up the magazine *Rumbos* (💻 rumbos delperu.com) but this is also written in Spanish.

There are nine main terrestrial **TV channels** in addition to a wide range of cable TV stations such as CNN and BBC World. The bulk of domestic television content is imported Spanish-language soap operas or locally made low-budget talk and news programmes. The main television networks are slowly regaining their news credibility in the wake of a series of scandals whereby the chief executives took money from Fujimori's spymaster, Vladimiro Montesinos, in exchange for positive coverage. These bribes were all caught on film and when the videos surfaced in 2001 the country was gripped by what became known as the 'Vladivideos' (see pp62-3).

Radio is a very popular form of entertainment and in the mountains is often the only way that people can keep abreast of the news. As well as the state run Radio Nacional there are three main national stations, all based in Lima.

Sport

Fútbol (soccer) is the most fanatically followed sport in the country, watched with an almost unparalleled zeal by hordes of spectators. The main teams, Alianza, Cristal and Universitario are from Lima (the classic local derby is Alianza versus Universitario), but Cusco giant killers Cienciano won the Copa de Sud America against Argentinean favourites Boca Juniors in 2004, sparking wild celebrations in the city. Unfortunately Peru hasn't qualified for the World Cup since 1982 and on two occasions has been squeezed out by local rivals Chile and Ecuador. Although most Peruvian teams and players will be unknown to you, key international stars such as Claudio Pizarro, the most-capped player in the current squad, have played in the UK, and can be seen in the European Champions League; Pizarro currently plays for Bayern Munich.

Other sports struggle to compete for attention, but **bullfighting** and **surfing** have dedicated followings.

PERU

Practical information for the visitor

DOCUMENTS AND VISAS

Citizens of the EU, USA, Canada, South Africa, Australia and New Zealand do not need a visa to enter Peru and are entitled to remain in the country as tourists for up to 183 days. Check with your local Peruvian embassy before departure to ensure that this is still the case as the situation does change periodically.

Before entering the country you will have to complete a *Tarjeta de Embarque/Tarjeta Andina de Migración* (**embarkation card/TAM**) on the plane or at the border crossing. In theory you must have a return ticket before being given a card but in practice this is rarely checked. Keep the card and your passport with you at all times when moving about the country, particularly in remote areas. The law also states that you must carry these documents on the Inca Trail. If you lose the card you may be fined.

As you enter the country the immigration officer will stamp your passport to authorize a stay of 30, 60, 90 or 183 days; note **that this cannot be extended within Peru** so ensure you request up to the maximum period if there's the slightest possibility you might need to stay longer.

If you need to **extend your stay**, you can cross one of Peru's borders and get a new tourist card when coming back in to the country.

Should you need a **tourist visa**, it will cost around US$38 or equivalent (prices vary according to your nationality), and you will need a valid passport, a fully completed visa application form, two passport photos, a return ticket and proof that you have enough money to finance your stay in Peru.

MONEY

Currency

There are **two currencies** in the Peruvian economy, the **nuevo sol** (s/) and the **US dollar** ($) and you can work with both. Use dollars for the big stuff (flights, international restaurants, big hotels, treks) but keep some soles for the small stuff (local shops/businesses, transport and restaurants especially in places outside Cusco and Aguas Calientes).

The Peruvian *nuevo sol* (s/), usually called just the *sol*, is broken down into 100 *céntimos* (cents). Whilst tied to the US$ the sol was, for many years, relatively stable and traded consistently at s/3.30-s/3.50 to US$1. However, in the aftermath of the 2011 election and as a result of uncertainty about the new government's policies and ability to maintain growth, it fell to s/2.59.

During the 1980s and early '90s Peru suffered very high inflation, running at thousands of percent at one stage, and the currency was devalued twice, changing from the sol to the *inti* and then again to the nuevo sol. Some of the old

PERU

notes may still be in circulation but they are worthless. Fortunately they look very different to the new notes, which have 'nuevo' clearly printed on them.

Notes in circulation are s/200, s/100, s/50, s/20 and s/10. Coins come in s/5, s/2, s/1, s/0.50, s/0.20 and s/0.10 denominations. Always ask for small bills when changing money or receiving local currency as the larger bills can be hard to break in remote communities or small towns. Make sure that all the notes are in good condition as some hotel owners or shopkeepers will refuse worn, torn or otherwise damaged currency.

❏ **Rates of exchange**

	PERU NUEVO SOL	US$
Au$1	s/2.58	US$0.95
Ca$1	s/2.68	US$0.98
€1	s/3.61	US$1.32
NZ$1	s/2.16	US$0.79
UK£1	s/4.25	US$1.56
US$1	s/2.73	–

For up-to-the-minute rates of exchange check 🖳 www.xe .com/ucc.

You will get a better rate if you withdraw dollars at an ATM and change them into soles rather than withdrawing soles.

Banks and casas de cambio
Banks are usually open during weekdays (9am-noon and 4-6pm). Generally, try to get to the bank earlier in the day and avoid going on Friday afternoons. Most banks have 24-hour ATMs which accept foreign credit and debit cards. Be sure to retrieve your card since there is no warning sound to remind you to do so.

Casas de cambio are generally open all day. Changing money here is straightforward as long as you have your passport with you to prove your identity. **Money changers** often loiter outside banks or congregate on street corners where there are banks or ATMs. Some wear jackets or badges with logos suggesting that they are official or regulated *cambistas* (money changers) licensed by the local municipality. However, they rarely offer better rates than those you can obtain from a bank and are far more likely to try and short-change you.

Using cards and travellers' cheques
There are lots of ATMs (cash machines) in Lima and Cusco where it is possible to withdraw money on your Visa or MasterCard. Using your **debit card** through an ATM that has Cirrus, Maestro or Plus system logos on it ought to give you access to your bank account. Cash withdrawals can usually be made in either US dollars or nuevo sol. Some banks charge for using this service so, before leaving home, check if this is the case with your bank. **Credit cards** are also widely accepted in moderate to expensive hotels, shops and restaurants in larger towns and cities although you should not rely on this means of payment once outside Lima or Cusco. Visa is the most commonly accepted card.

Travellers' cheques are a safe alternative to cash although they are now less widely accepted. Stick to US dollars for ease, convenience and the best exchange rate. American Express travellers' cheques are the most widely recognized and American Express has offices in Lima and Cusco.

❏ **Airport tax**
For most people this should now be included on their ticket but if not you may have to pay cash at the airport to cover an **international departure tax** of US$31 or the equivalent in local currency. On internal flights, such as the flight from Lima to Cusco, there is a **domestic departure tax** of US$6.80 (s/18).

GETTING AROUND

Travelling between cities

By air There are regular **flights** between Lima and Cusco as well as other major towns such as Arequipa, Iquitos, Puerto Maldonado and Trujillo. The domestic airline network is frequently in turmoil though and service providers often spring up and then fail. The most-established, reliable operators include: **LAN Peru** (🖳 www.lan.com) which flies to the most touristy destinations; **TACA** (🖳 www.taca.com) which has a regular service between Lima and Cusco; **Star Peru** (🖳 www.starperu.com) which has flights to Cusco and a handful of less obvious cities as well; and **Peruvian Airlines** (🖳 www.peruvian.pe) who operate between major centres and cities including Piura and Pucallpa. There's also a small quirky operator, **LC Perú** (🖳 www.lcperu.pe), which began life as cargo transportation company LC Busre but evolved into a passenger service, with a handful of scheduled flights to Andahuaylas, Ayacucho, Cajamarca and Huaraz amongst others, aboard small 19-seat planes. (See also box above and box p147).

Overland A popular alternative to flying is to travel overland by **bus**, the norm for most Peruvians. Services are regular and reasonably reliable although the buses can vary immensely in terms of quality from luxury coaches to scruffy ex-US school buses.

There are scores of competing companies with the biggest names operating the most frequent long-distance routes. The main companies are **Cruz del Sur** (🖳 www.cruzdelsur.com.pe) and **Ormeño** (🖳 www.grupo-ormeno.com.pe). Slowly Peruvian cities are adjusting to having a single bus terminal and centralizing the arrival and departure of the numerous operators, but these may still be clustered around a square. It is also possible that the departure point is in an entirely different place to the ticket office so make sure you check where the bus is leaving from. Arrival and departure times are loosely timetabled so take the journey times quoted with a pinch of salt.

Since the privatization of the railways in the late 1990s **train** services have ceased to be the cost-effective means of travel they once were. **PeruRail** (🖳 www.perurail.com) has daily services between Cusco (Poroy), Urubamba, Ollantaytambo and Aguas Calientes (below Machu Picchu) and between Cusco and Puno. The extension from Puno to Arequipa has been suspended but still occasionally runs as a charter service.

Competition on the popular Ollantaytambo to Aguas Calientes route comes from **Inca Rail** (🖳 www.incarail.com; see p371 & p373). There is also a weekly seasonal service operated by **Ferrocarril Central Andino** (🖳 www.ferrocarril central.com.pe) from Lima to Huancayo in the central highlands. This only runs from mid-April to the end of October but climbs to 4781m (15,685ft) in the course of the trip.

As a last measure it's possible to **hitch** a ride, although this isn't the safest way to travel and shouldn't be attempted alone. However, there aren't many private cars on the roads, buses are cheap and trucks often charge for giving a lift in rural areas, so hitching is a pretty impractical way of travelling.

Local transport

Walking is usually a safe and practical way of exploring a city. Alternatively jump in a **taxi**. Taxis don't usually have meters and will try to charge whatever they think they can get away with. Always ask what the fare is in advance and fix a price for the journey. If it seems outrageous don't be afraid to haggle: offer to pay half to three-quarters of the fare. Tipping is neither the norm nor expected. Official, regulated cabs called by telephone are usually more expensive than the private cars with a taxi sticker in the window flagged down in the street, but are generally more reliable.

People travelling alone, especially women, should always use a regulated taxi. Share taxis for longer trips often wait by main junctions or roundabouts to collect multiple fares.

Local **buses** are almost always beaten-up old bangers, but they are astonishingly cheap. *Micros* or *combis*, also known as *colectivos,* are minibuses or minivans that hustle for business on the streets of most towns. Stickers on the outside identify the route and the destination; although the system appears chaotic, they cover almost everywhere in a city. A conductor leans out of the door calling for business and once on board you must squeeze into place or risk standing for the entire journey. Fares are collected once you're on the move. Safety and personal health aren't usually top of the driver's priorities and you will often endure a pretty hair-raising ride.

Hiring a car

Driving in Peru is not for the faint hearted. It's a long way from place to place, traffic jams in Lima are horrendous, pollution is a real problem, the roads aren't especially good and other road users are often aggressive and bad-tempered. There are major car-hire firm offices in Lima and a handful of larger cities, including Cusco.

A driver's licence from your own country is usually sufficient unless you want to hire the vehicle for more than a month, in which case you will require an International Driving Licence. You will also need a credit card and usually have to be aged 25 or older.

Rates vary considerably from company to company and fuel is extra. For sound advice on motoring in Peru contact the Touring y Automóvil Club del Peru (🖳 www.touringperu.com.pe); however, the website is in Spanish.

PERU

ACCOMMODATION

Price

Prices in this book are split into three categories: **budget**, **mid-range** and **expensive**. Hotel prices are particularly changeable and may well vary in comparison to those quoted here. Nonetheless you will be able to make comparisons between the relative price brackets.

Prices are quoted for single/double/triple rooms (**sgl/dbl/tpl**); the description includes relevant information about whether bathrooms are attached (**att**) or shared/communal (**com**), other facilities and the availability of breakfast.

Budget rooms begin at US$5-35 for a room. Mid-range options are from US$35 to US$100. There has been a real explosion in this price bracket reflecting the growth in domestic and international tourism. Expensive hotels are defined as those charging more than US$100 per night and again there has been a raft of top-end, luxury hotel openings with prices to match. These hotels may also add 10% for service and 18% for tax. If you're travelling in the low season you may be able to negotiate a cheaper rate. Try asking '*tiene algo un poco más económico?*' (Have you got anything a bit cheaper?). Paying cash might also get you a discount.

Standards

Peru boasts the standard range of South American accommodation options, from five-star top-end hotels to basic rooms and shared dorms in hostels. Peruvian hotels are entitled to call themselves *residencials*, *hostals*, *hotels*, *pensións* or *hospedajes* and must identify themselves with a plaque posted outside indicating the type of establishment, even though this makes no difference to the standard of accommodation on offer. There is no universal standard of grading accommodation in Peru. When booking a budget place you might find yourself in a filthy, basic bolthole in a dangerous part of town overseen by an intimidating hotelier, or you could end up in a charming, atmospheric colonial mansion so your best bet is to actually look at a room to see whether it suits you before you hand over your money.

Camping is often possible and is usually free except in formal campsites. It is also possible to stay with local families on a homestay (see p167 and pp183-4).

FOOD

Peru has the most extensive menu on the continent and some of the world's top chefs, who are finally getting international recognition and are encouraging the spread of Peruvian food worldwide with restaurant openings across the Americas, Spain and in London. Yet mention Peruvian food to most people and the few that have heard of it might think of guinea pig. The country's cuisine is about so much more than that though. Lima is now one of the top gastronomic capitals of the continent with some world-class restaurants serving the *Novoandina* cuisine pioneered by the chef and restaurateur Gastón Acurio that blends indigenous, Spanish and Asian influences to mouth-watering effect. Other gastronomic centres include Arequipa, Chiclayo, Cusco and Trujillo.

Even in smaller regional restaurants Peruvian cooking can be very appealing; there's nothing finer than sitting in a darkened *picantería* (a traditional local restaurant often serving spicy food) with a steaming plate of *chicharrones* (fried pork and pork skin), and a mug of *chicha de jora*, the country's famous fermented maize beer. And *cuy* (guinea pig), be it fried, baked or barbecued, is actually very tasty.

Fish

Peru has excellent fish that includes *congrio* (conger eel), *corvina* (sea bass), *lenguado* (sole) and shellfish. Try the Peruvian version of fish and chips, *jalea* (fried whitebait) which is served with fried *yuca* (cassava or manioc), fried yellow peppers and a dollop of spicy *aji* sauce, *chupe de camarones* (traditional creamy prawn chowder), and that famous traditional Peruvian dish, *ceviche* (see box below).

Meat

Meat dishes are numerous and varied. Most common are *lomo cordon bleu* (beef loin steak stuffed with cheese and ham), *lomo milanesa* (beaten into a thin steak and fried in breadcrumbs), and *lomo a lo pobre* (fried with an egg on top). Chicken is also often served like this or simply roasted. *Parilladas* (a mixed grill and a restaurant that sells grilled meat) are generally very good.

More interesting dishes include *lomo saltado* (strips of beef stir-fried with onions, spicy orange peppers, tomatoes and soy sauce, served with rice and fried potatoes), *anticucho* (beef-heart kebabs cooked on a skewer over hot coals and served with a range of spicy sauces), *causa rellena* (a lightly spiced potato cake mixed with tuna or chicken), *aji de gallina* (shredded chicken stewed in a

---

❑ Ceviche

Ceviche (cebiche; fresh, raw white fish, marinated in lime juice, chillies and red onions and often served with two types of maize and sweet potato) is usually a lunch dish and is deliciously light and tasty. Many countries in South America lay claim to ceviche, but to suggest that it is anything but a Peruvian creation whilst in Lima or elsewhere along the coast is likely to get you into serious trouble.

How to make ceviche

- 1kg fresh raw white fish (lemon sole or halibut, alternatively mix half fish and half shellfish)
- 2 large red onions (known as *leche de tigre* or tiger's milk), sliced
- 1 or 2 chillies, chopped
- juice of 6 limes
- 1 tbsp olive oil
- 4 tbsp fresh coriander
- Seasoning to taste

Method: Wash and cut the fish into bite-sized pieces. Place in a dish with the onions, chilli and coriander. Mix up a marinade using the lime juice and olive oil and season to taste. Pour over the fish and store in a cool spot or refrigerator. How long you leave it for is a matter of taste. Some restaurants serve it after less than ten minutes, sashimi style; to 'cook' it through thoroughly will take about an hour. Serve with boiled sweet potatoes and corn on the cob.

PERU

rich, gently spiced cream sauce) and the coronary-inducing *chicharrones* (deep-fried chunks of pork or pork skin; the original hot pork scratchings).

Most unusual for many foreigners is the tradition of eating *cuy*, that popular childhood pet, the guinea pig. Considered a delicacy, it's usually fried or baked, prepared with *huarcartay* (an aromatic Andean herb), cumin and garlic and tastes a little like duck but with a unique gamey flavour. It is generally served whole, head, paws and all, as if it has just been run over in the traffic and peeled off a car wheel, and can be quite fiddly to eat.

Once scorned by the middle classes as being fit only for the poor peasant farmers, alpaca steak is now a staple on many *Novoandina* menus.

Other dishes

It was Viracocha's sons who discovered the **potato**, having been sent to Lake Titicaca by their Creator father to bring back the plants that grew there, so goes the Inca myth. It's not far from the truth, though, in that research shows that this is where the earliest potatoes evolved. Hunter-gatherers learnt to farm the tubers that grew there about 7000 years ago. Some 200 species of wild potato are found in South America and there are now an astounding 5000 varieties cultivated in the Andes.

Popular dishes include: *causa*, made with yellow potatoes, lemons, hard-boiled eggs, olives, sweet corn, sweet potato and cheese and served with an onion sauce; *papas a la Huancaina*, a cold appetiser of potatoes in a thick, spicy cheese sauce; and *papa rellena*, where a potato is baked then fried before being stuffed with meat, olives, onions, boiled egg and raisins.

You should also try *chuño*, freeze-dried potato. It was the Incas who developed freeze-drying as a way of preserving potatoes, which were then stored as a reserve if other crops failed. They freeze-dried them by leaving them out on winter's nights in sub-zero temperatures.

Quinoa used to be highly important within Andean civilizations, second only to the potato. In contemporary times its value is again being recognized because of its high nutritional and protein content, making it an unusually complete foodstuff.

In markets you'll see **maize (corn)** in an amazing variety of colours and sizes. Unlike the puny corn found elsewhere, Peruvian corn comprises giant white kernels bursting with flavour and juice. Corn has been planted in Peru for over 3000 years. The ancient farmers achieved a degree of sophistication in the selection and creation of new varieties that adapted to varying terrains and climates. Corn is cooked in a number of ways; on the cob, *choclo* or *choclo con queso* (with a piece of cheese), boiled, ground with a pestle and mortar, toasted or fermented into *chicha* (see p84). You'll find cornmash pastries (*tamales* and *humitas*), savoury or sweet and in a wide range of colours.

Soups are often hearty and filling. Try *yacu-chupe*, a green soup made from potatoes, cheese, garlic, coriander, peppers, eggs and onions or the pleasantly spiced *sopa a la criolla*, made with thin noodles, beef hearts and bits of egg and vegetables.

❏ **Health warning**
You should always be conscious of where your food has come from and how it has been prepared otherwise you run the risk of contracting food poisoning. Beware of tap water unless you are absolutely confident of the source, and if necessary boil or purify it before drinking. To be on the safe side, buy bottled water. Don't then get caught out by using ice that could have been made from contaminated water.

All food that can't be peeled or shelled should be washed in purified water. Stay clear of salads as they may have been washed in tap water. Ice cream from a reputable brand ought to be okay, unless the vendor has allowed it to melt and refreeze. Freshly, fully cooked food is generally safest, and try to stay clear of reheated dishes. That said *ceviche*, which isn't technically 'cooked' but marinated in lime, is perfectly safe if served fresh in a reputable restaurant.

As well as the wide range of Peruvian dishes you'll find excellent approximations of other cuisines: **pasta** is often freshly made and **Chinese food** (*Chifa*) is usually good.

Dessert
There's a wide range of options available for the sweet tooth, and the Peruvian tooth can be very sweet indeed. The most common puddings are *picarones* (light fried doughnuts with honey) and the jelly-like *mazamorra morada* (a sweet-tasting dish made from purple maize). When in Lima make sure to try Suspiro de Limeña (see p145), a classic dessert from the city.

In addition to all the standard citrus fruits and recognizable fruits such as bananas, guavas, pineapples, papayas, mangoes and passionfruits there are also four unusual varieties; the custard-ish *cherimoya* (custard apple), *guanabana* (soursop), the gloopy *granadilla* (similar to passionfruit) and the native powdery, peachy *lucuma* (eggfruit).

Taxes and tipping
Expensive restaurants will add 18% tax to the bill. They may also add a 10% service charge, which is meant to go to the waiter meaning that tipping is unnecessary. However, the money often doesn't reach the people who've earned or deserve it so you might want to consider leaving a cash tip as well. In budget or moderate restaurants tipping is normal although not obligatory.

DRINK

Non-alcoholic
Tea is widely drunk. It is usually served without milk but with sugar and lemon. Herb teas are also popular. *Mate de coca* (see box p84) made from coca leaves, is readily available in the cafés and restaurants in Cusco and helps to alleviate the symptoms of altitude sickness. **Coffee**, surprisingly for a coffee-producing country, is pretty poor and is either served as coffee essence, to which you add hot water, or instant coffee. Milk is again served separately. However, there are also plenty of places in Cusco that now serve a cappuccino or espresso.

PERU

❏ **Mate de coca**
This herbal tea is made by submerging the leaves of the coca plant in hot water or by using a pre-prepared tea bag. The tea is greenish yellow and has a slightly bitter flavour. Although legal in Peru, most countries do not distinguish between the coca leaf and any other substance containing cocaine, so the possession of coca leaf, even as a tea bag, is prohibited. If you try to take some home you run the risk of arrest and a possible prison sentence.

Bottled water is sold widely and should be drunk when you aren't confident of the water source or haven't had a chance to purify or boil the water yourself (see box p83). The usual range of **soft drinks** is available, with the addition of *chicha morada*, made from purple maize, and the ubiquitous, home-grown, iridescent Inca Kola, which outsells the imported American equivalent in Peru. Try it just once to discover the sickly sweet, bubblegum flavour.

Alcoholic

Peruvian **lager** is pretty drinkable. There are numerous bottled brands including Arequipeña, Cristal, Cusqueña and Pilsener that are all brewed to about 5% alcohol content and all taste quite similar. For a change try the sweetish dark ale Cusqueña Malta.

Peruvian **wine** is yet to reach the same heights as its South American neighbours, and the lack of infrastructure and poor marketing probably mean international sales are a way off; you're better off sticking to Chilean or Argentinean wine instead. If you are feeling adventurous try the Tacama, Ocucaje or Vista Allegre red or white wines from Ica.

Chicha is a maize wine that dates back to the time of the Incas but is still drunk today in the rural Andes. Nicknamed 'the champagne of the Incas', and made from a specific type of yellow maize called *jora*, it actually tastes like a type of cloudy pale cider. The name derives from the Spanish *chichal*, meaning 'saliva' or 'to spit', which refers to the Andean people's early methods of production: for centuries they found saliva an effective means of converting starches in the maize grains into fermentable sugars. Nowadays sugar is used to kick-start the process. Houses that brew and sell chicha can be identified by the red plastic bags hung outside on the end of long poles, not unlike pub signs.

Pisco is a potent clear spirit distilled from grapes. Usually drunk as part of a Pisco Sour cocktail, it can be deceptively strong.

Chileans also consider it their national drink and there is plenty of friction between the two countries over the origin of the drink.

❏ **Pisco Sour**
2fl oz Pisco
Half a lemon or one lime
1 egg white, whisked
1 tablespoon of sugar

Beat the egg white and sugar together. Add the Pisco and lemon juice and blend. Serve the cocktail over crushed ice and garnish with a dash of angostura bitters.

POST AND COMMUNICATION

Telephone

You can make **international phone calls** from public phones in the street operated by Telefónica-Peru, but only with a **phone card**. These are readily available from shops advertising *tarjeta telefónica* (telephone cards) or from touts hanging around phones selling them. There are standard phone cards or ones where you have to dial a number, usually ☎ 147, and then enter a PIN printed on the card – simply follow the instructions that follow from the opera-

> ❑ **Phone codes and numbers**
> To call Peru from abroad dial your international access code and then ☎ 51. Add ☎ 1 for Lima or ☎ 84 for Cusco.
>
> To make an international call from Peru dial 00 and then add your country code, STD and the number.
>
> | | |
> |---|---|
> | Operator | ☎ 100 |
> | Directory enquiries | ☎ 103 |
> | Emergency services | ☎ 105 |
> | International operator | ☎ 108 |

tor or recorded message to make the call. If you want to make calls from your mobile phone abroad, check with your phone provider what the charges and coverage are.

Often **internet cafés** also have private phone booths where it is possible to make cheap local and international calls.

Internet access

Although internet cafés open and close with alarming rapidity, there are usually lots to choose from in large towns and even in smaller places; many hotels and hostels now also offer internet access. There is free wi-fi for members of South American Explorers (see box p137) at their clubhouse in Lima.

Post

Post in Peru, branded Serpost, is slow but generally reliable. Letters to Peru take between 7-14 days whilst letters to Europe or the USA from Peru take between 10-21 days. **Stamps** are usually available in the same places that sell postcards.

Main *correos* (post offices) have **poste restante** and American Express offices will hold mail addressed to their customers. To pick up mail you will need your passport. When looking for mail check to see if it has been filed under any of the names on the envelope as post is not necessarily sorted by surname. To minimize confusion make sure all correspondents clearly print and underline your surname on the envelope.

ELECTRICITY

220 volts, 60Hz AC. Power cuts and surges are not unusual so it's worth bringing a surge protector for any valuable equipment such as laptops. Peruvian wiring often leaves a lot to be desired, particularly in bathrooms.

TIME

Peru is five hours behind GMT (UK winter time), in line with Eastern Standard Time in the USA.

PERU

HOLIDAYS AND FESTIVALS

Festivals are an intrinsic part of Peruvian life and take place with alarming regularity. The fiestas themselves are almost all vibrant, lively affairs that make for a great spectacle.

Hard partying, dancing and drinking disguise the fact that the reason for the frenetic festival is usually a practical one, be it a plea for favourable harvests or the health of livestock. The carousing, eating and drinking are considered to be ways of showing thanks for and celebrating the sun and the rain, which give rise to all life. Try to remember this when you awake after several days celebrating feeling rather the worse for wear.

January
- **1st New Year's Day** (all Peru but major fiesta in Huancayo)
- **6th   Fiesta de Ollantaytambo** (Cusco)
- **14th Feria de Pampamarca** Agricultural fair (Cusco)
- **18th Celebration of the founding of Lima** (Lima)
- **20th Procession of saints** (San Sebastián district of Cusco).

February/March
- Cusco hosts a wild and debauched **carnival**, with food and water fights in the streets and vast amounts of *chicha* is drunk (Cusco).

March/April
- **Semana Santa**, Holy Week – the week before Easter is a series of colourful, frequently raucous celebrations and processions; and Easter (all Peru)
- **Easter Monday** The blackened crucifix El Señor de los Tremblores (Lord of the Earthquakes) is paraded around Cusco, starting and finishing in Plaza de Armas where thousands of people gather to celebrate and make merry (Cusco).

May
- **1st Labour Day** (all Peru)
- **2nd/3rd** The **Vigil of the Cross** is held on any mountain top with a cross on the summit (Cusco).

June
- **7th-9th** The festival and pilgrimage of **Qoyllur Rit'i** led by the ukuku bear dancers (see box p103), is held on the glaciers north of Ausangate, the mountain 150km south-east of Cusco.
- **ninth Thursday after Easter Corpus Christi**: all the statues of saints from Cusco's many churches are paraded through the city and brought to the Cathedral, which is packed with revellers (all Peru, but Cusco in particular).
- **24th Inti Raymi** (the Resurrection of the Sun) is the ancient Inca festival of the winter solstice. Re-enacted at Sacsayhuaman, the lavish festival actually begins at the Coricancha, from where a procession makes its way through Cusco and up to the ruins above the city. The entire spectacle lasts all day and is a great family day out for locals (Cusco).
- **29th San Pedro y San Pablo** Festival of St Peter and St Paul (all Peru)

July
● **15th-18th** The **fiesta of the Virgen del Carmen** is held in Paucartambo, about 100km north-east of Cusco, during the Quechua month of Earthly purification. The statue of the virgin is paraded through the town amidst boisterous dancing, drinking and re-enactments of battles between mythical figures during which good triumphs over evil for another year (Paucartambo but also in Pisac and Pucara).
● **28th-29th Independence Day** In Lima this is marked with fireworks, live music and a lot of drinking in Plaza de Armas (all Peru).

August
● **Last Sunday** The Inca manhood rite of passage **Huarachicoy** is re-enacted at Sacsayhuaman (Cusco).
● **30th Fiesta de Santa Rosa de Lima** (Saint's day of Santa Rosa) (Lima)

September
● **8th** The **Day of the Virgin** is marked by parades and masked dancers performing in Plaza de San Francisco (Cusco).
● **mid** Lima hosts **La Mistura**, a giant gastronomy fair and celebration of Peruvian food with workshops and demonstrations by the leading local chefs (Lima).

October
● **4th Fiesta de la Virgen del Rosario** (Lima and Cusco)
● **18th-19th El Señor de los Milagros** (Our Lord of the Miracles): a venerated copy of this painting is paraded through Lima on an enormous silver litter weighing almost a ton (Lima).

November
● **1st Todos Santos**, All Saints' Day (all Peru)
● **2nd Dia de los Muertos**; day when Peruvians remember their dead (all Peru)
● **5th** Birth of the first Inca, Manco Capac; week-long festival centred on this date (Puno)

December
● **8th Immaculate Conception** Processions in honour of the Virgin Mary (all Peru)
● **8th** Everywhere shuts down around noon on **Cusco's national day** (Cusco).
● **24th Santurantikuy** This literally means 'saints for sale'. In Cusco this was originally a market where figurines for nativity scenes were sold, it is now a general market; elsewhere the day is a pre-Christmas holiday (Cusco).
● **25th Christmas** (all Peru)

SHOPPING

Fabrics
The Andean people have always placed great store by intricately woven textiles and fabrics have a long history amongst indigenous culture. Rugs, ponchos,

PERU

clothes and wall-hangings are all readily available from markets such as those at Chinchero, Pisac and Ollantaytambo.

Alpaca wool is widely used and most shopkeepers will proudly tell you that the fabric you're holding comes from 'baby alpaca'. The quality varies enormously. Modern dyes are less subtle than traditionally applied ones. If you singe a couple of fibres and it smells like burning plastic the material is acrylic. If it smells very bad when wet it's probably llama as alpaca is odourless whether wet or dry. The finest wool is from **vicuña**. The national animal of Peru was once hunted almost to extinction; in 1974 only 6000 remained but conservation has led to them being taken off the endangered list: there are now more than 350,000. Their wool is expensive because they can be shorn only every three years.

Arts and crafts
Andean crafts and folk art, ceramics, wood carvings, hand-tooled leather, gold and silver jewellery and *arpilleras* (appliqué pictures of Peruvian life) are all good buys and can be picked up at many of the markets or shops in larger towns. Never buy the framed insects seen for sale in Cusco, though. They are often endangered species and the trade in them depletes the resources of the Amazon. If you are tempted remember that if they are restricted or protected species customs will confiscate them from you. Genuine 'Inca' artefacts are often nothing more than cheap knock-offs; any actual relics you find must not be taken out of the country – it's illegal to export them.

Bargaining
Haggling and bargaining are often part of the ritual when shopping at markets and fairs. Foreigners, including those with backpacks, are seen as rich; in comparison to the many Peruvians who live below the poverty line, they really are. Prices can therefore sometimes be inflated. However, the vast majority of Peruvians are not out to take advantage of you. When buying hand-crafted goods remember that the seller has probably toiled to produce the exquisite textile or carving, and recognize the craftsmanship, skill and time that have gone into producing your souvenir. The tiny saving you might make by aggressive haggling could actually represent rather more to the person you are bargaining with. The seller may even be forced to sell their goods at any price in order to survive. Do not take advantage of this; only bargain when you feel that the price really is too high. Pay the fairest price, not necessarily the lowest price.

SAFETY

Pickpockets and opportunist thefts are the biggest problem for travellers. Usually thieves work in teams and target anyone who looks to have money. One of them will distract you using any number of ingenious techniques to get your attention. Most frequently, someone will trip or fall into you, an old lady might collapse in front of you or someone may spit or stick chewing gum to your clothes. Whilst you are distracted an accomplice relieves you of your wallet, by opening your bag with a razor or simply grabbing it and running. Muggings and assaults do happen too but are less common.

❏ **Tourist Protection Service**
If you think that you've been ripped off contact **Indecopi**, the government-run Tourist Protection Service (free ☎ 0800 4 2579) at Portal Carrizos 250 on Plaza de Armas in Cusco to report the incident and make a complaint. See p139 for details of the police service in Lima.

By not flaunting your valuables and staying alert in crowded or busy areas, such as markets, bus depots or railway stations, you can reduce the risk to yourself. Be careful when travelling at night and if necessary take a taxi rather than walk. A moneybelt is a good way of concealing your cash. Alternatively, make sure that you carry your cash in several different places in order to minimize the risk of losing it all. Some people go to the lengths of lining their packs with chicken wire or mesh to prevent bag slashers from opening up their packs.

Be on your guard when seemingly confronted by a policeman. Always ask to see identification and at no point simply hand over your passport or documents. If you can help it, avoid getting into a police car and instead insist on walking to the police station.

Should the worst happen, try to stay calm, remember that they are just after your money, and hand it over. It's not worth getting killed for. If you are a victim of crime, or do get ripped off, report it to the tourist police; they generally speak English and are usually helpful. Make sure that you get a police report for your insurance claim. Bearing all of this in mind, most people still have no problems when visiting Peru. Take care and you will probably be fine.

On the Inca Trail
A lot of agencies and guidebooks imply that the Trail is rife with opportunistic criminals and tent slashers waiting to steal your possessions. These tend to be exaggerated claims and theft itself is now uncommon on the Inca Trail, as long as you take a series of basic precautions. Don't take unnecessary valuables with you. Make sure not to take jewellery or large quantities of cash along (do remember to take your passport though as it must be shown at checkpoints). Carry any valuables that you do take in a safe pouch and make sure that you keep your camera in sight at all times, especially at meal times. When camping, remove temptation by ensuring that all your belongings are stored inside the tent, not outside or around it.

DRUGS
The possession of drugs in Peru, essentially marijuana or cocaine (see box p70), is considered a very serious offence and usually leads to draconian penalties. There is no bail for serious charges and you may be imprisoned for some time before coming to trial. If you are suspected or convicted of trafficking in drugs the sentence can be up to 15 years in prison. Avoid having any casual conversations with someone who offers you drugs, as the person you are speaking to may be a police informant or plainclothes officer.

PERU

3

THE INCAS

Hugh Thomson

The Imperial Landscape
A Reading of Inca History in the Sacred Valley

When the Inca emperor Atahualpa first met the Spanish conquistadors, he offered them a drink from a *qeros*, a drinking flask, in the
traditional ceremony of reciprocal toasting that had always been
practised in the Andes. The Spaniards refused, showing him a Bible
instead – which Atahualpa, insulted by
their refusal to drink with him, spurned.
What was this 'writing' anyway, these
scribbles on a piece of paper? Nor had
the Spaniards arrived with the traditional gifts, so the Inca emperor sent them
an insulting present of ducks gutted and
filled with straw. This, went the infer-
ence, was what he could do to the conquistadors whenever he wanted. The
Spaniards, in their turn, were outraged
at Atahualpa's insult to the Bible.

A more telling instance of the clash
and mutual misunderstanding of civilizations could not be imagined.

But before we become too self-
congratulatory and assume that we
understand such things in ways the brutal Spaniards did not, it is as well to
remember that an encounter with Inca
civilization is still almost the nearest we
can find to experiencing an entirely
alien mind-set – and as a result we can
misunderstand them just as easily.

Ancient Peru is one of the oldest

*Conqvista en los banos
estava Atagvalga Inga.*
Conquistadors (Sebastián de
Benalcázar and Hernando
Pizarro) confront Atahualpa
Inca at the royal baths,
(Cajamarca).

FELIPE HUAMÁN POMA DE AYALA,
FROM HIS *NUEVE CRÓNICA Y BUEN
GOBIERNO* (c1600)

civilizations on earth; yet it is also one of the most isolated. Until the
relatively late arrival of the Spaniards in 1532, the Incas and the many
cultures that preceded them had a unique way of looking at the world
– one that excluded writing, the wheel and many other necessities of
the so-called 'Old World', but managed to build magnificent monuments and a stable society in a terrifyingly unstable landscape.

And their relationship to that landscape is consequently very different. When you travel down the Sacred Valley and on towards Machu Picchu, you are passing through a region of extraordinarily stratified history. The eminent Andeanist Susan Niles has said that, given they were unable to record their history in writing, 'in many ways, the Incas sought to make history visible'; that is, the buildings they left behind were to remind their successors of their achievements. This is true of course of many monuments around the world, from the Pyramids to Les Invalides, but for the Inca Emperors it had the added urgency of being the only way they would be remembered: they carry no inscriptions.

Thus the so-called 'Sacred Valley' – the term was not used by the Incas themselves, as is often assumed, but was a marketing invention of 1950, designed to promote a driving rally held in the valley that year – could just as much be described as the Imperial Valley. From Huchuy Cusco, with its first essay at the architecture of the Inca 'royal estate', the *moya*, to the greatest example of all, Machu Picchu, the Urubamba valley is studded with calculated reminders of the imperial presence, and not just in the buildings but in the way the terraces and actual river have been landscaped and controlled; 'terraformed', as the archaeologists like to say.

Take Machu Picchu for instance: while almost certainly built by the emperor Pachacutec, probably as a winter retreat for the court from the rigours of more upland Cusco, it was also a reminder to new subjects he had conquered in the surrounding valleys that the Incas were here to stay; not only that, but as an additional humiliation those same new subjects were doubtless forced to build this new symbol of occupation by the Inca – and on a site that must have posed extreme engineering problems, as we know from the depths of the foundations and the bulwark terracing needed to support the spectacular city on a mountaintop.

Their labourers built with extraordinary facility and speed. When the Spaniards appointed a 'puppet Inca Emperor', having murdered his predecessor Atahualpa, they were astonished when a palace was constructed for him in what seemed to them little less than a day. But then the Incas were always a tribe in a hurry, and to understand them fully one needs to appreciate their historical imperative.

Amojonadores deste reino,
vna Cavcho Inga,
Cona Raqvi Inga.
Surveyors of this kingdom:
Una Caucho Inca and Cona
Raqvi Inca.

FELIPE HUAMÁN POMA DE AYALA,
(c1600)

The Incas were prodigious builders, accomplished engineers and skilled architects. Without the art of writing, they left their history in stone. They were able, however, to keep records of accounts and taxes using quipus, coloured knotted strings (see box p73).

THE INCAS

BIRTH OF THE INCA EMPIRE

It was only after 1400AD that the Incas began to expand out of their heartland around Cusco, so their empire lasted for little more than a century before being brutally cut short by the Spaniards. The Incas were the last in a whole series of cultures pre-dating the Spanish Conquest that stretched back to around 3000BC. The world has taken a while to appreciate the achievements of these more shadowy, earlier Peruvian civilizations, not least because the Incas downplayed the achievements of preceding civilizations and in some cases ignored them completely.

The Spanish chronicler Pedro de Cieza de León quoted his Inca sources as telling him that 'before them, there were only naked savages and that these natives were stupid and brutish beyond belief. They say they were like animals, and that many ate human flesh, and others took their daughters and mothers to wife and committed other even graver sins.'

This manipulative distortion of history was so successful – the same myth was repeated by other chroniclers like Garcilaso de la Vega in the early 17th century – that the truth has emerged comparatively recently.

Far from imposing order on an unruly bunch of savages, the Incas were the latest dominant tribe (and a short-lived one at that) in a series of Andean civilizations that had flourished over the preceding 4000 years: the Moche in the north of Peru, with their magnificent pottery, the Huari of the central states and the Tiahuanaco culture near Lake Titicaca were just a few of the cultures who had attained a high level and on whose achievements the Incas had often built.

The Incas were just one of a number of competing tribes in the area around Cusco, before beginning to build up their substantial empire under a series of dynamic and capable emperors. At its height Tahuantinsuyo, 'the land of four quarters' as their empire was called, spanned the Andean spine of the continent from Colombia to Chile.

To call it 'an empire' is strictly speaking misleading, if familiar – it was in some ways more like an extensive trading association controlled by the Incas. Nor were all Inca conquests military: Tahuantinsuyo can be compared to an aggressive modern corporation offering overwhelmingly compelling reasons to each client tribe why they should join – consumer benefits. The Incas also made it clear to any opponent that they would win whatever happened, because they always did. Cieza reported one Inca Emperor as saying to a prospective new

---

(**Opposite**) Unable to record their history in writing, the Incas sought to make it visible in the form of beautiful and dramatic buildings and stonework full of symbolism. **Top**: Dawn breaks over a typical trapezoidal archway amidst the ruins of Pisac (see p197), in the Sacred Valley. **Middle**: Vast concentric rings and agricultural terraces created by the Incas as an experimental farm at Moray (see p204). They were able to construct terraces for cultivation on even the steepest slopes, demonstrating their supreme engineering skills. **Bottom**: The Incas showed mastery over their medium in their use of stones of enormous size, dressed to fit perfectly together without the use of mortar. This wall is in Cusco on Hatun Rumiyoc (see p157). (Photos © Alexander Stewart).

tribe, 'these lands will soon be ours, like those we already possess.' Given the Indians' often fatalistic turn of mind, this proved effective diplomacy and many tribes capitulated without a fight. The Inca use of history to legitimize their leadership and facilitate such conquests was adroit.

Nowhere is this more evident than in their 'creation myths': one of these claims that the original Adam and Eve of the Inca line, Manco Capac and his sister, Mama Ocllo, had emerged from the Island of the Sun (now in Bolivia) on distant Lake Titicaca. This island, revered as the birthplace of the sun, had been a place of pilgrimage for the earlier Tiahuanaco civilization whose buildings were still so admired on the *altiplano*. By claiming that they too had come from the Island of the Sun, the Incas were harnessing the cultural power of an earlier mighty civilization, from the stones of whose great ruins, they implied, they somehow drew some of their own strength.

A SACRED LANDSCAPE

Stone was far more than just a building material for the Incas: they worshipped some of the great naturally occurring boulders in the region – like Chuquipalta, the 'White Rock' near Vitcos, or Q'enko – making them into *huacas* (shrines) with elaborate carvings. Such stone monuments were a reminder to themselves and others of their mountain origins and dynastic power.

In another Inca creation myth, Lord Viracocha formed the first man out of stone. Later, when the greatest of all Inca emperors, Pachacutec, successfully defeated the rival Chanca at the birth of his imperial Inca dynasty, he was said to have summoned 'the very boulders around Cusco' to rise up and fight with him in a desperate defence of the capital against the invaders.

There is an idea in the West that stone must imply some notion of permanence, but this is not necessarily true in the Andes, which is not a static landscape. In an area of incipient volcanic activity and landslides, with recurring and violent El Niño activity over the millennia, the landscape has always been changing. For the Incas, stone was a much more volatile, organic medium. This sense of stone as a life-force is crucial to understanding the Inca architectural and sculptural aesthetic. That old, tired phrase about 'the living stones' of some great site suddenly becomes a powerful, resurrected cliché when we look at Inca sites.

The sheer primacy given to monumental stonework by the Incas is remarkable. In doing so, they again claimed descent – and legitimacy – from the great Tiahuanaco civilization whose ruined city with its monoliths was still so admired across the Andes. Pachacutec even brought Colla stone

---

(Opposite) Top: The Coricancha in Cusco (see pp154-5) was the Incas' Temple of the Sun, the grandest building in the entire empire. After the Conquest the Dominicans built their monastery, Santo Domingo, right on top of it in a symbolic show of dominance of their religion. The superiority of the fine Inca masonry is obvious and it was also shown to be more technically advanced in the earthquake of 1950 when the monastery collapsed but the Inca stonework remained unharmed. **Bottom**: Somewhat fanciful giant mural in Cusco depicting the rise and fall of the Incas.

CORE OV·MAIOR·I MENOR
HATVNCHASQVICHVRV
~ MVLLO·CHAS QVI·CVRACA ~

Coreon major i menor.
Hatvn Chasqvi, Chvrv Mvllo
Chasqvi, Cvraca.
Couriers of greater and lesser
rank: Hatun Chasqui (chief
courier), Churu Mullu
Chasqui (the courier who
carries the conch shell),
Curaca (local chasqui).

The vast size of the Inca
empire meant that it required
efficient communications to
maintain control. The Incas
built a network of paved
roads covering more than
14,000 miles (22,500km) and
stretching from north of Quito
in modern Ecuador to south
of Santiago in Chile. Since
there was no knowledge of
the wheel or any horses,
transportation was by porter
or by using llamas as pack
animals. Communications
were provided by teams of
chasquis (couriers). They
would run in relays between
tambos (way stations) and it
is said that they moved so
quickly that they could bring
fresh fish from the sea up to
Cusco without it spoiling.

masons all the way from Lake Titicaca to try to
replicate the look of Tiahuanaco at some of the
ambitious sites he built, like Ollantaytambo; we
know because the masons rebelled against the
harsh working conditions.

GROWTH OF THE INCA EMPIRE

The phenomenal growth of the Inca Empire is
attributed by many chroniclers to the achievements of this one man: Pachacutec, who according
to these accounts, deserves to be as well known as
Alexander the Great or Napoleon.

Originally known as Inca Yupanqui,
Pachacutec was a younger son of the Emperor
Viracocha. During Viracocha's reign, in around
1438, the Chanca, a rival tribe to the north of
Cusco, attacked the Incas with such ferocity that
Viracocha and his designated heir, Inca Urcon,
fled the capital – some believe to the site of
Huchuy Cusco, the fascinating early estate built on
the hills above Calca, one of the least visited and
most evocative of the sites along the Sacred Valley.
Only a small band of captains led by Inca
Yupanqui remained to give a last-ditch defence.

It was now, according to the myth he later
assiduously propagated, that Pachacutec called 'on
the very stones of Cusco' to fight alongside them.
Not only were the Chanca sent packing, but Inca
Yupanqui (who then adopted the soubriquet
Pachacutec, 'Transformer of the Earth', and took
the throne from his disgraced father and brother)
embarked on an ambitious programme of conquest
that initiated the imperial phase of Inca culture.
Within a generation the Incas had grown from an
anonymous small tribe of the Cusco valley to
become the dominant force of the Andes.

During his long reign from c1438 to 1471,
Pachacutec's achievements seem almost to beggar
geographical comprehension: he led the first wave
of conquests over to Bolivia and Lake Titicaca; his
son Topa Inca, working under his direction, followed with further expansion north up to Ecuador,
until the empire stretched to an area the size of
Continental Europe.

Pachacutec was also acutely conscious of the need to create his own myth and legitimize his new dynasty. In the words of the chronicler Juan de Betanzos, 'he decreed the remembrance of history'. After his victory over the Chanca, he gathered the stones that were supposed to have helped him in his fight and set them up as carved rocks, or *huacas*, in places where they could be worshipped. He enthused the Incas with the idea that they were a people of power, of destiny, and created an elaborate hierarchy devolving down from his own position as the 'Sapa Inca', the emperor. The nobility became a separate tier in this hierarchy and were allowed to wear ear-plugs as a distinguishing feature. Tribes living close to Cusco were accommodated within this concept by being made *Incas de Privelegio*, 'Honorary Incas'.

El noveno Inga, Pachacvti Inga Ivpanqvi.
The ninth Inca, Pachacutec.
FELIPE HUAMÁN POMA DE AYALA, (c1600)

He also ensured that impressive monuments were erected – from stone of course – to this idea of an imperial destiny. Inca leaders had always been expected to build (one of the slurs perpetuated about the disgraced Inca Urcon, the brother that Pachacutec had usurped, was that he was too weak to leave a building to his name). But Pachacutec took this principle to new, grandiose extremes. He ordered the construction of Sacsayhuaman, of the temple-fortress at Ollantaytambo and, it seems probable, of Machu Picchu and Pisac. Any one of these sites would be a substantial monument; cumulatively they represent a quite exceptional achievement.

Pachacutec was said, according to later Inca accounts, to have laid down all the basic framework for the institutions of state over his long reign of approximately thirty years – institutions which his successors were ritualistically to preserve in his name. For the first time, the peoples of the coast and the mountains were given a unified administration that allowed peaceful trading and co-operation, with Quechua as the *lingua franca*. Where there had previously been darkness, so this story went, the Inca Empire brought order.

This account of Pachacutec, however, needs to be treated with some care. It is a seductive idea – an empire carved out by the sheer will-power of

Astrólogo Pveta Q save del sol y de la luna...
Astrologer and Shaman who studies the sun and the moon and the stars in order to know when to plant the fields. (Note that he carries a quipu, marking his astrological calculations with knots on the strings).
FELIPE HUAMÁN POMA DE AYALA, (c1600)

THE INCAS

Travaxa: Zara, Papa Hallmai Mita.
Work in January.
Maize, time of rain and digging. Month of the biggest feast.
FELIPE HUAMÁN POMA DE AYALA, (c1600)

Travaxa: Zara, Papa Apaicvi Aimoray.
Work in July.
Maize and potatoes. Month of the harvest and distribution of the lands.
FELIPE HUAMÁN POMA DE AYALA, (c1600)

one individual, single-handedly turning the tide of a nation's destiny – and as such appealing to Spanish chroniclers reared on just such chivalric exploits themselves.

Pachacutec was undoubtedly a dynamic and capable leader. But what has come down to us is very much the 'official version' of the history, carefully propagated by his own descendants; a usurping family, they had an interest in denigrating the achievements of their predecessors, who consequently may have received short shrift (just as the Incas were prone to ignore the influence of preceding civilizations). As the old English saying goes: 'Treason shall never prosper, for if it prosper it is no longer treason.'

While Pachacutec initially concentrated on the southern Andes and Bolivia, his son Topa Inca began the expansion into the northern ranges and Ecuador that was to have such a profound consequence for 'the land of the four quarters'.

The Incas had a prolonged love-affair with the warm climate of Ecuador: fertile land, the trade in exotic desirables like seashells and the attractions of the local girls combined to make it irresistible to the aesthetes from the highlands. Successive emperors spent more and more time campaigning there.

The rhythm of such campaigns allowed plenty of time to enjoy the place: the normal, very civilized practice of pre-Columbian peoples was for fighting to pause during harvest-time to allow both sides to gather in crops (when the Spaniards arrived, they disconcerted the natives by ignoring this convention). Cieza de León also reports that the Incas often found it too hot to fight in the summer.

Topa Inca, like his father, was a formidable builder: it is likely that he was responsible for Choquequirao, the spectacular site high above the Apurímac which emulates, or competes with, Machu Picchu; he also built an estate at Chincheros, the great walls of which support the later church plaza built by the Spaniards.

In Ecuador he founded the city of Tumipampa (modern-day Cuenca), where his son Huayna Capac, the future emperor, was born. When Huayna succeeded to the throne, Ecuador clearly appealed to him more than the harsher climate of the Inca heartland. He chose to stay for many years in his birthplace of Tumipampa, and was said to have preferred it to Cusco as a capital.

This did not stop him from ensuring that a substantial country palace, Quispiquanca, was built for him in what is now the town of Urubamba, beside the modern road ascending to the Chicón glacier; the site has recently been restored and is impressive if little visited, despite the nearby location of the best restaurant in the valley, El Huacatay (see p201).

By Inca standards Huayna seems to have been a bit of a *bon viveur*, perhaps because of his Ecuadorian upbringing: he was said to be able to drink three times as much as any of his subjects. When asked how it was that he never became intoxicated, he replied that 'he drank for the poor, of whom he supported many.'

Andas del Inga. Pillco Randa. The Inca's red litter, used in war. Here Huayna Capac is shown going to war with the Cañari in northern Ecuador.

FELIPE HUAMÁN POMA DE AYALA, (c1600)

Yet the push up into Ecuador by the Incas can with hindsight be seen as an expansion too far. In just three generations, under first Pachacutec, then his son Topa Inca and finally his grandson Huayna Capac, the Inca empire had grown from an enclave around Cusco to one that stretched right along the Andes. In the process it had become fatally distended.

The endless campaigns that Huayna waged in Ecuador had created a permanent standing army in the north, with powerful generals, a disruption to the normal Inca convention that armies were temporary and centred on Cusco; he had also fathered several sons there, which had serious dynastic implications.

In around 1527 came disaster: a fatal epidemic (opinions vary as to whether it was European smallpox that had swept down the South American coast from the north, or a local sand-fly disease, bartonellosis) killed as much as half the population of 25 million, including Huayna Capac himself.

The cracks in the Incas' new empire quickly started to show. Huayna had been away in the

Fiesta de los Ingas. Varicza, Aravi del Inga. Canta con sv pvca llama. Fiesta of the Incas. Dance, song of the Inca. He sings with his red llama.

FELIPE HUAMÁN POMA DE AYALA, (c1600)

north for over ten years. His legitimate successor and son, Huascar, was based back in Cusco. Now a contingent of Incas in Quito led by his son

THE INCAS

Conqvista preso Atagvalpa Inga.
Atahualpa in prison,
Cajamarca.
FELIPE HUAMÁN POMA DE AYALA,
(c1600)

'Do you eat gold?' asks the
Inca. 'I eat gold', replies the
Conquistador.
FELIPE HUAMÁN POMA DE AYALA,
(c1600)

Atahualpa (who may well have had an Ecuadorian mother) decided that they were far enough away both from Cusco and Huascar to declare independence.

The resulting civil war between the Ecuadorian and Peruvian sides of the Empire was devastating. It was the turning point in Inca fortunes, much more so than the Spanish Conquest of 1532, which simply exploited the wreckage it caused. The two sides were evenly matched: as the legitimate contender, Huascar had all the resources of the Cusco state behind him; Atahualpa was the more experienced soldier, with a strong Ecuadorian power-base and a ruthless streak – indeed far from being the passive and noble Indian sometimes portrayed, Atahualpa was one of the most brutal of all Inca emperors. Atahualpa eventually defeated Huascar and had him killed, but not before the country had been laid waste. Despite the civil war, Huascar still ensured that a country palace was built for him at Calca.

The epidemic and then the great Inca civil war so weakened Tahuantinsuyo that by 1532, when the Spaniards arrived, they could simply walk in and take it. The conquistadors, as so often, were incredibly lucky. After landing on the coast, at Tumbes, they travelled south down the Royal Road towards the Inca capital, moving through a civilization which had been fatally weakened by first disease and then internal divisions.

After the famous meeting with Atahualpa, in which the *barbudos*, the bearded ones, and the emperor so signally failed to understand one another, it was not long before Francisco Pizarro and his men kidnapped Atahualpa in the main square at Cajamarca; after extorting a huge ransom of gold and silver from the Inca, they executed him regardless and marched on Cusco to claim the Empire for themselves.

THE POWER OF THE MUMMY

The astonishing expansion of the Incas across a few generations before the arrival of the Spaniards can only partly be explained by dynamic leadership. Other factors contributed to their success: a facility for trade, their opportunism and an occasionally overlooked factor – the curious Inca laws of dynastic inheritance. When each Inca emperor died, his estate (or *panaca*) continued to maintain his household as if he were still alive – he remained 'resident' in his old palace as a mummy, to be brought out on feast days or for the coronation of his successors, and each of those successors would therefore have to build themselves a new palace. When a new emperor was crowned, the mummies of the whole previous dynasty of dead Inca emperors were carried in procession alongside him, along with their fingernail and hair trimmings, which had been scrupulously preserved while they were alive. The sense of a 'living' dynastic succession must have been overwhelming.

At the time of the Spanish Conquest there were 12 such *panacas* in existence. Each mummy would have its own litter, bearers and attendants from that *panaca*, and a pavilion would be erected for them on the main square where the coronation took place. In a ceremony that built on the traditional consumption of vast quantities of alcohol by the Inca's new subjects, the incoming emperor, the 'Sapa Inca', would also exchange toasts with each of his dead ancestors, with the mummy's attendants drinking on behalf of the corpse.

Entiero de Chinchaisvios.
Chinchaysuyu burial.

FELIPE HUAMÁN POMA DE AYALA,
(c1600)

Here a Chinchaysuyu mummy is being carried to its burial chamber. The Inca region of Chinchaysuyu was the northernmost part of the empire, in north Equador and southern Colombia. Atahualpa's mother was from this area.

It is clear that the 'mummy lobby' had grown very powerful towards the end of the Inca Empire and precipitated a bitter divide in Cusco. Huascar Inca, who had a reforming agenda during his brief tenure as emperor, tried to limit what he saw as the abuses that had grown up.

According to the chronicler Bernabé Cobo, 'So many nobles were involved in serving these dead bodies, and their lives were so licentious, that one day Huascar Inca became angry with them and he said that there should be an order to have all the dead bodies buried and to take all their riches away from them. He went on to say that the dead should not be a part of his court, only the living, because the dead had taken over the best of everything in his kingdom.'

It must have been particularly galling for each new emperor that the mummy of his predecessor got to keep all his land, wealth and particularly palaces, so that the incoming Inca would have to build a new one.

The main square of Cusco when the conquistadors arrived was witness to this: each side was lined with the palaces of past Incas, still inhabited by their mummies. Indeed there had been no space left for Huascar on the square itself and he had been forced, to his fury, to build a new palace on the hill above; he caused outrage at one point by threatening to confiscate one of the palaces of his dead forebears instead, according to Pedro Pizarro, one of the liveliest of Spanish chroniclers.

Much the same applied to the country palaces. One probable reason why Machu Picchu seems to have been abandoned by the time of the Spanish Conquest is that after the death of Pachacutec, it reverted to his panaca, not the incoming new Emperor, and therefore went into a gentle decline, without the imperial resources to maintain such a grandiose site.

And therein lies a powerful engine for continual Inca expansion: the fact that the mummy of a departed Inca and his panaca continued to own his palaces and land even after his death was a powerful incentive for every new emperor to go out and conquer new lands, since he would not simply be inheriting them.

THE GUERILLA CAMPAIGN AFTER THE SPANISH CONQUEST

The Incas did not just roll over and die after the arrival of the Spaniards in 1532, despite the initial success of the conquistadors. After Atahualpa's death, the Spaniards decided to install a puppet emperor on the throne, a brother of his called Manco; this proved to be a costly error. After a few years of obedience, Manco revolted, calling troops up from all over Tahuantinsuyo for one last blowing up of the fire from the dying embers.

Conqvista. Milagro del Señor Santiago major, após- tol de Jesu Cristo.
St James the Great, Apostle of Jesus Christ.
(St James comes to the aid of the Conquistadors and saves Cusco).
FELIPE HUAMÁN POMA DE AYALA, (c1600)

Pedro de Cieza de León described the conquistadors' dismay at suddenly seeing the strength of Manco's forces camped around Cusco: 'So numerous were the [Indian] troops who came here that they covered the fields, and by day it looked as if a black cloth had been spread over the ground for half a league.' Many of Pizarro's comrades had gone to Chile on an expedition, while others were in the newly founded city of Lima. The remaining Spaniards were taken by surprise and trapped in the streets of the town, while the Incas gathered outside the walls and in the great fortress above at Sacsayhuaman.

By setting fire to the roofs of Cusco and keeping up a punishing siege, the Incas came close to defeating the Spaniards. There were fewer than two hundred of the conquistadors, and of these, as Pedro candidly admits, only the cavalrymen really mattered, as the Spaniards on foot were no match for the agile Indians: 'the Indians hold the infantrymen in slight account'.

It was the European horses which were the Spaniards' only hope if they were to hold over 100,000 Inca soldiers at bay. On open ground, an armoured Spanish horseman with steel weapons against a native infantryman was like a tank against an archer. But in the cramped streets of Cusco, the horses were no longer so agile or effective. The Indians built palisades to contain them, and used slings to hurl burning cloth at the buildings where the Spaniards were sheltering. The defenders realized they were in an impossible position.

They mounted a despairing charge and rode up to take Sacsayhuaman, before Manco could assemble even more native troops for the siege. However much one might dislike the motives or morals of the conquistadors, this was a bold and brave move given how few of them there were and the overwhelming superiority of the Incas.

The Incas under Manco were forced to retreat. He led his men into the wild Vilcabamba area to the west of Cusco from where he and his successors remarkably managed to hold out against the Spanish for another forty years, waging intermittent guerrilla attacks.

It is in this area that some of the most deliberately inaccessible Inca ruins can still be found, like the settlement at Espíritu Pampa which more intrepid trekkers reach in a descent from Vitcos, a site originally built by Pachacutec but later reoccupied by Manco as a symbol that he was continuing in his ancestor's great tradition, however straitened his circumstances.

Manco used the emotive power of the mummies during his exile, carrying the surviving bodies of previous Inca emperors with him into the Vilcabamba, as well as the Punchao, the sun-shield. Even though the mummies were captured by the Spaniards and brought back to Cusco, they passed back into native hands and continued to be used by the underground resistance movement for the next 20 years.

In some ways, Manco Inca is the forgotten hero of Inca history. His predecessor Atahualpa is remembered as the emperor whom Pizarro and his men first seized and ransomed for rooms full of gold and silver before executing, while the name of Túpac Amaru, the very last Inca, lives on for its symbolic value and has been sporadically revived as the focus for later resistance groups.

La Preción de Topa Amao Ynga.
Túpac Amaru is led into Cusco.
FELIPE HUAMÁN POMA DE AYALA, (c1600)

But Manco was a more admirable character than either of them. When he was placed as a puppet on the throne by the Spaniards, he had already survived both a brutal civil war and the Spanish Conquest, which along with the epidemic had managed to lay waste one of the world's great empires in less than ten years. The world he had known had crumbled around him. Out of the ashes, and with some consummate political manoeuvring, he somehow managed to rally a rebellion which, if not ultimately successful, at least gave heart to his people.

MODERN PERU AND THE INCA LEGACY

The sense of landscape and buildings as important repositories of history still runs deep in the Peruvian psyche. When President Toledo – the first Peruvian president of Indian origin – was inaugurated, he chose to do so at Machu Picchu rather than as previously in Lima, a very deliberate nod to the Inca tradition.

Certain aspects of the Inca world-view – the belief in cooperative labour by communities, their superb agriculture and husbanding of shared resources, a spirituality rooted in stone and maize and the mountains, and in a sacred landscape – are still part of the Quechua inheritance, despite the intervening imposition of 300 years of Spanish rule.

Now the *indigenismo* movement of the early 20th century and recent political initiatives have sought again to place the Inca empire and its beliefs at the heart of Peru's sense of national identity, with a great national pride in their pre-Columbian achievements.

This has had one desirable outcome, in that the conservation and promotion of archaeological monuments has proceeded apace: from Choquequirao to Vitcos and even the formidably jungle-covered site of Espíritu Pampa, the visitor will see evidence of sustained reconstruction, if sometimes perhaps a little too over-enthusiastic. Only a few historic sites, like Huchuy Cusco, are still neglected, although these have the virtue of an atmospheric, overgrown setting as a result.

The recent work of historians and archaeologists such as John Rowe, Susan Niles, Brian Bauer and Richard Burger has given us more of an insight into the historical events that shaped the spectacular Inca architecture of their heartland around the Sacred Valley. But we still know less about the Incas and their predecessors than we do of other ancient civilizations, partly because of their illiteracy but also because we have come to a true study of their culture surprisingly late.

It would therefore be a mistake to underestimate the difference in outlook between the Incas and ourselves, and the difficulties in bridging that divide that still remain. When offered a cup by the Inca world, as the conquistadors were by Atahualpa, we should choose to drink deeply if we want to understand them.

Elements of the above article are drawn from Hugh Thomson's books on Peru: *The White Rock: An Exploration of the Inca Heartland* and *Cochineal Red: Travels through Ancient Peru* (both Phoenix).

In addition to writing the above books, Hugh Thomson has led several research expeditions to the area around Cusco and made the first reports of some previously unknown Inca sites. For more information see 🖥 www.thewhiterock.co.uk.

FLORA & FAUNA

4

The Machu Picchu Historical Sanctuary is a **UNESCO World Heritage Site** and, unusually, it's a World Heritage Site for both architecture and wildlife. The Sanctuary covers some 325 sq km in an area of wilderness banded to the north by the watershed of the Mt Veronica massif, in the east and west by the Cusichaca and Aobamba valleys, and in the south by the ridgeline of the Salkantay massif.

The area represents one of the world's most biologically diverse regions: 10% of Peru's entire **biodiversity** is represented within the confines of the Sanctuary alone. This includes around 200 species of orchid, more than 700 species of butterfly and over 400 species of bird. Of the 9000 or so registered bird species in the world, those found in Europe and North America account for around 1400. Peru accounts for almost 1800 on its own, of which 120 are endemic to Peru. The Sanctuary plays host to almost 5% of the world's known bird species.

The reason for this is the great variety of **ecosystems** generated by the wide range of altitudes found within the Sanctuary. The mouth of the Aobamba River lies at 1725m/5658ft, whilst a mere 20km away the peak of Mt Salkantay grazes 6271m/20,569ft. The high mountain ridges generate microclimates that are particularly

❑ **Qoyllur Rit'i (The Festival of the Snow Star)**
The **Andean bear**, known as *ukuku* in Quechua, is important in Andean folklore and plays a vital role in the Festival of the Snow Star at Qoyllur Rit'i, a village on Nevado Ausangate near Cusco. Once a year, typically in early June on the full moon before Corpus Christi, thousands of pilgrims gather high in the mountains. Each group is accompanied by an ukuku, a dancer in a wool mask and shaggy tunic who represents the bear. The ukuku is thought to live on the edge of two worlds. He is portrayed as a mischievous clown and a trickster, but is also a savage, supremely strong guardian sent to guide the pilgrims across the glaciers and protect them from the souls of the damned that wander the ice. According to legend the bear earns his manhood by confronting and defeating one of these souls, and the role of the ukuku is now seen as a traditional rite of passage for young men.

The festival dates back to the days when Peruvians made pilgrimages to placate the spirits or *apus* of the mountains with sacrifices. Legend has it that there's always a death during the pilgrimage and the apu is satisfied. It is the responsibility of the ukuku to bring down the healing properties of the apu in the form of glacial ice.

favourable to the evolution of certain species. The 4546m/14,911ft altitude span results in a broad scope of temperatures being available for different species to dwell in whilst regular rainfall and frequent cloud and mist mean that the region is also humid for much of the year.

The Sanctuary is classified into ten distinct '**Life Zones**', which range from the permanent snows of the high peaks through two types of high-altitude grassland to seven zones of forest. The best-known and most-recognized zones are the treeless, mountain grassland environment known as *puna* and the cloud forest, which harbours four Life Zones and is most commonly characterized by a dense and varied mass of trees, smothered in lichens, bromeliads and orchids, surrounded by tree ferns and bamboo. The Sanctuary is also home to some of the few remaining native Andean *Polylepis* forests, which are found on steep slopes and cliffs at higher altitudes; the classic Inca Trail passes through one such section during the ascent to Dead Woman's Pass (see p224).

See p44 for details of field guides to the region.

FLORA

In the Andes flowers and plants from the valleys and highland plains grow alongside each other as a result of the variations in altitude and climate found there. Consequently the region boasts a wide range of habitats and microhabitats, and features a huge diversity of wild species.

Trees

There are several beautiful trees found throughout the cloud forest. **Aliso** (*Alnus jorullensis*) grows up to 20m tall and is frequently found on the banks of rivers and streams between 2500m and 3800m. The Incas and the Spanish used its large trunks as beams and lintels in buildings. Today, doors, windows and fruit crates are made from its pale yellow wood.

The smaller **chacpa** (*Oreocallis grandiflora*) ranges in height from two to six metres. It has a host of pink flowered heads that can readily be seen in the Cusichaca Valley on the early stages of the Inca Trail. Baskets are made from the small, flexible branches and locals chew the leaves in order to prevent tooth decay.

The thorny **tara tree** (*Caesalpina spinosa*) is very common in the Cusichaca Valley. It is unusual in that it bears fruit year-round. These fruits contain tannin, used for tanning leather. They are also used to ease throat pain. The tara is most easily recognized by the characteristic orange/red seedpods it produces that resemble tough-skinned broad beans.

The **chamana** (*Dodonaea viscosa*) is also found in the Cusichaca Valley. It is a smaller shrub that grows to 2m and is covered in abundant foliage. It is the perfect plant for binding the soil along the steep mountainsides. The wood burns well even when fresh as it contains an oily substance that is flammable. The similar-sized **llaulli** (*Barnadesia horrida*) is a thorny bush that can be found in the ravines adjacent to the Urubamba Valley between 2900m and 3800m. The local farmers cultivate it as a hedge and use it to make a lattice on the roofs of their adobe huts upon which tiles are laid. The pink, daisy-like flowers are good for alleviating respiratory problems and bronchitis.

The town of Chilca, in the Urubamba Valley, gets its name from the **chilca bush** (*Bacharis latifolia*), which is abundant throughout the valley between 2500m and 3400m. Balls of white flowers form at the end of the branches in clusters. The leaves and flowers are used to make a yellow/green dye for wool. A ball of ash and calcium, called Llipta, which locals chew with coca leaves, is made from its ashes. The town Mollepata on the other hand, the start point for the treks over Mt Salkantay, is so called because the Incas cultivated molle trees in the region. The name literally translates as 'The place of the molles'. The **molle** (*Schinus molle*) is a 6-7.5m tall tree that is attractive enough to be used as an ornamental plant. The Incas used resin collected from it to embalm their mummified dead. Today, the tree's wood is used in carpentry and its ashes used for tanning and in the production of soap. Oil extracted from its leaves is used in perfumes and by the toothpaste industry. Honey, vinegar, tincture and condiments are all made from the small red fruits that the tree produces.

Other attractive ornamental trees include the **rata rata** (*Abutilon sylvaticum*), the pink and white conical flowers of which are used to decorate city plazas and gardens but is found wild in the Cusichaca Valley around Huayllabamba, and the **unca** (*Myrcanthes oreophyl*), which grows up to 15m tall and has very pretty, large white flowers with many filaments. The Incas used to make *keros*, ceremonial vases, from its heavy, white wood, whilst today it's used in furniture making.

The bright red splashes of colour visible around the towns of Pisac, Calca and Urubamba in the Sacred Valley are likely to be flowering **pisonay** (*Erythrima edulis*). This giant, leafy, 15m tall tree is native to the high jungle but the Incas acclimatized it to the highlands and considered it to be sacred. However, the real giant of the forest is likely to be the **eucalyptus** (*Eucaliptus globulus*). This imported tree grows up to 30m tall and is the most industrialized, commercialized and useful tree to the Andean people as it grows very quickly in comparison to Andean trees. Its wood is used in the building and mining industries and to make furniture, posts and railway sleepers. Its leaves are used to cure colds and to produce menthol on behalf of the drug and food industries.

Finally, keep your eyes peeled for the **kantu** (*Cantua buxifolia*), known locally as *Flor del Inca*, Peru's national flower. This red and yellow tubular flower, which opens out like a trumpet, grows on a shrub that stands up to 4m tall and grows between 2300m and 3800m. The Incas dedicated this plant to the Sun God and used the pattern of its flower on their pottery, textiles and ceremonial vases. Kantu are often grown as ornamental plants in town plazas, such as in Cusco and are a common sight throughout the Sacred Valley.

Orchids

The Machu Picchu Historical Sanctuary is famous for the quantities of orchids that flourish there. Over 70 genera and around 250 species thrive in the moist, humid confines of the Sanctuary. However, much of the region remains unexplored and there are undoubtedly more to be discovered, possibly for the very first time.

Although orchids abound, numbers around the Inca trail and in particular at Machu Picchu itself have dwindled significantly over recent years as a direct consequence of illegal collection by visitors. The biggest threats though are from deforestation and forest fires, which destroy valuable orchid gene banks and prime habitat as well as altering and annihilating entire ecosystems. A particular case in point is the unsympathetic and extensive clearing that occurred around Intipata (see box p232) on the Inca Trail, which resulted in the loss of unique habitat for the rare orchid *Telipogon papilio*, which now faces extinction in the Sanctuary. Conserving these orchids is everyone's responsibility. There is currently no single organization responsible for their preservation in Peru although INRENA (the Ministry of Agriculture), INDECOPI and PromPeru share the obligation. Until this commitment is taken seriously though it remains extremely difficult to manage the conservation of Peruvian orchids.

The observant or interested trekker should spot orchids at any time of year. The most-likely places to come across these exquisite flowers are off the beaten track though, especially in the cloud forest between 1800m and 3000m. Most flower during the rainy season, from October to March. The diversity of species on show is stunning.

The most widespread and populous genus is *Epidendrum*, of which there are around 30 species in the Sanctuary. The most common is *Epidendrum secundum*, known locally as **huinay huayna**, meaning 'forever young', a reference to the fact that this diminutive, striking orchid flowers almost all year. The small splashes of vibrant colour are most readily spotted around the ruins of Huinay Huayna on the Inca Trail, which is named after the plant. Its abundant flowers are red, pink, yellow or violet. Other species include the delicate and fragrant *Epidendrum ciliare*, which grows on trees and rocks at the lower elevations of the Sanctuary, and *Epidendrum coronatum*, which grows in open areas amidst other plants at altitudes between 2800m and 3200m.

Also commonly seen on the forest border and on open slopes are the *Odontoglossum sp*, whose bright yellow flowers are distinctively shaped and protected by brown or purple sepals.

Once widespread, *Masdevallia veitchiana*, known locally as **huakanki**, which means 'you'll cry', has been collected almost to extinction. One of the most striking orchids, its purple and orange flowers with three slight pointed petals are very distinctive and still sought after. The orchid requires open sunny areas and can still be seen at Huinay Huayna on the Inca Trail, where it clings to rocky outcrops carpeted in moss. It flowers from May to July.

The bamboo orchid, *Sobralia dichotoma*, also known as the **Inca orchid** or *Flor del Paraíso*, is visible around Machu Picchu by virtue of the fact that it grows so tall (up to 5m/15ft) and has large, showy, 8cm-diameter purple flowers that bloom from July to September and can easily be seen above the surrounding foliage. At the other end of the scale is one of the world's smallest orchids, a *Stelis* whose flower is barely 2mm wide.

Bromeliads, cacti and grasses

Bromeliads, relatives of the pineapple, can be seen throughout the Sanctuary. Several types of cacti are also common. The **agave cactus** (*Agave americana*) is a broad plant with bluish spiked succulent leaves that grows on the dry mountainsides. The Incas made ropes and knitted suspension bridges from the leaf fibres. They also made sandals from it. Local people now use it to form an impenetrable hedge and in the production of products such as soap. The **prickly pear cactus** is cultivated in order to obtain carmine, a natural red colourant used in food, and pharmaceutical and cosmetic industries. Carmine is obtained from the cochineal, a parasitic insect found in the cactus. The fruits of the cactus are delicious and are sold in many of the towns in the Sacred Valley.

There are two types of common **grasses**. *Stipa ichu*, the golden or brown stems of which grow in tussocks on the puna from 3000m to 4500m, is a tough, ubiquitous grass used to make roofs on huts, insulate beds and tents and as animal feed. The other is *Certaderia nitida*, which stands much taller and looks like a fox tail. A type of succulent grass, *Plantago rigida*, grows in round, rigid cushions. Inflexible leaves grow in star shapes in high swampy areas between 4500m and 4800m. Trekkers often use these cushions as stepping-stones across boggy areas. The Quechua name, *qachqa oku*, refers to the plant's texture (*qachqa* means 'rough') and habitat (*oku* means 'wet'). This plant is the favoured foodstuff of alpacas.

Shrubs and flowers

Familiar plants frequently seen whilst out walking in the UK, Europe and the US can be spotted in the Sanctuary, too. **Broom** (*Spartinum junceum*), a member of the sweet pea family, was introduced from Spain in 1580. This yellow flowering shrub grows well in grasslands up to 3500m. The plant is cultivated in order to produce dye, firewood and for use as decoration. Its bright flowers are used medicinally to treat rheumatism, oedema, liver diseases and abscesses. They also serve as makeshift confetti in parades.

Lupins (*Lupinus sp*) are another common shrub found throughout the grasslands in the area. Its blueish, lavender flowers are shaped like pea flowers and have bright yellow centres. The leaves, flowers and stems are used for a cream- or green-coloured dye.

Ladies' slipper (*Calceolaria engleriana*) is a member of the snapdragon family. The flowers of this 2m tall shrub resemble tiny 2cm slippers – the Latin name is derived from *calceolus*, meaning 'slipper'. In Quechua the plant is called *pucllu*, which means 'bag' or 'sack' and again refers to the shape of the flowers. Its Spanish nickname is *globitus*, meaning 'little balloons', because you can pop the flowers between your fingers. Various species are used by local people in tea as a cure for uterine problems or as a diuretic. Also readily identifiable are the flowers of the **wild potato** (*Solanaceae sp*). This erect, clambering herb has violet flowers with five points and protruding yellow anthers. There are some 135 species of this genus in Peru alone, growing in rocky or wooded areas.

A type of **lily**, *Bomarea dulcis*, grows around boulders in grassy areas. The plant produces between two and five dangling 2" flowers that resemble tubular bells. The sepals of these are reddish pink but have darker edges. The Quechua name for this plant is *milli milli*, meaning 'twins' and describes the two flowers often seen hanging together. The equally distinctive, purple-violet dangling flowers of *Brachyotum grisebachi* can be readily seen on the edges of the cloud forest near to water. This 2.5m shrub has many branches and produces masses of the distinctive flowers, which are occasionally worn by local people as ear decorations. **Begonias** (*Begonia bracteosa*) flourish within the Sanctuary and the red, white or pink flowers of various species can be seen on numerous dry, sunny, stepped slopes. **Bomareas** can be seen in two colours. The showy orange bracts of *Bomarea aurantiaca* and the deep red bracts of *Bomarea coccinea* are particularly visible in the humid cloud forest around Phuyu Pata Marca on the Inca Trail and in the jungle surrounding the Santa Teresa Valley.

Daisies, **fuchsias**, **elders** and **buttercups** are also prevalent. More unusual is the **datura** (**moonflower**), *Brugmansia arborea*; there are two types, which have white and red/green flowers respectively. Both are hallucinogenic and toxic if consumed.

FAUNA

Mammals

Although you may have heard of the **Andean (or spectacled) bear** (*Tremarctus ornatus*), the only member of its family found in South America, it is very shy and consequently difficult to see. Measuring 1.5-2m from head to tail, this black bear which gets its nickname from its creamy face markings and dark eye rings, is classified as 'vulnerable' because its territory has been reduced by deforestation, farming and other human activity. The bear survives in this hostile situation by being willing to eat anything, a policy that occasionally gets it into trouble when it raids maize crops at the edge of cloud forests. Typically though, these harmless animals feed on cacti, orchid bulbs, fallen fruit and assorted leaves, though they also prey on small animals such as rabbits, mice and nesting birds. However, the bear's favourite food is bromeliads; it will construct rudimentary platforms in order to clamber up trees, like Paddington reaching for marmalade, to be able to get at these plants. Having feasted, and without any natural predator (except man), the bear often just falls asleep. See also box p103.

Even more enigmatic and tricky to spot are **puma** (*Felis concolor*). These powerful, tawny cats are usually solitary animals that prefer habitats with dense underbrush and rocky areas perfect for stalking and ambushing prey. Once revered by the Incas as a symbol of power and elegance, their numbers have declined due to hunting and the loss of habitat and they are now rare in this region. The **culpeo fox**, known locally as *zorro*, is more common. This bold, versatile scavenger preys on rodents including Andean **skunks** and **weasels**, rabbits and birds, although it will also make do with carrion. There are two types of high-altitude grassland deer, the endangered **Andean huemal**, or *taruka* as it is called in Quechua, and the rather more common **white-tailed deer**.

Moonflower
Brugmansia arborea

Tailed Phragmipedium orchid
Phragmipedium caudatum

Ulluypiña
Eustephia coccinea

Begonia
Begonia bracteosa

*Odontoglossum
mystacinum* (Orchid)

Kantu/Cantuta
Cantua buxifolia

Bromeliad
Bromeliaceae

Huinay Huayna orchid
('Forever young')
Epidendrum secundum

Huakanki orchid
('You'll cry')
Masdevallia veitchiana

Llama llama
('Flames')
Oreocallis grandiflora

Flor del Paraíso
(Inca orchid)
Sobralia dichotoma

Lupin
(Tarwi, Chocho)
Lupinus sp.

Ladies' slipper
(Zaptitos: 'Little shoes')
Calceolaria engleriana

Wild potato
Solanum aloysifolium

Red datura/moonflower
Datura sanguinea

Broom (Retama)
Spartium junceum

The Sanctuary is also home to **pudu** (*sachacabra* in Quechua), secretive pygmy deer that are nocturnal and consequently rarely seen during the day.

Mountain **viscachas** (*Lagidium peruanum*) look a lot like rabbits but are in fact close relatives of the chinchilla. These bushy-tailed rodents with long furry ears are widespread, but blend easily into the background, their grey and brown fur perfect camouflage against the rocks that they like to sun themselves on. There are also large colonies living amongst the ruins at Machu Picchu.

Llamas (*Lama glama*) and **alpacas** (*Lama pacos*) are the most regularly seen animals in the Sanctuary. Relatives of the Old World camel, both species were domesticated many thousands of years ago by pre-Columbian Andean tribes who recognized these hardy creatures could carry substantial loads as pack animals and also represented a useful source of food and warm wool. Llamas are the most common and strongest of the Andean camelids. They stand 1.9m tall and can carry up to 60kg. The alpaca, known as *pacocha* in Quechua, has a smaller and more-rounded silhouette than a llama. In general alpacas have more and better-quality wool than llamas, the most desirable being from baby alpaca, which is soft and fine. Alpaca meat is also being promoted and many of the restaurants in Cusco serve it.

These two camelids have two wild relatives: the **guanaco** (*Lama guanicoe*), which stands just over a metre tall at the shoulder and has a grey face, short ears and a white belly, and the **vicuña** (*Vicugna vicugna*) which is a smaller, graceful-looking creature with inquisitive eyes, tawny brown fur on their upper parts and longer white fur on the throat and underside, reputed to be the finest animal wool in the world. Both of these are rarely seen in the Machu Picchu Sanctuary having been shot and trapped extensively by hunters and poachers, but are for-

---

❏ The Peruvian paso

The Spanish conquistadors were responsible for introducing the horse to South America. Initially used to intimidate the Inca troops who hadn't encountered horses in battle before, they were then used for transportation and breeding. Breeds included the jennet, an ideal light riding horse, the barb, which had great stamina and the Andalusian, an elegant, strongly built breed favoured as a warhorse. Horses with good endurance and a smooth gait were particularly prized; characteristics that led to the selective breeding of the Peruvian paso, noted for its good temperament and comfortable ride. Instead of a trot, the Peruvian paso performs an amble somewhere between a walk and a canter. The four beat lateral gait – right hind, right front, left hind, left front – accounts for the smooth ride since it causes none of the vertical bounce associated with trotting. The gait, which is natural and doesn't require training, also makes the horse very stable as there are always two and sometimes three hooves on the ground. The horses have great stamina and spirit, known locally as 'brio', and are able to cover great distances without tiring, travelling at a comfortable canter over uneven terrain. They are also willing to work and very biddable, making them an incredibly useful steed.

The past 30 years have seen a resurgence in the Peruvian paso's fortunes and the annual National Show just outside Lima to find the most elegant and beautiful horse in the country has developed into a major event in Peruvian cultural life.

tunately more common in the south. They are now protected species in Peru and although still vulnerable, their numbers have started to increase again.

Insects

Peru is justifiably famous for its **butterflies**: a fifth of the world's butterfly species is found here. Some 1300 species have been recorded in the community of Pakitza, in Manu National Park and over 1200 species have been noted at a community 145 miles/235km away on the Tambopata River. Incredibly, only 60% of these species overlapped. Scientists estimate that there must be more than 4000 species in the country, only about 3600 of which have currently been registered. Considering that North America boasts 679 species and Europe a mere 441 species, this is an astounding number.

The Andean highlands at more than 5000m/16,400ft are home to relatively few species. Those that do survive here are specially adapted to the rigorous environment. Tropical forests are the preferred habitat of most butterfly species. Trekkers on the Vilcabamba Trek are likely to see the most diverse array of butterflies, often encountering huge swarms congregating together.

Unfortunately, you are also likely to become very well acquainted with the **midges** that can be encountered throughout the Sanctuary, but most especially in the Santa Teresa Valley. They also plague the approach to Choquequirao.

Reptiles and amphibians

Few reptiles are known about, as the forest tends to be so dense and inaccessible. Keep a look out for **snakes**; coral snakes, bushmasters and the rare velvet fer-de-lance are endemic to the Sanctuary. They are all poisonous and should not be approached if encountered. Fortunately most snakes found in the Andes are non-venomous. Most frequently encountered are harmless whipsnakes: slender green snakes with yellow underbellies.

Frogs of the genus *Atelopus* also live in the forest above 2000m.

Birds

The Incas believed that birds were the messengers of the *apus*, the gods who lived on the summits of mountains. The condor, being the most impressive bird, was associated with the highest peaks whilst less-remarkable birds were considered to carry the thoughts and words of spirits residing on lower mountains.

The Sanctuary has an impressive array of avifauna for such a compact area. Many birds have relatively small altitudinal ranges, meaning that each of the Sanctuary's ten habitats is home to species that are found in no other zone. More than 400 species are known to exist in the Sanctuary and more than 200 of these can be readily observed along the Inca Trail or on the treks to Vilcabamba and Choquequirao.

The *Polylepis* woodland contains some of the rarest birds, including titspinetails and high-altitude hummingbirds, but the cloud forest is home to the greatest diversity and here you can expect to see tinamous, guans, parakeets, hummingbirds, wrens, jays, swallows, quetzals, woodpeckers, flycatchers and tanagers.

The best way to spot these birds is to look for them at the correct time of day. Although you can see birds at any time, your best chance is first thing in the morning or at dusk, when they are singing and most active. Be quiet as you walk through the forest and stop periodically to look around carefully. To improve your chances further, bring binoculars on your trip.

● **Andean condor** The emblematic Andean condor (*Vultur gryphus*) is actually an enormous vulture, boasting the largest wing span of any land bird. Some individuals have spans in excess of 3m/10ft and measure well over a metre from their bill to the tip of their tail. They can weigh up to 11kg. The adult plumage is uniformly black, with the exception of a white ruff surrounding the base of the neck. The head and neck are blackish red and bald, an adaptation for hygiene given that the bird primarily feeds on carrion and rotting meat. When in flight, it can be identified by its sheer size and characteristic silhouette: the finger feathers at the tips of its wings point forward. Condors prefer relatively open areas that allow it to spot carrion from the air and favour rocky cliffs and outcrops on which to nest. Although considered a mountain bird, it is more common on the coast.

ANDEAN
CONDOR

The Andean Condor is a national symbol of Peru and plays an important role in indigenous folklore and mythology. More recently it has endured a swathe of negative press, and stories abound of birds harrying travellers, killing livestock and even snatching small children whilst shepherds tended to their llama flocks. Writers including Bruce Chatwin (*In Patagonia*) and George Squier (*Peru – Travel and Exploration in the Land of the Incas*, 1877) documented instances where they came under attack from condors.

Hiram Bingham recounted in *Lost City of the Incas* that local shepherds had to wage a constant battle with condors that had no difficulty in carrying off a sheep. Even today some of the less-discerning newspapers occasionally run stories about condors snatching away unguarded infants. If you come across a condor in captivity or happen to see a stuffed specimen, a quick look at their ineffective, talon-free feet, akin to those of an enormous domestic chicken, which have been adapted for walking rather than holding or carrying objects, will debunk the notion that they could carry off anything substantial, let alone a small child or sheep wriggling to be free.

● **Birds of prey** The bigger birds in the high Andes are usually raptors or birds of prey. Look out for the **American kestrel** (*Falco sparverius*), a pair of **Aplomado falcons** (*Falco femoralis*) or a **mountain caracara** (*Phalcoboenus megalopterus*). The kestrel, colloquially known as a sparrow hawk, is a small falcon, averaging around 20cm from beak to tail, with blue-grey wings, a white head with blue-grey cap, white cheeks and a pair of vertical black face

MOUNTAIN CARACARA

markings. Its breast and tail are a brownish, rust-colour. The medium-sized falcon is 10-20cm longer but very slim. It has a dark blue-grey head, long, light brown pointed wings, a tapering tail with narrow white or grey bars and a paler breast. The caracara is larger still, measuring up to 50cm from beak to tail. It has characteristic black, white and grey wings, a black and white tail and the bare skin of its face is an orangey colour. A highly opportunistic scavenger, it can often be seen walking on the ground in search of carrion and can often be found near human habitation.

Other species to spot include a number of types of **hawk**, most common of which is the **red-backed hawk** (*Buteo polyosoma*), and the **black-chested buzzard eagle** (*Geranoaetus melanoleucus*). It is a big, bulky, powerful-looking bird measuring up to 80cm from beak to tail. Its plumage is predominantly a blue-hued grey colour, with black edges to its wings and a black neck and head. It is identifiable in flight by the short, wedge-shaped tail that scarcely protrudes from its broad wings.

BLACK-CHESTED
BUZZARD EAGLE

● **Guans** These large pheasant-like birds can be seen, or more frequently heard, crashing about in the trees of the humid montane forests. The most common is the **Andean guan** (*Penelope montagnii*). This turkey-sized bird, with orange-brown plumage and a red wattle, lives in the trees and feeds on fruit, seeds and other vegetable matter, rarely descending to the ground.

● **Motmots** These beautifully coloured birds are related to kingfishers. They occur in all types of forest as well as on open areas of grassland. Colourful, long and slender, they are medium-sized birds with long, broad bills that are somewhat curved down at the end. The most-distinctive feature though is their tail.

In most motmots, two central feather shafts grow much longer than the others. The **Highland motmot** (*Momotus aequatorialis*) grows up to 48cm and has a turquoise-blue forecrown and green underparts. It can be seen all along the Urubamba Valley, often perched on riverside boulders, and around Aguas Calientes. Similar, but slightly smaller and with brown underparts, is the **blue crowned motmot** (*Momotus momata*).

● **Tanagers** Amongst the forests' most common and visible birds, tanagers often congregate in small flocks near human habitation to feed in fruit trees. They are noted for their colourful plumage and few other species can compete with the broad spectrum of colours found on their feathers.

There are 135 species recorded in Peru, 60 of which can be seen around Machu Picchu; those most commonly spotted along the Inca Trail are the **blue-and-yellow tanager**, the **blue-grey tanager**, the **saffron-crowned tanager**, the **fawn-breasted tanager** and the **silver-beaked tanager**.

● **Trogons** Although less well known than other gaudy birds, trogons are often considered to be the most visually impressive. The largest of the species, the quetzals, are the most dazzling. Males are consistently more colourful than the females and have metallic or glittering green, blue or violet heads, backs and chests. Their breasts and undersides are contrasting bright red, yellow or orange. The females usually have darker brown or grey backs and heads, but they share the brightly coloured chests of the males. The long characteristic tail is squared off and striped black and white on the underside. Look out for the green-headed **collared trogon** (*Trogon collaris*) and the similar **masked trogon** (*Trogon personatus*), which can be distinguished by the thicker bars on its tail feathers.

● **Wrens** These are small, brownish birds that tend to skulk in thick under-growth. The Latin name of the genus, *Troglodytes*, refers to a cave dweller, a reference to the wren's predilection for nesting in holes and crevices. They are very vocal and have attractive singing voices. The typical sound heard at Machu Picchu is the song of the **Inca wren** (*Thryothorus eisenmanni*), which is native to Peru and whose distinctive spotted breast marks it out from other types of wren.

● **Hummingbirds** Almost everyone can identify hummingbirds, which evolved in the Andes. They are mostly tiny birds, usually clad in iridescent metallic greens, reds, violets and blues. These tiny, nectar-drinking birds rely entirely on their wings for locomotion since their feet and legs are too weak for anything but perching. There are more than 130 species of hummingbird in Peru, the majority of which are found in the Andes.

The most commonly spotted hummingbird along the Inca Trail or in Cusco gardens is the **sparkling violetear** (*Colibri coruscans*), which has a violet-blue chest and violet ear that extends to its chin. It is a tireless singer.

The slightly larger **green-and-white hummingbird** (*Leucippus viridicauda*) is regularly recorded around Machu Picchu, where it can be identified by its white chest.

The world's largest hummingbird is the surprisingly muted (at least in com-parison to its relatives) **giant hummingbird** (*Patagonia gigas*), which can measure more than 20cm from the tip of its long bill to the end of its tail.

You will also come across **sunangels**, **sapphirewings**, **coquettes**, **golden-throats**, **sunbeams** and **coronets**, each of which is as beautiful as its name promises.

● **Waterfowl** In mountain streams as well as along the Urubamba River, you can find **torrent ducks** (*Merganetta armata*). Uniquely adapted to swimming, diving and feeding in the fast rushing waters that cascade off the mountains, the ducks rarely stray far from the streams and even nest in crevices between boul-ders on the water's edge. Male torrent ducks have striking black and white striped heads and red beaks, and females have orange underparts, grey backs and a yellow bill.

Andean gulls (*Larus serranus*), the only gulls to be found in the high Andes, also live along the Urubamba or can be found on the higher elevation tarns. You can also see the **Andean (or ruddy) duck**, which is rust-red with a spiky black tail, and has a white face with a black cap and wide blue bill, and the **crested duck**, a sleek grey with a touch of red on the wings.

The heavily built **Andean Geese**, with white plumage and small pink bills, prefer being on land to swimming so that they can graze, whilst black and white **giant coots** are common on the water.

Elegant **puna ibis** (*Plegadis ridgwayi*), which have dark purplish-brown feathers and a chestnut face, can often be seen around Cusco and along the first stages of the railway trip to Machu Picchu foraging slowly and probing the shallow waters and mud with their distinctive long, curved bills.

● **Other birds**   The magnificent **cock of the rock** (*Rupicola peruviana*), with its prominent fan-shaped headdress of bright orange or scarlet feathers, is Peru's national bird. The female of the species is significantly darker and browner though. Frequently seen along the railway tracks around Machu Picchu, it is also common in the forests surrounding Espíritu Pampa, where gatherings of males compete for breeding females by displaying their gaudy plumage, bobbing and making a series of calls.

Other stunning, noisy birds often spotted are **parakeets**, which can often be seen and heard around Aguas Calientes or in the forests along the Vilcabamba trek.

On the ground you can see furtive **tinamous**, a type of partridge. Prior to the introduction of the chicken by the Spanish, the Incas domesticated tinamous for their meat and eggs. At one stage these birds were so common that they gave their name to the town in the Sacred Valley: Pisac means 'partridge'.

Swifts and **swallows**, with their distinctive swept-back wings and pointed tails, have easily identifiable silhouettes as they flash overhead.

Woodpeckers, such as the **bar-bellied woodpecker** (*Venilioris nigriceps*) and **crimson-mantled woodpecker** (*Piculus rivolii*), are recognizable due to their shape and habit of drilling in tree trunks.

The attractive **Andean flicker** (*Colaptes rupicola*), a fairly common, largish woodpecker (33cm from beak to tail) with a light brown head and black cap, grey and dark brown feathers and a yellow breast, lives in puna and scrubland where, rather unusually, it nests in earth banks and old adobe buildings.

Minimum impact trekking

Tourism is a vital source of income for Peru and, directly or indirectly, a great many Peruvians benefit from the increasing numbers of trekkers and tourists flocking to the country. However, there are undoubtedly problems along the Inca Trail and the other trekking routes in the region that are caused by the arrival of hordes of visitors. Litter, erosion, pollution and the destruction of the landscape and the Inca archaeological sites are all sadly the realities of large numbers of people visiting these areas.

The Instituto Nacional de Cultura (INC; see p165) does nominally try to keep the place clean, but unfortunately their actions aren't all that effective. Whilst it's easy to blame the authorities for the decline of the pristine wilderness, trekkers are equally at fault. People on the trails also have to take responsibility for their own litter and actions; each individual should remember that their thoughtlessness and self-ishness potentially has consequences for everyone else.

ENVIRONMENTAL IMPACT

Damaged vegetation, litter, polluted waterways, deteriorating facilities and an increase in erosion are all indications that trekkers have had a negative impact on the landscape. Fortunately, most people are now much more conscious of the potential impact that they have on the environment and are more likely to adopt a considerate, responsible attitude whilst trekking or otherwise enjoying the landscape. It's important that we all maintain this new-found responsibility.

Pack it in, pack it out

All waste must be carried off the mountain. Human detritus is one of the most significant threats to the natural environment. Unsightly and unhealthy, accumulated rubbish is a hazard for people and wildlife alike. If you are with an official group, in theory all you have to do is hand the litter to the team members who will then ensure that it is removed from the trail. Unfortunately this isn't always the case and more unscrupulous guides or porters may dump or drop rubbish along the route.

Keep an eye on your team and make sure they understand that it is important to you that they adhere to this rule. In addition, don't give them batteries to dispose of; keep hold of them and take them back home where there are proper facilities for getting rid of them. If you are trekking independently, take rubbish bags with you to carry all your waste and be conscious of the amount of litter you are likely to generate when preparing to trek. If you come across litter along the trail you should pick it up and remove it, if at all possible, in order to set a good example.

Bury your excrement

Where possible, always use the purpose-built toilet blocks along the trails or at the campsites. If you are trekking on one of the routes that doesn't have facilities, or are caught short on the trail, stick to the following rules: make sure you're at least 20m away from both the path and any water source or stream; take a trowel with you so that you can dig a small hole to squat over and cover the hole with plenty of soil once you're done; dispose of your toilet paper properly either by burning it or burying it deeply in the same hole. Better still pack it out along with everything else, having taken the precaution of double-bagging (preferably in a zip-lock bag) the offending article.

Don't pollute water

The Andean waterways and lakes are fragile ecosystems. Contamination can easily lead to deterioration in water quality. Equally, no-one wants to bathe in other people's bathwater. Or cook with it, do their laundry in it or indeed drink it. Yet this is the consequence for the local people if you wash your hair or body or clothes in the mountain streams, no matter how romantic an image this might conjure up. Your guide will almost certainly provide you with a bowl of warm water at the start and end of the day for you to wash with. Dispose of this carefully, at least 20m away from any other water source or stream, and wait until you finish the trek to have a proper wash.

Erosion

In general, the Inca trails are clearly marked and easy to follow. Try to stay on these paths wherever possible. The continued use of shortcuts, particularly on some of the steeper sections of trail, erodes the slopes. From the various passes it is very tempting to descend quickly and directly, and you may see people, especially guides, doing just that. Faster and possibly more fun, the shortcuts nonetheless destroy the fabric of the hillside and cause irreparable damage. Tedious as it may sound, stick to the marked paths.

Camping

When camping, try to have as little impact as possible on the countryside. Ask permission if near to a farm or small-holding. Confine yourself to as small a space as is realistic and do not spread yourself out unduly. Don't litter the area and when you strike camp make sure you tidy everything up and leave the site as you found it, undisturbed.

Campfires

Whilst a campfire sounds very appealing and the stuff of true camping expeditions, the reality of an out-of-control fire means that it just isn't worth the risk.

There's absolutely no need to light a fire on any of the treks described here: for cooking you or your guides ought to use a portable stove, whilst for heat you should simply put on another jumper or layer of clothes.

Don't camp in the ruins
The ancient stones have been badly damaged by trekkers in the past who liked the idea of spending a night amongst the Inca sites. Litter and human waste are not the only problems of this selfish action. Campfires damage the walls and clumsy campers dislodge and remove the stones themselves. Camping at the sites along the Inca Trail or at Choquequirao itself are banned and trekkers must adhere to these rules.

You do not belong amidst the ruins and you cannot stake a claim to them by sleeping amongst them.

Don't pick flowers or disturb fauna
Leave the flora and fauna alone. The Cusco region, a dedicated UNESCO natural World Heritage Site, is full of stunning flowers and some extraordinary bird and animal life. It is illegal to remove anything from the trails or the sanctuary, so leave it all where it belongs for others to enjoy as well.

ECONOMIC IMPACT

The economic importance of tourism for Peru is undeniable. However, not everyone benefits equally. If you book an organized trek through a foreign operator, the bulk of your money stays outside the country. Book a trek through an agency in Cusco, and a far greater proportion of the money remains in the city. The porters and trek team may not be from the city, although they will benefit from the opportunity to work. If you trek independently where possible, you will contribute far more to the local economy. Employ a local porter or *arriero*. Some independent trekkers feel that being burdened by their pack is part of the experience, but it is far more useful to the region if you hire help, and if arranged whilst there, can be a surprisingly simple, cheap way of putting something back and making your trip more enjoyable.

Pay a fair price for a fair service
Recognize the worth of a service to you and pay a reasonable rate for it. Do not attempt to bargain porters or arrieros right down and do not haggle overly aggressively. They are paid poorly for back-breaking work, yet are worth every sol to the success of a trek (see Porter welfare, pp22-3). However, do not believe the market traders and touts who tell you that goods have a fixed price!

CULTURAL IMPACT

The places that you are visiting are of great spiritual, historical and cultural importance. Show these places the respect that they deserve. To fully appreciate and understand the cultural history and value of the place that you are visiting you ought to spend some time learning about its people and history (see pp51-65).

Whilst you are trekking be considerate to other visitors and users of the countryside. Try to keep noise to a minimum. As a general rule, be selfless and remember that you are only visiting.

Encourage local pride
Encourage local pride by giving Peruvians a balanced view of life in your home country. In answer to queries about how much you earn, reply honestly but put the figures into context by comparing how much it costs to rent a flat or buy certain types of goods. Tell them what you think is good about their lifestyle – the extraordinary surroundings, the lack of real crime, the clean air – and comment on what appeals to you about their lifestyle. If you particularly enjoyed your stay or trek be sure to let them know.

To give or not to give?
Giving to beggars can perpetrate an attitude of dependency. Be careful not to load up with sweets or other gifts to answer the children's begging requests. Although handing things out might make you feel good in the short term, it can lead to a detrimental effect on the recipient, resulting in low self-esteem and an associated idea that the west and tourists hold the answer rather than their own culture. Additionally, there are no dentists in the rural communities and giving sweets to children here is not helpful.

If someone has done something helpful, consider rewarding them, but be careful as to how you do it. Requests for pens and other school equipment are harder to refuse, but donations should really be made to a school rather than an individual to ensure equal distribution.

You should also be wary of handing out medicines along the trails. Strong or prescription medicines may be taken incorrectly and do more harm than good. If you have additional or left over medicines, donate them to an agency or organization that can distribute them to a hospital instead.

Ask permission before taking a person's photograph
Respect their privacy and if they aren't comfortable or happy with the situation then leave them alone. Ideally you should not pay people for posing. If you offer to send someone a copy of the photo you've taken, make sure you get the address and follow through your promise.

Don't flaunt your wealth
Your wealth, however poor you may be by the standards of your home country, is far in excess of that of most Peruvians, so don't make a big issue of it and certainly don't flaunt it. Take care of valuables and put them away so as to remove temptation. When camping make sure that all your equipment is out of sight inside the tent, especially at night.

Don't lose your temper
Peruvians rarely lose their rag, and you should work hard to control your temper as well, even when things aren't working out as you might have hoped they would. Be polite and the chances are the courtesy will be returned.

Health and safety in the mountains

SAFETY

Although there are hazards in the mountains, a properly prepared expedition with the right equipment and a bit of common sense should not be troubled by them.

Weather
The weather in the Andes is very changeable. You should expect rain whatever the season and ought to carry warm clothing at all times, even if it seems to be a sunny day, since temperatures can plummet and conditions change very quickly. As a general guide, check the weather forecast with your agency or online before setting out and keep an eye on the weather as you walk. For more information about the climate, see p12.

Keeping on course
Although the majority of trails in the Cusco region are well trodden, there are also plenty of areas where you will come across very few people and where the track has disappeared, particularly on the Vilcabamba trek or longer routes linking Vilcabamba to Choquequirao, or Choquequirao to Machu Picchu. Bad weather can also mean that a path previously simple to follow becomes obscured and much harder to trace. In thick cloud or fog do not leave the path.

An accurate topographic map and a compass are helpful, as long as you know how to use them. Similarly, a handheld GPS (Global Positioning System) can help you to find your way.

Tell someone where you're going
If you are planning on trekking independently, before you set off on your trek, tell someone responsible, at your hotel or hostel for example, where you are going and when you expect to return. They should be aware of what to do if you don't come back, and how long they should wait before raising the alarm.

Beware of the dog
Rural dogs can be dangerous, some may even carry rabies, but are more often just a nuisance. If confronted by an angry, barking dog often just bending down as if to pick up a stone is enough to cause them to turn tail – this is what the locals do and the dogs are used to being pelted.

HEALTH IN THE MOUNTAINS

Trekkers often revel in the horror stories about the diseases encountered on treks and trips to the developing world. Whilst Peru does have a handful of serious health problems, you are very unlikely to be affected by them and if you follow simple guidelines you'll minimize the risk to yourself.

MINIMUM IMPACT & SAFE TREKKING

Acute mountain sickness (AMS)

Altitude sickness (or Acute Mountain Sickness, AMS) is a potentially fatal condition and must not be underestimated. The higher you go above sea-level, the lower the barometric pressure, resulting in less oxygen reaching your lungs with each breath. This in turn means that less oxygen is passed into your blood. It generally occurs above 3000m/10,000ft, but can affect people at lower elevations: it is the **speed of ascent** and not the actual altitude that causes AMS. The human body takes several days to acclimatize to an increase in altitude. There are no hard and fast rules as to how long this takes, as individuals are affected differently.

AMS and High Altitude Pulmonary Oedema (HAPE) and High Altitude Cerebral Oedema (HACE), the serious, life-threatening conditions that can occur as a result of it, are entirely preventable though, if certain precautions are taken:

- Don't exceed the recommended rate of ascent
- Drink plenty of liquid – at least four litres per day in some form
- Eat well – even if at altitude you find you lose your appetite
- Avoid overexertion by climbing slowly and steadily
- Look out for early symptoms of AMS and react to them.

Mild symptoms are uncomfortable, but not dangerous, and will pass in a couple of days. As well as breathlessness and an irritating dry cough, you will have a headache and feel nauseous. In more serious conditions you may start to vomit. Increasing tiredness, confusion and a reduction in coordination are more advanced symptoms. Initially ascend slowly, stopping frequently. Remember, it is the speed of ascent, not altitude itself that causes AMS. Drink plenty of liquids to prevent dehydration. Eat light meals and avoid alcohol. Use a light painkiller but do not take sedatives or strong painkillers, which may mask the onset of more serious symptoms.

If the conditions persist, or if you have any reason to suspect that you are suffering from AMS, you should consider descending at once. Even dropping down 500m/1600ft can have a beneficial effect. If you find yourself still struggling, descend further immediately, even during the night. See p47 for more on AMS.

Hypothermia

Also known as exposure, hypothermia develops as a result of someone being extremely cold. If they are hypothermic, they'll stumble, be confused, slur their speech, act oddly and be very cold to the touch. They may be oblivious to the fact that they are in danger. To try to prevent the onset of the condition or the deterioration of the casualty, try to warm them up, most usually by getting them out of wet clothing or by sharing bodily warmth.

Sunburn and sun-stroke

The strong Andean sun burns quickly. Protect against sunburn by wearing a hat, sunglasses and a shirt with a collar. You'll also need sunscreen as the sun is strong, and even an apparently cloudy day is no guarantee that you won't get burnt. Occasionally, if a person's temperature is driven dangerously high, they can develop sun-stroke. A victim of this will be delirious and confused, whilst their pulse will be racing and their breathing fast and erratic. Try to reduce their temperature gradually by fanning, sponging them with a damp cloth and shading them. If they lose consciousness you must try to get them to a doctor as quickly as possible.

Care of feet, ankles and knees
Whilst trekking, your feet are your most valuable tools. A twisted ankle, sore knee or septic blister can severely spoil your trek so take precautions to prevent them. Wear comfortable boots with good ankle support. Don't carry too much or over-stress your joints. Avoid walking in the dark. Wash and dry your feet thoroughly and change your socks regularly. If you do feel a blister developing, act immediately to prevent it from getting worse.

● **Blisters** Prevention is far better than cure when it comes to blisters. If you feel a tingling sensation or 'hot spot' developing stop at once and cover the irritated area with a piece of moleskin or Second Skin. If a blister does form either burst it with a sterilized needle and apply a dressing or build a moleskin dressing around the unburst blister to protect it.

● **Sprains** Reduce the risk of a sprain by wearing boots with good support. Mind your step as you walk over rough or uneven terrain too. If you do sprain an ankle, soak it in cold water and keep it bandaged. Aspirin is good for reducing swelling and easing the pain.

● **Knee problems** Sustained sections of steep downhill trail can result in sore, strained knees. When descending this type of trail take small steps and tread carefully to lessen the impact and jarring on the joints. Knee supports can give some assistance, and trekking poles can also help for long descents, particularly if you have a previous history of knee problems.

Chapped skin and lips
Carry moisturizer or Vaseline to apply to chapped skin. Use lip balm to soothe cracked or dry lips.

Food
To improve your chances of not getting sick when eating, maintain a high standard of hygiene. Essentially, if you can't cook it, peel it or wash it in clean, purified water you should be wary of it.

Water purification
Always boil, filter or purify your drinking water. This will help to reduce the risk of picking up a water-borne illness such as giardia, but will also reduce the number of non-returnable, non-reusable, non-biodegradable and very environmentally unfriendly plastic mineral water bottles found all over the routes. Iodine tablets or iodine drops are ideal for treating water; simply follow the instructions on the packet or bottle. A portable water filter chemically or mechanically cleans the water, but isn't necessarily thorough enough to remove all bugs or impurities. If you treat your water yourself you reduce the risk of it simply being warmed up in a kettle and can be absolutely sure that it has been purified.

LIMA

At the centre of the city lies the decaying hulk of a great colonial shipwreck. In flaking baroque these relics gaze, stained and weary, over the tin and concrete and electric wires. **Matthew Parris**, *Inca Kola*, 1990

Lima lies below a shroud of sea cloud for many months of the year and can look a little uninviting and uniform. It has also been subject to years of negative press, with reports of how the city has become shabby and unsafe, or simply boring. Consequently it became a simple stepping-stone for people travelling to the Andes or Amazon, a city to pass through, an overnight stop to endure rather than enjoy. Peru's capital has another side to it though; the former Spanish capital of South America, originally christened Ciudad de los Reyes (City of Kings), was once one of the continent's most alluring and impressive cities.

These days, it is in fact massively underrated and a wonderful introduction to what you'll see and find elsewhere. Archaeological sites stand amidst residential neighbourhoods whose architecture spans styles from the last 500 years. There are good museums, world-class restaurants and a burgeoning food scene, lively night spots and an irresistible energy and edge borne out of the multicultural mix found here. What's more, a resurgent local middle class are taking pride in their city and pioneering a renaissance that should ensure Lima's reputation is restored.

HISTORY

There's evidence of life and habitation in and around Lima dating back 7000 years. The earliest residents of the mouth of the Rio Rímac were settlers who came to the region to fish. They were followed by more sophisticated cultures who left their mark in the form of temples and pyramids.

These adobe structures, dating from around 3000BC, still stand although they have been assimilated into Lima's urban sprawl and now appear amidst residential districts.

Around 500AD the local oracle, Pachacámac, was established, meaning that it was ancient even before the Incas arrived in the 15th century. The Incas adopted the site into their society and developed a chain of temples along the coast, supported by peaceful communities. They never placed excessive emphasis on the region though, as the centre of their Empire lay east, in Cusco.

In contrast, the conquistadors recognized the need for a coastal capital, a link to the outside world and to Spain in particular. Having subdued Cusco, Francisco Pizarro established Lima in 1535, picking a site with a good natural harbour and reliable water supply to set up his capital. Almost immediately Lima came under threat as rebel Incas, led by Manco Inca, sought to cut off the Spanish supply line and link to the motherland by sacking the city. Although they staged a substantial siege, the Incas were broken by the Spanish cavalry, who easily dominated the Inca infantry on flat ground. With this defeat and failure to break the line of supply and communication, the rebellion was undone before it really got going.

Civdad La Villa de Callav.
City of Callao,
Gateway to Lima.

FELIPE HUAMÁN POMA DE AYALA, (c1600)

Under the rule of the Spanish, Lima became a thriving and important city. The viceroy of South America was based here and surrounded himself with the trappings of power associated with his position; there are documented reports of the celebrations that followed the arrival of a new viceroy that illustrate the wealth that was on show, with tapestries hung in the streets and individuals dressed in fine fabrics to attend bullfights and banquets. Other prominent institutions also established themselves here; the University of San Marcos, the oldest in South America, was opened in 1551, whilst the Spanish Inquisition also made Lima the centre of their operations in 1569. However, other, less-welcome visitors were also lured to Lima by the promise of wealth; privateers including Sir Francis Drake raided the city in 1579, whilst other pirate attacks followed. In response, the city rebuilt its defensive walls. The walls couldn't withstand a massive earthquake in 1746 though, which levelled many of the colonial buildings; 16,000 people died from the quake and the diseases that followed in its aftermath.

Such was the wealth and richness the city enjoyed under the Spanish that it resisted attempts to be liberated by San Martín. He in turn allowed the Limeños to continue as they were until they realized that there was no support forthcoming from Spain, at which point the viceroy fled into the mountains with a band of supporters and the city's residents switched allegiance to San Martín.

Unfortunately, Lima declined in post-independence Peru. What was once a spectacular city became shabby and untended, with streets unpaved and littered with filth that was picked over by vultures. Charles Darwin recorded in *The Voyage of the Beagle* in 1830 that 'Lima, the City of the Kings, must formerly have been a splendid town.' He declared though that at the time of his visit, it was, 'in a filthy state of decay.'

Nonetheless the city continued to grow and to such an extent that the outer walls were torn down to make space for new housing. This proved to be a costly mistake since without its defensive structures the Chileans easily overran the

LIMA

city in 1881, during the War of the Pacific. This latest batch of invaders didn't leave for two years.

More recently, the city saw spectacular growth during the early years of the 1920s, when large numbers of unskilled labourers arrived looking for work. Despite attempts to accommodate them and provide sewerage and open spaces, the city struggled under the weight of numbers, which increased to 170,000. Over-crowding has been a problem ever since; there are now more than eight million inhabitants in Lima, around a third of the total population lives here. Many of these are poor and live in *pueblos jóvenes* (shanty towns), where unemployment is rife.

The city does have another side to it though and many districts display the wealth and opulence of successful Limeños. First among these are San Isidro and Miraflores, where the emerging middle class make their homes. This group is also energizing and leading a renaissance in the city that sees them take pride in Lima's history and heritage. Run-down areas are being regenerated, infrastructure is being modernized and heritage sites are being preserved.

In 1991 the historic centre was recognized by UNESCO as a World Heritage site and by the end of the decade restoration work was underway on buildings, parks had been planted, streets cleaned, the police presence increased and even street vendors moved on. There are still plenty of problems, as there are in all world capitals, of poverty, race and class, but the multicultural mix of indigenous and Spanish influences, grime and glamour makes the city endlessly interesting. Increasingly positive press and exposure on the world stage also ensures that the city's stereotype is being transformed and it is being spoken of in the same terms as other more established cities on the continent previously considered far more desirable destinations.

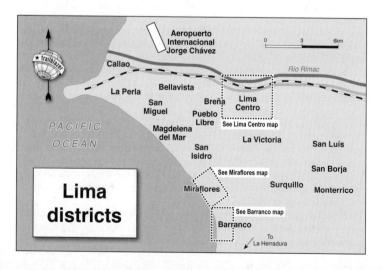

WHAT TO SEE AND DO

Lima Centro   [see map pp128-9]
At the heart of the city is **Plaza de Armas**, also known as Plaza Mayor. A bronze fountain from 1650 stands at the centre of the square, which was established on the site of an Inca market and meeting place. It was here that Pizarro founded the city in 1535. The northern end of the plaza is dominated by the imposing, gated **Palacio de Gobierno** (Government Palace; only open for occasional public events), which fills the entire length of one side; at noon it's possible to watch the changing of the guard.

On the right-hand side stands the **Archbishop's Palace**, which has an intricately carved wooden balcony. Adjacent to this is the **Cathedral** (Mon-Fri 9am-5pm, Sat 10am-1pm; entrance s/10, s/5 students). The cathedral has stood on this site since 1535 but as a result of numerous earthquakes has had to be rebuilt several times; the massive quake in 1746 in fact completely levelled the cathedral. The current building dates from 1758 and contains some elaborately carved choir stalls as well as a coffin that is reputed to hold the remains of Francisco Pizarro, who laid the first stone for the cathedral foundations and who was later assassinated in the plaza. There's also an impressive **statue of Pizarro** astride his horse in the square although, allegedly, he was a fairly mediocre rider.

Colonial architecture There are numerous examples of fine colonial architecture throughout Lima that have survived earthquakes, expansion and being damaged by the sea air; start by investigating the smart colonial buildings that surround Plaza de Armas and Plaza San Martín. Elsewhere, walk along Calle Ucayali, Conde de Superunda, Huancavelica or Jirón de la Union where you can see attractive *casonas* (large houses/mansions).

In particular, look out for **Palacio Torre Tagle**, Jr Ucayali 363, an 18th-century mansion considered one of the finest in the city, which is now home to the Foreign Ministry. Although a government building, it is possible to poke your head round the entrance in order to catch a glimpse of the delicate carvings and attractive Moorish balconies within. Across the street is **Casa Goyeneche**, Jr Ucayali 358, an impressive 18th-century mansion which has a distinctive European influence and characteristic carved balconies and ornate doors.

Iglesia de la Merced La Merced (cnr Jirón de la Unión and Jr Miró Quesada; Mon-Sat 8am-12.30pm & 4-7pm, Sun 7am-1pm & 4-7pm; free) stands on the site of the first Catholic mass in Lima, held in 1534. Built in 1541 but subsequently remodelled, it's one of the city's most important religious buildings. The imposing, ornate Baroque façade of carved granite gives the building a sense of grandeur whilst inside are masses of magnificent altars, varyingly in Baroque and Renaissance styles.

Santo Domingo church and convent The Santo Domingo church and convent (Jirón Camaná; Mon-Sat 5-8am, 9am-12.30pm & 3-6pm, Sun 9am-1pm; church free, convent s/5) is one of Lima's most striking religious buildings. It was established by the friar Vicente de Valverde, who accompanied Pizarro and the conquistadors; it was Valverde who had a hand in persuading Pizarro to execute Atahualpa. The pink façade is eye-catching and there are several attractive chapels and courtyards to explore and the skulls of two of the city's most venerated saints, Santa Rosa and San Martín de Porres, to discover, encased in glass in a dedicated shrine adjacent to the main altar. The saints' tombs are housed in the convent, surrounded by Baroque paintings and Spanish tile work.

San Francisco church and monastery The sizeable church of San Francisco (⌨ www.museocatacumbas.com; cnr Lampa and Ancash; daily 7-11am & 4-8pm; entrance s/7) was consecrated in 1673 and has endured despite the earthquakes. Although this Baroque building is attractive in its own right, with pretty yellow and white paintwork and a dramatic stone façade, the main attractions here include some spectacular artworks, pretty tile work and a vast 17th-century library containing 25,000 texts. Admission includes a guided tour (30 mins); tours leave when there are enough people.

The cavernous **catacombs** (9.30am-5.30pm) contain the bones of some 70,000 of the city's former residents; these are creatively if gruesomely arranged.

Museo de la Inquisición (⌨ www.congreso.gob.pe/museo.htm; Plaza Bolívar, Calle Junin 548; daily 9am-5pm; free) This colonial mansion was the one time headquarters of the Spanish Inquisition in South America, which operated from 1584 to 1820. The main tribunal room is wonderfully ornate and has a carved wooden ceiling, completely at odds with the dungeons elsewhere that have illustrations of the terrible types of torture conducted here in the name of eliminating heresy and blasphemy in the New World.

Museo de Arte de Lima (⌨ www.mali.pe; Paseo de Colón 125; Tue-Sun 10am-8pm, Sat to 5pm; entrance s/12) MALI, as it's sometimes referred to, contains everything from 3000-year-old pre-Columbian ceramics to post-conquistador paintings by the Cusco School and contemporary indigenous art. The eclectic collection, housed in a building designed by Alexandre Eiffel, is fascinating and the permanent exhibits provide an excellent overview of Peruvian art from all the important periods of the country's history.

Iglesia La Recoleta La Recoleta (daily 7am-7.45pm; free), on Plaza Francia, is an attractive blue-and-white-painted church. Founded in 1606 it has undergone extensive restoration and now boasts Gothic architecture and attractive stained-glass windows dedicated to important saints. It is sometimes referred to as the Church of the Sacred Hearts.

Parks and cliffs In the centre, **Parque de la Cultura** stages live music performances. One kilometre south of here, in **Parque de la Reserva**, is the **Circuito Mágico del Agua** (Magic Water Circuit; ⌨ www.parquedelareserva .com.pe; daily 4-10pm; s/4); it is a remarkable series of fountains backed by a light and music show; the largest fountain complex in the world, it features 13 separate jets, including one 80m high.

❑ Walking routes for central Lima and Miraflores

Although essentially Lima isn't a walker's city, within each district and especially in the centre, Miraflores or Barranco (see box p133), it's possible to enjoy exploring on foot, taking in the sights and atmosphere of the city and pausing *en route* to try out the cafés and restaurants you come across.

● **Lima Centro** (see map pp128-9) With a full day of exploration ahead why not start with a **buffet breakfast** at the **Sheraton Lima Hotel** (see p140).

When you are ready to start turn left out of the hotel and head straight up **Jirón Belén** (there's a pistachio-coloured building on the corner). After a block, look left to spot a blue church with a giant snowflake window (**Iglesia La Recoleta**; see opposite), which stands in **Plaza Francia**. Continue straight ahead until you reach **Plaza San Martín** which is ringed with white wedding-cake mansions and one pink one. In the centre of the plaza is a **statue of General San Martín** on a horse. The plaza is particularly delightful in October/November when the jacaranda trees are in bloom.

Keep to the left side of the plaza passing **Teatro Colón** (once a luxurious and respected theatre, it became a cinema in the 1950s and closed in 2003) and **Gran Hotel Bolívar** (see p140) on Plaza San Martín then head up Jirón de la Unión past **Iglesia de la Merced** (see p125).

At Plaza de Armas turn left for one block then right onto Jirón Camaná to come to **Santo Domingo** (see pp125-6). Head directly away from the church to re-join Jirón de la Unión, turn right and return to Plaza de Armas, turning left to walk along one side before turning left onto Jirón Carabaya to pass **Palacio de Gobierno** (see p125). A quick diversion to the route could be made to the **cathedral** (see p125).

At the junction with Jirón Ancash turn right and visit the **church of San Francisco** (see opposite) before walking another block and turning right onto Av Abancay. Pass Plaza Bolívar, marvel at the **Museo de la Inquisición** (see opposite) and turn right onto Jirón Junin for a block before a sharp right onto Jirón Ayacucho, which brings you to **Mercado Central**, a bustling market that occupies a whole block and sells just about everything. It is close to Bario Chino (Chinatown) so consider carrying on east for a block before turning right onto Jr Paruro where you'll find *Wa Lok* (see p146) which makes an ideal lunch stop. After lunch retrace your steps and head away from the market past a row of impressive colonial buildings including strawberry-pink **Palacio Torre Tagle**; look out for Toby jug faces peering down from an exquisite wooden balcony. Finally, turn left onto Jr Carabaya and continue to Plaza San Martín, which you can cut across to reward yourself with a Pisco Sour in Hotel Gran Bolívar. Allow a full day to take in everything along the route.

● **Miraflores** (see map p130) A gentle stroll taking several hours through **Miraflores** will allow you to enjoy this neighbourhood. Start by sampling **ceviche and seafood** at either Pescados Capitales (see p145) or La Mar (see p144) before making your way to the coast path and setting off south along the length of the cliff-top path, **Malecón de la Marina**, admiring the views and drama of the waves breaking on the beaches below.

As you walk off your lunch, enjoy the parks and public spaces you wander through and take advantage of lots of opportunities for people-watching, along with the chance to see paragliders jumping from the high points. Pass a **lighthouse** and come to the picturesque **Parque del Amor** (see p132) with its pretty mosaics before finishing at **Larcomar mall** (see p147), where you can sit and relax on one of the café terraces here; Mangos' has the best vantage point.

(Thanks to **Alison Roberts** for route planning)

LIMA

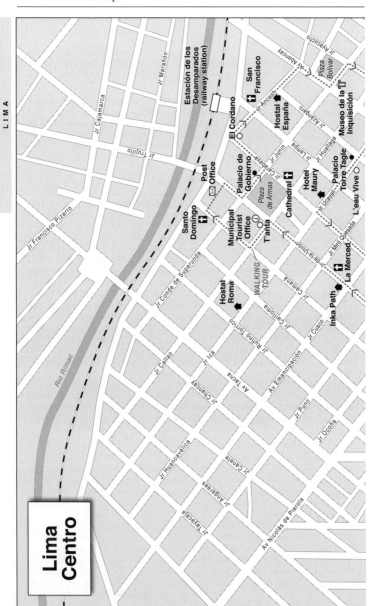

Lima
Centro

Río Rímac

Jr Francisco Pizarro

Jr Calamarca

Jr Marañón

Jr Trujillo

Estación de los
Desamparados
(railway station)

Post
Office

Santo
Domingo

Jr Conde de Superunda

Hostal
Roma

Jr Callao

Jr Ica

Jr Chancay

Av Tacna

Jr Rufino Torrico

Jr Cailloma

Av Emancipación

Jr Camaná

WALKING
TOUR

Jr Cusco

Inka Path

Jr Huancavélica

Jr Canete

Jr Angaraes

Jr Tajzala

Jr Puno

Jr Ocoña

Av Nicolás de Piérola

San
Francisco

Jr Ancash

Hostal
España

El Cordano

Palacio de
Gobierno

Jr Carabaya

Jr Junín

Plaza
de Armas

Municipal
Tourist
Office

T'anta

Jr Lampa

Cathedral

Jr Azángaro

Jr Abancay

Jr Ayacucho

Plaza
Bolívar

Museo de la
Inquisición

Jr Huallaga

Hotel
Maury

Palacio
Torre Tagle

L'eau Vive

Jr Ucayali

Jr Miró Quesada

Jr de la Unión

La Merced

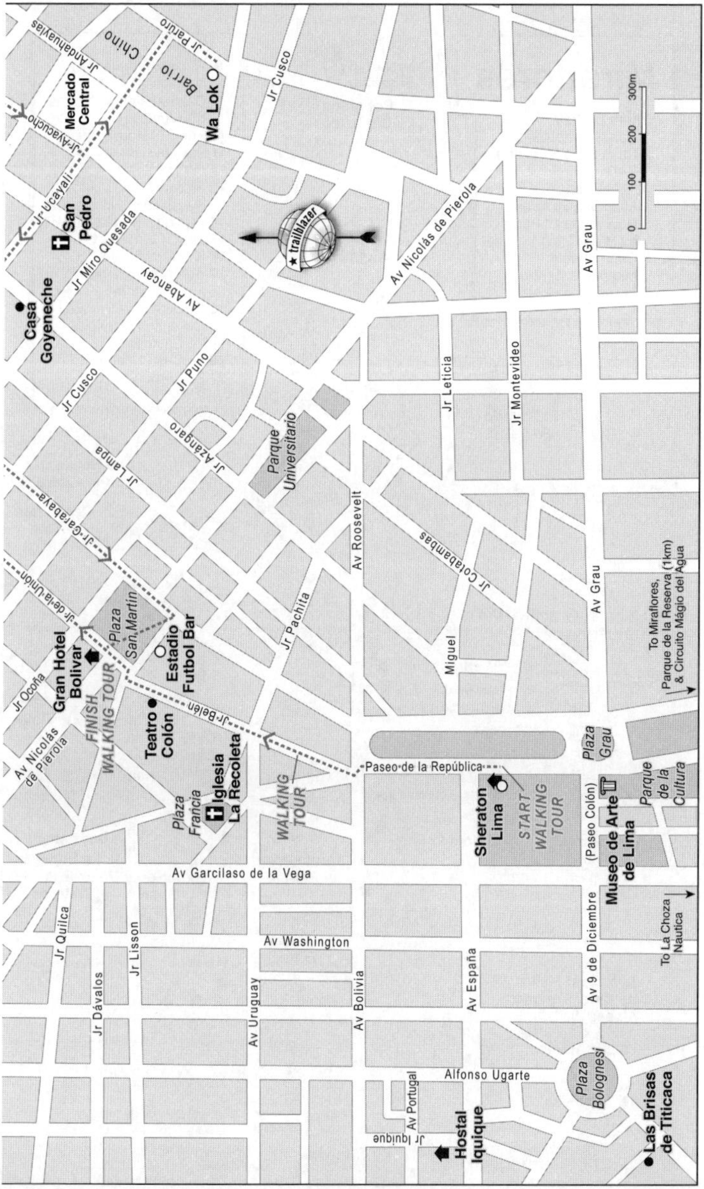
Jr Andahuaylas
Mercado Central
Barrio Chino
Jr Paruro
Wa Lok
Jr Cusco
Jr Ayacucho
Jr Ucayali
San Pedro
Jr Miro Quesada
Casa Goyeneche
Av Abancay
trailblazer
Av Nicolás de Pierola
Av Grau
0
100
200
300m
Jr Cusco
Jr Puno
Jr Azangaro
Jr Lampa
Parque Universitario
Jr Leticia
Jr Montevideo
Jr Garabaya
Jr de la Unión
Av Roosevelt
Jr Cotabambas
Plaza San Martín
Estadio Futbol Bar
Gran Hotel Bolivar
Jr Ocoña
FINISH WALKING TOUR
Teatro Colón
Jr Belén
Jr Pachita
Miguel
Av Grau
To Miraflores, Parque de la Reserva (1km) & Circuito Mágio del Agua
Av Nicolás de Pierola
Iglesia La Recoleta
Plaza Francia
WALKING TOUR
Paseo de la República
Sheraton Lima
START WALKING TOUR
Plaza Grau
(Paseo Colón)
Museo de Arte de Lima
Parque de la Cultura
Av Garcilaso de la Vega
Jr Quilca
Jr Lisson
Av Washington
Jr Dávalos
Av Uruguay
Av Bolivia
Av España
Av 9 de Diciembre
To La Choza Nautica
Alfonso Ugarte
Av Portugal
Jr Iquique
Hostal Iquique
Plaza Bolognesi
Las Brisas de Titicaca

Miraflores

Where to stay
1 Hostal Torreblanca
2 Casa Bella Miraflores B&B
3 Hitchhikers
4 Antigua Miraflores
5 Doubletree El Pardo by Hilton Lima
6 Casa Andina Miraflores Centro
7 Flying Dog Hostel

8 Radisson Decapolis Miraflores
9 Casa Andina Miraflores San Antonio
10 Friend's House
11 Bayview Hotel
12 JW Marriott
13 Flying Dog Backpackers Hostel
14 Flying Dog Hostel B&B
15 Hostal El Patio
16 K'usillu's Hostel
17 Sonesta Posadas del Inca Miraflores
18 Casa Andina Private Collection Miraflores
19 La Castellana
20 La Casa Nostra
21 San Antonio Abad

Choquenchanca
Mercado de Surquillo
START WALKING TOUR
Pescados Capitales
START WALKING TOUR
La Mar
WALKING TOUR
Cesar

Malecón de la Marina
Mendiburu
Cordova
Perez Aranibar
Merino
Av La Mar
Lord Nelson
Santa Cruz

Parque Grau
El Senorio de Sulco
Santa Cruz

PACIFIC OCEAN

0 100 200 300 400m

trailblazer

1 Plaza Morales Barros
Marqués de Torre Tagle
Bandelli
Lastres

Huaca Pucllana
Restaurant Huaca Pucllana

Túpac Amaru
Figueredo
Berlin
Ramón Zavala
Roma
Jorge Chávez
2 de Mayo
Julio Elcorrobarrutia
Enrique Palacios
Elias Aguirre
Primavera
Independencia

Lighthouse

Huaringas
3
Las Brujas de Cachiche
Plaza Bolgnesi
4
Germán
Av Grau
Recavarren
Bellavista

Aviación
José Gálvez
Madrid
Francia
Cisneros
Bolognesi
Italia
Tripoli
Venecia

Av José Pardo
General Borgoño
Piura
Coronel Inclán
Atahualpa

Plaza Republica

To Hotel Aleman, 400m
To El Peruanito, 500m

5
Panchita
Benchley Arms
Café Café
SAE
Post Office
Mercado Indio

Old Pub
7
Haiti
Olaya
Ovalo
Av Petit Thouars
Av Arequipa
6

Parque del Amor
Malecón Balta
Malecón 28 de Julio
Av Mariscal Oscar Benavides – Diagonal

La Rosa Nautica

Tourist Police
8
Parque Kennedy
13
Xocolati
Bar Habana
La Bodega de la Trattoria

FINISH WALKING TOUR

Craft stalls at Parque
14
Astrid y Gastón
15
Manuel Benilla
Diez Canseco

9
16
Alpaca III
17
18
Media Naranja

Larcomar Mall (Café Café, Mangos, Alpaca III, TIC, Cinema & PeruRail ticket office)
10
Colón
Pasaje el Suche

Killaii
19
20
Av La Paz
Schell
Av República

11
12

Alcan
Santa Isabel
San Fernando
Av José Larco
José Gonzales
Manco Capac
28 de Julio
Fores
Grimaldo
San Martín
del Solar

Juan Fanning
Ocharán
Porta

T'anta
Av Vasco Núñez de Balboa
Grimaldo
Paseo de la República
Av Reducto
Ramón Ribeyro
Benavides

Olcay
Alfaro
Parque Reducto
21

To Miraflores Park Hotel, 400m
To Fiesta, 200m

LIMA

Barranco

Where to stay
1 Aquisito
2 The Point
3 Second Home Peru
4 Kaminu
5 Barranco's
  Backpackers Inn
6 La Quinta de Allison

0 ___ 100m

Av-El-Sol-Oeste

Drca-Canes-co

Tacna

La 73

WALKING
TOUR

Centenario

Av-San-Martín

Garcia

Av Pierola

To Del Carajo

Av-Miguel-Grau

Paseo Sáenz Peña

Dédalo

Malécon-Pazos

Tacna

Martínez

San Antonio

Santa Rosa

Miraflores

Sargento
Pimiento

Circuito De Playas

Cavero

Colina

Canta Rana

Posada
del Angel

Ayahuasca

Junin

Domeyer

El-Libertador

Av Bolognesi

Union

La Bajado
de Baños

Bank
$

Sánchez
Carrión

La Noche

Juan Pazos

La Victoria

Statue of
Chabuca Granda

Ermita
Church

Bank $

La
Candelaría

Bars and
sunset
viewpoint

Paseo
Chabuca
Granda

Parque
Municipal

Juanito's

Puente de
los Suspiros

Museo de la
Electricidad

4

Museo Galeria
Arte Popular
de Ayacucho

trailblazer

5

Mariscal Castilla

Iskay

28 de Julio

Panama

Posada
del Angel

Av-San Pedro de Osma

Mochileros

6

Herrera

To Museo Pedro
de Osma, 350m
& Safe in Lima

Miraflores   [see walking route box p127, map p130]
Huaca Pucllana (Cnr General Borgoño and Tarapacá; Wed-Mon 9am-5pm; s/7) In the midst of a Miraflores residential area stands this large adobe pre-Columbian complex, centred on a pyramid and constructed by the Lima Culture some time in the 6th century. A ceremonial and administrative centre in its day, it has been quite heavily eroded by the elements but is still striking; the pyramid, which would have stood 23m high, is a powerful contrast to the contemporary buildings that sit immediately adjacent to the site. Excavations are ongoing but guided tours, mainly in Spanish, highlight the main features here.

Restaurant Huaca Pucllana (see p145), one of Lima's celebrated restaurants, can also be found on site; it affords diners incredible views of the illuminated ruins at night.

Parks and cliffs Stroll through **Parque del Amor**, which has elements of Gaudi's Parque Güell in Barcelona but was designed by Victor Delfín. Pick your way past amorous couples to find benches decorated with mosaics and covered in hearts and romantic writings along with a giant statue of two people caught in a clinch. There are good views from the tall cliffs too.

Barranco   [see walking route box opposite, map p131]
Puente de los Suspiros When walking around Barranco, look out for the attractive wooden footbridge known as Puente de los Suspiros (Bridge of Sighs), so named for the sounds of sighs that could be heard by people passing by the house of a noble's daughter who fell in love with a road sweeper but couldn't act upon it so would watch him from her window.

The bridge connects to a small cobbled passageway, **La Bajada de Baños** (The Bathing Path), which leads to a good sea view. There are steps down to the beach here but you shouldn't stray too far as this section of the beach isn't safe.

Museo Pedro de Osma (🖥 www.museopedrodeosma.org, Av Pedro de Osma 423; Tue-Sun 10am-6pm; s/20) Inside the ornate Palacio de Osma, the former beaux arts residence of the Osma family, is a private museum full of paintings by the Cusco School, colonial art, furniture and sculptures as well as silver pieces from the 16th to 19th centuries.

Pueblo Libre
Museo Nacional de Arqueología, Antropología e Historía del Peru
(Plaza Bolívar, Pueblo Libre; Tue-Sat 9am-5pm, Sun 9am-4pm; entrance s/10) This museum, in a colonial mansion, has a good range of exhibits and artefacts, including many originals, copies of which can be seen elsewhere as well.

Some of the most impressive pieces are Chavín artefacts from the Chavín de Huantar site close to Huaraz, including the Raimondi Stela, an elaborately carved statue that can be viewed both up and down to see a different image, and the Tello Obelisk, a carefully sculpted pair of caimans. There are rooms dedicated to individual pre-Hispanic cultures along with several mummies from the Paracas region, ceramics, metalwork, textiles and models of Inca archaeological sites.

❏ **Barranco walking route** [See map p131]

Barranco was once a seaside resort for Lima's wealthiest families wishing to escape the stifling summer heat downtown. Many of its magnificent mansions are still standing and, despite their neglected and crumbling appearance, provide a snapshot of what was once a very fashionable neighbourhood.

This **half-day walk** starts at **Parque Muncipal**, in front of lemon-coloured art café *Iskay* (see p144). Walk south down **Av San Pedro de Osma** passing **Museo Galeria Arte Popular de Ayacucho** (10am-6pm daily; free but you need to ring the bell) on the right and **Museo de la Electricidad** (🖥 museodelaelectricidad.blogspot .co.uk; 9am-5pm daily, free) on the left; in front of which is a tram which used to run between Barranco, Miraflores and Lima Centro.

You can continue walking for a couple of blocks, to No 423, to reach **Museo Pedro de Osma** (see opposite). Alternatively take a left up 28 de Julio (right if you're retracing your steps having visited the museum) and another left to bring you back to Parque Muncipal. Pop your head into *Juanito's* (Av Grau 274; p147) to see a traditional *bodega* (bar that also serves snacks) and try one of their sandwiches. Cross the park, stopping to admire the red biblioteca on your left, the equally red church on your right, the pool with Romanesque statue and fountain and locals promenading in the purple shadow of the jacaranda trees.

Follow pedestrianized **Paseo Chabuca Granda** straight ahead (passing the bodega on your left which has a display of plastic cocktails outside) and then take the steps down (don't cross the bridge). Follow cobbled **Bajada de Baños** (see opposite) towards the sea. This shady walkway is flanked by what were once grand houses and boughs of bougainvillea. It makes for an enjoyable stroll but turn back before reaching the end as this area has a nasty reputation for crime.

Climb back up the steps and cross the wooden **Puente de los Suspiros** (see opposite). Turn left and pass the raspberry-coloured, almost roofless, **Ermita Church**. Another legend suggests that fishermen, lost at sea in thick fog, had their prayers answered when a luminous cross appeared on the cliff top and guided them safely home. The church was later built on the very same spot. There are a number of bars here with great ocean views, perfect for admiring the sunset so maybe you'd prefer to end the walk here and wait for the show.

Back at the bridge there is a **Statue of Chabuca Granda**, a Peruvian singer and composer. One of the bars at the *mirador* is named after her best-known song *La Flor de la Canela*. Follow the steps up, cross the road and walk down **Junín** for a couple of blocks until you see the ocean. Follow the palm trees and strip of parkland along the cliff top. Ahead you can see Miraflores and its skyscrapers. Below are the beaches and surfers. Shortly you will see a blue and red tiled staircase on your right which leads to **Av Sáenz Peña**, a wide boulevard of some of Barranco's finest buildings. Usually the *D'Anafria* ice-cream men are here on their yellow tricycles, blowing their duck whistles in case you hadn't noticed them. It's a nice spot to sit or have a look around the craft gallery **Dédalo** (see p147) which has a garden *café*.

You can either return to Parque Muncipal along **Av San Martín** (the second right off Av Sáenz Peña) passing a couple of handmade clothing boutiques, or continue along the cliff top, weaving through the park and listening to the crashing waves below until you reach **Av El Sol Oeste**. Walk up the street for two blocks and stop for a snack at *La 73* (see p145).

Under no circumstances should you walk down to or back from the beach road. Alison Roberts

Next door stands **Quinta de los Liberatores**, once home to both the liberators San Martín (1821-2) and Bolívar (1823-6).

Santa Maria Magdelena church (Fri-Wed 7.30-9am & 6-9pm, Thur all day; free) Painted vivid orange, this church stands out in all senses of the phrase. Inside the colour scheme is equally strong, with dazzling altars against three of the walls. Below the church is a series of catacombs.

Museo Larco (🖳 www.museolarco.org; Av Bolívar 1515; daily 9am-10pm, to 6pm on public holidays; s/30) Within a privately-owned colonial mansion that once belonged to the viceroy, itself stood on top of the remains of a 7th-century pyramid, is a scholarly museum. Originally founded by Rafael Larco Hoyle in 1926, it houses his obsessively collected pre-Columbian trove. In the main house are hundreds of gold and silver exhibits along with textiles and an impressive array of pottery; there are thought to be more than 50,000 pots on display. More pieces are stored in a warehouse. A separate gallery is then given over to erotic-themed artefacts and earthenware that illustrate all manner of sexual activity. Many of the pieces were created by the Moche, Chimu and Chancay cultures, demonstrating that Peru's history is about more than just the Incas.

Elsewhere
Museo de la Nación (Av Javier Prado Este 2465, San Borja; Tue-Sun 9am-5pm; entrance s/10, students s/5) What looks like an ugly concrete monstrosity on the side of a motorway is in fact Lima's leading museum. Visit it so you can put the country's pre-Columbian history into context and to see scale models of many of the archaeological sites elsewhere in the country, including many of the Inca constructions close to Cusco. There's a lot to take in but the museum is well laid out and well signed; just leave enough time to get round all the exhibits.

Museo de Oro (🖳 www.museoroperu.com.pe, Calle Alonso de Molina 1100, Monterrico; daily 11.30am-7pm; entrance s/33) The Gold Museum is a vast private collection of pre-Hispanic gold. Unfortunately it has been tarnished by the discovery that a huge percentage of the items were fakes or copies; the museum maintains that what is now on display is authentic though. Take what you see with a pinch of salt – some of the exhibits are labelled as 'reproductions' – but also look out for some interesting weaponry as well as textiles and ceramics from the Moche culture that are on display too. There's little information available on the displays though.

Museo Andrés del Castillo (🖳 www.madc.com.pe; Jirón de la Unión 1030; Wed-Mon 9am-6pm; s/10) Inside a well-preserved 19th-century colonial house is an impressive collection of Nazca textiles and Chancay pottery that is well worth seeking out.

Huaca Huallamarca Within a residential section of San Isidro stands this temple (Calle Nicholás de Rivera and Av Rosario; Tue-Sun 9am-5pm; s/5), built

❑ **Pachacámac**
To the south of Lima, 30km away on the coast, stands the site of the ancient oracle and shrine to Pachacámac (Mon-Fri 9am-5pm; s/6), which operated at its height under the Huari culture in the 10th century. It was later assimilated into the Inca Empire and became a place of pilgrimage for them as well; they added the Temple of the Sun to the main citadel. Most of the pyramid structures here are heavily eroded and take some imagination to visualize at their height. However, there is some reconstruction to give you an impression of how significant a site this was before it was pillaged by the conquistadors and allowed to fall into disrepair.

by the Lima Culture around 200AD. The main adobe pyramid has been restored and a small site museum explains the huaca's history and contains a mummy found by archaeologists here.

PRACTICAL INFORMATION
Arrival
All flights, both international and from elsewhere in Peru, arrive at **Aeropuerto Internacional Jorge Chávez** (🖳 www .lap.com.pe), in the Callao district some 16km to the north-west of the city centre. Customs clearance is a bit of a lottery since, as you leave you must push a button and wait hopefully for a green light, indicating you're free to go. If the light is red, however, you must have your bags thoroughly checked. Inside the arrivals hall there are exchange bureaux and ATMs that accept all major credit cards; the exchange rates are better in town though. There are also car-hire desks belonging to most of the main international chains, an iPerú information desk (open 24 hrs), plus public telephones and internet access.

Taxis run from outside the arrivals hall; touts for official firms, wearing ID badges, will accost you the moment you emerge. Fares cost around s/40-50 depending on whether you go to the centre, San Isidro, Miraflores or Barranco. Cheaper, unlicensed cars can be hailed outside opposite the terminal although you'll have to haggle hard for a fair fare as they'll know that you're new in town.

If you are pre-booked at one of the smarter hotels or are on a tour a representative should meet you off the plane and have transport organized.

Orientation
Lima is built on a flat plain above a large arc of a bay. A sprawling city, it has many different neighbourhoods and districts (see map p124), the distances between which are often too big to walk. Within each district though there are some very attractive walking routes that you can follow to check off the main sites.

Lima Centro is the original heart of the city, several miles inland from the coast, on the banks of the Río Rimac. Plaza de Armas is the main focal point although other squares include Plaza Bolívar and Plaza San Martín. Amidst the chaotic, often snarled, centre there are a host of sights, museums and excellent restaurants to discover.

To the south-east is the industrial-commercial area of **La Victoria** and the suburbs of **San Luis** and **San Borja**, where Museo de la Nación can be found. Further out is wealthy **Monterrico**, setting for the Museo de Oro.

To the south-west in **Breña** are more residential streets. West of the centre is **Bellavista**, the coast and the port of **Callao**, overlooked by a fort. South of Callao, along the coast lie **San Miguel**, **Magdalena del Mar** and more affluent, smarter **San Isidro**, where many of the international embassies are. There are also several good hotels and decent restaurants plus an attractive park.

Beyond this is the well-to-do residential neighbourhood and shopping area of **Miraflores**, set above some vertiginous cliffs, and then the more bohemian district of **Barranco**, a one-time coastal retreat that has been absorbed into the city but which boasts hip bars, a lively night scene and a number of workshops that double as art galleries.

At the southern edge of the city is a hill, **El Morro**, from the top of which are good views over the coast and city. To the north are poorer suburbs.

Getting around

Taxis There are countless cabs plying their trade on the streets of Lima. Not all of these are registered, let alone regulated. For the safest ride and fairest fare, hail a yellow cab with a number painted on the door, as these are more likely to be reputable.

The journey from the airport to Lima Centro will set you back about s/15-20 and to Miraflores about s/30-35. From Miraflores to the city centre is about s/10-12 and to Barranco around s/5. If you want to get to Museo de la Nación or Museo del Oro from the centre, expect to pay around s/10-15.

Always agree the fare before you set off and, if there's more than one of you, clarify if the fare is for the journey or just per person.

Combis and collectivos

Lima's bus network of combis and collectivos, identified by their size, looks confusing to the untrained and uninitiated. However, it's actually pretty efficient, far-reaching and surprisingly cheap. Destinations are written on cards in the window; you can flag them down or ask them to stop anywhere along this route. Beware though, buses can be crowded and are often targeted by pickpockets.

The **most useful route** is the road that links Lima Centro with Parque Kennedy in Miraflores, Av Arequipa; buses are marked 'Todo Arequipa' and either list Wilson/Tacna or Larco/Schell/Miraflores depending on whether they're heading into or out of the centre.

To get to **Barranco** from the centre you'll need to travel on the Via Expresa, Lima's only urban highway, which goes from Plaza Grau to the northern tip of the suburb and is the fastest way to cross the city. There is also a service that travels to the **airport**; it's cheaper than a taxi but much slower.

Tours

A large number of agencies offer organized, guided tours of Lima; these are ideal if you find the sprawling city confusing or difficult to get around. Don't buy tours from touts at the airport or taxi drivers though and always get a receipt that details what is included in the tour.

Condor Travel (🖳 www.condortravel .com/peru/, ☎ 615 3000) in San Isidro has a good reputation for top-end tours that take in the main museums and sights.

Lima Vision (🖳 www.limavision .com, ☎ 447 7710) in Miraflores offers half-day tours of contemporary and colonial Lima, as do **Lima Tours** (🖳 www .limatours.com.pe, ☎ 619 6900), Jirón de la Unión 1040, who can also take you to Pachacámac.

Alternatively, hop on a **Mirabús** (🖳 www.mirabusperu.com), a red double-decker bus service with ticket offices at Parque Kennedy and Av Larco 345 that tours Lima's must-see sights.

To travel under your own steam, join a **bike tour** of lima (🖳 www.biketoursoflima .com, ☎ 445 3172, Calle Bolívar 150); it is an ideal way to spend a day exploring the city. There are several guided routes to choose from costing s/75-110.

Car rental

Many of the major international car-hire chains have offices in Lima. The companies listed below have branches at the airport as well as in Miraflores at the address listed.

Expect to pay around US$50 per day for a compact car, more if you want a bigger vehicle or an SUV.

Avis (🖳 www.avis.com.pe), Av Javier Prado Este 5233; **Budget** (🖳 www.budget peru.com), Canaval y Moreya 569; **Dollar** (🖳 www.dollar-rentacar.com.pe), Av

Cantuarias 341; **Hertz** (🖳 www.inkasrac
.com), Av Cantuarias 160. **Nacional** (🖳
www.nationalcar.com.pe), Av Costanera
No 1380.

Services
Tourist information There's an **iPerú
office** at the airport (☎ 574 8000) that's
open 24 hours. In town, if you need directions or want a straightforward answer to a
question, visit the iPerú office in Larcomar
(see map p130; ☎ 445 9400; Mon-Fri
11am-1pm & 2-8pm).

There is a more substantial **Municipal
tourist office** on Pasaje Ribera el Viejo in
Lima Centro (see map pp128-9) and half a
dozen or so **information kiosks** dotted
around Miraflores.

South American Explorers (see box
below) is another useful source of information, particularly in terms of planning a
trek.

Books & newspapers One of Lima's
leading **bookshops** (*librerías*), El Virrey
(🖳 www.elvirrey.com; Calle Bolognesi
510), has a range of speciality titles on subjects such as science and history. There are
smaller branches in San Isidro (Miguel
Dasso 141) and at Larcomar in Miraflores.
SBS (🖳 www.sbs.com.pe; Av Angamos
Oeste 301) has a good collection of guidebooks.

Worth trying too are Zeta (🖳 www.ze
tabook.com; Av Comandante Espinar 219)
and Delta Librería (Larco 970).
Alternatively, the SAE (see box below) has
a book exchange for members.

Day-old English-language **newspapers** can be bought from street vendors
operating in front of Café Haiti by the
Ovalo in Miraflores.

Maps City plans and **street maps** can be
picked up or bought from tourist shops and
kiosks. There's also a free map in the back
of the Páginas Amarillas (Yellow Pages).

If you're looking for **hiking maps**,
head to Instituto Geográfico Nacional (🖳
www.ign.gob.pe, ☎ 475 9960) on Av A
Aramburú 1190-1198, Surquillo, which
sells road maps of the entire country at
1:2,000,000 and hiking maps that cover the
treks described in this book at 1:100,000.
The SAE (see box below) also sell these to
members.

❏ South American Explorers (SAE)
South American Explorers (🖳 www.saexplorers.org) was founded as the South
American Explorers Club in 1977. Operating out of a head office in New York, the
non-profit organization intended to advance field exploration and research in South
America. It went on to achieve almost-legendary status with travellers for the support,
back-up services and assistance it provided when planning an expedition; in effect it
became a home away from home.

While the organization is no longer called a 'club' it runs a detailed website, pub-
lishes an online magazine and still has a number of clubhouses in South America.
Longest-running amongst these are the offices in **Lima** (Calle Piura 135, Miraflores;
Mon-Sat 9.30am-5pm, Wed till 8pm, Sat till 1pm) and **Cusco** (Atoqsaycuchi 670, San
Blas; Mon-Fri 9.30am-5pm, Sat till 1pm). It also still provides a wide range of assis-
tance to members, from storing kit to finding a trekking partner.

The clubhouses are staffed by knowledgeable volunteers so you'll be able to get
an answer to almost any question. There are also quiet communal spaces, free wi-fi,
complimentary hot drinks, a library of books and also the chance to buy information
packs compiled by staff and members. As a member you'll also be entitled to discounts on tours, hotels, language schools and guide services. Membership starts at
US$60 per year (US$90 per couple). It's possible to join on the spot at one of the
clubhouses.

❏ Bank branch locations
● **Banco Continental** Cuzco 286 in the city centre and on the corner of Larco and Tarata in Miraflores;
● **Banco Wiese** Larco 1123, Miraflores;
● **BCP** Lampa 499 in the city centre and several branches in Miraflores including Pardo 491, on the corner of Larco and Gonzales and on the corner of José Larco and Schell;
● **Interbank** Jirón de la Unión 600 in central Lima and Larco 690 in Miraflores;
● **LAC Dólar** Camaná 779 in the city centre and La Paz 211 in Miraflores.

Banks & casas de cambio There are 24-hour **ATMs** throughout Lima as well as at the airport in the international arrivals hall.

Several **banks** also have branches all across the city, with most represented on Av Larco at least.

Although the banks exchange currency, **casas de cambio** give a better rate. *Cambistas (* Street changers) may offer an even better rate but beware that these men, identified by the green bibs they wear and the wads of notes they clutch, are less scrupulous and there are plenty of scams associated with changing money this way.

Laundry Many hotels offer a laundry service. If this isn't available, *lavanderia* (launderettes) are easy to find throughout the city.

Communications
Internet There are internet cafés all across Lima, all charging similar rates, generally around s/2 per hour; try Av Larco if you're looking for somewhere to get online. Many of the hostels and hotels also have free internet access for guests.

❏ Embassies and consulates
Australia (🖳 www.embassy.gov.au/peru, ☎ 222 8281, Av V A Belaúnde 147, San Isidro); **Austria** (🖳 lima_ob@bmaa.gv.at, ☎ 442 0503, Av Central 643, San Isidro); **Belgian Consulate** (🖳 www.diplomatie.be/lima, ☎ 422 8231, Av Angamos Oeste 380, Miraflores); **Canada** (🖳 www.canadainternational.gc.ca/peru-perou, ☎ 319 3200, Bolognesi 228, Miraflores); **French Embassy** (🖳 www.ambafrance-pe.org, ☎ 215 8400, Av Arequipa 3415, San Isidro); **Germany** (🖳 www.lima.diplo.de, ☎ 212 5016, Av Arequipa 4210, Miraflores); **Ireland** (🖳 consul@irishperu.com, ☎ 242 9516 or 242 2640, Av Paseo de la República 5757B, Miraflores (The Embassy of Ireland in Mexico (🖳 www.irishembassy.com.mx) is also accredited to and represents Peru; **Israel** (🖳 embassies.gov.il/lima, ☎ 418 0500, Centro Empresarial, Platinum Plaza II, Av Andres Reyes 437, Piso 13. San Isidro); **Italy** (🖳 www.ambli ma.esteri.it/ambasciata_lima, ☎ 463 2727, Av G Escobedo); **Japan** (🖳 www.pe.emb-japan.go.jp, ☎ 219 9500, Av San Felipe 356, Jesús María); **Netherlands Consulate** (🖳 peru.nlembajada.org, ☎ 213 9800, Torre Parque Mar, Av José Larco 1301, Miraflores); **New Zealand Consulate** (🖳 cblume@cbconsultperu.com, ☎ 627 7778, Leonidas Yerovi 106, Oficina 42, San Isidro); **Spain Consulate** (🖳 www .maec.es/subwebs/Consulados/Lima/es, ☎ 513 7930, Calle Los Pinos, 490, San Isidro); **Sweden** (🖳 konslima@speedy.com.pe, 🖳 www.swedenabroad.com for general info, ☎ 442 8905, Psje La Santa María 130, cuadra 6 Av Conquistadores, San Isidro); **Switzerland** (🖳 www.eda.admin.ch/lima, ☎ 264 0305, Av Salaverry 3240, Magdalena); **UK** (🖳 www.gov.uk/government/world/peru, ☎ 617 3000, 22nd Floor, Torre Parque Mar, Av José Larco 1301, Miraflores); **USA** (🖳 lima.usembassy.gov, ☎ 618 2000, Av La Encalada 17, Surco).

Telephone The code for calling Lima when outside the city is 01. You can make calls using coin-operated phone booths coloured blue or green and marked Telefónica. Alternatively buy a pre-paid telephone card from a kiosk or shop; scratch off the silver colouring to reveal a code, dial the number and follow the instructions to make your call. You will be reminded how much money you have available and how many minutes remain.

Post The main post office (*correo;* Mon-Fri 7.30am-7pm, Sat 7.30am-4pm, Sun 8am-4pm) is at Jirón Camaná 195, just off Plaza de Armas.

In Miraflores there's a post office (Mon-Sat 8am-8pm, Sun 9am-1pm) at Petit Thouars 5201, Angamos Oeste. The SAE (see box p137 and map p130) also holds post for members.

Emergencies
Police If you are a victim of crime, contact the tourist police (☎ 243 2190; 24 hours) at Jirón Colón 246 in Miraflores.

Medical It shouldn't need saying, but make sure that before you travel to Peru you have medical **insurance** (see p47), just in case.

Pharmacies such as Inka Farma are open 24 hours and are usually well stocked. Look for them along Av Larco, Jirón de la Unión and Av Grau. In many cases you won't need a prescription to buy medicines.

If you need **medical help**, try Clínica Anglo Americano (🖳 www.angloamericana.com.pe, ☎ 616 8900) at Av Salazar or Clínica Internacional (🖳 www.clinicainternacional.com.pe, ☎ 619 6161) at Jirón Washington 1471.

Festivals
There are several significant annual events and festivals (see pp86-7) that it's worth targeting, as long as you book accommodation far enough in advance as the city can get very busy and popular places fill up.

WHERE TO STAY
Airport If you're determined to just fly in and out of Lima, stay at *Ramada Costa del Sol* (🖳 www.costadelsolperu.com, ☎ 711 2000, Av Elmer Faucett), which is immediately opposite the arrivals hall, within the airport perimeter. The hotel is quiet, despite the location, and many of its facilities, including its restaurant and spa, function 24 hours to cater for people arriving at all times of day and night. Expect to pay for the convenience though, with double rooms starting at US$275.

Lima Centro [see map pp128-9]
Budget *Hostal Roma* (🖳 www.hostalroma.8m.com, ☎ 427 7572, Jirón Ica 326) is a block and a half from Plaza de Armas. A little run down, the colonial mansion is nonetheless friendly and frequently full; rooms cost US$13/20/28 with shared bathrooms and US$16/25/35 for private facilities.

The popular traveller haunt *Hostal España* (🖳 www.hotelespanaperu.com, ☎ 428 5546, Jr Azangaro 105) stands close to the San Francisco church in a fine colonial building filled with statues and plants. There's a garden on the roof that's a great space to relax in. The rooms within the rambling house are basic but more than adequate, whilst guests have access to a café, complimentary wi-fi and an office with some tourist information. Dorm beds cost s/14 whilst rooms with shared bathrooms cost s/25/40/51 (sgl/dbl/tpl) and those with private facilities cost s/40/50/60 (sgl/dbl/tpl).

Hostal Iquique (🖳 www.hostaliquique.com, ☎ 433 4724, Jirón Iquique 758) is a straightforward, conveniently located hostel set in a safe street that has an attractively tiled lobby, clean, functional rooms, a small garden, free wi-fi and a helpful

Lima area code: ☎ 01. If phoning from outside Peru dial your country's international phone code and then ☎ +51-1.

attitude. There's also table football and pool on a rooftop-type terrace. The rooms with private bathrooms cost US$23/33/40 (sgl/dbl/tpl); those with shared facilities are US$16/26/33 (sgl/dbl/tpl). For quiet, ask for a room on the upper floors, at the back.

Inka Path (🖥 www.hotelinkapath .com, ☎ 426 1919, Jirón de la Unión 654) is a couple of blocks from Plaza de Armas and represents good value; the rooms are clean and cost s/70/90/120 (sgl/dbl/tpl) with shared bathrooms and s/105/135/180 for private bathrooms.

Mid-range *Hotel Maury* (🖥 mauryhotel lima.priorguest.com/en, ☎ 428 8188, Jirón Ucayali 201) is close to Plaza de Armas and the centre's main attractions. The communal areas are full of Victorian-style furniture whilst the restaurant has a good reputation and the bar boasts that it helped to invent the Pisco Sour (see box p84) in the 1930s, though there's plenty of competition for that honour. The rooms are spacious but a little tired; rates start at US$94 (dbl) although you can save up to a third by booking online.

Gran Hotel Bolívar (🖥 www.gran hotelbolivar.com.pe, ☎ 619 7171, Jirón de la Unión 958), on Plaza San Martín, is an institution in the city. A national monument dating from 1924, it has a wealth of interesting architectural features that include marble columns, high roofs and lamps imported from France that create an air of luxury despite the fact that the hotel is a little ragged round the edges.

The rooms are similarly opulent, whilst the bar is renowned for the quality of its Pisco Sour (see box p84), a far cheaper way to experience this venerable hotel than to actually overnight here. It's possible to get surprisingly good deals on rooms here but expect to pay around US$85 for a double.

Expensive *Sheraton Lima* (🖥 www.she raton.com.pe, ☎ 315 5000, Av Paseo de la Republica 170) is an imposing concrete structure dominating downtown that offers everything you might expect from a top-class hotel. There's also a casino, tennis court, health club and outdoor pool. Room rates vary widely depending on style and season but start at around US$200 and climb to about US$350.

Miraflores [see map p130]
Budget *Hitchhikers* (🖥 www.hhikerspe ru.com, ☎ 242 3008, Calle Bolognesi 400) stands in a pleasant residential area and has a fully equipped kitchen, BBQ area and lots of games and toys to keep backpackers occupied. Dorms cost s/28 whilst rooms start at s/65/70 (sgl/dbl) for shared bathrooms and rise to s/70/84 (sgl/dbl) for private bathrooms. There's also plenty of parking if you're driving or motorbiking in Peru; you can even sleep in your truck or camper at reduced rates and still use the hostel's facilities.

K'usillu's Hostel (🖥 www.kusillushos tel.com, ☎ 444 0817, Av Larco 655) is clean but plain. Service is efficient and welcoming though. Dorms are US$9 whilst rooms cost US$11/22/30 (sgl/dbl/tpl) and come with continental breakfast, internet access and use of the communal kitchen.

Flying Dog Hostel (🖥 www.flyingdog peru.com) has branches at: Diez Canseco 117 (**backpackers hostel**; ☎ 445 6745); Calle Lima 457 (**hostel and B&B**; ☎ 444 5753); and Martir Olaya 280 (**hostel**; ☎ 447 0673). Dorms cost s/30 and double rooms are s/66-90. The latter is the largest and has more private rooms.

Friend's House (☎ 446 6248, Manco Capac 368) is, as the name would suggest, a small, sociable place. Facilities are good and rooms are reasonably priced at s/35/48 (sgl/dbl, com) and s/40/70 (sgl/dbl, att).

Mid-range There's masses of choice in this category and some good deals to be had due to the competition.

La Casa Nostra (🖥 www.lacasanostra peru.com, ☎ 241 1718, Grimaldo del Solar 265), in a colonial complex, is a smart and well-turned-out place to stay with everything you might need in a cosy, albeit pretty generic environment. The rooms cost s/110/140/180 (sgl/dbl/tpl) and all have en suite bathrooms, free wi-fi and include breakfast.

Conversely, *Hostal El Patio* (🖥 www
.hostalelpatio.net, ☎ 444 2107, Diez
Canseco 341a) is full of character.
Comfortable, friendly and only a few minutes' walk from central Miraflores, there's
also a plant-filled patio that's great for
relaxing in and free wi-fi throughout.

The rooms cost s/126/156 (sgl/dbl) and
include private bathrooms, cable TV and
filtered water. Mini suites (s/186) have a
small kitchenette and minibar whilst suites
(s/231) boast a separate bedroom and living
room along with a fully equipped kitchen.
You can save s/15 by paying in cash.

Hotel Alemán (off map to north; 🖥
www.hotelaleman.com.pe, ☎ reservations
445 6999 or 446 4065, Av Arequipa 4704)
is a surprisingly quiet place to stay given
that it's on a busy main street. There's a
secure garage if you're driving and a café
where guests can take advantage of the buffet breakfast. The spacious rooms are
decked out in traditional textiles and cost
US$65/70/80 (sgl/dbl/tpl).

Hostal Torreblanca (🖥 www.torre
blancaperu.com, ☎ 447 0142, Av José
Pardo 1453) is a large terracotta-coloured
building on the edge of a park. A compact
lobby and reception area hint at the fact that
rooms are also fairly cramped but nonetheless nicely presented and complete with all
mod-cons. Rates are s/195/195/240 (sgl/
dbl/suite).

San Antonio Abad (🖥 www.hotelsan
antonioabad.com, ☎ 447 6766, Av Ramón
Ribeyro 301) is a large, justifiably popular,
yellow corner building close to parks and
attractions that lays on a free airport pickup if you reserve in advance. Rooms cost
US$60/75 (sgl/dbl); the rate includes a buf-
fet breakfast in the attractively tiled dining
room.

Bayview Hotel (🖥 www.bayview-ho
tel.com, ☎ 242 1953, Las Dalias 276) is a
colonial-style house in a quiet location that
has a shady garden and helpful information
desk as well as currency exchange. There's
a bar on site and 24-hour room service plus
free wi-fi. The rooms themselves are comfortable and well equipped. Rates are
US$65/75/88 (sgl/dbl/tpl).

La Castellana Hotel (🖥 www.castel
lanahotel.com, ☎ 444 3530, Grimaldo del
Solar 222) stands in an impressive hundred-
year-old manor house. The interior is a little disappointing in comparison, with dark
rooms and old-fashioned décor. There's lots
of space though and a decent, albeit expensive, restaurant attached. The rooms cost
US$68/80/95 (sgl/dbl/tpl).

Antigua Miraflores (🖥 www.antigua
miraflores.com, ☎ 201 2060, Av Grau 350)
is a pretty, Republican-era house full of
tasteful touches; the tiled floors, chande-
liers and woodwork are all well preserved
and give an impression of the house's history. Old fashioned, with the emphasis on
friendliness, it's a well-located, welcoming
place to stay. The hotel has colonial style
and traditional rooms. The former are
slightly larger and a little more comfortable
but consequently cost a little more; traditional rooms cost US$87/104 (sgl/dbl) and
Colonial rooms are US$104/119 (sgl/dbl).
Señorial rooms – junior suites with bigger
beds, Jacuzzis and kitchenettes – start at
US$119/142 (sgl/dbl).

The reliable **Casa Andina chain** (🖥
www.casa-andina.com) has several properties in Miraflores, two of which are in their
Classic category and fall in this price bracket: *Miraflores San Antonio* (☎ 241 4050,
Av 28 de Julio 1088) and *Miraflores
Centro* (☎ 447 0263, Av Petit Thouars
5444). Both are smart, modern and professional places with all mod-cons.
Comfortable and competitively priced, the
former is slightly cheaper, with prices starting from US$88 (dbl) as opposed to
US$106 (dbl) but rates vary depending on
the month.

Radisson Decapolis Miraflores (🖥
www.radisson.com, ☎ 625 1200, 28 de Julio
151) is a modern, international-standard
hotel often favoured by business travellers;
it boasts a rooftop pool, fitness centre, massage rooms, a restaurant specializing in
fusion foods, a Martini bar and a sushi bar.
Standard rooms are US$114, whilst superi-
or ones start at US$134 and junior suites
will set you back US$154.

Expensive You're spoiled for choice when it comes to blowing the budget in Miraflores but you do get some great hotels for the money.

Sonesta Posadas del Inca Miraflores (💻 www.sonesta.com/miraflores, ☎ 241 7688, Alcanfores 329) is popular with tour groups who come for the comfortable rooms and personal service. The rooms cost US$248/263 (sgl/dbl) and come with all the facilities and add-ons you'd expect for that price tag.

Doubletree El Pardo by Hilton Lima (💻 doubletree3.hilton.com, ☎ 617 1000, Independencia 141) is very centrally located and convenient. Facilities include an indoor swimming pool, fitness centre and a good Peruvian restaurant. Standard rooms cost US$230 whilst those with a king-sized bed are a bit more.

Casa Andina Private Collection Miraflores (💻 www.casa-andina.com, ☎ 213 4300, Av La Paz 463) one of the top-end properties in the Casa Andina chain. Close to Parque Central it has contemporary rooms, many with good views of the coast. Facilities include a heated pool, gym and lobby bar. The rooms cost US$320 (dbl) and US$350 (superior).

Miraflores Park Hotel (off map to south-east; 💻 www.mirafloorespark.com, ☎ 610 4000, Malecon de la Reserva 1035) is owned by Orient Express and as you'd expect from them, this place is opulent, with first-rate facilities and service. Set atop the Miraflores cliffs and amid some pretty gardens, it's a pleasant place to get your bearing and explore the city. The hotel also has an open-air, heated rooftop pool and spa and several excellent restaurants, making it a really attractive option in this price range. Double room rates start at US$290 for a city view and US$325 for a sea view, with suites costing US$480.

JW Marriott (💻 www.marriott.com, ☎ 217 7000, Malecon de la Reserva 615) also trades on its location, standing on the cliffs just by Larcomar Mall; every room has sea views. Ultra modern and set up to indulge guests, it has an outdoor rooftop pool and tennis courts along with a really good restaurant. The rooms start at US$260 making it reasonably good value as well.

Barranco [see map p131]
Budget *The Point* (💻 thepointhostels.com/peru/lima.html, ☎ 247 7997, Malecón Junín 300) is a spacious, sea-front house with high ceilings and wide corridors that attracts backpackers and travellers with its laidback attitude and tendency to host impromptu parties that move onto Barranco's nightspots after. Always busy, it can get a little overwhelming, with more than 50 beds in dorms (US$9-11) but also some single (US$18) and double ($24) rooms. Guests have access to free internet, cable TV, films and a weekly BBQ.

Barranco's Backpacker Inn (💻 www.barrancobackpackersinn.com, ☎ 247 1326, Malecón Castilla 260) is a quieter proposition, closer to the coast and with great ocean views. The rooms starting at US$30 for a double are cheery, as are the staff. Dorm beds are US$10.

Compact and bijou, *Kaminu* (💻 www.kaminu.com, ☎ 252 8680, Bajada de Baños 342) has a great location below Puente de los Suspiros. There's a roof terrace to relax on and a weekly BBQ. Bunk beds cost US$10-12 and double rooms are US$25.

For a quiet retreat, head to *Aquisito* (☎ 247 0712, Centenario 114), a charming bed and breakfast with basic, comfortable rooms equipped with cable TV and private bathrooms. Expect to pay s/50/80 (sgl/dbl).

Mid-range *La Quinta de Allison* (💻 www.hotelbarranco.com, ☎ 247 1515, Av 28 de Julio 281) is a pleasant retreat with fairly plain but functional rooms that cost s/50/70 (sgl/dbl). The setting on a busy road means some rooms are noisy but the location, just a block from Barranco Plaza, compensates.

Safe in Lima (off map to south; 💻 www.safeinlima .com, ☎ 252 7330, Alfredo Silva 150) might be overdoing it with the name but is in fact a quiet, homely place with simple but clean and comfortable rooms that also runs tours so has a wealth of information and advice to share with travellers. The rooms cost s/160/220 (dbl/tpl). From the main plaza in Barranco follow Av Pedro de Osma; the hotel is in Block 5 of Pedro de Osma.

Expensive *Second Home Peru* (💻 www .secondhomeperu.com, ☎ 247 5522, Domeyer 366) is an impressive Tudor guesthouse with just five bedrooms, each incredibly comfortable, equipped with luxurious linens and Louis XV tubs and individually decorated. Once the home of Peruvian sculptor Victor Delfin, it's tastefully and quirkily decorated with art and artefacts. It also has an outdoor pool, ocean and garden views. The rooms cost US$115/125 depending on the view, marking it out as great value as well.

San Isidro
Budget *Malka Youth Hostel* (💻 www .youthhostelperu.com, ☎ 442 0162, Av Javier Prado Este) is an affordable option in an often expensive part of town.

Run by a climber it's full of spectacular mountain photographs and has a small climbing wall in the garden along with all the usual facilities and add-ons such as cable TV, ping-pong tables and a café. Dorm beds with shared bathrooms cost s/30, whilst double rooms are s/70/85 with shared/private facilities.

Chez Elizabeth (mobile ☎ 9980 07557, Av del Parque Norte 265) is a quiet family house conveniently located close to Cruz del Sur bus station. The rooms with shared bathrooms cost s/65/80 (sgl/dbl) while those with private bathrooms cost s/80/100 (sgl/dbl).

Mid range *Casa Bella Peru* (💻 www .casabellaperu.net/sanisidro, ☎ 421 7354, Las Flores 459) is set in a renovated mansion from the 1930s just a block back from the golf course and Country Club. The rooms are simply decorated but come with the usual range of services including cable TV and wi-fi. They cost US$79/99 (dbl/tpl).

Libertador Lima (💻 www.libertador .com.pe/en/libertador/lima, ☎ 518 6300,

Los Eucaliptos 550), opposite the golf course, is part of this chain's portfolio of spa hotels.

A fairly small hotel, its rooms are a good size and equipped with everything the business traveller might require. The rooms start at US$132 but rates rise quite quickly if you upgrade to a superior room or suite.

Expensive *Country Club Lima* (💻 www .hotelcountry.com, ☎ 611 9000, Los Eucaliptos 590) is an exclusive, modern boutique hotel in a sprawling building held to be a national monument with lavish rooms, restaurants and a bar along with a garden. Communal areas are decorated with tiling, textiles and reproduction Cusco School paintings. There are five styles of room, which range from a Master room at US$239, through Governor rooms at US$319 to the Presidential suites, which start at US$1330.

Swissotel (💻 www.swissotel.com/ho tels/lima, ☎ 421 4400, Via Central 150) is one of the smartest hotels in Lima. Luxurious and well thought out, the rooms are stylish and complimented by cutting-edge amenities. The cheapest rooms, Premier, are US$215 with larger rooms boasting more facilities correspondingly more expensive.

The restaurants here provide a range of dining options whilst business travellers are especially well catered for.

Sonesta Hotel El Olivar (💻 www.son esta.com/lima, ☎ 712 6000, Pancho Fierro 194) overlooks Olive Grove Park. Large and comfortable, it's a great top-end option, complete with one of the finest Japanese restaurants (Ichi Ban; Mon-Fri & Sun 12.30-3.30pm, Mon-Fri 7-10.30pm, Sun to 10pm) in Lima. Rates start at US$446 (dbl).

WHERE TO EAT
Whilst in Lima, make sure you discover the food scene; local life revolves around food and it is chance to sample an emerging world cuisine in its original location. Countless eateries can rustle up versions of Peru's fusion food but look out in particular for ceviche, nutty stews, anticuchos and *causas*. See also pp80-3.

Eating in Lima is surprisingly afford-able but to really keep costs down and still enjoy a sensational meal, look out for the daily *menús* that are often available at local restaurants.

Fast food

There are lots of cheap eateries around Lima Centro. These include rotisserie chicken joints and safe international chains, especially around Parque Kennedy, but you're better off trying the local spots and discovering the traditional flavours of Peru.

Cafés

Miraflores area (see map p130) For a treat, head to *Xocolatl* (💻 www.xocolatl .pe, Manuel Bonilla 111; Mon-Sat 11am-8pm), a tasty specialist shop focusing on Peruvian sweets. Run by a pastry chef and chocolatier, it creates divine combinations that are ideal as desserts or indulgences.

For a simple, hearty sandwich, head to *El Peruanito* (Av Angamos Este 391), where roast meat is piled high on French bread; try the *chicharrón* (chunks of pork, with sweet potato).

To see the humble potato transformed, eat at *Cesar* (formerly called Mi Causa; Av La Mar 814), which boasts dozens of inventive hot and cold causa recipes, which combine potato with vegetables, meat and seafood to tantalizing effect.

Haiti (Diagonal 160) is stuck in a time warp with retro décor and formal waiters but serves up tasty sandwiches and pastries in an ideal spot for people watching.

Similarly good for whiling away time and watching the world, *Café Café* (Martin Olaya 250) has a sprawling drinks menu that includes two-dozen types of coffee and a range of inexpensive snacks, pizzas and sandwiches. There's also a **branch** in Larcomar mall.

However, if you are in the mall you should try *Mangos* (💻 www.mangosperu .com; buffets: Mon-Sat 4.30-8pm, daily 12.30-4pm, Sat & Sun 7.30-11.30am, happy hour Mon-Thur 7-10pm), one of the best of the cafés in the mall, with a broad deck and good views over the ocean as well as some decent food and drink.

Lima centro (see map pp128-9) A bit more upmarket, *T'anta* (Pasaje de los Escribanos 142; Mon-Sat 9am-10pm, Sun 9am-6pm), is part of celebrity-chef Gastón Acurio's stable of restaurants . The food in this café-bistro is an interesting mix of plates from Peru, Italy and elsewhere but also features salads and sandwiches. Prices are fuelled by the big name attached to the business but by and large dishes are tasty and a little unusual, whilst the wine list and cocktails are definitely superior to other places.

There are also branches in **San Isidro** (Panchio Fierro 115) and **Miraflores** (Av 28 de Julio 888; see map p130).

Barranco (see map p131) *Iskay* (Pedro de Osma 106; Mon-Sat 9am-11pm) is part café, part gallery but well worth visiting for either.

Cevicheria and seafood

Peru's national dish, ceviche, has to be tried and Lima is one of the best places in the country to sample the original or innovative variations of this classic.

There are plenty of authentic neigh-bourhood *cevicherías* but also a number of more sophisticated joints where it is given the fine dining treatment. In line with cevichería tradition, most restaurants only open till about 5pm.

Miraflores area (see map p130) There was no way celebrated chef Gastón Acurio wasn't going to tackle a local speciality like ceviche; stylish *La Mar* (💻 www.lamarce bicheria.com/lima/, Av La Mar 770; Mon-Thur noon-5pm, Fri-Sun to 5.30pm) is a high-end ceviche restaurant, popular with wealthy locals and visitors alike; many opt for the tasting menu to avoid having to choose between the mouth-watering dishes on offer.

La Rosa Nautica (💻 www.larosanau tica.com, Espigon 4, Costa Verde; daily noon-midnight) is superbly sited in a Victorian-style end-of-pier restaurant. Take a taxi to the boardwalk and then walk out, enjoying the views of the coast and cliffs. You might even spot a surfer or two riding the waves. Once *the* place for ceviche, the seafood is still good – try the ceviche or ask for the catch of the day – but other restaurants in town have caught up so you may want to drop by for just a drink instead. The location though is unparalleled. Don't confuse this with La Choza Nautica (see below).

Far better in terms of the food is *Pescados Capitales* (🖥 www.pescadoscapitales.com, Av La Mar 1337; daily 12.30-5pm & 8-11pm) in the far corner of Miraflores. The kitchen knocks up superb ceviche, served along with a wide range of South American wines in an airy restaurant; there's also a cool open-air terrace on which to have a drink.

Lima centro Although *La Choza Nautica* (south of map p129; 🖥 www.chozanautica.com, Av Breña 204; daily 10am-10pm) serves decent ceviche it is in a far less salubrious part of town compared to La Rosa Nautica (see opposite).

Barranco (see map p131) *Canta Rana* (Génova 101) has been in business for a quarter of a century despite the fact that it isn't properly signed and can be a little hard to find; look for the locals who flock to the Singing Frog to sample the 17 types of ceviche that the place is renowned for. Informal and simply decorated, it is in fact quite expensive but justifies it by being the epitome of the local *cevichería*.

Also well established and worth trying is *La 73* (Av El Sol Oeste 175, ☎ 247 0780; Mon-Sat noon-midnight, Sun and holidays to 10pm).

San Isidro You can also get excellent ceviche at *Restaurante de Conquistadores*

(🖥 www.segundomuelle.com, Mariana Caballero, Av Conquistadores 490; daily noon-5pm), part of the Segundo Muello chain. This place has been adopted by a younger crowd of up-and-coming Limeños who come for good fish dishes, seafood pastas and cocktails.

Peruvian
Miraflores area (see map p130) Set in a colonial house, *Astrid y Gastón* (🖥 www.astridygaston.com, Cantuarias 175; Mon-Sat 12.30-3.30pm & 7.45-11.45pm) is where the Peruvian food renaissance began. Chef Gastón Acurio and his wife Astrid pioneered *novoandina* cuisine, fusing traditional foodstuffs with Asian, African and Spanish flavours to startling effect. The grand dame of the scene now has plenty of competition but the colourful restaurant decked in modern art still packs a punch and creates innovative and unusual combinations that will tantalize and satisfy. As well as ceviche there are delicious lamb recipes and Peruvian curries of tubers, vegetables and grains.

Panchita (Av 2 de Mayo 298), one of Acurio's later projects, focuses on street food and captures authentic flavours such as flame-grilled anticuchos and *tamales*. It is not possible to book a table here so queues can be long.

Restaurant Huaca Pucllana (General Borgoño cuadra 8) is a smart restaurant alongside the Huaca Pucllana ruins (see p132); the views of the site are good especially in the evening from the covered terrace as the adobe ruins are illuminated.

The food is contemporary Peruvian, a reinterpretation of *criollo* cuisine, well-cooked and artfully presented, with a range

---

❏ **Suspiro de Limeña (Lima Sigh)**
This classic Peruvian dessert consists of a thick caramel bottom layer made from condensed milk, vanilla and egg yolks, topped with meringue combined with port syrup and a sprinkle of ground cinnamon as the finishing touch. Legend has it that it was named by the famous writer and poet Jose Galvez Amparo Ayarez, whose wife created it, because it was 'as sweet and soft as the sigh of a young woman from Lima.' First served in 1818, it epitomizes the Peruvian love of sweet things.

Alison Roberts

of dishes from typical chowders to *cuy* (guinea pig).

Las Brujas de Cachiche (🖳 www.bru jasdecachiche.com.pe, Jirón Bolognesi 460; Mon-Fri noon-midnight, Sun 12.30-4pm), the Witches of Cachiche, is a series of bars and dining rooms in an old mansion house. Elaborately and elegantly decorated, it's an exclusive albeit expensive place to try Peruvian and criollo dishes, especially if you tackle the lunchtime buffet. Ancient and pre-Columbian recipes are also reinvigorated with unusual accompaniments to great effect. They also host live criollo music shows.

El Señorio de Sulco (🖳 www.senorio desulco.com, Malecón Cisneros 1470; Mon-Sat 12.30pm to midnight, Sun 12.30-4pm) is a popular place, feted for its Criollo dishes, especially the seafood. Expensive, it is worth the extra cost for the clifftop views and atmosphere.

To try the flavours of the north, especially the region around Chiclayo, visit *Fiesta* (🖳 www.restaurantfiestagourmet .com, Av Reducto 1278), a deceptively simple set up that serves hearty, rich regional specialities such as *arroz con pato* (rice with duck) that'll have you considering an extension to your journey.

San Isidro *Malabar* (🖳 www.malabar .com.pe, Camino Real 101) is a consistently ranked destination restaurant in the heart of San Isidro. Up-and-coming chef Pedro Miguel Schiaffino is influenced by Amazonian foodstuffs and cooking techniques and prepares a seasonal menu that draws on these. Try catfish caviar, tiradito of sole, or carpaccio of pig's trotter. There's also a devilishly good cocktail list.

International

Lima centro (see map pp128-9) There are plenty of *chifa* (Chinese) restaurants but for something a little special, seek out *Wa Lok* (🖳 www.walok.com.pe; daily 9am-11pm; Jirón Paruro 864) in Barrio Chino (Chinatown); the Cantonese dim sum are especially delicious but the noodles and stir fries are also very good.

French-influenced food with a Peruvian twist is available at *L'Eau Vive* (Ucayali 370), opposite Torre Tagle Palace in an old building. It has a fixed-price lunch served in a simple dining room along with a broader à la carte menu available in a grand salon. Run by an order of nuns, there's a rendition of *Ave Maria* every evening at 9pm. Proceeds are donated to charity by the nuns.

Miraflores area (see map p130) *La Bodega de la Trattoria* (🖳 www.labodega delatrattoria.com, Manuel Bonilla 106) serves good approximations of Italian cuisine, especially ravioli, and also has a decadent list of desserts.

San Isidro *Matseui* (Manuel Bañon 260; Mon-Sat 12.30-3.30pm & 7.30-11pm) was once part owned by celebrity chef Nobuyuki Matsuhisa, who brought his brand of sushi to this part of San Isidro before he opened his chain of Nobu restaurants around the world. The restaurant is nothing special to look at from the outside but the sashimi and sushi rolls prepared here are the best in the city; try their take on a ceviche roll, stuffed with shrimp and avocado and soaked in a spicy ceviche broth. Walk south from Av Javier Prado Oeste on Av Camino Real and look for Manuel Bañon after one block.

BARS AND NIGHTLIFE

Lima has a more contemporary and happening nightlife than almost any other city in Peru. Barranco in particular has a lively atmosphere and a wide range of places in which to hang out.

Lima Centro

The many **bars** in the centre of Lima cater to all tastes. For old-world elegance head to the *Gran Hotel Bolívar* bar, on Plaza San Martin, to sip a Pisco Sour; for that essential sporting occasion try *Estadio Fútbol Bar* (Nicolás de Piérola 934).

The best **folklórica show** in Lima is at *Las Brisas del Titicaca* (🖳 www.brisasdel titicaca.com, Pasaje Walkuski 168), where folk and criolla are combined into an all-singing, all-dancing extravaganza.

Miraflores

Miraflores has a number of expat-style bars that are frequently full and boast a good atmosphere and range of international drinks. *Benchley Arms* (Atahualpa 174) and *Old Pub* (San Ramón 295) are two of the longest running. Alternatively, try *Bar Habana* (Manuel Bonilla 107), an artsy hangout run by a Cuban-Peruvian couple who combine each country's specialist cocktails.

Media Naranja (Schell 130), which has a Brazilian vibe, or *Huaringas* (Bolognesi 460), a busy lounge bar with a huge range of cocktails and a DJ on most weekends.

For a night that doesn't involve drinking or dancing, there's a **cinema** in Larcomar mall (⌨ www.larcomar.com/cine.html), which shows both Spanish- and English-language films.

Barranco

The hip and unofficial centre of the city's nightlife, Barranco is the district to descend on if you're after a good night out or the chance to enjoy the eclectic music scene in Lima.

Start your evening in *Ayahuasca* (San Martín 130), a fashionable bar in an old three-storey mansion, *Juanito's* (Av Grau; see box p133), where a bohemian crowd congregates, *Mochileros* (Pedro de Osma 135), which is in a turn-of-the-20th-century house that's often packed and hosts weekend events, or one of the branches of *Posada del Angel* (Pedro de Osma 164 & 218 and Av San Martín 157).

Afterwards, head to *tabernas* including *La Noche* (Bolognesi 307) in search of live Andean music, criolla or Latin jazz.

Finally, hit the *peñas* such as *Del Carajo* (San Ambrosio 328) and *La Candelaría* (Bolognesi 292) or clubs including *Sargento Pimienta* (Bolognesi 755) for the chance to dance.

SHOPPING

Lima boasts the widest range of shopping in Peru. The main precinct is **Jirón de la Unión**, which is full of boutique shops and big brands.

However, Miraflores has a wide variety of boutiques and brand-name shops so it is the best place to browse. On the clifftops at the end of Av Larco stands **Larcomar**, a large mall that's home to international brands as well as a varied food court. Interrupt your shopping for a coffee and a chance to look out over the ocean and watch the paragliders who jump off adjacent cliffs drift past. There are plenty of interesting outlets to discover selling handicrafts, clothes, bags and jewellery, although things are a little more expensive because of the location.

For an alternative experience, visit the **markets**, making sure to take your haggling skills with you. Gamarra in La Victoria is home to 20,000 stalls; **Mercado Indio** in Miraflores sells alpaca clothing and crafts and the **craft stalls** on Av Petit Thouars in Miraflores are good for art and souvenirs. Visit **Mercado de Surquillo** in Miraflores to see where Lima's restaurants source their produce.

For more expensive or bespoke pieces, head to **Dédalo** at Paseo Saenz Peña 295 in Barranco to pick up beautiful craft pieces and jewellery. **Killaii** on the corner of San Martín and Alcanfores, in Miraflores, also has a range of contemporary crafts, whilst **Agua y Tierra**, at Ernesto Diez Canseco 298, specializes in indigenous crafts from the Amazon. **Pasaje el Suche** is an interesting area to explore with a small number of souvenir shops to browse and a range of cafés and bars in which to relax.

The shops belonging to **Kuna by Alpacca III**, branches of which can be found at the airport, on Av Larco and in Larcomar mall amongst other venues, are ideal for woollen clothing in contemporary designs and colours.

MOVING ON

Lima is an effective gateway to the rest of Peru and it's possible to go to every corner of the country from the capital.

To get to Cusco, you can either fly or journey by bus. To fly is quick but more expensive and won't enable you to see the landscapes you're travelling over.

❏ **Domestic airline offices in Lima**
- **LAN Peru** (🖥 www.lan.com, ☎ 213 8200), Av José Pardo 513, Miraflores
- **Star Perú** (🖥 www.starperu.com, ☎ 213 8813), Av Comandante Espinar 331, Miraflores
- **TACA** (🖥 www.taca.com, ☎ 511 8222), Av Comandante Espinar 331, Miraflores
- **Peruvian** (🖥 www.peruvian.pe, ☎ 716 6000), Av José Pardo 495, Miraflores
- **LC Peru** (🖥 www.lcperu.pe, ☎ 204 1313), Av Pablo Carriquirry 857, San Isidro.

Air

The flight from Lima to Cusco takes just less than an hour; tickets are reasonable, starting at around US$120, and services are frequent. Flights depart in the morning because the weather is generally better. LAN (see box p147) is the main carrier but other competing airlines such as TACA operate the same route. Sit on the left-hand side of the plane for particularly good views of Mt Salkantay shortly before landing in Cusco.

Note that you may find that flying into Cusco from sea level leaves you poorly acclimatized and struggling to move around freely, at least for the first couple of days.

Bus

Lima doesn't have a central bus terminal so each operator manages its own departure points. Some even have several depending on the final destination so check carefully where you need to be to meet your ride. If you're travelling a long way it's also worth checking that you've a comfy seat; buses marked 'bus cama' have more generous, reclining seats.

There are two **overland routes to Cusco**. The majority of bus companies work their way south along the coast, via Nazca to Arequipa, where you have to change and board a bus that loops inland and north to Cusco. The journey takes some 20 hours to complete.

The alternative is to travel through the highlands, via Ayacucho, a route that is more direct but more precipitous and adventurous to travel although it is no longer plagued by the terrorists that held sway in Ayacucho during the 1980s and early '90s.

Reliable companies include Cruz del Sur (🖥 www.cruzdelsur.com.pe, ☎ 311 5050), which has several daily services that depart from either Quilca 531 in Lima Centro (economy Imperial and Ideal services to Cusco and elsewhere), or Av Javier Prado Este 1109 in San Isidro (luxury Cruzero and Cruzero suite services to Cusco and beyond). Tickets one-way are s/185; you can book online.

Ormeño (🖥 www.grupo-ormeno.com.pe, ☎ 472 1710) also have daily services leaving from Av Javier Prado Este 1057. Tepsa (🖥 www.tepsa.com.pe, ☎ 202 3535) also travel to Cusco, departing from Paseo de la República 151-A in Lima Centro and Javier Prado Este 1091. Fares are a little cheaper at s/125. These three companies also offer bus services to other parts of Peru.

Smaller companies travelling to cities other than Cusco include Flores (🖥 www.floreshnos.net, ☎ 332 1212), Empresa Molina (☎ 428 4852) and Movil Tours (🖥 www.moviltours.com.pe, ☎ 716 8000).

CUSCO & AROUND

Cusco
(Qosqo, Cuzco)

In the whole of old Peru, there was undoubtably no place that was as deeply revered as the imperial city of Cuzco, which is where all the Inca kings held court and established the seat of government.
Garcilaso Inca de la Vega *The Royal Commentaries of the Incas* (1609)

The cultural and religious centre of the Inca world, Cusco was once a truly awesome city. The seat of the God-king, the Inca, it was built to reflect the might of the Empire. Yet despite its brutal sacking by the Spanish conquistadors, Cusco remains an exciting and vibrant place, much more than just a tourist town. The capital of Cusco Department, it's also the undisputed archaeological capital of South America and a UNESCO World Heritage Site.

Spectacular colonial architecture stands astride monolithic ruined Inca palaces made of perfectly hewn stone, which line atmospheric, scorched cobbled plazas. White-washed alleys and terracotta-tiled roofs house a rich mix of history, lively nightlife and a vast array of museums, sights and scenery. Although it's embraced tourism and developed a sound infrastructure to support the influx of visitors, the city's magnificent historical past still has a powerful hold on its glorious present. The collision and fusion of indigenous Andean and imported colonial cultures is fascinating and always evident, even to those tourists who come to the city only as a staging post for the Inca Trail to Machu Picchu.

It would be a stretch to suggest that Cusco is anything but on the tourist trail these days, yet the city wears its celebrity lightly and retains an authenticity other must-see cities around the world lose. Although there are some tried and tested traveller haunts, and the cementing of the city's status has finally seen the arrival of global food chains and brands, there are also quirky finds, quiet corners and plenty of local eateries specializing in the country's indigenous flavours. Essentially, what was a backpacker Mecca has grown up. But it has done so in style as a rash of new boutique and top-end hotel openings demonstrate, which, coupled with the arrival of celebrity chefs from Lima, ensure that the city has a broader, more chic appeal than ever whilst the traditional reasons for visiting, the history, architecture, location and atmosphere, remain as relevant as ever. Much more than just a history lesson, Cusco now has a contemporary feel. To paraphrase the 17th-century chronicler of Inca life Felipe Huamán Poma de Ayala, it's 'un espacio mágico' (a magic space).

The city stands at 3360m (11,000ft) above sea level so the air is thinner here than you might be used to. Upon arrival spend a couple of days acclimatizing before you attempt anything too strenuous. This is especially important if you're flying in from Lima as your body will take a while to adapt to going from sea level to altitude in an hour. Consider travelling down to the Sacred Valley (see p194), some 500m lower, to aid acclimatization and to take in the superb sights here as well.

HISTORY

Origins and early history

Legend states that the city was founded around AD1100 when the original Inca Manco Capac, having descended from the sun and risen from Lake Titicaca, plunged a staff into the soil and declared it fertile enough to support a city, a city he called Cusco (popularly thought to mean 'navel of the earth').

With no written records, the history of Cusco before the arrival of the Spanish is unclear. There is, however, archaeological evidence to suggest that other tribes lived here long before the arrival of the Incas. The Killke were probably the first but they were subjugated by the powerful and successful Huari culture, which came to dominate the area, with the Sacred Valley forming part of their northern highland frontier. Eventually the Huari moved away and the Killke resumed control of the region and secured it with hilltop fortifications. However, they never built in the Cusco valley, leading archaeologists to believe that by the 12th century there were already stable, sizeable settlements there. These weren't strong enough to resist the Incas though, and by the 13th century most had been subdued by the new arrivals, although it wasn't until the early 15th century that Cusco enjoyed its great expansion and rise to prominence.

Inca capital

During its heyday, as the Inca capital, the city must have looked dazzling with gold, silver and precious stones adorning its fine buildings, truly awe-inspiring to the visitor. It was the centre of political power and the cultural and religious heart of the society. All roads led to Cusco: the main roads to each of the four corners of the empire led away from the main plaza, whilst sacred and religious lines from other spiritually significant sites convened on the Coricancha. Built to reflect the enormity of the Incas' achievements and visibly demonstrate their superiority, the city ranked alongside many of the great European buildings when it came to elaborate architecture and sheer opulence.

The city was allegedly constructed on the orders of the Inca Pachacutec, who oversaw the destruction of the original simple structures found there after the conquest and demanded a city of stone be built in their place. Legend tells that Pachacutec went on to design the city in the shape of a puma, one of the Incas' sacred animals: the river Tullumayo forms the spine, the river Huatanay the belly and Sacsayhuaman (see p190) is laid out in the shape of the animal's head. The success of the city was down to Pachacutec's skills as a sophisticated urban planner. The city's superb infrastructure and a series of channels that diverted streams across the city provided fresh drinking water and ferried waste away, making it clean and hospitable.

Sadly the city was gutted in the wake of the Spanish conquest and now appears as a pale imitation of itself. The gold, silver and jewels that adorned the buildings were all looted, whilst the most significant and impressive buildings were all torn down. The infrastructure was damaged and the city allowed to become squalid and dirty. In a final desperate bid to oust the Spanish, the rebel Incas set fire to their own city and torched what was left of their once-magnificent capital.

Cusco after the conquest

Once the Spanish had definitively added Peru to the realms of Charles V, they realized that they needed a capital by the sea in order to support their new conquest. Since Cusco was set inland and moreover had strong associations with the past, it wasn't a suitable seat for government. With the transference of power to Lima, Cusco's influence inevitably waned.

The city was rebuilt, using stones pillaged from once-great Inca buildings to construct new colonial structures. Often these new buildings rose phoenix-like from the foundations of the Inca buildings, a not-so-subtle visual reminder of the dominance of the Spanish over their subjects. Unfortunately the colonial buildings were less robust than their predecessors and the occasional earthquakes that Peru experiences inevitably reduced them to rubble, leaving the remnants of the Inca architecture still standing.

Despite taking a back seat in determining the country's future and direction, Cusco still enjoyed moments in the headlines. During the 17th and 18th centuries the Cusco School of painting developed here and attracted a worldwide reputation. In 1780 it was the centre for the revolution staged by José Gabriel Condorcanqui, who took on the name Túpac Amaru II. In 1825 Bolívar arrived in the city and later the first royal oath of independence was sworn before the giant blackened crucifix nicknamed *El Señor de los Temblores*, now kept in the cathedral (see p152).

More recently, with the uncovering and popularization of Machu Picchu and other Inca ruins, the city has developed a role as Peru's most important tourist centre, a fact which has ensured its renaissance and re-emergence as one of the country's most vital, important cities.

WHAT TO SEE AND DO

Plaza de Armas

The main square has always been the city's focal point although during the time of the Incas it was twice as large. Once called Aucaypata ('the square of war or weeping'), it was a ceremonial site surrounded on three sides by huge Inca mansions. Along one side, in a stone ditch, ran the river Huatanay. On the far side

of the river stood Cusipata ('the joyful square'), which is where modern-day
Plaza Regocijo now stands. Cusipata was the setting for Inca celebrations and
feasts. Nowadays, colonial arcades full of shops and restaurants line the square,
and the balconies that overlook the original heart of the Inca capital are used by
cafés and restaurants to provide exceptional views.

There are usually two flags flying in the square: the red-and-white-striped
Peruvian national flag and the rainbow-striped Quechua flag, which bears a
striking resemblance to the gay pride banner, and from which it can be distinguished by an additional blue line.

The Cathedral
(Mon-Sat 10am-6pm, Sun 2-6pm; entrance through Iglesia de Jesús María;
s/25, free with religious ticket; see map p160) Built between 1556 and 1669 on
the site of the Inca Viracocha's palace, the monolithic renaissance-style cathedral dominates one side of the plaza and acts as a significant statement of religious superiority, designed to awe the local population.

The cathedral (Cathedral of Santo Domingo) stands between the church of
Jesús María (to the left as you look at the cathedral) built in 1733, and Cusco's
oldest church, El Triunfo (to the right), which dates from 1536 and is the resting place of the historian Garcilaso de la Vega. The main doors, which are dis-
creetly marked with a carved puma head, are open first thing in the morning for
genuine worshippers. This is an excellent time to slip in and see the cathedral,
and to appreciate the stunning works of art in rather better light than the gloom
that pervades once the doors are shut again.

Full of treasures, the cathedral is one of the city's best repositories of colonial art, particularly from the Cusco School, and has a sacristy full of portraits
of priests from the past. There are also wonderful murals, gilded altars and a
very finely carved choir representing 80 saints and dating from the 17th century by Martín Torres and Melchor Huamán, as well as a solid-silver high altar
backed by a *retablo* that's considered a masterpiece of indigenous carving.
Elsewhere, look for the blackened crucifix, *El Señor de los Tremblores* (the Lord
of the Earthquakes) that was paraded around Cusco in 1650 to stop a giant earthquake and which now stands in an alcove adjacent to the entrance to El Triunfo.

The parade worked and the event has been commemorated in a giant can-
vas that stands facing the entrance of El Triunfo. The colouring of the cross is
a result of decades of exposure to candle smoke. In the north-east corner of the
cathedral there's also a very famous painting of the Last Supper by Marcos
Zapata, painted with an Andean audience in mind, so with Christ and his disci-
ples feasting on roast *cuy* (guinea pig) and drinking chicha. Some people hold
that the face of Judas is actually a portrait of Pizarro.

The three buildings are periodically restored and worked on, meaning that
sections may be shut off or various works of art covered or moved into storage.

La Compañía (Jesuits' Church)
(Daily 9am-noon & 3-5.30pm; s/15, free with religious ticket; see map p160)
This Jesuit church is the other massive building on Plaza de Armas. Built on the

ruins of the palace of the Inca Huayna Capac, described by chronicler Pedro Sancho as the greatest Inca palace, it is a grand building complete with decorative baroque façade and a pair of impressive belfries.

Work began in 1578 but a giant earthquake in 1650 practically demolished the building and it wasn't finished until 1668. The Jesuits intended the church to outshine the neighbouring cathedral, but Pope Paul III intervened and declared it must not. Unfortunately by the time the message filtered back to Peru the work had already been completed. The two buildings are quite similar, although some believe that La Compañía eclipses its neighbour.

❑ **Boleto Turístico Unico (BTU) – Visitor's Ticket**
Admission to many of Cusco's museums and archaeological sites can only be achieved by using the **Boleto Turístico Unico** (BTU or Visitor's Ticket; 🖳 www.bo letoturisticocusco.net), which costs s/130 (US$45) for adults and s/70 for students with a valid ISIC card; it is valid for 10 days and is sold at the **Oficina Ejecutiva del Comite** (**OFEC**; Mon-Sat 8am-5pm, Sun 8am-8pm) office that is on the corner of Garcilaso and Plaza Regocijo, and also at the OFEC office at Av El Sol 103 (Mon-Sat 8am-6pm, Sun 8am-1pm).

It is also possible to buy a ticket at most of the sites featured although this is a gamble as they may have run out; ideally, buy the ticket in advance of visiting the sites from the offices or online.

Sites covered within Cusco and the surrounding region are the Santa Catalina Monastery, Municipal Museum of Contemporary Art, Regional History Museum, Coricancha site museum, Popular Art Museum, Centre of Native Music and Dance, Pachacutec monument, Sacsayhuaman, Q'enko, Puca Pucara, Tambo Machay, Tipon, Pikillacta, Pisac, Ollantaytambo and Chinchero.

The ticket allows only one entrance to each of these 16 sites; this is tiresome if you want to go back to any but if you paid entrance fees for all the sites separately it would cost much more than s/130. Note that the ticket does not cover the Coricancha-Santo Domingo complex (see pp154-5), merely the small museum in the grounds whose entrance is on Av El Sol. Nor does it include any religious sites or access to Machu Picchu.

If you want to go to any of the religious sites it is worth considering a **religious buildings ticket** (s/50). This secures entry to most of Cusco's churches and Museo de Arte Religioso.

Alternatively, there are three **partial boletos**, divided as circuits, which can be bought separately and which enable you to visit a selection of the sites. Each of these costs s/70. **Circuit 1** (valid for one day) combines Sacsayhuaman, Q'enko, Puca Pucara and Tambo Machay; **Circuit 2** (two days) combines the Museum of Contemporary Art, Museum of Regional History, Museum of Popular Art, Coricancha site museum, the Pachacutec monument, Centre of Native Music and Dance, Tipon and Pikillacta; **Circuit 3** (two days) combines Pisac, Ollantaytambo, Chinchero and Moray.

Several of the major sites, including Ollantaytambo, Sacsayhuaman, Pisac and Chinchero, can only be accessed with a boleto turistico. Other, smaller sites such as Tipon and Moray can be seen by buying individual tickets at the site.

Overall the best buy is the full Boleto Turistico as it offers the widest range of access.

The interior is cool and dark, the shadows hiding interesting paintings of local weddings that show plenty of period detail, including a representation of the marriage of Martín García de Loyola to the Inca princess Ñusta Beatriz. The baroque style, gold-leaf-covered altar is vast and impressive. The catacombs beneath the church are worth exploring and the view from the 2nd floor choir area is worth climbing a set of rickety steps to see. Often illuminated at night, the church is visible from many of the hotels and hostels high on the surrounding slopes.

Museo de Historia Natural

(Mon-Fri 9am-noon & 3-6pm; s/2) This motley collection of stuffed local fauna is hidden off Plaza de Armas on the same side as La Compañía. There are also a number of birds, reptiles and snakes from Manu National Park, but the specimens are pretty poor and presentation is disappointing.

Inca walls

The Inca walls that line the north-western side of the plaza are reputed to be part of Pachacutec's palace, whilst those in the northern corner belong to the palace of Sinchi Roca. There is also some fine Inca masonry (walls) on Calle Loreto; see map p173.

Coricancha (Temple of the Sun) and Santo Domingo

(⌨ www.qorikancha.org; Mon-Sat 8.30am-5.30pm, Sun 2-5pm; s/10, s/6 for students, not on the Visitor's Ticket)

'All the Incas enriched this city and, among its countless monuments, the Temple of the Sun remained the principal object of their attention. They vied with one another in ornamenting it with incredible wealth, each Inca seeking to surpass his predecessor.' **Garcilaso Inca de la Vega** *The Royal Commentaries of the Incas* (1609)

To the south-east of Plaza de Armas, the Inca Sun Temple, Coricancha (also written as Koricancha or Qoricancha) is Quechua for 'Golden Enclosure' and it was the centre of the Inca religion, having previously been the site of a Huari sun temple. The building comprised four small sanctuaries set around a central courtyard and was once lavishly decorated with gold plates and precious stones. Writing 50 years after the conquest, the historian Garcilaso de la Vega described the awe-inspiring magnificence of the main sanctuary, dedicated to the Sun:

'The four walls were hung with plaques of gold, from top to bottom, and a likeness of the Sun topped the high altar. This likeness was made from a gold plaque twice as thick as those that paneled the walls, and was composed of a round face, prolonged by rays and flames, the way Spanish painters represent it; the whole thing was so immense that it occupied the entire back of the temple, from one wall to the other.'
Garcilaso Inca de la Vega   *The Royal Commentaries of the Incas* (1609)

The Spanish Conquistadors pillaged the site and stole the lot.
    The other sanctuaries within the temple, which boast some of the most exceptional stonework and polished jointing in the city, were dedicated to various deities including the Moon (the bride of the Sun); Venus, the Pleiades and the stars; Thunder and the Rainbow. Garcilaso de la Vega noted that, 'They

called the rainbow *cuichu* and revered it very specially. When it appeared, they immediately put their hands over their mouths through fear, they said, that it might make their teeth decay. I can't say why'.

The mummies of previous Incas were kept here, as were the kidnapped principal idols of tribes that the Incas defeated. 'They were', wrote Garcilaso, 'so well preserved that they seemed to be alive. They were seated on their golden thrones resting on plaques of this same metal, and they looked directly at the visitor.' He went on to describe the astonishing garden outside the temple:

> 'In the time of the Incas, this garden, in which today the convent brothers cultivate their vegetables, was entirely made of gold and silver; and there were similar gardens about all the royal mansions. Here could be seen all sorts of plants, flowers, trees, animals, both small and large, wild and tame, tiny, crawling creatures such as snakes, lizards and snails, as well as butterflies and birds of every size... quinoa as well as other vegetables and fruit trees... very faithfully produced in gold and silver... and large statues of men and women and children made from the same materials.'
> **Garcilaso Inca de la Vega** *The Royal Commentaries of the Incas* (1609)

The Spanish looted almost everything from here too.

Conquering Cusco, Juan Pizarro, the younger brother of Francisco, took control of the Coricancha. Fatally wounded at the siege of Sacsayhuaman, he bequeathed the temple to the Dominicans, who built the Monastery of Santo Domingo here. Constructing the monastery on the foundations of the Inca building was meant to demonstrate the superiority of Christianity over the indigenous beliefs. An earthquake in 1950 destroyed the monastery but left the Inca stonework, some of the finest masonry in Peru, undamaged.

The **Chapel of Santo Domingo** (Mon-Sat 7am-7.30pm, Sun 7-11am & 6-8.30pm) also merits a visit, with intricate carvings, the priest's fine clothing and other fabrics on display. The graves of the rebel Incas, Sayuri Túpac and Túpac Amaru, and of the conquistador Juan Pizarro are also here. Black and white photographs in the entrance to the complex catalogue the damage sustained by the chapel during the various earthquakes.

Outside the temple is a set of grassy gardens with a pre-Inca spring and bath dating back to the Huari culture. **Coricancha Museum** (Mon-Sat 9am-5pm, Sun 8am-2pm; Visitor's Ticket) is under the gardens and can be accessed by walking downhill from the complex on Avenida El Sol. Although small this archaeological museum boasts some interesting pieces including pre-Inca ceramics and stonework, Inca crafts and carvings, some found in the Coricancha, and a mummy.

West and south of Plaza de Armas
This constitutes the area south of Plateros and north of Avenida El Sol, behind the Portales de Comercio and Confiturías.

● **La Merced** (Mon-Sat 8am-noon & 2-5pm; s/6, s/3 students; not included in the religious ticket) Originally built in 1534 this grand church, Cusco's third most important colonial church, was largely reconstructed after the 1650 earthquake in a combination of baroque and renaissance styles. Inside are riches to rival those contained in the Cathedral, with the ornate white-stone cloisters and large collection of Cusco School religious art a special highlight.

The church's most prized possession – a metre-tall solid-gold *monstrance* (vessel) covered in precious stones, diamonds and pearls – is kept in a locked cloister. Because the church faces on to the market the priests were able to preach directly to the milling crowds of Indians and espouse their message to a large audience. Buried here are the conquistadors Gonzalo Pizarro and Diego de Almagro.

● **Museo y Convento de San Francisco** (Mon-Fri 6.30-8am & 6-8pm; s/5, not included in the religious ticket) This forbidding building, dating from the mid 17th century, dominates Plaza San Francisco. Inside are: the oldest cloister in Cusco, a carefully crafted choir, suitably bloodthirsty decorations, paintings by local artists as well as two crypts piled high with bones.

● **Iglesia de Santa Clara** (Irregular opening hours; free) This 16th-century church is only rarely open, but worth a visit if you are lucky enough to come upon it whilst a service is in progress.

If you do go during a service, the nuns sometimes sing from behind a substantial metal grille. Inside the church are huge mirrors; originally intended to lure curious Indians into the building, they now multiply and reflect the candlelight magnificently.

● **Museo Historíco Regional y Casa Garcilaso** (Mon-Sat 8am-5pm; the only way of visiting is with a Visitor's Ticket) Originally inhabited by the historian Garcilaso de la Vega, the building was rebuilt by the famous Peruvian architect Víctor Pimentel after the 1986 earthquake reduced it almost to rubble.

The museum offers a basic overview of Peruvian history and has a token collection of pre-Inca ceramics, pottery, arrow heads and other Inca weaponry, architectural tools and agricultural implements, a Nazca mummy and some gold jewellery found at Machu Picchu.

The main attractions, though, are the colonial furniture and copious examples of the Cusco School of Art, many drawn by Cusquenian artists including Marcos Zapata, Bernando Biti and Antonio Huillca. There are also some black and white photographs that capture the aftermath of the 1950 earthquake.

● **Mercado San Pedro** (Daily) An essential stop on any tour of the city, the central market is opposite San Pedro train station. Everything is for sale, from fruit and veg to meats you recognize and some you won't. Noisy, busy, smelly and something of a sensory overload, it's a great place to people-watch. Keep an eye on your wallet and bag as pickpockets and bag slashers operate here and prey on the distracted.

● **Santa Teresa** (Irregular opening hours; free) This is a rather nondescript building from the outside but it is set in an attractive square that has interesting illustrations of the life of the saint on the walls inside. The stone wall bordering Calle Saphi is a very good example of polygonal masonry.

East and south of Plaza de Armas

These are the streets north of Avenida El Sol and south of Triunfo, which lie behind La Compañía.

● **Calle Loreto** The finely crafted stone work of this renowned Inca alley, which runs south-east alongside La Compañía, is well worth a look. The left-hand wall was part of the Acllahuasi, a convent of Inca nuns drawn from the most beautiful women throughout the empire.

● **Scotiabank** (open during bank hours; free) The bank that now stands on Calle Maruri occupies the site of the palace of Túpac Inca Yupanqui. The elegantly cut and finely sculpted stone walls are still hugely impressive although somewhat at odds with the modern operation inside them. There is also a small **museum** inside that explains the history of the building and exhibits local artwork. On the first floor is a fascinating permanent exhibition of black and white photographs by the Peruvian photographer Martin Chambi (see p74).

● **Museo de Arte Religioso y Palacio del Arzobispal** (Mon-Sat 8am-5.30pm, Sun 2-5.30pm; s/15, free with religious ticket) Standing on the remains of an original Inca building, the colonial mansion that houses the museum and Archbishop's Palace is striking. Inside is a large collection of religious art from the Cusco School including paintings by Marcos Zapata and the Corpus Christi collection by an unknown artist, as well as a number of intricate mosaics and the first organ to arrive in Peru.

The museum and palace is situated at one end of **Calle Hatun Rumiyoc**, the narrow alley that boasts the famous 12-sided stone that has become something of a symbol for Cusco and can be seen throughout the city and advertised on the side of Cusqueña beer bottles. The original Inca wall in which the stone is set used to be part of the palace of Inca Roca. At the far end of the wall is a small side street that runs along what would have been the back of the palace. This, too, boasts beautifully moulded stones. These intricately worked blocks conceal the outline of a puma, which the locals sitting round it will happily point out to you, for a small fee, if you're struggling to make it out.

● **Monasterio de Santa Catalina de Sena** (🖳 www.monasteriosantacata linacusco.org; Mon-Sat 8.30am-5.30pm, Sun 2-5pm; free with Visitor's Ticket, s/8 without, or s/15 if combined with Convento Santo Domingo) This small convent is a beautiful building but the contents of the museum, a handful of dioramas and some religious art, are relatively disappointing in comparison.

● **Museo de Casa Concha** (Mon-Sat 9am-5pm; s/20) Covering two floors of a large colonial building, the 'Shell House' is now the repository for some of the 4000 artefacts removed from Machu Picchu by Hiram Bingham and shipped back to the USA. After years of high-profile petitioning to Yale University, many of these pieces were returned in 2012 and can now be seen in Peru for the first time. See also box p158.

A series of rooms around a large courtyard contain historical photographs and original documentation of early exploration and the approach to Machu

❏ **Grand Museum of Tawantinsuyo**
As the book went to press the President of the Cusco region, Jorge Acurio Tito, announced a plan to create the Grand Museum of Tawantinsuyo, which will become a bespoke repository for objects found at Machu Picchu, removed by Bingham and subsequently returned by Yale University.

The museum, which will cost US$100 million to build, will stand at the heart of a 500-acre cultural park, close to the ruins of Sacsayhuaman. The design for the museum will be decided by an international competition and the building is planned to open at the end of 2014.

As well as artefacts from Machu Picchu, the museum will house art works currently stored in various places around Cusco. Once open, it should be widely advertised; enquire at the tourist office for up-to-date information.

Picchu, a giant-scale diorama of the site complete with narration, pottery and ceramics found there and a number of objects connected to daily life at Machu Picchu. There's also an examination of the practice of cranial deformation, an examination of the Incas interest in archaeoastronomy and the way that they understood the seasons and skies, a fascinating quipu and a selection of pre-Inca musical instruments. Most of the exhibits are described in Spanish.

There's also a very impressive interactive **3D tour of Machu Picchu** that you can control, bringing up photographs taken by Bingham and a commentary on what you're looking at. As the museum beds in, more pieces are also promised and the collection housed here should grow, affording visitors an even-more comprehensive history of Machu Picchu.

● **Iglesia de San Blas** (Mon-Sat 10am-5.30pm, Sun 2-5.30pm; s/15) This simple adobe church contains a breathtakingly intricate carved cedar-wood pulpit dating from the 17th century, the detail of which includes an angel, a sun-disc, some faces and bunches of grapes. At the top is St Paul with his foot on a skull believed to be that of the craftsman responsible for the carving. The church also has a baroque gold-leafed altar.

North of Plaza de Armas
● **Iglesia de San Cristóbal** (Irregular opening hours; free) Set high above Cusco, this church is thought to have been built on the site of the palace of Manco Capac, the first Inca. Surrounded by a massive Inca stone wall, the church was built by Inca Paullu as a means of demonstrating his new Christian faith.

● **Museo Inka** (Mon-Fri 8am-7pm, Sat 9am-4pm; s/10) This impressive colonial house stands on Inca foundations, on the corner of Ataud and Tucumán. Inside is a massive stairway, guarded by sculptures of mythical creatures, and an attractive courtyard.

The building, originally belonging to Admiral Don Francisco Maldonado, was badly damaged by the 1650 earthquake but was rebuilt and is still a striking structure. Most importantly, the museum houses the finest collection of Inca artefacts in the city and the largest collection of Inca objects in the world. Metal- and gold-work, jewellery, pottery, ceramics, textiles and paintings are all on display and laid out in an easy-to-follow and informative fashion although the English-language explanations are a little basic. There is also a reconstructed burial chamber containing several mummies.

High-quality, expensive weavings are for sale in the courtyard of the house and you can often find craftsmen working here on the beautiful fabrics.

● **Palacio Nazarenas Hotel** This building, on Plazoleta de las Nazarenas, was formerly called **House of the Serpents** because of the snakes carved into the door lintels. The house is reputed to have once belonged to the man responsible for stealing the golden disc of the sun from the Coricancha. Garcilaso de la Vega describes how he lost it:

> 'When the Spaniards entered Cuzco, this likeness of the Sun, as the result of a division of property, fell into the hands of one of the early conquistadors, who was a man of noble birth by the name of Mancio Serra de Leguisamo, whom I knew very well before I came to Spain. He was a great gambler and he had no sooner acquired this treasure than he gambled and lost it in one night; and we might even say, echoing Father Acosta, that this is the origin of the expression "to gamble the Sun before it rises".' **Garcilaso Inca de la Vega** *The Royal Commentaries of the Incas* (1609)

These days, it has been converted into a luxurious hotel (Palacio Nazarenas; see pp170-1). It's possible to step inside even if you aren't a guest, in order to admire the original features of this exceptional building. Through the imposing stone doorway is a tiled reception and a courtyard ringed by original frescoes that tell a series of stories and depict nuns, bullfights and daily life. Also ask to see the library and its stock of original books.

● **Museo de Arte Precolombino/Casa de Cabrera** (daily 9am-10pm; s/20, student s/10) This small yet fascinating museum is set within the grand, spacious confines of the Earl of Cabrera's colonial mansion. Cabrera was responsible for founding Ica on Peru's coast.

The museum covers the artistic achievements of the various ancient Peruvian cultures and houses a superb collection of artefacts from the Moche, Chimú, Paracas, Nazca and Inca cultures. Dating from 1250 to 1532, these archaeological treasures include carvings, ceramics, and gold- and silver-work, all of which are superbly lit and well presented with both English and Spanish text explaining what you are looking at.

● **Hotel Monasterio** This hotel (see p170), Cusco's finest, was converted from the elegant old **Seminary of San Antonio Abad**. Although a very upmarket establishment, it is possible to visit if you drop in for a beer at the bar. Once through the Inca-colonial doorway you look onto a spacious courtyard, which is only slightly spoiled by the glassed-in cloisters surrounding them.

map

159

CUSCO

To Sacsayhuaman
and other local Inca sites
(see 'Around Cusco' map)

To Sacsayhuaman
(see 'Around Cusco' map)

trailblazer

0   100   200m

Pumacchca

South American Explorers

San Blas

Plazoleta de San Blas

Museo de Arte Religioso y Palacio del Arzobispal

Museo de Arte Precolombino/ Casa de Cábrera

Museo Inka

Plazoleta de las Nazarenas

San Cristóbal

Santa Teresa

Town Hall

Iglesia de Jesús María

Cathedral

El Triunfo

Plaza de Armas

See 'Plaza de Armas area' map

La Compañía

Museo de Historia Natural

Museo de Casa Concha

Santa Catalina

iPeru office

OFEC

Museo Histórico Regional y Casa Garcilaso

Museo y Convento de San Francisco

Streets: Pumacchca, Tres Cruces, Pasñapata, Tandapata, Carmen Bajo, Chihuanpata, Tullumayo, Carmen Alto, Atoqsaycuchi, Angelitos, San Blas, Choquechaca, Ladrillos, Ese, Pumacurco, Concepción, Colcampata, Waynapata, Ataud, Purgatorio, Tucumán, Resbalosa, Suecia, Procuradores, Plateros, Coricalle, Tecsecocha, Saphi, Amargura, Tandapata de Monjaspata, Siete Cuartones, Teatro, Arones, Meloc, Nueva Alta, Calle Fierro, Sta Ana, Apurimac, Nueva Baja, Tordo, Granada, Garcilaso, Heladeros, Espinar, Plateros, Sta-Teresa, S Juan de Dios, Mantas, Maruri, Loreto, Arequipa, Triunfo, Calle-Herrajes, Hatun Rumiyoc, San-Agustín, Sta Mónica, Ruinas, Palacio, Culebras, Herrajes, Plaza Regocijo

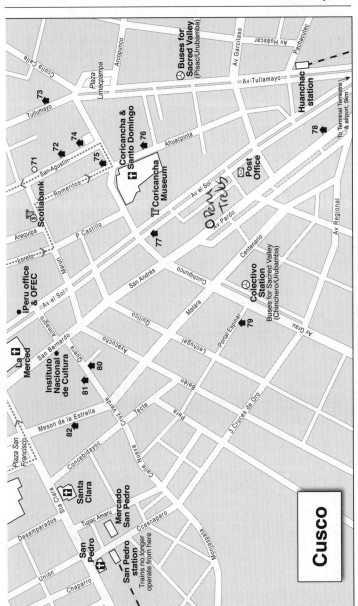

Cusco

CUSCO

□ **CUSCO WALKING ROUTES** **[see map pp160-1]**
The best way to explore Cusco and get a feel for both its past and present is to set out on foot and wander through the labyrinthine streets, from plaza to plaza and past Inca sites and colonial treasures. Below are two recommended circuits that take in a handful of the key attractions. Allow about **two hours** for each.

● **North and west** From **Plaza de Armas** stroll north-west up Procuradores, also nicknamed Gringo Alley. At the far end turn right, north-east, climb a set of steps and take the second left, Calle Suecia, which ascends steeply in a roughly north-westerly direction. At the first junction take the broad tarmacked road that sweeps right and climbs around a bend to arrive below **Iglesia de San Cristóbal** (see p158), which stands to your left.

Below the church, on the apex of the bend, is a narrow alley, **Resbalosa**, which descends steeply in a roughly southern direction, giving you unparalleled views over the city. At the T-junction turn right on to Waynapata and head south-west, retracing your earlier steps past the entrance to Procuradores. Turn right onto Tecsecocha, first left on to Tigre and cross over Plateros to join Siete Cuartones; the church of **Santa Teresa** (see p156) is on the corner of Plateros and Siete Cuartones.

Beyond the church, the first road to the left is Santa Teresa; it descends south-east from here and brings you to Plaza Regocijo. On your left as you enter the square is the Town Hall. In the south-west corner of the square stands the renovated house of Garcilaso de la Vega, which is incorporated in the **Museo Histórico Regional y Casa Garcilaso** (see p156). Turn right on to Av Garcilaso, which runs alongside the house, and one block later emerge in Plaza San Francisco. **Museo y Convento de San Francisco** (see p156) is immediately opposite. The plaza is bordered on its southern side by Santa

Clara, a busy, main artery that leads south-west to the convent of the same name as well as the main market and San Pedro station.

To return to Plaza de Armas simply follow Santa Clara north-east for four blocks from Plaza San Francisco.

● **South and east** From the southern side of Plaza de Armas pick up Calle Loreto (see p157); it runs away from the square in a south-easterly direction, alongside La Compañía. At the far end of this narrow, historic alley turn left onto Calle Maruri. Immediately on your left is **Scotiabank** (p157), with its original Inca walls. Continue north-east along Maruri, then take the first right, Romeritos, and walk south-east one block to emerge next to Hotel Libertador in a small square that looks onto the **Coricancha** and **Santo Domingo Monastery** (see pp154-5).

From the Coricancha take the road leading north-east which ultimately leads you to Plaza Limacpampa. Before then though, take the first left and climb north-west along San Agustín. The fourth road to the right is Hatun Rumiyoc, on the corner of which stands the **Museo de Arte Religioso** (see p157). Turn right (north-east) here and walk down Hatun Rumiyoc and then Cuesta San Blas to reach Plazoleta de San Blas and the **church** (Iglesia de San Blas; see p158) that stands here.

From the plaza pick up Carmen Alto heading north-west from the western corner of the square before taking the first left and zigzagging your way to Plazoleta de las Nazarenas, which is the setting for **Museo de Arte Precolombino** (see p159), **Casa de Cabrera**, **Palacio Nazarenas Hotel** (formerly the House of the Serpents; see p159) and **Hotel Monasterio del Cuzco** (formerly the Seminary of San Antonio Abad; see p159).

To return to Plaza de Armas continue straight on (south-west) and walk down Cordoba de Tucumán past **Museo Inka** to arrive once again in the main square.

CUSCO MAP KEY – see previous pages for map

Where to stay

1 Hostal Familiar
2 El Balcón Inn
3 Loki Backpackers Hostel
4 Hotel Fierro
5 Hotel Meloc
6 Hotel Picoaga
7 Hotel Royal Inka II
8 Hotel Royal Inka I
12 Casa Andina Classic Cusco Plaza
13 WalkOn Inn
14 Hostal Corihuasi
16 Hostal San Isidro Labrador
17 Hostal Suecia II
18 Hostal Rojas
25 Del Prado Inn
26 Hostal Suecia I
27 Hostal Resbalosa
28 Albergue Muncipal
29 Fallen Angel
30 Palacio Nazarenas
32 Hostal Cartagena
33 Hostal Arqueologo
34 Hostal Rumi Punku
35 Los Apus Hotel y Mirador
37 Casa de Campo Hostal
38 Hospedaje Familiar Kuntur Wasi

39 Hostal Pensión Alemana
40 Hostal El Grial
42 Casona los Pleiades
44 Amazonas Hostal
45 Marani
46 Hospedaje Sambleño
49 Boutique Hotel Casa San Blas
53 Amaru Hostal
58 Hotel Monasterio
63 Emperador Plaza Hotel
64 Casa Andina Classic Cusco Catedral
66 Novotel Cusco
67 Albergue Casa Campesina
68 Hotel Ruinas
69 Orquidea Real Hostal
70 Casa Andina Classic Cusco San Blas
72 Casa Andina Classic Cusco Koricancha
73 Estrellita
74 Casa Andina Private Collection Cusco
75 Hotel Libertador Palacio del Inka
76 Hostal Pascana
77 Maison de la Jeunesse

78 La Posada del Abuelo
79 Sonesta Posada del Inca Cusco
80 Los Aticos
81 Hostal Machu Picchu
82 The Point

Where to eat and drink

9 Chicha
10 El Truco
11 Kin Taro
15 Victor Victoria
19 Los Perros
20 Chez Maggy
21 Sumaq Misky
22 La Tertulia
23 Chez Maggy
24 Kusikuy
29 Fallen Angel
31 MAP Café
36 La Quinta Eulalia
41 7 Angelitos
43 Km0
47 The Muse Too
48 Pachapapa
50 El Buen Pastor
51 Macondo
52 Granja Heidi

54 Jack's
55 Kushka...fe Deli
56 Café Cultural Ritual
57 Kushka...fe
58 Hotel Monasterio
59 Uchu Peruvian Steakhouse
60 Marcelo Batata
61 Cicciolina
62 La Bodega 138
65 Rosie O'Grady's
71 Moni

cusco

PRACTICAL INFORMATION
Arrival
As a result of its position high in the Andes, **you will need to take a couple of days to acclimatize** once you have arrived in Cusco, especially if you arrive from Lima or other low-lying places. Do not attempt anything too strenuous whilst your body adjusts. Acclimatization is quicker if you do not eat or drink excessively.

By air   Aeropuerto Alejandro Velasco Astete (information ☎ 222611) lies 5km from the main Plaza de Armas at Quispiquilla. A 10-minute taxi ride will cost about s/10-15 from the airport car park or about half that from the street outside as drivers here don't have to pay the waiting fee levied by the car park. *Colectivos* to the centre cost even less and can also be hailed from the street outside the airport. You could walk to the plaza in around an hour but this isn't particularly safe.

By rail   Trains from Juliaca and Puno arrive at **Huanchac station**, at the south-eastern end of Avenida El Sol, about a 20-minute walk from Plaza de Armas. Taxis from outside the station cost s/5 to the centre of town.

Trains to and from Machu Picchu or Ollantaytambo operated by PerúRail arrive and depart from **Poroy**, over a hill from Cusco on the road to Urubamba. Those run by Inca Rail start and finish at Ollantaytambo.

Sadly trains no longer operate from Cusco's oriental and historic station, San Pedro.

By bus   Long-distance buses arrive and depart from **Terminal Terrestre** on Avenida Vallejo Santoni, close to the giant statue of Pachacutec, south-east of the city centre. A taxi from here to Plaza de Armas costs around s/5-10 whilst a colectivo to the centre will charge s/1.

Orientation
Cusco is divided into five districts, each centred on a square or temple. At the heart of the city lies Plaza de Armas. The majority of sights are within easy walking distance of here. South of the Plaza, Avenida El Sol runs past Coricancha. Heading uphill and south-west from Avenida El Sol there are Plaza San Francisco, Mercado San Pedro and Iglesia de Santa Clara. One block west of Plaza de Armas is Plaza Regocijo which has Inca origins and contains some of the city's finest mansions and municipal palaces.

From the north-east corner of Plaza de Armas, Calle Triunfo climbs steeply through a stunning Inca-walled street to the artisan quarter of San Blas, centred on an attractive church. Uphill and north-west from Plaza de Armas, Calle Plateros climbs towards the Inca fortress Sacsayhuaman and the giant statue of Christ that overlooks the city.

Getting around
The centre of Cusco is fairly compact and easy to explore on foot, though for trips after dark or longer journeys consider taking a **taxi**. These can be found throughout the city, particularly around Plaza de Armas. They ought to charge a flat fare of s/3-4, rising to s/5-6 after 9pm, for journeys in the city, but if they suspect you've just arrived or aren't on the ball they may try to charge extra. For longer journeys always agree a price in advance as the cabs don't have meters. In the past there have been reports of taxi drivers robbing people.

If you are uncomfortable flagging one down in the street, ask your hotel to arrange

❏ **Word of warning**
Cusco has a deservedly mixed reputation for robbery. The areas around the markets and the old San Pedro train station are notorious. San Blas at night is also potentially dangerous. Take care when walking after dark, or hail a licensed taxi. Similarly be streetwise if visiting out-of-the-way ruins, especially if going alone or late in the day.

a taxi or call one of the licensed operators: Aló Cusco (☎ 222222) and Radio Taxi (☎ 222000) are both reliable and have good reputations. Alternatively, catch a communal **colectivo**, which will inevitably be cheaper but less comfortable, and which aren't allowed within two blocks of Plaza de Armas.

There is also a hop-on, hop-off tourist **tram** service, Tranvia (🖳 www.tinti.pe/tranvia-del-cusco/, ☎ 223840) which operates on a 90-minute city circuit (s/20) beginning and ending in Plaza de Armas; services depart at 8.30am, 10am, 11.30am, 2pm, 3.30pm, 5pm and 6.30pm.

Those on a larger budget may choose to **hire a car**. Most agencies have an office at the airport although some, including Localiza (☎ 242285/263448; Av El Sol 1089), can be found on Av El Sol.

Tourist information

There is a very helpful **iPeru** tourist information office in the arrivals hall of the airport; there is also one on the ground floor at Av El Sol 103 (☎ 252974; 24hr help line ☎ 01 574 8000, 🖳 www.peru.travel/en; Mon-Sat 8.30am-7.30pm), which provides tourist information and assistance. Free maps are also available.

OFEC (see box p153) have an office in the same building on the opposite side of the entrance hall.

South American Explorers (🖳 www .saexplorers.org; see box p137) have a clubhouse (☎ 245484; Mon-Fri 9.30am-5pm & Sat 9.30am-1pm) at Atoqsaycuchi 670, San Blas. It is a veritable treasure trove of information, and members receive discounts at many of the hotels, sights and entertainments in Cusco.

Entrance tickets for Machu Picchu (see p347) are available from the **Instituto Nacional de Cultura** (INC; ☎ 236061; Mon-Fri 9am-1pm & 4-6pm, Sat 9-11am) office on Calle San Bernardo, south-west of Plaza de Armas.

Banks and cambios

Most of the **banks** are strung out along Avenida El Sol. These all have ATMs with 24-hr access and security protection, from which you can withdraw US$ and soles. Queues are common and service can be slow. Banks typically shut 1-3pm.

BCP (Av El Sol 189) and **Interbank** (Av El Sol 380) both have Visa ATMs, handle Amex and can convert travellers' cheques. **Banco Continental** (Av El Sol 459) also has a Visa ATM and changes travellers' cheques but charges commission. **Banco Latino** (Av El Sol 395) has ATMs for MasterCard. **Scotiabank**, at Calle Maruri 315, is a good alternative if you aren't on Av El Sol.

In addition to the ATMs at the banks, there are some on Plaza de Armas, Av La Cultura and in the San Blas district.

There are **cambios** all over Cusco, especially on the western side of Plaza de Armas, and it's difficult to pick out any one over the other. These tend to charge slightly higher commission than those on Av El Sol, the best of which is **LAC Dólar** at Av El Sol 150. The street changers tend to congregate outside the major banks, particularly at the top end of Av El Sol. **DHL/Western Union** (☎ 224167) is at Av El Sol 627A and at Maruri 310 (☎ 248028).

Try to save your small change and lower denomination bills as you will need these once outside Cusco, since there is usually a shortage of change in the smaller villages and people will not be able to break a large note for you.

Bookshops

There several places around Plaza de Armas where you can pick up English-language books; look on Portal de Comercio and Portal de Confiturías. Elsewhere, try **Jerusalén**, at Helaferos 143 (south-west of Plaza de Armas), for guidebooks, postcards and music CDs, or **Librería CBC** (🖳 www

---

☐ **Emergencies**
Fire: ☎ 103;   Police: ☎ 105;
Tourist Police: ☎ 249654 or ☎ free 0800 4 2579 (24 hours), Saphi 510, and an office (9am-6pm) on Plaza de Armas at Portal Carrizos 250, near the Compañía.

.cbc.org.pe), at Av Tullumayo 274, for material on Peru's history, local anthropology and archaeology. The **585 Bookshop** at Av El Sol 781A isn't very large but has a wide range of foreign-language books, including English.

Communications
● **Telephone and fax** There are public pay phones everywhere, and it's easy to ring abroad with a Telefonica phonecard that can be bought from almost any of the small shops lining Plaza de Armas. Alternatively, you can get someone else to do it for you in one of the numerous internet cafés, where you can usually also send and receive faxes.

● **Post** For letters, the **correo** (post office; Mon-Sat 7.30am-8pm, Sun 8am-2pm) is on the west side of Av El Sol, No 800, on the fifth block downhill from Plaza de Armas. Poste Restante services are free. DHL have an office at Av El Sol 627A if you want to send packages overseas.

● **Internet access** Internet cafés open and close around Cusco with alarming regularity but you're never far from one; there are a great many to choose from, the main difference being the speed of connection and other facilities on offer: the best places will also have scanners, webcams, CD burners and knowledgeable staff. Rates are fairly standard (s/1.50-2/hour).

Festivals
See pp86-7 for details of the main festivals and events in Cusco.

Medical services
Hospitals: Regional ☎ 227661 or 223691 in emergencies, Av de la Cultura, Clinica Pardo ☎ 240997, Av de la Cultura 710; **Tourist Medical Assistance** ☎ 240768; **Pharmacy** Millenium (☎ 241784), Calle Santa Catalina Angosta 163 and Inka Farma (☎ 240167), Av El Sol 210 (24 hours).

Equipment rental
Equipment and trekking gear can be hired from the travel agencies along Procuradores or from a number of shops on Platores. Make sure you check everything

carefully in advance as it has been known for bits to be missing and the standard of stuff available can be pretty poor. Butane and other cooking stove fuel can also be bought from these places. To hire anything you will have to leave a deposit and a copy of your passport.

Soqllaq'asa Camping Services (☎ 252560), at Plateros 365, have down sleeping bags, ThermaRest sleeping mats and gas stoves for hire. Cutlery, pots and pans are usually thrown in free. They will sometimes buy your old kit from you too.

Tatoo, on Calle del Medio 130, has high-quality gear available at appropriately high prices. Big brand-name hiking, climbing and camping gear is on offer alongside the own-brand clothing.

International-brand **North Face** also has a couple of concessions, including one on Plaza de Armas at 194 Portal de Commercio.

Trekking provisions
Mercado San Pedro (San Pedro Market), opposite San Pedro station, is the best place to stock up on basic supplies.

Alternatively there are supermarkets on Avenida La Cultura, including **Supermercado D'Dinos** which is open 24 hours. Alternatively try **Supermercado Gato** at Portal Belén 115.

Laundry
You won't have any trouble finding someone willing to take in your laundry for a small consideration. **Lavaclin** at Suecia 400 and **Splendor** at Suecia 326 both collect and deliver your laundry. Also recommended are **Adonai** and **Lavendería Louis** on Choquechaca and **Easy Wash** and **Inka Laundry** on Calle Ruinas.

Otherwise there are several *lavandarías* on Procuradores and Plateros. Most places are open 7.30am-8pm.

Language courses
Peru has become an increasingly popular country in which to study Spanish.

Most organizations run classes for 20 hours a week. It is cheaper to study for a longer period of time or in a group though.

One-to-one sessions cost US$15-20 whilst group classes cost US$5-10 per hour.

Of all the language schools in Cusco, the best is probably **Academia Latino-americana de Español** (🖳 www.latinosch ool.com) at Plaza Limacpampa 565, which can also arrange for you to stay with a host family. Also try: **Amauta** (🖳 www.amauta spanish.com), Suecia 480, 2nd Floor; **Amigos Spanish School** (🖳 www.spanish cusco.com), Zaguan del Cielo B-23; **Trilogia Tourist Services** (🖳 www.cusco spanishschool.com), Calle Carcilaso 265, 2nd Floor; **Excel** (🖳 www.excel-spanishlan guageprograms-peru.org), Calle Cruz Verde 336; **San Blas Spanish School** (🖳 www .spanishschoolperu.com), Carmen Bajo 224.

Embassies and consulates
Austria (☎ 227339 or 246595), Urb Magisterio K-1, Casilla 14; **Belgium** (☎ 261517), José G Cosio 307; **France** (☎ 233610), Av Micaela Bastidas 101, Diagonal, 4th Floor, Huanchac; **Germany** (☎ 235459), San Agustín 307; **Holland** (☎ 224322), Av El Sol 954; **Ireland** (☎ 243514), Av Pardo 827; **Italy** (☎ 224398), Av Garcilaso 700, Huanchac; **UK** (☎ 239974), Barry Walker, Calle Clorinda Matto de Turner 330; **USA** (☎ 231474), Av Pardo 845.

WHERE TO STAY   [see map pp160-1]
Cusco is extraordinarily well equipped for tourists and has an enormous number of places to stay that should suit all tastes and budgets. Whilst rates are proportionally more expensive than elsewhere in Peru, they still tend to represent remarkably good value for money. Quoted prices also tend to be negotiable, as they are seasonally affected and driven by demand.

The city gets busiest during July and August, particularly during the run-up to Inti Raymi (see p86), when rates rocket by as much as 20%, but outside of peak season you ought to be able to negotiate a good deal.

Plaza de Armas is understandably the focus for most people when looking for places to stay, but the hotels here tend to be those with the most inflated prices and therefore often represent the worst value for money. Step away from the plaza, though, and there are good deals aplenty, particularly in the hilly streets that lead up to Sacsayhuaman or up towards the San Blas district. Bear in mind that many of the very cheap places to stay are often in the less salubrious, less safe parts of town.

Breakfast is not always a given so it is included in the description where it is available. Many of the places below now have **wi-fi**.

Host Family Peru (☎ 741636, 🖳 www.hostfamilyperu.com) has been set up to help people looking for accommodation with local families. Peru Treks (see pp183-4) also operates an Andean homestay programme and arranges places to stay in the mountains surrounding Cusco.

Note: Abbreviations used are: **sgl/dbl/tpl** = single/double/triple room, **att** = room with attached bathroom, **com** = room with common (shared) bathroom.

Plaza de Armas area
Budget A good budget bet in a central location is the youth hostel **Albergue Municipal** (☎ 252506, 🖳 albergue@muni cusco.gob.pe), at Kiskapata 240, which is spanking clean, has a café and good views from a sunny concrete balcony. It costs s/17 per person and is a great place to stay if you're in a group. The dorms have bunk beds for four to eight people.

Also recommended is **Hostal Resbalosa** (☎ 224839, 🖳 www.hostalresba losa.com), Calle Resbalosa 494, which has a bright friendly courtyard, beautiful 180° views over the town towards Mt Ausangate, and costs just s/20/30/45 (dorm/sgl/dbl, com). The rooms with private facilities are around s/20 more. Avoid the rooms around the entrance, which are older and noisier.

Taxis can only reach within about 100m of the hostel as it is set on a steep, cobbled, pedestrian-only street.

Another good-value place is ***Hostal Rojas*** (☎ 228184, 🖳 www.hostalrojas .com), Calle Tigre 129, with a pleasant green courtyard behind enormous front doors; rates are s/60/90 (sgl/dbl, att). Try to get the top floor rooms, which have a view and are slightly quieter.

Other places worth looking at in this area include the two Hostals Suecia run by the same friendly people and popular with foreigners. ***Hostal Suecia I*** (☎ 233282, 🖳 www.hostalsuecia1.com) is at Calle Suecia 332. The plain rooms surrounding the courtyard cost s/60/90/120 (sgl/dbl/tpl, att) from January to May and s/10 more from June to December. ***Hostal Suecia II*** (🖳 www.hostalsuecia2cusco.com, ☎ 239757), at Tecescocha 465 and set in a colonial-style building with a pretty courtyard, costs s/30/40 (sgl/dbl, com) and has some rooms with attached bathroom for s/40/60 (sgl/dbl).

There's also ***Hostal Machu Picchu*** (☎ 231111), Calle Quera 282, with its two colonial courtyards, tiled floors and flower-filled courtyard, s/40/70/100 (sgl/dbl/tpl, com).

Up the hill near San Cristóbal and on a corner that catches the sun, is ***WalkOn Inn*** (☎ 235065, 🖳 www.walkoninn.com), Calle Suecia 504, with great views, a family atmosphere and smart internal décor. Dorm beds are s/25 whilst private rooms cost s/65/75 (sgl/dbl, com) or s/75/85 (sgl/dbl, att). Breakfast isn't included but is very cheap and as such great value.

The Point (☎ 252266, 🖳 www.the pointhostels.com), at Mesón de la Estrella 172, is part of a well-respected small chain that provides secure, clean, comfortable surroundings for backpackers at reasonable rates, although they tend to be raucous, party-fuelled places: Horny Llama Bar here does little to dispel this and the hostel revels in its reputation as one of the premier party places for backpackers. Dorms in the spacious colonial house cost s/22-30 depending on the number of beds; just don't expect an early or especially quiet night.

Mid-range ***Loreto Boutique Hotel*** (see map p173; ☎ 226352, 🖳 www.loretobouti quehotel.com; US$75/95/115 sgl/dbl/tpl, att), Calle Loreto 115, deserves a mention because some of the rather dark rooms have genuine Inca walls; it's also very conveniently located, right on the plaza, down an alley adjacent to La Compañía.

Much better value is ***Hostal Corihuasi*** (☎ 232233, 🖳 www.corihuasi.com), Calle Suecia 561, which charges US$45/56/68 (sgl/dbl/tpl, att, breakfast) during low season and US$12 more for each type of room during the high season. This labyrinthine, larger hotel set on the slopes north of the plaza is favoured by some adventure-tour companies and can get fully booked easily. The good-sized rustic rooms are equipped with alpaca blankets and woven textiles. Try to get the room directly above reception (No 1), which has the best view in all Cusco. The rate includes complimentary pick up from the airport.

If you fancy something a little more central there's ***Emperador Plaza Hotel*** (☎ 261733/227412, 🖳 www.emperadorplaza .com), Santa Catalina Ancha 377. It's clean, has cable TV in the rooms and costs from US$55/58/68 (sgl/dbl/tpl, att, breakfast); the balcony rooms are best.

Los Aticos (☎ 231710, 🖳 www.losati cos.com), Calle Quera 253, is a good bet for longer stays. Small and simple, it has a free self-service laundry room and kitchen facilities. Complimentary Peruvian cookery classes are also taught here; you simply pay for the ingredients. The rooms cost US$50/50 (sgl/dbl, att) although you can get a 10% discount by booking online.

Another good option is ***Del Prado Inn*** (☎ 224442, 🖳 www.delpradoinn.com), Calle Suecia 310, a smart hotel charging US$75-85/110-130/135 (sgl/dbl/tpl, att) depending on whether the room has a balcony or not (the balcony rooms can be noisy though). You can save 15% by booking online. Towards the top end of this price bracket but it's worth the money if you're looking for an efficient, friendly place to stay in a superb central location. The dining room boasts original Inca walls.

Expensive *Hotel Ruinas* (☎ 260644, ☐ www.hotelruinas.com), Calle Ruinas 472, is a well-sited place popular with business travellers and tour groups that has little real character although the rooms are spacious and well presented. Those with outside views are the best. It is well run but is a little overpriced at US$100/125/155 (sgl/dbl/tpl, att, breakfast).

Hotel Picoaga (Lima ☎ 711 2020, ☐ www.picoagahotel.com), Santa Teresa 344, was once the colonial home of the Marques de Picoaga and is now a much better bet as somewhere to stay. The large contemporary and colonial double rooms around the attractive, shady courtyard of this fine building cost upwards of US$135/145, whilst suites start at US$300.

Sonesta Posada del Inca Cusco (☎ 227061, ☐ www.sonesta.com/CuscoPosadas), at Portal Espinar 108, is a very accommodating, hospitable place to stay with rooms on the upper floors looking out on to the plaza and its own restaurant. Advertised rack rates start at US$250/265/290 (sgl/dbl/tpl, att) but substantial discounts are possible throughout the quieter part of the year and if you book well in advance.

San Blas area
Budget *Hospedaje Familiar Kuntur Wasi* (☎ 227570), Tandapata 352A, is run by a very considerate, friendly local family. Regular hot water, access to a decent kitchen and the great atmosphere make this a good choice; it will only set you back s/25/40 (sgl/dbl, com) or s/40/80 (sgl/dbl, att).

The recommended, rickety *Hospedaje Sambleño* (☎ 262979, ☐ www.barnmed .com/hostalsambleno/), Carmen Alto 114, which is built around a maze of staircases, has cable TV in the lobby and is a bargain at US$7/14/18 (sgl/dbl/tpl) for a room with attached lavatory.

Mid-range There are numerous options in this bracket in this area.

Amaru Hostal (☎ 225933, ☐ www .amaruhostal.com), Cuesta de San Blas 541, is an old house with a sociable green courtyard filled with geraniums in rusty cans. Some of the rooms off the courtyard boast original Inca walls. It also has a free book exchange, piano and oxygen. They charge US$27/33 (sgl/dbl, com), US$40/55/75 (sgl/dbl/tpl, att).

If you're after a pleasant little bed and breakfast joint try *Casona los Pleiades* (☎ 506430, ☐ www.casona-pleiades.com), Calle Tandapata 116; it has compact, tidy rooms in a renovated colonial house overlooking the city and costing US$60/75 (sgl/dbl, att, breakfast). The staff here are helpful, friendly and keen to offer advice.

At Calle Tandapata 660, *Amazonas Hostal* (☎ 236770, ☐ www.amazonhotel cusco.com) is a bright, friendly place run by Amazon Trails Peru (a trekking and tour agency, see p180). It offers reasonable rooms for US$35/50/60 (sgl/dbl/tpl, com, breakfast) and has a garden and terrace with panoramic views where you can unwind after your trek.

Hostal El Grial (☎ 223012, ☐ www .hotelelgrial.com), Carmen Alto 112, is attached to a neighbouring Spanish school with whom they can arrange lessons at discounted rates. The rooms are modern and well-kept, as is the cosy lounge. Rates are US$30/50/60 (sgl/dbl/tpl, att, breakfast).

Marani (☎ 249462, ☐ www.hostalma rani.com), Carmen Alto 194, is full of character and run by a knowledgeable couple who are heavily involved in the local community: in the decade or so they've been in business they've built schools in the surrounding rural areas, trained teachers and helped out at Cusco hospital. The rooms vary in size and shape but are generally large and high ceilinged; all provide a haven from the hustle and bustle outside. They cost US$33/52/72 (sgl/dbl/tpl, att, breakfast).

Hostal Pensión Alemana (☎ 226861, ☐ www.cuzco.com.pe), Calle Tandapata 260, is a Swiss-German hostel whose clean, European décor looks as if it would be more at home in the Alps. Popular with European travellers, it is a comfortable, attractive place to stay and at US$55/66/83 (sgl/dbl/tpl, att) during the low season and around US$9 more during the high season it won't break the bank either.

Cheaper but less atmospheric is *Orquidea Real Hostal* (☎ 221662, 🖳 www .orquidea.net), Alabado 520, which is owned and run by a package tour company, but has pleasant rustic rooms with modern amenities that enjoy views across the city. Rates start at US$41/55/69 (sgl/dbl/tpl, att, breakfast).

Hostal Rumi Punku (☎ 221102, 🖳 www.rumipunku.com), Choquechaca 339, is instantly identifiable because of the giant Inca stonework around the main door. This stylish colonial house has good-quality but pricey rooms costing US$80-120/100-130/130-170 (sgl/dbl/tpl, att, breakfast) depending on the season. Suites cost US$200. There is also a rooftop terrace as well as attractive gardens and the staff are particularly helpful.

For those who want to get away from it all, *Casa de Campo Hostal* (☎ 244404, 🖳 www.hotelcasadecampo.com), at the very northern end of Calle Tandapata (No 298) in San Blas, is just delightful. Built on a slope overlooking the town, the rooms and terrace are simply gorgeous, the location so peaceful, and they'll even throw in an airport pickup if you book in advance. The rooms start at US$45/55/80 (sgl/ dbl/junior suite), though bargaining is distinctly possible.

Expensive *Hotel Arqueologo* (☎ 232522, 🖳 www.hotelarqueologo.com), Calle Pumacurco 408, is named after the Inca stonework in the street leading to the entrance. A favourite with the French, it's pleasant enough and the inner courtyard and fireplace lounge are great places to hang out but at US$97/120/160 (sgl/dbl/tpl, com, breakfast) you can do better for your money.

Similarly priced but better value is *Boutique Hotel Casa San Blas* (☎ 237900, 🖳 www.casasanblas.com), Tocuyeros 566; it was Cusco's first boutique hotel. Set in an 18th-century colonial mansion and centred round a courtyard are some spacious but simple rooms costing US$120/120/190-240 (sgl/dbl/suite, att, breakfast). Service here is polished and personalized.

Also worth a look is *Los Apus Hotel y Mirador* (☎ 264243, 🖳 www.losapushotel .com), at Atocsaycuchi 515, an atmospheric, airy Swiss-run establishment full of distinctive features, varnished wood and classy furnishings. The best views are from the breakfast lookout on the top floor. All this comes at a price: rooms are expensive at US$114/140 (sgl/dbl, att).

Many of Cusco's finest hotels can be found in this area. *Novotel Cusco* (☎ 581033, 🖳 www.novotel.com), Calle San Agustín 239, has evolved from the earthquake-damaged ruins of the home of the conquistador Miguel Sanchez Ponce and now includes elegant stone archways, a glass-roofed courtyard and a central fountain. The rate (US$200-240; sgl/dbl, att) depends on whether the room is in the contemporary or more characterful older, colonial wing.

Once the stand-out hotel in Cusco *Hotel Monasterio* (☎ 604000, 🖳 www .monasteriohotel.com), Calle Palacio 136, Plazoleta Nazarenas, remains incredibly impressive but is no longer alone in this category. The hotel is a sensitive conversion of the old Seminary of San Antonio Abad (see p159) that retains a sense of its roots and original purpose. Along with everything you'd expect from an international five-star hotel it also has a gilded baroque chapel, peaceful courtyards, elegant cloisters, a Michelin-starred chef and oxygen-enriched air in the rooms (additional US$40). Being one of Cusco's finest hotels it is not cheap – US$385-515 (dbl, att, breakfast, suites US$565-2140) – but you may be able to negotiate a better rate. Spa packages are also available.

Competition comes in the form of *Palacio Nazarenas* (☎ 458222, 🖳 www.pal acionazarenas.com), which stands next door at Plaza Nazarenas 144. History is superimposed on history in this luxurious hotel inside a converted colonial building (see p159). The original courtyard and many features remain, including a beautiful set of frescos from the 18th century. Amidst the labyrinthine interior is a secret garden, spa, swimming pool and several herb gardens plus an 18th-century library complete with original books. World-class chef Virgilio Martinez runs the kitchen. The Palacio and

Nazarenas Suites are the finest, with stunning architectural elements, all mod-cons and good views. Prices start at around US$600 and climb to around US$1500.

A little more affordable is the achingly hip *Casa Cartagena* (☎ 224356, 🖥 www.casacartagena.com), at Pumacuco 336, on the street leading away from Plazoleta Nazarenas. Another sympathetically restored colonial mansion, it has original frescos and balconies but also Italian design touches with pieces of sculpture that stand 4-6ft high, a pool, spa and flagship royal suite that includes a giant imported Italian marble Jacuzzi. Suites range from US$520 to US$2100. Additional oxygen is s/150.

If it's cool you're after, try *Fallen Angel* (☎ 258184, 🖥 www.fallenangelincusco.com) in the corner of Plazoleta Nazarenas (No 221). Best known as a bar (see Bars and nightlife), the venue is also a guesthouse with four uniquely designed rooms, costing US$350-400, which have an eclectic, contemporary style and masses of character.

Plaza Regocijo area
Budget To the west of the main plaza there are fewer options, but still some gems to be found. *Loki Backpackers Hostel* (☎ 243705, 🖥 www.lokihostel.com/en/cusco), Cuesta Santa Ana 601, is a historic viceroy's residence transformed into a funky backpacker's haven, with mixed or single-sex dorms, a shared kitchen, free internet access, a bar sporting superb views over the city and a lively atmosphere. Dorms cost US$21-34 and rooms US$75-85 (twin or dbl, att).

Mid-range At Saphi 440, *Hostal San Isidro Labrador* (☎ 226241, 🖥 Labrador @qnet.com.pe) is an elegant, unpretentious place in a decent location. Simply furnished, it has colonial arches, two patios and comfy rooms at US$35/45/55 (sgl/dbl/tpl, att).

One of the most impressive hotels in this category is *El Balcón Inn* (☎ 236738, 🖥 www.balconcusco.com), Tambo de Montero 222, housed in a restored pre-colonial house dating back to 1630. All 16 rooms are en suite, many with magnificent views of the city, and the staff are incredibly

friendly. It's a bit of a climb to get here, but it's worth every step: room rates are US$60/80/95 (sgl/dbl/tpl, breakfast) and suites are US$125-145.

Expensive *Hotel Royal Inka I* (central reservations ☎ 263276, hotel ☎ 302763, 🖥 www.royalinkahotel.pe), Plaza Regocijo 299, is built on the foundations of Pachacutec's palace and has front rooms with colonial furnishings overlooking the plaza as well as a bar and restaurant. Rates (US$68-72/90-95/100-110 sgl/dbl/tpl, att, breakfast) depend on the season. It's slightly better than its similarly priced sister, *Hotel Royal Inka II* (same contact details), which is just up the road at Santa Teresa 335 and has a sauna and Jacuzzi.

Casa Andina (🖥 www.casa-andina.com) is part of an upmarket Peruvian chain. There are five hotels in Cusco: *Classic Cusco Catedral* (☎ 233661) at Santa Catalina Angosta 149, close to the Cathedral; *Classic Cusco Plaza* (☎ 231733), Portal Espinar 142, between Plaza de Armas and Plaza Regocijo; *Classic Cusco Koricancha* (☎ 252633), San Agustín 371, near to the Coricancha; and *Classic Cusco San Blas* (☎ 263694), Chihuampata 278, in San Blas. The flagship branch, *Private Collection Cusco* (☎ 232610), Plazoleta Limacpampa Chico 473, is in a smart colonial mansion with four courtyards, a gourmet restaurant and a pisco bar.

Service is exemplary at all Casa Andina's hotels and rates (including breakfast) for the modern, well-equipped rooms start from US$78 and rise to over US$400 for those in the Private Collection. However, discounts are often available.

Elsewhere
Budget There are also some good options dotted elsewhere in the city, particularly south of the plaza.

Estrellita (☎ 234134), Av Tullumayo 445, is a basic option with a compact communal area, simple kitchen and rather rudimentary rooms, but it is clean, handily positioned and excellent value at US$6/11 (dbl, com/dbl, att).

Hostal Familiar (☎ 239353, 🖳 hostal familiar@hotmail.com), Saphi 661, is a well-established rickety old guesthouse away from the centre whose well-tended courtyard, rudimentary rooms and family atmosphere are perennially popular. Rates, which start at US$15 (com), are flexible when the place is quiet.

Maison de la Jeunesse (☎ 235617, 🖳 hostellingcusco@hotmail.com) is down a small side street, 5 Pasaje Grace, off Av El Sol, opposite the Coricancha. Affiliated to Hostelling International (🖳 www.hihostels .com), this is a good-quality hostel with kitchen facilities, communal rooms and a balcony. Dorms cost US$11 whilst rooms start from US$20/35 (sgl/dbl, com).

Mid-range If you're looking for somewhere south of the plaza consider tranquil *Albergue Casa Campesina* (☎ 233466), Av Tullumayo 274. It is a pleasant hostel with rooms costing US$36/49 (sgl/ dbl, com). The money generated here goes to support the Casa Campesina organization that in turn works to promote and help local *campesina* communities. The **Store of the Weavers** (see p179) is on the same site.

Hostal Pascana (☎ 225771, 🖳 www .hostalpascana.com) is hidden away on a side street, Ahuacpinta (No 539), behind the Coricancha. Well-run and reasonably priced (US$35/45/55 sgl/dbl/tpl, att); it is a well-kept secret in this part of town.

Down near Huanchac Station, *La Posada del Abuelo* (☎ 221332, 🖳 www.la posadadelabuelocusco.com), Av Pardo 975, is a good bed and breakfast bet. The rooms are cosy and comfortable and cost US$45/55/65 (sgl/dbl/tpl, att).

North of the plaza two places worth looking at are run by **Niños Unidos Peruanos Foundation** (🖳 www.ninosho tel.com), which was established by a Dutch couple to support neglected and underprivileged street kids; the couple have adopted a dozen street children themselves. The hotels are: *Hotel Meloc* (☎ 231424), Calle Meloc 442, a 17th-century colonial house which has been converted into a stylish, spotless place to stay, with gorgeous rooms set around a pretty courtyard. Service is

fabulous and the breakfast is sumptuous though it costs extra. The rooms cost s/60/ 120 (sgl/dbl, com) or s/132/192/240 (dbl/ tpl/tpl, att). *Hotel Fierro* (☎ 254611), a little further from the centre on Calle Fierro (No 476), follows a similar design. The proceeds from both are used to fund the charity.

Expensive *Hotel Libertador Palacio del Inka* (☎ 231961, 🖳 www.libertador.com .pe), Plazoleta Santo Domingo 259, is an enormous converted colonial building, once a palace called Casa de Los Cuatro Bustos. Not quite as luxurious as the Monasterio or the other top-end hotels, this award-winning place nonetheless offers the full five-star package, an excellent restaurant and is a little more welcoming to dirty trekkers. It costs upward of US$235 (dbl, att, breakfast) and suites start at US$300.

WHERE TO EAT
There's almost too much choice in Cusco when it comes to picking a place to eat. From cheap steaming *anticucho* barrows on the street to five-star, white-linen restaurants where you have to book in advance there's something for everyone and every budget. If you're just after a drink and a snack wander along Calle Procuradores or Calle Plateros and you'll inevitably stumble on somewhere that takes your fancy. San Blas also has an up-and-coming scene with various cafés and good-quality restaurants now open here. Many of the Bars and clubs (see Bars and nightlife) also offer food.

For more details of some of the restaurants mentioned here see 🖳 www.cusco restaurants.com.

If you're after very cheap meals there are plenty of fixed menu places offering three courses for s/5 on Pampa del Castillo near the Coricancha and south of Plaza de Armas. Alternatively, **Mercado San Pedro** (see map p161) is a good bet, offering the finest, freshest juices squeezed in front of you, soups and main dishes in the heart of a traditional, boisterous setting. Beware though, your stomach should be attuned to local food before you go and some of the sights and smells in the market might just put you off your meal.

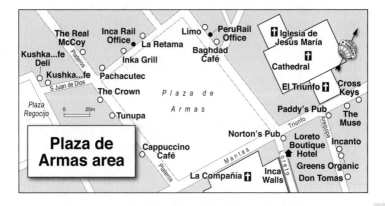

Plaza de Armas area [see map above]
There are plenty of places immediately around the plaza where you can hang out and snack throughout the day. *Cappuccino Café*, Portal de Comercio 141, has three small balconies directly opposite the Cathedral that overlook Plaza de Armas. It has a relaxed atmosphere, board games, good breakfasts and 30 different types of coffee. Larger meals are also available. There is also internet access here.

The Real McCoy at Plateros 326, 2nd Floor, is a stylish yet relaxed place to spend time. They also serve fabulous big breakfasts, toast and Marmite, cauliflower cheese, Branston pickle and puddings with custard as well as staples such as sandwiches and salads. They also do a great roast with sage and onion stuffing and gravy, ideal for Brits missing the taste of home.

Kushka…fe (🖥 www.kushkafe.pe), Espaderos 142, is a relaxed literary-style café where you can feel completely at ease as you enjoy a selection of pastries and a coffee, or come for the generous sandwiches, which include traditional *butifarra* (pork and sweet onion salsa sandwich), and smoked ham and chicharron with sweet potato. Just around the corner on Plaza Rejocijo is a *Kushka…fe branded deli*, where you can buy regional Peruvian specialties. There's a second branch of both the café and the deli at Choquechaca 131-A (see map pp160-1).

For traditional Peruvian fare or contemporary *Novoandina* dishes try *Inka Grill* (🖥 www.cuscorestaurants.com) at Portal de Panes 115 on Plaza de Armas; it is a decent place in which to treat yourself. They try to give Peruvian dishes a contemporary twist, so you could have Novoandina dishes such as *pollo relleno prosciutto* (chicken stuffed with prosciutto ham), or a good *aji de gallina* (spicy, creamy chicken stew). There's also homemade pasta and a wide vegetarian selection.

Also on the plaza, on Portal de Carnes, to the left of the cathedral as you look at it, are several first-floor restaurants; *Limo* (🖥 www.cuscorestaurants.com; at No 236) is a Peruvian cookery and pisco bar that rustles up high standard ceviches and causas as well as sushi rolls and a range of tempting seafood mains. As the name suggests there's also a large number of pisco-based drinks to try.

Baghdad Café has a good balcony view over the plaza from which to enjoy *adobo de chanco* (pork stew), trout ceviche or baked cuy. It's also worth trying their alpaca steaks, which come with fennel, rosemary or thyme sauce.

On Portal de Belen, which runs away from the south-east corner of the plaza, look for *Greens Organic* (🖥 www.cuscorestaurants.com), an atmospheric 1st floor restaurant at Santa Catalina Angosta 135, with an innovative chef and changing menu. Dishes

CUSCO

are always fresh, organically grown and carefully sourced; look out for trout and mango ceviche, wholewheat pastas, campesino sandwiches and, in the evenings, grilled trout or alpaca. Desserts include mango ravioli and a rich pecan cheesecake. On the ground floor is *Incanto* (💻 www.cus corestaurants.com), a fine Italian-style restaurant known for its pastas. Nearby, *Don Tomas* offers Peruvian staples such as aji de gallina, anticuchos, chicharron and *lechon con tamales* (baked piglet with corn patties).

La Retama, Portal de Panes 123, is a popular place serving Novoandina fusion food. It's often booked up by people who come to enjoy the balcony and lively music and dance performances.

On the same stretch is *Pachacutec*, Portal de Panes 105, that serves typical Peruvian fare along with international staples and good Italian dishes to packed tables filled with travellers waiting to catch the nightly folk shows.

Equally busy is elegant *Tunupa*, Portal Confitura 233; its narrow glassed-in balcony provides panoramic views of the plaza and it serves first-rate international and traditional food from a menu or buffet. Popular with tour groups, the cavernous interior often reverberates to the sound of live music.

Cusco and around [see map pp160-1]
La Tertulia, at Procuradores 44, is justifiably popular thanks to the classical music that accompanies every breakfast, the efficient service and the superior quality of its scrambled eggs. A vegetarian buffet and set menu are available during the day.

Although there are plenty of pretenders, the queen of pizzerias remains *Chez Maggy* (💻 www.pizzeriaschezmaggy .com). With no fewer than three establishments on Procuradores (at Nos 344, 365 and 374), another on Plateros (No 348), and a further outpost in Aguas Calientes, Maggy's has come to dominate the city's pizza industry, producing wood-fired pizzas for every taste. They also run a delivery service (☎ 246316).

Victor Victoria, at Tecsecocha 466, is another perennially popular place offering good-sized portions of cheap vegetarian and Israeli-influenced food as well as some Peruvian staples.

Kin Taro, at Heladeros 149, serves delicious sushi, using Peruvian trout, and other Japanese staples such as miso soup and sake.

If you're after one of Cusco's most famous dishes and want to try guinea pig (*cuy*), consider *Sumaq Misky*, Plateros 334 (2nd floor); the entrance is concealed up an alley of souvenir stalls. Once you've found your way in and upstairs, there is a small bar and a large dining room with an open kitchen serving traditional Peruvian fare (alpaca steaks, aji de gallina, *lomo saltado*) and more adventurous dishes. They specialize in guinea pig though. They also hold weekly Sapo tournaments (see box below). *Kusikuy*, Suecia 339, is reputed to be one of the best places to try cuy, although it also offers other traditional

---

❑ **Sapo**

This game of skill involves throwing a disc into a series of holes in the top of a box, worth different amounts of points, with a series of obstacles designed to make these targets more challenging. The most valuable hole is guarded by an ornate metal frog and to score the highest points you must throw the disc into the frog's mouth, at which point the player typically yells 'Sapo!'.

The game, similar in many ways to the British Pitch Penny, evolved from a game where the Incas would toss a gold coin into a lake in the hope that a frog, which was considered powerful, would take the piece in its mouth. If the frog (El Sapu) took the piece, the player was instantly granted a wish and the frog turned into solid gold. In reality the frog is rarely gold and the wishes made rarely come true, but it is still an exciting, entertaining way to pass the time over a couple of Pisco Sours.

Peruvian dishes on its short menu. The set lunch is remarkably good value too.

El Truco, Plaza Regocijo 261, is stylish and has good service although it is popular with tour groups who come for the generous buffet lunches and nightly folk music shows, so can be very busy. *Chicha*, on the 2nd floor here, is renowned chef Gastón Acurio's first Cusco restaurant and features his take on regional highland cooking. The results are full of bold flavours, although his Lima staples, such as ceviche, are also available. The bar here also makes a mean pisco sour.

For somewhere truly unique, head to *Fallen Angel* (see Where to stay), in the corner of Plazoleta de las Nazarenas. Run by the same individual who owns Macondo (see p176), it uses aquariumesque Perspex-topped baths full of fish and coral as tables and is crammed full of glitter and kitsch. The food is sumptuous though, especially the steaks, and the cocktails are devilishly good. Another of Cusco's best restaurants is found next door. *MAP Café* (🖥 www.cusco restaurants.com) in **Casa Cabrera**, home to the Museum of Pre-Columbian Art, Plazoleta de las Nazarenas 231, is run by the same people as are in charge of several of Cusco's good-quality restaurants. Set in a beautifully sited restaurant in the courtyard of a restored colonial house, it serves a creative menu of excellent Peruvian cuisine including trout with ginger potatoes, Andean pesto-stuffed chicken and guinea pig confit with peanut-tossed potatoes. An excellent range of European and New World wines is available to wash your meal down with. Quality comes at a price though and it isn't cheap (main course s/27-60, wine s/66-120, cocktails s/10-25). There's live music most evenings to accompany supper.

Hotel Monasterio (see Where to stay) pioneered fine dining in Cusco. With food this exquisite being served in suitably sumptuous surroundings – the dining room is where monks once sang – you could be in any one of the finer restaurants in Europe, an illusion that the bill will do nothing to dispel.

San Blas area On the road up to San Blas the superb *El Buen Pastor*, at 579 Cuesta San Blas, has everything you could ask for from a bakery: great, great bread, fantastic *empanadas*, drool-inducing gateaux and low prices. What's more, this place is a charitable concern, helping to finance a home for girls from disadvantaged backgrounds.

Equally good first thing in the morning is *Cicciolina*, Calle Triunfo 393. Set off the main street adjacent to a courtyard this two-storey building caters to different tastes: on the ground floor is a bakery doling out generous breakfasts and fresh, tasty pastries whilst upstairs is a highly-rated sophisticated tapas bar and Spanish-themed restaurant that cleverly fuses Andean and Mediterranean food and styles of cooking with an impressive range of wines available. As befits a bakery, the desserts are also excellent.

Around the corner at Palacio 135 is *Uchu Peruvian Steakhouse*, which serves delicious meat a myriad of ways in a fine dining surrounding. A mixed meat plate gives you a bit of beef, lamb and alpaca, although the stone-cooked alpaca with a selection of sauces and chili peanut mash is the standout. If you want something other than steak, there are also prawn kebabs and fish although vegetarians will have to console themselves with the extensive wine list. Further up Palacio is *Marcelo Batata* (see Bars and nightlife), which is run by the same people and has a range of contemporary Peruvian dishes and a fine panoramic view from the roof terrace across the terracotta tiles of the city. It's only open 2-11pm though.

La Bodega 138, Herrajes 138, is another laid-back and friendly place that cooks good Italian food with great pizza. *Jack's*, on the corner of Choquechaca and Cuesta San Blas, is also a good bet for decent coffee, fresh juices and large internationally themed comfort food such as pancake stacks, burgers and enormous breakfasts in a smart venue with friendly staff; popular with backpackers, there's often a long queue.

CUSCO

Overlooking Plazoleta de San Blas, *The Muse Too*, Tandapata 917, is the sister property of the bar on Triunfo (see Bars); it's a bohemian café that serves coffee and snacks as well as main meals and some superb cocktails. They have a range of vegetarian and vegan dishes and also have daily films, games and live music.

Café Cultural Ritual, on Choquechaca 140, offer a tasty, largely vegetarian, menu of Andean specialities such as fried yucca and quinoa pancakes, although there are some meat dishes too.

La Quinta Eulalia, at Choquechaca 384, is another decent local option at the budget end of the scale. Only open for lunch, its small terrace is an ideal place to enjoy local fare, traditional music and traditionally brewed chichi.

Moni, San Agustín 311, is a familiar, atmospheric vegetarian place recommended for its innovative takes on Peruvian staples as well as for the chilled ambience in the café-bar and the puddings on offer.

Swiss-run *Granja Heidi*, at Cuesta San Blas 525, serves half-litre jugs of authentic, piping-hot chocolate for just s/2.5. During the day they offer freshly sourced and prepared food, yoghurt and delicious crêpes. The contemporary Peruvian dishes, such as *seco de cordero* (lamb in coriander sauce), *carapulcra con pollo* (sun-dried potatoes in a mild chilli sauce) and vegetarian options like *loqro* (mashed pumpkin with fava beans, cheese, potato and rice) and *rocoto relleno* (chillies stuffed with vegetables), on offer in the evenings are also well worth trying.

For more unusual dishes try *Macondo*, at Cuesta San Blas 571, which is one of the coolest and campest restaurants in Cusco, and run by one of its most flamboyant citizens. The walls are decorated with regularly changing art exhibitions, sofas are made out of bedsteads and cushions litter the surfaces. The food is contemporary Andean and Amazonian, based on local recipes that are given a twist. Desserts are first-rate and the cocktails dangerously good.

Classic Peruvian food can be found at *Pachapapa* (🖳 www.cuscorestaurants .com), Plaza San Blas 120. Dishes range

from commonplace roast *cuy* (guinea pig) to the more exotic alpaca steaks; a very pleasant evening can be had munching on the native wildlife. The outdoor seating around an open fire pit is a bonus too and there's often live harp music playing.

Elsewhere
For those in search of an authentic dining experience, the finest *cevichería* in Cusco is reputed to be *Las Machitas*, at Av Peru F-9 Urb Progresso; it is a dirt street and is some way from the centre of town. However, the huge portions of ceviche are reasonably priced and very tempting; their other Peruvian specialities are also recommended.

BARS AND NIGHTLIFE
Other than Lima, no Peruvian city can match Cusco for places to drink and dance. The city has a huge range of venues, to suit all tastes; you just need to listen out for the latest thing. The plaza is a hive of activity from early to late, whilst those in the know head to less obvious parts of the city to find the latest hip hangout.

Bars
Plaza de Armas area [see map p173]
The famous Cross Keys' (see below) place on the plaza has been taken over by *The Crown*, which shares the same location but none of the atmosphere of the original.

Norton's Pub, which previously reveled in the name Norton's Rat Tavern, also overlooks the plaza; the entrance is on Santa Catalina Angosta 116. It's almost a North American biker bar and has TVs, darts and pool tables as well as a balcony from which to watch the world go by. The food is simple but filling and wholesome.

Paddy's Pub (formerly Paddy Flaherty's), at Triunfo 124, is a compact Irish bar complete with Guinness, that's usually absolutely heaving with travellers, although largely devoid of locals. There are TVs, games and a generous happy hour.

Cross Keys, a long-term Plaza de Armas institution, has been relegated to the 1st floor of 350 Triunfo by pressure on rents and properties on the main square. What was probably the most-established pub in town has simply relocated exactly as it was, right down to the dart board and football memorabilia that compete for space on the walls with photographs, maps and other oddities. Local beers such as Cusqueña are on offer alongside home UK favourites including Speckled Hen, IPA and Boddingtons. There's also a short but tasty food menu.

Also on Triunfo at 338 (1st floor) is *The Muse* (see Where to eat), a large café-lounge-restaurant with a hip atmosphere and regular live music acts.

Cusco and around [see map pp160-1]

Los Perros, on Tecsecocha 238, is a very comfortable place to kick back and while away an afternoon or evening. One of Cusco's favourite watering holes, it is renowned for its magnificent salads, wontons to die for, curries, stir fries and puddings such as sticky fig cake. There's also a book exchange, board games and stacks of out-of-date magazines to keep you entertained.

South of Plaza de Armas, *Rosie O'Grady's*, at Santa Catalina Ancha 360, is a vast Irish bar that's a lot less crammed than Paddy's Pub. Open late, it has some pretty tasty food and a decent happy hour.

Marcelo Batata (see Where to eat), on the 3rd floor of Palacio 121, is a funky hangout with a great roof terrace that has unprecedented views across the roof of the Cathedral and surrounding buildings. To go with the views are great pisco mixes including infused ginger, purple corn and eucalyptus, shots of flavoured pisco and a range of classic cocktails. There are also tempting snacks and well-made mains complete with food and wine pairing suggestions.

A very small haunt set above the city on a hillside close to San Blas, *7 Angelitos*, Siete Angelitos 638, attracts a young, cool crowd looking for live music, DJ sets, quality mojitos and a funky atmosphere when it all kicks off.

Km0, Tandapata 100, just off Plaza San Blas, is a Mediterranean-themed bar. An expat favourite, it's a convivial place to spend time, snack on tapas and listen to live jazz or Latin bands.

Cult favourite *Fallen Angel* (see Where to stay & Where to eat), on Plazoleta Nazarenas, is popular with a hip crowd of discerning locals and adventurous visitors. It occasionally hosts outrageous parties but consistently serves decidedly devilish cocktails, as does its sister bar, *Macondo* (see p176), at Cuesta San Blas 571.

Clubs

You will have no trouble finding a club in Cusco; the difficult part is trying to avoid them. Touts used to swarm around Plaza de Armas handing out flyers and free drink tokens, but even now it's possible to spend an entire evening touring the clubs without once paying for your drink; beware though, the rum is cheap and the Cuba Libres handed out are often potent. The clubs themselves tend to be located on the corners of the plaza. Although clubs come and go and the names change, the venues and addresses usually remain the same.

The longest-running venue is *Mama Africa*, Portal Harinas 191 (2nd Floor), which plays something for everyone and is usually packed, particularly for its happy hour (8.30-11pm).

On the opposite side of the plaza above Gatos market on Portal Belén is *Uptown*, which caters to a similar crowd, but which although slightly larger is generally hot and smoky, owing to the lack of windows or ventilation.

Extreme, Portal de Carnes 298, is a long-standing Cusco mainstay that's similarly busy and plays contemporary dance music as well as techno and R'n'B (Rhythm and Blues). It also has a big screen for films and sport and a couple of bars that seem to give out an awful lot of free drinks.

Kamikase, Plaza Regocijo 274, lies in a cavernous basement and plays rock music as well as hosting daily live acts. It has a happy hour (8-10pm) and is frequented by locals as much as tourists.

Mythology, Portal de Carnes 298, plays '80s and '90s tunes.

Ukuku's, at Plateros 316, plays the widest selection of music, including reggae, rock, techno, salsa, samba, blues, jazz and Huayno and is consistently popular. It also has live acts every evening and a happy hour (8-10.30pm).

Other entertainment

Peliclub, at Tecsecocha 458, is a small independent **cinema** that shows some classic old movies (s/5, s/2 students). Just down the road is Indigo, a lounge bar that's part of Hotel Royal Qosqo (Tecsecocha 2), which shows three films a day (entrance free but you have to buy food or drinks), and many of the pubs and nightclubs (Mama Africa's, Ukuku's, Extreme) also show movies in the afternoon.

There's a regular, nightly folk music and dance show at **Centro Qosqo de Arte Nativo** (Av El Sol 604), which was founded by a group of artists in 1924. Entrance to the energetic, authentic shows, which run from 7 to 8.30pm, is free with a Visitor's Ticket (see box p153).

Nightly dance shows are held at the **Teatro Municipal**, on Calle Mesón de la Estrella 149; it occasionally hosts plays and dance classes too. **Teatro Kusikay**, on Unión 117, hosts a spectacular traditional dance show (Mon-Sat 7.30pm), which draws its inspiration from local festivals and costumes. **Teatro Inti Raymi**, at Saphi 605, has one of the best live music shows, every evening from 6.45pm.

If you fancy doing something a little more active, some of the clubs (see p177) have **salsa lessons** starting at 9pm, followed by **samba lessons** at 10pm. Salsa Perú (☎ 255745) offers group and one-to-one salsa, merengue and cha-cha classes for people of all abilities.

Finally, if you're just back from your trek there's no better way to pamper yourself than to visit Siluet at Calle Quera 253, down an alley by the Chinese restaurant, a **health spa** with a sauna, Jacuzzi and masseur/se. It's open every day 10am-10pm.

Therapeutic **massage** is also available at a number of outlets. Avoid the ones touting for business around the plaza; ask your hotel for a recommendation or try Nueva Vida at Produradores 341, Samana Spa on Calle Tecsecocha 536, or a place associated with a hotel or hostel.

SHOPPING

Cusco has some of the finest craft markets and authentic souvenirs anywhere in Peru. Sadly in a bid to clean up Cusco, the authorities have moved on the artisans so often seen in the streets and plazas and relocated them to the giant **Centro Artesanal** at the end of Av El Sol. Not many tourists actually trek all the way down here, which is very bad for the local craftsmen but very good for those who do make the trip as they can expect a bargain if prepared to haggle. There are, however, a handful of much smaller **markets** dotted about and a number of weekend fairs.

San Blas is Cusco's traditional artisan district and several workshops here are worth visiting. **Taller Olave**, Plaza San Blas 651, **Taller Merida**, Carmen Alto 133, and **Taller Mendivil** on the plaza have striking treasures, sculptures, colonial religious images and icons, ceramics and earthenware.

In addition there are the many souvenir shops that line the main streets and tend to feature similar produce, at similar prices.

General souvenirs

There are loads of places to choose from around Plaza de Armas. One of the better, more-discerning places is **Jatum Maqui**, just up from the plaza at Tecsecocha 432, which keeps prices down without compromising the quality of the goods.

La Mamita, at Portal de Carnes 244, has a very good collection of pottery, but also sells jewellery, wickerwork, baskets and textiles.

Jewellery

Ilaria, Portal Carrizos 258, is part of a nationwide chain of high-quality jewellers. There are also branches in El Monasterio, the Libertador and at the airport.

Aldo is another chain with outlets in Hotel Libertador, Plaza de Armas, and at the airport selling Incan and contemporary designs in addition to watches and porcelain.

For more unusual, unique designs in gold, silver or using semi-precious stones check out **Calas**, at Siete Angelitos 619-B, **Mullu**, at Triunfo 120, and **Spondylus** at

Cuesta San Blas 505. Some of the best stuff can be found at **Inka Treasure** at Triunfo 375 and on Plazoleta Nazarenas.

Alpaca and llama woollens
Kuna (🖳 www.kuna.com.pe), with branches in Plaza Regocijo 202, Monasterio Hotel, Libertador Hotel and the Museo de Arte Pre Colombino, has good-quality alpaca coats, scarves and other knitwear but note that there's a cheaper branch of the same shop in the departure lounge of the airport. **Alpacas Best**, Portal Confitura 221 and Plaza Nazarenas 197-199, have a selection of handmade sweaters, jackets, coats and accessories.

The **Center for Traditional Textiles of Cusco** (🖳 www.textilescusco.org), Av El Sol 603A, is a non-profit organization set up to aid the survival of Incan textile traditions and to provide support to those communities with a history of weaving. By researching and documenting complex styles and techniques the Center helps to ensure that 2000-year-old textile traditions will not be lost. Examples of the fine work are available for sale in the Center but bear in mind that work of this quality does not come cheap. They can also arrange tours to workshops in Chinchero and elsewhere in the Sacred Valley.

The **Store of the Weavers** (🖳 www.cbc.org.pe), at Av Tullumayo 274, is a local co-operative run by a handful of communities promoting traditional techniques. The superb textiles produced are expensive as you are paying for exquisite craftsmanship; all the money raised goes to the actual artisans, many of whom can be seen working on site.

T-shirts and clothing
For something a bit different from the common-or-garden Peruvian football shirt, the ubiquitous Cusqueña and Inca Kola shirts (*'La Bebida del Peru!'*) or the less appealing 'I love Cusco' numbers, look out for the unique designs in **Andean Expressions** at Choquechaca 210.

For more upmarket attire, visit **Werner and Ana**, Plaza San Francisco 295A, a top-end showroom offering innovative and unusual alpaca clothing from the chic Dutch-Peruvian duo.

Handmade leather shoes and boots are available from **Away** at Procuadores 361.

Ponchos and textiles
The shop at Portal Comercio 173, on Plaza de Armas, has the widest range of antique and new ponchos in Central Cusco. A little expensive but it's worth coming here to see some of the fabulous old blankets, *mantas* (shawls) and ponchos they have in the store even if you don't want to buy.

Tankar Gallery, Calle Palacio 121, has a variety of tapestries produced by local artists that are representative of Andean traditions and customs. They also produce handmade ceramics.

Ceramics and pottery
Maky, at Carmen Alto 101, has a fine collection of tea sets, incense holders and other pottery decorated with pre-Hispanic and Inca motifs. Slightly more expensive and better quality are the goods at **La Mamita**, at Portal de Carnes 244.

Instruments and Andean music
Anyone interested in Andean music should head to **Taki Museo de Musica de los Andes** at Hatunrumiyoc 487. The knowledgeable owner runs a workshop and shop here producing and selling typical musical instruments.

For Andean CDs try **Flutes of Peru**, at Av El Sol 230, which offers both traditional and more modern Peruvian music.

TREKKING AGENCIES
Listed here are some of the better-established agencies with good reputations and a solid history of delivering services of a high standard, in line with the regulations and requirements to look after porters and crew. Inclusion in the list is no guarantee of quality, though; you should do your own research before settling on a group to guide you.
● **Amazonas Explorer** (☎ 252846, 🖳 www.amazonas-explorer.com, Av Collasuyo 910, Miravalle) A specialist white-water rafting (see p184) and mountain-biking (see p185) company owned by British and Swiss

CUSCO

expats living in Cusco that is renowned for its adventure tours but which also runs decent, small-group, fixed-departure Inca Trail trips as well as treks on the Choquequirao to Huancacalle route. Has a good reputation for treating its porters and staff well and paying proper salaries.

● **Amazon Trails Peru** (☎ 437374, 🖳 www.amazontrailsperu.com, Calle Tandapata 660) German-Peruvian outfit that runs jungle trips (see box p185), has their own accommodation, Amazonas Hostal, in

Cusco (see p169) and organizes a handful of trips and treks in the Cusco and Sacred Valley area including the Inca Trail, Salkantay and Choquequirao to Machu Picchu trek.

● **Andina Travel** (☎ 251892, 🖳 www.andinatravel.com, Plazoleta Santa Catalina 219) Recommended American-Peruvian outfit committed to supporting local communities through sustainable development and which runs good-quality Inca Trail, Santa Teresa, Salkantay and Choquequirao

---

❏ TREK AGENCIES, LICENCES AND WHAT THEY REALLY REPRESENT

Background Over the last decade the Peruvian government has introduced a series of rules and regulations designed to control and regulate access to the Inca Trail and so reduce the environmental impact of thousands of trekkers descending on the trail every year. The rules are stringently adhered to, so you must be aware of them (see box pp216-17 for a comprehensive list of Inca Trail regulations).

One of the requirements is that for **any trek that uses a stretch of the classic Inca Trail you must have a licensed guide and a trekking permit, both of which must come from a regulated agency**. Consequently this is also a requirement for the short Inca Trail from Km104 and for the Salkantay Trek. At the time of writing this wasn't a requirement for the Santa Teresa, Vilcabamba or Choquequirao treks, but the situation may change and there have been various whispers about proposed alterations to the regulations to include some or all of these routes.

Licence requirements In theory a licence means that the agency has satisfied a series of criteria and been deemed professional and responsible enough to organize treks. They should have good equipment, provide a reasonable standard of food and service and employ properly qualified guides. However, there are still a lot of frankly poor companies in Cusco who are allowed to operate. The cheaper deals they tend to offer aren't necessarily the best value and almost certainly mean a compromise in standards. These agencies have a reputation for: cutting corners; pairing up groups with others; failing to provide a Spanish-speaking, let alone English-speaking, guide; being environmentally insensitive and not clearing up after themselves; and for failing to look after their porters. On top of this, the food's likely to be pretty grim, the equipment dodgy and there are usually hidden costs that make the whole unpleasant experience more expensive than it was first advertised. Essentially, you get what you pay for.

At the time of writing over 170 agencies licensed to operate Inca Trail treks were competing for business. The list is reviewed every year, with licenses renewed or revoked, so before handing over any money make sure to check carefully that the agency you are considering is still allowed to operate and has the requisite paperwork. Be aware that **licences are only issued to Peruvian companies**, not to overseas outfits or foreign tour operators. For the most comprehensive list of up-to-date licensed agencies check out 🖳 www.andeantravelweb.com. To check the availability of Inca Trail trek permits visit 🖳 www.machupicchu.gob.pe; Direccion Regional de Cultura Cusco, DRCC) or click on the links shown on the Andean Travel website.

treks as well as 10-day trips from Choquequirao to Machu Picchu and 6-day treks from Huancacalle to Machu Picchu. They can also arrange jungle trips (see box p185) and bespoke treks. Prices are dependent on group size.

● **Apumayo** (☎ 246018, 💻 www.apumayo.com, Jr Ricardo Palma Ñ-11, Santa Monica) Professional, high-quality whitewater rafting specialist (see box p184) with a strong environmental agenda. Also run trips and tours in the Sacred Valley region

as well as Inca Trail, Salkantay and Choquequirao treks.

● **Big Foot** (☎ 233836, 💻 www.bigfootcusco.com, Calle Triunfo 392) Tends to focus on tailor-made itineraries but does run a 10-day Vilcabamba trek that isn't readily available elsewhere in addition to the more standard Inca Trail, Salkantay, Santa Teresa and Ausangate Circuit treks.

● **Ch'aska Tours** (☎ 240424, 💻 www.chaskatours.com, Calle Garcilaso 265) Cultural and nature tours available but also

---

Costs There is a wide range of prices quoted for trekking the Inca Trail – from about US$500 to virtually whatever you're prepared to part with. Realistically a classic four-day trek will set you back US$540-600. Although there are deals out there for less than this, simple arithmetic combining all the individual food and transport costs, entrance fees, permits and equipment hire shows that it just isn't possible to run a good-quality trek for less than US$500 (see box p14). Don't allow agencies to fob you off with 'estimates' either, get a definite quote to prevent a nasty surprise later.

At the upper end of the scale, charging upwards of US$800 are the exclusive agencies such as **Condor Travel**, **Explorandes**, **Inka Natura** and **Inca Explorers**. Good-quality mid-range outfits selling treks from US$540 to US$650 but still offering a high-level of service and a responsible attitude towards their porters include **Peru Treks**, **Q'ente**, **SAS** and **United Mice**. At the cheaper end of the market but still capable of delivering an all-round good service without compromising standards or porter welfare is **Wayki Trek**.

When it comes to buying a trek, always pay for it at the agency's office and demand a written receipt and contract. There have been various instances where people claiming to be representatives of big agencies have taken money for a place on a trek at a bus station or airport and simply disappeared with the cash.

Arriving in Cusco without a booking It hasn't been possible to pitch up in Cusco and arrange to walk the Inca Trail for some time now, but still people arrive expecting to do this. At the very slowest times of year (Dec-Jan) it might be possible to pull something together within a couple of weeks, but usually you have to book a place on a trek at least three months in advance of the departure date. During the high season (Jun-Aug) you should consider signing up five to six months in advance to guarantee availability, especially if you aren't able to be flexible about departure dates.

Should you arrive in Cusco without anything arranged though, don't despair. There are plenty of alternatives to the classic Inca Trail and it is possible to organize a trek on the Santa Teresa route (which actually finishes at Machu Picchu) at shorter notice. However, because this trek isn't regulated there is scope for unlicensed operators and guides to be used, so again, be careful when booking. Other treks that are currently unregulated and so easier to arrange are the Vilcabamba and Choquequirao treks. You might also want to consider the Ausangate Circuit or Lares Valley trek, or multi-day white-water rafting, mountain-biking or jungle trips.

If you are interested in activities other than trekking see the box on pp184-5.

❑ **Private guides**
A few private guides are registered with Inrena, the government agency committed to managing and conserving the national parks and archaeological sites. It can be difficult to track these people down because they are usually affiliated to a larger agency and don't want to spoil the relationship they have with their employers. However, a list can be obtained from the Asociación de Guías Oficiales de Turismo (☎ 233457, ▭ www.agoturcusco.org.pe), though the website is in Spanish. The website ▭ www.leaplocal.org also recommends local people qualified to lead treks and tours.

good-value treks on the Inca Trail and routes through the Lares Valley from Salkantay to Machu Picchu.

● **Condor Travel** (☎ 225961, ▭ www.condortravel.com) Expensive, top-end agency offering high-class tours and trips throughout Peru. Slick and professional operation with regular departures on the Inca Trail as well as other treks in the Cusco area. Well-connected and the local representative for a number of international airlines if you are after plane tickets. The head office is at Armando Blondet 249, San Isidro, Lima.

● **Ecotrek Peru** (DYF Expediciones; ☎ 247286, ▭ www.ecotrekperu.com, Urb Quispicanchi F-3) Decent, porter-friendly outfit run by an ex-manager of the South American Explorers Club that specializes in jungle trips to the Pongo de Mainique but which also arranges single and multi-day mountain-biking tours and cultural trips as well as treks in the Cusco region, including the Inca Trail, Salkantay, Choquequirao and a 9-day Vilcabamba trip.

● **Enigma** (☎ 222155, ▭ www.enigmaperu.com, Jr Clorinda Matto de Turner 100) Smaller, quality operator based away from the city centre in a residential part of town offering reasonably priced mid-range treks supported with good equipment and some knowledgeable guides on the Inca Trail, Salkantay, Santa Teresa and Choquequirao treks as well as the Ausangate Circuit and cultural treks such as the Lares Valley hike.

● **Eric Adventures** (☎ 272862, ▭ www.ericadventures.com, Urb Santa Maria A1-6) Offer a number of treks including variations on the Inca Trail, Salkantay and Choquequirao to Machu Picchu. They also offer several activities (see box pp184-5).

● **Explorandes** (☎ 238380, ▭ www.explorandes.com, Paseo Zarzuela Q-2 Huancaro) Well-established major tour operator at the top-end of the market, with correspondingly high prices, that offers a superb range of treks throughout Peru including the classic Inca Trail, Salkantay, Santa Teresa, Choquequirao and 10-day Choquequirao to Machu Picchu trek in addition to expeditions to the Colca Canyon and Cordilleras Blanca and Huayhuash. Departures are flexible and group sizes are kept small. Also ecologically aware, committed to preserving the environment and conscious of the need for the further development of ecotourism.

● **Inka Natura** (Lima ☎ 440-2022, ▭ www.inkanatura.com, Manuel Bañon 461, San Isidro, Lima) Pricey, professional outfit that specializes in jungle trips (see box p185), but also has various Inca Trail, Salkantay, Choquequirao and Choquequirao to Machu Picchu treks and Cusco regional hikes that are similarly well supported and expensive.

● **Llama Path** (☎ 240822, ▭ www.llamapath.com, Calle San Juan de Dios 250) Mid-range outfit operated by a Peruvian-English partnership that has a wide range of treks, including the Inca Trail, Santa Teresa, Salkantay and Choquequirao treks, at reasonable rates. They also run a Vilcabamba to Machu Picchu trip. Inclined to try and keep group numbers small they have dependable, fixed departure dates and are committed to sustainable tourism.

● **Machete Tours** (☎ 224829, ▭ www.machetetours.com, Triunfo 392) Budget operator run by a Peruvian-Danish pair that's more often associated with jungle trips to Manu or climbing and hiking expeditions around Huaraz but who also run Inca Trail, Salkantay and Vilcabamba outings as well as regular treks to Choquequirao and nine-day treks between Choquequirao and Machu Picchu.

● **Mayuc** (☎ 232666, 🖳 www.mayuc.com, Portal Confituras 211) White-water-rafting specialist (see box p184) but also runs private and group treks on the Inca Trail, Salkantay/Choquequirao, Choquequirao to Machu Picchu, and Vilcabamba Trail.

● **Mountain Lodges of Peru** (☎ 262640, 🖳 www.mountainlodgesofperu.com, Av El Sol 948, Of 403) This is the only agency offering lodge accommodation on a trek to Machu Picchu thus enabling you to trek in style. Four private, scenically sited, eco-lodges line the Santa Teresa trail that accesses Machu Picchu via a backdoor route. Each lodge (Salkantay Lodge & Adventure Resort, Wayra Lodge, Colpa Lodge, Lucma Lodge) boasts friendly, attentive staff and excellent facilities. Rooms are double, twin or triple and all have en suite facilities, including hot showers. The rooms at Salkantary are a mix of Andean and colonial architectural styles.

Saunas are available at no extra cost. Three of the lodges (Salkantay, Wayra and Colpa) also have an outdoor Jacuzzi that you can sink into at the end of the day. To further help ease the strains of trekking a professional massage service is offered for a small charge at each overnight stop. Should you feel the need, you can also communicate with the wider world via the satellite phone and internet access available at each lodge. Each lodge has a well-trained chef and kitchen capable of producing surprisingly refined three-course meals given its location; alcoholic drinks are available every evening too along with complimentary filtered water and soft drinks.

The prospect of an evening of relative comfort and good food is a great incentive when trekking. However, for the pleasure of not camping you'll have to pay a princely sum.

● **Peru Treks & Adventure** (☎ 222722, 🖳 www.perutreks.com, Av Pardo 540) Peruvian-English trekking specialist that focuses on the Inca Trail and which has an excellent reputation for looking after their porters and crew. They are also heavily

❏ The Inca Jungle Trek

You may come across an increasingly large number of agencies in Cusco offering another 'back door' route to Machu Picchu. The Inca Jungle Trek, created by Cusco agencies, is an activity-filled approach to the ruins that avoids any regulations but which also offers little in the way of Inca history until you arrive at your final goal. The trip sees you initially driving from Cusco to Abra Málaga. You then travel by bike and on foot to Machu Picchu.

The first day involves a straightforward 4- to 5-hour 2-wheeled descent from the high pass at Abra Málaga (4350m) to Santa María. The following day is a 6- to 7-hour trek through the cloud forest from Santa María to Santa Teresa that is fairly taxing if a little unspectacular, although there is a section of authentic Inca trail along the way; some operators opt to drive you over this section. Having recuperated overnight in Santa Teresa and at the hot springs nearby, or gone in search of more thrills at the nearby zipline (see box p261), you spend six hours walking from Santa Teresa to Aguas Calientes, much of it along railway tracks.

The fourth and final day is spent exploring the ruins at Machu Picchu. The trip details vary considerably according to operator, with different levels of accommodation and equipment offered. Side-trips and excursions, such as white-water rafting from Santa Teresa, can also be added to the journey. Make sure to check what your trip price includes before you sign up but expect to pay around US$350-400 for a decent tour, safety equipment, access to Machu Picchu and a return train fare and transfer back to Cusco.

involved with sustainable tourism, and plough much of their profit into schemes and projects set up to help local people and communities. They also run a **homestay programme** where you can stay with families in Chinchero (see p199) or Amaru

(north of Pisac) and experience their way of life and culture.

● **Q'ente** (☎ 222535, 🖳 www.qente.com, Calle Choquechaca 229, 2nd Floor) Upmarket mid-range agency whose name is Quechua for 'hummingbird'. Their helpful

---

❑ AGENCIES SPECIALIZING IN ACTIVITIES OTHER THAN TREKKING

Although synonymous with world-class trekking, plenty of other activities are available; some people like the idea of horse trekking around the Sacred Valley but many take the chance to indulge their passion for adrenalin sports. Whether you want to ride the rapids through the Sacred Valley, float high over the landscape or crash through it on two wheels, there's something for all levels of ability and experience. Equally if you want to retreat to the forest in search of some of Peru's enormously diverse flora and fauna, there are agencies that are particularly good in putting together jungle itineraries.

For a one-stop adrenalin fix visit **Action Valley** (☎ 240835, 🖳 www.actionvall eycusco.com, office in Cusco at Calle Santa Teresa 325), 11km outside Cusco on the road to Urubamba and Abancay, where you can try bungee jumping, slingshot (the reverse of a bungee jump), bridge swinging or use their climbing wall.

White-water rafting

White-water rafting is an exhilarating rush and Cusco boasts access to several rivers with world-class runs and rapids. The sport is inherently dangerous so make sure you check out the company you sign up with carefully and bear in mind that budget outfits may have sub-standard equipment or poorly trained guides. In the Cusco region there are five main options for rafting: the Río Urubamba is a scenic float through the heart of the Sacred Valley with grade 2-3 rapids; the Cusipata is slightly more thrilling with more grade 3 rapids; the Chuquicahuana offers grade 3-4 rapids. Multi-day trips are made on the Río Apurímac, which features some of Peru's finest white water and the Río Tambopata, which allows you to explore the jungle in an unusual way.

Companies to consider are: **Amazonas Explorer** (see p179), a professionally run and popular agency headed up by a British-Swiss partnership that specializes in adventure activities but is best known for its exhilarating multi-day white-water rafting expeditions on the Apurímac and Tambopata rivers. Also runs an epic 16-day trip from Lake Titicaca to the Amazon using canoes, rafts and 4x4s as well as standard Inca Trail and Choquequirao treks; **Apumayo Expeditions** (see p181) offers excellent, adventurous outings according to a fixed timetable with day trips on the Urubamba and multi-day trips on the Apurímac (4 days), Cotahuasi and Tambopata (12-day safari). They are sensitive to the impact they have on the rivers and are heavily involved in programmes to maintain the cleanliness of the Rio Urubamba; **Eric Adventures** (see p182) a white-water specialist with a lot of adventure activities such as mountain biking, climbing, paragliding and horse riding on their books; **Mayuc** (see p183) another white-water-rafting specialist that operates day trips on the Urubamba, Cusipata or Chuquicahuana as well as 4-day expeditions on the Apurímac; **SAS Travel** (see opposite) and **United Mice** (see p186).

Paragliding and ballooning

For an alternative view of the Sacred Valley consider taking to the air and flying or floating across the countryside. The valley provides exciting but challenging flying conditions; if the wind isn't just right your trip will, very sensibly, be postponed.

and accommodating staff, knowledgeable guides and wide range of treks make them a good bet. Treks include the Inca Trail, Santa Teresa, Salkantay, Choquequirao, Vilcabamba and Ausangate Circuit in addition to a 9-day Choquequirao to Machu Picchu route and a 17-day Choquequirao to Espíritu Pampa trip. They also boast numerous city and Sacred Valley tours.

● **SAS Travel** (☎ 249194, 🖳 www.sastrav elperu.com, Calle Garcilaso 270) Large, well-organized agency with a plenty of

● **Eric Adventures** (see p182) offer a three-day paragliding course in Chinchero and a 900m tandem jump as a single-day activity.

● **Wayra** (see *Sol y Luna*, p200) For a thrilling alternative view of the Sacred Valley consider taking one of the tandem flights offered by this Urubamba-based outfitter. Flights launch from two sites in Chinchero and cost US$100. They also offer three- and eight-day courses for people who want more than a brief introduction to the sport.

Mountain biking

Cusco is an excellent base for mountain biking and there are masses of well-used farm roads, tracks and dirt trails through the surrounding mountains and countryside. Facilities are pretty basic and hire equipment isn't great so serious cyclists should bring their own bikes. However, a number of agencies in Cusco offer mountain-bike tours in and around the Sacred Valley, the most popular being day trips to Maras, Moray and Salineras (see p204), or to the Inca ruins at Pikillacta and Tipon (see pp213-14). Multi-day tours explore the Lares Valley or even venture into the jungle.

Companies to consider include: **Amazonas Explorer** (see p179); **Ecotrek Peru** (see p182); **Eric Adventures** (see p182); **SAS Travel** (see above); **United Mice** (see p186).

Climbing

The Cordilleras Vilcabamba and Vilcanota provide some challenging routes for mountaineers with experience and their own gear. There are few opportunities for inexperienced climbers though and hire kit is often barely adequate.

Few guides or companies capable of leading expeditions are in Cusco; most are based in Huaraz. **Eric Adventures** (see p182) offer a half-day rock-climbing course near Sacsayhuaman and a full-day canyoning expedition near Pisac. Also consider **Machete Tours** (see p182).

Jungle trips

The rainforest and jungle within easy reach of Cusco is some of the finest in Peru. Without too much effort it's possible to swap the Andes for the Amazon and immerse yourself in an entirely different landscape.

Companies to consider include: **Amazon Trails Peru** (see p180) A German-Peruvian outfit that runs multi-day tours to Manu and owns their own private nature reserve situated to the south-east of Manu; **Andina Travel** (see p180); **Ecotrek Peru** (see p182) specializes in jungle trips to the Pongo de Mainique; **Inka Natura** (see p182) offers trips to Manu where you stay either in their own Manu Wildlife Centre or a luxury tented camp alongside Cocha Salvador, one of the area's most stunning oxbow lakes; **Machete Tours** (see p182); **Manu Expeditions** (☎ 225990 or 224235, 🖳 www.manuexpeditions.com, Calle Clorinda Matto de Turner 330), a brilliant, well-established outfit set-up by self-confessed 'birding bum' Barry Walker that organizes and runs group and tailor-made trips to the Manu biosphere.

CUSCO

staff and guides meaning that it is able to offer regular Inca Trail departures as well as treks to Salkantay, Choquequirao and the Lares Valley. Justifiably popular and a little more expensive because of it, especially if you want to travel in a small group. Also offers white-water rafting, mountain-biking and horse-riding expeditions.

● **United Mice** (☎ 221139, 💻 www.united mice.com, Av Pachacuteq 424) This outfit has the most memorable name. It offers a range of budget treks including some limited departures on the Inca Trail, Salkantay, Choquequirao and Choquequirao to Machu Picchu treks. Popular and good-value, although the treks aren't as cheap as they once were, the company also offers mountain-biking and rafting trips. A small percentage of their profit is donated to a foundation supporting street kids in Cusco.

● **Wayki Trek** (☎ 224092, 💻 www.wayki trek.net, Av Pardo 506, Paseos de los Héroes) Small budget agency, whose name is Quechua for 'brother', with a reputation and popularity that belies their size. On offer are good-value Inca Trail treks but also Salkantay, Choquequirao and 9-day Choquequirao to Machu Picchu treks in addition to the Ausangate Circuit, all in groups around half the size of most other operators. Wayki also offers the chance to spend a day with a porter prior to the trek, to visit their village and to learn a little more about their lives as a way of showing how closely they work with their teams.

MOVING ON
Air
The airport is a few kilometres south of Plaza de Armas. It takes five minutes by taxi from there. From here you can fly to most major Peruvian towns. See box p78 for information about departure taxes.

Airlines include: **LAN** (💻 www.lan .com), Av El Sol 627B; **Star Perú** (💻 www .starperu.com), Av El Sol 627; **TACA** (💻 www.taca.com), Av El Sol 602B.

There are seven flights daily to Lima. The cheapest leaves early in the morning. Fares start at around US$88 but can easily

rise to US$175. There are spectacular views of Salkantay out of the right-hand side windows, about 10 minutes after take off. The flight takes 50 minutes. You should try and catch as early a flight as possible since there is a higher risk of flights being delayed or cancelled later in the day.

Bus
All international and long-distance buses use the main bus terminal (Terminal Terrestre), 2km south of Plaza de Armas, near the airport. Agencies on Av El Sol and in Plaza de Armas sell tickets for a healthy commission; you will get far cheaper tickets at the terminal itself. It isn't necessary to book far in advance; if you arrange your tickets the day before you can usually choose your seat.

International services operate to La Paz and Copacabana in Bolivia, or to Tacna by the Chilean border.

The route to **Lima via Abancay** and Ayacucho takes 20-25 hours and costs between US$20-37. The alternative is to go **via Arequipa**, which also takes around 20 hours and costs US$20-50.

Buses to **Quillabamba** leave from Santiago bus terminal in the west of the city.

Regional services to **Pisac** (s/3-5; 1hr, approx 4/hr) leave from Av Tullumayo (buses to Calca) or Calle Puputi (buses to Urubamba).

Services to **Urubamba** (s/3; 2hrs) leave frequently throughout the day from Av Tullumayo. Alternatively try to catch a *colectivo* (s/5, 2hrs) from Av Grau near Centenario.

To get to **Chinchero** catch a bus to Urubamba from Av Tullumayo (about s/2-4, 1hr); the bus tends to leave early in the morning.

The furthest destination in the Sacred Valley is **Ollantaytambo** (s/5; 3hrs). Direct buses (4/day) leave from Av Grau or Tullumayo (about s/5; 2-3hrs). At other times you will have to take a bus to Urubamba and get an onward connection from there.

Other destinations include: **Nazca** (US$20; 14hrs); **Abancay** (US$5; 5hrs), take this bus for **Cachora**, see p301; **Juliaca** (US$3-4; 5-6 hrs); **Puno** (US$5-10; 6-7hrs); and **Arequipa** (US$10-25; 10-12hrs).

Local buses leave from a variety of departure points.

The cheap way to Machu Picchu
In the past you had no choice but to take the train to Aguas Calientes and were at the mercy of the expensive fares levied by the train operator. However, there is an alternative, cheaper route as a result of the bridge that was built across the Urubamba.

From Terminal Terrestre catch a bus to Quillabamba (s/20; depart 7pm) but ask to be dropped off at Santa María. Pick up a minibus to Santa Teresa (s/7.50), two hours away, arriving around sunrise. Here you can now cross the Urubamba on the new bridge. Turn right on the far bank and hike the 6km to La Hidroeléctrica on an even, graded road, although there is a possibility of catching a lift on the back of a passing truck. From the train station at La Hidroeléctrica you can ride to Aguas Calientes (s/30). Alternatively carry on walking along the tracks and after 2-3 hours you will come to the town.

If you start to flag, there is overnight accommodation at *Hospedaje Mandor*, about 2km downstream from the bridge back across the Urubamba that leads to Machu Picchu.

To return to Cusco either retrace your steps via Santa Teresa and catch the 10am bus from here to Santa María, in time to meet the 1pm bus to Cusco which arrives 6-7 hours later. Alternatively catch the train from Aguas Calientes to Ollantaytambo or direct to Cusco.

Rail [see pp370-3]
Trains for Juliaca and Puno leave from **Estación Huanchac** on Av Pachacutec. Tickets must be bought at the station.

Trains for Aguas Calientes (for Machu Picchu) leave from **Poroy**, just outside Cusco, or from Ollantaytambo, depending on the train operator. Tickets for these routes must also be bought in advance (see below).

Pay close attention to timetables, opening hours and ticket prices as these change frequently.

To get to Machu Picchu as cheaply as possible see column opposite.

Buying tickets The main office for **PeruRail** can be contacted on Cusco ☎ 581 414 or via 🖳 www.perurail.com. They have an office on Plaza de Armas at Portal de Carnes 214. Estación Huanchac is open for ticket sales Monday to Friday 7am-5pm, Saturday & Sunday 7am-noon.

Rival company **Inca Rail** (🖳 www.incarail.com), whose trains leave from Ollantaytambo for Aguas Calientes and Machu Picchu, also have an office on the Plaza, at Portal de Panes 105, ☎ 233030. Make sure you have ID, preferably your passport, when buying tickets. It is also possible to buy tickets in advance online with a credit card. This generates an e-voucher that is not valid for travel; it must be converted into a proper ticket at least an hour before departure.

Taxi
A taxi to Pisac will set you back about s/30.

CUSCO

Around Cusco

RUINS NEAR CUSCO (DAY HIKE)   [see map p191]

The landscape around Cusco is dotted with small, interesting archaeological sites, many within easy walking, horse-riding or mountain-biking distance of the city. Five of the main sites can be visited in the course of a half-day's trek, which allows you plenty of time at each ruin. A gentle stroll across the rolling grasslands is also an ideal way to acclimatize to the altitude here. Access to four of the five is with the Visitor's Ticket (BTU, see box p153). The fifth, Salapunco, is free anyway. If you do not have a Visitor's Ticket it is possible to buy a separate ticket for just these four sites; the **Boleto** covering this 'circuit' is Circuit 1 (see box p153) which costs s/70.

The 8km (5-mile) route detailed below is the most commonly trekked path in the vicinity of Cusco and gives access to Tambo Machay, Puca Pucara, Salapunco, Q'enko and Sacsayhuaman. The trek can be done in either direction but it is simpler to catch a taxi out to the furthest point and then walk back. This way each site builds in magnificence too, until you arrive at Sacsayhuaman, one of the most spectacular standing stone sites anywhere in the world. Taxis from Plaza de Armas to Tambo Machay cost around s/20 one way. Alternatively take a bus bound for Pisac and ask to be dropped off at Tambo Machay (about s/2). See p192 for details of returning to Cusco from Sacsayhuaman.

In the past there have been robberies and muggings around the ruins close to Cusco, so keep your wits about you, leave all your valuables in your hotel and don't try to visit these places after dusk. It is always much safer to walk in small groups rather than on your own.

Tambo Machay

Tambo Machay is set back from the road from Cusco to the Sacred Valley. From the corner where you are deposited, walk up the gravel track for about 200m until you reach the site (7am-5.30pm; only possible with Visitor's Ticket). The name Tambo Machay translates as 'Inn Cave', but is more frequently referred to as Los Baños del Inca ('The Inca's Baths'). The carefully cut stones frame and channel a fresh water spring which issues from high on the slope above the site and is channelled from one terrace to another, vanishes underground and re-emerges in twin cascades. The precise purpose of the site is unknown but it is likely that it was used in the worship of water.

● **Route to Puca Pucara** From Tambo Machay walk back to the main road. There is an alternative trail that climbs over the hill above the site, but this is periodically closed to visitors. Cross the road and begin to walk back towards Cusco, following the signpost to Puca Pucara which is visible ahead of you. About 200m later veer left from the main road and drop down to the entrance to Puca Pucara.

Puca Pucara

This collection of stone buildings (7am-5.30pm; Visitor's Ticket) perched on a promontory overlooking a deep valley was probably a private hunting lodge connected to one of the Inca's private estates. It has also been suggested that it used to be a military fort or checkpoint along an Inca Road, since the literal translation of the name means 'Red Watchtower' or 'Red Fort'.

● **Route to Salapunco** Beyond Puca Pucara walk parallel to the road heading back to Cusco and briefly follow it for 50m before cutting away left. A faint track sets off parallel to the road and descends to a small hamlet with a football pitch on your right. Descend south beyond the adobe houses for about half-an-hour, negotiating some boggy patches and marshy depressions as the path traces the route of a seasonal stream.

Having curved left then right, the path splits. The two clearer trails, on each flank of the valley that has begun to form, stay high but you want to take the central path which sticks to the valley floor and descends amidst scrub and small trees. As you get lower, keep an eye out for Andean flickers (see p114), a type of woodpecker, which live in the surrounding area.

The path winds between some rocky outcrops and beneath several cliffs pocked with niches and caves. The last of these, on your right as you descend, is a 50m-high, split cliff-face, sometimes called Laqo, which conceals two caves. The area has been partially excavated to reveal carvings and engravings in the rock as well as what could be an altar. Following a dog-leg left immediately after this cliff you should be able to see the monolithic rock of Salapunco ahead. Walk towards the giant boulder sitting in the centre of a rolling plain. As you pass a seasonal pond and approach the site you will start to see carved rocks and carefully flattened surfaces, evidence of Inca activity.

Salapunco

Salapunco (also known as **Cusilluchayoc**; always open; free) is a giant lime-stone boulder that is riddled with passages and carvings, many representing animals. The Quechua name translates as 'place of the monkeys', from the Quechua *kusillo*, meaning monkey. Cut steps lead to the top of the rock, where there are polished surfaces and smoothed seats giving excellent views out over the surrounding countryside.

Off the beaten path, the site is usually deserted. Over the years there has been a fair amount of excavation here; archaeologists have discovered remnants of Inca walls and other structures buried beneath the site. In fact, it appears that there may be several metres of interesting features here below ground level, although nobody knows why this might be the case.

● **Route to Q'enko** If you stand on top of Salapunco and look toward Cusco, you can see a faint trail heading diagonally across the grassland towards a cluster of houses, Villa San Blas, backed by a stand of eucalyptus. Follow the diagonal path west across the field. After 100m you drop briefly into a creek bed. Around 400m further on the path passes to the left of a small sculpted outcrop of rock that has finely cut and polished platforms. As you approach the houses, keep them to your left. Cross a dirt road and turn left (south) and pass in front of the houses, descending into a shallow gully alongside a stone wall. Walk downhill briefly, turn right (west) and cut through a gap in the wall and stroll 50m through a eucalyptus copse before emerging at a car park adjacent to the main road, in front of the next site: Q'enko.

Q'enko

Q'enko (7am-5.30pm; Visitor's Ticket) is a second large limestone outcrop, the name of which translates as 'zigzag' or 'labyrinth'. Smaller than Salapunco, it has far more designs cut into it, many of which are very detailed. The site is a *huaca* (sacred site) and many of the carvings have special significance. A llama, a condor and snakes have all been identified, although unfortunately most of these are on the upper surface of the rock and it is now forbidden to climb on the stone. Channels and rivulets have been cut into the stone and may have been used to course *chicha* during ceremonies.

At the front of the site, a standing stone enclosed by a finely sculpted niched wall has also been identified as casting a shadow shaped like a puma's head when the sun rises on the winter solstice (21st June). Inside the huaca is a tunnel that leads to what appears to be a beautifully sculpted altar.

● **Route to Sacsayhuaman** From Q'enko rejoin the road and turn left towards Cusco. Follow the road as it passes to the right of a mound, **Q'enko Chico** (Little Q'enko), which is built above a stone wall that includes a fitted block with 21 angles. As the road bends left, veer right and join a dirt track which passes through a scruffy wood. Beyond this it eases past a straggle of souvenir shops and emerges on a wide open plain. Continue towards a hut. Turn left (west) and present your Visitor's Ticket at the ticket office. From here continue downhill gently towards a car park. To your right is the awesome ruin of Sacsayhuaman (see below) and to your left you'll see the **Christ Statue** (Cristo Blanco) with his arms outstretched. Donated by Palestinian refugees to express their thanks in 1944, the statue is clearly visible from Cusco during the day and at night it is brilliantly illuminated.

Sacsayhuaman   [see map p193]

To avoid the worst of the crowds at Sacsayhuaman (7am-5.30pm; Visitor's Ticket) consider getting here early, before the tour buses arrive, or later in the afternoon once they have moved on.

The size of the stones here really is incredible and historian Garcilaso de la Vega was massively impressed but quite at a loss for an explanation as to the construction of Sacsayhuaman:

'A Spanish monk, who recently visited Peru, told me on his return, that he would never have believed what people tell him about this fortress if he hadn't seen it with his own eyes, because it is even more difficult to imagine than one can say; and that, in reality, it seemed hardly possible that such a project could have been successfully carried out without the help of the Evil One. Those were his very words. If we think, too, that this incredible work was accomplished without the help of a single machine, it is too much to say that it represents an even greater enigma than the seven wonders

Around Cusco

RIDGE
OF HILLS

TAMBO
MACHAY

TO SACRED
VALLEY, PISAC,
ETC.

THE TREK FROM TAMBO
MACHAY TO SACSAYHUAMAN
TAKES AT LEAST TWO
HOURS BUT IS BEST TREATED
AS A MORE LEISURELY
OUTING, IDEAL FOR HELPING
THE BODY ACCLIMATIZE

FARMS

PUCA
PUCARA

FOOTBALL
PITCH

FIELDS &
FARMED
LAND

★ trailblazer

IGNORE PATHS
THAT STAY HIGH TO
DESCEND INTO
VALLEY

SACSAYHUAMAN
SEE SACSAYHUAMAN
MAP

CLIFF/
LÂQO

SCULPTED
ROCK

CAN BE
BOGGY

SALAPUNCO

TICKET
OFFICE

SOUVENIR
SHOPS

WALL

TICKET
OFFICE

CAR
PARK

POND

TICKET
OFFICE

CHRIST
STATUE

Q'ENKO

DIRT
ROAD

TO SAN
BLAS

SAN
CRISTÓBAL

Q'ENKO CHICO

TO CUSCO VIA
RESABALOSA,
20-30MINS

TO CUSCO &
CALLE
PUMACURCO,
20-30MINS

0   ½ mile

0   1km

APPROX SCALE

AROUND CUSCO

of the world?... One sees how the Egyptian pyramids were constructed, with the combined forces of time and countless workers... But how may we explain the fact that these Peruvian Indians were able to split, carve, lift, carry, hoist and lower such enormous blocks of stone, which are more like pieces of a mountain than building stones, without the help of a single machine or instrument. An enigma such as this one cannot be easily solved without seeking the help of magic, particularly when one recalls the great familiarity of these people with devils.'

Garcilaso Inca de la Vega *The Royal Commentaries of the Incas* (1609)

This prepared the way for theorists such as Eric von Daniken who was convinced that this was the work of visitors from outer space.

The Spanish nicknamed the site 'the Fortress'. However, current research and the discovery of Inca tombs containing the bodies of priests in the area suggest that it was more likely to have been a temple. The layout of the site makes it likely that it was used as a sanctuary and place to worship the sun. Regardless of the original reason for its construction, the massive stone walls were used as a fort by the armies of Manco Inca as he fought to evict the Spanish from Cusco (see p100).

The site itself is one of the most impressive stone monuments left standing in the world and is awe-inspiring in its stature and form. Enormous stone blocks stand solemnly in three tiers of zigzag **walls** that stretch 360 metres. John Hemming calculated in *Conquest of the Incas* that the largest stone in the structure stands 8.5m high and weighs 361 tonnes. The massive blocks curve into one another as if squashed together like clay. For structural strength the largest stones are set at the apexes of the zigzags that form the wall. Unfortunately the site has been used as an unofficial quarry for cut stones over the years and many of the smaller stones have been pillaged by people for use in construction elsewhere. The structure used to be topped by three giant towers, called **Salla Marca**, **Paunca Marca** and **Muyu Marca**, which were razed to the ground following the defeat of Manco Inca. The foundations and concentric ringed outlines of these three giants are slowly being uncovered and renovated.

Across a broad, flat space known as the Esplanade, stands a giant mound called the **Inca Throne**, where an altar has been carved out of the rock. It is thought the Inca or other high-ranking individual oversaw ceremonies from here. Nearby are numbers of seats cut into the stone. Nowadays, however, the smooth grooves and polished slopes on the far side of the mound are used by children as a **slide**, giving the mound the nickname *el rodadero* (literally means rolling easily). Beyond the mound is a small amphitheatre and a section of hill riddled with **tunnels**. Some of these remain open, but you'll need a torch to make your way through them.

● **Returning to Cusco** From Sacsayhuaman it takes about 20-30 minutes to stroll gently downhill to Plaza de Armas. Although there are several routes, the simplest is to descend from the car park on the dirt path that drops through a gully to eventually join the tarmac road on a hairpin bend. There is an OFEC ticket office here that checks Visitor Tickets for people walking up to the site.

Join the road and follow it carefully around a set of S-bends to reach the

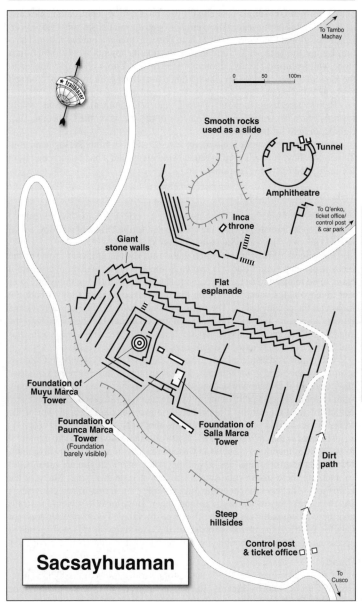

To Tambo
Machay

0   50   100m

Smooth rocks
used as a slide

Tunnel

Amphitheatre

To Q'enko,
ticket office/
control post
& car park

Inca
throne

Giant
stone walls

Flat
esplanade

AROUND CUSCO

Foundation of
Muyu Marca
Tower

Foundation of
Paunca Marca
Tower
(Foundation
barely visible)

Foundation of
Salla Marca
Tower

Dirt
path

Steep
hillsides

Control post
& ticket office

Sacsayhuaman

To
Cusco

church of **San Cristóbal**. This church was built by Cristóbal Paullu Inca and dedicated to his patron saint. The church is open during the day and free to visit. Inside the gloomy interior it is just about possible to make out the restored atrium. Lining the back wall of the terrace outside the church is an original Inca stone wall featuring 11 large, doorway-sized niches. This wall once belonged to the Palacio de Colcampata, in which Manco Inca lived prior to his rebellion and flight to Vilcabamba.

Below here there is a set of steep stairs (**Resbalosa**) that drop rapidly towards Plaza de Armas, emerging on one of the streets by the Cathedral. Turn right from here for the plaza.

If you choose to walk the route in reverse and trek from Sacsayhuaman to Tambo Machay, you will need to retrace your steps, hail a bus or *colectivo* from the main road or try to flag down a taxi.

THE SACRED VALLEY

The road north from Cusco climbs up to a pass, undulates across the pampa and then descends dramatically into the spectacular, fertile Urubamba Valley, which is also known as the **Valle Sagrado** (Sacred Valley).

The mighty river that flows through the valley was considered sacred by the Incas. Upstream from Pisac it is known as the Vilcanota, whilst downstream it tends to be referred to as the Urubamba. The region is dotted with historic sites and archaeological ruins, signifying the importance of the valley to both the Incas and the conquistadors. The Incas built their palaces, religious centres and retreats alongside this giant tributary of the Amazon: highlights include the citadels at Pisac and Ollantaytambo, but less well-known sites such as Salineras and Moray are also here to be discovered.

The region is considered sacred because of its vital importance to Cusco as a source of food and grain. Quechua legend also holds that when the sun sets it slips through the underworld beneath the Urubamba, where it draws deeply from the chill waters and rises the following morning refreshed. A separate legend claims that the earthly Urubamba is a mirror for the celestial river of the Milky Way, and that the two flow into one another.

The area is rich in history so it's worth allocating several days to explore it fully. Most of the travel agencies in Cusco offer day or half-day trips to a number of sites and traditional markets in the valley, although you are often better off tackling these under your own steam and at your own pace. Many of the towns and villages throughout the Sacred Valley are set up to receive visitors and there are plenty of places to stay and linger. There are also several Inca trails and more recent paths cut into the flanks of the valley. For inspiration look for Charles Brod's *Apus & Incas* in one of the bookshops in Cusco. In order to access most of the sites though you will need a Visitor's Ticket (see box p153).

Pisac

Pisac, which is named after the Quechua for partridge (*pisaca*), lies 32km northeast of Cusco. Built by Viceroy Toledo, the man responsible for crushing the

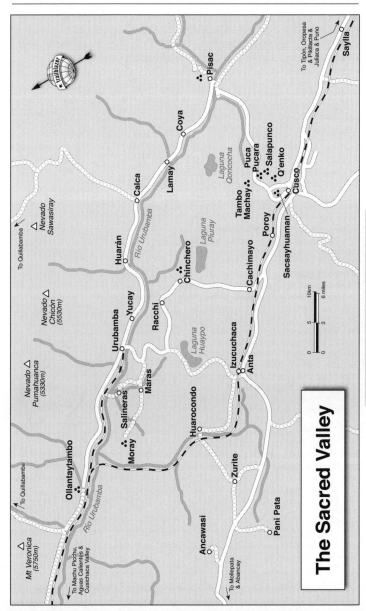

To Quillabamba

△ Nevado Sawasiray

Pisac

Coya

Lamay

Calca

Rio Urubamba

Laguna Qoricocha

Puca Pucara

Tambo Machay

Salapunco

Q'enko

Cusco

To Tipon, Oropesa & Pikillacta & Juliaca & Puno

Saylla

Poroy

Sacsayhuaman

Huarán

Chinchero

Laguna Piuray

Cachimayo

Yucay

Racchi

Urubamba

Nevado Chicon (5530m)

Nevado Pumahuanca (5330m)

To Quillabamba

Laguna Huaypo

Izcuchaca

Anta

Maras

Salineras

Moray

Huarocondo

Zurite

Ancawasi

Pani Pata

To Mollepata & Abancay

Mt Veronica (5750m)

Ollantaytambo

Rio Urubamba

To Machu Picchu, Aguas Calientes & Cusichaca Valley

The Sacred Valley

0   5   10km
0   3   6 miles

AROUND CUSCO

trailblazer

last Incas, on the site of an Inca settlement, the village is divided into two parts. On the valley floor sits the colonial village with its traditional Andean markets, whilst high above on a spur stands the citadel, a lofty Inca site set above a series of giant sweeping terraces that presides magisterially over the valley.

Services

Lively, traditional **markets** in Pisac are held on Plaza de Armas. The most significant one takes place on Sunday, when you can see traditionally dressed locals buying and selling crops, foodstuffs and craftwork, and smaller affairs on Tuesday and Thursday. This is an ideal opportunity to pick up a well-made souvenir; the ceramics and rugs here are particularly high quality though they're not the cheapest. Locals pack the plaza early on and the chaotic scene unfolds throughout the morning, before easing down around lunchtime.

There is an **ATM** (cashpoint) on Plaza de Armas.

Where to stay

There are a few options if you are tempted to stay in Pisac: *Hospedaje Beho* (☎ 203001), 50m north of Plaza de Armas, on the path to the ruins, is a small shop offering simple bed and breakfast (US$10/15, sgl/dbl, com) in rooms set around a courtyard and garden; *Hospedaje Familiar Semana Wasi* (☎ 203018) on the eastern edge of the plaza has basic but clean rooms (US$11/15, sgl/dbl); *Pisac Inn* (☎ 203062, 🖳 www.pisacinn.com) in the south-west corner of the square has an attractive courtyard, bright, bold hand-painted murals, a relaxed ambience and renovated rooms (s/143/182, sgl/dbl, att) as well as a **restaurant** (see Where to eat) and a natural rock-heated sauna, making this the best bet in a central location.

A little further out are two smarter outfits. The first, *Paz y Luz* (☎ 203204, 🖳 www.pazyluzperu.com; s/110/170/240 sgl/dbl/tpl, suites for s/220, breakfast), is 1km east of the centre, close to the river, with a homely feel, a well-kept garden and impressive views of the surrounding hills.

The expat owner also offers healing courses drawn from Andean and international traditions, meditation classes, Reiki and yoga sessions.

The other one is *Royal Inka Hotel Pisac* (☎ 203064, 🖳 www.royalinka hotel.com; US$58/80/100, sgl/dbl/tpl, breakfast) set in a converted hacienda and boasting its own restaurant, bar, swimming pool, sauna and tennis courts. The hotel also has bicycles for rent. The hotel is part of a chain with other branches in Cusco (see p171).

Where to eat

Should you get hungry, there is a giant *Clay Oven Bakery* on Mariscal Castilla that is used to bake traditional flatbreads and empanadas or sometimes to roast guinea pig. Alternatively, there are several decent **cafés** adjacent to the plaza on which the market is held.

Laid-back *Mullu* stands on the 2nd floor of a house opposite the church and has a rickety balcony from which to watch the activity whilst enjoying a selection of juices and smoothies, sandwiches and other Novoandina snacks. There's also an **art gallery** downstairs. Close by is *Doña Clorinda*, a café which serves mostly Peruvian staples.

The Blue Llama is good for coffee, breakfast, juices and sandwiches; these can be consumed on the 1st floor balcony overlooking the square. They also have a tasty range of vegetarian dishes and a daily menu at s/19. *Ulrike's Café* has a rooftop terrace, wi-fi and book exchange although the coffee and cakes are better reasons to visit. They too have a good selection of vegetarian food and a daily menu (s/17).

Cuchara de Palo, in Pisac Inn, is a very good restaurant; it serves more café staples than available elsewhere and specializes in Novoandina cuisine.

Transport

Buses to Cusco leave from close to the bridge outside the main centre; services operate roughly every quarter of an hour up until around 8pm, the journey takes up to an hour and the fare is s/3-5.

Pisac ruins (see map p198) The **citadel** is open 7am-5.30pm and entry is with a Visitor's Ticket (see box p153). Guides charge US$5 for a tour of the ruins. It is a large site and you should allow a couple of hours to explore the terraces, water ducts, ruins and hidden chambers as well as to take in the superb views of the valley, the patchwork of patterned fields, sheer cliffs and jagged ridges.

These ruins, some of the most spectacular in the Sacred Valley, are thought to have been built during the reign of Pachacutec. Narrow paths edge above steep drops and have to pass through **giant stone archways** and a short stretch of **tunnel** to reach the ceremonial centre at the heart of which stands a rare intact **Intihuatana** – a sacred sculpted rock or 'hitching post of the sun', the vast majority of which were decapitated by the conquistadors. A number of tombs have been uncovered in the cliff faces behind the site, on the far side of the Qitamayo Gorge, but have been plundered and are now closed to visitors.

The stiff climb up to the site from the valley floor takes 1-1½ hours. If you aren't already acclimatized to the altitude you will have to take it even more slowly. From the market in the heart of the village pick up the path to the north of the square, which sets off west of the church.

After 10 minutes the path forks. The upper branch is a longer, gentler ascent alongside the Rio Quitamayo to **Hanan Pisac**, the northernmost sector of the site. The lower branch crosses the river and climbs more directly and aggressively through a set of terraces to the lookout post above the valley, from where it is a short walk to the heart of the site and the Intihuatana. If you'd rather not walk, a 15-minute taxi ride from Pisac to the ruins costs s/15-20. Alternatively you can hire horses in the village (look around the plaza) and ride to the top for s/10 per person.

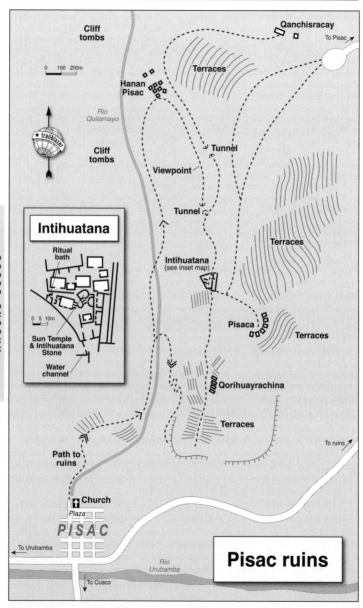

Cliff tombs

Qanchisracay

To Pisac

Terraces

0   100   200m

Hanan Pisac

Río Quitamayo

Cliff tombs

trailblazer

Tunnel

Viewpoint

Tunnel

Terraces

Intihuatana

Ritual bath

Intihuatana (see inset map)

0 5 10m

Sun Temple & Intihuatana Stone

Water channel

Pisaca

Terraces

Qorihuayrachina

Terraces

To ruins

Path to ruins

Church

Plaza

PISAC

To Urubamba

Río Urubamba

Pisac ruins

To Cusco

AROUND CUSCO

Chinchero

This small town north-west of Cusco is set amidst the Anta plains, overlooking the Sacred Valley. The village mostly comprises adobe houses, but there is also a split-level plaza at the top of a steep winding street, with an impressive Inca wall inset with large trapezoidal niches separating the two sections. Beyond here there are also **Inca remains and terraces** (7am-5.30pm; Visitor's Ticket). Further down the valley there are also interesting examples of channels and stairs cut into the rocks.

The attractive **colonial church**, built on the upper level of the plaza and dating from the early 17th century, was constructed on Inca foundations and has been unusually decorated inside with red and blue floral patterns. It also has paintings from the Cusco School. The colourful **Sunday market** (crafts as well as local produce) is worth coming for as it attracts fewer tourists than the Pisac markets and is considered to be more traditional.

Where to stay

There are very few places to stay in Chinchero. Your best bet, other than a handful of rather basic hospedajes, is *La Casa de Barro* (☎ 306031; US$40/55/70, sgl/dbl/tpl, breakfast), a modern hotel with hot water, a bar and its own restaurant.

However, Peru Treks & Adventure (see p183), in partnership with Andean Travel Web (see box p43), have a well-established **homestay** programme, where you can stay with a local family (s/20 per person). Facilities at the house are generally very basic and the family only speak Quechua and Spanish, but you are able to gain a brief insight into their daily lives. Contact the agency to arrange a visit.

❏ **New Cusco Airport proposal**

The latest controversial project to raise its head in Peru's pursuit of growth and development is the decision to relocate the main airport for Cusco from the city to the high plain adjacent to Chinchero. The airport in Cusco is deemed to have served its purpose, largely because it can't accommodate international flights. The land it currently stands on is also prime real estate in a city that struggles for space because of the natural barriers to expansion all around it. The idea of moving the airport has been mooted for years but few thought it would be allowed to proceed. However, in 2012 it was announced as a done deal and large amounts of money as compensation were paid to a handful of communities on whose farmland the airport will be constructed. Other inhabitants on the vast open area aren't scheduled to receive anything.

The high-volume airport won't start to be built until 2015 and isn't scheduled for completion for four years but the impact on the region could be colossal; the wild, empty plain will be tragically developed and the views over the Chincheros plain to Mt Veronica past lakes and fields will be impacted not only by the airport itself but also all the ancillary buildings and developments that will inevitably follow. Whether the airport, which will be 400m higher (a lot at these altitudes), will work as an international destination remains to be seen. The pampa here is also often cold and obscured with cloud, conditions that hardly suit large aircraft, making the project and choice of location seem even riskier. Opponents have proposed using Pampa de Ante instead as it's several hundred metres lower, closer to Cusco and much less damaging to local communities. Currently the suggestion has fallen on deaf ears.

Transport
To return to Cusco catch the bus (about s/2-4; 1hr) from the main road. Take any bus that cross the high pampa rather than those that go to Cusco via Pisac.

Urubamba

This sprawling transport hub at the junction of the roads from Pisac and Chinchero is often a necessary stepping stone to somewhere else in the Sacred Valley. Urubamba's not a particularly attractive town, although it has a palm-filled plaza and grand colonial church, but the setting is magnificent, beneath a set of fine snow-capped peaks.

Many of the **adventure activities** run by agencies in Cusco (see box pp184-5), such as white-water rafting, hot air-ballooning and horse riding, begin from Urubamba. It also hosts a local **market** one block west of the plaza and is home to a number of artisans including weavers, ceramicists, potters, sculptors and artists. It is quite possible to spend half a day wandering about the **studios and workshops** watching the workers create their wares. One of the most interesting is Seminario-Behar Ceramic Studio (☎ 201002, 🖥 www.ceramicaseminario .com; open daily; free), at Av Berriózabal 450; it specializes in producing ceramics using pre-Colombian techniques. World renowned, the studio produces exquisite but expensive pieces. There are three **ATMs** here.

Where to stay
There are plenty of hotels in Urubamba but also some cheaper places.

Quinta los Geranios (☎ 201093), Cabo Conchatupa, has clean, bright rooms (s/45/60/70, sgl/dbl/tpl), a garden and an open-air restaurant. *Hostal Urubamba* (☎ 201062; s/20/30 sgl/dbl, com; s/30/40 sgl/dbl, att) on Jirón Bolognesi, one block east of Plaza de Armas.

Many of the **hotels** are lined up along the main road running along the south-western edge of the town. Most luxurious is *Tambo del Inka* (☎ 58 1777, 🖥 www.liber tador.com.pe; US$220, dbl, att), Av Ferrocarril, which has large colonial-style rooms in expansive grounds and a world-class spa. There's also a private railway station in the grounds where the PeruRail service to Machu Picchu stops. The grounds are spacious and attractive and service is exemplary.

Just west of town is the charming *Sol y Luna Lodge Spa* (☎ 201620, 🖥 www .hotelsolyluna.com; US$242/242/320/393, sgl/dbl/tpl/quad, breakfast), which has luxury bungalows set in a pleasant garden full of eucalyptus and cypress trees, its own restaurant that hosts folk shows, tennis courts and a spa. The hotel's **activity centre**, Wayra (🖥 www.wayrasacredvalley .com) organizes horse-riding with Peruvian Paso ponies, mountain-biking, paragliding and white-water rafting.

On the road to Ollantaytambo, 3km from Urubamba, is a handful of colourful, rustic cottages complete with small kitchen, terrace and balcony, to rent at *K'uychi Rumi* (☎ 201169, 🖥 www.urubamba.com; s/400/440/610, sgl/dbl/tpl); cottages that can sleep up to six people cost s/850.

San Agustín Urubamba (☎ 201444, 🖥 www.hotelessanagustin.com.pe; US$105/120/190, sgl/dbl/junior suite, breakfast) lies 1km east of town in spacious grounds and with a swimming pool, sauna and Jacuzzi. There is a 15% discount for online booking.

On the outskirts of Urubamba at **Jirón Recoleta** and part of the same chain is *San*

AROUND CUSCO

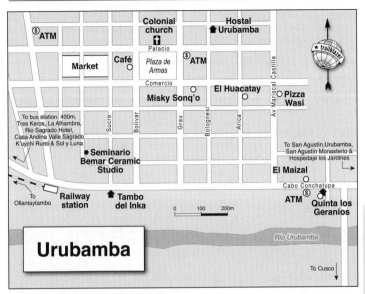

Urubamba

Agustín Monasterio de la Recoleta (☎ 201666, 🖥 www.hotelessanagustin.com .pe; US$145/170/200, sgl/dbl/junior suite, breakfast, 15% discount if booked online). Set in a converted 15th-century monastery, this striking hotel offers standard rooms and more luxurious suites but also retains the chapel and cloistered courtyards of its original incarnation.

Best of all though is *Rio Sagrado Hotel* (☎ 201631, 🖥 www.riosagradohotel .com; US$600/800, sgl/dbl), set just above the river with a tranquil garden and raft of facilities including a sauna, Jacuzzi and well-tended bar and restaurant. The rooms are extravagant and elegant, with giant panoramic windows that look out over the garden and river below.

Not quite as decadent but a very good choice at the price is *Casa Andina Valle Sagrado* (☎ 765501, 🖥 www.casa-andina .com; US$200), which is further away but very quietly sited, set back from the main road in attractive, expansive grounds. Tiers of two-storey cottages feel homely and are kitted out in traditional textiles. There's a

large restaurant and more intimate bar area along with a spa, gym and sauna. There's even a planetarium on site, although this isn't open all year-round.

Hospedaje Los Jardines (☎ 201331), Jr Convención 459, has a handful of rooms around a pretty garden. Rooms cost US$30/ 38 sgl/dbl with breakfast for US$3.

Where to eat

If you're not eating in your hotel and want to head out for food, there's a *café* on the western side of the plaza. Just to the east of the plaza is *Misky Sonq'o* where you can buy breakfast, toasties and other snacks.

There are a few **pizza restaurants** on Av Mariscal Castilla, the best of which is *Pizza Wasi*; it offers lasagne and ravioli in addition to the standard fare.

Some of the best food is at *El Huacatay* (🖥 www.elhuacatay.com), Jr Arica 620, a smart atmospheric place that serves great Novoandina staples with a contemporary flourish.

On the main road you'll find the rustic *El Maizal* which also serves Novoandina dishes from an extensive buffet. Alternatively, head to **Tres Keros**, 500m west of town on the main road, where the chef smokes his own trout and serves a range of steaks and Novoandina dishes.

Just over a kilometre further on is **La Alhambra**, a buffet joint popular with tour groups who descend on its gardens over lunchtime, lured by the good-quality food and pleasant environment.

❏ **Hugh Thomson describes living in the small market town of Urubamba**
'While writing a book on Peru, I wanted to find a quiet base where I could live with my family. Cuzco itself does not have the healthiest climate for kids, as the high mountain bowl can trap the car pollution and they can find the altitude hard, whereas the town of Urubamba seemed more easy going and had a good school. I remembered the American traveller Ephraim George Squier's comments in the 19th century:

Although only 2500 feet lower than the Cuzco Basin, the Yucay [Urubamba] Valley, protected on all sides, enjoys a much more benign climate, similar to that of Nimes and other parts of the south of France. Both healthy and fertile, easily accessible from the capital, and with a vegetation unrivalled in the Sierra, this sweet and tranquil valley, surrounded by some of the highest mountains of the Continent, quickly became the favourite place of recreation for the Incas. The soil is rich and the climate, in spite of the fact that the Valley is enclosed by high snow-capped mountains, is soft and agreeable. A more beautiful place than this does not exist in all of the Andes...'

We found a house on the outskirts of Urubamba, at a place called K'uychi Rumi which means 'rainbow stone' in Quechua: the houses shared a communal garden, a riot of hibiscus, abutilon, poinsettias and roses, with arum lilies growing alongside the small irrigation ditches that ran through the property; the owners, architect Carlos Rey and his wife, Claudia, had also introduced some pre-Columbian plants – *polylepis* trees and *quinoa*. A line of yellow broom led along paths to a large stand of eucalyptus at the far end of the property where the children would spend many happy hours swinging over the stream; immediately beyond rose the ravine up to Pumahuanca, one of the passes leading to the Amazon.

The rhythm of such small market towns had always appealed to me and I now quickly found it seductive: the Post Office that never seemed to open; the old men moving around the benches in the Plaza to keep getting the sun – I overheard one telling another: 'get it written down on paper because you know that words can be blown away by the wind'; a shoe shine boy playing his Gameboy while he waited for customers; the café on the corner of the square called, with the utmost simplicity, 'The Corner Café'.

But Urubamba was a mountain as well as a market town: like a settlement in the old West where the main drag is only a temporary slowing of a longer route through the wilderness, the high street past the gas station turned into a country lane which led directly up to the Chicón glacier.

We rode up there sometimes from the town, picking our way through the cobbled streets nervously as the odd mototaxi could shoot without warning from an alley and scare the horses, the drivers treating them as if they were errant pedestrians. By riding, we could get glimpses over the high patio walls of hidden courtyards, orchards and market gardens. The surrounding fields were a reminder too that Urubamba was organized not around its streets but around its water supply: there was a complicated series of irrigation canals, which could be diverted at different points during the day under a tightly regulated system. Woe betide the *campesino* who 'forgot' to divert a canal back

Transport
Minibuses to Cusco leave throughout the day going via Pisac or Chinchero respectively (about s/5; 2 hrs). The journey to Chincherro costs approximately s/2-4.

Quicker *colectivos* depart from Calle Pavitos. Urubamba bus station is just to the west of the town, on the main road. There's also a tourist train service between Urubamba and Aguas Calientes (see p372).

to his neighbour at the appointed hour – or for that matter the three-year-old boy like ours, Leo, who enjoyed damming or diverting them at 'inappropriate' moments.

Within a few weeks of arriving we were invited to a local wedding and realized that we already knew most of the congregation. The bride and groom emerged from the town hall registry office to a full band playing in the town square, a band in which the bridegroom usually played himself.

I had met Joyo several times at the Corner Café, eating empanadas with a saxophone slung over his shoulder. He was an architect who had travelled in France, been an active revolutionary during the 1968 Sorbonne uprising, and had since settled in Urubamba with Lola, his French girlfriend and now bride, to play music; they were getting married to regularize both their own nationalities and those of their adopted children.

Unfortunately, as Joyo had told me, the Peruvian authorities had made a mistake and thought initially they wanted to get divorced, not married. Peruvian bureaucracy, once started, will move in only one direction: Joyo's protests that they could not get divorced because they weren't married had fallen on deaf ears; it had taken six months of bureaucratic confusion before their 'divorce' had come through and they could get 'remarried'.

Joyo unslung his sax and was leading his own wedding procession around the town square and up to their house for a wedding party that would last all day and all of the night. One of his band had played with the Grateful Dead. There were fond memories of the time Keith Richards had passed through with the Stones on one of their Peruvian adventures and busked in the Corner Café (it had been a country that had always appealed to Mick Jagger, not least because when in the Amazon to film *Fitzcarraldo*, no one had recognized him).

Indeed over the months that we lived there, I began to realize that there was a bohemian diaspora around Urubamba of pony-tailed hippies and Peace Corps veterans of a certain age, who had fetched up here in the cheap land and low regulations of the '70s, when dope could be grown in your back garden. The valley had changed considerably since then. In recent years the beginnings of the tourist boom engulfing Peru had spilled over from Cuzco and hotels were being built at an alarming rate, usually with our landlord Carlos Rey as architect. There were also many exiled Limeños, like Carlos, who had moved here for the good life. Some had put Jacuzzis into their haciendas. Even the taxi drivers now had mobile phones.

It intrigued me that the picture I had always had of Urubamba from afar – the small market town in the heart of the Sacred Valley, the grain basket of the Incas – should have such a touch of Laurel Canyon about it. Of course there were still plenty of local villagers still keeping horses, minding their small plots and threatening to shoot the neighbours if the irrigation canal wasn't turned over to them at the appointed hour. But just when you least expected it, with the wood-smoke drifting past the eucalyptus stands and the sun setting on the Chicón glacier, a four-wheel drive would flash past blaring out rap music'.

Hugh Thomson wrote, while based in Urubamba,
Cochineal Red: Travels through Ancient Peru

Around Urubamba

● **Salineras** West of Urubamba, high on the flank of the valley, is the unusual site of Salineras (9am-4.30pm; s/7) where mineral-rich, salty water from a hot spring higher up the valley is channelled into thousands of large, flat, shallow pans and allowed to evaporate so that salt is produced. This is then collected intensively by hand, just as it has been for hundreds of years, and continues to provide work for the locals.

To get here it's a 45-minute walk from Urubamba, or catch a bus (s/2) back to Chinchero and ask to be dropped off at the junction to Maras (see map p195). You may then be able to pick up a taxi from the junction to the site, otherwise walk west for about 2½ miles and take the right-hand track that cuts north across the pampa for a further three miles to descend to the site (1hr).

From the site it's possible to descend the levels of salt pans to emerge at the bottom; walk down a narrow valley until you reach the Urubamba River, turn right and walk upstream a short while to reach a bridge. Cross this and climb through some houses to reach the main road, from where it's easy to pick up a lift to Urubamba and beyond.

● **Maras** A shabby colonial-era village that once supported a thriving community. Evidence of past glory can be seen in the decorated stone arches and intricate lintels that still adorn some of the run-down houses. When the nearby silver mines ran dry, the town was virtually abandoned and has been allowed to become a poor, rural community. There is very little left here except for a barely standing colonial church, a dusty, empty plaza and a set of market stands with nothing to sell.

● **Moray** If you were to continue west from Maras on an unpaved, dirt track for 9km though, you would come to the unusual, atmospheric site of Moray (dawn to dusk; s/10). Three large concentric depressions in the earth have been cut and shaped into circular terraces of varying sizes. Hidden from sight until you are virtually on top of them, these giant amphitheatres are very striking. If you clamber up the hill behind the deepest depression you get a view of all three amphitheatres and can see the entire site in context. Thought to be an Inca farm, this extraordinary place was used to test the effects of altitude on different plants. The deepest depression is around 30m from rim to floor and temperatures within the bowl can vary by up to 10°C. It is thought that the terraces, built over containing walls filled with fertile earth and watered by complex irrigation systems, each had their own micro-climate enabling the Incas to grow more than 250 species of plants.

If you don't fancy walking all the way up to the site, catch a Chinchero-bound bus (s/2 from Urubamba) and ask to be dropped off at the road to Maras. It's a 2½-mile walk from here to Maras (1½hrs) and a further four miles to Moray (2½hrs), although you may be able to hitch a lift or pick up a taxi from the junction (typically s/5 to Maras and s/20 for a return trip to Moray).

Ollantaytambo   [see map p206 & p208]

The historic town of Ollantaytambo stands at the far end of the Urubamba Valley, 68km from Cusco. Here the fertile valley narrows and the river flows into a gorge. In this strategic spot the Inca Pachacutec built the fortress and religious complex of Ollantaytambo having subjugated the valley's former residents. The massive ruins set above a compact town are some of the most striking and impressive in the whole of the Sacred Valley.

The town itself is a relaxing, easy-going alternative to Cusco and a good way of escaping some of the bustle associated with the larger city. However, since PeruRail started using Ollantaytambo as the start and end point for its train services to Machu Picchu, the town periodically becomes congested with lorries and buses that battle through the narrow streets; the latter are trying to meet the trains and the passengers they disgorge. The resulting queues can choke the access roads and main plaza – they were never designed to accommodate such large, or so many, vehicles – spoiling the relaxed Andean ambience here.

It is about 150 metres from the plaza to the ruins (see p207).

The old town The photogenic town set in the shadow of the illustrious ruins is one of the finest examples of Inca town planning. In most towns the original Inca streets and housing have been knocked down and built over, but in Ollantaytambo there are still plenty of original examples of each. The town is laid out in a grid and the corners of the main streets are marked by giant stone blocks. The Incas arranged their towns in communal blocks called *canchas*, which housed a number of families. The double-jamb doorways to these canchas indicate that the residents must have been part of the Inca elite. Simpler structures that would have belonged to poorer, less-important citizens employed to work for the Incas can be found in the northern part of the town.

El Museo CATCCO (☎ 204204; daily 9am-7pm; entrance by donation) is one block west of Plaza de Armas on Patacalle. Inside this well-kept museum dedicated to ethnography and regional history are superb displays of historical and cultural artefacts. Local artisans, weavers and ceramicists also work on the premises; their wares are on offer for sale in the museum shop or in the Casa Ecologica shop next door to the restaurant Mayupata. Guides trained by the museum can be hired here and they can also arrange tours of the surrounding area. For a fascinating, detailed examination of the Inca stonework here, read *Inca Architecture and Construction at Ollantaytambo* by Jean-Pierre Protzen (1993).

The **market** consists of souvenir stalls for tourists and **Mercado Central** sells food and goods for the locals. There is a small **tourist information point** on the plaza and an **ATM**, though it is expensive to withdraw money here.

Where to stay
Hostal Ollanta (☎ 204116; US$7.50/15, sgl/dbl, com) on the southern side of the plaza has a good location and rooms which are a decent size, albeit rather rudimentary.

Better though is *Casa de Wow* (☎ 204010, 🖳 www.casadewow.com; s/45/70/90, sgl/dbl/tpl, com, s/100 dbl, att) a couple of minutes' walk away from the plaza on a quiet side street, which is great value and

very friendly. Run by a creative local, the place is decorated in traditional style and has beds built by the owner himself. There's wi-fi throughout and a pretty roof terrace as well.

Hostal Munay Tika (☎ 204111, 🖳 www.munaytika.com), Av Ferrocarril 118, on the road to the station, is an attractive guesthouse with a bar and sauna as well as quiet, spacious rooms (US$40/50, sgl/dbl, breakfast) with access to the kitchen for guests. Nearby, *Las Orquídeas* (☎ 204032) is a reasonably priced hostel with basic rooms (US$25/35, sgl/dbl, breakfast) and a pleasant courtyard in which to lounge.

On the road between the ruins and Plaza de Armas is the excellent *KB Tambo* (☎ 204091, 🖳 www.kbperu.com), which has good-sized comfortable rooms. The garden-view rooms in the older part of the building are US$22/44/66 (sgl/dbl/tpl, att) whilst Superior rooms with larger windows and better views cost US$29/58/87 (sgl/dbl/tpl, att). There's wi-fi throughout as well as a pretty garden and roof-top deck complete with bar and Jacuzzi along with views of the ruins and a restaurant.

The excellent North American-owned *El Albergue* (☎ 204014, 🖳 www.elalbergue.com; US$70/100, sgl/dbl, att, breakfast, Superior rooms slightly more), Casilla 784 Cusco (entrance on the platform of the station), has 16 elegant rooms set around a courtyard, a sauna and a shop/gallery selling handicrafts. Good discounts are available during the low season. The building is a characterful cottage, adjacent to the platform. Handy for the trains, it is some 800m to the town though.

The modern terracotta-coloured *Hotel Pakaritampu* (☎ 204020, 🖳 www.pakaritampu.com; US$166/173/221, sgl/dbl/tpl, att, buffet breakfast), on the road just up from the station, is comfortable and friendly, has a bar and restaurant as well as internet service for visitors and a TV room.

Hostal Sauce (☎ 204044, 🖳 www.hostalsauce.com.pe; US$89/98/145, sgl/dbl/tpl, att, breakfast) has the best location, overlooking the Inca ruins and close to the main plaza. The rooms are comfortable though service is sometimes brusque.

Where to eat

The Coffee Tree on the western side of Plaza de Armas has a range of coffees and cakes. Also on Plaza de Armas is *Esquina*,

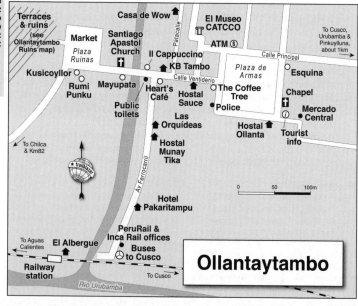

which is the perfect spot for a plum brownie, hot chocolate and chance to watch the activity in the square.

Hearts Café (🖥 www.heartscafe.org), on Avenida Ventiderio, opens early for breakfast and specializes in vegetarian and wholefood dishes cooked with a local twist but also has a range of international dishes. The profits are ploughed back into the community and go towards children's and women's projects in the Sacred Valley.

For coffee and breakfasts also try *Il Cappuccino*, just before the bridge, which offers a slightly more up-market service. The same owners run *Kusicoyllor*, on Plaza Ruinas, which dishes up pizza and pasta in generous portions.

Set back a little is *Rumi Punku*, which serves superior dishes including great steaks with mash and blue cheese sauce and generous burritos. *Mayupata*, on Jr Convención by the bridge, serves good Peruvian food in addition to international dishes and has an open fireplace and bar overlooking the river.

Transport

From here there are **trains** to Aguas Calientes. Having caught the train back from Aguas Calientes it is very easy to pick up an onward bus to Cusco. See pp370-1 for details of the tourist train service from Cusco to Ollantaytambo. The station is about a 10- to 15-minute walk from Plaza de Armas.

Buses and **colectivos** depart for Urubamba (s/1), Chilca and Km82 from the main plaza and outside the station. Direct buses to Cusco (s/10) depart from outside the station, where they meet the incoming trains. To avoid the scrum you may be better taking a colectivo to Urubamba and catching a bus on to Cusco from there.

Ollantaytambo ruins   [see map p208]

The daunting **fortress** was described by Pedro Pizarro as 'so well fortified that it was a thing of horror'. It was to this mighty castle that Manco Inca retreated following his uprising. Pursued by the Spanish, he holed up in the fortress high above the surrounding plain and faced the conquistadors. After two days of heavy fighting he forced the Spanish to retreat, the first time that the colonial army had been bested in combat by the Incas. Manco realized he wouldn't be able to maintain his superiority so close to Cusco and sadly abandoned the fortress to move over the mountains to Vilcabamba.

The fortress (7am-5.30pm; Visitor's Ticket) still looks much as it once did and it's easy to see how the Spanish would have been appalled at the prospect of throwing themselves against the 16 great walled terraces that hug the contours of the hills and bar the route up to the unassailable fortress.

More than 200 **steps** lead steeply through the terraces from the plaza below. Giant walls rise from the almost sheer cliff-faces preventing any attacker from flanking the site.

At the top of the steps stands the **unfinished Sun Temple**, which is made up of six enormous, mortarless monoliths cut from pink porphyry and mottled with orange lichen. These upright stones have been carefully fitted together aligned east to west. Double-jambed archways on the approach to this point indicate that this was a very important centre.

From the top you can see the quarry Cachicata, 3.5km south-west of the site at the foot of Yana Urco (the Black Mountain), where a huge rockfall provided loose stones of huge size. From the top of the fortress you get a very good impression of the Herculean task required to haul the stones all the way from

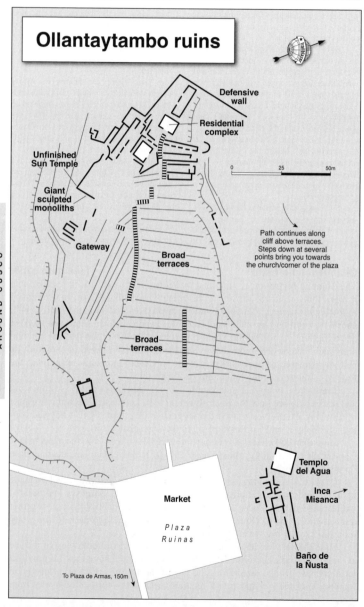

Ollantaytambo ruins

Defensive wall

Residential complex

Unfinished Sun Temple

Giant sculpted monoliths

Gateway

Broad terraces

Broad terraces

0   25   50m

Path continues along cliff above terraces. Steps down at several points bring you towards the church/corner of the plaza

Templo del Agua

Inca Misanca

Baño de la Ñusta

Market

Plaza Ruinas

To Plaza de Armas, 150m

AROUND CUSCO

the quarry to the temple. In order to cross the Urubamba, it is thought that the Incas simply diverted the river around the blocks positioned on its banks.

A handful of giant blocks, known poetically as *piedras cansadas* ('tired stones'), litter the valley floor, lying where they were presumably abandoned whilst being transported from the quarry.

Work your way along the terraces north-east and descend again to a point just behind a church set on the side of the small plaza. There are a few smaller Inca ruins here including a small temple or observatory called **Inca Misanca**, and 200m below, the **Baño de la Ñusta**, a site associated with ritual bathing and the worship of water.

Opposite the main site, on the eastern edge of Ollantaytambo, is a steep cliff known as **Pinkuylluna** (off map p206). High on this cliff-face are the remnants of a number of *qolqas* (storehouses). There is a faint path that climbs to the storehouses, but you need to be careful and should take a guide rather than set off alone.

Cusichaca Valley
Some 26km from Ollantaytambo is the Cusichaca Valley. This area has been at the heart of a series of excavations carried out by the archaeologist Ann Kendall over the last 30 years (🖳 www.cusichaca.org). The organization also pioneers integrated rural development projects in tandem with local communities, promoting the use of local resources, traditional skills and appropriate modern techniques to benefit the communities involved.

The Inca Fort **Huillca Raccay** (see box p236) was uncovered in the late 1970s before work focused on the ruins at **Patallacta** (see box p220), at the start of the classic Inca Trail. Subsequent excavation has been done in the Patacancha Valley to the north-east of Ollantaytambo.

Aguas Calientes (Pueblo Machu Picchu) [see map p211]
Officially known as Pueblo Machu Picchu, this village is very much the end of the line now that the track that used to run on to Quillabamba has been destroyed. Really just a dormitory town for the ruins themselves, it's an ugly rash in the pristine forest of the Sanctuary and has in the past been described as the 'Armpit of Peru'. The town is, however, undergoing something of a renaissance and amidst all the development work there now stands one of the finest hotels in the entire valley and a very good restaurant. Information is available from the **iPeru branch** (☎ 211104) on Av Pachacutec, in the same building as the **Machu Picchu ticket office** that sells entrance tickets to the ruins.

For a while regulation changes have meant that you can no longer buy entrance tickets for Machu Picchu upon arrival at the site itself but must buy them in advance in Aguas Calientes. Even if this situation has changed it's far better to **get your ticket in advance in Aguas Calientes** rather than waste precious time in a line at the ruins. Similarly, if you want to climb Huayna Picchu or Machu Picchu peak you must buy a ticket in advance, as these can no longer be arranged at Machu Picchu. If you are travelling with a trekking agency or tour group they should ensure that you are provided with an entrance ticket and any additional tickets. Tickets are available from the INC/Machu Picchu Cultural Centre in Aguas Calientes, which is adjacent to the main plaza in the same building as the iPeru office. The office opens at 5.15am and payment for the ticket must be in exact money only. Buy your ticket the day before – they are valid for three days from the date of purchase, but only for a single entry to the site. If you want to return to Machu Picchu you will have to buy a second ticket. Tickets are also available in Cusco (see p165).

There are plenty of **internet cafés** and **cash machines** on Av Pachacutec, around the plaza and throughout the town. Trawl the **market** adjacent to the main station for textiles, T-shirts and other souvenirs.

The **hot springs** after which the town is named comprise a series of rather pungent communal baths several minutes' walk north from town. These are open daily 5am-8.30pm and cost s/11 to visit. If you are tempted, the pools are cleanest and most pleasant first thing in the morning.

On the road to Machu Picchu it's worth visiting **Museo de Sitio Manuel Chávez Ballón – Machu Picchu Museum** (Carreterra Hiram Bingham; 10am-5pm; s/22) a small museum displaying a number of objects uncovered at Machu Picchu. There are interactive displays and a wealth of information on excavations, Inca building methods, cosmology and other cultural bits and pieces. There's also an interesting **botanical garden** here.

The trail up the mountain called **Putucusi** also starts here. Follow the railway track 250m west of the local railway station on Av Imperio (not the main station for Cusco) to pick up a steeply ascending path that climbs for two hours to the top (ask at Gringo Bill's if you're having trouble locating the path). Parts of the trail have long sections of fixed wooden ladder that aren't for the faint-hearted, even though they are solid and in good condition, and in others you may have to scramble. If it has been raining the path can be very slippery and treacherous. The views during the ascent and the panoramic sight of Machu Picchu when it is revealed at the top are stupendous, though.

Where to stay

Cheapest of all is the *municipal campground* (s/15 per person; cold water shower) about 1km downhill from the centre of town towards Machu Picchu and adjacent to the bridge over the Urubamba. Take great care of your possessions here.

In an alley off Pachacutec, is *Hospedaje Joe*, where rooms can cost as little as s/20/40 (sgl/dbl, com). On the plaza just before Gringo Bill's, *Hospedaje Bromelias* (☎ 211145) is rough and ready but cheap as a result (US$7.50/12, sgl/dbl, att). *Hospedaje los Caminantes*, at Av Imperio de los Incas 140, alongside the railway tracks, is clean and friendly enough to make up for the basic rooms (US$7.50/15, sgl/dbl, att) and noisy location.

For other cheaper accommodation, head up the hill towards the hot springs; this street, Av Pachacutec, is dotted with places to stay including the efficient and comfortable *Ima Sumac* (☎ 232111; US$20/35 sgl/dbl, breakfast).

A mid-range option close to the train tracks is *Machupicchu Hostal* (☎ 211034; US$55/65/70 sgl/dbl/tpl) which is tidy and efficient, boasts a pretty interior courtyard and has rooms which are good value but with paper-thin walls.

The bohemian *Rupa Wasi* (☎ 211101, 🖥 www.rupawasi.net; US$69-109, dbl, breakfast) is a rustic eco-lodge hidden up Huanacare, a small alley off Collasuyo. Ridiculously laid-back it's a haven for

Aguas Calientes

To hot springs

La Cabaña Hostal

Ima Sumac

Govinda

El Manu

Clave de Sol (Chez Maggy)

Inca Yupanqui

Wiracocha

Hostal Wiracocha Inn

Football pitch

Av Pachacutec

El Mapi Hotel Machu Picchu

Av Hermanos Ayar

Walsicha Pub

Indio Feliz & Captain Bar

Hotel Machu Picchu Inn

Yupanqui

Hospedaje Joe

Rupa Wasi & Tree House

Hospedaje Bromelias

Gringo Bill's

Av Pachacutec

Centro Cultural Machu Picchu iPerú & INC office

Pueblo Viejo

María Capac

Market

Railway station

Machu Picchu Pueblo Hotel & Café Inkaterra

Plaza de Armas

Collasuyo

Colla Raymi

Sinchi Roca

Ticket office & buses to Machu Picchu

Toto's House

To Putucusi

Hospedaje Los Caminantes

Local railway station

Police station

Train ticket office

Av Imperio de los Incas

Hostal Presidente

Machu Picchu Hostal

To Municipal Campground, Museo de Sitio Manuel Chávez Ballón & Machu Picchu

Hatuchay Machu Picchu Hotel

Río Urubamba

trailblazer

AROUND CUSCO

50m

25

0

those who just want to chill out, although cooking classes, birdwatching trips and other treks can be arranged by the knowledgeable, friendly owners as well.

Hostal Wiracocha Inn (☎ 211088, 💻 www.wiracochainn.com; from US$65/65/85, sgl/dbl/tpl, att), on Calle Wiracocha, is small and helpful. The rooms, with large windows and good views, are smart and well tended and service is good. A Junior suite costs US$120.

Gringo Bill's (☎ 211046, 💻 www.gringobills.com) is at Calle Colla Raymi 104, just off the plaza. The place is something of an institution in Aguas Calientes and still maintains its high standards, remaining friendly, easy-going and offering reasonable value at US$97/136 (dbl/tpl, att). There's a restaurant, a bar and a rooftop Terraza Lounge; the latter is a great space to relax in or catch up with other travellers.

Also recommended are the smart *Hotel Machu Picchu Inn* (☎ 211011, 💻 mapiinn@terra.com.pe; US$105, sgl & dbl), on Pachacutec 101, amidst the hostels and cheap eateries, and the good-value *Hostal Presidente* (☎ 211065, 💻 presiden te@terra.com.pe; US$75/80/85, sgl/dbl/tpl, breakfast), situated by the railway tracks on Imperio de los Incas.

Hatuchay Machu Picchu Hotel (☎ 211201, 💻 www.hatuchayhotelsperu.com), at Carretera Puente Ruinas 4, is a smart, modern place opposite the river and just down from the old station. Although soulless and lacking any real character, the rooms are luxurious and have balconies (US$250/270/450, sgl/dbl/tpl, att). Buffet breakfast, dinner and collection from the station are included in the rate.

El MaPi Hotel Machu Picchu (Lima office ☎ 01 422 6574, 💻 www.elmapihotel .com), at Pachacutec 109, is a smart, stylish hotel full of restored and recycled materials that is part of Inkaterra's more affordable arm. It's all relative though and the rooms still cost US$250. For the money, the rooms, adorned with slogans on the walls are small but the general ambience is relaxed and the restaurant is good. The bar also makes a decent pisco sour.

The top hotel is *Machu Picchu Pueblo Hotel* (reservations in Lima ☎ 01 510 0400, 💻 www.inkaterra.com), where beautiful colonial-style bungalows are set in 12 acres of exquisite, enclosing forest, five minutes' walk east from the rest of town; to get here follow the basic path next to the railway line. There is also a pool, a sauna, spa and an expensive restaurant. Room rates begin around US$430 and rise sharply depending on the style of room and the season; the Inkaterra Suite tops the bill at more than US$900.

There's also an expensive *hotel* at the ruins themselves (see p348).

La Cabaña Hostal (☎ 211048), on Av Pachacutec, is a quiet cosy place with rustic décor and a homely atmosphere. Standard/ superior rooms cost US$130/150; both rates include breakfast.

Where to eat

The best restaurant is the outstanding French-run *Indio Feliz* (☎ 211090, 💻 www .indiofeliz.com), Calle Lloque Yupanqui Lt 103. The restaurant incorporates *Captain Bar*; it's a great spot for a drink as it is decked out with antiques and objects representing travel, the navy and piracy. Dishes here include Urubamba trout, ginger chicken, beef skewers and a wide range of delicious desserts. The wine list is well chosen and prices are reasonable.

Café Inkaterra at Machu Picchu Pueblo Hotel (see Where to stay) gives Indio Feliz a run for its money with high-class Peruvian fusion food and good views over the river.

The vast *Toto's House*, overlooking the river at the south-eastern corner of the village on Av Imperio de los Incas, offers an 'all-you-can-eat' international and Peruvian buffet for US$12, while *Pueblo Viejo*, on Pachacutec, owned by the same group, serves grilled meats and pizzas from its open wood-fired grill.

Govinda, on Pachacutec, serves good-value vegetarian food. You can also get decent veggie food at *El Manu*, which is one of the town's best-value eateries.

Cusco's Chez Maggy (see p174) has a branch at Pachacutec 156, called *Clave de*

Sol, selling decent oven-baked pizzas and other international fare.

The tiny *Tree House Restaurant* (🖥 www.rupawasitreehouse.com; Calle Huancacare 180) has just a couple of tables so it is often full but everyone has come to sample the fusion food served in an inviting setting.

For **live music** in a good atmosphere visit *Waisicha Pub* on Calle Lloque Yupanqui.

Transport
Aguas Calientes boasts two **railway stations**: the modern one, surrounded by wire fencing and policed by armed guards, serves the expensive tourist trains. The ticket office here is open from 6.30am-5.30pm.

Local trains set off from the stretch of tracks running beneath the police station, to the south of the main square. There's no indication that this is a station, for it's little more than a rail track with pizza restaurants either side. All train tickets must be bought from the ticket office (8.30am-6pm) to the east of the police station. See pp370-3 for details and timetables of the train service. This is also where the train from La Hidroeléctrica, at the end of the Santa Teresa trek, stops (see p371).

The **buses for Machu Picchu** leave from the bus 'station', just a patch of concrete where the train tracks pass over a small stream, every 15-30 minutes from 6.30am-1pm. You can buy tickets for the 20-minute journey (US$6 one way) at a concrete house near where the bus leaves.

See p348 for more information on transport from Aguas Calientes and Machu Picchu.

SOUTH AND EAST OF CUSCO

For many people the focus of a trip to Cusco is the Sacred Valley and Machu Picchu. However, there are also several fascinating ruins to see to the south and east of the city.

A paved road runs south-east from Cusco to **Sicuani**, following the upper reaches of the Río Urubamba. There are some ruins scattered across the altiplano here, indicating the spread of the Incas towards Lake Titicaca, where the road eventually arrives at Puno.

Just outside Cusco, making it virtually a suburb, stands **San Jerónimo**, which hosts an enormous fruit and veg market on Saturdays. South-east from here the valley narrows as you approach Oropesa, before which lie the ruins of Tipón and after which the ruins at Pikillacta.

Tipón (7am-5.30pm; s/10; free with Visitor's Ticket) is 25km from Cusco and 2km before Oropesa, around an hour's walk away from the main road, hidden at the head of a small valley beyond the remains of the hacienda Quispicanchi. The extensive Inca ruins here include a series of agricultural terraces, ceremonial baths, fountains and stone-lined irrigation channels. Above the last terrace a trail leads to a temple complex built around a *huaca*. An enormous reservoir collected water from a spring, which was then distributed to the terraces along a series of channels. Behind and to the left of the main site a faint trail leads to a further series of ruins and well-preserved Inca terraces that are now in use by local people. So extensive are the terraces here that archaeologists have suggested the site may have been an experimental farm, much like Moray (see p204).

Historians counter that Tipón could have been a palace but the accounts left by chroniclers make it difficult to say whose it was. Garcilaso de la Vega believed that it was the royal house of Viracocha whose father, Yáhuar Huácac, was defeated by the Chancas. Viracocha stood up to and later defeated the Chancas, and was subsequently crowned Inca in place of his father. Garcilaso wrote that, 'It was determined that the son, as most of the court decided, would be the head of the kingdom; and to avoid riots and civil wars, they accepted everything the prince wanted. After it was agreed, they obtained a Royal House, between Muyna and Quepicancha, in a pleasant place with all the gifts, fields, gardens and other royal amusements for hunting and fishing.' Other chroniclers, such as Pedro Cieza de León and Juan de Betanzos, claim that it was actually Viracocha's son Pachacutec who defeated the Chancas after his father and older brother Inca Urcon had fled Cusco.

Further on from Tipón are the villages of **Oropesa** and **Huacarpay**; the latter stands on the shores of Laguna Huacarpay. Dotted around the lake are several pre-Columbian sites. Foremost of these is **Pikillacta** (7am-5.30pm; s/10, free with Visitor's Ticket), whose name translates rather unfortunately as 'City of Fleas'. The substantial site, 32km from Cusco and 7km from Oropesa, is the largest provincial outpost of the Ayacucho-based Huari (AD600-1000) and is the only major pre-Inca site around Cusco. The large complex, which is surrounded by a defensive wall, is thought to have been a storehouse or centre for collecting tributes and supplies. There were also adobe buildings and *tambos* here, many of them more than one storey tall, and many whose rough walls were treated with lime. Unusually the doors to these buildings appear to be on the 1st floor and in theory they must have been entered via ladders. Not much is known of the history of the site, but the small turquoise figurines in Museo Inka (see pp158-9) were found here. The Incas subsequently modified the site and possibly built the aqueduct that links Pikillacta to Rumicolca.

Around 1km beyond Pikillacta stands the beautifully crafted, enormous Inca archway and defensive passage at **Rumicolca** (open all day; free). Built on top of an original Huari site, the Inca stonework is vastly superior to the cruder, original construction. The archway itself rears up from the altiplano in a series of four tiers and stands a full 12m/40ft above the plain. During Inca times all traffic on the road to and from Cusco had to pass through the giant, imposing archway, which acted as a checkpoint, regulating the passage of goods and people.

To get to any of these sites from Cusco catch a bus to Urcos, departing from Av de la Cultura. For Tipón ask to be dropped off at Oropesa and then walk back down the Cusco road for 2km, until you come across the signposted path to Tipón and follow this for an hour as it climbs through a gully to the ruins. For Pikillacta or Rumicolca, both of which are on the main road, ask to be dropped by the entrance to the site. Alternatively, you can catch a taxi from Cusco, or take an organized tour run by one of the agencies in town (see pp179-86).

ROUTE GUIDE & MAPS   8

Using this guide

ROUTE DESCRIPTIONS

Directions in the following chapter are shown as an instruction to go left or right and as a compass point. For instance, if the instruction stated 'turn right (west)', it would indicate that west is to your right.

Direction

The trails described in this book are laid out as they are usually walked, from the traditional start point to the typical finish point. In a number of instances it is possible to walk the trail in either direction. The exceptions are that you are not allowed to start at Machu Picchu and hike the Inca Trail in reverse, meaning that you can't finish at Km104, Km88, Km82, Chilca (Km77) or Mollepata. The Choquequirao trek is typically done as a there-and-back hike along the same route, although it is possible to connect it to other treks and complete a linear hike, finishing at Machu Picchu or Vilcabamba.

ROUTE MAP NOTES [See pp28-9 for route planning map]

Scale and walking times

Most of the trekking maps in this guide are drawn at the same scale, roughly 1:50,000 (20mm = 1km; 1¼ inches = one mile). Many of the trails are uphill and downhill so the length of a trek is not an accurate reflection of the time it will take you to complete. The times included on the maps are there only as a guideline. They refer to **walking times only** and do not include any stops for breaks or food. To calculate the total time it will take to complete a section you will need to make allowances for these and add on a few minutes. Overall you may find that you need to **add between 10% and 30%** depending your walking speed and average length of time taken at each break.

Gradient arrows

There are gradient arrows marked on the trekking maps throughout the book. The arrows point uphill; two arrows close together mean that the hill is steep, one on its own means that it is a gentler gradient. If, for example, you are walking between A (at 3100m) and B (at 3300m) and the path between the two is short and steep, it would be illustrated as follows: A – – – >> – – – B.

Place names

The Quechua names for many of the ruins and archaeological sites along the various treks can be spelt in several ways as the original language had no alphabet or written guide. The more common Hispanic versions have been used here as they appear on most maps in this form. However, there has been a movement to reclaim a lot of colonial names for the indigenous language; this has caused confusion and ensured that in some cases there are now two or three versions of a name.

Where there's the potential for confusion all names are shown so, for instance, Llactapata is also referred to as Paltallacta – but this shouldn't be confused with Patallacta (no first 'l') as that is an entirely different place.

GPS waypoints

If you're following the **Inca Trail** there's very little opportunity to get lost. The Inca Trail would be a straightforward path to follow even without being accompanied, such is the quality of the path.

❏ Inca Trail regulations explained

The Inca Trail is governed by a series of complex and convoluted regulations, which are enforced stringently. They also change frequently and prices are hiked from time to time. Before booking check the latest information with Andean Travel Web (🖳 www.andeantravelweb.com/peru) where there are links to the Spanish-language only DRCC (Direccion Regional de Cultura Cusco) website (🖳 www.machupicchu.gob .pe) showing permit availability. South American Explorers (🖳 www.saexplorers .org) also has good information.

● **Permit** The key elements to remember are that **you must have a permit before embarking on the trek to Machu Picchu**. A maximum of 500 people including guides, cooks and porters are allowed to start the trail each day. In reality this means that only around 200 tourists per day can begin the trek. This daily limit covers not only the classic Inca Trail but also the extended routes from Km77 and Km82, the Salkantay Trek that joins the Inca Trail at Huayllabamba and the two shorter routes from Km104. The result is that there is fierce competition for the permits, and in order to secure a preferred departure date you will have to **book well in advance**, especially during high season (Jun-Aug) when you should try to secure your permit five to six months ahead.

To book a permit you must use a **licensed agency** based in Peru; they are not issued directly to tourists. In order to obtain a licence, the agency must prove that they provide professional, licensed guides, good-quality camping equipment, radio equipment and first-aid supplies including oxygen. Licences are reviewed annually in February. Agencies can only take groups of up to 16 people at any one time, and must provide two or more guides for groups of more than eight people (seven on the routes from Km104).

See pp179-86 for information on arranging treks in Cusco and for a list of well-established companies with sound reputations. You will need to provide the agency with your name and passport details, and pay the entrance fee in advance. Permits are issued for an individual and are not transferable. Nor are they refundable. Once issued, it is also impossible to change the start date. Agencies have to make the booking for an entire group in one go and can't make alterations so they prefer to wait as long as

Similarly, the **Salkantay, Santa Teresa and Choquequirao** routes are easy to follow, especially if you are trekking with a licensed guide. The latter is clear because there's just a single route descending into and climbing out of a sheer valley. Should you find yourself erring from a path, the chances are a steep drop or a thick forest will deflect you back in the right direction.

Given this, modern Wainwrights may scoff at the idea of using GPS whilst more open-minded walkers will accept that GPS technology can be an inexpensive, well-established if non-essential navigational aid. In no time at all a GPS receiver with a clear view of the sky will establish your position and altitude in a variety of formats.

The majority of maps in the route guide include numbered waypoints based around landmarks or objectives along the trail; these correlate to the list on pp374-6, which gives the latitude/longitude position in a decimal minute format as well as a description. You can download the complete list of these waypoints for free as a GPS-readable file (that doesn't include the text descriptions) from the Trailblazer website: 🖳 www.trailblazer-guides.com (click on GPS waypoints).

---

possible to secure as many trekkers as they can before committing themselves to a set of permits as it is more profitable.

Regulations have also been imposed to try and improve the plight of **porters** working on the Inca Trail, whose permits are paid for by the agency that employs them (see pp22-3).

● **Entrance fees** The fee for the **classic Inca Trail** is s/254 (US$99; see note below) for adults and half price for children and students (see note below). The fee is payable by anyone trekking to Machu Picchu via Huayllabamba regardless of where their trek starts. There is a fee of s/146/83 (US$57/32) for adults/children or students (see note below) using the **Salkantay Trek** to simply hike over Salkantay and out via Km88. The entrance fee for the shorter routes from Km104 is s/146/83 (US$57/32) for adults/children and students. The fee does not include the s/126/63 (US$49/24.50) one-day entrance charge to Machu Picchu. People on the **Santa Teresa trek** need to pay s/129 (around US$50) for an INC permit when they get to Soray Pampa. For those tackling the **Vilcabamba Trail**, be aware that there is a s/108 (around US$42) fee that includes access to the ruins themselves.

Notes: In all cases the dollar rate quoted is approximate as it depends on the exchange rate at the time. **Children** aged 8-17 and **students** under 28 who can present a valid International Student Identity Card (ISIC) at the time of booking pay half the rate; under 8s are free.

● **Documents** Whilst on the Inca Trail, trekkers must carry their actual **passport** with them; a photocopy is not sufficient. You will be required to present your passport at various checkpoints with your trek permit and, if relevant, your **ISIC card**.

● **Banned items** As part of an attempt to conserve the trail the following are banned: **plastic bottles** (although evidence along the trail suggests that this isn't being enforced properly); **pets** and **pack animals** (although llamas are allowed as far as Huayllabamba); and **walking poles with a sharp tip** (they are OK if the tip is covered by a rubber bung as that will minimize damage to the Inca paths).

The exception are the maps for the routes that travel through the **Vilcabamba region**. At the time of writing there were disturbances and unrest in the area (see box p32), meaning that independent trekking here was not recommended so GPS data has not been made available.

Bear in mind that the vast majority of people who trek the Inca Trail or other associated routes do so perfectly well without a GPS unit. Instead of rushing out to invest in one, consider putting the money towards good-quality footwear or kit instead.

Getting to the trailheads

For the Inca Trail you are almost certain to be trekking with an agency, which means that you will be collected in Cusco and taken to the trailhead either by bus or by train. Many agencies use minibuses to transport trekkers to Km82, as they are quicker and can depart at any time whereas trains operate to a schedule. The **trains** to Aguas Calientes, which go via the trailheads at Km77, 82, 88 and 104, leave regularly each day though; most trekkers using the train start walking from Km88. See pp370-3 for details of times and prices.

It is also possible to catch a ride on a **tourist bus** from Cusco to Chilca (Km77) or Km82. These are cheaper and since they are usually packed with fellow tourists you will inevitably start walking as a group. You are far better off overnighting in Ollantaytambo and catching an early bus from there to the trailhead, to arrive well before the first bus from Cusco.

Buses from Cusco to Mollepata leave early from Calle Arcopata. Buses to Abancay that also depart from here can drop you off at the road that leads up to Mollepata although it's a long walk from there to the actual trailhead.

For information on how to get to Huancacalle for the Vilcabamba Trail see p271; for Cachora for the Choquequirao Trek see p301.

The classic Inca Trail

This is the undisputed draw for most people coming to Cusco and is by far the most popular and over-subscribed trek in the region. Given that you can get to Machu Picchu in four hours on a train, there has to be something intrinsically exciting and rewarding about the Inca Trail to merit spending four fairly grueling days walking to the same destination.

Passing through outstanding scenery, dramatic landscapes and encountering a series of increasingly spectacular ruins, it is in fact a spellbinding way to arrive at Machu Picchu and a walk that absolutely lives up to its billing as one of the finest in the world.

The Inca Trail &
Variant Routes
Overview

KM88 (QORIHUAYRACHINA) TO HUAYLLABAMBA   [MAP 1, p222]

The train from Cusco only stops briefly at Km88, sometimes also referred to by its Quechua name Qorihuayrachina, so watch the kilometre markers after Km82 and be ready to disembark. Once off the train continue to walk west along the tracks, in the same direction as the train was heading. A path leads away from the tracks and down to the river, where there is a substantial bridge and a **warden's hut**. A guard here will check your permit and passport before letting you cross the river and begin the trail proper.

Once on the far side of the bridge bear left (east) and climb gently through a stand of eucalyptus trees above the southern bank of the Urubamba.

Three-quarters of an hour after setting off from the bridge you will come to the mouth of the Cusichaca Valley, down which flows a river by the same name. At the junction of the two valleys lie the sprawling ruins of **Patallacta** (see box below). A small round tower, **Pulpituyoc**, stands on a ridge by the river. It is possible to *camp* on the banks of the river in the lee of the ruins.

Passing to the east of Patallacta, the trail continues gently gaining height whilst continuing south before crossing over the Cusichaca and climbing steeply up the opposite slope for 10-15 minutes. It settles on the eastern bank and begins to head upstream towards Huayllabamba. In places the path divides briefly before coming together again. Follow the broader, most obviously used track (usually the lower branch) in these instances.

❏ Patallacta and Pulpituyoc

Although first uncovered by Hiram Bingham in 1911 and partially excavated by him in 1915, it wasn't until the late 1970s when Ann Kendall and the Cusichaca Trust extensively excavated the site that people realized just how substantial **Patallacta**, sometimes called Llactapata, was; it's one of the largest settlements in the region.

The site, on a crescent-shaped bluff where the Cusichaca joins the Urubamba, is laid out in a typical Inca fashion and dates from the mid 15th century. There are 116 buildings and five baths laid out in a regular pattern. A canal feeds the main baths but appears to have fallen into disuse shortly after the invasion of the Spanish conquistadors, implying that the site was abandoned around 1540.

Extensive terraces surround the buildings, suggesting that the site used to be primarily an agricultural station responsible for the production of crops such as maize that would have been used to supply other Inca sites in the region, and a distribution centre for those crops produced higher up the Cusichaca valley such as potatoes. Ann Kendall oversaw the excavation and restoration of around six miles of Inca irrigation channels, which helped to transform the farming possibilities in the region. The site probably also had a strategic function as it sits at the junction of a number of Inca paths, and was ideally placed to regulate traffic and monitor who was moving where.

The round tower standing close to the main ruins, **Pulpituyoc**, whose name means 'containing a pulpit', was the religious centre for the site. Here there are eleven buildings, two baths and a carefully sculpted rock, reminiscent of the one close to Vitcos and enclosed by a curved wall, which acted as a shrine. Although the exact purpose and use for the buildings isn't known, the fact that they have curved walls signifies that this was a place of great spiritual importance to the Incas.

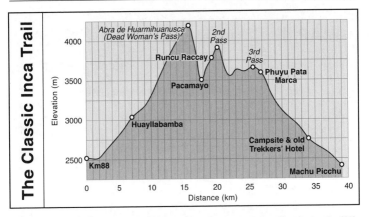

The path climbs gently but steadily for an hour, passing first beneath cliffs covered in bromeliads and then through gentler terrain. Several terraces are visible on the far side of the river. Ignore the lesser tracks leading down to the river, one of which crosses a bridge to a small settlement on the far, western bank. Stay on the eastern bank; is possible to *camp* on this side opposite the houses on the western bank. Continue past a signboard exaggerating the steepness of the route ahead and a hut where you can buy soft drinks. From this point there are good views back down the Cusichaca valley to Mt Verónica, which is visible as a pyramid in the middle of the valley.

Beyond the huts the path arrives at a second bridge (**Puente**). Cross the Cusichaca here and climb sharply to a small settlement called **Hatun Chaca**, where there are some flat pitches for a *campsite*; you can also buy soft drinks or chicha here.

Half an hour and 2km (1¼ miles) after Hatun Chaca cross another bridge, over the Llulluchayoc, a tributary of the Cusichaca, at the outskirts of Huayllabamba. **Huayllabamba**, a sprawling place built above Inca terraces, is the largest village on the trail and it's the last place where you can buy basic food supplies. There are a number of *campsites* here with toilet blocks and cold running water. Huayllabamba used to have a reputation for theft but it is much improved and is one of the few sites along the trail where you can camp within a community, chat with locals and even join a game of football on the local pitch (though it is exhausting work at this altitude).

At the top of the village is a **warden's office** where you must register and where porters have their loads checked and weighed before they can progress.

☐ **Important note – walking times**
Unless otherwise specified, **all times in this book refer only to the time spent walking**. You will need to add 10-30% to allow for rests, photography, checking the map, drinking water etc. When planning the day's hike count on 5-7 hours' actual walking.

ROUTE GUIDE AND MAPS

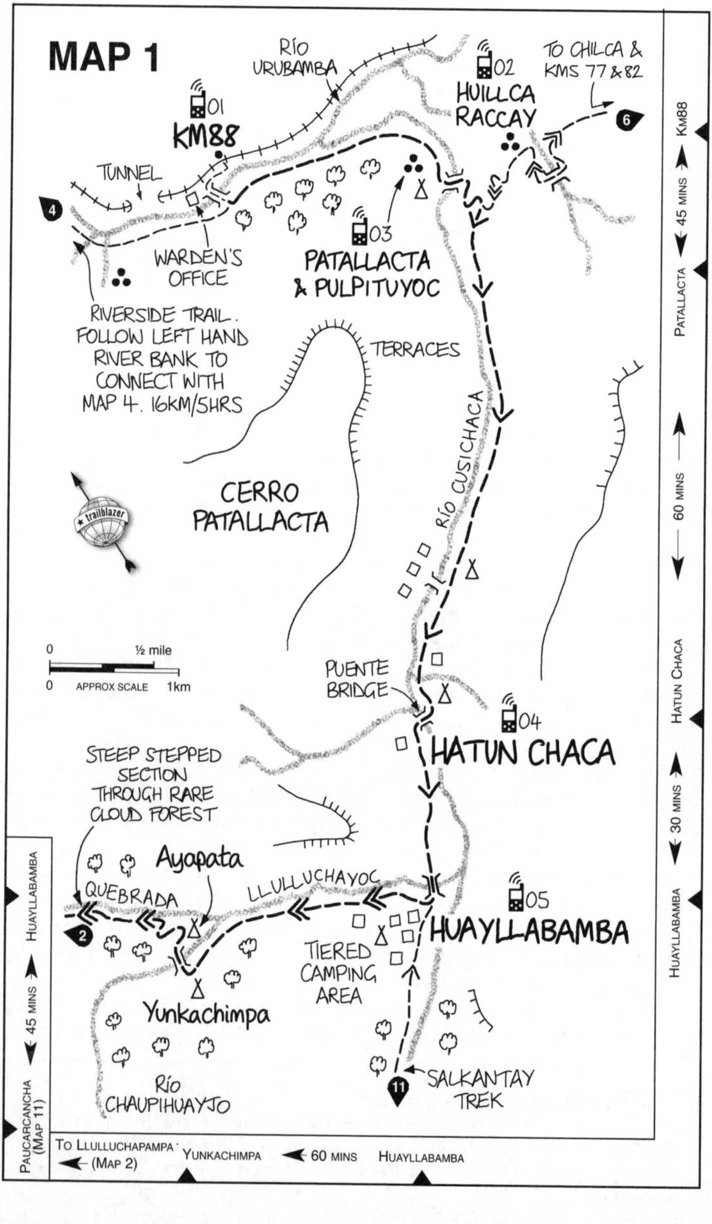

MAP 1

Río URUBAMBA

TO CHILCA & KMS 77 & 82

⌂02 HUILLCA RACCAY

6

⌂01 **KM88**

TUNNEL

4

WARDEN'S OFFICE

⌂03 **PATALLACTA & PULPITUYOC**

RIVERSIDE TRAIL. FOLLOW LEFT HAND RIVER BANK TO CONNECT WITH MAP 4. 16KM/5HRS

TERRACES

CERRO PATALLACTA

Río CUSICHACA

0   ½ mile
0   APPROX SCALE   1km

PUENTE BRIDGE

⌂04 **HATUN CHACA**

STEEP STEPPED SECTION THROUGH RARE CLOUD FOREST

Ayapata

QUEBRADA

2

LLULLUCHAYOC

⌂05 **HUAYLLABAMBA**

TIERED CAMPING AREA

Yunkachimpa

Río CHAUPIHUAYJO

11

SALKANTAY TREK

KM88

↑ 45 MINS ↓ PATALLACTA

↑ 60 MINS ↓ HATUN CHACA

↑ 30 MINS ↓ HUAYLLABAMBA

ROUTE GUIDE AND MAPS

PAUCARCANCHA (Map 11)   ↑ HUAYLLABAMBA

↑ 45 MINS ↓

TO LLULLUCHAPAMPA
◄ (MAP 2)   ▲ YUNKACHIMPA   ◄ 60 MINS   HUAYLLABAMBA

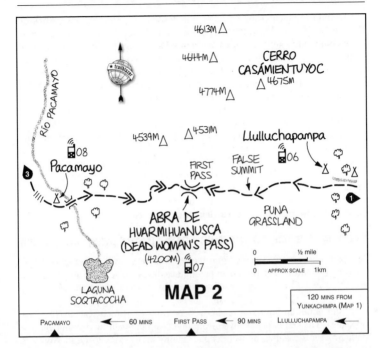

HUAYLLABAMBA TO PACAMAYO CAMP [MAP 1; MAP 2]

From the bridge over the Llulluchayoc follow the trail on the river's left-hand (south-west) bank, heading uphill. At a hairpin bend it quickly gets much steeper; after about an hour of climbing you reach *Yunkachimpa campsite* alongside the Río Chaupihuayjo (also shown as the Río Huayruro on some maps). Small and set on two tiers, the campsite itself is OK, but the surrounding area is badly littered and has in places been used as an al fresco toilet by inconsiderate trekkers.

Pass through the campsite and over a **bridge** across the river. Then head steeply uphill through a clearing and small campsite called *Ayapata*, before following the left-hand (south-west) bank of Quebrada Llulluchayoc as it veers to the west. Lupins and snapdragons line the path and you soon enter a beautiful cloud forest or *polylepsis* woodland, rare in the Andes because it's self-contained. The path climbs through the forest alongside the course of a river, occasionally close to the water and at other times high above it, on a series of steep steps.

As you reach the fringe of the forest there is another *campsite*, but 20 minutes beyond this, above the treeline, is a better one. *Llulluchapampa* has running water, a toilet block set on the top tier of terraces and exceptional views down the valley. It is exposed though and can get very cold at night; after torrential rain the ground becomes boggy here.

Beyond Llulluchapampa it is possible to make out the first pass. **Abra de Huarmihuanusca (First Pass)** is sometimes spelled Warmiwañusqa but is more commonly known as **Dead Woman's Pass**. It isn't known who the dead woman was or even if there was actually a dead woman at all, with many putting the name down to the fact that the pass resembles a woman lying on her back as if dead. The ascent to the pass looks deceptively simple. Although it is a gradual, steady climb parallel to the river, up to its source and then across the puna and over a section of paved path (laid in 1998 to protect the mountain from erosion), it will take 1½-2 hours to reach the high point (4200m/13,775ft).

From the broad saddle that marks the pass, the path descends steeply and swiftly into the neighbouring valley, plummeting 800m/2625ft in the course of just over a mile. At the bottom of this dizzying descent is *Pacamayo campsite*, a vast, sprawling campsite set amidst some scrubby trees, adjacent to the Río Pacamayo. It is popular with large tour groups and although the facilities here are reasonably good, with two toilet blocks, it is often noisy and crowded. Guides have to register at the **warden's hut** in the centre of the site.

PACAMAYO CAMP TO THE THIRD PASS [MAP 2 p223; MAP 3, p229]

The path climbs very steeply from the Pacamayo camp up a series of steps, crossing two bridged sections over precipitous drops where the original trail has crumbled away. Take the opportunity during the climb to admire the viewpoints over the valley below whilst pausing for breath on the way up.

After about an hour you reach the Inca ruins of **Runcu Raccay** (see box opposite). The site is best viewed from higher up the path, where you can see both structures together as well as outstanding views back to Dead Woman's Pass. Camping is not permitted around the ruins.

The **second pass** (3950m/12,955ft), sometimes called Abra de Runcu Raccay, is another hour up, beyond a series of false summits and at the top of a series of steep staircases. Just before the real pass, the path winds between two **lakes** where Andean gulls sometimes gather. The ground around the lakes is boggy. Don't stray from the dirt-gravel path as you risk damaging this very fragile eco-system. By the tarns there's a sign saying 'Deer Area', but you'll be very lucky to see any. You are no longer allowed to camp alongside the lakes or at the pass itself. The second pass is another broad saddle and boasts exceptional views of Pumasillo (6072m/19,915ft) and the Vilcabamba range. Below it the path again falls away steeply into an adjoining valley.

Having descended through a **short tunnel** the trail begins a series of tight switchbacks, dropping height quickly until it reaches a small viewpoint atop a promontory. Beyond here the descent is more gradual and the path curls and coils across the slopes. To the right (north) of the pass lies a large, algae-covered lake, whilst ahead of you (west) Sayac Marca is visible straddling a rocky spur high above the cloud forest. The path tumbles down a stretch of hillside towards a hairpin bend. Just before this dog-leg right is a staircase that branches left (south-west) and climbs 50m/150ft to the entrance of **Sayac Marca** (see box p226). Camping is not permitted here.

Around the hairpin bend and sitting in the shadow of Sayac Marca is the small set of ruins at **Concha Marca**. Tucked in a little valley and perched atop a series of tall, rounded terraces, these ruins were only uncovered in the early 1980s. The small stream here is a good place to fill up with water as there isn't another water source until the Third pass. However, purify the water carefully.

Beyond the ruins lies a stretch of very attractive trail. The path skirts a series of precipices on stone slabs, most of which are of Inca origin, and contours

❑ Runcu Raccay

The compact ruins at Runcu Raccay, perched precariously above a vertiginous chasm on a large terrace, were found by Hiram Bingham. Given its location on the Inca Trail and the fact that it had superlative views across the valley to Abra de Huarmihuanusca, Bingham decided that it must have been a fortress or watch tower. The archaeologist Dr Paul Fejos examined it in 1940 and concluded that it was a *tambo* for passing travellers or *chasquis*.

The site consists of two structures: a larger, round building with a double skin and walls indented with niches and a smaller, lower, rectangular structure. Both are completed in fairly basic, rustic style and the stonework is rough and ready in comparison to what the Incas could really do. The popular theory is that the site is a transitional building, taking travellers from the purely practical buildings in the Cusichaca Valley to the far more elaborate, significant structures closer to Machu Picchu. Its location would have been very deliberate though, with the Incas keen that people passing this way had the chance to venerate their surroundings.

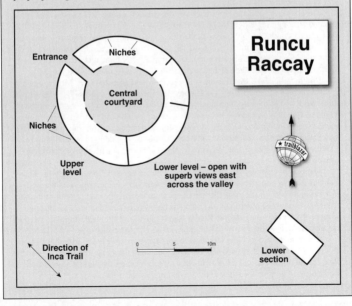

Runcu Raccay

Entrance

Niches

Central courtyard

Niches

Upper level

Lower level – open with superb views east across the valley

★ trailblazer

Direction of Inca Trail

0   5   10m

Lower section

ROUTE GUIDE AND MAPS

through some very beautiful cloud forest. If you find yourself tackling this stretch in cloud or mist you would do well to wait it out, itinerary and time allowing, in order to enjoy the drama and beauty around you. Twenty minutes' easy walk from Sayac Marca is an open section of hillside called **Chaquicocha** where you are allowed to pitch *camp*. There are a number of flattened, grassy pitches and a toilet block. If it has been raining the ground can be boggy.

From the campsite the path snakes steeply uphill, past two **viewpoints**. At the second of these the trail forks, with a faint, disused and heavily overgrown side path leading off right (north). This path avoids the Inca tunnel and used to rejoin the main route around a kilometre (half a mile) further along the trail.

The main trail continues, rounding a spur and turning from north-west to north-east. A section of intricately laid Inca paving leads down to an **Inca tunnel**. This 16m long corridor exploits a fault in the seemingly sheer cliff that blocks the way ahead. Emerging from the impressive tunnel the path climbs again towards the third pass.

❑ **Sayac Marca**

The dramatically sited ruins of Sayac Marca are protected on three sides by sheer cliffs that fall away to the jungle far below. Hiram Bingham again first found the site, but it was Dr Paul Fejos who gave it the appropriate, descriptive moniker Sayac Marca, meaning 'Inaccessible Town', in the 1940s. The ruins, made up of a dozen chambers, passages and retaining walls, overlook the Aobamba Valley and stand at a fork in the original Inca road.

The classic Inca Trail continues on one branch of the fork whilst the other descends through the jungle to the river Aobamba that flows along the bottom of the valley, then climbs steeply up the other side of the valley to the ruins at Llactapata (see box pp262-3), before dropping off the far side of the next ridge and descending to the river Santa Teresa. Fifteen kilometres from Sayac Marca it clambers once more to the ruins at Ochopata before becoming completely subsumed by the jungle.

Bingham believed that the site was a fortress and an outpost for Machu Picchu. Fejos disagreed saying that it wasn't impressive enough to be a fortress. Neither is the stone work of sufficiently high quality for the site to be a religious centre although there are ceremonial water channels at the base of the outcrop. Nor are there enough terraces or agricultural land in the vicinity for it to have been a farming outpost. With the compact **Concha Marca** ruins just below, it is also unlikely to have simply been a tambo, meaning that no-one is actually sure what these superb ruins were originally used for.

The building appears to grow organically out of the rocky promontory on which it stands and the entire shape of the structure emphasizes and exaggerates the natural features and shape of the prow that sticks out from the hillside. At the heart of the site is a large, unadorned outcrop of rock that juts up from the foundations. The stonework is more impressive than that at Runcu Raccay, marking the next stage on the pilgrimage to Machu Picchu, but is still quite rustic in appearance.

Bingham drew particular attention to the 'eye-bonders', holes drilled in corners of walls, which were used to fasten thatched roofs onto the stone structures. The elaborate layout of the site and the way in which it incorporates the natural terrain has led archaeologists to date the ruins to the second half of the 15th century.

Sayac Marca

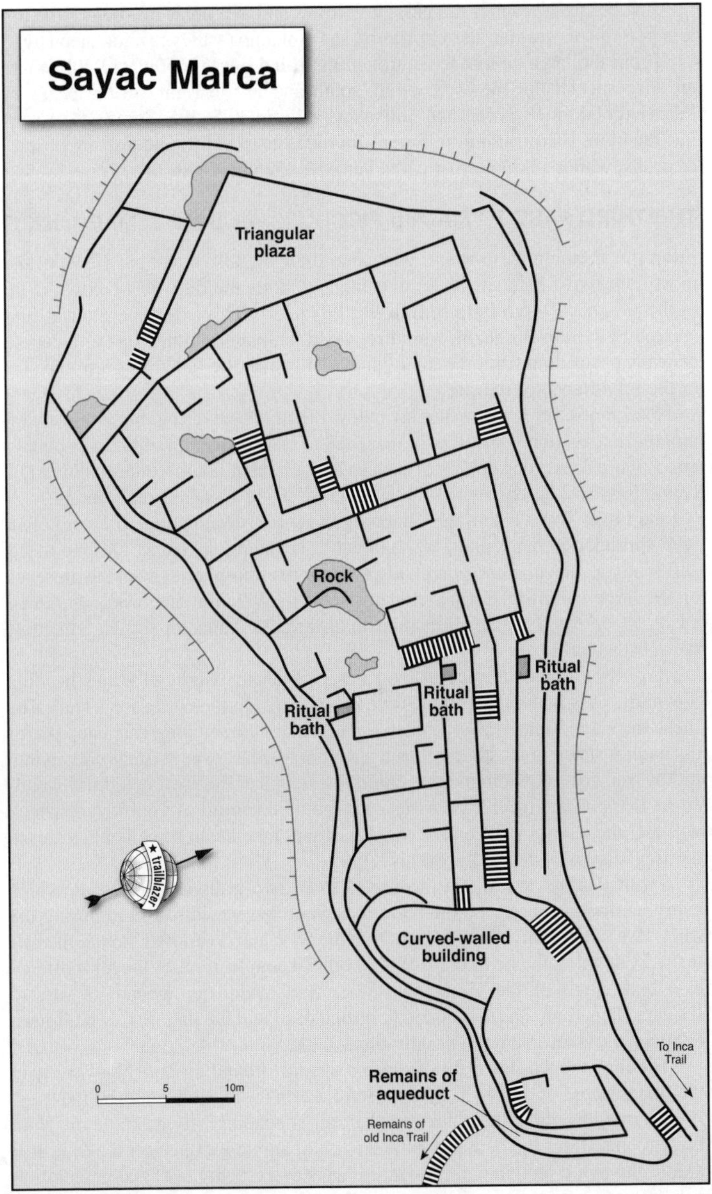

Triangular plaza

Rock

Ritual bath

Ritual bath

Ritual bath

Curved-walled building

Remains of aqueduct

Remains of old Inca Trail

To Inca Trail

0   5   10m

Just before it reaches the pass, it narrows and at a point just before the top it is possible to see into the Urubamba and Aobamba valleys simultaneously.

From the large *campsite* set around the **third pass** (3650m/11,970ft) there are also spectacular views. Looking south and left to right are the peaks of Palcay (c5600m/18,370ft) and Salkantay (6270m/20,565ft). Some 35km west lies the high, sharp summit of Pumasillo (6072m/19,915ft) and a string of lesser peaks, whilst 15km north-west is Veronica (5750m/18,860ft).

THE THIRD PASS TO MACHU PICCHU   [MAP 3; MAP 4, p231]

From the stunning eyrie where you camp there are also excellent views of the most impressive Inca site so far encountered along the trail. Just below the lip of the pass lies **Phuyu Pata Marca** (see box p230). This extensive site was first spotted by Hiram Bingham, who discovered the baths and the tops of a couple of walls protruding from the thick jungle. However, he failed to grasp the size or the importance of the site.

Paul Fejos did realize what lay below the jungle covering, but after several months' excavation had still only managed to clear a fraction of the site, uncovering two plazas, four groups of houses and a hidden house concealed in a terrace. However, he christened the site whose name translates appropriately as 'Cloud Level Town'. With the site prone to swirling Wagnerian mists and often seen shrouded in blankets of white cloud, it is an apt nickname. Despite this it still looks spectacular and potentially even more atmospheric; even the presence of the large campsite just above can't spoil it. What's more, when the cloud clears, the views from the Urubamba up towards Mt Yanantin and Mt Salkantay are spectacular.

From the lowest terrace of the ruins pick up the **flight of stairs** heading downhill. This is the most impressive set of steps on the entire Inca Trail. The Incas turned a 500m (1500ft) hillside into a staircase, etching each step out of the natural shape of the bedrock: one giant boulder has over 30 steps carved into it. The trail coils down into dense cloud forest, one of the most delightful wooded sections on the trek. It's a lovely walk, but be careful of your knees, which will feel the strain by the end of the day. It will take about three hours to reach the final campsite and old Trekkers' Hotel.

From Phuyu Pata Marca there used to be two trails. The old trail, which everyone took up until the dramatic Inca Staircase was discovered during the early 1980s, left Phuyu Pata Marca from the west and contoured around the valley side, hugging the lie of the land. Although a couple of miles longer it offered excellent views of the Urubamba valley and eventually wound its way to Intipata. This route has subsequently been closed and the majority of it allowed to become overgrown and virtually impassable.

Having stepped down the Inca staircase for around an hour you will gain the first glimpse of the old Trekker's Hotel, its tin roof visible amongst the trees. It is to this unsightly shambles that the trail is heading. About 2½ hours from Phuyu Pata Marca the path passes to the left of a pylon set just off the trail. Just before the pylon though a narrow trail breaks away right (east) and descends to

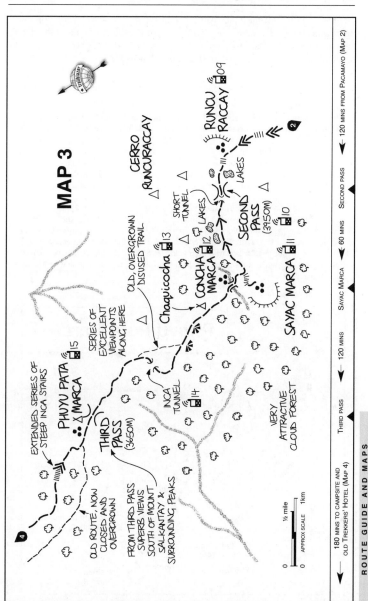

MAP 3

SERIES OF EXCELLENT VIEWPOINTS ALONG HERE

CERRO RUNCURACCAY

OLD OVERGROWN DISUSED TRAIL

Chaquicocha 🏚13

EXTENDED SERIES OF STEEP INCA STAIRS

PHUYU PATA △MARCA 🏚15

SHORT TUNNEL

LAKES

CONCHA MARCA 🏚12

RUNCU RACCAY 🏚09

THIRD PASS (3650M)

SECOND PASS (3950M) 🏚10

LAKES

OLD ROUTE, NOW CLOSED AND OVERGROWN

INCA TUNNEL 🏚14

SAYAC MARCA 🏚11

FROM THIRD PASS SUPERB VIEWS SOUTH OF MOUNT SALKANTAY & SURROUNDING PEAKS

VERY ATTRACTIVE CLOUD FOREST

½ mile   1km

0   APPROX SCALE

←— 180 MINS TO CAMPSITE AND OLD TREKKERS' HOTEL (MAP 4)   THIRD PASS ←— 120 MINS —→ SAYAC MARCA ←— 60 MINS —→ SECOND PASS ←— 120 MINS FROM PACAMAYO (MAP 2)

the hotel within half an hour, losing height rapidly through a series of short, tight switchbacks. However, the shortcut doesn't really save you all that much time and it is in fact far less scenic than the traditional route, which pushes on beneath the pylon cables towards **Intipata** (see box p232).

❏ **Phuyu Pata Marca**
The site is thought to date from the late 15th century and is attributed to Pachacutec or his successor Túpac Yupanqui (Topa Inca). It is built in an atypical style, unlike the more structured Inca sites elsewhere. However, the stone work is very good in parts, particularly on the upper terraces.

The ruins occupy a pyramid of seven terraces that hug the contours of a spur, linked by a fine stairway. The long, straight staircase descends between several tiers of buildings. To one side are six 'Inca baths' (five ceremonial baths and one principal one) that were probably not actually used to wash in, but are more likely to have been used in conjunction with the ritual worship of water.

The function of the site is again unclear and the handful of basic Inca ceramics found in the ruins give no clues as to its purpose. The most likely theory states that the site was connected with the ritual worship of water, but other suggestions range from a guard house to a private hunting lodge. Similar structures can be seen at Tambo Machay and further along the Inca Trail at Huinay Huayna and at Machu Picchu itself.

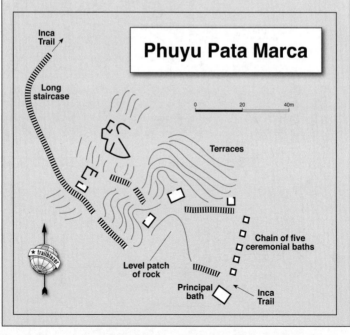

Phuyu Pata Marca

Inca Trail
Long staircase
Terraces
0   20   40m
trailblazer
Level patch of rock
Chain of five ceremonial baths
Principal bath
Inca Trail

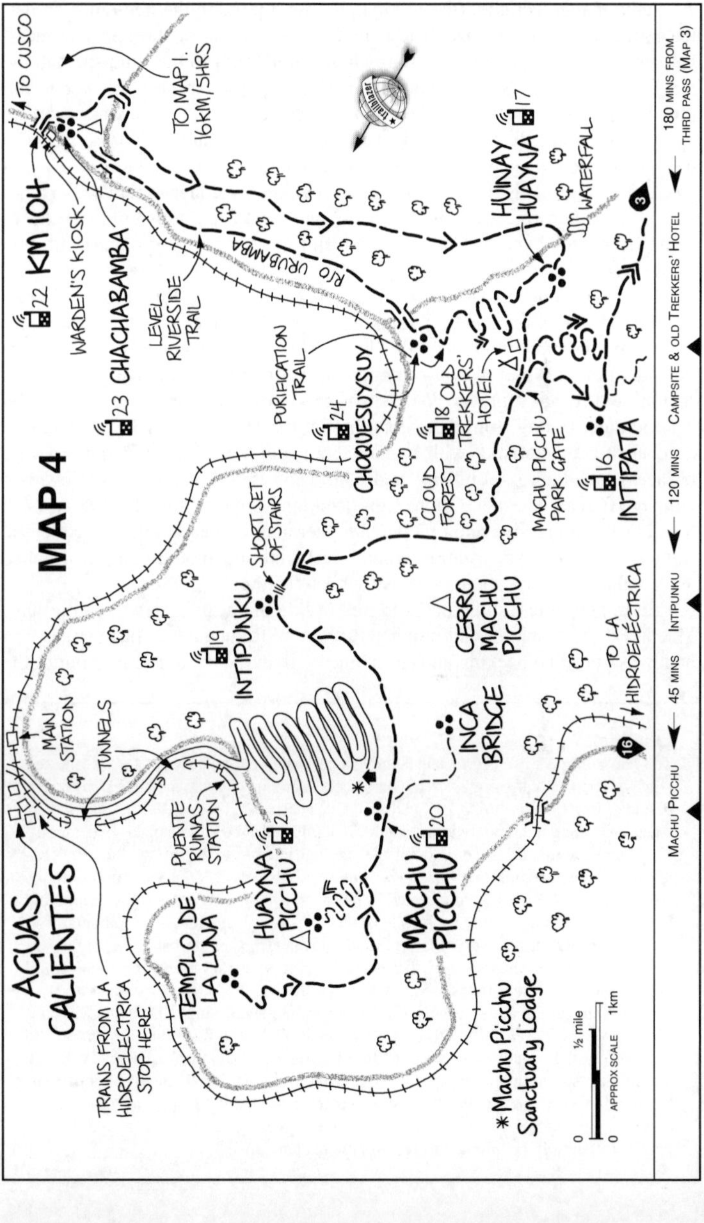

MAP 4

TO CUSCO

TO MAP I.
16KM/5HRS

180 MINS FROM
THIRD PASS (MAP 3)

🏠22 KM 104

WARDEN'S KIOSK

🏠23 CHACHABAMBA

LEVEL
RIVERSIDE TRAIL

RÍO URUBAMBA

HUINAY
HUAYNA 🏠17

WATERFALL

3

PURIFICATION
TRAIL

🏠24
CHOQUESUYSUY

🏠18 OLD
TREKKERS' HOTEL

CLOUD
FOREST

MACHU PICCHU
PARK GATE

🏠16
INTIPATA

SHORT SET
OF STAIRS

🏠19

INTIPUNKU

CERRO
MACHU
PICCHU

INCA
BRIDGE

TO LA
HIDROELÉCTRICA

16

MAIN STATION

TUNNELS

PUENTE
RUINAS
STATION

🏠21
HUAYNA-
PICCHU

🏠20
MACHU
PICCHU

AGUAS
CALIENTES

TRAINS FROM LA
HIDROELÉCTRICA
STOP HERE

TEMPLO DE
LA LUNA

*Machu Picchu
Sanctuary Lodge

MACHU PICCHU — 45 MINS — INTIPUNKU — 120 MINS — CAMPSITE & OLD TREKKERS' HOTEL — 180 MINS

½ mile

0   APPROX SCALE   1km

ROUTE GUIDE AND MAPS

As you approach the site you first glimpse it through the trees and can better gauge its enormous size. The path emerges on one of the upper terraces. Descend to the lowest terrace, from where a trail leads to the campsite and the old Trekkers' Hotel. Sadly the hotel is now closed and has been allowed to fall into disrepair. This is, though, the last place before Machu Picchu where you are allowed to *camp*. Because of this it is always full, meaning you are likely to have a crowded, noisy night wherever you end up. There are a number of toilet blocks in the grounds. If you don't mind standing in a queue there's also a hot shower although the water is unreliable and frequently runs cold. If you've come from Mollepata or Chilca and haven't already bought your permit, you must do so here.

From the campsite a short 10-minute trek takes you to the ruins of **Huinay Huayna** (see box opposite), a stunning terraced complex, 500m and a world away from the modern mess you've just left. The name Huinay Huayna (sometimes written as Wiñay Wayna) belongs to an attractive orchid that grows in the region, and means 'forever young. It is the most impressive site on the Inca Trail to date. Dating from the second half of the 15th century, the site shares a number of characteristics with Intipata: both comprise a series of fine, curving terraces spread across a hillside and both were used to grow crops. However, Huinay Huayna is a much more significant and important site; the stonework here is very impressive and of a much higher quality than at Intipata. Note: the ruins are locked every evening around dusk and you should be careful not to leave valuables lying about your tent whilst visiting.

From here it takes two hours to trek to Intipunku (the gateway to the sun). Machu Picchu is another 45 minutes further on. Remember to have your torch handy as you'll be packing and starting to walk in the dark. The gate out of the

❏ **Intipata**

The name Intipata literally means 'sunny slope' and is particularly apt for this massed range of terraces that seem to stretch on endlessly. Whilst clearing the huge steps over a period of four months during 1940, Dr Paul Fejos despairingly described in his diary terraces 'extending indefinitely to the south'. In total he cleared and mapped 48 terraces.

There are no plazas, ceremonial sites or fortifications to disturb the broad sweeping terraces suggesting that the site was used exclusively as an agricultural outpost. However, three houses are concealed in hollow terraces. Given the broad panoramic views down into the valley to the site of Choquesuysuy and across the mountains to the lookout platform on top of Cerro Machu Picchu, the site probably had some sort of strategic importance as well. By using Intipata as a mid-point, messages could have been transmitted from the valley floor all the way to Machu Picchu.

Despite cutting and removing 40,000 square metres of jungle, Dr Fejos was convinced that there was still more to be uncovered. Although historians are anxious to try and reveal as much as possible, naturalists are concerned that insensitive clearing and blunt restoration techniques have damaged prime habitat favoured by a particular breed of very rare orchid. In order to preserve the habitat and protect the flower, there are frequent rumours that the site will be closed and left uncleared, and that the jungle will simply be allowed to reclaim the ancient stones.

❏ Huinay Huayna (Wiñay Wayna)

This complex's sweeping terraces lead round to a series of buildings with high-quality masonry, a *double-jamb* doorway and a curved structure that looks out over Mt Verónica. The finest examples of Inca stonework can be found in these buildings, which are constructed out of some of the largest and most perfectly fitted blocks along the Inca Trail. There are also lots of gables and exterior pegs used to secure thatched roofs. From this upper cluster a staircase descends to a second level, alongside a sequence of 10 stone baths, down which flows water from a spring that originates at Phuyu Pata Marca. The likelihood is that these were involved in the ritual worship of water and that the site had an important role as a ceremonial or religious centre.

From the last structure at the lowest level, there's a trapezoidal window that frames a nearby waterfall, reinforcing the idea that the site was connected with the veneration of water.

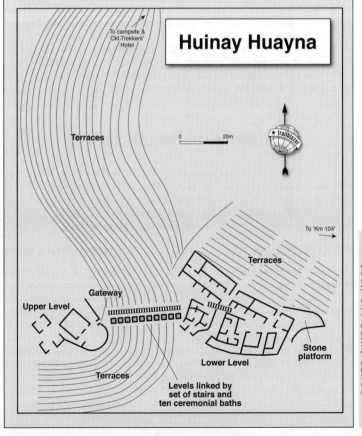

Huinay Huayna

To campsite &
Old Trekkers'
Hotel

Terraces

0   25m

To 'Km 104'

Terraces

Gateway

Upper Level

Terraces

Stone
platform

Lower Level

Levels linked by
set of stairs and
ten ceremonial baths

campsite opens at 5.30am and closes at 3.30pm. Most trekkers crowd by the gate in the dark, hoping to get the earliest start to Machu Picchu when it opens. The result is a convoy of bobbing headlamps in the mad dash to reach Intipunku by sunrise. You may consider delaying your departure from the campsite by 15-30 minutes to enjoy an emptier path, better light and the very attractive final section of the Inca Trail. After all, sunrise over Machu Picchu is often hazy or shrouded in light cloud, so the chances are you won't miss much by arriving a little later; you'll still get to enjoy the ruins before the tours and trainloads of day-trippers arrive.

The trail to Intipunku is easy and very straightforward to follow. It undulates a little, then passes a couple of steep rock faces, before climbing about 14 **very steep steps** to what you assume is Intipunku. It's actually the remains of a watchtower commanding superb views south back to Intipata, Huinay Huayna, Phuyu Pata Marca and to Choquesuysuy at the start of the Purification Trail. Intipunku is, in fact, just around the corner, at the top of a short set of rather gentler stairs. This is an awe-inspiring approach, the architecture reinforcing your sense of anticipation. When you finally arrive at **Intipunku**, the view across the wide bend of the Urubamba explodes before you and you can at last see, sheltering under the sugar-loaf mountain of Huayna Picchu (see pp352-3), your journey's end, **Machu Picchu** (see pp339-62).

Variations on the classic trail

These variations are up to four hours longer than the first day of the classic Inca trail and provide alternative start points. They are particularly popular with trekking agencies, which tend to begin all their trips from Km82. You won't gain much from starting at Chilca instead, although it is a scenic, simple stroll to the main trail that allows you to ease in to the trek proper.

FROM CHILCA (Km77)   [MAP 5; MAP 6, p237]

The small hamlet of Chilca stands at Km77 on the railway. It is also readily accessible by road; indeed many of the trekking agencies drive here to start their organized hikes. If you're arriving by bus make sure you tell the driver you want to get off here as they will assume you are bound for Km82, the more popular starting point. Although little more than a collection of adobe houses and shacks, Chilca is still more substantial than anything found at Km82 or Km88.

From the railway station head south and wind through the houses towards the road and bridge across the Urubamba. Cross the river here and turn right (west). Follow the clearly defined dirt track along the southern bank of the river as it descends towards a stand of eucalyptus trees. Bromeliads, wild pepper trees and chilca bushes, from which the village gets its name, also line the path. Beyond the small copse the path bears north-west and undulates through a patch

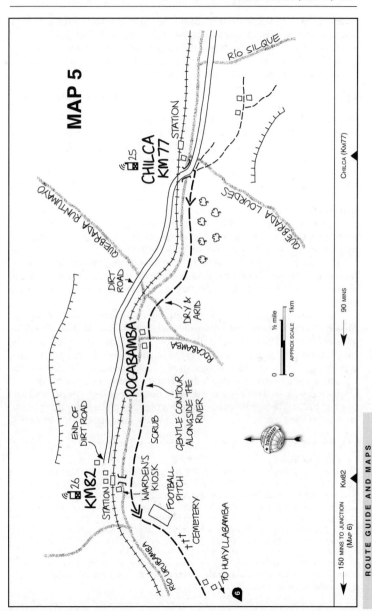

MAP 5

RÍO SILQUE

STATION

25
CHILCA
KM 77

QUEBRADA RUNTUMAYO

DIRT ROAD

QUEBRADA LOURDES

DRY & ARID

ROCABAMBA

ROCABAMBA

GENTLE CONTOUR
ALONGSIDE THE
RIVER

SCRUB

END OF
DIRT ROAD

KM82

STATION

26

WARDEN'S
KIOSK

FOOTBALL
PITCH

CEMETERY

RÍO URUBAMBA

TO HUAYLLABAMBA

6

0   ½ mile
0   APPROX SCALE   1km

← CHILCA (KM77)

← 90 MINS

← KM82

← 150 MINS TO JUNCTION
(MAP 6)

of dry scrub dotted with cacti, crossing the small Quebrada Runtumayo, to reach the village of **Rocabamba**, where there is a stream but no facilities.

Bearing west, the path crosses the stream and weaves through a further patch of scrub to arrive at the Km82 bridge, 1½ hours after leaving Chilca.

For the continuation of the route see below.

FROM KM82   [MAP 5, p235; MAP 6]

This is the end of the road for tourist buses and the furthest point along the Urubamba Valley accessible by road. Most tour agencies pull into the car park to the north of the houses here and start the trek from this point. There are precious few amenities here, but a couple of enterprising individuals sell last-minute supplies and cold soft drinks. You must present your passport and register at the **warden's kiosk**. The trail is only fractionally longer than the classic Inca trail as the routes join somewhere approximately mid-way between the two start points.

If starting here head south-west from the houses and walk down towards the river bank. Cross the bridge here and on the south side of the Urubamba turn right (west), ignoring the path left that goes to Chilca.

If coming from Chilca, ignore the river crossing and continue west. Immediately the path climbs steeply away from the river. It evens out and heads south-west past a **football pitch** and a cemetery before passing through a small village.

As the river curves west, so the path follows it and arrives at the village of **Miskay**. At the far end of the village the path divides. Take the less-substantial left-hand fork (south) and head briefly towards a rocky cliff before veering right (west). Follow the path as it ducks into and scrambles out of a small gully, having crossed a stream. Just beyond here, commanding the mouth of the Cusichaca Valley, stands the Inca hillfort **Huillca Raccay** (see box below).

Further west on the far side of the valley lies the sprawling site of Patallacta (see box p220). The path descends in a series of gentle zigzags towards the eastern bank of the Cusichaca river, where it joins the main Inca trail from Km88,

ROUTE GUIDE AND MAPS

> ## ❑ Huillca Raccay
> It doesn't look like much but this fort is thought to be one of the earliest built in the region. Between 1978 and 1980 it was extensively excavated by Ann Kendall who discovered that people inhabited the area long before the Incas arrived. Once they had subdued the original residents of the valley, the Incas built the fort to maintain control and assert their dominance over the local tribes.
>
> The ruins comprise a complicated collection of gate-houses, lofts and what are thought to be barracks. In total there are 37 Inca buildings here and some 70 pre-Inca constructions scattered on the flatter land behind. From this vantage point the Incas commanded exceptional views up and down the Urubamba and managed access to the Cusichaca. Later, once Llactapata had been built, the fort protected and controlled the agrarian settlements further down the valley.

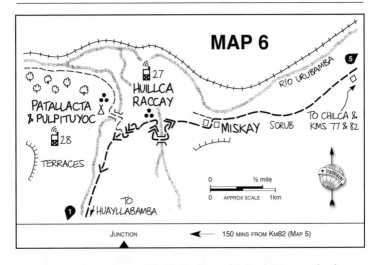

some 2½ hours after leaving Km82. Lupins and broom overgrow the descent and it is easy to lose the way, but you should have no problem in picking up the trail if you continue westwards and downhill towards the valley bottom. At this point turn left and head up the valley (south) towards the village of Huayllabamba on the broad, well-worn trail.

See p221 for the continuation of the route to Machu Picchu.

The shorter trails

For those people who don't have the time or inclination to tackle a four-day walk there are various alternatives. It's only a half-day hike uphill to Huinay Huayna and the old Trekkers' Hotel from Km104 on the railway line (Map 4) and just a couple of hours' gentle stroll along the classic Inca Trail from here to the first glimpse of Machu Picchu and the ruins themselves.

Alternatively, follow the southern bank of the Urubamba downstream for a couple of hours to the ruins at Choquesuysuy and then climb more steeply towards Huinay Huayna, from where you join the Inca Trail for the final push to Machu Picchu. Both of these treks are open year-round so they are ideal for people who would rather trek to Machu Picchu than simply catch the train and a bus but who arrive during February when the Inca Trail is shut.

People using these trails can't stay on the trail or camp at Huinay Huayna but have to push on to Machu Picchu in order to descend to stay overnight in Aguas Calientes, before returning the following day to fully explore the ruins.

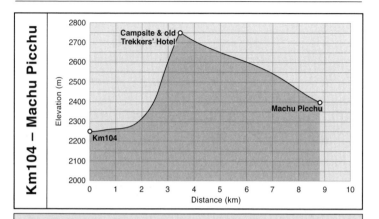

❏ Chachabamba

Amongst the buildings on the site is a natural shrine and 14 ceremonial baths. This is more than almost anywhere else along the Inca Trail, suggesting that the site must have been an important religious centre and associated with water worship. It probably also fulfilled a function as a watchtower, controlling access to Machu Picchu.

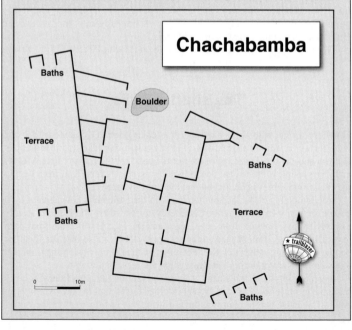

KM104 TO HUINAY HUAYNA (PURIFICATION TRAIL) [MAP 4, p231]

The train takes 3½-4 hours to travel from Cusco to Km104, where it pauses briefly to let people disembark. A **warden's kiosk** stands adjacent to the bridge across the Urubamba, where you must present your passport and register.

On the far side of the river turn right (west) and shortly come to the ruins at **Chachabamba** (see box opposite). Dating from the late 15th century, it is a sophisticated site set on an old Inca road. Uncovered in 1940 by Dr Paul Fejos, the site had lain undisturbed despite the construction of the railway on the opposite bank of the river some time earlier. Since then it has been cleared and a number of buildings uncovered.

From the ruins the path divides: the right-hand path follows the river west towards **Choquesuysuy** (see box below) before scrambling steeply up to the ruins at Huinay Huayna alongside the old Trekkers' Hotel.

❏ **Choquesuysuy**
Built on either side of a tributary of the Urubamba at Km107, Choquesuysuy comprises six groups of buildings, totalling 18 houses, a series of seven ceremonial baths and a number of well-crafted terraces and walls. The site is ideally placed to oversee traffic along the valley floor and commands the approach to Machu Picchu, although the hydroelectric power station now blocks the path. The quality of the stonework and the presence of the baths suggest it was also a religious centre.

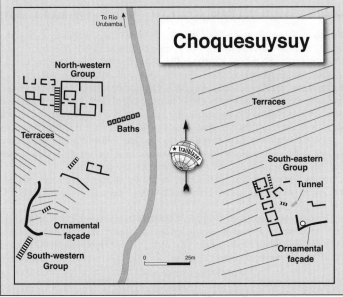

To Río
Urubamba

Choquesuysuy

North-western Group

Terraces

Baths

Terraces

★ trailblazer

South-eastern Group

Tunnel

Ornamental façade

South-western Group

Ornamental façade

0   25m

ROUTE GUIDE AND MAPS

Picking up on the perceived religious function of the site, the steep track has been dubbed the Purification Trail. It takes 2-3 hours to climb from the valley floor to Huinay Huayna (see box p233). Pass through the site on a staircase adjacent to a series of ceremonial baths and pick up the path from the upper level of the site that undulates for a further 15 minutes to reach the abandoned Trekkers' Hotel, which is still used as the final **campsite** (see p232) on the classic Inca Trail.

Alternative route from Choquesuysuy

A slightly gentler alternative than the vertical ascent from Choquesuysuy is to take the left-hand fork that crosses a stream and passes through a patch of forest and underneath two electricity cables before climbing more evenly across an exposed slope in a westerly direction. This stream is the last water source before the ruins and since the climb is exposed and exhausting in direct sunshine you should make sure to fill up all water bottles.

After a mile you gain your first glimpse of the hotel and the massed terraces of Intipata (see box p232) beyond it. A little after this, good views of Huinay Huayna come into focus whilst far below Choquesuysuy is also visible.

The narrow path continues to climb up and across the mountainside before levelling and finally descending briefly through some woods. Rounding a small spur it passes a waterfall and a number of Inca walls and bits of building still shrouded in vegetation before emerging at the foot of Huinay Huayna. Climb the staircase through the site and then up past the stone baths to the upper level. Turn right (north-west) and leave the site on a well-trodden trail that leads to the campsite (see p232) after 15 minutes.

KM88 TO KM104 (RIVERSIDE TRAIL) [MAP 1, p222; MAP 4, p231]

Instead of following the classic Inca Trail, there is the option to escape the crowds and the majority of the stiff climbs by following the river as it flows downstream from Km88 to Km104 before ascending to Huinay Huayna and the campsite and old Trekkers' Hotel. Rarely done and consequently not nearly as well-worn as the classic trail, this gentle riverside stroll is an excellent way of accessing the major ruins at the end of the trek and allows you to explore some interesting sites along the way, including Machu Q'ente and Huayna Q'ente and the Inca compound Torontoy which boasts a 44-angle stone in one of its walls.

The trail typically takes **two days** to complete. You will need a **permit** for the trek though and because it overlaps with the final section of the classic Inca Trail the route is subject to the same regulations and restrictions.

Note: The start and end of the route are shown on Map 1 and Map 4 respectively. The intervening section is not mapped but is very easy as you simply follow the river bank.

Having registered at the **warden's kiosk** before the bridge at Km88, cross the Urubamba but instead of turning left for the classic Inca trail, turn right and having headed south for 50m bear west along the southern bank of the river in the lee of several sheer cliffs. The 16km (10-mile) path is clear and reasonably well maintained, but as a result of the reduced traffic it receives can occasionally be overgrown.

❏ **Huayna Q'ente and Machu Q'ente**
The exact purpose of these two sites isn't known, but they are thought to have multiple functions, including being resthouses or inns, religious sites and agricultural posts.

Huayna Q'ente is the more impressive structure. Dating from the second half of the 15th century, it is thought to have been built either during the reign of Pachacutec or that of his successor Túpac Yupanqui (Topa Inca). It is an intricately constructed site with plenty of fine stonework on display, suggesting that it was used as a *tambo* (a type of inn) by people making pilgrimages to Machu Picchu. There are two stone baths connected with the worship of water and two sacred rocks thought to be *huacas* (sacred sites). Extensive terraces support the site and a clever canal system supplies the various levels of agricultural land with water.

In contrast, **Machu Q'ente** is plainer, suggesting that it had a primarily agricultural function, although there are also the remnants of a large building thought to have perhaps been a barracks. Close by is a large, peculiarly carved stone that looks similar to Ñusta España (see p274), the sculpted boulder close to Huancacalle.

Around 20 minutes after crossing the Urubamba you come to the rarely visited ruins of **Huayna Q'ente** and **Machu Q'ente** (see box above). These two sites stand on the Inca road to Chachabamba, although the road actually follows the river all the way to the Amazon.

There are *campsites* just two hours down from Km88 and at Chachabamba, five hours from Km88. From Chachabamba you have the option of ascending to Huinay Huayna via the standard route (see p232), or via Choquesuysuy and the Purification Trail (see pp239-40).

The Salkantay/Mollepata Trek

This is essentially an extension of the Inca Trail that allows you to experience a fantastic section of wilderness free from most of the crowds before committing to the final three days of the classic Inca Trail culminating at Machu Picchu. The **6- to 7-day trek** from the watershed of the Apurímac to the Urubamba is quite arduous, as you must cross a high pass at almost 5000m/16,400ft. The views of the Vilcabamba range and the proximity to the bulk of Mt Salkantay more than compensate for the effort required.

This trek is advertised under various names, and although you may see it listed as the **Mollepata Trek**, or even the **High Inca Trail**, the most common moniker and spelling is the one used here.

MOLLEPATA TO SORAY　　　　　　　[MAP 7, p245; MAP 8, p246]

See box p242 for details about Mollepata. The trail leaves from Mollepata's Plaza de Armas and follows the dirt road that winds all the way to Soray via the small settlement of Marcocasa (also known as Cruzpata). Since the road was

ROUTE GUIDE AND MAPS

improved, almost every agency now drives at least as far as Marcocasa to begin the trek, with many continuing all the way to Soray. There is no public transport along this stretch of road, which is quiet and rarely travelled but not particularly exciting or interesting to trek along.

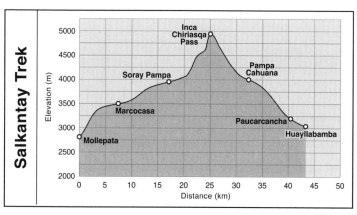

❑ Mollepata

Mollepata lies 3½ hours' drive west of Cusco, at the end of a dirt track off the main Cusco to Abancay road. Described by E G Squier as 'a collection of wretched huts on a high shelf of the mountain with a tumbledown church, a drunken governor... a place unsurpassed in evil repute by any in Peru', it has fortunately evolved since 1877 into a pleasant mountain town perched on a hillside overlooking the deep citrus-producing valley of the Apurímac. This small huddle of houses is the start point for two increasingly popular treks, the Salkantay trek and the Santa Teresa trek, each of which passes beneath the imposing glaciated peak of Mt Salkantay (6271m/20,569ft).

The early **bus** from Cusco (5am and 1pm from opposite the western end of Calle Arcopata; s/8-15; 3½hrs) will take you all the way to the plaza in the village, but some of the later ones drop you only at the bottom of the dirt track, down by the Apurímac river. Alternatively take the bus from Cusco to Abancay, departing from Terminal Terrestre and get off at the road junction for Mollepata. From the main road to the village is a fair walk, which whilst feasible over the course of several hours isn't very interesting or scenic. It's usually possible to hitch a lift from the junction to the village though.

There are a couple of **hostels**, the better one, *Hospedaje Mollepata* (☎ 832103; s/25 per night) being one block to the west of the main plaza, behind the church. Breakfast in the attached restaurant costs just a couple of sols and a simple *cafecito* will set you back just s/1.5. *Restaurant Salkantay* on the same street is very popular with locals and the food is fresh. It is also reasonably priced – dinner costs s/3-5.

There are a few small **stores** where you can buy some basic last-minute provisions. There are also **arrieros** for hire. In addition to the wages and the hire of the mules, you are responsible for paying for the arrieros' return trip, which from Huayllabamba should only be one day, whilst from Santa Teresa or La Hidroeléctrica takes two days.

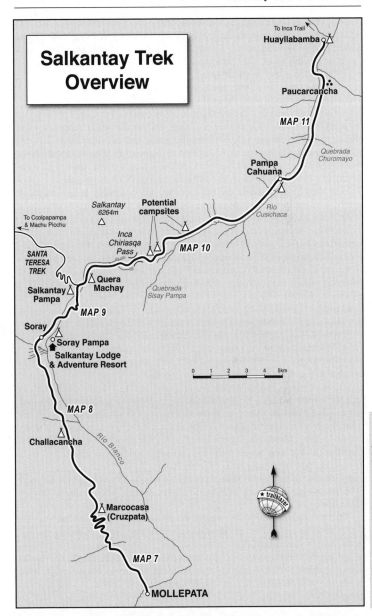

Salkantay Trek Overview

Huayllabamba

To Inca Trail

Paucarcancha

MAP 11

Quebrada Churomayo

Pampa Cahuana

Salkantay 6264m

Potential campsites

Rio Cusichaca

To Ccolpapampa & Machu Picchu

Inca Chiriasqa Pass

MAP 10

SANTA TERESA TREK

Quera Machay

Quebrada Sisay Pampa

Salkantay Pampa

MAP 9

Soray

Soray Pampa

Salkantay Lodge & Adventure Resort

MAP 8

0 1 2 3 4 5km

Challacancha

Rio Blanco

Marcocasa (Cruzpata)

MAP 7

trailblazer

MOLLEPATA

Take the concrete road that leaves from the plaza's north-west corner and follow it as it snakes through the houses. Ignore the dirt track branching left and continue until the concrete runs out at a T-junction after 200m. Turn right (north-east) onto a dirt and cobble road before veering round to the left (north-west) through a **grove of eucalyptus**.

The road from the village eases along the left (west) side of a valley that's heading roughly north-west. Should you wish to avoid this rather tedious section of the trail there is a faint track that drops into the Pumachupán valley to the right of the road, contours roughly north towards the head of the valley and climbs to Marcocasa, cutting between the bends and switchbacks of the road until it reaches the hamlet. It is difficult to pinpoint exactly where the track branches right, so check with your arriero. Don't drop too low into the valley as a number of trails simply lead to cultivated farm plots further below.

The road leads towards the head of the valley, gaining height gently. It curves left and steepens before crossing a **bridge** and coming to a pleasant glade. After the glade the road bends right and climbs past a farm and some cultivated plots of land before beginning a series of long switchbacks. A concrete **irrigation channel** carrying snowmelt from Salkantay bisects the road. Having crossed this irrigation channel on a bridge the road arrives on the crest of a ridge at the small settlement of **Marcocasa** (3500m/11,480ft). It takes 2½-3 hours to reach the village from Mollepata. A **large blue cross**, sometimes swaddled in different coloured cloths, stands to the left of the road and there is a cleared level patch of ground 100m to the right where you can *camp*. Fill up your water bottles at a spring behind some houses at the back of the cleared area (where the power lines lead to), because the streams are unreliable on the way to Soray. From Marcocasa there are some superb, expansive views of the snow-capped Huarohuirani (to the north behind the hill), the village of Qurawasi away in the distance to the west, and Mollepata off to the south.

Beyond Marcocasa the directions are simple – follow the road all the way to Soray Pampa (Map 8). Less than two hours after leaving Marcocasa the road passes **Challacancha**, which consists of two huts with thatch and tin roofs and a small *campsite* to the right-hand side of the road. There are plenty of water sources nearby. About 1-1½ hours after leaving Challacancha the path passes a **ramshackle hut and small holding**, and after another 30 minutes or so it arrives on some high puna fields – Soray Pampa. By now you will have excellent views of the bulk of Mt Humantay and to its right as you look at it the sheer pyramid of Mt Salkantay (6264m/20,551ft), whose name means 'Savage Mountain'.

The pampa is latticed with small concrete drainage canals and streams that you'll have to cross (though these disappear in dry years). Keep to the left (west) side of the pampa, close to the rock wall if you want to remain dry footed. At the far (north) end of the pampa stands **Soray** itself, on the far (north) side of a stream – often there's a simple bridge of tree trunks but you might have to use stepping-stones if this has been washed away. This is a good place to *camp*.

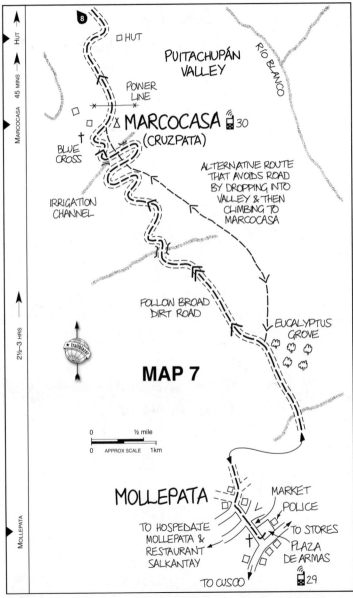

HUT →

45 MINS →

MARCOCASA

2½-3 HRS →

MOLLEPATA

8

□ HUT

PUITACHUPÁN VALLEY

RÍO BLANCO

POWER LINE

△ MARCOCASA 📱30
(CRUZPATA)

BLUE CROSS †

IRRIGATION CHANNEL

ALTERNATIVE ROUTE THAT AVOIDS ROAD BY DROPPING INTO VALLEY & THEN CLIMBING TO MARCOCASA

FOLLOW BROAD DIRT ROAD

EUCALYPTUS GROVE

★ trailblazer

MAP 7

0   ½ mile
0   1km
APPROX SCALE

MOLLEPATA

MARKET

POLICE

TO STORES

TO HOSPEDAJE MOLLEPATA & RESTAURANT SALKANTAY

PLAZA DE ARMAS

📱29

TO CUSCO

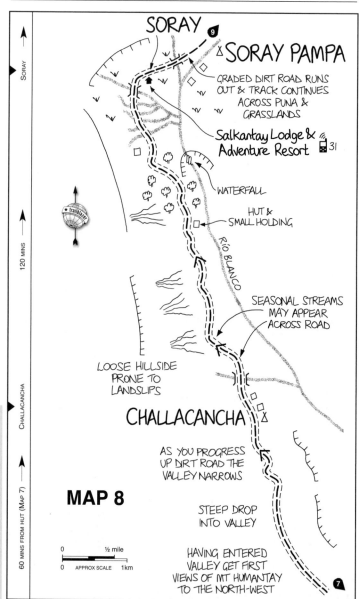

SORAY

△ SORAY PAMPA

GRADED DIRT ROAD RUNS
OUT & TRACK CONTINUES
ACROSS PUNA &
GRASSLANDS

Salkantay Lodge &
Adventure Resort 31

WATERFALL

HUT &
SMALL HOLDING

RÍO BLANCO

SEASONAL STREAMS
MAY APPEAR
ACROSS ROAD

LOOSE HILLSIDE
PRONE TO
LANDSLIPS

CHALLACANCHA

AS YOU PROGRESS
UP DIRT ROAD THE
VALLEY NARROWS

MAP 8

STEEP DROP
INTO VALLEY

0   ½ mile

0   APPROX SCALE   1km

HAVING ENTERED
VALLEY GET FIRST
VIEWS OF MT HUMANTAY
TO THE NORTH-WEST

SORAY

120 MINS

CHALLACANCHA

60 MINS FROM HUT (MAP 7)

ROUTE GUIDE AND MAPS

The lodge here, **Salkantay Lodge & Adventure Resort**, is run by Mountain Lodges of Peru (see p183) and can only be used by people on the lodge to lodge trek to Santa Teresa.

SORAY TO PAUCARCANCHA
[MAP 9, p248; MAP 10, p249; MAP 11, p251]

The trail heads up the valley to the north-east (right). The path starts on the left-hand side of the valley and crosses the **Río Salkantay**, a tributary of the Río Blanco. In the lee of the mountains on this side of the valley is *Camping Humantay*, a large shelter with a corrugated iron roof, under which people can camp. Other huts (lean-to structures) act as kitchens and dining rooms.

There's an interesting detour from here that climbs north-west away from the campsite to a pretty glacial, turquoise tarn below the slopes and shrinking glaciers of Mt Humantay, which itself often has impressive cornices and over-hanging snowy ridges. The ascent to the tarn takes around an hour whilst the return journey lasts half that time.

The main path climbs uphill on the other side of the valley though. Pass through a **gap** in a tumbledown stone wall and begin a series of zigzags to ascend the valley. Direct shortcuts between switchbacks are easy to follow, although steep and occasionally muddy. Half an hour after Soray Pampa you pass through a rudimentary **gate** set in a stone wall in order to enter **Salkantay Pampa**. Mt Salkantay, the sacred mountain of the Incas, is ahead of you. Descend to Río Salkantay and cross a number of branches to the left-hand side of the pampa, where the path becomes boggy and the track indistinct. As long as you continue following the stream north-east, however, you'll be fine.

At the head of the valley is a massive wall of scree – the **terminal moraine** (end debris) of a glacier. The flat ground before the moraine is a great place to *camp*. The path divides here; the left-hand fork bearing north-west around the moraine towards a V-shaped valley is the way for the Santa Teresa Trek. To continue on the Salkantay Trek take the right-hand fork (east), crossing back over the stream, towards the pass at Inka Chiriasqa.

A series of steep switchbacks climbs sharply up the eastern shoulder of Mt Salkantay. A short distance into the climb the path passes a flat patch of hillside called **Quera Machay** which makes for a decent *campsite*. Beyond here the path heads north and then east, continuing to climb all the while. Alternative trails branch off and descend to the lateral moraine of the glacier. Ignore these and keep the river between you and the glacier.

As you gain height and climb through **Pampa Japonés** the valley narrows dramatically. From the high point there are good views back over the wall of lateral moraine to a pair of lakes. At this point the ridge is visible ahead and the pass can be made out above a very steep slope. It is tempting to cut out the last climb and nip over the watershed by the glacier instead, but this is potentially very dangerous. **Inka Chiriasqa** (aka Chiriaska/ca/q'ua; 4950m/16,235ft), which translates as 'the place where the Inca cools down', is a narrow (barely a metre wide) knife-like pass.

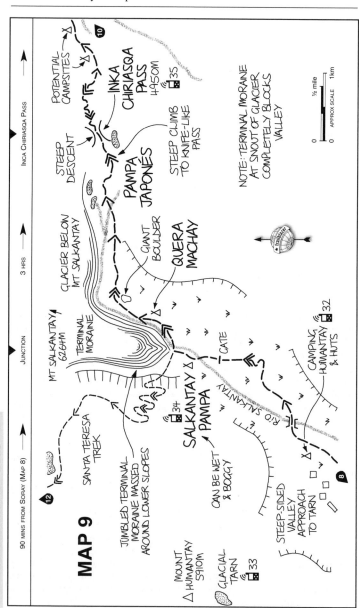

MAP 9

90 MINS FROM SORAY (MAP 8)

JUNCTION   3 HRS   INCA CHIRIASQA PASS

MOUNT HUMANTAY 5910M

GLACIAL TARN 📷33

STEEP-SIDED VALLEY APPROACH TO TARN

CAN BE WET & BOGGY

TUMBLED TERMINAL MORAINE MASSED AROUND LOWER SLOPES

SANTA TERESA TREK

SALKANTAY PAMPA 📷34

MT SALKANTAY 626HM

TERMINAL MORAINE

GLACIER BELOW MT SALKANTAY

GATE

RÍO SALKANTAY

CAMPING HUMANTAY & HUTS 📷32

GIANT BOULDER

QUERA MACHAY

PAMPA JAPONÉS

STEEP DESCENT

STEEP CLIMB TO KNIFE-LIKE PASS

POTENTIAL CAMPSITES

INKA CHIRIASQA PASS 4950M 📷35

NOTE: TERMINAL MORAINE AT SNOUT OF GLACIER COMPLETELY BLOCKS VALLEY

0   ½ mile   1km
APPROX SCALE

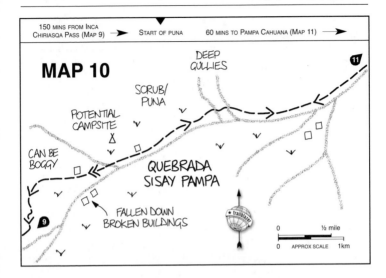

MAP 10

DEEP GULLIES

SCRUB/ PUNA

POTENTIAL CAMPSITE

CAN BE BOGGY

QUEBRADA SISAY PAMPA

FALLEN DOWN BROKEN BUILDINGS

★ trailblazer

0   ½ mile
0   APPROX SCALE   1km

From the pass there are stunning views of both the valley behind you and the one that lies ahead. The path drops quickly from the high point, descending swiftly into the adjoining valley passing two *potential campsites*. The path is clear and easy to make out – it simply follows the valley down. Initially it crosses puna heading south-east but soon bends north-east and becomes increasingly steep. There is another *campsite* 1½ hours beyond Inka Chiriasqa, just before a ridge, but it is popular with tour agencies and frequently fully occupied.

A little further on, beyond the ridge, the path tracks across a patch of glacial outwash and begins to follow the northern bank of the river. This is **Quebrada Sisay Pampa** (Map 10) and is also used as a *campsite*. Follow the left-hand (north) bank of the river and continue downstream. The path skirts around two gullies that have seasonal streams and continues to descend whilst the surrounding hillsides become increasingly steep. A broad river joins from the south.

Almost immediately after this the valley turns north-east. From here you can make out an Inca canal below you. This area, 3½ hours from the pass, is **Pampa Cahuana** (Map 11). The path meanders between a clutch of houses, farms and a football pitch before crossing a bridge to the eastern (right-hand) bank of the **Inca-built canal**. Constructed to drain the flat upper valley and prevent the river meandering lazily here, the well-engineered canal was used to irrigate this section of the basin and still carries melt water into the valley bottom. There are some good flat places to *camp* here.

At the far end of a narrow gorge the valley and canal, which develops into Río Cushichaca, turn north and continue to descend through changing vegetation until, 1½ hours from the bridge, the path arrives at the small hamlet and ruins of **Paucarcancha** (see box p250).

❏ Paucarcancha

This partially renovated ruin, also sometimes referred to as **Incarajay**, stands guard over the Cusichaca river, dominating the valley and protecting an approach to Machu Picchu from the Apurímac to the south. The Incas were not native to this valley, but this imposing fort built following the submission of the indigenous tribes sometime in the second half of the 15th century, would have served as a potent reminder of the new rulers of the region. It would also have served as a strategically sited tambo.

The fort contains 16 buildings, some of which are thought to be barracks. Trapezoidal windows look out over the countryside and large sets of terraces adorn the surrounding hillsides, presumably providing crops and foodstuffs for the inhabitants.

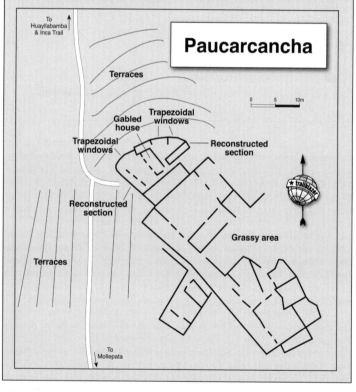

Paucarcancha

To Huayllabamba & Inca Trail

Terraces

0 5 10m

Gabled house

Trapezoidal windows

Trapezoidal windows

Reconstructed section

Reconstructed section

Grassy area

Terraces

★ trailblazer

To Mollepata

Beyond the ruins and the small village continue the trek to Huayllabamba (45 mins; see p221). Once there you can join the classic Inca Trail, or walk down the Cusichaca Valley and either catch a train back to Cusco or onwards to Aguas Calientes from Km88; alternatively you can walk to Km82 (Chilca), or even trek along the river to Machu Picchu.

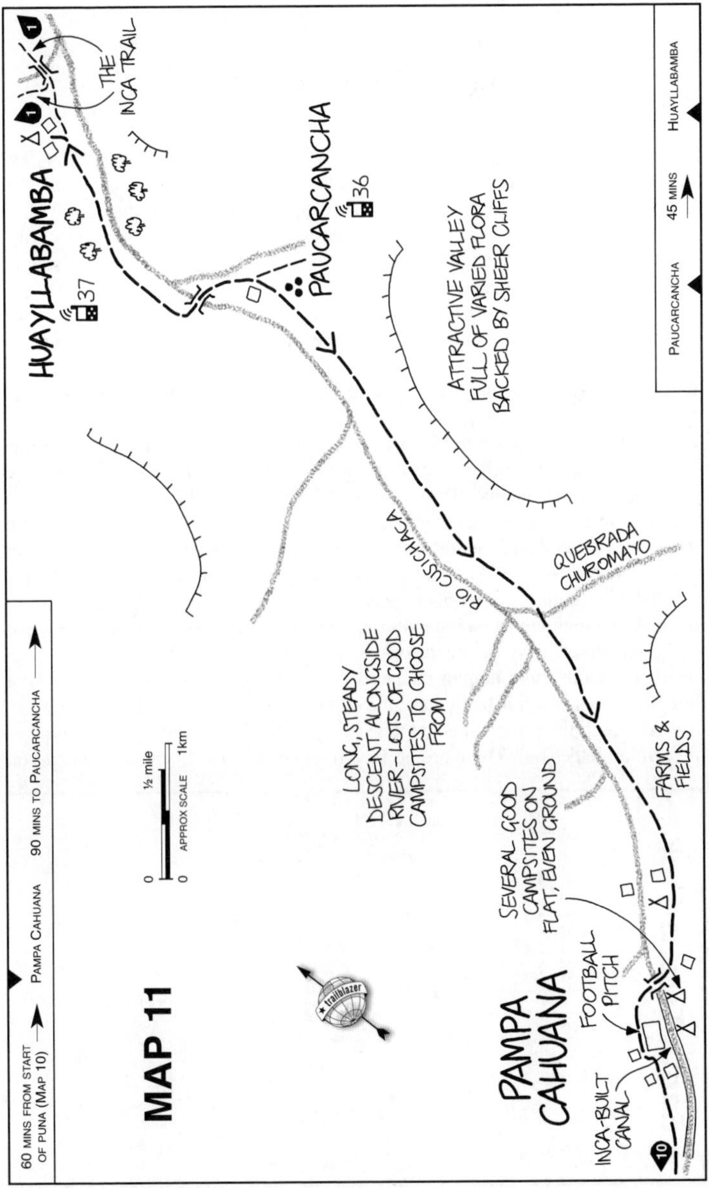
MAP 11
60 MINS FROM START OF PUNA (MAP 10)
PAMPA CAHUANA
90 MINS TO PAUCARCANCHA
PAUCARCANCHA
45 MINS
HUAYLLABAMBA
0 ½ mile
0 APPROX SCALE 1km
trailblazer
HUAYLLABAMBA
37
THE INCA TRAIL
1
PAUCARCANCHA
36
ATTRACTIVE VALLEY FULL OF VARIED FLORA BACKED BY SHEER CLIFFS
RÍO CUSICHACA
QUEBRADA CHUROMAYO
LONG, STEADY DESCENT ALONGSIDE RIVER – LOTS OF GOOD CAMPSITES TO CHOOSE FROM
FARMS & FIELDS
SEVERAL GOOD CAMPSITES ON FLAT, EVEN GROUND
FOOTBALL PITCH
PAMPA CAHUANA
INCA-BUILT CANAL
10

The Santa Teresa Trek

This route is the only 'back door' approach to Machu Picchu (see overview map). Closed for a number of years in the wake of the massive landslide in 1998 that wiped out the village of Santa Teresa (see box p261) and the nearby railway line, it was only re-opened by the authorities to ease the pressure on the Inca Trail and provide an alternative for those short of time, money or simply caught out by the complex regulations.

However, its growing popularity meant that it was only a matter of time before the government imposed a set of rules in line with those already in place on the classic Inca Trail; the INC have now determined that it should only be undertaken with an agency so you need to purchase a permit (see box p217) at Soray Pampa (s/129, approx US$50) for the section from Soray Pampa to Lucmabamba. If you are trekking with an agency check to make sure that this fee is included in the price of the trek. However, I have still encountered people tackling the route independently and simply bypassing the checkpoint, which may not be possible in the long term if the INC decide to apply the rules more vigorously. Check with South American Explorers (🖥 www.saexplorers.org) or Andean Travel Web (🖥 www.andeantravelweb.com/peru) for the latest status.

All this means it is no longer the deserted, remote route it once was and since there are no regulations on the number of people beginning the route each day it can get relatively busy during the peak season. However, there are still fewer people on it than its more famous counterpart so rather than camp amidst crowds of other trekkers, you'll actually have the opportunity to interact with the locals.

Although the routes finish at the same point, this is a very different type of trek to the Inca Trail. There are no Inca ruins, except for Llactapata, when you

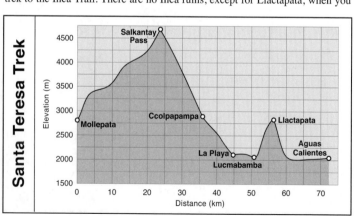

ROUTE GUIDE AND MAPS

Santa Teresa Trek

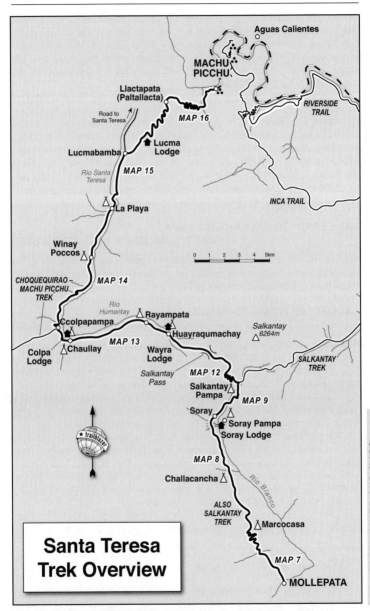

Aguas Calientes

MACHU
PICCHU

Llactapata
(Paltallacta)

RIVERSIDE
TRAIL

Road to
Santa Teresa

MAP 16

Lucma
Lodge

Lucmabamba

MAP 15

Rio Santa
Teresa

INCA TRAIL

La Playa

Winay
Poccos

0 1 2 3 4 5km

CHOQUEQUIRAO –
MACHU PICCHU
TREK

MAP 14

Rio
Humantay

Rayampata

Ccolpapampa

Huayraqumachay

Salkantay
6264m

Colpa
Lodge

Chaullay

MAP 13

Wayra
Lodge

SALKANTAY
TREK

Salkantay
Pass

MAP 12

Salkantay
Pampa

MAP 9

Soray

Soray Pampa
Soray Lodge

MAP 8

Challacancha

Rio Blanco

ALSO
SALKANTAY
TREK

Marcocasa

Santa Teresa
Trek Overview

MAP 7

MOLLEPATA

ROUTE GUIDE AND MAPS

are in sight of Machu Picchu. However, the scenery is stunning and the varied range of landscapes that you pass through make the Santa Teresa route an excellent outing in its own right. You'll explore a wider range of landscapes, climb closer to the snow line and descend further into the subtropical forest than you would on the Inca Trail, meaning that you'll have a much better chance of seeing a wider range of birdlife and flora.

The best time to tackle the trek is during the dry season (May to September), as the high pass can be blocked by snow during the wet season.

The trek begins from Mollepata and traditionally takes four days. You should factor in a fifth to explore Machu Picchu properly. The trek is relatively strenuous since it climbs from the watershed of the Apurímac (2800m/9185ft) to cross a 4700m/15,415ft pass below Mt Salkantay, tumbles back down into the thickly forested Santa Teresa valley (2300m/7545ft), breaches another pass as 2850m/9350ft and descends 600m/1970ft into the Aobamba valley to finish at Aguas Calientes, at the foot of Machu Picchu mountain.

MOLLEPATA TO SALKANTAY PAMPA
MAP 7, p245; MAP 8, p246; MAP 9, p248]

For information on getting to the trailhead at Mollepata see box p242. For details about the first stage of the trek follow the directions from Mollepata on the Salkantay/Mollepata Trek (see pp241-7).

SALKANTAY PAMPA TO RAYAMPATA
[MAP 9, p248; MAP 12; MAP 13, p257]

At Salkantay Pampa, the trail divides. The Salkantay trail branches right (northeast) around the moraine at the foot of Mt Salkantay towards the Inka Chiriasqa pass and Huayllabamba. For the Santa Teresa trek you want to bear left (northwest) around the left-hand side of the moraine towards the Salkantay Pass.

The path begins to climb steeply up seven tight switchbacks (Map 12), known as **Siete Culebras** (the Seven Serpents), and crests a small knoll after which it undulates north, parallel to the moraine, gradually gaining height.

Having scrambled through a boulder field, you snake across a level pampa and arrive at a small lake, **Laguna Salkantaycocha**, at its western end. **Soroyccocha**, the area of flat, clear ground just before the lake, makes for a good *campsite*; high and exposed it can get cold here but there's some protection from the nearby moraine ridge and the setting, backed by hills and looking directly onto the face of Mt Salkantay, is superb.

The track passes to the left (south) of the lake and climbs above it for a further 20-25 minutes, during which time you cross a series of ridges and pass a

---

❏ **Important note – walking times**
All times in this book refer only to the time spent walking. You will need to add 10-30% to allow for rests, photography, checking the map, drinking water etc.

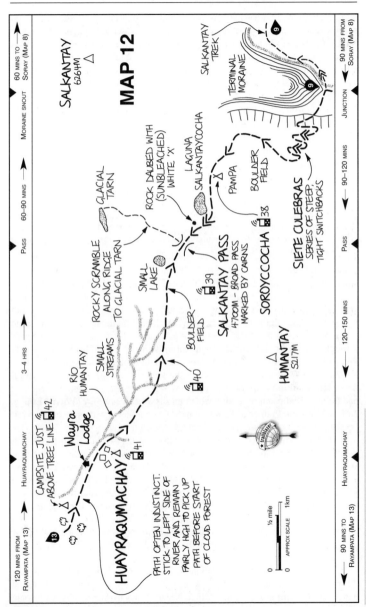

MAP 12

SALKANTAY
6264M △

60 MINS TO → Soray (MAP 8)

MORAINE SNOUT →

60–90 MINS →

PASS →

3–4 HRS →

HUAYRAQUMACHAY →

120 FROM Rayampata (MAP 13) →

9

SALKANTAY TREK

TERMINAL MORAINE

9

JUNCTION

90 MINS FROM → Soray (MAP 8)

GLACIAL TARN

ROCK DAUBED WITH (SUNBLEACHED) WHITE 'X'

ROCKY SCRAMBLE ALONG RIDGE TO GLACIAL TARN

LAGUNA SALKANTAYCOCHA

△

PAMPA

BOULDER FIELD

SIETE CULEBRAS
SERIES OF STEEP, TIGHT SWITCHBACKS

90–120 MINS →

SMALL LAKE

SOROYCCOCHA 🏠 38

SALKANTAY PASS
4700M – BROAD PASS MARKED BY CAIRNS

🏠 39

HUMANTAY
5217M △

120–150 MINS →

PASS →

Río Humantay

SMALL STREAMS

BOULDER FIELD

🏠 40

Wayra Lodge 🏠 42

△

🏠 41

CAMPSITE JUST ABOVE TREE LINE

△

13

HUAYRAQUMACHAY

PATH OFTEN INDISTINCT. STICK TO LEFT SIDE OF RIVER AND REMAIN FAIRLY HIGH TO PICK UP PATH BEFORE START OF CLOUD FOREST

½ mile
APPROX SCALE 1km
0

90 MINS TO → Rayampata (MAP 13)

★Trailblazer

large rock daubed with what was once a red 'X' that has now faded and been sun-bleached white. A further 5-10 minutes' easy scrambling brings you to **Salkantay pass** (4700m/15,415ft), which is variously known as Humantay Pass or Apacheta Pass. The pass is marked by a series of cairns (*apachetas*) up to 6ft tall, built to honour the *apus*, the more ghoulish of which include bones and skulls. It takes 3-3½ hours to get to the pass from Soray Pampa.

The pass is part of the shoulder of Salkantay, which rises to the north-east. If it is clear you should be able to see across the south face of the mountain to the high pass Inka Chiriasqa in the distance. To the south stands Tucarhuay whilst to the south-west lie the glaciated twin peaks of Humantay and to the north-west stands Pumasillo.

Diversion to a glacial tarn

From the pass there's a rough scramble along the ridge, over giant boulders, towards the lower slopes of Salkantay that affords excellent views of the mountain and its fluted face, before a glacial tarn fed by meltwater becomes visible below. Stark and barren, it's nonetheless beautiful, with the chalky blue of the lake contrasting strongly with the surrounding rock and scree. On warm days listen out too for the sound of avalanches, as slabs of snow let go of the steep slopes across from you.

Beyond Salkantay pass the path descends steadily west, dropping past a small tarn and through a **boulder field** that chokes the narrow valley. As the valley broadens, the track frequently vanishes in muddy mires where a number of small streams cross the route. Stick to the left-hand (west) side of the valley and you will pick up the path further down. In places simple stone walls span the width of the valley, but there are gaps or gates along them allowing you to pass through. The bogs and streams eventually give rise to **Río Humantay**, which you follow on its left (west) bank, crossing small tributaries as you go.

About two hours from the pass on the left bank (west) of the river, you'll reach **Huayraqumachay** or 'Eye of the Wind'; there are a couple of farm huts and a flat, raised patch of ground which makes a good *campsite*. **Wayra Lodge**, part of Mountain Lodges of Peru (see p183), is on the opposite side of the river, perched above a cliff with spectacular views down the valley.

After Huayraqumachay the path is fairly imprecise, but keep to the left (west) of the river and remain fairly high on the valley. You'll pass a number of simple farm plots amidst some giant boulders. There's also a *campsite* here with a number of large, leveled pitches and assorted covered structures under which you can cook or eat. Below these the valley sides steepen and the puna gives way to scrub. Just above the treeline is a large, well-prepared *campsite*. The path then descends into the cloud forest, which is draped with moss and lichen although there also lots of bomaria and orchids to spot as well. Look out too for parakeets and hummingbirds. Although frequently muddy and often churned up by mules, the main path can be found quite easily.

This track continues to descend gently through the cloud forest and around 90 minutes after Huayraqumachay, you'll pass some gravestones marking the fringes of **Rayampata** (Map 13), which is also shown as Arayan Niyoc on some

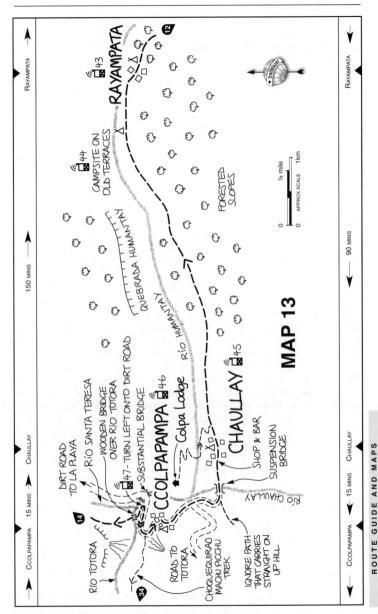

MAP 13

maps. Several huts are adjacent to the track and there are a few small terraces where you can **camp**. Water can be collected from the river below the huts. The families occasionally have soft drinks for sale. The views from the huts down the valley, of the snow-capped range ahead, are excellent.

RAYAMPATA TO CCOLPAPAMPA   [MAP 13, p257]

From Rayampata you descend through thickly forested slopes. The skies are often clear first thing in the morning and an early start means that you'll be able to enjoy outstanding views. You'll also be able to hear the spectacular dawn chorus, as there is a wealth of birdlife in the upper reaches of the cloud forest. A quarter of an hour after leaving Rayampata you pass a small **campsite** that takes advantage of the flat ground on top of broad terraces for tent pitches.

After an hour the path passes a pair of *collpas* (small earthen cliffs), clay licks used by parakeets, and in about 30 minutes you reach the village of Chaullay. Just prior to entering the village a small trail breaks right from the main path and quickly zigzags down a steep slope to reach the Río Humantay. On the far side a corresponding path ascends to **Colpa Lodge**, owned by Mountain Lodges of Peru (see p183); the lodge has an attractive front lawn that acts as a panoramic viewpoint overlooking Ccolpapampa and the valley ahead.

Chaullay (not to be confused with the ruins of the same name on the Vilcabamba Trail) is an attractive settlement at the junction of two valleys with a handful of rudimentary stores selling basic provisions. There are also several covered areas where you can eat and a basic shop advertising itself as a bar. Greener and cleaner than Rayampata, it would make an excellent **campsite** were it not for the clouds of mosquitoes. If the pests are out in force there are several good alternative campsites a further 15 minutes along the path.

Pass through the village and cross the Río Chaullay on the concrete suspension bridge and turn right (north) on the far bank, ignoring the well-trodden trail that zigzags west up the side of the valley to pick up the broad, graded road that now reaches from Santa Teresa as far into the mountains as here.

Follow the road downstream along the left (west) bank of the river to **Ccolpapampa**, a slightly larger community than Chaullay where there are a number of level pitches on which to **camp**. Nowadays, Ccolpapampa is well connected to the outside world, with the road extension from Santa Teresa bringing trucks to the rough and ready collection of tin-roofed huts. There are also a couple of basic places to pick up a beer or soft drinks.

CCOLPAPAMPA TO LA PLAYA   [MAP 13, p257; MAP 14]

The onward road can be picked up on the far side of the grassy central square and continues down the valley. The road soon bends left (west) into the **Quebrada Totora**. Follow it down a sweeping bend, with an eye on the land-slip scars that mark the steep slopes all around. A smaller path branches off left from the apex of the bend but ignore this, it actually leads to Choquequirao and is part of the route that links Choquequirao to Machu Picchu. Instead double

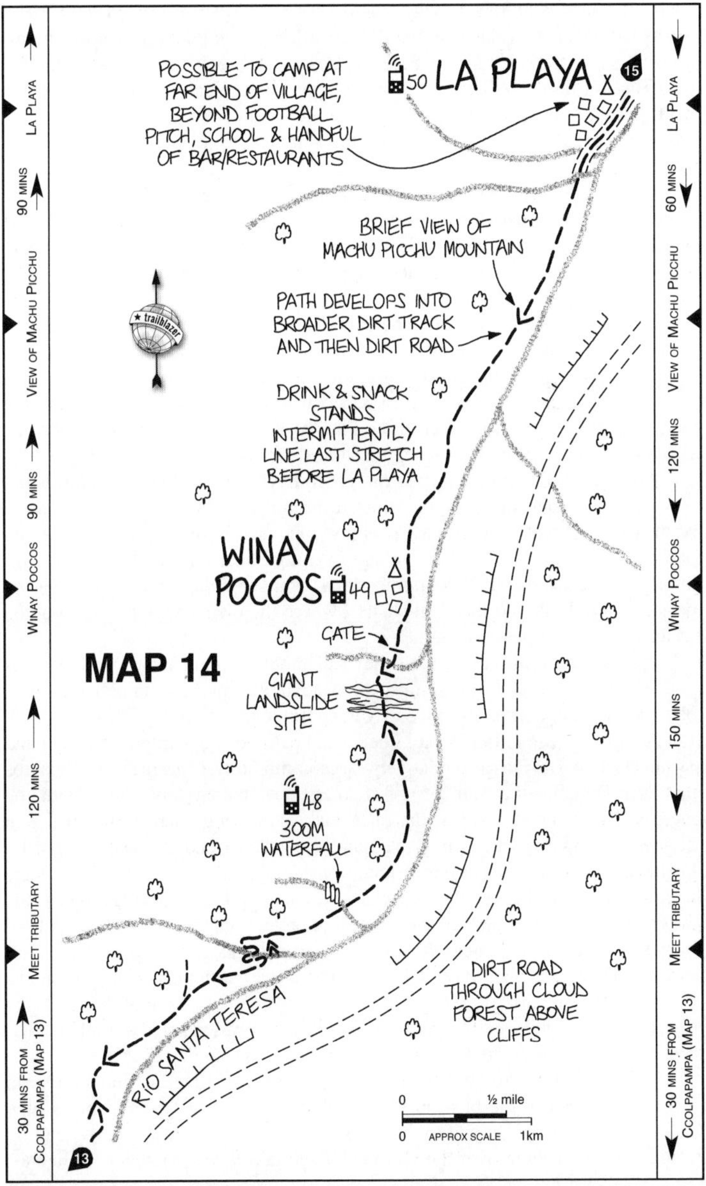

POSSIBLE TO CAMP AT FAR END OF VILLAGE, BEYOND FOOTBALL PITCH, SCHOOL & HANDFUL OF BAR/RESTAURANTS

📶 50 LA PLAYA 15

BRIEF VIEW OF MACHU PICCHU MOUNTAIN

PATH DEVELOPS INTO BROADER DIRT TRACK AND THEN DIRT ROAD

DRINK & SNACK STANDS INTERMITTENTLY LINE LAST STRETCH BEFORE LA PLAYA

★ trailblazer

WINAY POCCOS 📶 49

GATE

MAP 14

GIANT LANDSLIDE SITE

📶 48
300M WATERFALL

DIRT ROAD THROUGH CLOUD FOREST ABOVE CLIFFS

RÍO SANTA TERESA

13

0   ½ mile
0   APPROX SCALE   1km

Left margin (bottom to top): LA PLAYA → 90 MINS → VIEW OF MACHU PICCHU → 90 MINS → WINAY POCCOS → 120 MINS → MEET TRIBUTARY → 30 MINS FROM CCOLPAPAMPA (MAP 13)

Right margin (top to bottom): LA PLAYA → 60 MINS → VIEW OF MACHU PICCHU → 120 MINS → WINAY POCCOS → 150 MINS → MEET TRIBUTARY → 30 MINS FROM CCOLPAPAMPA (MAP 13)

back on yourself before curving round above the river. Before a large steel, wood and concrete bridge over the Río Chaullay, which joins Río Totora, there's a turning left and a small dirt trail that descends steeply to a **wooden bridge** over Río Totora itself. There used to be a pair of scenically sited cement baths here that had hot spring water channeled into them from higher up the valley but they were destroyed by an avalanche, which also blocked the waterway.

On the far side of the wooden bridge the trail leads along the left (west) side of the river, now the **Río Santa Teresa**, in a north-easterly direction. On the opposite bank the road continues down the valley but is quickly lost amidst the thick vegetation and you're able to continue trekking, unaware of the main access route. Where the path divides take the lower (right-hand) branch to make a slow descent through the cloud forest.

Half an hour before entering the Santa Teresa Valley the path reaches a **tributary**. Head upstream here along the tributary for about 8m before crossing it in order to pick up the path on the far side. A little further on the path crosses beneath the thundering course of a **300m waterfall**, which plunges from the cliff tops through the forest, crashing into the river below in six great bounds. Cross the falls on a series of stepping stones, watching your footing.

About 2km (1¼ miles) further on, you'll have to scramble over a **landslide** that has devastated the path and scarred the hillside, although vegetation and scrub has begun to grow back. Cross a second stream on stepping stones and pass through a **gate** before descending to **Winay Poccos**, a village of a few simple houses and some strips of farmed land. You can *camp* in a grassy clearing beside a small hut and thatched shelter, where the owner will sell you bottled water and bags of passion fruit.

The path continues down the valley and about 1½ hours from Winay Poccos you'll get your first brief glimpse of Machu Picchu Mountain before it is obscured by an intervening ridge as you continue to descend.

About 2½ hours after Winay Poccos the path develops into a dirt road and meanders into **La Playa**, a relatively large community of farmers and arrieros that is embracing the numbers of trekkers now taking this route. With the increased number of visitors, the once makeshift bridge across the river that divides the town has been improved and the road extended, meaning that La Playa has been able to develop quite considerably. As you enter the village there's a series of shacks selling drinks and snacks and some *tent pitches*. At the far end of the village, beyond the football pitch and school, are also a couple of **bars/restaurants**, and small kiosks selling soft drinks as well as a cold water shower. There are also several houses that allow *camping* in their grounds. However, the quietest place to pitch your tent is on the far side of the river that runs through the village; the campsite is on a slightly raised patch of ground adjacent to the old square, looking back across the village and up the valley.

This is also where you can get transport to the village of **Santa Teresa** (see box opposite); the bus journey (s/3) takes an hour. Some agencies pick you up here and shuttle you to the hot springs at Santa Teresa, before leading you across the bridge over the Urubamba and taking you to Aguas Calientes.

❏ **Santa Teresa**
Santa Teresa used to be a small, subtropical village connected to Aguas Calientes, and therefore Machu Picchu, by a short train ride. The railway represented the main link between the town and the outside world. In spring 1998 both the village and the railway line were destroyed by an enormous landslide that swept down from the surrounding mountains. Torrential El Niño rainstorms loosened the soil on the mountainside, releasing a colossal landslip into the Río Urubamba. Around 15 people died and over 350 families were affected. Almost 80% of the buildings in the old part of Santa Teresa were destroyed or partly damaged. The railway line was mangled beyond use and at the time of research still hadn't been repaired. The power station, La Hidroeléctrica, was also badly damaged.

The reconstruction and regeneration of Santa Teresa has been taking place slowly ever since although further floods in 2010 set the redevelopment back. However, the 'back door' route to Machu Picchu and the bridge across the Urubamba are bringing more people into the valley. Nonetheless, it remains a fairly plain settlement, with a smattering of basic hostel accommodation and cheap chicken restaurants, of little real interest to the casual visitor.

If you're staying overnight try *Albergue Municipal* (☎ 984-145049), which has dorm beds for s/20 and double rooms for s/60, or *Eco Quechua* (🖳 www.ecoquechua .com, ☎ 630877 or ☎ 984 756855), an atmospheric lodge outside the town, which allows **camping** at s/12 per tent and has rooms from US$65 (sgl and dbl). In town, **internet access** is sporadically available in a few cafés. There are no banks or cash points though.

Some 4km (2½ miles) from Santa Teresa, the **Cocalmayo hot springs** (s/5) are a genuine attraction, with warm water pools and a café. Also popular is **Cola de Mono Canopy zipline** (🖳 www.canopyperu.com; US$60), about 2km (1¼ miles) from Santa Teresa. Billed as South America's highest zipline, it whisks people through the air above the Sacsara Valley. There are 2500m of cable in total over six runs; the longest ride is 400m, the highest 150m and riders on the line reach speeds of 60kph (37mph).

This option prevents you from completing the trek on foot and actually deprives you of the bulk of the final stage, a stage that includes the recently rediscovered and partially uncovered ruins of Llactapata (see box pp262-3).

LA PLAYA TO AGUAS CALIENTES
[MAP 15, p265; MAP 16, p267; MAP 4, p231]

On the far side of the **bridge** that bisects the village, join the gravel road that runs above the river towards Santa Teresa. After 3km (2 miles) there is a large **faded blue 'INC' sign** on the right-hand side (east) of the road, next to the small community of **Lucmabamba**. Turn right (east) here on to a grassy track and a short section of restored, broad Inca steps, which climb past coffee **plantations**, houses with concrete slabs for drying coffee beans and plots of lemon and passion-fruit trees. Thirty minutes from the junction, on the right-hand side of the track, stands the thatched, modern **Lucma Lodge** belonging to Mountain Lodges of Peru (see p183). (continued on p266)

ROUTE GUIDE AND MAPS

❏ Llactapata (Paltallacta)

Despite their proximity to Machu Picchu, the ruins of Llactapata (also known as Paltallacta) have been little investigated since they were initially uncovered by Hiram Bingham in 1912. The site, situated on and below a long ridge, lay untouched for more than 70 years after this discovery, until being 'rediscovered' in the early 1980s. Since then, studies have shown the site to be far larger and more significant than previously imagined.

The first account of the ruins was published by Bingham. An initial foray into the Aobamba Valley by Bingham's assistant had met with 'almost insuperable difficulty' as a result of the dense, impenetrable forest that clad the hillsides. Bingham himself explored the region 10 days later and recorded that he '... found some interesting ruins ... The end of that day found us on top of a ridge between the valleys of the Aobamba and the Salcantay.' The small collection of structures he then loosely described is part of Llactapata, which, owing to its strategic location overlooking Machu Picchu's western flank, and the clear and unrivalled view of the city from here, he decided was 'the ruins of an Inca castle'. He went on to attribute its construction to one of Manco Inca's captains.

In total, Bingham spent just five daylight hours at the site and failed to properly explore or map the ruins. His expedition was sorely handicapped by an unhelpful team of *arrieros* who had been press-ganged into service; his account of the trip in fact spends more time lamenting the deficiencies of his team than describing the ruins. The *arrieros* later abandoned him.

Unfortunately Bingham's imprecise notes regarding the location were too vague for anyone to be able to retrace his steps, and slowly the forest closed back over the ruins. In truth his descriptions of the ruins, published alongside news of the uncovering of Machu Picchu, Vitcos and Espíritu Pampa, failed to inspire people to follow in his footsteps. It wasn't until the early 1980s that Hugh Thomson rediscovered them, and not until the early part of the 21st century that any serious archaeological investigation was carried out, with extensive excavation and mapping undertaken by Thomson.

The site, whose name means 'High Town' in Quechua, is considerably larger than first thought, although it is still hard to tell where the ruins begin and the cloud forest ends. The complex faces Machu Picchu, which lies 5km (3 miles) to the east, on the far side of the Aobamba valley. The sacred peaks of Mt Veronica and Mt Salkantay are also visible from here.

The site consists of several interrelated high-status building groups including a feature thought to be a **sun temple**, which has uncanny similarities in terms of structure, size and alignment to the Coricancha (see pp154-5) in Cusco. There are also residential sectors here that might have served as high-status *tambos*, and agricultural areas thought to have been used to grow crops to supplement food production at Machu Picchu.

Although the stonework is generally less impressive than at Machu Picchu because of the metamorphic rocks available, the solid buildings, multiple niches, shaped corner stones and **double-jamb doorways** are indicative of a place of great importance. Evidence shows that the crude walls were in fact coated with light-coloured clay that would have concealed the rough stonework beneath a smooth, striking façade.

An Inca path uncovered by Hugh Thomson and Gary Ziegler leads from the site towards Vilcabamba and Vitcos, whilst the Inca path that starts at the Inca drawbridge behind Machu Picchu and runs across the head of the valley to Llactapata would have provided a suitably elaborate and spectacular entrance to the site. This would have allowed the Inca to visit the site for particular ceremonial occasions, such as the June solstice.

A unique feature is a 45m/145ft long **sunken corridor** set 1.8m/6ft into the earth and aligned so as to point directly at Machu Picchu. During the summer solstice, the sun rises over the Torreón in Machu Picchu, and falls directly along this channel. The building thought to be a sun temple and various viewing platforms throughout the site lend further weight to the ritual significance of Llactapata.

In his report on the site, Hugh Thomson suggests that the careful alignment (see p264) of the key buildings and features in relationship to Machu Picchu indicate that Llactapata was 'part of a carefully designed network of interrelated administrative and ceremonial sites supporting the regional administrative and ceremonial centre at Machu Picchu'.

Underlining the importance of the site and its ritual significance are the facts that a number of key buildings in Machu Picchu are set to look over the Aobamba valley towards Llactapata. The Intihuatana and the small structure at the summit of Huayna Picchu are both aligned to look east across the valley. The house on Huayna Picchu also contains a *huaca* that replicates the Llactapata ridge.

So far much of the site is off-limits to the public whilst investigations and excavations are carried out. Just a handful of buildings have been restored and since the pace of excavation is so slow, the forest has reclaimed some previously cleared areas, meaning that it takes no small amount of imagination to visualize the grandeur of the sprawling site and imagine the significance of the spectacular view of Machu Picchu spread out across the horizon to the west.

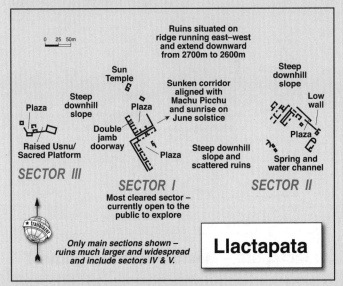

Ruins situated on ridge running east–west and extend downward from 2700m to 2600m

0   25   50m

Sun Temple

Sunken corridor aligned with Machu Picchu and sunrise on June solstice

Steep downhill slope

Low wall

Plaza

Steep downhill slope

Plaza

Plaza

Double jamb doorway

Plaza

Raised Usnu/ Sacred Platform

Steep downhill slope and scattered ruins

Spring and water channel

SECTOR III

SECTOR I

SECTOR II

Most cleared sector – currently open to the public to explore

Only main sections shown – ruins much larger and widespread and include sectors IV & V.

Llactapata

Llactapata – Machu Picchu alignment

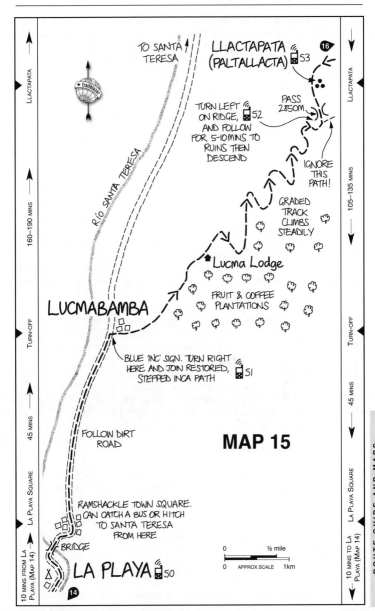

TO SANTA
TERESA

LLACTAPATA
(PALTALLACTA) 53

16

★ trailblazer

TURN LEFT
ON RIDGE, 52
AND FOLLOW
FOR 5-10 MINS TO
RUINS THEN
DESCEND

PASS
2,850M

IGNORE
THIS
PATH!

Río Santa Teresa

GRADED
TRACK
CLIMBS
STEADILY

Lucma Lodge

LUCMABAMBA

FRUIT & COFFEE
PLANTATIONS

BLUE 'INC' SIGN. TURN RIGHT
HERE AND JOIN RESTORED, 51
STEPPED INCA PATH

FOLLOW DIRT
ROAD

MAP 15

RAMSHACKLE TOWN SQUARE.
CAN CATCH A BUS OR HITCH
TO SANTA TERESA
FROM HERE

BRIDGE

LA PLAYA 50

14

0   ½ mile
0   APPROX SCALE   1km

LLACTAPATA

160-190 MINS

TURN-OFF

45 MINS

LA PLAYA SQUARE

10 MINS FROM LA
PLAYA (MAP 14)

LLACTAPATA

105-135 MINS

TURN-OFF

45 MINS

LA PLAYA SQUARE

10 MINS TO LA
PLAYA (MAP 14)

(Continued from p261) Continue ascending for 2-2½ hours on a wide, even path, as plantations give way to scrub which in turn gives way to cloud forest that thickens as you climb around a series of spurs before entering dense, virgin forest. Finally, go up a short section of steps and arrive at a **ridge-pass** (2850m/9350ft).

Ignore a wide, slightly overgrown path heading east and instead follow the narrower, muddier track that branches left (north) and runs along the ridge for 5-10 minutes, before it begins to descend into the Aobamba Valley. There are now tantalizing glimpses of Machu Picchu sprawled across the ridgeline 5km (3 miles) ahead, shadowed by the unmistakable shape of Huayna Picchu.

The path runs down the hillside past the partially cleared ruins of **Llactapata** (Paltallacta; see box pp262-3), which remain largely hidden under moss and leaves, and weighed down by a dense tangle of twisted tree roots.

Immediately below the ruins is a clearing boasting exceptional views of Machu Picchu sprawled across a ridge, where it is possible to *camp* (Map 16). There are some makeshift shelters here and a local farmer who sometimes has soft drinks or water for sale. The next accommodation is in Aguas Calientes.

From the campsite, the descent begins in earnest for 1½ hours, plunging 600m (1968ft) down a remorseless series of switchbacks to enter a **coffee plantation** and emerge at a **suspension bridge** across the Río Aobamba. On the far side of the river turn left (north) and follow the right-hand side (east) of the valley downstream towards the confluence of the Aobamba and Urubamba rivers. To your right and high on the cliff above, a huge stream of water spews from a hole in the cliff; it's part of the hydroelectric project (La Hidroeléctrica).

Cut over a low hillock and enter the Urubamba valley. Join the broad gravel road running adjacent to the river and head upstream towards La Hidroeléctrica and the small **railway station** next to it. Ignore the bridge over the Urubamba and instead stop at a **checkpoint** where you must show your passport. Then push on to the station, which is signposted below some power station buildings. The platform, up a series of steps to the left of the road, is lined with makeshift stalls and shabby *cantinas* selling drinks and snacks. The **ticket building** is one of the last buildings on the right; it opens around 3pm and the train to Aguas Calientes (s/20) departs around 4pm.

Diversion to Sector Intihuatana
If you find you have plenty of time to kill at the station, there is a small but interesting set of sculpted stones at Sector Intihuatana, a short walk along the line. Head down the tracks towards Machu Picchu and take the unmarked track that climbs briefly between two shacks. Cross the railway line as it doubles back on itself and climb a further short slope into a patch of forest. Scattered here, surrounded by banana and avocado trees, is a series of terraces, walls, archways, fountains, scooped stones and carefully sculpted boulders, all within site of Machu Picchu and the Inca drawbridge. The lack of signs and restoration here mean it is rarely visited.

The site lies on the site line between Llactapata and Machu Picchu (see map p264); this suggests that the various ruins are interlinked and shared ceremonial roles, particularly during the summer and winter solstices.

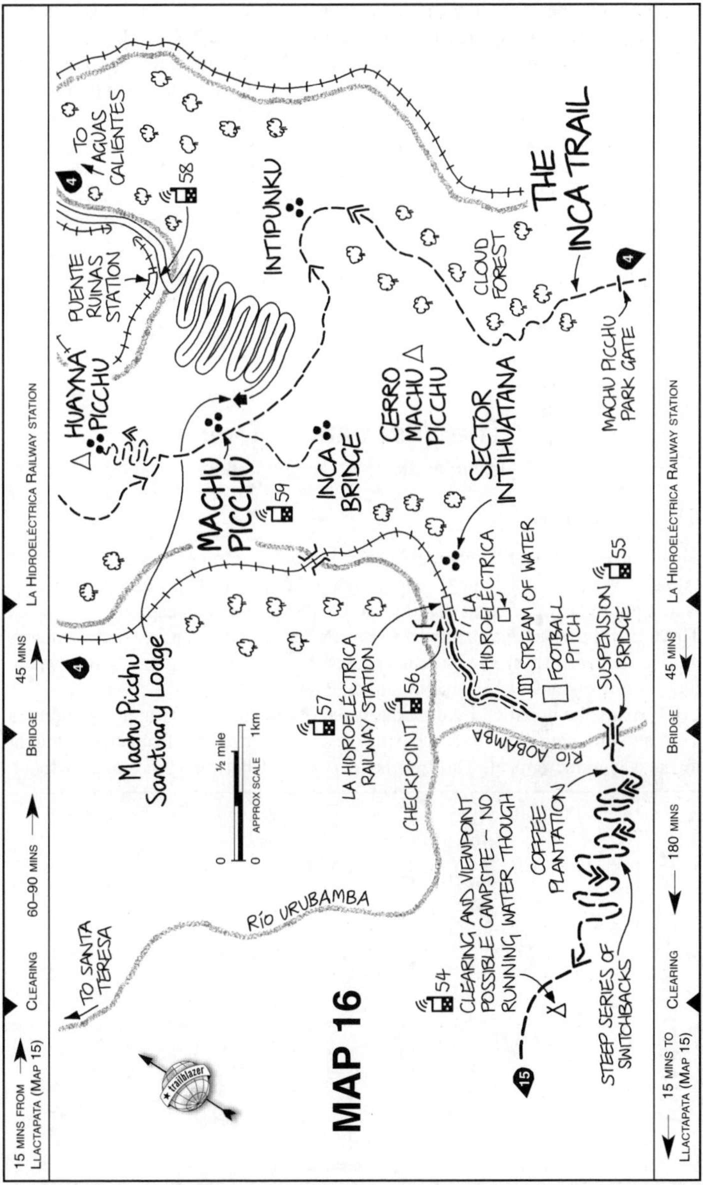

MAP 16

Once on the train it takes almost an hour for it to trundle across the Urubamba, clatter past **Puente Ruinas** at the foot of Machu Picchu and squeal to a stop in Aguas Calientes (see pp209-13) at the old local railway station on Avenida Imperio de los Incas. Alternatively, you can walk the 10km (6¼ miles) to Aguas Calientes in about 2-3 hours by simply following the railway tracks. Along the way there are several places where enterprising locals have set up stalls to sell soft drinks and snacks and you are treated to great views of the newly uncovered lower terraces at Machu Picchu. As you near Aguas Calientes, the tracks pass through two tunnels and a path that climbs left to **Putucusi** (see p210), before arriving in the lower part of the town.

From **Aguas Calientes** you can catch a shuttle bus up to Machu Picchu, something you'll most likely want to do first thing the following morning to get a full day exploring the site. For details on moving on from Aguas Calientes to Machu Picchu see p348.

The Vilcabamba Trail
Alexander Stewart & Henry Stedman

INTRODUCTION

This is an exceptional, rarely tackled trek through the forest between the remote villages of Huancacalle and Chaunquiri, via the ruins of Espíritu Pampa, which is thought to be the remains of Vilcabamba, the last city and capital of the Incas. The trail follows a route believed to be similar to that taken by Manco Inca as he fled the Spanish in 1537 and later taken by the conquistadors themselves in their two invasions of Vilcabamba in 1539 and 1572.

For anyone horrified by the tidal wave of humanity surging along the Inca Trail and breaking over Machu Picchu, this remote trek free from crowds ought to have genuine appeal. The trek is best tackled between May and October.

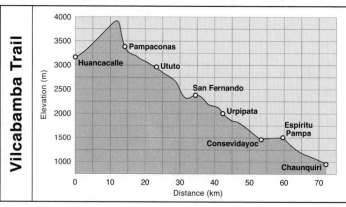

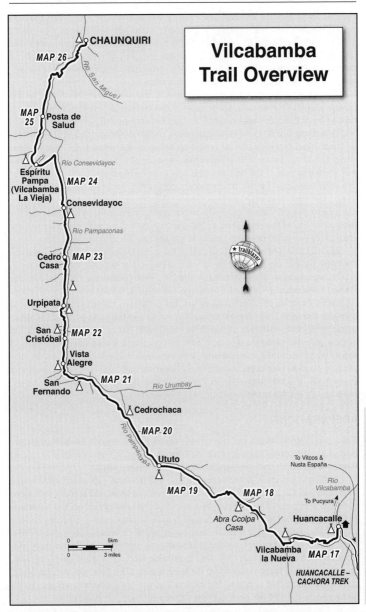

Vilcabamba Trail Overview

CHAUNQUIRI

MAP 26

Río San Miguel

MAP 25 Posta de Salud

Espíritu Pampa (Vilcabamba La Vieja)

Río Consevidayoc

MAP 24

Consevidayoc

Río Pampaconas

Cedro Casa MAP 23

Urpipata

San Cristóbal MAP 22

Vista Alegre

San Fernando MAP 21

Río Urumbay

Cedrochaca

MAP 20

Río Pampaconas

Ututo

MAP 19 MAP 18

To Vitcos & Nusta España

Río Vilcabamba

To Pucyura

Huancacalle

Abra Ccolpa Casa

Vilcabamba la Nueva MAP 17

HUANCACALLE – CACHORA TREK

0   5km
0   3 miles

Outside these months the trail can be very wet and muddy – at times the narrow, slippery paths are virtually impassable – and you will struggle to find a guide or *arriero* happy to take you. At the time of writing you could tackle the trail independently, but it is expected that the INC will impose rules and fees on the trail sooner rather than later, in line with proposals to implement similar regulations on the Salkantay and Santa Teresa treks.

This 3- to 4-day trek takes approximately the same amount of time as the classic Inca Trail, but it is more strenuous and taxing. Depending on how many people have used the trail recently, it can be very heavily overgrown too. In addition, there are no designated campsites and no facilities such as flush toilets or wash blocks, which can be found on some of the other treks. You'll even struggle to find locals selling soft drinks and snacks. The weather also wreaks havoc on this part of the region and it appears to almost always be the wet season with rain never far off. Bridges often get washed away by the swollen rivers during the rains and landslips loosened by the wet weather invariably obliterate the trail in places. This is certainly no straightforward walk in the park and for those who found the Inca Trail a little too easy, this is a much more significant challenge; the sense of achievement in completing the trek is immense.

Having endured and overcome all of these obstacles you might be forgiven for thinking that the goal and the reward at the end of the trek would be immediately spectacular. This isn't really the case though and the ruins at Espíritu Pampa (Vilcabamba La Vieja), although substantial, do not bear close comparison with those on the Inca Trail or at Choquequirao. However, for those who consider the Inca Trail sites excessively restored and thus a little artificial, these partially uncovered ruins, cloaked by tree roots, lianas and thick vegetation offer a glimpse of how early explorers and pioneers would have encountered them. In addition, the route, an original Inca trail that retains some of its distinctive giant paving slabs, is stunningly beautiful and takes you through almost every type of ecological zone in Peru, offering excellent opportunities to see flora and fauna not usually encountered elsewhere.

PREPARATIONS

This trek is fairly tough but there's no reason why someone with average fitness, decent stamina and a desire for adventure shouldn't be able to complete it, though a bit of advance preparation and thought is required.

Although you can currently trek the trail independently there are some issues over safety in the area (see box p32), with reports of increased activity by narcotraffickers in parts of the jungle. As a result you should **check on the situation before setting out** and also hire an arriero to help carry your equipment and act as a guide. Experienced arrieros can be engaged in Huancacalle (see p273). Before you begin the trek ensure that you have agreed an exact itinerary and price and be aware that you may need to provide food and shelter for your guide. In addition to the fee you should tip the team if they did a good job. Alternatively, there are a handful of agencies that run treks on this trail, who will supply guides and mules as part of the package you sign up for (see pp179-86).

There is no accommodation or opportunity to resupply along the trail so all equipment and food must be brought from Huancacalle. You will need a tent and camping gear, although if you are trekking with an agency they will usually be obliged to provide these – check that they do. No special equipment is required, although a machete might come in handy if the trail is overgrown: your arriero ought to have one of these. Make sure you have plenty of wet-weather gear and that your kit is stored in waterproof bags as there is a higher than usual chance of it getting soaked in this part of the region. Insect repellent is also essential as the trail can be plagued by mosquitoes, and you must have some sort of anti-malarial medication.

To get the most out of your trek and fully appreciate the history and significance of the region and the ruins, you should also read up about the Vilcabamba district (see p44).

GETTING TO AND FROM THE TRAILHEAD

The trek begins in Huancacalle, which can be reached by bus from Cusco, via Quillabamba (see below). At the end of the trek onward transport from Chaunquiri (see p295) is rather erratic, so to maximize your chances of picking up a bus aim to reach the village in time for the weekend markets, after which you should be able to find a ride.

Bear in mind it takes a long time to travel to the Vilcabamba region and that you may want to spend a day in and around Huancacalle, exploring the nearby ruins and archaeological sites. So, you should allow at least a week for the entire trip and possibly as many as nine days.

Cusco to Quillabamba

Buses leave throughout the day from Santiago Bus Terminal (see p186) and run via Ollantaytambo. The road trip is spectacular and takes you across the Abra de Malaga, which affords outstanding views of the Veronica Range. If you take the overnight bus you will, of course, miss these. Beyond here the tarmac runs out. The journey, pot-holes, punctures and traffic permitting takes around seven hours and costs s/25-35. A few bus companies ply this route, the best of which are Ampay (☎ 245734) and Selva Sur (☎ 247975).

Around 1½ hours before Quillabamba is **Chaullay** (see box below); here the historic Choquichaca Bridge, built on Inca foundations, crosses a gorge and the road continues parallel to the Río Urubamba until it reaches Quillabamba.

❏ **Chaullay**
Chaullay, not to be confused with the settlement of the same name on the Santa Teresa Trek, was once the site of the strategically important Inca rope bridge Choquichaca, which provided access to the Vilcabamba valley. If the Incas anticipated an invasion they simply cut the bridge and withdrew into the protected valley, safe in the knowledge that the gorge was too precipitous to cross any other way. It was here that Inca warriors fatefully killed the Spanish envoy Atilana de Anayo, an atrocity that sparked the final invasion of the region in 1572.

Quillabamba

Set at the confluence of the Chuyapi and Urubamba rivers, Quillabamba is the most important town in the region. Known as La Ciudad de Eterno Verano (the 'City of Eternal Summer'), Quillabamba was a thriving jungle town with a decent food market at its centre, whose prosperity derived from the coffee industry. Goods such as fruit and coffee are still shipped to Cusco, but the town is now better known as a stepping stone on the way to Vilcabamba, or the Pongo de Mainique (canyon) and beyond that the Amazon.

The **bus stations** for Huancacalle and Cusco are several blocks south of Plaza Grau. There are a couple of **internet cafés** on and around the plaza and **banks** can be found on Jr Libertad and Jr Bolognesi.

The cheaper **accommodation** options are around the main market and Plaza de Armas. Try the clean, friendly *Hostal Alto Urubamba* (☎ 281131; s/20/30/40 sgl/dbl/tpl, com, or s/45/75/85, att), at Jr 2 de Mayo 333, which has a pleasant courtyard and a small restaurant attached but can be very noisy.

Alternatively, well worth considering is the spotless, two-storey colonial *Hostal Don Carlos* (🖳 www.hostaldoncarlosquillabamba.com, ☎ 281150; s/75/110/120 sgl/dbl/tpl, att) to the west of the plaza on Jr Libertad 566; it has hot

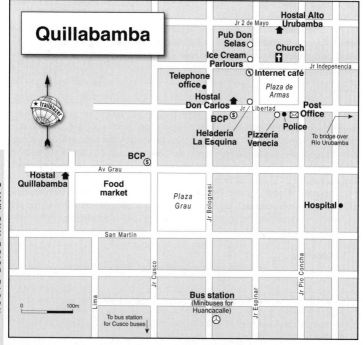

showers, a bar and restaurant. A little more expensive is the smarter *Hostal Quillabamba* (☎ 281369), on the corner of Prolongación and Av Grau, just behind the main food market. Large, kitsch and a little out of place, the rooms all have private bathrooms and cost s/120-180 (sgl/dbl). There is also a swimming pool, parking spaces and a restaurant here.

For fast, wholesome **food** try one of the chicken restaurants strung out along Av San Martín. *Pub Don Selas*, at Jr Espinar 235, serves sandwiches and other snacks whilst *Heladería la Esquina*, on the corner of Espinar and Libertad, is a retro joint that does café staples, ice cream and good juices. *Pizzeria Venecia* on the plaza and *Pizzeria Alamos* on Espinar serve just what the names imply. On the west side of the plaza are also several decent *ice-cream parlours*. For local fare and superb, freshly squeezed juices try the main **food market**.

A short drive from the centre is Sambaray, a popular complex of outdoor swimming pools, playing fields and gardens on the banks of the Urubamba, where there's also a *bar* and a decent *restaurant*. If the water's not too rapid it's also possible to go tubing on the Urubamba. Elsewhere, there's an attractive waterfall, **Siete Tinajas**, about a 45-minute bus ride from town.

Quillabamba to Huancacalle Minibuses depart for Huancacalle at 9am and at noon. The bumpy journey takes 4-5 hours and costs around s/10. You may be able to find a service that goes all the way through to Vilcabamba La Nueva, although these are infrequent and, despite saving you time on the trek, would mean you miss the fascinating ruins around Huancacalle.

Just before Huancacalle is the larger village of **Pucyura**; this was the location of the first church built in the valley. Constructed by Friar Diego Ortiz in the wake of the peace treaty between the conquistadors and Titu Cusi in 1568, the original has long since been torn down, and a modern church now stands on the same site.

Huancacalle   [see map p275]
Huancacalle is a simple, typical Andean town set in a very pleasant part of the Vilcabamba valley. It essentially comprises a single street, along which all life is visible, with pigs, chicken and donkeys roaming loose and locals sat watching the world go by. The traditional start point for people trekking to Espíritu Pampa and nowadays for those tackling the route that links Huancacalle to Choquequirao or even Machu Picchu, the town is used to trekkers – you can hire arrieros and guides and pick up a smattering of last-minute provisions – but there are few other facilities and there aren't really any restaurants.

The best **accommodation**, *Sixpac Manco Hostal* (☎ 812714) at the far end of the village, is run by the Cobos family. This family are also the best-known and most reliable guides in the region. Beds in this tranquil, pleasant hostel cost s/20 and the owners will also prepare meals (s/3-5).

Another option is the simple but functional *Hospedaje los Koyas* on the main street, which has dorm beds for s/10. Alternatively you can *camp* by the road opposite the abandoned visitor's centre.

Side trip to Vitcos

On the prow of a promontory poised between the Río Vilcabamba and Las Andenes stream are the ruins of Vitcos (see box p276), Manco Inca's first capital in Vilcabamba and another of Hiram Bingham's discoveries. Easily accessible from Huancacalle, you can make a very pleasant half-day trip to the ruins and surrounding sites. The paths are clearly defined and you should have no problem following the broad tracks. Alternatively, you can hire a guide in Huancacalle for a small fee.

Opposite Sixpac Manco Hostal on Huancacalle's main street is a trail that crosses two rivers. Just after the second river the trail divides. Take the left-hand fork and begin to climb north along the flank of a hill known as **Rosaspata** (3050m/10,004ft), passing the remains of an old Spanish mill. The entire hill is dotted with the remains of Inca structures, though most remain covered in scrub and unrestored.

On the crest of the hill, surrounded on three sides by sheer cliffs and overlooking the valleys below and the town of Pucyura to the north-west, is **Vitcos**, the centre of operations for the Incas whilst in exile.

Unlike the other ruins, the modest complex here has been partially restored. The main site stands on a promontory, the narrow neck of which is blocked by a long rectangular building. Beyond this is a plaza. On the far side of this plaza stands a series of finely crafted ashlars and gateways some 76m (250ft) long, the double-jamb entrances of which open onto large rooms filled with niches. This structure is backed by an upper level that comprises residential buildings and storage facilities. There are superb panoramic views from here of not only the valley but also the passes that lead into it. On the lower level, on the far side of the plaza is a finely carved stone throne.

A second path descends the eastern side of Rosaspata, heading south and losing height as it passes through a light **eucalyptus grove**. The valley floor is marked by a series of broad agricultural terraces, or *andenes*, atop which stand a number of **carved boulders**.

From the valley floor the path begins to climb again and after 10-15 minutes, at the southern end of Rosaspata, comes to the site known variously as **Ñusta España**, Yurac Rumi (White Stone), or Chuquipalta. Sculpted boulders, carved stone seats, water channels and baths surround an enormous granite boulder more than seven metres tall and fifteen metres wide. The smallness of this sheltered side valley exaggerates and draws attention to the size of the rock.

The sweeping curves and smooth top of this giant *huaca*, the spiritual centre of the exiled Inca state, are relatively untouched but the side wall has been straightened and other surfaces are carved with a series of bosses, steps, protrusions and other decorations, some of which are reminiscent of the Southern Cross. Under the stone is a spring, the waters from which are carefully channelled through a small ceremonial bath before being carried away. The stone work is outstanding and the various features are illuminated as the sun tracks over the sacred site. Thatched buildings would originally have surrounded the rock.

A Spanish priest, Antonio de la Calancha, described the site as 'the principal *mochadero* – the common Indian word for their shrines – in these *montañas*'. He also recorded that a devil 'captain of a legion of devils' used to inhabit the rock. Such was the fear of this creature and the dislike of the Inca habit of worshipping natural objects such as stone that in 1570 two

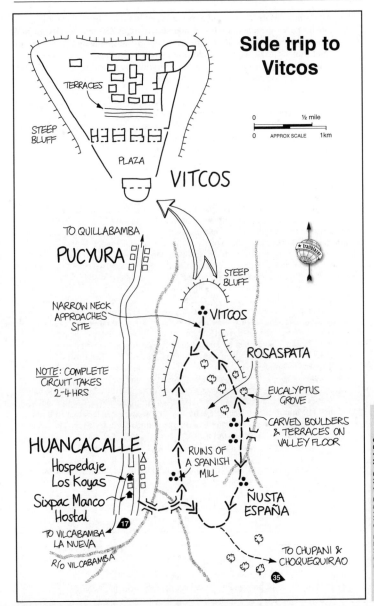

Side trip to Vitcos

TERRACES

STEEP BLUFF

PLAZA

VITCOS

0   ½ mile
0   APPROX SCALE   1km

TO QUILLABAMBA

PUCYURA

STEEP BLUFF

NARROW NECK APPROACHES SITE

VITCOS

ROSASPATA

EUCALYPTUS GROVE

NOTE: COMPLETE CIRCUIT TAKES 2-4 HRS

CARVED BOULDERS & TERRACES ON VALLEY FLOOR

HUANCACALLE

Hospedaje Los Koyas

Sixpac Manco Hostal

RUINS OF A SPANISH MILL

ÑUSTA ESPAÑA

TO VILCABAMBA LA NUEVA

17

RÍO VILCABAMBA

TO CHUPANI & CHOQUEQUIRAO

35

Augustinian friars exorcized the rock and had it burnt. They also destroyed as much of the surrounding temples and structures as they could. The toppled stones and razed walls are the result of this assault, although they were of course unable to do anything much to the rock itself. Legend also records that during Inca times a girl could prove her virginity by urinating at the top of the rock: if the urine precisely followed the grooved channel across the surface she was deemed to be chaste.

From here the path climbs westwards before eventually dropping back down, past the junction with the trail you initially took, to cross the river below Huancacalle. The complete circuit takes around two hours to trek, but you should factor in a couple of hours exploring the various sites along the route.

❏ Vitcos

Constructed by Manco Inca in 1537 following the Incas' retreat from Cusco, the new capital was only briefly occupied before a raid by the conquistador Orgóñez caught the Incas unaware. Routed, Manco was forced to quit the site and flee further into the jungle. Orgóñez was subsequently summoned to Cusco and forced to abandon the pursuit, meaning that Manco was able to return from the jungle to reclaim Vitcos. A further attack by Gonzalo Pizarro meant the Inca once again had to temporarily quit his capital before returning when the Spanish returned to Cusco. From here Manco went on to mount raids and guerrilla attacks on the Spanish, who were now embroiled in a civil war between those who supported Almagro and those who backed Pizarro. Gonzalo Pizarro was eventually executed and his brother Francisco assassinated. Manco welcomed the seven Spanish renegades responsible for the assassination on the basis that any enemy of Pizarro was a friend of his and gave them shelter at Vitcos. Manco's friendship was to be his undoing and after several years, in 1544, the Spanish murdered him in a final act of treachery. The soldiers, supporters of Almagro's cause, thought that by slaying the Inca they could curry favour with the victorious Pizarrists and earn their right to return. Manco's son, Titu Cusi, witnessed the attack and recorded it in his chronicles: 'One day with much good fellowship they were playing at quoits with him: only them, my father, and me, who was then a little boy … Then just as my father was raising the quoit to throw, they all rushed upon him with knives, daggers and some swords … he fell to the ground covered with wounds, and they left him for dead. I being a little boy, and seeing my father treated in this manner, wanted to rush over to help him. But they turned furiously on me and threw a lance which only just failed to kill me too.'

The assassins made their escape, but were tracked down, caught and burnt to death by Manco's supporters. The Inca himself survived for a further three days, long enough to learn that his attackers had all been killed. The assailants' severed heads were paraded at Vitcos and staked there for more than 20 years as a gruesome reminder of their fate.

Titu Cusi went on to become Inca in his turn and later also died at Vitcos, following a severe illness.

❏ Important note – walking times

All times in this book refer only to the time spent walking. You will need to add 10-30% to allow for rests, photography, checking the map, drinking water etc.

HUANCACALLE TO UTUTO
[MAP 17, p278; MAP 18, p279; MAP 19, p281]

Overview
From the centre of Huancacalle a dirt road coils and snakes westwards across the hillside beyond the village, gaining height steadily but evenly in the course of 2½ hours to arrive at the Abra Ccolpa Casa, which marks the boundary between the Andes and the Amazon basin.

Route
At the far end of the village look for the fork in the road and take the right-hand branch. Rather than follow the road all the way to the pass, which would be time consuming and tedious, look for the path that cuts between the loops and climbs the hill in a more direct fashion. Keeping a **crucifix**, one of the 14 Stations of the Cross lining the road side, on your left follow the path as it zigzags and then rejoins the road before leaving it again immediately before a bridge, close to the **VIIth Station of the Cross**. Cross the subsequent bridge and forge ahead, keeping the Río Vilcabamba on your right.

Cutting between the next set of switchbacks, you pass the VIIIth and IXth Stations of the Cross. (The Xth station would have been on the bend between the IXth and XIth but it is missing.) Rejoin the road close to the **XIth Station**, where the gradient eases and the land begins to resemble farmland, and pass through the village of San Francisco de la Vitoria de Vilcabamba, more often simply referred to as Vilcabamba or **Vilcabamba La Nueva** in order to distinguish it from the Inca's final capital city.

Originally built in the 16th century adjacent to Vitcos by the first Spanish settlers, the town was moved up the valley to its current exposed location by the source of the Río Vilcabamba to support a silver mine nearby and became the capital of the region. The Spanish were never fully able to settle this region though as it was too high and too remote to appeal to many of the new arrivals. The settlers quickly exhausted the land and once the mine ran dry in the late 18th century, they abandoned it. Intended to be a symbol of Spanish success, Vilcabamba La Nueva once again became a backwater. Straggling along the road, the modern town is centred on the ruins of a 16th-century chapel, whose ancient **belltower** is all that remains, and a large modern **Catholic mission** and its church that now stands where the original once did. The town is not geared up for visitors and there is nowhere to stay though you should be able to *camp* on the far side of the river. Ask permission first though. Nor are there many shops or places to pick up anything more than the most basic supplies.

Beyond the town enter the wide valley to your right and follow the road which struggles on northwards across small-holdings and arable land dotted over the mountainside before petering out (Map 18) just before the **Abra Ccolpa Casa** (3900m/12,792ft). A shrine to **Santa Rosa de Lima** stands here close to the remains of an **Inca plaza**, in the south-eastern corner of which are heaped the remains of an Inca shrine. The views of the surrounding peaks are spectacular in clear weather; Bingham described the view as he came over the pass as 'a great wilderness of deep green valleys and forest-clad slopes'.

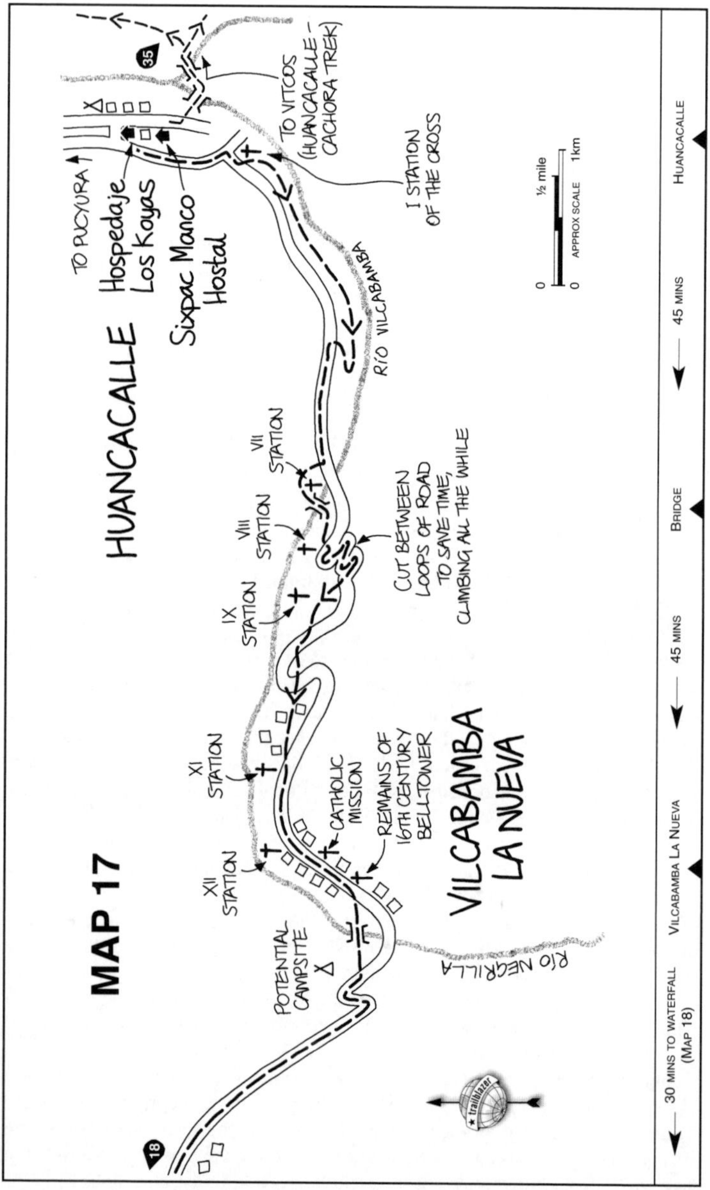
MAP 17
HUANCACALLE
TO PUCYURA
Hospedaje Los Koyas
Sixpac Manco Hostal
35
TO VITCOS (HUANCACALLE – CACHORA TREK)
I STATION OF THE CROSS
RÍO VILCABAMBA
VII STATION
VIII STATION
IX STATION
CUT BETWEEN LOOPS OF ROAD TO SAVE TIME, CLIMBING ALL THE WHILE
XI STATION
XII STATION
CATHOLIC MISSION
REMAINS OF 16TH CENTURY BELLTOWER
VILCABAMBA LA NUEVA
POTENTIAL CAMPSITE
RÍO NEGRILLA
18
0 ½ mile
0 APPROX SCALE 1km
trailblazer
30 MINS TO WATERFALL (MAP 18)
VILCABAMBA LA NUEVA
45 MINS
BRIDGE
45 MINS
HUANCACALLE

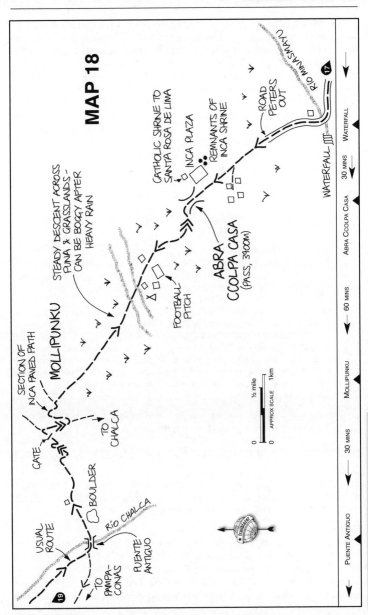

MAP 18

SECTION OF INCA PAVED PATH

MOLLIPUNKU

STEADY DESCENT ACROSS PUNA & GRASSLANDS— CAN BE BOGGY AFTER HEAVY RAIN

GATE

TO CHALCA

BOULDER

RÍO CHALCA

USUAL ROUTE

PUENTE ANTIGUO

TO PAMPA-CONAS

19

FOOTBALL PITCH

ABRA CCOLPA CASA (PASS, 3910M)

CATHOLIC SHRINE TO SANTA ROSA DE LIMA

INCA PLAZA

REMNANTS OF INCA SHRINE

ROAD PETERS OUT

RÍO MINASMAYU

17

WATERFALL

0   ½ mile
0   1km
APPROX SCALE

trailblazer

ROUTE GUIDE AND MAPS

PUENTE ANTIGUO ◀ 30 MINS ▶ MOLLIPUNKU ◀ 30 MINS ▶ ABRA CCOLPA CASA ◀ 60 MINS ▶ ABRA CCOLPA CASA ◀ 30 MINS ▶ WATERFALL ◀ WATERFALL ▶

On the far side of the pass descend gently north-west, sticking to the left-hand side of the long valley. There is evidence of a road being built here, and the path cuts between the wide bends. The path passes a **football pitch** – adjacent to which there is a good spot to *camp* – and undulates across the puna to the crossroads at **Mollipunku**. Great slabs of Inca paving and original steps descend from here towards the Río Chalca and the bottom of the valley, which you reach within half an hour.

Cross the river on the **Puente Antiguo**, after which the trail forks. Both branches lead to Ututo in roughly the same amount of time although the lower one is the simpler, gentler path.

The **lower path** descends from the bridge to the left bank of the river and follows it, passing a number of scenic spots that would make attractive campsites. As the trail progresses the vegetation becomes increasingly wild and dense. Small plots of farmland stand partially hidden amongst the tangle. As you near the small hamlet of Ututo the ground becomes increasingly boggy, with small streams, some of which aren't bridged, flowing off the hillside and across the path to join the main river.

Alternative (higher) route
This path for this route goes via the village of **Pampaconas** (Map 19), which lies on the far side of a large, deep bog known as **Oncoy Cacha**. **Pampaconas** (3340m/10,955ft) is an exposed, fairly inhospitable place, but there are the **remnants of an Inca plaza** and platform here that were used by the Incas for ceremonial sun worship. Eventually Titu Cusi gave permission for the first Christian cross in the region to be erected here.

Beyond the village the countryside used to be heavily forested, so much so that the Spanish invaders in 1539 and 1572 were forced to leave their horses at Pampaconas and progress on foot. Bingham suffered the same misfortune in 1911 whilst exploring the region. Nowadays the way is clear though and descends evenly along stretches of Inca staircase and original path to reach the small settlement of Ututo.

The dry patches of ground that can be found around the collection of rudimentary houses at **Ututo** make excellent *campsites*.

UTUTO TO VISTA ALEGRE   [MAP 19; MAP 20, p283; MAP 21, p285]
Overview
This gentle, wonderfully scenic section of the trail makes for an excellent day's walking, with plenty of flora and birdlife to keep you enthralled as you amble largely downhill through increasingly verdant cloud forest.

Route
Cross the large **orange bridge** at the western end of the village and begin to walk on the right-hand (eastern) bank of the river. Fields and tended pastures give way quickly to **forest** (Map 20). The path rises and falls above the river, occasionally on original **Inca stairs**. Vincent Lee has suggested that the Spaniards were oblivious to the Inca trail here and tried to hack out another trail

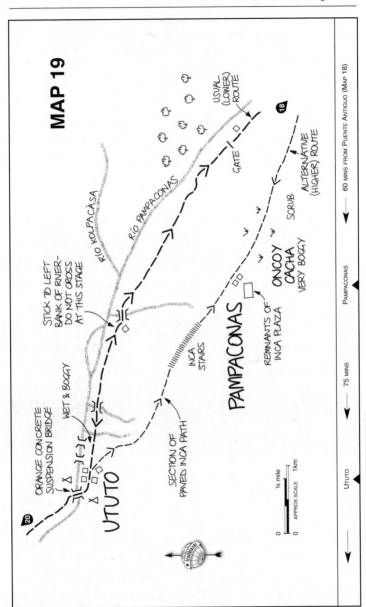

MAP 19

USUAL (LONER) ROUTE

GATE

18

ALTERNATIVE (HIGHER) ROUTE

SCRUB

RÍO PAMPACONAS

RÍO KOLPACÁSA

STICK TO LEFT BANK OF RIVER- DO NOT CROSS AT THIS STAGE

WET & BOGGY

ORANGE CONCRETE SUSPENSION BRIDGE

20

UTUTO

SECTION OF PAVED INCA PATH

INCA STAIRS

PAMPACONAS

ONCOY CACHA VERY BOGGY

REMNANTS OF INCA PLAZA

½ mile   1km

APPROX SCALE

0   0

trailblazer

60 MINS FROM PUENTE ANTIGUO (MAP 18)

PAMPACONAS   75 MINS   UTUTO

on the far side of the river, which explains how it took them eight days to march to Vilcabamba, whilst modern trekkers complete the same route in just two.

As you descend, the trail crosses several small streams issuing into the river to your left, which steadily grows in size. Following a particularly scenic stretch of cloud forest the path reaches **Cedrochaca** (Puente de Cedro), an orange suspension bridge. It is possible to *camp* on the bank adjacent to the bridge.

Cross the bridge and begin to climb on the left-hand bank of the river, gaining height briefly through a further forested stretch, although swathes of trees have been cut or burned to create more potential farming patches. Having lost the accumulated height slowly and evenly the path bends north-west and enters the clearing of **Tambocarahuina** (Map 21). Bingham noted that in this part of Peru 'any little natural breathing space at the bottom of a canyon is a *pampa*'. The clearing itself is pretty unremarkable, except that it has views of the narrow ridge above, upon which, in 1984, Vincent Lee identified the Inca fort **Huayna Pucará** (see box below).

Beyond the clearing, pass through a **gate** and cross a small stream before working your way through a small settlement, past patches of hillside that have been slashed and burnt, and converted into homestays and cultivated plots. A series of zigzags bring you down to the Río Zapatero and the single house here.

A second series of switchbacks climbs away from the river before the gradient lessens and the path climbs more gently towards the village of **San Fernando**, where it is possible to *camp*. Shortly beyond here are two streams in quick succession. The Sucsu Chincana is crossed via a **blue suspension bridge** whilst the Ounay has to be breached using a **rickety wooden bridge**. If you're not confident on the slippery, makeshift bridge and the stream isn't too high or fast, simply ford it. On the far side of the bridge stands **Vista Alegre** (Happy View), which comprises a scattering of houses and a football pitch, on which it is possible to *camp*.

❏ Huayna Pucará

The narrow ridge of Huayna Pucará dominates this section of trail. The Spanish friar, Martín de Murúa, who chronicled the conquest of Vilcabamba, described the ridge as 'a knife edge which two men could not walk along side by side'. The name of this strategic spot literally translates as New Fort.

Unfortunately the site didn't really live up to its name. As the Spanish pushed into the region during 1572, the Incas planned to stage an ambush here, using the vertiginous ridge as the ideal place from which to launch an attack on the troops below. The plan was to hurl enormous boulders down on the enemy, whilst archers picked off any survivors. The surprise was lost though when a defector betrayed the position of the fort and warned the Spanish of the trap.

During the night the Spanish scaled the hillside to higher ground, outflanking the fort and turning the tables to give themselves the advantage. Realizing the hopelessness of the situation, the Incas fought a determined rearguard action as they retreated, before fleeing into the forest below. The Incas had lost their last effective chance to defeat the Spanish and subsequently they offered little further resistance. It is not known what eventually happened to the Inca traitor.

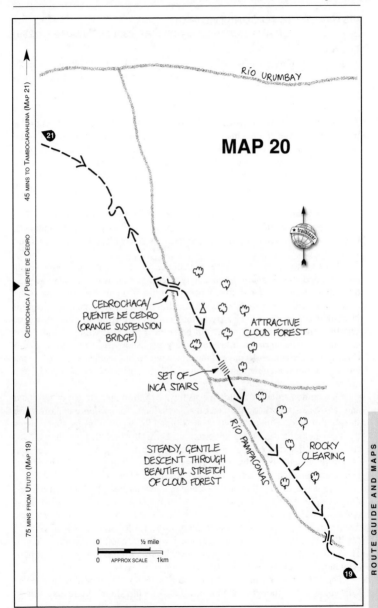

RÍO URUMBAY

MAP 20

21

45 MINS TO TAMBOCARAHUINA (MAP 21) →

CEDROCHACA / PUENTE DE CEDRO

75 MINS FROM UTUTO (MAP 19) →

CEDROCHACA/
PUENTE DE CEDRO
(ORANGE SUSPENSION
BRIDGE)

SET OF
INCA STAIRS

ATTRACTIVE
CLOUD FOREST

RÍO PAMPACONAS

ROCKY
CLEARING

STEADY, GENTLE
DESCENT THROUGH
BEAUTIFUL STRETCH
OF CLOUD FOREST

trailblazer

0   ½ mile
0   APPROX SCALE   1km

19

ROUTE GUIDE AND MAPS

VISTA ALEGRE TO CONSEVIDAYOC
[MAP 21; MAP 22, p286; MAP 23, p287; MAP 24, p289]
Overview
This section begins much as the previous one finished, with a walk across small streams and through scenic forest as you hug the western flank of the valley, descending all the while.

Route
The narrow path beyond Vista Alegre crosses the Río Vista Alegre on an unstable wooden bridge and begins to undulate in a northerly direction, hugging the flank of the valley and climbing into and out of the folds in the hillsides (Map 22). The vegetation here is potentially very thick and the trail can be overgrown in places. Rainfall also loosens the steep-sided slopes and landslides are frequent, so you may have to improvise a path or climb further up the hillside to pick your way carefully across the scar before rejoining the main path.

Just over an hour beyond Vista Alegre is the farm of **San Cristóbal**, where a small grassy clearing doubles as a *campsite*. After here the path undulates through thick forest, passing occasional farms as you walk along the steep-sided valley flank.

After an hour, set beneath the crest of the hill, but high above the river, is another good spot to *camp*. Immediately after, cross the Río Urpipata and pass through the village of **Urpipata**. Vincent Lee has also identified this site as the location of Machu Pucará (the Old Fort), although all that remains is a handful of tumbledown walls, which may or may not be part of the original structure. The Incas fought a highly successful battle here in 1539, killing a number of conquistadors in an ambush. Their victory was short lived though as Pedro Pizarro returned within 10 days of the attack with reinforcements and seized the hill. By the time of the second invasion in 1572 the site had been abandoned and offered no resistance to the invading army.

Descending from the hilltop the path weaves through a stretch of farmland and crosses a slippery log path passing a small area for *camping* and dropping steeply to the Río Tunqul Mayu (Map 23) and the wooden bridge that crosses it. There are limited camping opportunities here, although the pools in the river are good for dunking yourself in. Cross a boggy patch of ground on the far side of the stream and climb sharply to **Huaynapata**, a small clearing in the forest, before dropping back down to cross the Río Luca Mayu.

A series of steep switchbacks ascend to a few farmed plots at **Cedro Casa**. At this point the path begins to follow a pattern, descending steeply west towards the river before climbing aggressively east away from it again. An hour further on is a vast, bare rock outcrop known as **La Roca**, from where you can catch the first tantalizing glimpses of Consevidayoc, another hour to the north. The intervening countryside is scarred with farmed plots and slash-and-burn clearances as well as by the landslips.

The scattered settlement of **Consevidayoc** (Map 24), sometimes written as Consebidayoc, is thought by Vincent Lee to be the site of Marcanay, where

Friar Diego Ortiz was martyred for failing to cure the Inca Titu Cusi with medicine he had given him. You can *camp* in the school compound here if you get permission from the school director, who lives on site. Pitches cost s/10-15 depending on group size and the number of mules you have.

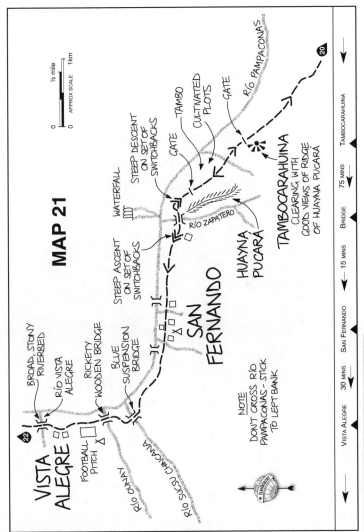

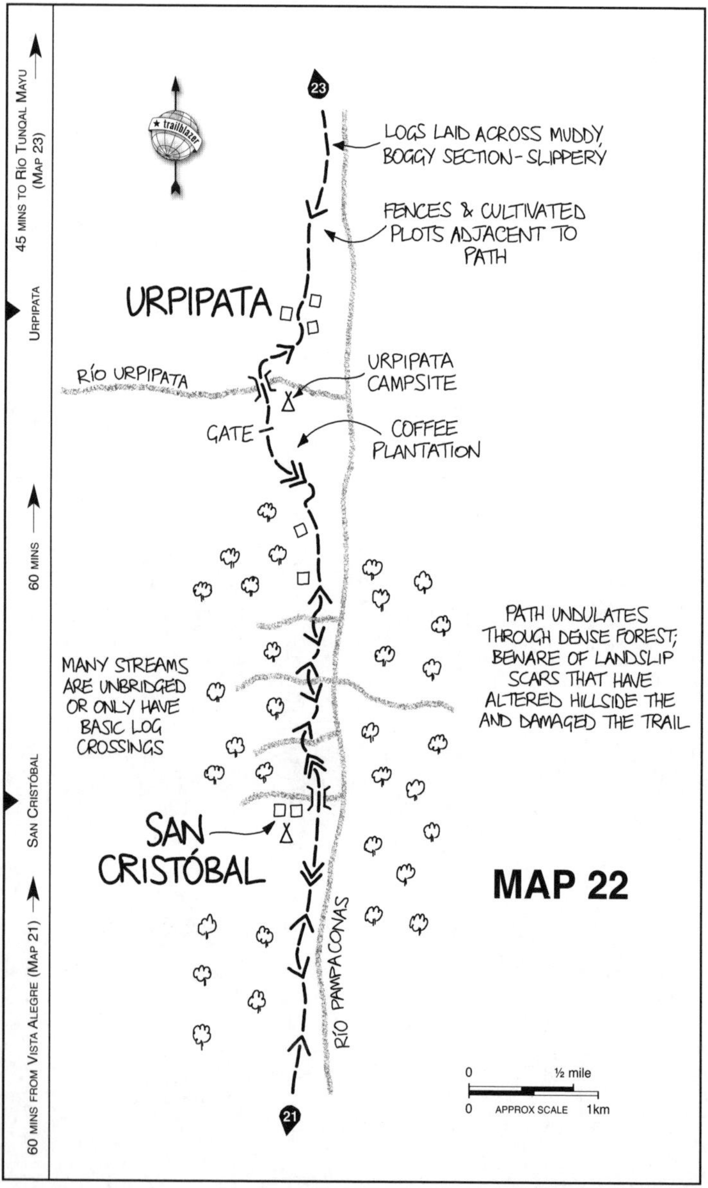

★ trailblazer

LOGS LAID ACROSS MUDDY, BOGGY SECTION - SLIPPERY

FENCES & CULTIVATED PLOTS ADJACENT TO PATH

URPIPATA

RÍO URPIPATA

URPIPATA CAMPSITE

GATE

COFFEE PLANTATION

PATH UNDULATES THROUGH DENSE FOREST; BEWARE OF LANDSLIP SCARS THAT HAVE ALTERED THE HILLSIDE AND DAMAGED THE TRAIL

MANY STREAMS ARE UNBRIDGED OR ONLY HAVE BASIC LOG CROSSINGS

SAN CRISTÓBAL

MAP 22

RÍO PAMPACONAS

0   ½ mile

0   APPROX SCALE   1km

ROUTE GUIDE AND MAPS

23

21

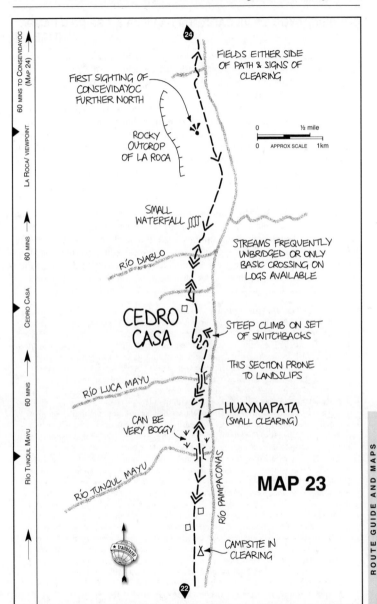

60 MINS TO CONSEVIDAYOC (Map 24)

La ROCA/ VIEWPOINT

60 MINS

CEDRO CASA

60 MINS

RIO TUNQUL MAYU

24

FIELDS EITHER SIDE OF PATH & SIGNS OF CLEARING

FIRST SIGHTING OF CONSEVIDAYOC FURTHER NORTH

ROCKY OUTCROP OF LA ROCA

0   ½ mile
0   APPROX SCALE   1km

SMALL WATERFALL

STREAMS FREQUENTLY UNBRIDGED OR ONLY BASIC CROSSING ON LOGS AVAILABLE

RÍO DIABLO

CEDRO CASA

STEEP CLIMB ON SET OF SWITCHBACKS

THIS SECTION PRONE TO LANDSLIPS

RÍO LUCA MAYU

HUAYNAPATA (SMALL CLEARING)

CAN BE VERY BOGGY

RÍO TUNQUL MAYU

RÍO PAMPACONAS

MAP 23

CAMPSITE IN CLEARING

trailblazer

22

ROUTE GUIDE AND MAPS

CONSEVIDAYOC TO VILCABAMBA LA VIEJA & ESPÍRITU PAMPA
[MAP 24]

From Consevidayoc the path climbs through yet more plantations and farm plots to a junction. Ignore the right-hand fork that descends to the river as it goes directly to Chuntabamba, avoiding the ruins at Espíritu Pampa completely.

Instead, take the **left-hand fork** and climb again for almost an hour to reach the top of a forested hill. Ascending a set of steps and passing a pretty waterfall en route, you reach the top of the hill. Here there are the remnants of a small Inca building thought to have been a **watchtower**; it looks out over the broad, restored Inca steps that sweep down towards Vilcabamba La Vieja – the Incas always knew how to make an entrance.

Descend the **grand ceremonial staircase** into the lush valley for 15-20 minutes to reach **Vilcabamba La Vieja**, a small settlement centred on a church-cum-school. There's a farm, a few houses, a small shop and some decent places to *camp*.

The ruins of **Espíritu Pampa** (literally translated as the Plain of the Spirits) are a 10-minute walk through the forest; some 400 ruins lie concealed by jungle and vegetation. Bingham gave a good indication of the thickness of the vegetation and the challenge in spotting, let alone uncovering, the ruins when he wrote that: 'Nothing gives a better idea of the density of the jungle than the fact that the savages themselves have been within five feet of these fine

---

❏ The Lord of the Huari (Wari)
The history of Espíritu Pampa was thrown into turmoil by the discovery of a Huari leader's tomb amidst the Inca ruins by a team of Cusco archaeologists, led by Javier Fonesca, in 2010. The discovery implies that Espíritu Pampa has a far older history than previously believed. In total, the team uncovered 16 tombs within a 450 sq metre area, half of which have subsequently been excavated. The discovery was remarkably surprising given that the Huari, a pre-Inca culture, were never thought to have reached the jungle and will require historians to re-examine the extent of Huari expansion and their possible relationship with the Incas.

The Huari thrived from 600AD to 1100AD, and according to preliminary studies, the tomb dates from around 1000AD, towards the time the civilization would have been at its height. Typically, Huari tombs were associated with extended funerary rights and have been found within a larger complex; excavations over time may reveal such a centre. Due to the humidity of the jungle, the tombs contained little evidence of bones or textile other than fragments. The high-ranking noble though, dubbed the Lord of the Huari and sometimes referred to as the Lord of Vilca, was found with a silver death mask, large Y-shaped silver breastplate, two gold arm cuffs embossed with anthropomorphic feline figures, two wooden staffs sheathed in silver, several hundred large sequin-like silver pieces and necklaces decorated with lapis lazuli, turquoise and other stones. Pottery discovered includes Nazca designs, which hint at contact with coastal civilizations. Revised theories suggest that the Huari had a far larger empire than previously thought and a presence at Espíritu Pampa, which the Inca knew about. When it came to retreating from the conquistadors, the Inca established themselves on the site of this habitation and built their own structures. What is clear though is that this discovery complicates our understanding of how Peru's civilizations spread and how subsequent cultures repurposed existing settlements.

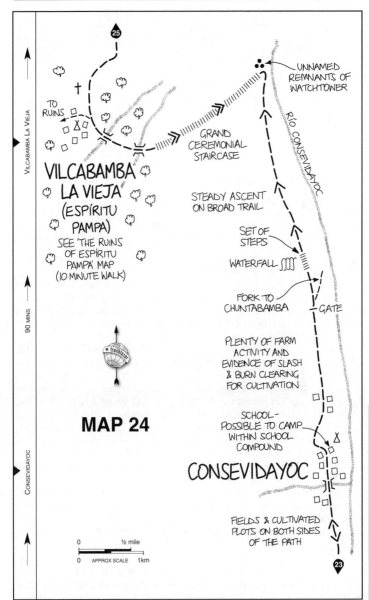

25

TO RUINS

VILCABAMBA LA VIEJA

UNNAMED REMNANTS OF WATCHTOWER

RÍO CONSEVIDAYOC

VILCABAMBA LA VIEJA (ESPÍRITU PAMPA)

GRAND CEREMONIAL STAIRCASE

STEADY ASCENT ON BROAD TRAIL

SEE 'THE RUINS OF ESPÍRITU PAMPA' MAP (10 MINUTE WALK)

SET OF STEPS

WATERFALL

90 MINS

FORK TO CHUNTABAMBA

GATE

PLENTY OF FARM ACTIVITY AND EVIDENCE OF SLASH & BURN CLEARING FOR CULTIVATION

MAP 24

SCHOOL—POSSIBLE TO CAMP WITHIN SCHOOL COMPOUND

CONSEVIDAYOC

CONSEVIDAYOC

FIELDS & CULTIVATED PLOTS ON BOTH SIDES OF THE PATH

0   ½ mile
0   APPROX SCALE   1km

23

ROUTE GUIDE AND MAPS

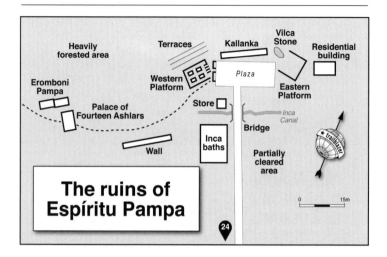

Heavily forested area

Terraces

Kallanka

Vilca Stone

Residential building

Eromboni Pampa

Western Platform

Plaza

Eastern Platform

Palace of Fourteen Ashlars

Store

Inca Canal

Bridge

Wall

Inca baths

Partially cleared area

The ruins of Espíritu Pampa

0   15m

★ Trailhead

24

walls without being aware of their existence'. It also explains why he failed to uncover the extent of the city or recognize its true scale and importance. Gene Savoy, 50 years after Bingham, is in fact responsible for the early work and revised view of the ruins. Only a handful of the most important structures have been uncovered, with very little reconstruction having taken place. However, a surprising discovery in 2010 forced archaeologists to reconsider their understanding of the site and its origins (see box p288).

A further tranche of work was conducted in 2011 in conjunction with the centenary celebrations at Machu Picchu. In a superhuman effort the authorities cleared the central plaza and a larger area that radiated away from here, allowing visitors to appreciate the size of the site. They also partially reconstructed a number of walls and structures, identifying a great hall and an alleged Temple of the Sun as well as a two-storeyed structure, with pole holes high in a wall indicating where the upper floor would have been fitted, which archaeologists have speculated would have been Manco's palace. Giant trees still overgrow this building and dominate the entrance. Unfortunately the number of visitors doesn't justify the cost of maintaining the clearance, so it's likely that over time the jungle will reclaim the stones.

Beyond this, the outskirts of this considerable city are subsumed by the jungle, providing a fascinating 'before and after' feel to the site. The still buried ruins await discovery by you; be careful moving vegetation though so as to not disturb any of the stones. Although the structures and the site in general aren't immediately impressive, with a bit of effort and imagination you can fully appreciate the scale of this spectacular abandoned city. For those who find the overly reconstructed ruins at Machu Picchu a little fake, these structures, found just as early explorers would have uncovered them, offer an atmospheric alternative. Stones are held in the muscular embrace of vines and creepers whilst roots burst through the walls like buttresses. Moss and lichen mottle the masonry and the whole lot is stained green. It's a charming, moody place to spend time and even basic exploration of the site is immensely rewarding.

Although archaeologists have discovered that the Incas weren't the first culture to reside here (see box p288), Espíritu Pampa was built according to an Inca template and the layout is reminiscent of other sites. However, there's a lot about it that is different, due in large part to its lower location, away from the mountains, on the edge of the Amazon.

The central section where you first arrive is the most carefully cleared and exposed part of the site. The trail to the impressively large central plaza passes several carefully carved **baths** and crosses a **bridge** over an Inca canal. In the **plaza** several giant kapok trees still stand; an indication of just how much vegetation subsumed the site. The plaza is backed by a long **kallanka** and **terraces** surround it. There are also lots of shards of imitation Spanish roof tiles, scattered around the site along with stone pegs and eye-bonders that would have been used to secure the thatched roofs. A sculpted stone phallus found at the site is also displayed in the main plaza, although where this would have originally been sited or what its purpose was, is unclear. Other features include a number of crumbling walls that have niches in them; another has three carved water spouts jutting from it, which would have created small fountains.

In the north-east corner of the plaza is a huaca; the **Vilca stone** is a giant, uncarved boulder leaning slightly on its side and described as looking 'like a great egg' by Gene Savoy. A couple of minutes to the south of the plaza is a lengthy striking stone wall now covered in moss. Beyond this lies the section originally uncovered by Bingham, called **Eromboni Pampa**, where the **Palace of Fourteen Ashlars** stands. Bingham describes being guided to them in 1914:

> While we were wondering whether the Incas themselves ever lived here, there suddenly appeared the naked figure of a sturdy young savage, armed with a stout bow and long arrows, and wearing a fillet of bamboo. He had been hunting and showed us a bird he had shot. Soon afterwards there came the two adult savages we had met at Saavedra's, accompanied by a cross-eyed friend, all wearing long tunics. They offered to guide us to other ruins. It was very difficult for us to follow their rapid pace. Half an hour's scramble through the jungle brought us to a pampa or natural terrace on the banks of a little tributary of the Pampaconas. They called it Eromboni. Here we found several old artificial terraces and the rough foundations of a long, rectangular building 192 feet by 24 feet. It might have had twenty-four doors, twelve in front and twelve in back, each three and a half feet wide. No lintels were in evidence. The walls were only a foot high. There was very little building material in sight. Apparently the structure had never been completed. Near by was a typical Inca fountain with three stone spouts, or conduits. Two hundred yards beyond the water-carrier's rendezvous, hidden behind a curtain of hanging vines and thickets so dense we could not see more than a few feet in any direction, the savages showed us the ruins of a group of stone houses whose walls were still standing in fine condition.
>
> **Hiram Bingham** *Inca Land – Explorations in the Highlands of Peru* (1922)

There are few terraces as the uneven terrain was difficult to farm and yet, according to various chroniclers, the Incas wanted for very little. Martín de Murúa, a Spanish friar, recorded that: 'The Incas enjoyed scarcely less of the luxuries, greatness and splendour of Cusco in that distant land of exile. For the Indians brought with them whatever they could get from outside for their contentment and pleasure. And so for that time they enjoyed the good life there'.

The jungle also gave up fruits, coca, sugar, honey and various fowl on which the Inca dined. The reality of course was that Manco retreated to the jungle as a last resort, because it was militarily expedient to do so and because, following his last stand at Ollantaytambo he had nowhere else to go. The Incas consequently had little choice but to endure the humidity, insects, snakes and

❏ **Manco's capital?**
There have been very few excavations of note at Vilcabamba despite the ruins being uncovered by **Hiram Bingham** in 1914. Bingham in fact refused to believe that the small collection of buildings he found was the last capital of the Incas and got himself into all sorts of intellectual knots arguing, against all the evidence, that Machu Picchu must have been the last city of the Incas simply because it looked more suitable and spectacular. He also argued that the Incas 'would not have cared to live in this hot valley'. In fact, it wasn't until 1964 that **Gene Savoy** realized the extent of the ruins and exposed the true scale of the site.

The limited archaeological research that has been conducted, whilst only just scratching the surface of this giant site, has proved conclusively that the ruins are of Inca origin. Less spectacular or well-crafted than other major Inca sites, they can appear rather mundane and uninspiring to the casual visitor, hence Bingham's belief that the site couldn't possibly be the last capital. However, the distinctive layout, style of craftsmanship and stonework coupled with the features found at the site including canals, baths, ashlars and sacred rocks are all indicative of Inca architecture and conclusively prove that Espíritu Pampa is of Inca origin.

Debate has raged as to whether the site constituted Manco's final capital, though. The sheer scale of the site means that it must have been of some importance. Even in exile, the Incas created a number of extravagant signature pieces. The giant sweeping staircase that descends to the site is one such feature. The Vilca stone, positioned to dominate the plaza and eerily reminiscent of the celebrated *huaca* Ñusta España (see p274), lends weight to the theory that the site also had a special ceremonial significance.

The key discovery when it came to dating the site was the uncovering of a number of terracotta roof tiles. These imitations of Spanish roof tiles can only have been seen by the Incas in Cusco, and then copied. Prior to the Conquest, the Incas only used straw or turf to roof their houses. Therefore the site must have been built after the arrival of the Spanish conquistadors. The most likely architect is therefore thought to be Manco Inca. The type of structures built, allied to the date when they would most likely have been constructed, suggests that the site is indeed the last Inca capital, Vilcabamba.

There is, however, no absolute proof that this is the case and some doubts do still remain. Evidence to support descriptions in some of the chronicles of the time is inconclusive; although modern-day Pampaconas still bears the same name as that used by the conquistadors, Marcanay may or may not be the modern village of Consevidayoc; Huayna Pucará is more than likely the site of the Inca ambush that went horribly wrong, but Machu Pucará may or may not be the actual site of the Inca Old Fort. As John Hemming wrote in *Conquest of the Incas*, 'Unless someone can discover another ruin that so exactly fulfils the geographical and topographical details known about Vilcabamba, and that also contains imitation Spanish roofing tiles, the lost city of Vilcabamba has finally been located as Espíritu Pampa'.

diseases rife in the jungle, as well as the constant threat posed by the conquis-tadors, who were never more than a couple of days' march away from the exiles.

For a fuller picture of the site, check out Vincent Lee's book *Forgotten Vilcabamba*, which contains maps and drawings of the ruins.

VILCABAMBA LA VIEJA & ESPÍRITU PAMPA TO CHAUNQUIRI
[MAP 24, p289; MAP 25, p294; MAP 26, p295]

Overview
The final stage of the trek is the shortest, but also one of the most taxing, as the combination of exertion and heat can be debilitating.

Route
A path leads away from the church, over a sturdy **orange suspension bridge** (Map 25) that breaches the Río Santa Isabel and heads north-east down the left bank of the river. Within half an hour it reaches the bridge over the Río Chuntabamba and then the junction with the path from the Río Consevidayoc. A short, sharp climb takes you into an area of well-tended fields and farmland, past a concrete house and **Posta de Salud** (a health station). The introduction of agriculture here has meant that sections of the forest have been cut down to accommodate the coffee, orange and maize plantations that line the path as you descend evenly along the flank of the valley for almost an hour, crossing a **sus-pension bridge** over a tributary as it goes (Map 26).

The path then drops quickly to the river and crosses it on the **Azul Mayo** sus-pension bridge. On the far side a dirt road has been graded and pushed up the valley; some trekking operators will arrange to collect you here and drive you the final distance in a minibus; however, occasional landslides make this road impassable for vehicles. Somewhat alarmingly, rumour has it that the road is set to continue making its way back on the downriver side, pushing further into the jungle, which would have dramatic implications for the area. If you're continu-ing on foot, after the bridge a set of **switchbacks** carry you quickly back up the far side of the river before a long looping bend brings you back on yourself.

The path begins to gain height as it follows the river in a north-east direc-tion, before becoming much steeper and tougher to ascend. It's a steady, unre-lenting climb until you reach the highest point on the trail, where there is a view of Chaunquiri on the right-hand side of the valley. Beyond here the path starts to go back down equally steeply in order to cross the Río San Miguel on a robust bridge, the **Puente La Resistencia**. It's then a 45-minute walk, much of it uphill, on the dirt road that eventually leads to Chaunquiri.

Chaunquiri
Untidy, shabby and centred round a football pitch, Chaunquiri is not the sort of place you'd usually seek out. It is, however, the only way out of the area. There is no accommodation here although you can *camp* in the centre; alternatively you may be able to persuade a local family to let you stay in their house but you should expect to contribute something so negotiate a rate. A couple of cheap, basic **cafés** set around the plaza sell drinks and simple fare.

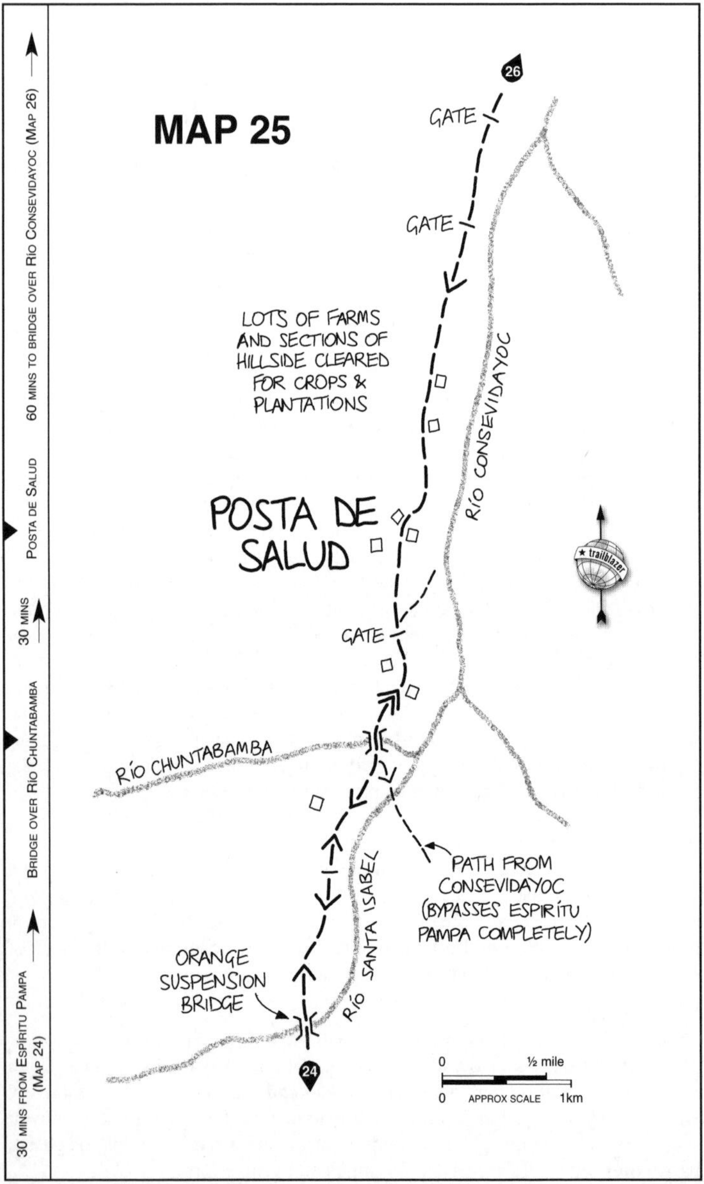

MAP 25

GATE

GATE

LOTS OF FARMS
AND SECTIONS OF
HILLSIDE CLEARED
FOR CROPS &
PLANTATIONS

RÍO CONSEVIDAYOC

POSTA DE
SALUD

GATE

RÍO CHUNTABAMBA

PATH FROM
CONSEVIDAYOC
(BYPASSES ESPÍRITU
PAMPA COMPLETELY)

RÍO SANTA ISABEL

ORANGE
SUSPENSION
BRIDGE

0   ½ mile

0   APPROX SCALE   1km

60 MINS TO BRIDGE OVER RÍO CONSEVIDAYOC (MAP 26) →

POSTA DE SALUD

30 MINS

BRIDGE OVER RÍO CHUNTABAMBA

30 MINS FROM ESPÍRITU PAMPA (MAP 24) →

ROUTE GUIDE AND MAPS

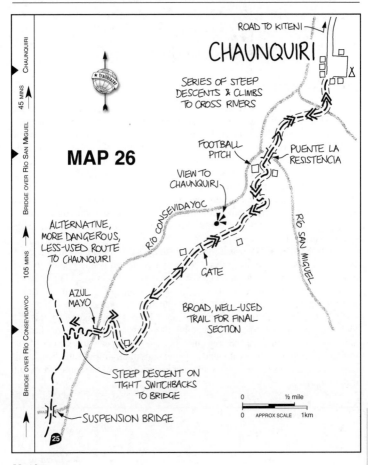

ROAD TO KITENI

CHAUNQIRI

SERIES OF STEEP
DESCENTS & CLIMBS
TO CROSS RIVERS

MAP 26

FOOTBALL
PITCH

PUENTE LA
RESISTENCIA

VIEW TO
CHAUNQIRI

RÍO CONSEVIDAYOC

RÍO SAN MIGUEL

ALTERNATIVE,
MORE DANGEROUS,
LESS-USED ROUTE
TO CHAUNQIRI

AZUL
MAYO

GATE

BROAD, WELL-USED
TRAIL FOR FINAL
SECTION

STEEP DESCENT ON
TIGHT SWITCHBACKS
TO BRIDGE

SUSPENSION BRIDGE

0   ½ mile
0   APPROX SCALE   1km

25

CHAUNQIRI

45 MINS

BRIDGE OVER RÍO SAN MIGUEL

105 MINS

BRIDGE OVER RÍO CONSEVIDAYOC

Moving on

From Chaunqiri catch a bus to Kiteni, 34km (21 miles) and two hours away. (It is possible to walk there, but this is a long, dry, full-day's trek.) Buses don't go all that regularly so it is best to target the trucks going to market there on Wednesday and Sunday. **Kiteni**, which is rumoured to be where Túpac Amaru was captured, is little more than a jungle town, but does at least have a couple of places to stay in the centre and southern section of town. Basic *hospedajes* here cost s/10-25.

From Kiteni you can pick up a bus or truck to **Quillabamba**, which is 7-9 hours away (s/10-15). If you are lucky you may even find a direct truck from Chaunqiri to Quillabamba, particularly if you are trying to travel on Sunday.

The Choquequirao Trek

INTRODUCTION

Regarded by many as the original 'lost city' of the Incas, Choquequirao was the first fabled set of ruins to be uncovered. People had been aware of its existence from at least the 18th century but it was rarely visited and despite several acclaimed 'rediscoveries' over the years, it wasn't until Hiram Bingham arrived here in 1909 that it really came to people's attention. For Bingham it was the discovery that fired his passion to uncover Machu Picchu and Espíritu Pampa.

Set in a remote part of wilderness, on a ridge spur around 1750m/5740ft above the Apurímac River and surrounded by sheer, snow-capped peaks, it is an awe-inspiring destination that requires a degree of effort to reach. Choquequirao is a pretty good substitute for Machu Picchu; the main features of both are similar in many respects.

As archaeologists increasingly recognize the site's importance to the Incas, and awareness of the ruins grows, Choquequirao has gained in popularity as a trekking destination. A donation by the French government in 2003 (see p299) has also meant that further archaeological work at the site has been undertaken and further discoveries made that simply enhance the appeal of these ruins.

As the rules on the classic Inca Trail are enforced more rigorously this trek looks set to continue to offer a genuine alternative. Although the authorities have moved to simplify the trek and increase its appeal, the drama of the region's uncompromising wild landscape remains undiminished and Bingham's classic descriptions of the rigours and scenic attractions of the approach remain true to this day.

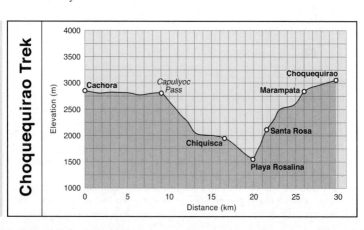

Despite the increase in popularity and attention that Choquequirao has enjoyed, you are still unlikely to encounter many other people on the trek.

The standard trek takes four days to complete; it's a two-day trek from Cachora to the Choquequirao ruins, and two days back again. However, there is more than enough of interest at Choquequirao to justify spending a day exploring the site. This would entail incorporating an extra day into your schedule, but

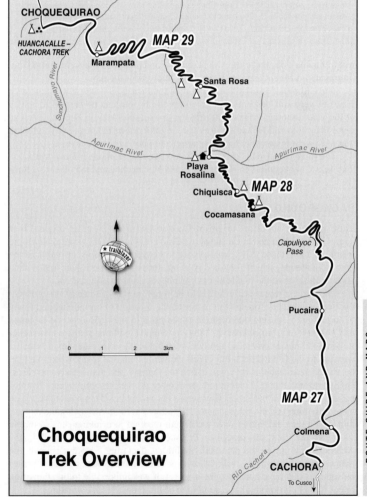

❏ **Choquequirao route – oroya (cable car) river crossing**
In 2012 the Choquequirao route was shut when a series of massive landslides destroyed the concrete bridge that provided the only crossing point over the Apurimac River.

At the time of writing the installation of an oroya (see p305) means the route can be used though not by mules. As a result operators have to arrange for a new mule team to meet groups on the far side of the river. This is obviously an additional expense, as is making the first mule team wait at Playa Rosalina for your return, assuming you're going out from Choquequirao the way you came in. Consequently, many agencies initially opted not to run the Choquequirao Trek, as they couldn't offer the same level of service. You need to continue to check the situation (see box p33).

would enable you to see the site at sunrise and watch as the light shifted and illuminated different aspects of the ruins throughout the day.

The entire trek is slightly tougher than the Inca Trail because it comprises a series of very stiff descents and gruelling climbs, but can be tackled for much of the year although it is best during the dry season (May to September). The route is easy to follow and the trek can be undertaken independently although you may want to consider hiring an arriero to help lighten your load.

The route can also be incorporated into two longer, more arduous treks: one that links Choquequirao to Huancacalle and Vilcabamba and the other that links the site to Machu Picchu. However, see box above.

BACKGROUND

Little is known about the origin of Choquequirao, not even its original Inca name. Its Quechua name translates as 'Cradle of Gold'. Only marginally more is known about those early explorers who uncovered the ruins, in search of the gold of its name, which they believed the Incas had buried there rather than allow it to fall into the hands of the grasping Spanish conquistadors.

The earliest report of the site is to be found in the writings of the prospector Juan Arias Diaz Topete who recorded the location of an uninhabited town, 'Chuquiquirao', during one of three expeditions to the region that he mounted in 1710. Over a century later, in 1834, the French explorer and treasure-seeker Eugene, Comte de Sartiges, approached the site. A village headman issued a warning to the Comte, declaring, 'Tell the white men that to get where we live, the roads are so bad that they will die on the journey, and that we have no chicken eggs to give them.' Undeterred, the Comte de Sartiges employed a team of porters to hack and burn their way across the mountains from Mollepata via an incredibly long and circuitous route. He endured great hardships on the expedition, lost a man and mules over a cliff and resorted to drinking rum all day to stave off the cold. He described the scenery as some of the finest in the Americas, but cursed the path and conditions, declaring 'I do not believe that man could ever live in this valley, however fertile it is, because of the voracious mosquitoes that have taken possession of it. It was impossible to breathe, drink or eat without absorbing large quantities of these insufferable creatures.'

Although he reached Choquequirao, the Comte de Sartiges' expedition produced neither detailed documentation of the site nor any gold. But this failed foray didn't deter the many treasure seekers that subsequently visited Choquequirao. However, none of them ever found any gold either.

The first-known drawings of the site were produced in 1847 by the French Consul in Peru, Léonce Angrand, although the originals of these maps languished in the vaults of the Bibliothèque Nationale in Paris until eventually being published in 1972. For a long time academics wrongly declared Choquequirao to be the site of Manco Inca's final capital, Vilcabamba.

Paramount in perpetuating this idea was the Peruvian naturalist and cartographer Antonio Raimondi, who spent the late 1860s scouring the upper Vilcabamba valley for the ruins of the capital. Upon finding nothing, Raimondi lent his prestige and academic weight to the theory that the site had already been found at Choquequirao, the only major Inca ruin known in the area at that time.

Hiram Bingham forged a path to the site in 1909 whilst travelling through Peru, an experience that inspired his search for Machu Picchu. Although largely uninterested in the accounts of the ruins hidden in the mountains – Bingham admitted that he 'had never heard of Choqquequirau' – he allowed himself to be persuaded by a local official, the prefect of Abancay, to mount an expedition to the site and there undertake some serious documentation of the ruins. Bingham pioneered a new and much more direct approach to the site from the south, which avoided the mountain ranges but did involve crossing the Apurímac river on an 80m-wide wire bridge: 'The bridge was less than 3 feet wide but 273 feet long. It swayed in the wind on its six strands of telegraph wire. To cross it seemed like tempting fate. So close to death did the narrow cat-walk of the bridge appear to be, and so high did the rapids throw the icy spray, that our Indian bearers crept across one at a time, on all fours and obviously wishing they had never been ordered by the prefect to carry our luggage... It must have seemed to them the height of folly for any one voluntarily to use this bridge' *(The Lost City of the Incas).*

His route reduced to a matter of days an approach that had previously taken weeks to accomplish and has been used as the way to Choquequirao ever since. To further simplify the trek, the authorities replaced the old cable bridge with a concrete and steel suspension bridge in 1994. A giant landslip destroyed this bridge in 2012 (see box opposite) but the authorities are planning to replace the temporary oroya crossing with a more substantial, permanent bridge.

Despite developments, for much of the 20th century Choquequirao was overshadowed by Machu Picchu; it wasn't until the mid 1980s that the clearance and restoration of the ruins even began. Owing to its remoteness and lack of infrastructure, the site remained off most people's radar. Ongoing exploration and excavation has resulted in the site being opened up though. In 2003 the French government donated €5 million (US$5.7 million) to Peru's government to fund the study of the ruins and the development of tourist facilities at the site. This coincided with a promotional push, designed to ease the pressure on the Inca Trail, ensuring that Peru's 'second Machu Picchu' came to greater prominence.

PREPARATIONS

The trek can be undertaken through an agency or done independently. Either way, **you'll need a tent and adequate food** as there are no stores or huts along the length of the route. Campsites are shown on the maps.

If you undertake the trek independently you should **consider hiring an arriero** and mules to accompany you since climbing the sheer valley sides in the dry heat is tough enough without being laden down with equipment and food. Arrieros can be hired in Cachora (see opposite) or Colmena (see p302).

Although the trek to Choquequirao is marginally harder than the classic Inca Trail, most averagely fit individuals with a degree of experience and a little preparation should be able to reach the ruins with nothing more than a dull ache in their calves.

The trek requires no special equipment. You should, however, make sure you have the **capacity to carry several litres of water** since the points at which you can refill bottles are far apart and the heat and humidity of the Apurímac valley will cause you to dehydrate very quickly once you begin to exert yourself. You should also carry sufficient **insect repellent**, since large sections of the track are plagued by sand-flies and mosquitoes.

The **fee** for visiting the ruins (s/36 per adult) will be included in the price you pay your agency if trekking with a guided group, but you will have to pay that yourself if undertaking the trek independently.

❏ Sayhuite (Saywite)
Some 45km (28 miles) east of Abancay, set back from the road opposite the junction for Cachora, lies the community of Concachaca. In the midst of this hamlet, open to the elements, is the enigmatic Sayhuite (sometimes written as Saywite) monolith, one of several huacas scattered around this area. This sizeable, elaborately carved boulder is approximately 4m (13ft) in diameter and stands over 2m (6½ft) high. The delicate reliefs etched into the top surface represent aspects of Andean culture and appear to show a complex map of some kind: some rumours allege that it represents the construction plans for Tahuantinsuyo, the Inca Empire and the author Hugh Thomson describes it in his book *Cochineal Red* as, 'a meteorite shot from the past containing the Inca world in capsule form'.

Elaborately carved buildings, terraces and geometrical patterns can be made out amidst the intricate sculpture, which has unfortunately been damaged by exposure to the elements and by souvenir hunters and vandals. There are also numerous figures including humans armed with arrows and a variety of llamas, vicunas, pumas, snakes, monkeys and lizards. Channels on the stone hint at the rituals and ceremonies that may have been connected with it. The rim has notches around it, thought to once have held an elaborate textile or gold cladding. Stones such as Q'enko in the Sacred Valley have a similar sculpted surface. However, none is as elaborate as Sayhuite or as isolated within the landscape; nor does any have as intimate a relationship with their surroundings. It costs s/10 to visit this boulder. Close by are wells, canals and several large boulders that have been split in half, suggesting that Sayhuite stood at the heart of a larger religious complex. One such monolith, at the bottom of the hill, has steps that seemingly lead nowhere carefully cut into it.

As a final piece of preparation, **read** about the ruins in advance to get the most from your visit. Vincent Lee's excellent *Forgotten Vilcabamba* and Hugh Thomson's *The White Rock* are good places to start.

GETTING TO THE TRAILHEAD

To reach **Cachora**, catch an early morning bus from Cusco (see p186) to Abancay and ask to be dropped off at the Cachora turn-off. Buses leave throughout the early morning until around 7am. The drive takes 3½-4 hours and follows the Apurímac river through a spectacular, sheer-sided gorge.

Two hours from Cusco the road crosses the Cunyac bridge over the Apurímac, the border between the departments of Cusco and Abancay. The road climbs up and away from the river, passing Sayhuite (see box opposite) to arrive at the signposted junction for Cachora. Expect to arrive by 11am. There is a large sign for Choquequirao at the junction. Occasionally taxis wait to ferry people (30-45 mins) along the winding dirt track to Cachora (s/5 fare), 4km (2½ miles) away. Alternatively, it's a two-hour walk downhill through eucalyptus groves dotted with cacti, or an hour if you cut across the bends in the road.

CACHORA   [see Map 27, p303]

Cachora sits in an idyllic spot cupped on three sides by steep sloping ridges at the head of the Cachora valley. It is a picturesque Andean town that enjoys fertile soils, a reliable water supply, reasonably temperate weather and stunning views north of the snow-capped peaks of the Vilcabamba range on the far side of the Apurímac river, including the imposing Padrayoc (5482m/17,990ft).

On the southern edge of the plaza is the **Comisaria PNP building**, where you should consider registering if trekking alone or without the back up of an agency (although it is not obligatory to do so). You can **hire arrieros** from around the central plaza and buy a small quantity of basic provisions from the handful of **hole-in-the-wall shops** on the main street.

Unfortunately, most people simply pass through the town, arriving early with their tour or trekking operator and hitting the trail immediately. Consequently Cachora hasn't benefitted from the influx of visitors and the infrastructure here remains very basic.

There are a few **hospedajes** (whose names frequently change), where families offer cheap double rooms, usually with a basic breakfast. The simplest just have mattresses on the floor, whilst the better ones also have hot water and may offer evening meals.

Look out for the established, charming, rustic *Los Tres Balcones* (🖵 www .choquequirau.com, ☎ 984-897566; US$20pp, breakfast), on Jr Abancay, which was refurbished in 2013. The name comes from the three carefully carved balconies set above an intricately embossed front door. It is possible to *camp* here; otherwise there are good-value double rooms with hot showers. The restaurant here serves pizzas, parrilladas and other traditional dishes. The owners can also arrange guides and mules on your behalf.

Also well worth considering is the small, friendly, family-run *Casa de Salcantay* (☎ 984 281171, 🖳 www.salcantay.com; US$30/60 sgl/dbl, breakfast), situated just outside the main village. The house has hot water and free internet access; evening meals cost US$6. The owner, a Dutchman with a wide knowledge of the area and experience of mountaineering in Peru, also organizes horse rides, guided treks to Choquequirao and hires out mules and drivers to independent trekkers.

Around the town are a number of small, anonymous-looking hole-in-the-wall **cafés** that serve simple meals at very reasonable rates – look for one that's popular with the locals and stick your head round the door to see what's cooking. You can also pick up a small amount of fruit and vegetables from simple **shops** on the streets off the main plaza but don't expect to stock up for a multi-day trek from here.

CACHORA TO CHIQUISCA   [MAP 27; MAP 28, p306]

In the north-western corner of the plaza a small road heads down the valley, directly towards the snow-capped peak of Padrayoc on the far side of the Apurímac valley. After the last house branch left and follow a small track as it descends for 10-15 minutes towards a **blue 'INC' sign**. Turn left here and descend on a series of tight, dusty loops, crossing an irrigation channel as you lose height. Carry straight on and climb gently through stands of eucalyptus to get up onto the left-hand side (west) of the valley, crossing a stream as you do. This track is narrow and often muddy; it may be impassable to small minibuses or 4WD vehicles after heavy rain.

Shortly after a gate the track divides. The lower branch descends for 1km (half a mile) to **Colmena**, where several families live in ranch-style farmhouses. You can hire arrieros and horses here. From Colmena, you can cross the Cachora river and climb up the western side of the valley to rejoin the original road heading north. Eventually it will be extended all the way to Capuliyoc, but at the time of writing it peters out beside the lone hut at **Pucaira**, 8km (5 miles) from Cachora, beyond the giant boulder marking the start of Choquequirao National Park.

The stream in a deep U-shaped hollow shortly after Pucaira is the last place to refill water bottles until Chiquisca, at least four hours away. The track then passes through a **gate** and curves around a rocky promontory, which gives outstanding views of the surrounding valleys and ridges (Map 28). A battered sign warns of rockfall here, so take care. From this point it is also possible to make out Capuliyoc pass ahead, around half an hour away at the top of a sharp final push. Sometimes you can buy soft drinks and water at a shack up here.

❏ **Important note – walking times**
All times in this book refer only to the time spent walking. You will need to add 10-30% to allow for rests, photography, checking the map, drinking water etc.

ROUTE GUIDE AND MAPS

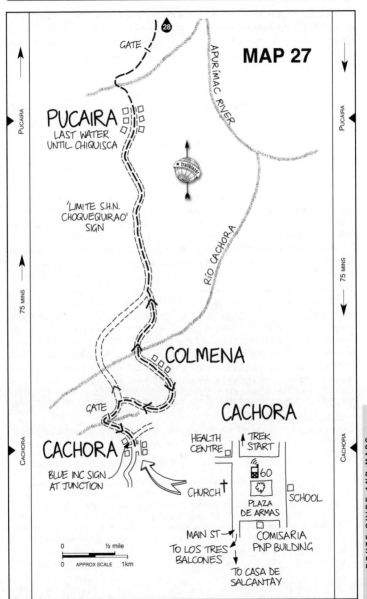

MAP 27

GATE

PUCAIRA
LAST WATER
UNTIL CHIQUISCA

APURÍMAC RIVER

'LIMITE S.H.N.
CHOQUEQUIRAO'
SIGN

RÍO CACHORA

trailblazer

COLMENA

GATE

CACHORA

CACHORA
BLUE INC SIGN
AT JUNCTION

HEALTH
CENTRE

TREK
START

CHURCH †

60

PLAZA
DE ARMAS

SCHOOL

MAIN ST

COMISARIA
PNP BUILDING

TO LOS TRES
BALCONES

TO CASA DE
SALCANTAY

PUCAIRA

PUCAIRA

75 MINS

75 MINS

CACHORA

CACHORA

0   ½ mile
0   APPROX SCALE   1km

ROUTE GUIDE AND MAPS

Capuliyoc pass (2800m/9185ft) is a narrow wind-beaten arête, whipped by clouds which frequently shroud the vertiginous cliffs and jagged peaks nearby. However, on clear days and with binoculars, you can just make out the hazy outline of Choquequirao, perched high atop a forested ridge away to the west. With the naked eye you can also feast on dramatic views of the canyon-like Apurímac valley, one of the deepest ravines in the Americas.

From the pass at Capuliyoc, the path drops steeply into the Apurímac valley on a series of **switchbacks**, descending amidst tough grasses and cutting across the remnants of a large rockfall. About 2km (1¼ miles) after the pass the path edges around a rocky prow and across a concrete ledge with handrail to a spectacular viewpoint at **Cocamasana**. From here you can make out the campsite at Chiquisca and, beyond that, the crossing point for the Apurímac river. Rather depressingly, you can also pick out the steep zigzags up the apparently sheer valley opposite – part of the route ahead.

Just beyond the viewpoint, on a narrow terrace below a hillside of blue agave cacti, is the Cocamasana *campsite*, which has a flimsy thatched shelter and room for a handful of tents that are treated to spectacular views straight down the valley.

As the path descends for the next 4km (2½ miles) you'll notice a change in vegetation, as trees festooned with bromeliads replace scrub and cacti, and a rise in temperature. There are also several landslip scars on the slopes here; rockfalls are frequent though rarely of sufficient magnitude to affect the route.

Passing a rock indicating the 16km (10 miles) mark, the path curves right and goes by a thatched shack on a small knoll, adjacent to which you could *camp*, although there's no water supply. A much better bet is **Chiquisca**, in the wooded area just below, where a local family will let you *camp* (for free) beneath cherimoya, lemon and papaya trees in a clearing adjacent to their house or on a series of terraces behind the house. There's running water, toilets and even a cold shower (s/1); the family sells soft drinks and bottled water and can

---

❏ **The Apurímac**

'The sound of the Apurímac rises faintly from the gorge, like a murmur from outer space...

'Apurímac River! Apurímac River!' the Runa children repeat with tenderness and a touch of fear.'   **José María Arguedas**, *Los Ríos Profundos*

The Apurímac river rises near Arequipa and eventually flows into the Amazon as a raging torrent 250ft wide and 80ft deep. The rapids and churning water along its length led to the Indians giving it its Quechua name, Apu-rimac, which literally translates as 'The God Who Speaks', or 'Great Speaker'.

During Inca times a famous rope bridge spanned the canyon where an Inca road crossed from one bank to the other. When threatened, the Incas simply cut the bridge, knowing the river was usually too violent to risk crossing any other way. Unfortunately, when the conquistadors marched on Cusco and the Incas cut the bridge, the invading Spanish were able to ford the river as the usually torrential Apurímac was particularly low.

rustle up a cooked meal for a small charge. There's a more spacious *campsite* where large tour groups tend to stay about 50m further down the track; there's water here too.

CHIQUISCA TO CHOQUEQUIRAO   [MAP 28, p306; MAP 29, p307]

An early start will give you the most of the shade and morning cool; the valley bottom becomes unbearably hot later and the ascent of the far side of the valley can be exhausting in direct sun.

Beyond Chiquisca the path descends steeply for half an hour in a series of hairpin bends for 2km (1¼ miles) to the riverside and **Playa Rosalina**, where a rudimentary *lodge* with dorm rooms, toilets, showers and a *restaurant* stands amidst boulders and stubby trees. You can also *camp* here but the place is infested with sand-flies. The **Apurímac** is very strong, but you can get water and wash in the sheltered spots. Nearby there is a **checkpoint** where you must sign in.

An orange concrete suspension bridge used to span the Apurímac and link the departments of Abancay to the south and Cusco to the north but a giant landslip destroyed this in 2012. At the time of writing there still wasn't a timetable for the bridge's reconstruction so the *oroya* set up by local people was the only way to cross the river. The **oroya** consists of a small cage which is slung below a cable spanning the river; it can hold two people and their packs at a time. The cage is sturdy and perfectly safe but there's plenty of movement as it is hauled manually, using a sequence of ropes, over the water; it is a dramatic way to cross a large river and is certainly not for the faint-hearted. What's more, it's hard, physical work to lift the cage and its occupants up to the landing platform on the far side of the river. A local, or someone from the lodge at Playa Rosalina, will probably be happy to work the oroya but you may find you have to get involved if no-one is about. The crossing is the lowest point on the trek; once on the far side you must begin the long climb to Choquequirao.

On the north side of the Apurímac, the ascent begins gently before succumbing to a series of sweeping **switchbacks** (Map 29). These become progressively shorter and tighter as they weave beneath a cliff and climb swiftly past slopes scarred by recent rockfall.

About two hours beyond the bridge the path climbs above a crop of bright green sugar cane cultivated for the production of *cañazo*, the lethal spirit beloved by the local people. There is a traditional sugar-cane press just below the main terrace here. Above this field is **Santa Rosa**, a cleared area and settlement that overlooks the valley. The land belongs to a local family but it is possible to *camp* here; there's a water source nearby, but the pitch is sometimes plagued by sand-flies.

Push on for 10 minutes beyond the small shrine on the other side of Santa Rosa to a second slightly larger, more pleasant *campsite*, **Santa Rosa Alta**, next to a narrow stream and free from sand-flies, which boasts sumptuous views of the valley and the previous day's walk. At the farm here, you may be able to hire mules if you haven't already done so, but they are more expensive than at the trailhead and you'll probably be too exhausted to haggle.

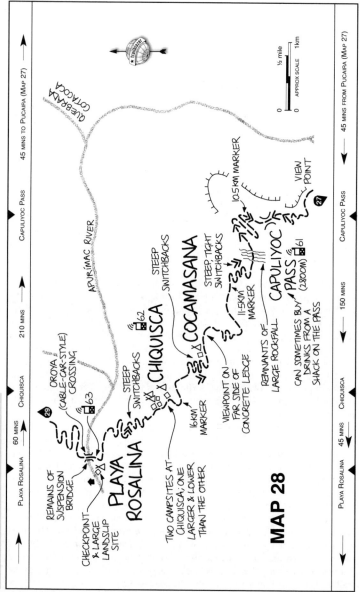

MAP 28

PLAYA ROSALINA — 60 MINS — CHIQUISCA — 210 MINS — CAPULIYOC PASS — 45 MINS TO PUCAIRA (MAP 27)

PLAYA ROSALINA — 45 MINS — CHIQUISCA — 150 MINS — CAPULIYOC PASS — 45 MINS FROM PUCAIRA (MAP 27)

trailblazer

0   ½ mile   1km
0   APPROX SCALE

QUEBRADA COTACOCA

APURIMAC RIVER

REMAINS OF SUSPENSION BRIDGE

CHECKPOINT & LARGE LANDSLIP SITE

PLAYA ROSALINA

OROYA (CABLE-CAR-STYLE) CROSSING

63

STEEP SWITCHBACKS

CHIQUISCA

62

STEEP SWITCHBACKS

TWO CAMPSITES AT CHIQUISCA; ONE LARGER & LOWER THAN THE OTHER

16KM MARKER

VIEWPOINT ON FAR SIDE OF CONCRETE LEDGE

COCAMASANA

STEEP TIGHT SWITCHBACKS

11.5KM MARKER

REMNANTS OF LARGE ROCKFALL

10.5KM MARKER

CAPULIYOC PASS (2800M)

61

CAN SOMETIMES BUY DRINKS FROM A SHACK ON THE PASS

VIEW POINT

27

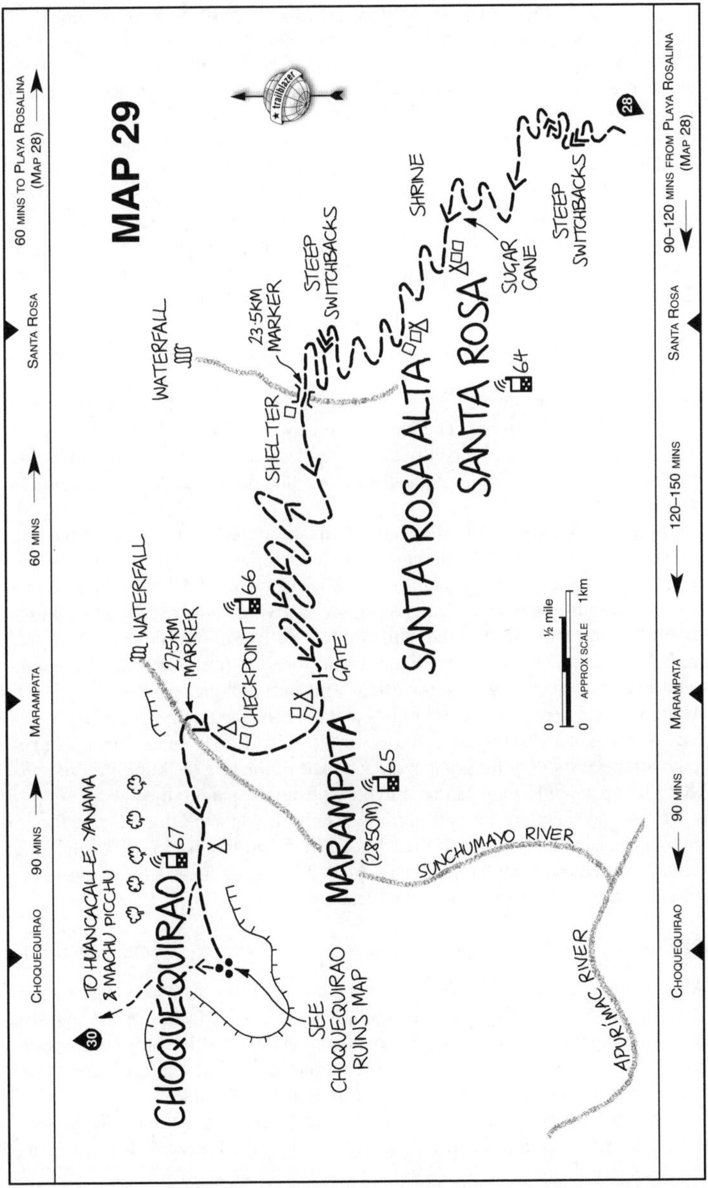
MAP 29
60 MINS TO PLAYA ROSALINA (MAP 28)
SANTA ROSA
60 MINS
MARAMPATA
90 MINS
CHOQUEQUIRAO
90–120 MINS FROM PLAYA ROSALINA (MAP 28)
SANTA ROSA
120–150 MINS
MARAMPATA
90 MINS
CHOQUEQUIRAO
trailblazer
28
30
TO HUANCACALLE, YANAMA & MACHU PICCHU
CHOQUEQUIRAO
67
SEE CHOQUEQUIRAO RUINS MAP
WATERFALL
27.5KM MARKER
CHECKPOINT
66
GATE
MARAMPATA
(2850M)
65
SUNCHUMAYO RIVER
APURÍMAC RIVER
WATERFALL
23.5KM MARKER
SHELTER
STEEP SWITCHBACKS
SANTA ROSA ALTA
SANTA ROSA
64
SHRINE
SUGAR CANE
STEEP SWITCHBACKS
0
½ mile
0
APPROX SCALE
1km

The long, strenuous climb continues past the **23.5km rock**, where the track crosses a stream and zigzags up a forested ridge that rises ahead of you. This lengthy ascent can seem endless in the absence of landmarks or features by which to gauge your progress. After 2-2½ hours of toil from Santa Rosa the path passes through a rustic gate and rounds a wooded prow to emerge at **Marampata** (2850m/9350ft), a village on a steep hillside that is home to two families. You can *camp* on the terraces by the houses for free and enjoy the exceptional, panoramic views. By now the valley is too steep to see the Apurímac at its foot; a series of hanging valleys block out each succeeding drop, hiding the true extent of the chasm. You can, however, see the outline of Choquequirao on an adjacent ridge top. Also in the settlement is a toilet and you can buy bottled drinks and basic snacks from one of the houses.

From Marampata the path undulates westwards before turning into a sub-sidiary valley. Here you'll find the **Choquequirao checkpoint**, although it's still 1.5km (one mile) to the ruins where the warden is likely to be; he'll soon find you when you pitch *camp*. The ruins themselves are clearly visible from this point across the gorge. The Upper and Lower Plaza straddle a ridge about 500m above a number of recently uncovered terraces that merge into thick forest; they seem to be clinging to a sheer slope that disappears into a bottomless ravine.

Skirt around the side-valley and at its head pick your way across the Sunchumayo River, which tumbles down in a series of giant shelves, on the boulders acting as giant stepping stones. After heavy rainfall this section can be very precarious and the river can rise significantly making the crossing complicated. Beyond the waterfall the path climbs briefly before dividing. The right-hand fork continues to climb through cloud forest to the ruins, whilst the left-hand branch descends gently for 500m to a pair of long, narrow terraces on which you can *camp*. There are toilets and cold showers here. Use of the facilities is free when you buy an entrance ticket (s/36) for the ruins. Tickets ought to be arranged by your trekking agency as part of the trek fee but if you're travelling independently they can be purchased from the gate to the site.

From the junction the path climbs evenly through the thick forest for 15 minutes before emerging from the trees on to the north-eastern end of the long curved terraces beneath the Lower Plaza. A 2m-wide stone road runs along the base of these terraces to a rough path leading up to the Lower Plaza.

CHOQUEQUIRAO   [see map p311]

Although only about a third of the site at Choquequirao has been cleared, there is still plenty to see. The site is potentially larger than Machu Picchu, but has fewer buildings. Despite the degree to which the area is still overgrown, or perhaps even because of it, the site is utterly spectacular and reinforces the belief that the Incas chose locations in part for their aesthetic value.

The terraces you could see on the way from Marampata are the lowest feature at the site. **Paqchayoc** lies about 350m below the Pikiwasi (Ridge Group) ruins, on a steep slope of between 35° and 45°. Ongoing restoration work here has revealed sweeping terraces over 450m wide and 250m high.

The tumbledown walls have been cleared and repaired and the single building at the heart of them restored. **Casa de la Caida de Agua** (House of the Waterfall) has several small rooms marked with niches and double-jamb doorways, leading archaeologists to suggest that it was connected in some way to religious ceremonies or the worship of water. There are superb views from here of the Sunchumayo River cascading down the head of the valley, and a broad, **smoothed ceremonial rock** just below the building. The terraces are well irrigated and it is likely that the Incas grew crops on them to support the main site.

Above the terraces and beyond a stretch of forest are the subtly **curved terraces** beneath the Lower Plaza where you first entered the site. A similarly gently curved **stone road**, known as the **Avenue of the Cedars**, runs the length of the 350m long terraces. The slight degree of curvature accommodates the contour of the slope and draws the eye left towards the Truncated Hilltop (Usnu), the focal point of the site, set to the south of the Lower Plaza.

Four sets of steps link the three broad, high terraces although there is no apparent stairway connecting either the stone road or the terraces to the **Lower Plaza**, where the majority of the high-status ceremonial and residential buildings are located. A great hall looking out over the Apurímac valley, a lesser hall and three double-sided two-storey buildings stand at the northern end of the

---

❏ **So whose was it?**
Unfortunately this enigmatic site is yet to give up all its secrets and until the material gathered by the current archaeologists is analysed fully there is no conclusive evidence suggesting who may have built Choquequirao or why. To further complicate things there appears to be no reference to the site in any of the Spanish chronicles.

The sweeping, stacked terraces are reminiscent of those at Huinay Huayna on the Inca Trail, whilst the site most closely resembles Inca country estates and ceremonial centres such as Pisac and more pertinently, Machu Picchu. There are plenty of comparisons to be made between these two sites. Vincent Lee points to the ridge-top location and the way that the Apurímac relates to Choquequirao in the same way as the Urubamba does to Machu Picchu. He observes that although the setting of Choquequirao is probably more spectacular, being three times as far above the Apurímac as Machu Picchu is above the Urubamba, the latter remains the finer site by virtue of its superior architecture. Nonetheless, Choquequirao does exhibit high-status architecture designed for royal occupation, as evidenced by the large number of double-jamb doorways. Both places also exhibit the attributes of royal estates with watercourses and fountains, sacred outcrops and kallankas. In summary, Vincent Lee observed that, 'both sites evoke much the same feeling of reverence for and celebration of wild Nature and the splendours of the high mountain world.'

If, as is widely thought, Pachacutec built Machu Picchu, it's fair to surmise that Choquequirao was either also built during his reign or by someone powerful who admired his work. Based on the architectural style and the prevalence of double-jamb doorways, Lee himself concluded in his report into recent work at the site that Topa Inca, who succeeded Pachacutec, was 'the probable suspect' responsible for the site.

plaza. High status is conveyed by the extensive use of double-jamb doorways on these principal buildings. The stonework is inferior to some of that found at Machu Picchu, something US explorer Gary Ziegler attributes to the frangible metamorphic rock found at Choquequirao, which is an inferior building material to the granite and andesite of Machu Picchu.

An intricate **water channel** runs along the western edge of the ridge to a 'fountain', probably the site's water supply, on the Upper Plaza. From the Lower Plaza a rough path also climbs alongside the channel 50m north-west to the Upper Plaza. Rustic structures at the southern end of the plaza face an array of terraces and niched retaining walls. Their lesser stonework and the absence of any double-jamb doorways implies that they are less significant than those found around the Lower Plaza.

On the western edge of the Upper Plaza stands an impressive retaining wall above a terrifying cliff-drop that plummets over 1750m/5740ft to the Apurímac river. At the south-western end of this group is the structure called the **Giant Stairway**. This peculiar set of eight small terraces is built around a large outcrop of bedrock and a number of big boulders. Like many of the features at Choquequirao its purpose remains unknown.

A path on the western edge of the Lower Plaza descends through the forested slope below the site to some of the most unusual discoveries at Choquequirao. A frighteningly steep Inca staircase drops off the plaza and plummets down the hillside to a set of terraces. Uniquely, these tall terraces are decorated with patterns. The first you encounter have white zigzags set amidst the dark stones, whilst a little lower down are the **llama terraces**. Images of 22 llamas, both adult and young, have been uncovered here, either singly or in pairs.

Unusually, the terraces were built using vertical rather than horizontal stones, so that craftsmen were more easily able to insert shapes and patterns into them. The white rocks used for the patterns clearly stand out and the result, which is clearly visible from a distance, is a striking visual celebration of one of the Inca's most prized animals. Quite what the true purpose of this decoration was, no-one is entirely sure. A rough track leads from the far side of one of the upper terraces to a makeshift viewing platform that gives the best views of the uncovered stretch of hillside.

Back at the southern end of the Lower Plaza is a collection of what appears to be small shrines featuring double-jamb niches. Next to these is a sizeable double-jamb doorway through which a path climbs to the top of what Bingham described as the **Truncated Hilltop**. This ceremonial square, or *usnu*, was undoubtedly the focus of the site, as demonstrated by its elaborate entrance and the ring of stones around it. The platform, which would have required an enormous amount of effort to create, has stunning panoramic views of the surrounding ridges and peaks. Its use is unknown although people have speculated that it may have been a celestial observation platform or a place from which to communicate with other sites.

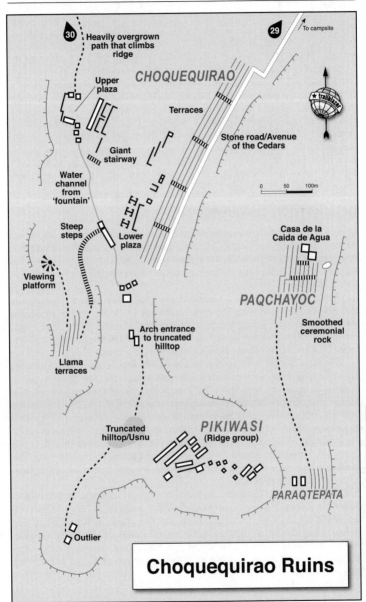

Choquequirao Ruins

To the south-west of the Truncated Hilltop is a narrow ridge, above vertiginous drops on either side; a faint track leads along this ridge to the **Outlier**, where two well-crafted oblong buildings stand opposite each other across a small courtyard. The purpose of these buildings is also unknown, although the higher-quality stonework suggests that they were important.

Below the Truncated Hilltop, 50-100m to the south-east, is large collection of buildings and terraces called **Pikiwasi** (**Ridge Group**). This area was only explored and mapped in 1996 by Vincent Lee and still remains uncleared. Below here, and currently accessible only from Paqchayoc, is **Paraqtepata**, a further set of steep terraces poised above a sheer cliff. These terraces are the steepest on the site and have poor irrigation, suggesting that their main purpose may have been to reduce erosion. The surrounding slopes are still heavily forested but outlines of dilapidated structures and further terraces are clearly visible, hinting at what might lie beneath.

OPTIONS FROM CHOQUEQUIRAO

From Choquequirao you essentially have **three options** as well as one that at the time of writing was only theoretically possible. The first and most common is to **retrace your steps to Cachora**. Back at the main road, you can catch a bus (departs around 5.30am and 11am) or flag down a *colectivo* or taxi to Cusco, four hours away.

Alternatively, you have a **choice of two trek extensions**: to Huancacalle and Vilcabamba following the route described on pp326-38; or to Machu Picchu via the Santa Teresa valley, which is described on pp313-25. Both routes are very beautiful, but they're also strenuous, isolated and should only be undertaken by more experienced trekkers after thorough preparation.

The final option is to **return to Cusco via San Ignacio and Abancay**. However, the **path was rendered impassable** and the San Ignacio bridge severely damaged by landslips in 2012, meaning that the route was closed. The bridge is unlikely to be rebuilt quickly given the remoteness of the crossing but you may still see this option advertised on some agency websites. If you intend to tackle it, check well in advance whether the route has been reopened.

Assuming this route is possible it starts with a steep descent from the ruins to the Río Apurímac; after a walk of at least four hours you would reach San Ignacio Playa, where a river crossing would let you ascend to San Ignacio where it's possible to *camp*.

A walk along the Tambobamba Valley, through an attractive forest, leads to *Villa los Loros* (🖳 www.choquequiraolodge.com, ☎ 83 816052/816053; US$43/86 sgl/dbl with dinner and breakfast, free camping, restaurant). From here you can hike out to Huanipaca, 17km (10½ miles) away; alternatively you can arrange for an agency to come and collect you. You can then easily access the larger town of Abancay, from where it's possible to pick up a bus heading back to Cusco.

Choquequirao to Machu Picchu

INTRODUCTION

For people with time, the trail from Choquequirao to Machu Picchu is one of the finest outings in the Cusco region and a superb way of combining two Inca sites with a genuine wilderness experience. Traversing the entire Vilcabamba range from the Río Apurímac to the Río Urubamba, the path is strenuous and spectacular.

Steep ascents and equally punishing descents quickly follow one another as you trek across the grain of the land and are forced to climb and fall from pass to pass. Extraordinary vistas await at the top of each crossing; the great peaks – Choquetecarpo, Chaupimayo, Sacsarayoc, Padrayoc and Salkantay – that line the path are all clearly visible in the course of the trek. The trail follows an original Inca road, which in parts is still visible and well preserved. There is also a handful of colonial-era sites along the route such as the mines at La Victoria, and a number of contemporary hamlets where you can camp.

The trek essentially links the Choquequirao Trek to the Santa Teresa trek via a section of very scenic, secluded countryside. The route is tougher than the Inca Trail owing to the terrain but walkers with a reasonable degree of stamina and fitness shouldn't find it unduly taxing. Although it links the major ruins which can be busy, the vast majority of the trek is spent in rarely visited stretches of remote countryside and you will see precious few trekkers. It is best tackled during the dry season (May to September), but can be attempted at any time of year. Bear in mind though that the highest pass is just shy of 4800m/15,750ft and the weather up there can be very inhospitable: the pass may even be blocked by snow at some times of year.

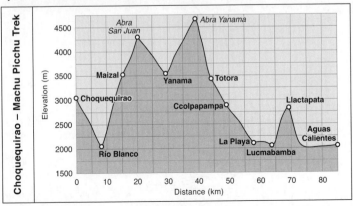

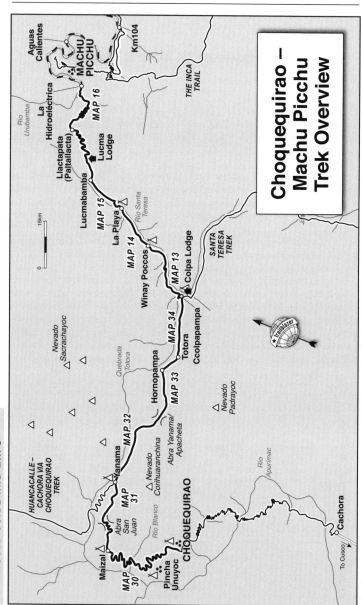

Choquequirao – Machu Picchu Trek Overview

At present it is perfectly feasible to tackle the route independently and no charges or permits are required, although you have to pay entrance fees for both Choquequirao and Machu Picchu. You should take a guide though and consider hiring *arrieros* to help carry the weight of a week-long expedition.

There are very few places to buy food or drink along the route and you are far better off taking everything you think you will need from Cusco. Guides and arrieros can be organized in Cusco or hired locally in Cachora, at the start of the trek. Slowly agencies in Cusco are recognizing the potential and appeal of this route and a number now offer fully guided, organized treks (see pp179-86).

The trek can be done in either direction, but typically people finish at Machu Picchu. If this is the case, the trek actually begins in Cachora (for details on getting to the trailhead see p301, for details on Cachora see p301) and usually takes seven days; you'll need a further day at both Choquequirao and Machu Picchu in order to fully explore the ruins, so should realistically allow nine days for the entire trip.

CACHORA TO CHOQUEQUIRAO
[MAP 27, p303; MAP 28, p306; MAP 29, p307]

For information on getting to the trailhead, the village of Cachora and the first two days of the route, from Cachora to Chiquisca and Chiquisca to Choquequirao see pp302-8. For details of the features at the ruins and an explanation of Choquequirao's history see pp308-12.

CHOQUEQUIRAO TO MAIZAL [MAP 30, p317]
Overview
Following a day exploring the ruins at Choquequirao and relaxing after the haul there from Chiquisca, the trail resumes with a long, tiring day. This is potentially the toughest day of the entire trek if completed in one go, as you are required to descend very steeply into the Quebrada Victoria (also known as the Quebrada Blanco), past the partially restored ruins at Pincha Unuyoc, then climb equally aggressively up the far side of the valley to regain all the lost height.

One alternative and a way to reduce the total trekking time for this section is to leave Choquequirao late in the afternoon and hike to Pincha Unuyoc, around three hours away, where it is possible to camp. This will save time the following day, but could curtail your time spent exploring the ruins at Choquequirao.

Route
From the campsite at Choquequirao, follow the trail that ascends through the forest towards the ruins. Just above the campsite the path branches; take the right-hand fork and follow a series of steep switchbacks as they clamber through the dense vegetation towards the ridge ahead.

An alternative is to begin from the Upper Plaza of the ruins. Pick up a heavily overgrown trail that heads straight up the ridge behind the ruins. The path here is steep and poorly marked and you must clamber over roots and push through the vegetation to make headway. As you climb there are several stone walls, channels and outlines of structures hidden tantalizingly in the jungle. After 10-15 minutes the path joins the main route ascending from the campsite and the two continue to climb gently through the cloud forest, switching from the right- to left-hand side of the ridge.

The path crosses the ridge one more time and then contours around 50m across the forested face of the mountain above a precipitous drop. From here you have your final view of Choquequirao, as well as an impressive plunging view into the Apurímac gorge, before crossing a further ridge and dropping below it to lose sight of the ruins. As you descend (briefly steeply) you leave the cloud forest and emerge onto a hillside swathed in high puna grasses. The views ahead are breathtaking; the Río Yanama plunges through a gorge straight ahead of you, whilst the Río Blanco, which is also sometimes shown as the Río Victoria on maps, courses through the steep-sided valley that you are now standing directly above.

Having contoured across the grasslands, a series of long switchbacks brings you swiftly off the mountainside and lead towards the corrugated roofs of the archaeologists' huts visible far below, adjacent to Pincha Unuyoc. Just above the camp and the ruins is a flat, clear shelf that looks over the surrounding valleys. This makes a decent *campsite*, but very little water is available here.

A further 10-15 minutes' descent on a gentler dirt track through scrub and matted vegetation brings you to the massed terraces of **Pincha Unuyoc** (2470m/8100ft; see box p318). Below the terraces the path continues its long, hot, exposed descent on a series of increasingly loose and sandy switchbacks towards the valley bottom. In direct sunshine this can be a very tiring section to tackle.

Río Blanco, at the bottom of the valley, issues from the upper slopes of Corihuaynachina (5404m/17,725ft) at the head of the valley and has gouged out a trench in the soft soil here. The path tumbles into this to finally emerge on the broad flood plain. The width of the flood plain is indicative of just how much water pours off the surrounding glacier-capped mountains during the wet season – at this time of year or during flash floods, the river can be impassable.

On arriving on the floodplain head downstream on the rocky, boulder-strewn banks briefly and look for the makeshift log bridges that act as crossing points. Cross to the right-hand side of the river and continue downstream for a further 200m. Although plagued by sandflies, this area makes an excellent rest stop, and gives you the opportunity to take a deserved dip in the icy meltwater.

Pick up the path that climbs away from the river and edges into the forest to begin to scale the flank of the valley. The gradient is relentless and you climb steeply for the next 3½-4 hours. The path is clear and relatively even, so not too taxing. Gaps in the increasingly tall and dense vegetation reveal stunning views, giving you reason to pause and draw breath.

The path gains around 1300m/4275ft in the course of the climb and eventually brings you to a small ledge, **Maizal**, where a local family has a rudimentary farm. It is possible to *camp* on a small terrace here and the family may be able to sell you soft drinks. Alternatively, there is a second campsite (see p319) 20 minutes further on.

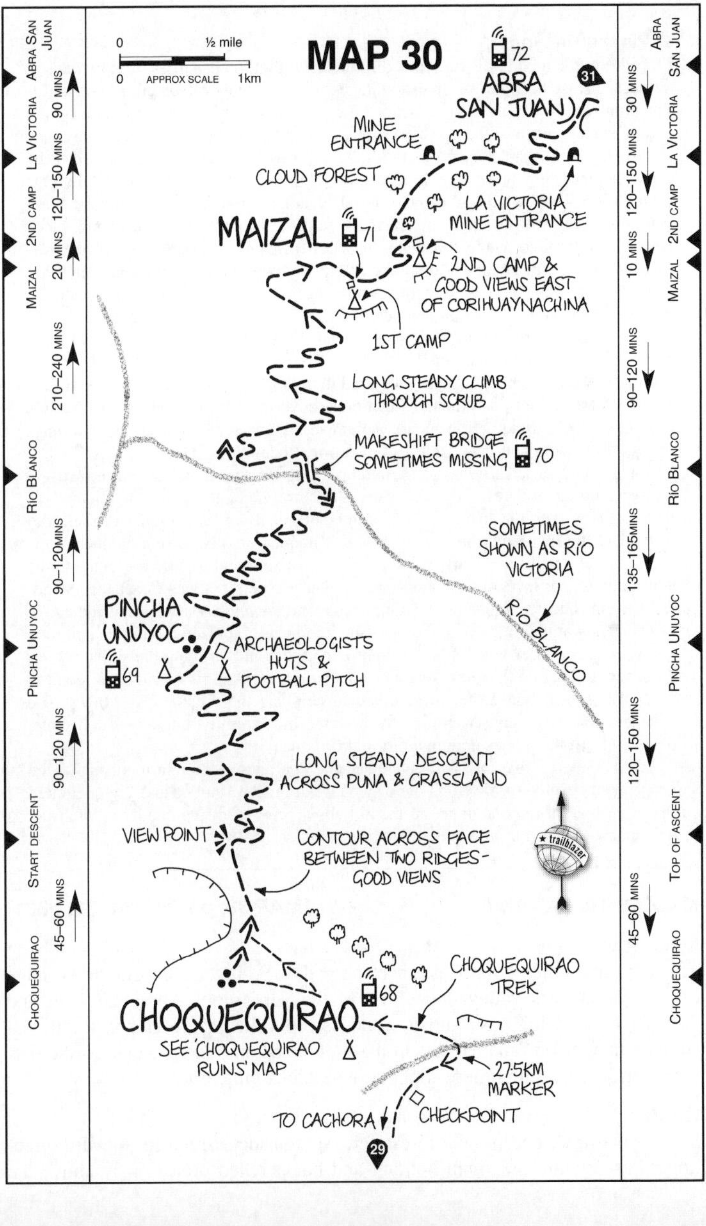
MAP 30
0 ½ mile
0 APPROX SCALE 1km
72
31
ABRA SAN JUAN
MINE ENTRANCE
CLOUD FOREST
LA VICTORIA MINE ENTRANCE
MAIZAL
71
2ND CAMP & GOOD VIEWS EAST OF CORIHUAYNACHINA
1ST CAMP
LONG STEADY CLIMB THROUGH SCRUB
MAKESHIFT BRIDGE SOMETIMES MISSING
70
SOMETIMES SHOWN AS RÍO VICTORIA
RÍO BLANCO
PINCHA UNUYOC
69
ARCHAEOLOGISTS HUTS & FOOTBALL PITCH
LONG STEADY DESCENT ACROSS PUNA & GRASSLAND
VIEW POINT
CONTOUR ACROSS FACE BETWEEN TWO RIDGES - GOOD VIEWS
trailblazer
68
CHOQUEQUIRAO TREK
CHOQUEQUIRAO
SEE 'CHOQUEQUIRAO RUINS' MAP
27.5KM MARKER
CHECKPOINT
TO CACHORA
29
ABRA SAN JUAN
90 MINS
LA VICTORIA
120–150 MINS
2ND CAMP
20 MINS
MAIZAL
210–240 MINS
RÍO BLANCO
90–120MINS
PINCHA UNUYOC
90–120 MINS
START DESCENT
45–60 MINS
CHOQUEQUIRAO
30 MINS
120–150 MINS
10 MINS
90–120 MINS
135–165MINS
120–150 MINS
TOP OF ASCENT
45–60 MINS

❏ **Pincha Unuyoc**
Etched into the broad hillside above the Quebrada Victoria is a mass of more than 50 terraces that spill down the forested slopes. Pincha Unuyoc (sometimes shown as Pinchiunuyoc or Espa Unuyoc) means 'Water bursting forth' and is a reference to a natural spring (now a silted-up cave) which once provided the site's water via a canal. Uncovered by Hugh Thomson in 1982, the site was later detailed and described by Gary Ziegler and Vincent Lee. In size and scale, Pincha Unuyoc resembles Intipata on the Inca Trail. A large number of terraces, aligned roughly east–west to benefit from the sunshine all day, are currently cleared, creating an enormous, steep amphitheatre; stand at the top of the terraces to appreciate the drama of the surrounding landscape and the scale of the enterprise required to create these structures. Work is continuing at the site, with yet more terraces being uncovered and restored; the suggestion is that at one time much of this vast hillside was actually terraced and used to cultivate crops. Only one structure has been uncovered on the site so far, a small building of unknown function in the centre of one of the upper terraces, set on a giant boulder. The building has a recessed double-jamb doorway, but it is unclear if the structure had any ceremonial function. Above the site on a section of hillside unsuitable for agriculture there are a number of uncleared, unrestored buildings thought to be storehouses or rudimentary accommodation.

The site itself clearly has an agricultural function and the advanced Inca irrigation system meant that the flow of water was controlled and directed to each of the terraces. However, the site isn't thought to be originally of Inca origin. It is believed to predate the Incas and the construction of Choquequirao because a number of architectural details are clearly not Inca, but are reminiscent of sites attributed to the Chacapoyas. For instance, the stones are laid at geometric angles rather than standing upright. This technique of 'weaving with stone', *tejando con piedra*, is indicative of Chacapoyan buildings. The theory is that the Incas colonized the region and took control of existing structures before improving them and bringing the skills of their engineers to bear on the sites. When Choquequirao was built it would have required a support site to house the workers and to cultivate the crops for the Incas. The Chacapoyas would have been used to serve the Inca nobility, but kept at a discreet distance from the priests and dignitaries at Choquequirao.

It is believed that an Inca trail linked the two sites. Although this hasn't been properly uncovered or traced all the way between Pincha Unuyoc and Choquequirao yet, it is thought to contour round the hill above, cross the ridge under an archway and access Choquequirao via the Llama terraces (see p310).

MAIZAL TO YANAMA [MAP 30, p317; MAP 31, p321]
Overview
This is a far simpler, but no less spectacular day. From the campsite on the edge of one precipitous valley you climb to the vertiginous Abra San Juan and descend beyond the pass into a second steep valley to reach the traditional Andean hamlet of Yanama, lost in the mountains and unconnected to the outside world by anything more sophisticated than a mule track.

Route
Several paths are cut into the forest here, so consider asking for onward directions. Pass behind the small holding and hut perched precariously above the

gorge and contour towards the head of the valley before continuing to climb (for about 20 minutes) on a narrow track until you arrive at a smaller ledge, where another farmer has a house. It is possible to *camp* on a pair of terraces beneath the basic hut; terraces that boast spectacular views of the valley and snow-capped peak Corihuaynachina at its head. There are also good views back across the *quebrada* to Pincha Unuyoc.

If not staying here pass below the campsite and continue towards the head of the valley, gaining height as you go. There is evidence here of slash-and-burn farming, with locals desperately cutting back the jungle to create small plots of land on which to grow maize and other crops.

The path hugs the hillside and follows it into a large bowl, climbing in zig-zags to gain height. The vegetation is lush and there is a lot of birdlife here. The trail itself is clear, but can be very muddy. If it has been raining the mules will cut up the track quickly and turn it into a quagmire, so take care.

Ninety minutes from the campsites the path undulates past the **entrance to a mine**. It continues to rise and fall across the valley side until a series of switchbacks takes you rapidly up through a very attractive stretch of cloud forest. Around 2-2½ hours from the campsites the path has gained sufficient height to emerge above the treeline. As it passes through small stands of scrub and tus-socks of ichu grass it climbs a mound of red-orange rubble to reach the entrance to **La Victoria mine**, an 18th-century silver mine that has long since been worked dry. The mine entrance is open and it is possible to creep inside. Take a torch and mind your head. By creeping along the shaft for 50m you can access a central junction where it is possible to stand upright. Three further tunnels descend into the darkness from here. Iron rails dug into the floor of the left-hand tunnel were designed for trolleys carrying rock to be pushed along.

Back outside, the path coils across the puna, in places following original Inca paving. The hillside is now exposed and if the weather is clear, you are treated to panoramic views. The path continues to climb gently towards the broad saddle ahead. Around 4-4½ hours from Maizal you reach a slight notch in the saddle, the **Abra San Juan** (4170m/13,680ft). The far side of the pass is much steeper than the one you have just climbed up and the sheer drop that greets you at the top is breathtaking. Looking back there are good views of Corihuaynachina and Padrayoc. Ahead stand a number of massed mountains, most prominent of which are Choquetecarpo and Sacsarayoc (sometimes referred to as Pumasillo). In the lee of these giants lies the Yanama valley, along the bottom of which flows the Río Yanama. Machu Picchu lies in a roughly easterly direction, whilst the faint path seen heading north-west on the far side of the valley eventually leads to Huancacalle and the start of the Vilcabamba Trail. Keep an eye out for condors, often spotted surfing the thermals rising up the cliff faces here.

The path edges around a precipitous promontory and clings to the cliff side (Map 31). Just beyond here is a **larger mine entrance** and a short tunnel that burrows under the mountain. By now the trail is well graded and relatively gentle. A series of long switchbacks brings you down from the pass and beneath a cliff face. **Three smaller mine entrances** are cut into this section of

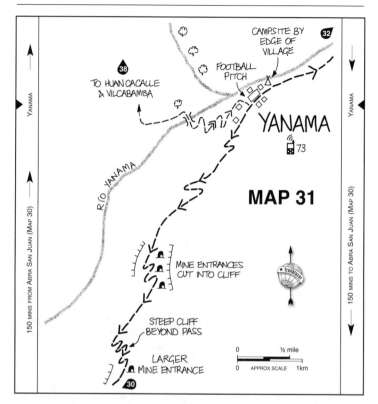

the mountain. The trail inches round an exposed spur on a narrow balcony path set above a sheer drop before the switchbacks begin again. Follow these across puna and pasture, amidst wild flowers and clumps of grasses, keeping an eye ahead for the hamlet of Yanama, now visible on the valley floor. Meander down the hillside between stone-walled corrals and fields until, 2½ hours from the pass, you reach the hamlet.

Set above the Río Yanama, the small community of **Yanama** is home to around 20 families. The well-tended village is centred on a school and a foot-ball pitch, whilst houses and farms growing potatoes, quinoa and okra are scat-tered along the valley floor. Some families let you *camp* by their houses and some may be able to sell you soft drinks, beer or occasionally basic supplies; if you are lucky the family may lay on a *pachamanca*, the traditional feast cooked in an earth oven beneath hot stones. You may also be able to hire guides and arrieros here. Fields are farmed in the traditional manner and the only conces-sion to modernity is a solar-powered satellite phone, which works irregularly;

the connection is best earlier in the day. You can buy phone cards for it from the family whose house it is in for s/1 more than the value printed on the card.

YANAMA TO TOTORA [MAP 31; MAP 32; MAP 33, p323]

Overview
This is a long but stunning day that sees you traverse a section of attractive, windswept puna before crossing the route's highest pass, beneath the imposing snow-fields of Padrayoc. Beyond here you descend into the verdant Quebrada Totora and work your way downhill past a handful of scattered hamlets to arrive at the settlement of Totora.

Route
From Yanama, ignore the trail heading north-west towards Choquetecarpo and ultimately to Huancacalle; instead pick up the path heading east, which climbs alongside the Río Yanama towards the head of the valley.

Stick to the right-hand (southern) bank of the river as the path climbs evenly above it through pasture and farmland. Cross two streams issuing from higher on your right (Map 32), using logs and strategically placed stones to reach the far side.

As you gain height the valley starts to broaden and the 'V' shape gives way to a flat bottomed 'U' shaped valley, with waterfalls springing from the cliffs. High above are the glacier-topped peaks of Sacsarayoc (to the north) and Padrayoc (to the south-east), the mountain so clearly visible from Cachora, where it is seen looming over the Río Apurímac. Cross a third stream and pass

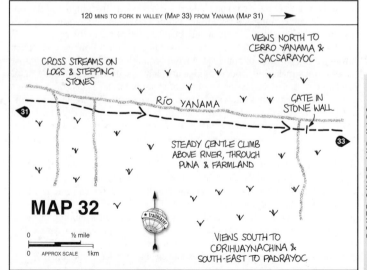

120 MINS TO FORK IN VALLEY (MAP 33) FROM YANAMA (MAP 31) →

VIEWS NORTH TO
CERRO YANAMA &
SACSARAYOC

CROSS STREAMS ON
LOGS & STEPPING
STONES

RÍO YANAMA

GATE IN
STONE WALL

STEADY GENTLE CLIMB
ABOVE RIVER, THROUGH
PUNA & FARMLAND

MAP 32

0   ½ mile
0   APPROX SCALE   1km

VIEWS SOUTH TO
CORIHUAYNACHINA &
SOUTH-EAST TO PADRAYOC

through a gate in a rustic stone wall before continuing to climb. After two hours you arrive at a **fork in the landscape**, where two valleys come together (Map 33). Continue straight on, ignoring the left-hand branch which leads the eye up to the massed snows and glaciers higher on the mountain. The path now enters a bowl full of rolling hillocks and grassy knolls. The path is indistinct here and there are no obvious landmarks, but if you stick to the right-hand side of the bowl and the stream that flows through it, you should be fine.

At the head of the bowl is a **rock wall with a waterfall** cascading down it. Cross the stream flowing through the bowl and aim at the wall, but look for a path that bears left and climbs up the narrow valley to the left (east). A series of easy switchbacks gain height quickly and the glacier hanging from the upper slopes of Padrayoc rapidly comes into view. Cross a stream issuing from the snout of the glacier and follow the zigzagging path as it climbs, occasionally ducking behind a ridge or moraine wall before re-emerging beneath the glacier. An hour after you began climbing, the path scrambles up a final steep section and arrives at a small, narrow saddle between two rocky points, the **Abra Yanama** (4700m/15,750ft), which is also sometimes referred to as the Apacheta Pass. From here there are exceptional views of Padrayoc to the south and Salkantay and Humantay to the east.

On the far side of the pass the path drops steeply into another bowl, where **loose scree** quickly gives way to a **boulder field**. Stick to the right-hand side of the corrie initially, before following the path as it cuts back towards the centre of the bowl and begins to descend a ridge, the right-hand side of which falls away sharply. Looping switchbacks bring you off the ridge; as you lose height the path gradually broadens and begins to weave through scrub and low vegetation. It crosses to the right-hand side of a river issuing from higher in the valley and descends alongside it until just before two small huts, where it crosses back to the left bank and enters an attractive swathe of cloud forest.

The river quickly swells in size and volume as you follow it downstream towards a small huddle of houses at **Hornopampa**. Just before the houses, cross the river on a makeshift wooden bridge and continue downstream on the right-hand side of the river, passing a couple of small homesteads and farmed plots as you go. Totora comes into view further down the valley, straggled across the hillside. The path undulates past scattered houses, then meanders through a stand of eucalyptus trees and breaches two stone walls before crossing a football pitch and climbing a short way to arrive in Totora 3-4 hours after dropping off the pass.

Totora is a larger village than Yanama. For a long time it too was cut off from the rest of the world. However, the road from Santa Teresa that used to go as far as La Playa and then Ccolpapampa on the Santa Teresa route has been pushed on further and now snakes as far as Totora; in the future it may even go deeper into the mountains. Centred on a ratty blue and white building that doubles as a community centre and sometime clinic, it is spread across the valley above the Río Totora. Adjacent to the community centre clinic is a broad flat area where you can *camp*. There is also a very basic toilet block here.

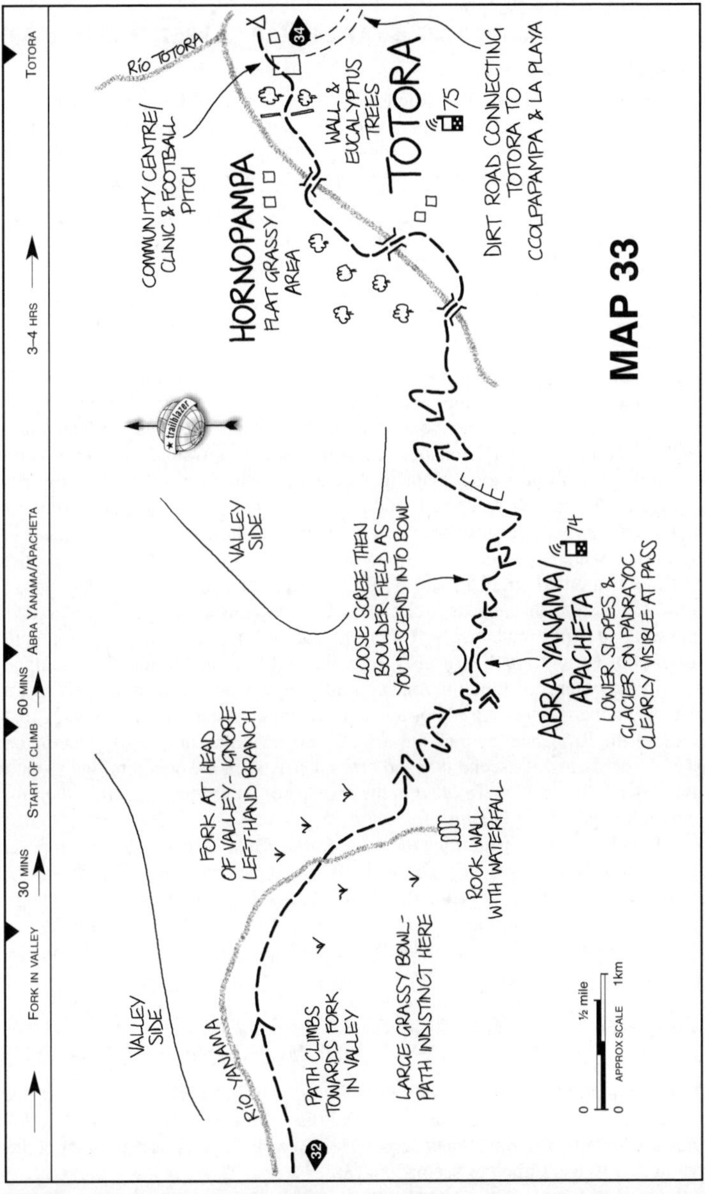

MAP 33

TOTORA

RÍO TOTORA

34

COMMUNITY CENTRE/
CLINIC & FOOTBALL
PITCH

HORNOPAMPA
FLAT GRASSY
AREA

WALL &
EUCALYPTUS
TREES

TOTORA

75

DIRT ROAD CONNECTING
TOTORA TO
CCOLPAPAMPA & LA PLAYA

ABRA YANAMA/APACHETA

VALLEY
SIDE

LOOSE SCREE THEN
BOULDER FIELD AS
YOU DESCEND INTO BOWL

ABRA YANAMA/
APACHETA

74

LOWER SLOPES &
GLACIER ON PADRAYOC
CLEARLY VISIBLE AT PASS

FORK IN VALLEY   30 MINS   START OF CLIMB   60 MINS   ABRA YANAMA/APACHETA   3-4 HRS

FORK AT HEAD
OF VALLEY - IGNORE
LEFT-HAND BRANCH

ROCK WALL
WITH WATERFALL

VALLEY
SIDE

RÍO YANAMA

32

PATH CLIMBS
TOWARDS FORK
IN VALLEY

LARGE GRASSY BOWL -
PATH INSISTINCT HERE

½ mile

0   APPROX SCALE   1km

TOTORA TO LA PLAYA
[MAP 33 p323; MAP 34; MAP 13, p257; MAP 14, p259]

Overview
This part of the trail links the remote wilderness section of the route with the second half of the Santa Teresa trek. From Totora the path follows the Río Totora through an impressive, ravaged valley before reaching Ccolpapampa, where it joins the onward route down the Santa Teresa valley, to arrive at La Playa.

Route
Head downstream from Totora and immediately make your way across two **unbridged streams** before easing along the hillside high above the Río Totora and crossing a small landslip. The steep soil slopes are particularly prone to landslips here and there are several sections where the eroded cliffs have collapsed, making the path rather precarious in places. As you progress downstream the valley deepens into a 'V'. Cross a second and then a third deep, plunging landslip, taking the time to gawp at the views of the river far below.

Contour along an attractive balcony path, which loses height gradually and affords good views of Humantay away to the east. Around 1½ hours from Totora and opposite a giant landslip, a series of switchbacks drop you towards the river. The path then curves round to the right and follows the river around a bend, from where you can see the confluence of the Río Totora and the Río Chaullay, which combine and flow onward as the Río Santa Teresa. Here, the path joins a broad, graded road. If you turn right upon joining the road, you'll follow it a short distance as it climbs to **Ccolpapampa** (see p258) where it is possible to *camp* and buy soft drinks. **Colpa Lodge,** owned by Mountain Lodges of Peru (see p183), is also close by, on the far side of the Río Chaullay.

In the other direction, the road continues down the valley, ultimately to La Playa and then Santa Teresa. Follow it briefly and just before a large bridge that crosses the Río Chaullay pick out a small dirt track that drops left towards the Río Totora below. Descend this and cross the river on a wooden bridge around two hours after leaving Totora. On the far side of the bridge is a small shelf on which it is possible to *camp*.

Beyond here the path joins the route of the Santa Teresa trek (see Map 13, p257) and follows a gently descending trail down the Santa Teresa valley, through cloud forest, above the Río Santa Teresa. The path passes under a large waterfall and then through the small village of Winay Poccos (see Map 14, p259). Around 2¾ hours beyond here and some 5 hours from Ccolpapampa the path enters **La Playa** (see p260).

LA PLAYA TO AGUAS CALIENTES
[MAP 14, p259; MAP 15, p265; MAP 16, p267]

For information on the final day of trekking and the partially uncovered but nonetheless spectacular and interesting ruins at Llactapata see the route description and details under the Santa Teresa Trek (see pp262-3). For details about the village of Aguas Calientes see pp209-13.

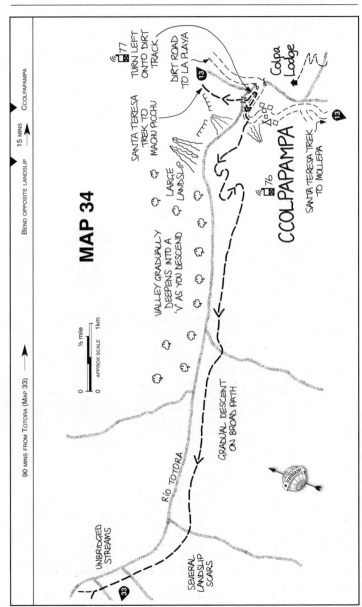

MAP 34

0   ½ mile
0   APPROX SCALE   1km

TURN LEFT
ONTO DIRT TRACK

77

13

DIRT ROAD
TO LA PLAYA

Colpa
Lodge

13

SANTA TERESA
TREK TO MACHU PICCHU

LARGE
LANDSLIP

VALLEY GRADUALLY
DEEPENS INTO A
'V' AS YOU DESCEND

76

CCOLPAPAMPA

SANTA TERESA TREK
TO MOLLEPA

GRADUAL DESCENT
ON BROAD PATH

Río TOTORA

33

UNBRIDGED
STREAMS

SEVERAL LANDSLIP
SCARS

Huancacalle to Cachora via Choquequirao

INTRODUCTION

This route traverses a huge section of the Vilcabamba range and links Vitcos, Manco Inca's temporary palace whilst in exile, to Choquequirao. The path follows an original Inca trail that is still evident in many places. It is a wild and scenic trek for those looking for a little more adventure than the classic Inca Trail offers. In fact the route was opened up in response to the pressures on the classic routes and as an attempt to generate employment and income in these poor, remote parts of the region. The hope is that the advent of tourism will persuade people to stay in their traditional farming communities rather than settle for a slum in Cusco and the prospect of working in the city as a menial labourer or taxi driver.

The route is an excellent way of linking two historically important sites and exploring a stretch of undamaged wilderness. It also means you can trek to and from Choquequirao without having to retrace your steps, as you do on the standard approach to the ruins. However, the trek is quite taxing; you are crossing the entire Vilcabamba range and it is impossible to exaggerate the amount of ascending and descending involved. Typically it takes 7-8 days to complete. In addition you should allocate a day to fully explore the ruins at Choquequirao.

Currently the route can be done independently; no fees, other than to access Choquequirao, or permits are applicable. You should hire a guide though as the route is arduous and in parts fairly indistinct. Arrieros and mules are also a good idea so that you aren't shouldering all the equipment and gear yourself. Several agencies are now offering variations of this route, so it is possible to sign up for a fully guided, kitted trip (see pp179-86).

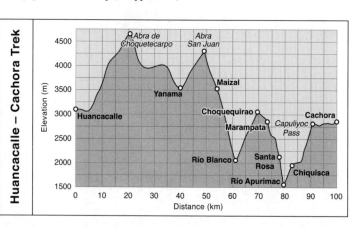

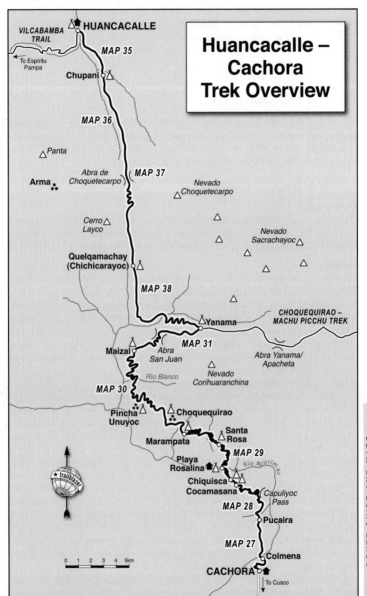

VILCABAMBA TRAIL

HUANCACALLE

To Espiritu Pampa

MAP 35

Chupani

Huancacalle – Cachora Trek Overview

MAP 36

Panta

Arma

Abra de Choquetecarpo

MAP 37

Nevado Choquetecarpo

Cerro Layco

Nevado Sacrachayoc

Quelqamachay (Chichicarayoc)

MAP 38

Yanama

CHOQUEQUIRAO – MACHU PICCHU TREK

MAP 31

Maizal

Abra San Juan

Abra Yanama/ Apacheta

Rio Blanco

Nevado Corihuaranchina

MAP 30

Pincha Unuyoc

Choquequirao

Marampata

Santa Rosa

MAP 29

Playa Rosalina

Rio Apurimac

Chiquisca Cocamasana

Capuliyoc Pass

MAP 28

Pucaira

MAP 27

Colmena

CACHORA

To Cusco

0 1 2 3 4 5km

★ trailblazer

ROUTE GUIDE AND MAPS

The route can be done in either direction, but is normally tackled, and is described here, from Huancacalle to Cachora, via Choquequirao. The exception is if you are planning to combine the route with the Vilcabamba Trail for one great, epic adventure, in which case you would begin at Cachora, trek to Choquequirao and then on to Huancacalle before joining the trail to Vilcabamba La Vieja and the ruins at Espíritu Pampa.

GETTING TO HUANCACALLE

The trek starts from Huancacalle. For information on accessing the trailhead from Cusco see p271 and for details of the village itself see p273. For information on the nearby ruins of Vitcos and the half-day walk that allows you to explore these and the *huaca* at Ñusta España see p274.

HUANCACALLE TO CHUPANI   [MAP 35]

Overview
This is a gentle, fairly short first day's walk that sees you head up valley and ease into the mountains in preparation for the longer days ahead. Given the short trekking time, you could easily fit in a trip to Vitcos (see pp274-5).

Route
From the main street in Huancacalle, walk downhill until you come to Sixpac Manco Hostal at the southern end of the village. Bear left (east) and cross a pair of rivers here. Ignore the path that branches left and climbs north along the flank of Rosaspata towards Vitcos, unless you wish to explore the ruins, and instead continue roughly east. The path climbs stiffly along a section of Inca stairway and rounds the southern end of Rosaspata. In an open clearing there is a second fork. The left-hand branch drops down the eastern flank of Rosaspata to Ñusta España. Ignore this and instead take the right-hand fork, heading south-east, which begins to climb gently through a small copse.

After five minutes the path emerges from the trees and approaches a stretch of cultivated hillside, the farmed plots of which are marked out with stone walls. The path is vague and unclear for this early stage, but if you bear in mind that you are basically heading in a south-easterly direction and aiming for the adjacent valley you ought to be able to make your way there. Climb between a couple of farms and push on alongside a rustic wall, climbing evenly. Pass between two walls and bend round to the right to follow the wall as it contours across the hillside. A scrubby hedge also stands to your right at this point. Keep the wall on your right as you climb past a small clutch of houses with thatched and corrugated iron roofs. As the wall bends round to the right cut away from it and continue straight on through a patch of low scrub. Bear left towards the mouth of the adjoining valley but watch out for boggy ground here. Pass to the left of a further pair of buildings and 15 minutes after the junction for Ñusta España enter the broad U-shaped valley.

Traverse the left (east) flank of the valley, pushing through scrub. The path is clear but can be very muddy. Head up the valley for around half an hour then

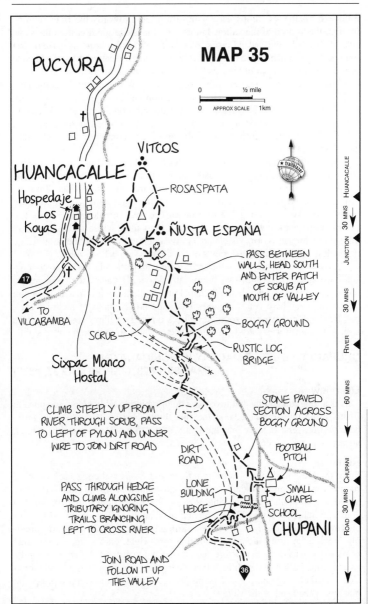

MAP 35

PUCYURA

0   ½ mile

0   APPROX SCALE   1km

VITCOS

HUANCACALLE

ROSASPATA

Hospedaje
Los
Koyas

17

ÑUSTA ESPAÑA

PASS BETWEEN
WALLS, HEAD SOUTH
AND ENTER PATCH
OF SCRUB AT
MOUTH OF VALLEY

TO
VILCABAMBA

SCRUB

BOGGY GROUND

RUSTIC LOG
BRIDGE

Sixpac Manco
Hostal

CLIMB STEEPLY UP FROM
RIVER THROUGH SCRUB, PASS
TO LEFT OF PYLON AND UNDER
WIRE TO JOIN DIRT ROAD

STONE PAVED
SECTION ACROSS
BOGGY GROUND

DIRT
ROAD

FOOTBALL
PITCH

PASS THROUGH HEDGE
AND CLIMB ALONGSIDE
TRIBUTARY IGNORING
TRAILS BRANCHING
LEFT TO CROSS RIVER

LONE
BUILDING

HEDGE

SMALL
CHAPEL

SCHOOL

CHUPANI

JOIN ROAD AND
FOLLOW IT UP
THE VALLEY

36

HUANCACALLE

30 MINS

JUNCTION

30 MINS

RIVER

60 MINS

CHUPANI

30 MINS

ROAD

ROUTE GUIDE AND MAPS

follow the path as it drops across marshy ground towards the river running through the bottom of the valley. Ignore a trail heading south-east on the same side of the river and instead cross over to the far bank (west) on a **rustic log bridge** at a point where the river boils through a narrow cataract. On the far side of the river follow a set of zigzags that climb steeply west, away from the river towards a stretch of scrub and other vegetation. Upon entering the scrub pass under and just to the left of an **electricity pylon** and emerge onto a **dirt road**, which actually comes from Huancacalle. Turn left along the road and head up the valley. At a hairpin bend pick up a trail that cuts between loops in the road, and rejoin the road slightly higher, turning left and continuing to head south-east, up the valley.

After 50m, at another hairpin bend, leave the road as it prepares to double back on itself and instead join a path that heads straight on. Contour along the western side of the valley. Just above a small farm the path divides. Take the lower, left-hand fork and cross a section of farmland to join a stone-paved avenue that crosses a boggy bit of ground. The path now descends gently and evenly towards the river and the far end of the valley, which forks. The small village of Chupani is now visible on a raised shelf to the left, at the point where the valley divides, with good views of the countryside behind you.

Cross a river issuing from the right-hand valley, the Quebrada Cayco, on a solid wooden bridge and, two hours after leaving Huancacalle, bear left to meander between a school, small chapel and football pitch to reach the centre of the village, where you can *camp*. There are no amenities or facilities here, but the site does have very good views back down the valley; Rosaspata can be seen to the north-west, although Vitcos and Huancacalle are both out of sight.

CHUPANI TO QUELQAMACHAY (CHICHICARAYOC)
[MAP 35, p329; MAP 36; MAP 37, p333]

Overview
This is a long, tough day that involves you climbing steadily across the puna to finally cross the Abra de Choquetecarpo, the highest point on the trek. From here you descend quickly into the cloud forest to reach a campsite set in an attractive grove.

Route
From the previous night's campsite retrace your steps and cross back over the river before turning left (south) this time and continuing up the valley. The way ahead is wild looking and the ring of peaks that tower above are daunting and at this point appear inviolable. Having climbed up the valley for around 10 minutes on a broad track, there is a **lone building** to your right. Just after the building break away from the broad path that turns right, onto a smaller trail that bears left, ducks through a **hedge** and cuts away towards a tributary feeding the river below. Follow the path as it then bears right and begins to ascend alongside the tributary, gaining your first proper views of the snow-capped peaks and glaciers at the head of the valley.

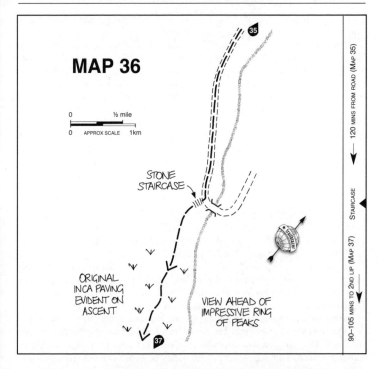

MAP 36

0   ½ mile
0   APPROX SCALE   1km

STONE
STAIRCASE

ORIGINAL
INCA PAVING
EVIDENT ON
ASCENT

VIEW AHEAD OF
IMPRESSIVE RING
OF PEAKS

35

37

← 120 MINS FROM ROAD (MAP 35)

◄ STAIRCASE ►

90–105 MINS TO 2ND LIP (MAP 37) ▼

Ignore trails branching left, which cross the stream to reach farms on the far side, and instead zigzag up the nearside of the stream until you emerge onto a **dirt road** half an hour after striking camp. Turn left and walk along the road as it makes its way gently up the valley.

Follow the road for around two hours as it climbs up the valley (Map 36). As the road shapes up to curve left and descends to cross the river below, look on the right-hand side of the road for a **stone staircase** that climbs a small bluff steeply. Above the bluff there is a path that winds through scrub and then contours up the side of the valley towards a bowl at its head ringed with an impressive selection of peaks. The path at this point is part of an old Inca trail and the original paved stones are still visible in places. Follow them as they climb gently, crossing a stream issuing from your right on a **wooden bridge** as you do (Map 37).

The path gains height and edges round a **spur** angling from the right before climbing a **flight of steps** to breach the lip of a vast, deeply scooped bowl. The path continues to hug the right-hand side of this basin, the bottom of which is laced with streams and waterways. It then gains height as it climbs towards the head of the valley. A short section of downhill path leads to a water channel and is quickly replaced by a series of enervating steps that climb steeply. A little

ROUTE GUIDE AND MAPS

over four hours after leaving Chupani you crest a **second lip** and enter a much smaller bowl set beneath a craggy ring of peaks.

There is a further lip to attain. The path that climbs to this is particularly fine and has been built up on one side to provide a level, even staircase on which to ascend. Around 30 minutes of steep ascent bring you to the **third lip**, where just to the left of the path lie the **ruins** of an old *tambo*. Enter a third bowl, where once again the path sticks to the right-hand wall.

The final climb to the pass, which isn't visible from this point, is long and steep. The steps that have been created are again ingeniously built and initially provide a broad, even staircase on which to climb. As you get to the head of the valley the gradient increases and the steps become narrower and steeper. As you push on up through increasingly rocky surrounds the stairs become especially steep. Eventually the path levels out though and you can make out the cairns and apachetas that decorate the pass, which you gain 5-6 hours after setting out.

The **Abra de Choquetecarpo** (4550m/14,925ft) is very dramatic and divides the Urubamba and Apurímac watersheds. The pass, a narrow notch in a stony ridge, is quite slight and the ground falls away on both sides. The view ahead of the sheer-sided U-shaped valley is breathtaking and full of drama. It is into this valley that you are about to plummet.

From the pass an initially steep, tight set of switchbacks plunges into the valley and you lose height rapidly. A long traverse right (west) brings you beneath a set of **crags** before you continue to descend on an evenly angled path. The path then bears left and passes beneath a rocky bluff before joining a stretch of **paved Inca path**, half an hour and several hundred metres below the pass.

The road ahead is an excellent, broad Inca trail that has weathered remarkably well. The going underfoot is solid and straightforward and you are able to take in the views along the length of the valley of which you now find yourself at the bottom. After 15 minutes you head down a series of steps to cross a stream on a wooden bridge. Beyond here the paving deteriorates and eventually gives way entirely to a grass track.

This path descends the right-hand (west) side of the valley, whilst waterfalls cascade down the left-hand (east) flank and glaciers are visible above the dark, sheer walls and impressive granite spires that line the way. The going is easy, and you can relax as you pass through a stand of trees and then a large boulder field to arrive adjacent to the river. Follow the river downstream. The path braids here, but stick to the stream. All the threads eventually come together in order to cross the stream on a simple bridge before pushing on downstream on the left-hand (east) bank.

As you descend the valley sides steepen and the vegetation begins to grow in height. The humidity also increases and you enter some attractive cloud forest. The path then crosses to the right-hand (west) bank of the river briefly where a stretch of particularly muddy track brings you to a bridge that crosses back over to the left-hand (east) bank. A couple of tributaries issue from high above to the left and have to be forded or crossed on rudimentary log bridges. Eventually, three hours below the pass and some 8-9 hours since you first set

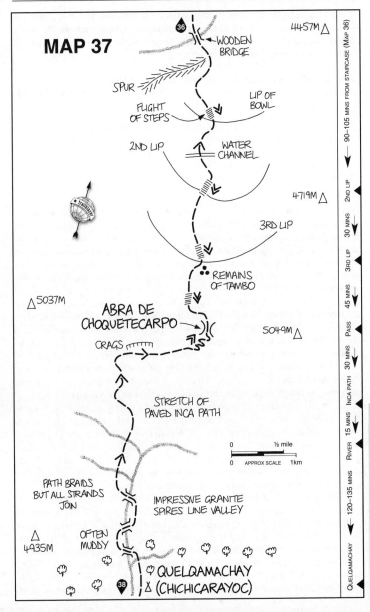

MAP 37

36

WOODEN BRIDGE

4457M △

SPUR

LIP OF BOWL

FLIGHT OF STEPS

2ND LIP

WATER CHANNEL

4719M △

3RD LIP

REMAINS OF TAMBO

△ 5037M

ABRA DE CHOQUETECARPO

CRAGS

5049M △

STRETCH OF PAVED INCA PATH

0 ½ mile
0 APPROX SCALE 1km

PATH BRAIDS BUT ALL STRANDS JOIN

IMPRESSIVE GRANITE SPIRES LINE VALLEY

△ 4935M

OFTEN MUDDY

QUELQAMACHAY
△ (CHICHICARAYOC)

38

90–105 MINS FROM STAIRCASE (MAP 36) ◄ 2ND LIP ◄ 30 MINS 3RD LIP ◄ 45 MINS PASS ◄ 30 MINS INCA PATH ◄ 15 MINS RIVER ◄ 120–135 MINS QUELQAMACHAY ◄

ROUTE GUIDE AND MAPS

off, you arrive in an attractive clearing adjacent to the river, where it is possible to *camp*. This area is known as **Quelqamachay** (or **Chichicarayoc** depending on who you talk to) and makes for an appealing place to pass the night although there are no amenities or facilities here.

QUELQAMACHAY (CHICHICARAYOC) TO YANAMA
[MAP 37, p333; MAP 38]

Overview
The onward section is a very pleasant walk through attractive cloud forest. The path clings to the hillside and is spectacular, level (even as it climbs and falls), and relatively straightforward to follow. A final stiff ascent brings you to the small village of Yanama, from where an Inca trail strikes off east towards Machu Picchu; the continuing path to Choquequirao sets off south.

Route
From the campsite you start by heading downstream through lush cloud forest. The valley, the Quebrada Otiyoc (also sometimes referred to locally as the Quebrada de Quelqamachay), steepens and the river below falls away as the gorge narrows. Having undulated through the forest for 15 minutes follow a set of long switchbacks that strike off up the left-hand (east) flank of the valley before contouring evenly along it. After ducking into a gully to pass beneath a **waterfall**, a pattern develops whereby the path alternatively contours and climbs. There are several good viewpoints from spurs overlooking the valley and the forested ridges on the far side. The forest itself is thick and full of birdlife.

As you progress down the valley the path drops gently into gullies and then climbs out of them to round a spur and ease into the next ripple in the hillside. Around two hours after setting out a steep climb brings you to a level patch of ground from where you can see a T-junction ahead where the Quebrada Otiyoc intersects with the Río Yanama. The flat ground here would make a scenic *campsite*, although there are meagre water supplies in the vicinity.

A steep climb above this plateau gives way to a long diagonal haul across an exposed area of puna during which time you gain height steadily on a superb balcony path with outstanding views. The path crosses a broad, barely discernable ridge and begins to lose height on the far side. A short switchback leads to a path heading almost due south that descends past a small farm and then bends left to enter the Yanama valley. From high on the hillside here there are further exceptional views of the wild landscape ahead of you.

Dropping below the treeline, you lose height steadily as the path descends towards the Río Yanama, which gets louder as you get closer. Passing a couple of farms and walled plots set aside for cultivation, the path continues to work its way off the mountain, until after an hour you reach the river. Turn left (east) and walk upstream on the left-hand (north) bank for 15 minutes. Cross the river adjacent to a series of rapids and a small cascade, on a wooden bridge, before beginning a final gruelling climb. For 30-60 minutes ascend a series of switchbacks that carry you away from the river. Once at the top roughly contour along

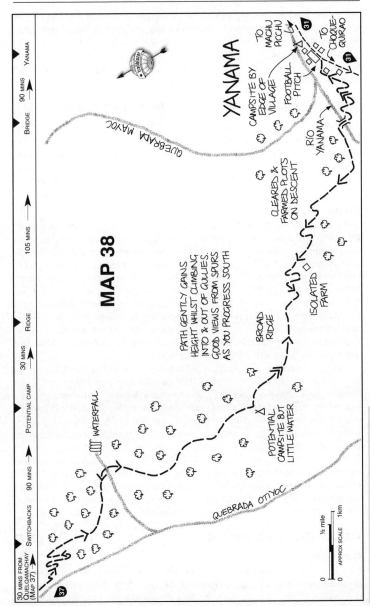

MAP 38

the valley, heading east and gaining height slowly. Rounding a bend you lose sight of the way you've just come and enter a cluster of eucalyptus trees. Scattered amongst the trees are a number of farm buildings and houses.

Continue to ease across the hillside and about six hours after setting out you arrive in the small village of **Yanama** (see p320) where it is possible to *camp* adjacent to some of the local houses.

YANAMA TO MAIZAL   [MAP 31, p320; MAP 30, p317]

Overview

The next section, from Yanama to Choquequirao is detailed in the description of the Choquequirao to Machu Picchu trek (see pp313-25). Essentially you are following this route, but in the opposite direction. This stage involves climbing from the valley floor to the Abra San Juan and crossing into the adjoining valley to descend back into the cloud forest to reach the campsite at Maizal.

Route

From Yanama look for the path that zigzags south-west through the outskirts of the village and then climbs the hill to the south, passing through scrub and small trees (Map 31). After an hour the gradient eases and you contour across the hillside towards a sheer cliff. Pass below this, above an airy drop, and climb a set of steps worn into the rock. The first of a series of entrance tunnels to disused mine shafts appears on your left. After the third tunnel the path cuts away from the cliff but continues to wind up the hillside in a roughly south-westerly direction.

Having passed a **larger mine entrance** where it is possible to walk in upright, the path struggles up a last short section and rounds a rocky, precipitous promontory to reach the pass (Map 30). The narrow, steep-sided **Abra San Juan** (4170m/13,680ft) is 2½ hours from Yanama.

Drop off the far side of the pass and ease across an exposed section of puna to pick up an old paved Inca path. Half an hour's descent brings you to La Victoria mine entrance marked by an enormous slagheap of red-orange scree and rubble dug out from underground. Drop below this and descend into the cloud forest on a muddy, rutted stretch of path that has been badly dug up by mules. A number of zigzags and long diagonals lead downhill through the trees. Follow the path as it hugs the contours and creases in the hillside, ducks into and out of gullies, crosses exposed sections of landslip-damaged hillside and explores the dense jungle. Finally, three hours from the pass you reach the first of two *campsites* at Maizal. The second is a further 20 minutes downhill. Both are adjacent to farmer's houses and have superb views but no other facilities. The lower site has a small shack that occasionally sells soft drinks though.

MAIZAL TO PINCHA UNUYOC   [MAP 30, p317]

Overview

This is a very straightforward but tiring day that sees you cover an enormous distance but make very little progress as the crow flies, since you are simply descending all the way into the plunging valley below you in order to scale the far side again and reach the campsite you can see from the start point, adjacent to the partially restored ruins at Pincha Unuyoc.

Route
Initially, descend through the cloud forest on a clear, even path for 1½-2 hours, losing height as the track zigzags downhill. A final switchback brings you to the Río Blanco, sometimes referred to as the Río Victoria, at the bottom of the Quebrada Victoria. Walk upstream briefly. You can plunge into several pools along this stretch but beware, the meltwater is icy cold.

Cross the river on an unstable wooden bridge and begin to regain all the height you've just lost via a punishing collection of long diagonal sections of track that weave uphill through dry scrub. In direct sunshine this can be a very tiring, dusty exercise although the views of the valley and surrounding mountains make up for the effort. After 2-2½ hours you arrive at the massed terraces of Pincha Unuyoc (see box p318), where it is possible to *camp*. If the site here is busy, there is another *campsite* a little further up, on a broad shelf above the ruins, overlooking the valley.

PINCHA UNUYOC TO CHOQUEQUIRAO   [MAP 30, p317]

This short stretch takes you from the terraces at Pincha Unuyoc to the ruins at Choquequirao, which are set several hundred metres higher, overlooking the neighbouring Apurímac valley.

The path climbs above the site of all the excavation and restoration at Pincha Unuyoc and passes by the archaeologists' hut and temporary residence. It then zigzags through scrub and crosses a football pitch overlooking the valley; woe betide anyone who kicks the ball too far into touch here. The ascent takes 2-2½ hours after which you arrive at a stunning *mirador* with views along the Río Apurímac to the west and Río Yanama to the north-west. Around 10-15 minutes contouring across the face of the mountain between two sharp ridges gives you the first tantalizing glimpses of Choquequirao just below and strung out along a knife-like ridge. Having crossed the second ridge the path descends through dense cloud forest for 10 minutes to reach a junction adjacent to a tumbledown stone building. The faint, heavily overgrown trail to the right descends to the Upper Plaza of the ruins themselves. The more usually used left-hand fork continues downhill gently and easily for a further 20-30 minutes. Follow the signposts and arrows that indicate the way to the official *campsite* for Choquequirao (see p308), which you reach 3-3½ hours after leaving Pincha Unuyoc.

For full descriptions of the ruins and the features of the site see pp308-12.

CHOQUEQUIRAO TO CHIQUISCA   [MAP 29, p307; MAP 28, p306]

Overview
From here until the end of the trek you are retracing the route described in more detail in the Choquequirao trek (see pp296-312). The first section is seemingly straightforward and almost all downhill, but the descent into the Apurímac canyon is long and strenuous; your knees will take a pounding as you drop into

one of the deepest gorges anywhere in the world. Having reached the bottom and crossed the river, you are faced with the onerous task of having to climb out again, and you must trek uphill until you reach the campsite at Chiquisca.

Route
From Choquequirao (Map 29) head into a deep gully and cross the Sunchumayo river as it tumbles down the hillside. Climb back out of the gully and ascend to the **Choquequirao checkpoint**, from where there are exceptional views of the terraces far below the main ruins and strung out along the ridge. Beyond here the path contours around the hill and arrows across the high puna to reach **Marampata** 1½ hours after leaving Choquequirao. There is a house selling soft drinks here as well as basic snacks, a toilet block and an area to *camp*.

After Marampata the descent begins in earnest and a long section of dusty, exposed switchbacks takes you across the cliff face and down into the valley. The path is steep and the descent is surprisingly taxing. After an hour you reach **Santa Rosa Alpa** and then the small farm at **Santa Rosa** where you can draw breath and buy soft drinks or water. A further 30- to 60-minute' steep descent brings you to the Río Apurímac, which was straddled by a large suspension bridge until this was destroyed by a landslip in 2012. A traditional oroya (see box p298) now spans the river and is the only means of crossing, at least until the more substantial bridge is rebuilt; at the time of writing there was no timetable for this being completed. On the far (southern) bank stands Playa Rosalina (see p305 and Map 28), where you can *camp*. There is also a *lodge* here.

Having reached the lowest point of the trek, you are now faced with the unenviable task of climbing out of the valley. The path begins by contouring upstream briefly, then launches into a sequence of switchbacks, alternately long and short, that carry you up the flank of the valley. After an hour of continual ascent you reach **Chiquisca** (see pp304-5), where there are two *campsites*, the first lower and larger than the second, a toilet block and the opportunity to buy soft drinks, water and beer from the accommodating family that lives here.

CHIQUISCA TO CACHORA   [MAP 28, p306; MAP 27, p303]
Route
From Chiquisca continue climbing the side of the valley on a broad, level path that gains height remorselessly. After 1-1½ hours you arrive at **Cocamasana**, a narrow ledge facing directly down the valley with superb views, where it is possible to *camp*. Two hours' climbing on long zigzags brings you to **Capuliyoc**, a dramatic, narrow pass with breathtaking views of Padrayoc and its neighbouring peaks towering above the valley that you've just emerged from. You are now into the home straight; an easy, essentially downhill trudge that begins on a narrow balcony path and develops into a broad dust road brings you to the farm at **Colmena** in 1-1½ hours (Map 27).

The path takes you through a section of eucalyptus forest towards the head of the valley, where you finally climb briefly to enter Cachora, some two hours after leaving the pass. For information on the town, its services and how best to continue on to Cusco, see pp301-2.

MACHU PICCHU

Sophie Campbell, Alexander Stewart & Bryn Thomas

In the variety of its charms and the power of its spell, I know of no place in the world which can compare with it. Not only has it great snow peaks looming above the clouds more than two miles overhead; gigantic precipices of many-colored granite rising sheer for thousands of feet above the foaming, glistening, roaring rapids; it has also, in striking contrast, orchids and tree ferns, the delectable beauty of luxurious vegetation, and the mysterious witchery of the jungle.
Hiram Bingham *Inca Land – Explorations in the Highlands of Peru* (1922)

Romance swirls about Machu Picchu like the mists that suddenly roll in from the mountains, bringing with it an equal degree of obfuscation. Why are these majestic ruins perched on a saddle ridge high above the Urubamba Valley? Who lived in them and what did they do? The briefest of visits to the site shows that the one thing everyone agrees on is that nobody knows for sure. That doesn't stop them having theories. From the most learned of academics to the youngest of guides, everybody has a hypothesis; just stop and listen to passing tours and you will hear the same place described in a dozen different ways. It adds greatly to the charm of the place – and it is unlikely that we will ever know the truth.

The fame that the 20th century brought to Machu Picchu has been a mixed blessing. It has fascinated the world since its rediscovery in 1911; tourism figures have risen steadily – to around 900,000 visitors a year – and are now capped at a 2500 maximum per day. In 1983 it achieved international cultural status by joining the list of UNESCO World Heritage Sites. In 2007 it was chosen, by online public vote, as one of the world's 'New Seven Wonders'.

A dispute over the ownership of the land rumbles on. Two brothers, Edgar and Adolfo Abrill, are seeking compensation from the Peruvian government, claiming that the land was expropriated from their grandparents in 1935. Other issues include erosion of the Inca Trail and ruins from sheer numbers of enthusiastic visitors, and some controversial restoration programmes. However, a long-running dispute about the return of Machu Picchu artefacts from Yale University was settled in 2010 and the university has begun to return the 'goods, pieces and parts' that were taken from the ruins between 1911 and 1915 by Hiram Bingham and his team of archaeologists. Some of these are now displayed in Cusco (see pp157-8).

But flawed beauty or not, whether it is your first time or your fifth, and whether you come by train, bus or on foot, you cannot fail to be amazed by the sheer, glorious improbability of Machu Picchu.

Historical background

Whoever they were, whatever name be finally assigned to this site by future historians, of this I feel sure – that few romances can ever surpass that of the granite citadel on top of the beetling precipices of Machu Picchu, the crown of Inca Land.
Hiram Bingham *Inca Land – Explorations in the Highlands of Peru* (1922)

WHO BUILT MACHU PICCHU?

Myths aside, the Inca Empire evolved over a period of around 300 years (see pp90-102), from modest tribal beginnings in a village to the south of Cusco, sometime early in the 12th century, to its demise at the hands of the

Conquistadors. When the ninth Inca, Pachacutec (Pachacuti Inca Yupanqui), took the throne in 1438, he began the great expansion of Inca territory. A 16th-century document found by the archaeologists Luis Miguel Glave, María Remy and JH Rowe seems to confirm that it was Pachacutec who rebuilt Cusco, in a manner befitting an imperial capital. He probably built Machu Picchu, as well, in the mid 15th century.

A CITY ABANDONED

Sometime early in the Spanish Conquest, however, it was abandoned for reasons we do not know. This did at least protect it from the Spanish who clearly knew nothing about it. This mysterious withdrawal from public life was probably caused by a combi-

Statue of Pachacutec
Aguas Calientes

nation of disease and vicious factional fighting amongst Inca clans. Whatever the reason, the collection of pale granite buildings on its ridge – a masterpiece in architecture and setting by any standards – was left to succumb to the encroaching foliage, much in the manner of Cambodia's Angkor Wat.

It is interesting that Machu Picchu's superbly constructed agricultural terraces, too good to abandon, were used for centuries by local farmers, who always knew about the ruins.

THE GREAT REDISCOVERY – 24TH JULY 1911

It was one of these farmers who in 1911 led the ambitious young explorer Hiram Bingham up the densely overgrown, snake- and insect-infested path to the ruins. Funded by Yale University, he was actually searching for Vilcabamba, or 'The Lost City of the Incas', which he believed had been built by the penultimate Inca after his defeat at the hands of the Spanish.

In *Inca Land – Explorations in the Highlands of Peru* (1922) he recounts the events of that historic day, 24th July 1911:

'We had camped at a place near the river, called Mandor Pampa. Melchor Arteaga, proprietor of the neighboring farm, had told us of ruins at Machu Picchu... The morning of July 24th dawned in a cold drizzle. Arteaga shivered and seemed inclined to stay in his hut. I offered to pay him well if he would show me the ruins. He demurred and said it was too hard a climb for such a wet day. When he found that we were willing to pay him a sol, three or four times the ordinary daily wage in this vicinity, he finally agreed to guide us to the ruins. No one supposed that they would be particularly interesting'.

Indeed, the other members of his team, naturalist Harry Foote and team doctor William Erving, declined to go. Foote set off to catch butterflies and Erving's excuse was that he had to 'wash his clothes'. Bingham left accompanied by the police sergeant who'd been allotted to them and the farmer, Melchor Arteaga. They followed the Urubamba upstream for 45 minutes and then crossed the 'foaming rapids' on some slender logs.

'Leaving the stream, we struggled up the bank through a dense jungle, and in a few minutes reached the bottom of a precipitous slope. For an hour and twenty minutes we had a hard climb. A good part of the distance we went on all fours, sometimes hanging on by the tips of our fingers. Here and there, a primitive ladder made from the roughly hewn trunk of a small tree was placed in such a way as to help one over what might otherwise have proved to be an impassable cliff. In another place the slope was covered with slippery grass where it was hard to find either handholds or footholds. The guide said that there were lots of snakes here. The humidity was great, the heat was excessive, and we were not in training'.

They reached a hut where 'two pleasant farmers, Richarte and Alvarez', gave them gourds of cool water. As they rested the farmers said they had come up here to use the old terraces and had been living here for about four years. They added that there were many more terraces and even some ruins nearby. Hot and exhausted by the climb Bingham was in no hurry to move on...

'Furthermore, the view was simply enchanting. Tremendous green precipices fell away to the white rapids of the Urubamba below. Immediately in front, on the north side of the valley, was a great granite cliff rising 2000 feet sheer. To the left was the solitary peak of Huayna Picchu, surrounded by seemingly inaccessible precipices. On all sides were rocky cliffs. Beyond them cloud-capped mountains rose thousands of feet above us'.

The farmers said that soon after they had come up here they had cleared some of the ruins and rethatched some of the houses to live in but they were too far from the water sources. The aqueduct which had brought water into the buildings was blocked with earth from the terraces so they had abandoned the Inca houses and built their own. They continued to farm the old terraces, growing maize, potatoes, sugar cane, beans, peppers, tree tomatoes and gooseberries. When Bingham finally left the cool of the hut to investigate further, he found that:

'Hardly had we rounded the promontory when the character of the stonework began to improve. A flight of beautifully constructed terraces, each two hundred yards long and ten feet high, had been recently rescued from the jungle by the Indians. A forest of large trees had been chopped down and burned over to make a clearing for agricultural purposes. Crossing these terraces, I entered the untouched forest beyond, and suddenly found myself in a maze of beautiful granite houses! They were covered with trees and moss and the growth of centuries, but in the dense shadow, hiding in bamboo thickets and tangled vines, could be seen, here and there, walls of white granite ashlars most carefully cut and exquisitely fitted together. Buildings with windows were frequent'.

Amazed at the quality of the masonry Bingham soon began to realize the significance of the ruins. Seeing the structures that became known as the Torréon and the Temple of Three Windows he wrote:

'To my astonishment I saw that this wall and its adjoining semicircular temple over the cave were as fine as the finest stonework in the far-famed Temple of the Sun in Cuzco. Surprise followed surprise in bewildering succession. I climbed a marvelous great stairway of large granite blocks, walked along a pampa where the Indians had a small vegetable garden, and came into a little clearing. Here were the ruins of two of the finest structures I have ever seen in Peru. Not only were they made of selected blocks of beautifully grained white granite; their walls contained ashlars of Cyclopean size, ten feet in length, and higher than a man. The sight held me spellbound.'

'It did not take an expert to realize, from the glimpse of Machu Picchu on that rainy day in July, 1911, when Sergeant Carrasco and I first saw it, that here were most extraordinary and interesting ruins. Although the ridge had been partly cleared by the Indians for their fields of maize, so much of it was still underneath a thick jungle growth – some walls were actually supporting trees ten and twelve inches in diameter – that it was impossible to determine just what would be found here'.

One of Hiram Bingham's photographs of Machu Picchu in 1911 before excavations began. (From *Inca Land – Explorations in the Highlands of Peru* (1922)

He returned to his university, Yale, raised funds and came back in 1912 with several projects in mind, including a more extensive investigation of Machu Picchu. He transported many of his finds – not gold, as is widely believed, but mainly potsherds and stone fragments – back to America, with the permission of the then government of Peru. It is now fashionable to disapprove of Bingham, who was one in a long line of post-colonial explorers discovering, or plundering, the world at the time – but nothing can take away from him what he must have seen that first time, peering beneath the undergrowth and realizing the extent and quality of the ruins and their extraordinary position.

And it is Bingham who is responsible, for good or bad, for the second age of the Incas, the tourism age, which has brought so many people to Peru.

❏ Who really discovered Machu Picchu?

You'll hear various claims that it wasn't Hiram Bingham but a Peruvian landowner, an English missionary or a German entrepreneur who was the true discoverer of Machu Picchu.

Although the Conquistadors certainly didn't get here, Bingham soon realized he wasn't the first outsider to see Machu Picchu. Amongst the ruins he found graffiti left by Peruvians Enrique Palma, Gabino Sánchez, and Agustín Lizárraga that they had made on their visit on 14th July 1901. Other visitors may have been Thomas Payne and Stuart McNairn, English missionaries whose descendants claim they visited the ruins in 1906, having been informed about them by an engineer named Franklin.

From the middle of the 19th century, as the South American rubber boom got under way, the whole area had to be opened up. Gold miners and prospectors also came searching this way. In the 1860s the land around Aguas Calientes was bought by Augusto Berns, originally from Germany, who set up a sawmill to make railway sleepers. Indeed, in 1911 Bingham noted this rusting machinery mistakenly identifying it as a press for sugar cane. It is claimed that in the 1880s Berns tried to get investors interested in an excavation business to search for gold and other treasures on Inca sites in the area. Although Machu Picchu isn't mentioned as one of them, 'Picchu' mountain is actually marked on a map dating from 1874.

In the 1890s the Peruvian government pushed a road up the Urubamba right below Machu Picchu, bringing more people into the area. It was this road that Bingham followed in 1911.

So Bingham was not the first person to see Machu Picchu but what he did after seeing it was very different from what everyone else did: he recorded his visit scientifically and organized expeditions to study the site. As historian Daniel Buck says in an article published in *La Republica* (31 Aug 2008): 'There can be no doubt that Bingham is the site's "scientific discoverer," an honorific bestowed on the Yale professor by José Gabriel Cosío, a Cuzco academic and official delegate to Bingham's second expedition. It is also true that others had known of the ruins long before Bingham. One can make the case that Machu Picchu was never totally lost. It was periodically known and unknown, there and not there – visited, lived in, farmed, and even bought and sold – from the 16th century until Bingham permanently removed it from obscurity.'

THE RE-BIRTH OF A LEGEND – BINGHAM'S THEORIES

Unfortunately he was also, often unwittingly, responsible for some of the myths and misunderstandings that have grown up around the site. He was, after all, not a trained archaeologist (though he was a history lecturer at Yale) but an explorer and treasure hunter, and one should not forget that he did go on to become a politician, elected as a US senator in 1922.

He was also a talented photographer, and when the National Geographic Society devoted an entire issue to the story it ignited world interest. It was sheer romance: the geographical setting, the sun worship, the mythical gold of the Incas, the brutal Conquistadors. Reading the article you can quite see why it's said that the character *Indiana Jones* is based on Bingham:

'There was nothing for us but to run, and we did that, tearing through the jungle down hill in an effort to get around the side of the fire... the grass and soil under my feet let go, and I dropped. For about 20 feet there was a slope of about 70 degrees, and then a jump of about 200 feet, after which it would be bump and repeat down to the river. As I shot down the sloping surface I reached out and with my right hand grasped a mesquite bush that was growing in a crack about 5 feet above the jump-off'. *In the Wonderland of Peru* **Hiram Bingham**, **National Geographic Society** (April 1913).

He wrote several books about Machu Picchu and the Incas, the best known being *Inca Land – Explorations in the Highlands of Peru* (1922) and, in 1948, the best-selling *Lost City of the Incas* (he simply transferred the label from Vilcabamba; it was too good a title to lose). The three conclusions that he reaches in the first book and develops in the second are certainly sensational but have lost their credibility over the last hundred years.

Bingham was most excited to find a fine building with windows at Machu Picchu, the building he called the Temple of Three Windows, as he considered that it fitted a description of the temple at Tampu-tocco, **the birthplace of the first Inca**, **Manco Capac**, who lived around 1200AD. There are, however, sev-

eral other more likely contenders for the site of Tampu-tocco, Chokepukio near Cusco among them. Furthermore, in the historical description of the site it's difficult to separate myth from reality.

In his mind this was not just a lost city of the first Inca but **the** Lost City, the final refuge of the Incas who had fled in the path of the Conquistadors. This was also **Vilcabamba**, the city of gold that the Spanish had been looking for. It was the position of Machu Picchu, on a promontory that afforded such good protection from attack and was easily defensible, that made him believe that it was their final stronghold. Actually Bingham did discover the true lost city when he found the ruins at Espíritu Pampa but the setting of Machu Picchu made it infinitely more romantic cast as a final refuge for this doomed civilization. He ends the books with his most fanciful theory:

Detail of exterior of Temple of Three Windows. (Hiram Bingham, from *Inca Land – Explorations in the Highlands of Peru* (1922).

'In its last state it became the home and refuge of the Virgins of the Sun, priestesses of the most humane cult of aboriginal America. Here, concealed in a canyon of remarkable grandeur, protected by art and nature, these consecrated women gradually passed away, leaving no known descendants, nor any records other than the masonry walls and artifacts...'

Early excavations revealed that over 80% of the skeletons discovered in Machu Picchu were female. The Incas dedicated their most beautiful daughters to the service of the sun god and Bingham suggested that these skeletons might be **Virgins of the Sun**, the chosen women who had escaped from Cusco when the Spanish arrived. Indy would certainly have found Virgins of the Sun here but, of course, miraculously still alive. Hiding from the evil Conquistadors they'd have discovered the secret of eternal life from the seeds of a vine found only on the top of Huayna Picchu. Disappointingly, more recent studies have shown that male and female remains were found in almost equal numbers.

SO WHY WAS MACCHU PICCHU BUILT?

In the century that has elapsed since Bingham's rediscovery of Machu Picchu the body of knowledge about the Incas has grown considerably as this and other sites have been more thoroughly excavated, the study of archaeology has evolved and more credible theories have emerged.

It was clearly not a conventional city. Built between 1450 and 1470, during the reign of Pachacutec, it's thought that Machu Picchu would have accommodated only 750-1000 people so it was actually quite small. It was certainly at least agriculturally self-sufficient; the Incas had long since mastered the art of making a little land go a very long way and the ruins are skirted by steep terraces with stone holding walls and efficient drainage systems. In fact, the area occupied by terraces should have been able to produce a surplus of foodstuffs.

Bingham emphasized Machu Picchu's military characteristics, keen to make it fit as the last citadel of the Incas. He identified some of the buildings as barracks, but also recognized distinct areas that he labelled agricultural, spiritual or residential (for nobility or priests, and more humbly, for artisans, farmers or servants). Those divisions, loosely speaking, still hold today. It is certainly true that Machu Picchu's position on the promontory in a bend in the Urubamba would have made it easy to defend. It would have made an excellent lookout station but the quality of the buildings suggest it was very much more than this.

Near one of the trade routes out of the lowland forests to Cusco, could Machu Picchu have been an administrative centre? The Incas kept tabs on their sprawling empire by constant stock- and census-taking. The tallies were knotted into strings (*quipu*) and carried along the trails by swift-footed relay runners (*chasquis*). There could have been a way station here but the buildings seem too grand for it to have been an administrative centre. It's certainly not like any others the Incas built specifically for this purpose.

The setting is important: Machu Picchu is laid out roughly on a north-south axis, which means that it gets the full benefit of sunrise on its main flank and a clear view both of significant peaks around it and the moon, stars and planets in the sky above. There is also the sacred river far below. For the Inca and his people, animists and sun-god worshippers, such a position would not have been a coincidence.

Machu Picchu as a spiritual centre?

To a Western eye, the ruins bring to mind a mediaeval monastic complex, combining spiritual, ceremonial and agricultural elements with a degree of fortification. Some of the most significant buildings are obviously for religious use.

In Machu Picchu: The Sacred Center, Johan Reinhard examines the sacred and symbolic aspects of the landscape archaeology of the region. The site is spread across a saddle between the two peaks, Machu Picchu and Huayna (Wayna) Picchu. Huayna Picchu is the furthest point of a long spur running north from the snow-capped sacred mountain of Salkantay. In Reinhard's words: 'At Machu Picchu we find a unique combination of landscape and cosmological beliefs which together formed a powerful sacred center which united religion, economics and politics. These factors led to the construction of one of the most impressive ceremonial sites of the ancient world'. He suggests, furthermore, that Machu Picchu would have been an important place of pilgrimage.

While it's undeniable that the sacred buildings of Machu Picchu are carefully aligned and of a high quality suggesting their importance, surely a place of pilgrimage would not have been so quickly forgotten.

The most credible theory – a royal retreat

Imagine that you're standing on the top of Machu Picchu peak looking down on the view as shown in Hiram Bingham's photograph on p342, but that the overgrown terraces that can just be discerned in the picture do not exist. There's nothing here but virgin jungle and you have all the money in the world to build your dream retreat. Where's the perfect site? You wouldn't put it down in the deep dark valley but on that saddle between the two peaks, just where Machu Picchu is now. Richard L Burger and Lucy Salazar-Burger (just as Bingham, both from Yale) have put forward the theory that Machu Picchu was just that: a royal retreat and hunting lodge.

They noted that the site does not resemble any of the five main types of Inca settlement. It's far too small to have been a provincial capital; also too small and lacking the adequate proportion of types of building to have been an administrative centre; unlikely to have been built as a way station or *tambo* or rest stop along the Inca road network because of the fine religious buildings; not a government-established agricultural settlement and obviously not a non-Inca village that paid tribute to the empire. Within the 1% of other known Inca settlements is that of the royal estate, and some of the characteristics and features of these can also be found at Machu Picchu.

Royal estates were outside the state administrative system and owned and operated by *panacas* (royal corporations) for a particular Inca king and used by him as a country getaway for relaxing and entertaining.

The relatively small size of the settlement at Machu Picchu, the high quality of the stonework and the fact that its location and extent indicate it wasn't built for economic reasons together suggest that it probably was a royal estate. The archaeological evidence is backed up by a historical reference. In a document written in 1568, historian John Howland Rowe found a reference to a site named Picchu that was within Pachacutec's estate.

Examined as a royal retreat, the type and style of the buildings of Machu Picchu seem to make much more sense. There are groups of buildings obviously designed for high-status households and others which must have housed their retainers. The fact that there were fine religious buildings of particular significance here is not surprising since the royal retinue would have required rituals, sacrifices and astronomical observations needing numerous priests and attendants. The location is idyllic but also safe, defensible and very private – the perfect royal hideaway.

Practical information

OPENING TIMES & TICKETS

The site is open daily from just before dawn (around 6am) until 5pm but last entry at 4pm.

Tickets (s/128/64 adults/students and children) must be purchased in advance as they cannot be bought at Machu Picchu; a maximum of 2500 people are allowed into the site per day. To ensure you are able to visit on the day you want, buy your ticket well before arriving at the site; during the busiest times of year **consider buying it up to a week in advance**. Tickets can be purchased from the offices in Cusco (see p165) or Aguas Calientes (see pp209-10); take your passport and cash (either soles or dollars), or a Visa or MasterCard. In theory you can also book online (🖳 www.machupicchu.gob .pe) but sometimes the English version of the website doesn't work for payments and you'll need to revert to the original Spanish-language site; only Visa credit cards are accepted.

If you also want to climb **Huayna Picchu** (see box pp352-3) or **Machu Picchu mountain** you need to buy a combined entrance and climbing ticket. Tickets for the former cost s/152 (s/128 for Machu Picchu and s/24 for Huayna Picchu) and for the latter s/142 (s/128 for Machu Picchu and s/14 for Machu Picchu mountain). Student and child rates are half price.

You'll find the ruins slightly less crowded on Sunday when package tourists head off to the market at Pisac; Tuesday and Thursday are also less busy. Very early in the morning and late afternoon is the quietest time of day to be here.

If you're walking the Inca Trail your permit should include entry into the ruins and if you don't want to look round Machu Picchu on the day you arrive it may be possible to do so the next day. Check when you arrive that this still applies.

WHAT TO BRING

The site is exposed, so can get very hot when the sun is out. Conversely, if the cloud has rolled in, it can get very cold. It also rains unpredictably. You'll need clothes suitable for a variety of conditions including **waterproofs** and **sunscreen**. It's worth bringing **insect repellent** in case there are midges, and a **flashlight/torch**.

As no backpacks larger than 20 litres (a small daypack) are allowed into the ruins you must leave them at one of the two **left luggage offices**. The one inside the entrance is the cheaper. Also forbidden are food, disposable plastic drink bottles and walking sticks. You'll need a metal or durable plastic water bottle (not a disposable plastic bottle) so that you can have water with you as you look round.

GETTING THERE AND AWAY

On foot

On the **Inca Trail** trek you reach Machu Picchu via **Intipunku**, the Sun Gate. From here it's a walk of less than 30 minutes, gently down hill. The first walkers from the last camp at Huinay Huayna tend to arrive in a rush in a bid to see sunrise.

Walking from **Aguas Calientes** takes 1¼-2 hours depending on your fitness. Turn right over the bridge and follow the road. When it begins to zig-zag up the hill you'll find the path that shortcuts straight up. The first 15 minutes are along the flat then it's steeply uphill. Coming back down takes around 50 minutes.

By bus from Aguas Calientes

A large fleet of buses ferries day-trippers (adult/child one-way US$12/5, return US$17/9) up to the ruins. The first buses leave at around 5.30am or half an hour before dawn and then every 10-20 minutes. The bus ticket office in Aguas Calientes opens 15 minutes before the first bus leaves. Don't buy a return ticket unless you're positive you're going to take the bus back as it's a pleasant walk down along the trail through the trees.

WHERE TO STAY

The only accommodation here is at *Machu Picchu Sanctuary Lodge* (☎ +51 16 10 8300, 💻 www.sanctuarylodgehotel.com), scandalously close to the ruins. It's the kind of place which these days they'd never allow to be built in such an environmentally and archaeologically sensitive position. None of the rooms looks over the ruins themselves but you can see Huayna Picchu from some. Well equipped and comfortable, they cost upward of US$975 a night, with those looking out on the mountain costing US$1180 and suites starting at US$1400. If you can afford to stay here you may as well go the whole way and book a wedding package – from US$2450 all in, including the services of a shaman to officiate as you take your vows before an undeniably spectacular backdrop.

Most people stay in **Aguas Calientes** (see pp209-13).

WHERE TO EAT

Food isn't allowed in the ruins and if the snack lunch in your daypack is discovered they'll probably make you leave it in a locker at the entrance.

Tampu Restaurant in Machu Picchu Sanctuary Lodge serves breakfast (5.30-9am), lunch (noon-3pm) and dinner (6.30-9.30pm). A buffet lunch (11.30am-3pm) of international and Peruvian staples is available in *Tinkuy Buffet Restaurant*.

There's also an overpriced *snack bar* by the entrance to the ruins. They sell hamburgers, hot dogs, pizzas, empanadas, sandwiches, beer, water, tea and coffee. A hamburguesa macchupicchu is about US$10. You're far better off bringing your own water and food.

MACHU PICCHU GUIDE

Above all, there is the fascination of finding here and there under the swaying vines, or perched on top of a beetling crag, the rugged masonry of a bygone race; and of trying to understand the bewildering romance of the ancient builders who ages ago sought refuge in a region which appears to have been expressly designed by Nature as a sanctuary for the oppressed, a place where they might fearlessly and patiently give expression to their passion for walls of enduring beauty.
  Hiram Bingham *Inca Land – Explorations in the Highlands of Peru* (1922)

In the 21st century the ruins absorb visitors in numbers that would, no doubt, amaze the Incas. Until now, incredibly, you can still wander freely within many of the buildings here – quite aside from potential damage to the ruins, it is surprising that there aren't more accidents, especially when it rains – and the site swarms with people photographing both the ruins and the picturesque llamas that have been re-imported for the purpose. It remains to be seen what restrictions the future holds for visitors; in the meantime, enjoy the freedom.

❏ **Top tips for making the most of your visit to Machu Picchu**

❶ **Try to visit on a Sunday** as many tour groups visit the Sacred Valley markets instead; Tuesday and Thursday are also typically a little quieter.

❷ **Get here as early as possible**. If you're staying in Aguas Calientes make sure you get your entry ticket the day before (see p347), check the time the first bus leaves and get there early to get a bus ticket. At the height of the season consider buying your bus ticket the day before.

❸ **Climb Huayna Picchu** but if tickets for that have gone climb Machu Picchu Mountain. The views are superb but you can only buy tickets for each ascent in advance (see p347), not in Machu Picchu.

❹ You're allowed to take only **a small 20-litre day-pack** into the ruins. Make sure you have adequate water (in a metal or camping type bottle, not in a disposable plastic bottle); sunblock, suncream and a hat; a waterproof jacket and sweater in case it turns wet or cold; and a torch/flashlight can be useful. Officially food isn't allowed but some people try to sneak in a snack for lunch, given the prices in the café and restaurant. You may be made to leave this in a locker at the entrance.

❺ **Spend as long as possible at the ruins** You'll need at least a full day to explore the site but allowing two days is much better so that you can see it at different times of day, as the sun and light affect the atmosphere and appearance of the site. Stay as long as you can; it's busiest between 9am and 4pm. Avoid the bus and walk back down to Aguas Calientes.

Machu Picchu
Viewed from Huayna Picchu

Inca Trail to Intipunku

Trail to Machu Picchu Mountain

N

Hotel & Entrance

Start

21

3

8

9

20

19

Eastern Terraces

Inca Trail to
Drawbridge

1 Viewpoint & Guardhouse
2 Kallanka
3 Agricultural Sector
4 Dry Moat
5 City Gate
6 Quarry
7 Fountains Street
8 Temple of the Sun
9 Tomb of the Princess
10 Royal Quarter
11 Western Terraces
12 Principal Temple
13 Temple of Three Windows
14 Intihuatana
15 Central Plaza
16 Plant Collection
17 Sacred Rock
18 Group of Three Doorways
19 Industrial District
20 Temple of the Condor
21 Storage Huts

Entry to Huayna/Wayna Picchu hike

❏ CLIMBING HUAYNA PICCHU (WAYNA PICCHU)

[Buy tickets in advance: see p347; limited to 400 people] To sit on the 2700m/ 8860ft shaggy crest of Huayna Picchu on a clear morning, with the ruins laid out below you and the sun sliding up behind the mountains like a new *centavo*, is probably the most magnificent experience that Machu Picchu can offer. But it takes planning and shouldn't be attempted if you are unfit, struggling with the altitude or suffer from vertigo. Since only 400 tickets a day are available they sell out well in advance, so book early. Half this number are allowed to climb the peak between 7am and 8am and must be down by 10am; the second half are allowed to begin the ascent between 10am and 11am and must return by 1pm. A certain amount of scrambling is involved and you'll need good shoes.

Huayna Picchu stairway. Slip here and you could land up in the Urubamba River.

On the steep route from the summit of Huayna Picchu to the Temple of the Moon.

Huayna Picchu summit

The vertiginous walk up takes anything from 40 minutes to 1½ hours depending on how busy it is and your state of fitness. The path zig-zags relentlessly upwards; after 15-20 minutes there's a junction: **take the right path for the top**; the left path is the Gran Caverna Trail to other side of the peak. Near the top and some narrow terraces, there's **another fork**: to the right leads up eventually through a short tunnel to the summit and to the left also leads to the summit but via terraces and some small ruins including an intact, though roofless, building which catches the morning sun on its impossibly steep crag. No doubt offerings to the sun god would have been made from up here and the building may have been a **temple**. The **terraces** up here are really too small for growing anything useful and it has been suggested that they may have been planted with bright flowers to provide a splash of colour that could be seen from the royal estate below. It's also likely that some royal guards would have been posted up here as it would make the perfect lookout station. This area is sometimes roped off, particularly after wet weather when the stairs are treacherous. The **summit** is surprisingly roomy and the views from up here are truly spectacular.

Temple of the Moon & Gran Caverna Trail

From the top you can take the fantastically steep trail, some parts of it by makeshift ladder, down the far side, amongst birds, butterflies and beetles. After a 30-40 minute descent to a point lower than Machu Picchu itself, you reach a clearing and a fine double wall of masonry appears, with alternating windows and niches. The cave behind contains the **Temple of the Moon**: a beautiful double-lintel door fits into the cave, along with walls, niches and a fine throne or platform of white granite. This is some of the finest

ORIENTATION

Machu Picchu is at 2350m/7708ft (main plaza) and most of the buildings are spread across a saddle between two mountains, Machu Picchu ('Old Peak', 3060m/10,040ft) and the soaring sugarloaf of Huayna/Wayna Picchu ('New Peak', 2700m/8860ft) – with the Urubamba river and Aguas Calientes far below at 2000m/6560ft. If you've bought tickets in advance you can climb either **Huayna Picchu** and visit the Temple of the Moon below it (see p352) or **Machu Picchu mountain** (see p362). Other excursions include the **Inca draw-bridge** (20 minutes each way, see p362).

The sites below are keyed to the overview map on p350-1.

VIEWPOINT & GUARDHOUSE [1]

That first sight, so familiar from a thousand posters and brochures, of the whole of Machu Picchu spread out before you has all the more impact if you come upon it suddenly as you do when approaching on the Inca Trail. To get something of this effect if you've come up by bus from Aguas Calientes, after passing through the checkpoint and walking 100m, don't continue into the ruins but

Inca stonework in Machu Picchu; obviously an important ceremonial building, it may have contained mummies. It's unlikely to have had anything to do with the observation of the moon, though; it faces the star cluster known as the Pleiades. About 50m below is **another group** of caves and buildings. The stonework is less impressive and in places defaced with graffiti.

To return, walk anti-clockwise along what is known as the **Gran Caverna Trail** around the mountain for 40-60 minutes to rejoin the trail at the junction 15-20 minutes from the entry kiosk. This can also be done in reverse but the climb up from the Temple of the Moon to the summit is very steep: it's easier to approach the summit the normal way.

Inkaraqay Archaeologists are currently clearing these ruins, lower down the steep north face of Huayna Picchu. Covering about 4500 square metres mainly of terraces, it appears that Inkaraqay was mainly agricultural in nature, supplying food for Machu Picchu. It is hoped that it will eventually be opened to visitors. A near vertical, snake-infested trail leads from Inkaraqay to the summit of Huayna Picchu.

The Temple of the Moon

Lower buildings, Gran Caverna

Guardhouse (aka Watchman's Post) with the kallanka at the back (right)

Funerary Rock: a mortician's slab?

take the path to the left that climbs steeply through the trees and brings you out at the top of the agricultural zone by the guard-house. You're rewarded with a magnificent view of the ruins, Huayna Picchu and the spinach-green peaks beyond. This is a good place to come to watch the sunrise or take that classic picture.

The **Guardhouse [1]** (*Recinto del guardian*) looks too grand to be a restored thatched sentry box, but its position overlooking the entire site suggests some sort of surveillance role. Above it is a low, carved boulder known as the **Funerary Rock**. Since human bones were found in this area Bingham assumed it was a cemetery. Perhaps the rock was a mortician's table for the evisceration of bodies during the process of mummification, or a sacrificial altar; the hole on the side of the rock could have been for tying up the llama that was waiting to be sacrificed.

Across the open area here at the southernmost extent of Machu Picchu is a large unremarkable building (the largest building on the site) with eight openings in its walls. This is probably a **kallanka [2]**, a hall which provided lodgings for a large number of people. As it is right beside the Inca Trail which runs in here from Intipunku and out to the drawbridge it may also have been used as a rest stop.

Below the Guardhouse are the extensive terraces of the **agricultural sector [3]** (*zona agricola*). These had to be very carefully constructed to allow adequate drainage given the very high rainfall in this region. Each terrace had a base layer of stones followed by gravel sand and then topsoil. Given the number of terraces at Machu Picchu, which is increasing as more are uncovered (4500 square metres recently at Inkaraqay, see p353), it's clear

The Dry Moat divides the agricultural sector from the urban sector.

that they could have produced far more food than would have been needed by the city's population of about 750 people. It's been suggested that some of the terraces may have been given over to the cultivation of the sacred coca leaf, which flourishes in this climate and altitude. It would have been in high demand in Cusco.

At the northern side of the agricultural sector and across the **Dry Moat [4]** you reach the main buildings of the city. As well as providing an obstacle that could have provided some defence if Machu Picchu were under attack it also served as the main drain for the city's carefully constructed drainage network.

CITY GATE [5]

There's usually a bottleneck at this handsome trapezoid entryway, partly because people want to admire the fine stonework with its lintel of one hefty stone slab, and partly because it's instinctive to want to stop on stepping through and absorb the view. Look back as you do so to see the stone eyelet that probably served as some sort of lock for a door hinged into the stone. The sturdy construction, widening towards the base, is classic Inca design; beautifully-fitted stones, no mortar and a form that is said to weather earthquakes. Its size is interesting; this is a doorway, not a magnificent entry to a city – it appears deliberately discreet and low key.

City gate

QUARRY [6]

The source for Machu Picchu's stone is within the city itself: you pass the large area of boulders shortly after going through the city gate. To carve their building blocks without iron tools the Inca masons probably employed the labour-intensive neolithic technique known as flaking, using a hammer stone. They may have split stones using wooden wedges hammered into natural cracks. Bingham attempted to show that the Incas used boiling water to split

Work in progress at
the quarry.

stones but the experiment was unsuccessful. The whackiest suggestion is that the Incas cut the rocks using solar power reflected off large parabolic reflectors made of gold but it's certainly true that such objects were found by the

Conquistadors who promptly melted them down into ingots.

Some rocks have clearly been worked on but it's said that the one that's usually pointed out by the guides (photo above) was actually a modern experiment by the archaeologist Manuel Chavez Ballón.

This is a good place to come back to when you want a place to sit and rest; you'll find lots of viscachas, rabbit-like rodents, sunning themselves on the rocks.

Viscacha

Machu Picchu's water
supply still functions

FOUNTAINS STREET [7]

Follow the steps down Fountains Street (*Fuentes*), so named for the 16 watercourses (not actually fountains) that flow along it. Water from the main spring runs for 750m to feed into the topmost of these square cisterns, which descend the hill in a series, getting progressively less fancy as they go. The highest and grandest tank was 'no doubt reserved for the Inca himself so he would get the cleanest water.

Near the bottom of the street is an open-fronted building, known as a *wayrana*, with its thatched roof restored so you can get an idea of how all the buildings would have looked. It shows how the stone pegs protruding at the top of many of the walls were used to secure the roof struts. This wayrana may have been the focus of ceremonial activities involving worship of the water that flowed past it.

THE TEMPLE OF THE SUN [8]

This tower (*El Torréon*), which curves inwards like a snail shell and encloses a mysterious, tomb-like rock, is surely the most beautiful structure here. Currently

Perfect stonework on the tower of the
Temple of the Sun

The Temple of the Sun, just after the
winter solstice

roped off, you may only be able to view it from above or below. Bingham went into raptures when he first glimpsed it:

'Owing to the absence of mortar, there are no ugly spaces between the rocks. They might have grown together... The elusive beauty of this chaste, undecorated surface seems to me to be due to the fact that the wall was built under the eye of a master mason who knew not the straight edge, the plumb rule, or the square. He had no instruments of precision, so he had to depend on his eye. He had a good eye, an artistic eye, an eye for symmetry and beauty of form'.

Its stonework is darker and finer than that of the surrounding buildings, it has narrow windows towards the top of the wall and one larger window has holes drilled around the edges, though nobody can be sure of their exact function. It may have been that astronomical instruments were attached to them as this temple was used as an astronomical observatory. At the winter solstice (21st June), the rays of the sun as it rises align perfectly with the rock on the floor of the temple. Niches around the walls of the temple would have held offerings and idols. Animal sacrifices may have taken place on the carved central rock.

Stairs lead from the temple down to the fine two-storey building which Bingham fancifully misnamed as the **Palace of the Princess** (*Ñusta*). Its position suggests that it was a kind of sacristy used by the high priest presiding over ceremonies in this temple.

The entrance to this area is through one of finest examples of an Inca gate.

THE TOMB OF THE PRINCESS [9]

Right underneath the Temple of the Sun is a strik-ing triangular cave, formed by the hewn edge of the

Entrance gate to the Palace of the Princess and Temple of the Sun

massive supporting boulder and carefully fitted masonry. Inside, a set of steps carved into the natural rock and markedly pale against the darkness, ascend to nowhere. This classic step symbol is often found at Inca sites. It's said to rep-resent the three levels of the world: heaven, earth and the underworld. Again, the 'Princess' title is not based on fact and Bingham found no evidence of bod-

ies buried here and probably didn't expect to as burial was only for the masses; nobles were mummified. It may, however, have been used as a temporary mau-soleum for the mummies of important ancestors of the Inca king, which he would have brought with him when he was staying here.

You may overhear guides telling their tour groups that the four sites above (the fountains, the wayrana, the Temple of the Sun and this tomb), symbolize the four elements of water, air (the wayrana being open on one side), fire and earth. The Incas certainly worshipped the elements but whether they identified these particular four sites as a symbolic group is debatable.

Directly beneath the Temple of the Sun is the Tomb of the Princess

THE ROYAL QUARTER [10]

The Inca class system was clearly expressed in stone – the better the dress-ing, the grander you were – as well as in the distinct division between *hanan* (upper

Apartments in the Royal Quarter

class) and *hurin* (lower class) districts. The fine ashlars used in these buildings, their size and finesse, show that they belonged to the elite. The Royal Apartments are laid out as a classic *kancha* (group of rooms for an extended family), with two large rooms and two wayranas around a central patio. One of the open-sided wayranas would have been used as a kitchen. Attached to one of the large rooms is an addition known as the 'Inca's bathroom' which has a drain in the corner.

WESTERN TERRACES [11]

Walk back up the hill, over and around the quarry, to peer over the back wall at the precipitous terraces. Recent research has shown that in Inca times more varieties of maize and potatoes could be cultivated at altitude than today. Whatever they grew, the engineering is impressive: few slopes are so steep that they have not been terraced. Along the top of the terraces runs the path leading to what was once an Inca bridge, probably made of timber and vines, which crossed a sickening drop and continued down the mountain.

THE PRINCIPAL TEMPLE AND SACRED PLAZA [12]

The small open patch of ground often referred to as the Sacred Plaza (*Sector de los Templos*) is surrounded by buildings which, from their elevated position and sophisticated stonework, obviously had religious significance. The **Principal Temple** is in the wayrana style (open on one side) and has an impressive row of niches all along the back wall. There's some evidence of subsidence here with a large gap opening up on the right-hand side of the temple back wall. In front is a

The Sacred Plaza and the Principal Temple

huge block of stone, rising altar-like out of the ground; this may have been a roof support. There is much speculation about the building; certainly the sun does enter during the winter solstice along an identifiable course and broken pottery remains have been found in the plaza, suggesting some sort of ritual involving the breaking of vessels. Just outside the temple, on the ground, is a kite-shaped rock which is said to be a representation of the stars of the Southern Cross, astronomically important to the Incas. It does, indeed, point south.

Behind the Principal Temple is a separate structure which may have had a priestly function – Bingham named it the **Sacristy** and it's also known as the Ornaments Chamber; it contains a famously elaborate stone, with 32 edges carved into the raw

Rock in the shape of The Southern Cross

rock, to the left of the doorway. The one on the right has 28 corners.

Just below the Principal Temple is the **Temple of Three Windows [13]** (*Templo de las Tres Ventanas*), with a wall of perfectly-finished masonry pierced by three trapezoid windows, overlooking the ruins below. It was this building that convinced Bingham that he'd located Tampu-tocco, the birthplace of the first Inca, Manco Capac (see p344). The temple actually has five windows, two of which have been

Temple of Three Windows
(viewed from outside)

blocked up. Opposite the wall of windows and the remains of the roof pillar is a rock carved with the step symbol representing heaven, earth and the underworld.

INTIHUATANA – THE HITCHING POST OF THE SUN [14]

Steps lead up to this startling carved stone, carved in situ into a wide step and squared-off post aiming skywards, the focus of the highest and perhaps the most significant part of this religious section of Machu Picchu. Similar stones were found at many of the Inca ruins and early archaeologists called them *inti-huatana* meaning 'place where the sun is tied'. In winter, with the sun furthest from the earth, the Incas believed they needed to ritually secure it to hitching posts such as this one lest the life-giving sun desert them. The festival of Inti Raymi was (and still is) held at the winter solstice (21st June). Realizing their importance to Inca culture, the Spanish settlers damaged every intihuatana they found by breaking off the post; this is the sole complete survivor.

Visitors under the guidance of a local shaman offer prayers to the setting sun, beside the Intihuatana

The archaeologist Johan Reinhard has shown that Machu Picchu was carefully aligned with sacred peaks, the intihuatana being at its very centre. The top of Huayna Picchu, for example, is due north. The position of the sun and stars was important to the Incas both for religious reasons and, more prosaically, in order to chart the progress of the seasons which was important to farmers so that seeds were planted at the right time to allow for the best harvest. At the equinoxes the sun rises behind the summit of Veronica. The careful alignment of the intihuatana means that it was probably used as an observatory. It has also been suggested that the stone was a sundial but this is unlikely as the Incas had no concept of time in terms of hours and minutes.

Reinhard has also done some fascinating work on structures built to replicate significant mountains. From the south of the stone, look north towards

Huayna Picchu and the shape of the intihuatana does appear to be a conscious imitation of the mountain behind it. If ever there was a stone with presence, however, this is it – which only added to the national fury when it was damaged during a beer commercial shoot in the year 2000.

THE CENTRAL PLAZA [15]

This huge rectangle of flat green grass is a welcome breathing space amongst all the steep steps and stones and is generally grazed by a llama or two. It must have been significant with so little space available and was probably used for commerce and wider ceremonial purposes. Anyone who has seen the (now colossal) Inti Raymi celebrations in Cusco or at Tiahuanaco at the winter solstice can imagine a smaller version of the event happening here.

In the south of this plaza, near the Temple of Three Windows, is a small collection of **plants [16]** that would have grown here in Inca times. As well as various orchids, *yuca* (the cassava root and foodstuff, not yucca the decorative plant), strawberries and moonflower there are coca plants, all helpfully labelled.

THE SACRED ROCK [17]

The Sacred Rock

Beside the entry gate to Huayna Picchu this large rock faces a small open square with two thatched wayrana on opposite sides of it. The rock itself is a huge slab, again made significant by its enclosure by its neighbouring buildings and the plaza. Its very position shows it was an object of veneration and its surface may well originally have been polished like the sacred rocks found at Ollantay-tambo. Its shape seems to mimic the mountains behind it.

GROUP OF THE THREE DOORWAYS [18]

You are now in the residential area to the north east of the site that was probably occupied by less elevated inhabitants – perhaps the people who did the work, fed and looked after the nobility, maintained the terraces and harvested the crops. It is so called because there are three fine doorways to be seen. Below it is another cemetery area, east facing, and outside the Machu Picchu equivalent of the city limits.

EASTERN TERRACES

Covering an area of four hectares, this is the most extensive set of terraces at Machu Picchu. Not quite as steep as their western counterparts but impressive nonetheless, there are two sections: a smaller run set below the lower residential area and a whole hillside of them, facing due east below. The terraces were constructed between 1470 and 1530 and include ceremonial watercourses.

Part of the newly excavated and restored section that lies between Machu Picchu and Aguas Calientes will be opened to visitors in 2011. Entry to the lower terraces will probably be from the road leading up from Aguas Calientes.

INDUSTRIAL OR MORTAR SECTOR [19]

Bingham quite understandably believed, when he saw that one of the buildings in this more crowded, commercial zone had mysterious, crater-like protrusions on the floor of its courtyard, that they were mortars for grinding corn. It is now thought that the surfaces are too flat for the purpose. It is possible that they may have had some sort of astronomical function; water may have been poured into them, for example, and celestial events such as eclipses observed in reflection.

TEMPLE OF THE CONDOR [20]

This is one of most mysterious structures at Machu Picchu. On the ground is a piece of dark granite, unmistakably polished and wrought into the shape of a condor seen from above, with its distinctive head and white collar formed by a separate piece of stone. If you have a very vivid imagination you may be able to identify the swoops of natural rock behind as wings. The Incas worshipped the *Apu Kuntur* (Condor God) and even today some Andean villages such as Cotabambas celebrate the Yawar Fiesta. In this a captured condor, the spirit of the Incas, is tied to the back of a bull symbolizing the Spanish Conquistadors. The condor overpowers the bull, lashing at it with its beak, drawing blood and gouging out the bull's eyes. The bull dies and the condor is released, the Inca god triumphing over the Spanish to bring good fortune to the village.

Temple of the Condor
(red lines showing how the rocks behind may be seen as the wings)

The rock beneath the natural rock has been hollowed into small vaults, sometimes referred to, with wistful relish, as 'jails'. This idea was first suggested by Bingham who referred to these buildings as the Prison Group. Some guides will tell you that prisoners may have been held here and in the buildings behind. In the so-called **jail** there are human-sized niches with holes in the stones halfway up each side to which the arms of the prisoners could have been bound. This is unlikely as it's believed that the Incas didn't have prisons; wrongdoers were dealt with immediately: either by being put to death or by losing their privileges.

The Jail

Agricultural sector and
storage huts

STORAGE HUTS [21]

Cross the terraces of the agricultural sector again to
return to the entrance. Bingham referred to these
huts as barracks, but being located conveniently at
the end of the agricultural terraces, it is likely that
they functioned either as housing for farmers or
storage huts for tools and supplies, or both. Some
have been rethatched.

SIDE TRIPS

The best of the side trips is the climb up **Huayna/
Wayna Picchu** (2700m/8860ft, see p352).

As an alternative, however, you can climb
Machu Picchu peak (3060m/10,040ft), the peak
opposite. **A ticket must be bought in advance**
(see p347); unlike climbing Huayna Picchu, there are no time restrictions. There
tend to be far fewer people here than atop Huayna Picchu. The climb takes up
to two hours (plus an hour to walk down) and is steady if not especially difficult. Head up the path towards Intipunku, away from the main site. After 150m
look for a signposted turning to the right and join a series of broad steps that
ascend through trees and scrub. Along the way are viewing platforms and, close
to the top, a long curved stone staircase. On the summit itself there are some terraces and a small building. The views are spectacular: to the east are Putucusi
and Veronica; the San Miguel Range lies to the west whilst to the south is Mt
Salkantay.

A considerable feat of Inca engineering, the **drawbridge** is another worth-
while (short) excursion. The main Inca Trail skirts through the southern end of

Inca drawbridge

the ruins via the guardhouse and the kallanka to
reach the drawbridge. A stone wall was built
against the cliff face with planks to cross the gap in
the middle. These could have been withdrawn to
close this entrance to the city. Since a visitor
plunged to his death from the bridge the path has
been closed a short distance before it but you can
get a good view of the drawbridge from the viewpoint. It takes about 20 minutes each way from the
guardhouse; the path climbs steeply for the first
five minutes and then levels out, clinging to the
cliff edge with superb views across the valley. The
trail may be closed in the afternoon.

If you didn't reach Machu Picchu by following
the main Inca Trail it's well worth walking up it to
Intipunku, (The Sun Gate). The robust stone paving on the path is still intact
after all these years. Allow 1-1¹/2 hours to walk there and back, with some time
at the gate to sit and enjoy the superb views back over the ruins.

APPENDIX A – QUECHUA & SPANISH

Although Spanish is the main language of Peru, you will find that Quechua, also known as *Runasimi*, is widely spoken in the Andes. Although spoken by a number of Andean tribes prior to the spread of the Inca empire, the language was adopted by the Incas to unify their multilingual subjects and consolidate their empire.

After the Spanish Conquest, Quechua continued to be used largely as the general language and main means of communication between the Spanish and indigenous people, so continued to expand its range, but all administrative use of the language was banned in the late 18th century in the wake of the Túpac Amaru II revolution. Despite a brief revival post-independence the language has generally declined and is increasingly restricted to rural areas but it is still one of the most widespread indigenous languages in the Americas. It remains a largely oral language as there is a lack of written material. There is, though, a realization of Quechua's value as a national symbol and vehicle for promoting native culture.

QUECHUA

Quechua and Spanish have become intermixed over the years and there are lots of Spanish loan words in Quechua. There are also a number of Quechua loan words in English, via Spanish. These include ayahuasca, coca, condor, llama, puma, quinoa and vicuna.

Until the 20th century Quechua was written using Spanish spelling (eg Inca, huayna, collasuyu, quipu, condor), making it more familiar to Spanish speakers and also easier to use for borrowings into English. In 1975 the Peruvian government adopted a new orthography eg Inka, wayna, Qollasuyu, khipu, kuntur. The different spellings are still highly controversial in Peru. The Spanish system, which is largely used in this book, is more readable, makes Quechua easier to learn and is how place names are usually depicted on maps. The newer form is, however, thought to be a better phonology of Quechua.

The only readily available book is *Quechua Phrasebook*, published by Lonely Planet.

SPANISH

The conquistadors brought their language with them to South America. Over time Castillian Spanish evolved into Latin American Spanish, an arbitrary name for the idiomatic and native expressions and specific vocabulary of Spanish spoken in Latin America. The version of the language spoken here is a dialect of Castillian Spanish as opposed to a distinct language, even though it contains various features that distinguish it from European Spanish. The differences are akin to those between British English and US English. Apart from slang or extreme colloquialisms, the main differences are in pronunciation, rhythm, grammar and unique vocabulary.

Particular pitfalls are 'll', pronounced 'y', 'hu' pronounced 'w', 'q' pronounced 'k' and 'ce' or 'ci' pronounced 's' rather than with the 'th' lisp and 'v' as in English rather than as 'b'.

Stress goes on the penultimate syllable unless there's an accent to indicate an alternative stress.

ENGLISH	QUECHUA	SPANISH
General words and phrases		
Hello / Good day	*¡Napaikulyaiki!*	*¡Buenos días!*
Goodbye	*Hokhkootikama*	*Adiós*
See you	*Ratukama*	*Hasta luego*
Mr / Sir	*tayta*	*señor*
Madam	*mama*	*señora*

ENGLISH	QUECHUA	SPANISH
How are you?	*¿Allillanchu?*	*¿Cómo está usted?*
What's your name?	*¿Iman sutiyki?*	*Cómo se llama?*
I'm ...	*... -n sutiy*	*Me llamo ...*
Please / Thank you	*Allichu / Añáy*	*Por favor / Gracias*
Excuse me	*Munayniykimanta*	*Con permiso*
Sorry (apologies)	*Pampachayuay*	*Disculpe*
Where are you going?	*¿Maytataq rishanki?*	*¿Adónde vas?*
What's this called?	*¿Imatataq kaypa sutin?*	*Qué es esto?*
Can I stay here?	*¿Puñupayukuykimanchu?*	*¿Puedo pasar la noche aquí?*
Yes / No	*Arí / Mana*	*Sí / No*
impossible	*mana atina*	*imposible*
good / bad	*allinmi / manan allinchu*	*está bien / no está bien*
beautiful	*añañá*	*bonito*
hot / cold	*ruphay / ch'ulli*	*calor / trío*
rain / snow	*para / rit'i*	*lluvia / nieve*
wind	*wayra*	*viento*

Directions

left / right	*lloq'e / paña*	*izquierda / derecho*
here / there	*kaypi / chaypi*	*aquí / allí, allá*
over there	*haqay*	*por ahí*
up / down	*wichay / uray*	*arriba / abajo*
near	*sispa*	*cerca*
far (far off)	*karu*	*lejos*
straight ahead	*dirichu*	*derecho*
everywhere	*maypipas*	*en todos partes*
Where is a / the ...?	*¿Maypin ...?*	*¿Dónde está ...?*
... bus / truck / minibus	*... omnibus / karro*	*... el bus / el camión / el minibus*
... bus station	(N/A)	*... estacíon de autobuses*
... hotel / hostel	*... qorpa wasi*	*... el hotel / hostal*
... house	*... wasi*	*... la casa*
... pass	*... q'asa*	*... la abra*
... path	*... ñan*	*... el camino, el sendero*
... railway station	*...ferrocarril*	*... el estacíon de ferrocarril*
... river	*... mayu*	*... el río*
... toilet	*... bañu*	*... los baños*
... village	*... llaqta, marka*	*... el pueblo*
... water / ... food	*...unu /... mikuna*	*... agua / ... la comida*

When?

When?	*¿Hayk'aq?*	*¿Cuándo?*
soon	*kunan*	*pronto*
right now	*kunallan, kunanpacha!*	*ahora mismo*
later	*qhepata*	*más tarde*
never	*manan hayk'aqpas*	*nunca*
today	*kunanmi*	*hoy*
tomorrow	*qayantin*	*manana*
yesterday	*qayna*	*ayer*

Help!

Help me!	*!Yanapaway!*	*¡Socorro!*
Take me to a hospital	*Uspitalman pusaway*	*Lévame al hospital*

ENGLISH	QUECHUA	SPANISH
It hurts	*Nanan*	*Me duele*
I'm cold	*Chiriwashan*	*Tengo frío*
I'm hungry	*Yarqawashan*	*Tengo hambre*
I'm thirsty	*Ch'akiwashan*	*Tengo sed*
I'm tired	*Sayk'usqa kan*	*Estoy cansado*
I'm hot	*Q'uñi*	*Estoy caliente*
I've got a headache	*Umaimi nanawan*	*Tengo un dolor de cabeza*

Numerals

	Quechua	Spanish		Quechua	Spanish
1	*u'/ huk*	*uno*	18	*chunka pusaqniyuq*	*dieciocho*
2	*iskay*	*dos*	19	*chunka isqunniyuq*	*diecinueve*
3	*kinsa*	*tres*	20	*iskay chunka*	*viente*
4	*tawa*	*cuartro*	21	*iskay chunka hukniyuq*	*vientiuno*
5	*pisqa*	*cinco*	30	*kinsa chunka*	*trienta*
6	*suqta*	*seis*	40	*tawa chunka*	*cuarenta*
7	*qanchis*	*siete*	50	*pisqa chunka*	*cincuenta*
8	*pusaq*	*ocho*	60	*suqta chunka*	*sesenta*
9	*iskun*	*nueve*	70	*qanchis chunka*	*setenta*
10	*chunka*	*diez*	80	*pusaq chunka*	*ochenta*
11	*chunka hukniyuq*	*once*	90	*iskun chunka*	*noventa*
12	*chunka iskayniyuq*	*doce*	100	*pachak*	*cien*
13	*chunka kinsayuq*	*trece*	101	*pachak hukniyuq*	*ciento uno*
14	*chunka tawayuq*	*catorce*	200	*iskay pachak*	*doscientos*
15	*chunka pisqayuq*	*quince*	1000	*waranqa*	*mil*
16	*chunka suqtayuq*	*dieciséis*	2000	*iskay waranqa*	*dos mil*
17	*chunka qanchisniyuq*	*diecisiete*	1,000,000	*hunu*	*un millón*

Money and costs

money	*qolqe*	*dinero*
How much is ...?	*¿Maik'ata'g ...?*	*¿Cuánto cuesta ...?*
... that one	*... haqay, chay*	*... eso/a*
more / less	*aswan / aswan pisi*	*más / menos*
a little	*chika, pisi*	*un poco, poquito*
big, large	*hatun*	*grande*
small, little	*huch'uy*	*pequeño/a*
How does it cost to hire ...?	*¿Maik'ata'g ...?*	*¿Cuánto cuesta...?*
... a guide	*... pusawasqaykimanta*	*... arrendar un guía?*
... a horse	*... caballoykikunamanta*	*... arrendar un caballo?*
... a llama	*... llamaykikunamanta*	*... arrendar una llama?*
... for a week / day	*... sapa semanan / p'unchay*	*... por semana / día*
Do you sell ...?	*¿Icha ... ta bendiwankiman?*	*¿Me vende ...?*

Food and drink (see pp80-4)

beer	*sirwisa*	*cerveza*
bread	*t'anta*	*pan*
chicken	*wallpa*	*pollo*
coca	*kuka*	*coca*
egg	*runtu*	*huevo*
fish	*challwa*	*pescado*
fruit	*ruru, añawi*	*fruta*

ENGLISH	QUECHUA	SPANISH
Food and drink (*cont'd from p365*)		
maize (corn)	*choqllo (sara)*	*maíz (choclo)*
meat (dried)	*aycha (ch'arki)*	*carne (charqui)*
potato	*papa*	*papa*
soup	*chupi*	*sopa*
roast	*kanka*	*asado*
boil	*t'impuy*	*hervir*
fry	*theqtichiy*	*freír*
raw	*hanku*	*crudo*
cooked	*chayasqa*	*cocido*
fizzy drink / pop	*bebida gaseosa*	*bebida gaseosa*
hot (temperature)	*q'oñi*	*caliente*
spicy	*haya*	*picante*
cold food	*kharmu*	*comida fría*

Food and drink glossary

aji hot pepper from which a spicy sauce is made

aji de gallina shredded chicken stewed in a rich, gently spiced cream sauce

anticucho beef-heart kebabs cooked on a skewer over hot coals and served with a range of spicy sauces

bodega wine shop or bar that also serves snacks

butifarra pork and sweet onion salsa sandwich; the pork is cooked with pepper, garlic, cumin, achiote and oregano

cafecito small black coffee

cañazo strong alcoholic spirit distilled from sugar cane

cantinas a bar room

causa / causa rellena a lightly spiced potato cake mixed with tuna, egg, shrimp, avocado or chicken

ceviche / cevichería (also cebice / cebicheria) raw fish marinated in citrus juice and spiced with chilli / restaurant that serves ceviche

chicha / chicha morada a drink made from purple maize (corn) and spices; *chicha de jora* is Peru's famous fermented maize beer

chicharron(es) deep-fried pork and pork skin

chuño type of traditional freeze-dried potato

cuy guinea pig

huarcartay an aromatic Andean herb

leche de tigre literally 'tiger's milk', a mixture of lime juice, salt and hot pepper used to 'cook' classic ceviche

llipta a mixture of lime or quinoa and potash taken with a plug of coca leaves and chewed together to release the active ingredients in the leaves

lomo cordon bleu beef loin steak stuffed with cheese and ham

lomo milanesa beef loin beaten into a thin steak and fried in breadcrumbs

lomo a lo pobre beef loin fried with an egg on top

lomo saltado strips of beef stir-fried with onions, spicy orange peppers, tomatoes and soy sauce, served with rice and fried potatoes

mercado market

moraya freeze-dried potato

Novoandina Style of fusion cuisine that combines modern techniques, traditional raw materials and both Peruvian and Asian culinary ideas

pachamanca traditional feast cooked in an earth oven beneath hot stones

parrillada BBQ/grill method of cooking, also a plate of grilled meat and a restaurant that serves this kind of meat

picantería a traditional local restaurant often serving spicy food

pisco sour drink made from pisco (Peruvian spirit), lemon and egg white

quinoa an Andean grain-like crop grown for its edible seeds

tamales steamed or boiled dough stuffed with meat, veg, cheese or fruit.

APPENDIX B – GLOSSARY

AMS acute mountain sickness

abra high mountain pass

aclla a 'chosen woman' of the Inca, an Inca nun

acllahuasi convent or nunnery

alpaca type of domesticated camelid resembling a small llama, bred for its wool

altiplano literally 'high place', an area of high-altitude plateau

amauta Inca oral historian who cultivated their myths and legends

andene broad agricultural terrace or set of terraces built on Andian slopes

andesite igneous volcanic rock common in mountains of North and South America, including the Andes, after which it is named

Antis collective term for tribes living in Antisuyu and the rainforest

Antisuyu the eastern part of Inca empire, bordering the upper Amazon

apacheta cairn; pile of stones

apu / apus god(s) or spirit(s) of the mountains that protect local people in high areas

arpilleras appliqué pictures illustrating Peruvian life and traditions

arriero muleteer, wrangler of pack animals

ashlar sculpted square blocks of stone or any dressed stonework

altiplano steppe alpine zone; high Andean grassland

audiencia a seat of government of Spanish South America; also type of court set up to administer royal justice

awaska type of cloth garment worn daily by ordinary people

ayllu Inca kinship group

Aymara ethnic group living to south and east of Lake Titicaca and their language

baño (when used archaeologically) a ceremonial bath

barranca ravine

cabildos town councils

cacique leader of indigenous tribe

calle street

cambista money-changer

cambio (bureau de change) place to exchange money

campesino Peruvian peasant or worker of the land

cancha small plot of land or block of houses in an Inca town

casonas large houses/mansions

caudillos the military leaders at the time of Peruvian independence

cejas de la selva literally 'eyebrows of the jungle' (the eastern slopes of the Andes, fringed with forest)

ceques sacred lines radiating from the centre of the Sun Temple in Cusco and passing through a set of huacas or shrines

cerro mountain

ceviche / cevichería see opposite

chacos royal hunts

chasqui messenger or courier usually operating as part of a relay

Chinchaysuyu the northern quarter of the Inca Empire

chullo type of traditional woolly hat

chullpa tomb or burial chamber

ciudadela high-walled enclosure housing a series of storage rooms, a large platform cum burial place and a number of *audiencias* or audience rooms

coca plant used by Peruvians to ease altitude sickness and for stamina and health; the basic ingredient of cocaine

colectivo / combi type of public transport that is part bus, part taxi

Collasuyu south-eastern province of the Inca Empire

collpas clay licks ie areas of exposed clay where parakeets congregate to eat the soil in order to get salt

Condesuyu the south-western quarter of the Inca Empire

Convención (La) the district to the east of Machu Picchu

conquistadors Spanish explorer soldiers who conquered South America in the 15th and 16th centuries

Coricancha Inca Sun Temple

corregidores chief magistrate appointed by the king of Spain; local, administrative and judicial position

correo post office

costa coast

Coya the Inca's sister, his official wife and high priestess

Creole Peruvian-born person of European descent

Criolla Creole-style music and cooking predominately found along the coast

Curaca Inca name for local noble

double-jamb an entrance or doorway framed by two jambs (vertical columns) indicating an important access point

El Niño A weather phenomenon where a band of anomalously warm ocean water temperatures sometimes develops off the western coast of South America and can cause climatic changes across the Pacific Ocean

encomendero name given to the owner of an *encomienda*

encomienda plot of land governed by a Spaniard whose native inhabitants paid tribute to an encomendero

eye-bonder archaeological term for the pierced stones found in Inca buildings, often round or protruding from walls or gables; probably used for securing thatched roofs and hanging doors

fuente(s) fountain(s); source of water

garúa low level cloud formed on the coast during cooler months of the year

gnomon a carved vertical stone

guanaco type of wild camelid related to the llama and alpaca

guano sea bird excrement used as a fertilizer

HACO/HAPO rare condition of high-altitude sickness caused by ascending too quickly, which can be fatal

Hanan Inca clan division, also a part of an Inca town, more powerful/prestigious than *Hurin* (see below)

hospedajes lodging, accommodation

huaca sacred spot, usually a sculpted stone or feature in the landscape

huaqueros tomb-robbers or treasure-hunters

huayna small or young, opposite of *machu*

huayno form of Peruvian Andean music with high-pitched vocals

Hurin an Inca clan division, also a part of an Inca town, less powerful/prestigious than *Hanan* (see above)

INC Instituto Nacional de Cultura, the government department responsible for managing and preserving archaeological sites

Inca see Sapa Inca

Indios Indians

Indigenismo early 20th century political movement

Inti the sun, and the name of the Sun God

Intihuatana ritual stone, literally the 'hitching post of the sun'

Inti Raymi Inca religious festival to observe the winter solstice and honour the god Inti; now recreated and a major tourist attraction

jirón (jr) street

kallanka Inca meeting hall

llama a South American camelid (relative of the camel) used in Andean countries as a pack and food animal

machay cave

machu old, big, opposite of *huayna*

mamacona mother superior in a convent that is dedicated to serving the Inca

mestizo person of mixed Indian and European blood

micros also known as *combis* or *colectivos*

mirador viewpoint

mit'a Inca tax, often paid in compulsory community labour

mitimaes Inca settlers transplanted to perform *mit'a* in another part of the country

mochadero common Indian word for their shrines

nevado mountain peak, usually covered in snow

orejones literally 'big-ears', slang term used to refer to Hispanics and by the Inca to refer to *conquistadors*

oroya traditional cable-car style river crossing using a cage attached to a zip line and manoeuvred over the river by a series of ropes

Pachamama goddess revered by Andean Indians, literally Earth Mother

pampa plain, or occasionally any small, flat area

panaca the tradition of preserving the estate of a dead person

peña a bar or club featuring live folkloric music

picka basic method of Inca construction

polylepis type of shrub/tree species endemic to the mid and high elevation areas of the Andes

posta de salud health station

pucará Inca fort

pueblos jóvenes shanty town or slum

puna high-altitude grassland, usually above the treeline

Punchao a sacred idol of the sun from Cusco's Sun Temple, looted by the conquistadors

Qenko sacred sculpted stone near Cusco

qeros a drinking vessel, especially for chicha

quebrada deep, sheer-sided river valley

Quechua native South American language spoken primarily in the Andes and used by the Incas, also refers to the Incas' descendants currently living in Peru

quipus literally 'talking knots', a recording device of knotted strings used by the Incas; could only be read by skilled interpreters, the quipucamayos

qollqa Inca storehouse

qompi fine fabric woven for the Inca

raccay ruins

Runasimi the Quechua word for the language, literally 'people's speech'

Sapa Inca the Great Inca, the Inca emperor and ruler of Cusco and the empire, also known simply as 'the Inca'

sapo traditional Peruvian game

sierra highland region

selva jungle

sol(es) unit of Peruvian currency

soroche altitude sickness

suyua division of the Inca empire

Tahuantinsuyu name of the Inca empire

tambo an inn or rest-house

tarjeta telefónica telephone card

taxista taxi driver

Tiahuanaco a pre-Inca Peruvian culture

tumi a ceremonial Andean knife

urpu traditional fat-bellied pot with a curved base and long spout

usno raised ceremonial square in an Inca city

vicuña undomesticated camelid living in high alpine areas of the Andes that is related to the llama and alpaca, with very fine wool

Valle Sagrado Sacred Valley of the Incas; lies along the Urubamba River, north of Cusco

Vilcanota alternative name for the upper Urubamba River

Villac Umu chief of the caste of priests in the Inca state religion

Viracocha the creator of the Incas and a key figure in Inca mythology, also the name of one of the early Incas

Wayrana style of building with one of its long sides open

APPENDIX C – RAIL INFORMATION

Traditionally, buses have been the cheapest and easiest way of getting around Peru, even if journeys take a long time and aren't always comfortable. However, there is no road access to Aguas Calientes, the gateway to Machu Picchu. Thus the only alternatives are to walk in or take the train. Not surprisingly the train emerges as the only real option for many visitors. However, around the end of the 20th century the privatization of the rail network saw the new owners, PeruRail, introduce restricted tourist services and much higher fares. Competition was finally introduced in the form of rival firms Inca Rail and Machu Picchu Train, although they ran a much-reduced range of services.

To offer a more meaningful alternative service, these two operators subsequently merged and are called Inca Rail. There's also a subsidized train service for local people; although Peruvian citizens from outside the area can occasionally use it, foreigners may not.

RAIL SERVICES

Timetables can change at short notice and occasionally there are enforced changes due to track damage or bad weather meaning that departure points, particularly from Cusco (Poroy) can also vary. In most instances, if the train can't run from a particular station, a replacement bus service will shuttle you to a new departure point. Before travelling, make sure to check operator timetables for up-to-date information and advice.

● **PeruRail** Currently PeruRail (⌨ www.perurail.com) operates three services of their **blue-liveried tourist train** from the station at Poroy, 13km (8 miles) outside downtown Cusco (about a 20-minute drive; taxi s/30), through the Sacred Valley to Aguas Calientes. Sadly the trains no longer leave from the main station in Cusco meaning you miss out on the slow, scenic zigzag as the train ascends a series of switchbacks to leave the city. However, the majority of their services operate from Ollantaytambo in the Sacred Valley. A taxi here costs around s/80.

The 'budget' **Expedition service** (previously called the Backpacker) is the cheapest, see opposite. The **Vistadome service** has panoramic windows, complimentary drinks and snacks and takes slightly less time to complete the route but costs a little more.

The top-of-the-range ride is aboard the **Hiram Bingham** which runs Monday to Saturday. The exorbitant fare (see opposite) entitles you to brunch and dinner in the opulent dining car, cocktails and live entertainment en route as well as guides, bus transfers from Cusco to Poroy and from Aguas Calientes to Machu Picchu, entrance to the ruins and afternoon tea in the plush Machu Picchu Sanctuary Lodge. That's still a lot of money for a day trip, though. The Hiram Bingham service doesn't run on Sundays.

Tickets can be bought from the main office at Portal de Carnes 214 on Plaza de Armas in Cusco, or from a subsidiary office at Calle Regocijo 202 on Plaza Regocijo; both are open daily 7am-10pm. PeruRail also has a stand at Jorge Chavez International Airport in the National Departures area on the 2nd Floor between gate 13 and 14 (daily 4am-8pm) and in Larcomar Mall on Malecon de la Reserva in Miraflores, Lima (daily 11am-10pm).

Tickets can also be bought at the stations in Poroy, Urubamba, Ollantaytambo and Aguas Calientes or **online** with a credit card. Print the e-voucher and take it along with your passport to the station at least an hour ahead of departure, where you can exchange it for a ticket. The e-voucher alone is not valid for travel.

PeruRail also run the train service that connects Aguas Calientes to La Hidroeléctrica. Tickets (from US$18 one way) can only be bought from the station in Aguas Calientes – though the service sometimes operates from the local railway station on Av Imperio de los Incas – or from the ticket office adjacent to the tracks at La Hidroeléctrica.

• **Inca Rail** (💻 www.incarail.com) operates six departures daily from Ollantaytambo to Aguas Calientes aboard their smart **white and green trains**. Their **Tourist service** features seats with access to fold-away dining tables and panoramic windows whilst their **Executive Service** also includes a selection of artisan chocolates. **First Class services** include a gourmet meal.

Tickets can be bought from their office on Calle Portal de Panes 105 on Plaza de Armas in Cusco (☎ 233030) or from the station in Ollantaytambo (☎ 204211) and Aguas Calientes (☎ 211052). You can also buy tickets online.

TIMETABLES AND FARES

Bear in mind that the **timetables** below are subject to change at very short notice and are a guide rather than a rule. To get the most up-to-date information check locally at the railway stations or try visiting the respective company's website.

Unfortunately there aren't any ways of making these journeys cheaper. In real terms the **fares** are representative of what you might expect to pay for such a spectacular ride elsewhere in the world; they just seem hugely inflated by Peruvian standards.

PERURAIL
Cusco (Poroy) to Machu Picchu (Aguas Calientes)
Services are daily, except for the Hiram Bingham which does not run on Sundays.

SERVICE NAME	TRAIN No	FARE (US$) ONE-WAY FROM	DEP CUSCO (POROY)	ARR MACHU PICCHU (AGUAS CALIENTES)
Vistadome	31	$82	06.40	09.52
Expedition	33	$68	07.42	10.51
Vistadome	203	$80	08.25	12.11
Hiram Bingham	11	$378.50	09.05	12.24

Machu Picchu (Aguas Calientes) to Cusco (Poroy)
Services are daily, except for the Hiram Bingham which does not run on Sundays.

SERVICE NAME	TRAIN No	FARE (US$) ONE-WAY FROM	DEP MACHU PICCHU (AGUAS CALIENTES)	ARR CUSCO (POROY)
Vistadome	32	$84	15.20	19.05
Expedition	34	$68	16.43	20.23
Vistadome	604	$84	17.27	20.40
Hiram Bingham	12	$378.50	17.50	21.16

La Hidroeléctrica to Machu Picchu (Aguas Calientes)
Note: This service uses the local railway station in Aguas Calientes.

SERVICE NAME	TRAIN No	DEP LA HIDROELÉCTRICA	ARR MACHU PICCHU (AGUAS CALIENTES)
Expedition	72	07.54	08.35
Vistadome	504	15.00	15.47
Expedition	22	16.35	17.50

Machu Picchu (Aguas Calientes) to La Hidroeléctrica
Note: This service uses the local railway station in Aguas Calientes.

SERVICE NAME	TRAIN No	DEP MACHU PICCHU (AGUAS CALIENTES)	ARR LA HIDROELÉCTRICA
Expedition	71	06.44	07.29
Expedition	21	12.35	13.30
Vistadome	501	13.30	14.22

Ollantaytambo to Machu Picchu (Aguas Calientes)

Most train services operate from Ollantaytambo; trekking operators generally transfer clients from Cusco to Ollantaytambo by minibus if they're not already based in the Sacred Valley. PeruRail lays on occasional special trains between Ollantaytambo and Urubamba.

SERVICE NAME	TRAIN No	FARE (US$) ONE-WAY FROM OLLANTAYTAMBO	DEP OLLANTAYTAMBO	ARR MACHU PICCHU (AGUAS CALIENTES)
Expedition	71	$56	05.07	06.34
Expedition	81	$56	06.10	07.40
Vistadome	301	$80	07.05	08.27
Expedition	83	$62	07.45	09.15
Vistadome	601	$81	08.00	09.24
Vistadome	501	$79	08.53	10.29
Vistadome	203	$77	10.32	12.11
(fare plus buffet at the Sanctuary Lodge costs $114)				
Expedition	73	$54	12.58	14.24
Vistadome	303	$66	13.27	14.49
Vistadome	603	$57	15.37	17.02
Expedition	75	$57	19.00	20.43
Expedition	51	$66	21.00	22.50

Machu Picchu (Aguas Calientes) to Ollantaytambo

SERVICE NAME	TRAIN No	FARE (US$) ONE-WAY FROM	DEP MACHU PICCHU (AGUAS CALIENTES)	ARR OLLANTAYTAMBO
Expedition	50	$53	05.35	07.44
Expedition	72	$54	08.53	10.52
Vistadome	302	$72	10.55	12.32
Vistadome	204	$74	13.37	15.04
Expedition	74	$71	14.55	16.31
Vistadome	304	$85	15.48	17.29
Vistadome	504	$78	16.22	18.01
Vistadome	604	$87	17.27	18.56
Vistadome	606	$81	18.10	19.45
Expedition	84	$67	18.45	20.18
Expedition	76	$63	21.30	23.01

Between Cusco and Puno (Lake Titicaca)

This is possibly the highest passenger railway route in the world: at its highest point, La Raya, the altitude is 4313m/14,146ft. The luxurious **Andean Explorer** train, decorated in the style of the Pullman trains of the 1920s, leaves Cusco for Puno from Huanchac Station on Monday, Wednesday and Saturday at 8am and gets to Puno at 6pm. During the high season (Apr-Oct) there is an additional departure on Friday.

Trains from Puno to Cusco also depart on Monday, Wednesday and Saturday at 8am and arrive in Cusco at 6pm. Again, during the high season there is an additional departure on Friday.

Tickets cost US$255 from Cusco to Puno and US$153 from Puno to Cusco and include a three-course lunch.

Between Puno and Arequipa

Once a popular route, this stretch of track is currently only available for private charters. For the latest information see 🖥 www.perurail.com.

INCA RAIL

Ollantaytambo to Machu Picchu (Aguas Calientes)

CLASS	TRAIN No	FARE (US$) ONE-WAY	DEP OLLANTAYTAMBO	ARR MACHU PICCHU (AGUAS CALIENTES)
Tourist / Executive	41	$55 / $70	06.40	08.01
Tourist		$60	07.20	08.48
Tourist / Executive / First class	43	$55 / $70 $215	11.15	12.45
Tourist / Executive	45	$55 / $70	16.36	18.09

Machu Picchu (Aguas Calientes) to Ollantaytambo

CLASS	TRAIN No	FARE (US$) ONE-WAY	DEP MACHU PICCHU (AGUAS CALIENTES)	ARR OLLANTAYTAMBO
Tourist / Executive	42	$45 / $60	08.30	10.10
Tourist / Executive	44	$55 / $70	14.30	16.05
Tourist		$60	16.12	17.50
Executive / First	46	$70 / $215	19.00	20.32

APPENDIX D – GPS WAYPOINTS

Each GPS waypoint below was taken on the route at the reference number marked on the map as below. This list of GPS waypoints is also available to download from the Trailblazer website – 🖥 www.trailblazer-guides.com. Owing to security problems in the Vilcabamba area at the time of research we were unable to cover that region so waypoints are not provided for Maps 17-26, or for Huancacalle to Cachora via Choquequirao trek (Maps 35-38).
See pp216-18 for more information.

MAP	REF	LATITUDE	LONGITUDE	LOCATION
The classic Inca Trail and variations				
1	01	13° 13'34S	72° 26'10W	Km88 – disembark from the train and cross the bridge
	02	13° 14'08S	72° 25'24W	Huillca Raccay
	03	13° 13'53S	72° 25'30W	Patallacta
	04	13° 15'25S	72° 26'34W	Hatun Chaca
	05	13° 15'51S	72° 26'49W	Huayllabamba
2	06	13° 15'01S	72° 28'18W	Llulluchapampa campsite
	07	13° 14'32S	72° 29'03W	Abra de Huarmihuanusca (First Pass)
	08	13° 14'01S	72° 29'53W	Pacamayo campsite
3	09	13° 13'42S	72° 30'06W	Runcu Raccay
	10	13° 13'36S	72° 30'18W	Second Pass
	11	13° 13'41S	72° 31'01W	Sayac Marca
	12	13° 13'36S	72° 30'57W	Concha Marca
	13	13° 13'21S	72° 31'10W	Chaquicocha campsite
	14	13° 12'37S	72° 31'38W	Inca Tunnel
	15	13° 12'24S	72° 31'56W	Third Pass and Phuyu Pata Marca
4	16	13° 11'13S	72° 32'28W	Intipata
	17	13° 11'35S	72° 32'10W	Huinay Huayna
	18	13° 11'24S	72° 32'13W	Old Trekker's Hotel
	19	13° 10'13S	72° 32'06W	Intipunku
	20	13° 09'57S	72° 32'44W	Machu Picchu
	21	13° 09'21S	72° 32'45W	Huayna Picchu
	22	13° 11'09S	72° 30'30W	Km104 – disembark from the train and cross the bridge
	23	13° 11'10S	72° 30'37W	Chachabamba
	24	13° 11'15S	72° 31'51W	Choquesuysuy
5	25	13° 13'23S	72° 20'25W	Km77 – disembark from the train or bus and cross the bridge over the Río Urubamba
	26	13° 12'57S	72° 23'02W	Km82 – disembark from the train or bus and cross the bridge over the Río Urubamba
6	27	13° 14'08S	72° 25'24W	Huillca Raccay
	28	13° 13'53S	72° 25'30W	Patallacta

MAP REF LATITUDE LONGITUDE LOCATION

The Salkantay Trek

MAP	REF	LATITUDE	LONGITUDE	LOCATION
7	29	13° 30'32S	72° 31'40W	Mollepata Plaza de Armas
	30	13° 27'16S	72° 32'21W	Marcocasa
8	31	13° 23'40S	72° 34'28W	Salkantay Lodge & Adventure Resort
9	32	13° 23'11S	72° 34'19W	Camping Humantay
	33	13° 22'40S	72° 35'04W	Glacial lakes beneath slopes and glaciers of Mt Humantay
	34	13° 21'59S	72° 33'35W	Salkantay Pampa
	35	13° 21'26S	72° 32'22W	Inka Chiriasqa Pass
11	36	13° 16'49S	72° 27'00W	Paucarcancha
	37	13° 15'51S	72° 26'49W	Huayllabamba

The Santa Teresa Trek

MAP	REF	LATITUDE	LONGITUDE	LOCATION
7	29	13° 30'32S	72° 31'40W	Mollepata Plaza de Armas
	30	13° 27'16S	72° 32'21W	Marcocasa
8	31	13° 23'40S	72° 34'28W	Salkantay Lodge
9	32	13° 23'11S	72° 34'19W	Camping Humantay
	33	13° 22'40S	72° 35'04W	Glacial lakes beneath slopes and glaciers of Mt Humantay
	34	13° 21'59S	72° 33'35W	Salkantay Pampa
12	38	13° 21'28S	72° 33'67W	Soroyccocha campsite
	39	13° 20'88S	72° 33'78W	Salkantay Pass
	40	13° 20'58S	72° 34'68W	Pampa opens out after boulder field
	41	13° 19'78S	72° 36'12W	Huayraqumachay campsite
	42	13° 19'34S	72° 36'47W	Campsite just above treeline
13	43	13° 18'70S	72° 38'16W	Rayampata
	44	13° 19'02S	72° 38'47W	Campsite on old terraces
	45	13° 19'51S	72° 39'81W	Chaullay and Colpa Lodge access
	46	13° 19'10S	72° 40'14W	Ccolpapampa
	47	13° 18'99S	72° 40'10W	Turn left onto dirt track from road
14	48	13° 18'18S	72° 39'81W	Cross under waterfall
	49	13° 17'80S	72° 38'96W	Winay Poccos
	50	13° 13'59S	72° 37'66W	La Playa town square
15	51	13° 12'81S	72° 37'04W	Lucmabamba, turn right off road at blue 'INC' sign
	52	13° 11'16S	72° 35'36W	Ridge top – turn left
	53	13° 11'14S	72° 35'07W	Llactapata
16	54	13° 11'13S	72° 34'88W	'Clearing, viewpoint and campsite'
	55	13° 11'22S	72° 34'32W	Cross Rio Aobamba on a suspension bridge
	56	13° 10'24S	72° 33'44W	Checkpoint
	57	13° 10'28S	72° 33'24W	La Hidroelectrica railway station
	58	13° 09'15	72° 31'36W	Puente Ruinas railway station
	59	13° 09'57S	72° 32'44W	Machu Picchu

MAP REF LATITUDE LONGITUDE LOCATION

The Choquequirao Trek

MAP	REF	LATITUDE	LONGITUDE	LOCATION
27	60	13° 30'43S	72° 48'46W	Cachora Plaza de Armas
28	61	13° 26'36S	72° 48'38W	Capuliyoc Pass
	62	13° 25'46S	72° 50'29W	Chiquisca campsite
	63	13° 25'19S	72° 51'12W	Playa Rosalina campsite & river crossing point
29	64	13° 24'49S	72° 50'54W	Santa Rosa
	65	13° 23'59S	72° 51'28W	Marampata
	66	13° 23'55S	72° 51'33W	Checkpoint
	67	13° 23'35S	72° 52'25W	Choquequirao

Choquequirao to Machu Picchu trek

MAP	REF	LATITUDE	LONGITUDE	LOCATION
30	68	13° 23'35S	72° 52'25W	Choquequirao
	69	13° 22'23S	72° 53'02W	Pincha Unuyoc
	70	13° 21'53S	72° 53'07W	Cross Rio Blanco
	71	13° 21'04S	72° 53'08W	Maizal
	72	13° 19'53S	72° 51'56W	Abra San Juan
31	73	13° 19'19S	72° 50'40W	Yanama
33	74	13° 20'14S	72° 46'08W	Abra Yanama
	75	13° 19'53S	72° 43'06W	Totora
34	76	13° 19'10S	72° 40'14W	Ccolpapampa
	77	13° 18'99S	72° 40'10W	Turn left on to dirt track from road

Route map key

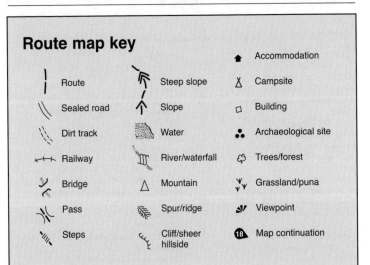

	Route		Steep slope	♠	Accommodation
	Sealed road		Slope	⋀	Campsite
	Dirt track		Water	▫	Building
	Railway		River/waterfall	⁘	Archaeological site
	Bridge		Mountain		Trees/forest
	Pass		Spur/ridge		Grassland/puna
	Steps		Cliff/sheer hillside		Viewpoint
				18	Map continuation

INDEX

Page references in **bold** type refer to maps

TRAILBLAZER TREKKING GUIDES
Europe
Corsica Trekking – GR20
Dolomites Trekking – AV1 & AV2
Scottish Highlands – The Hillwalking Guide
Tour du Mont Blanc
Walker's Haute Route: Mt Blanc to the
  Matterhorn

South America
Inca Trail, Cusco & Machu Picchu

Africa
Kilimanjaro
Moroccan Atlas – The Trekking Guide
Australasia
New Zealand – The Great Walks
Asia
Nepal Trekking & The Great Himalaya Trail
Sinai – the trekking guide
Trekking in the Everest Region
Trekking in Ladakh

New Zealand – The Great Walks
Alexander Stewart, 2nd edn, £12.99
ISBN 978-1-905864-11-9, 272pp, 60 maps, 40 colour photos
New Zealand is a wilderness paradise of incredibly beautiful landscapes. There is no better way to experience it than on one of the nine designated Great Walks, the country's premier walking tracks. Also includes detailed guides to Auckland, Wellington, National Park Village, Taumarunui, Nelson, Queenstown, Te Anau and Oban.

The Walker's Haute Route – Mt Blanc to the Matterhorn
Alexander Stewart, 1st edn, £12.99
ISBN 978-1-905864-08-9, 256pp, 60 maps, 30 colour photos
From Chamonix to Zermatt, the 180km (113-mile) Walker's Haute Route traverses one of the finest stretches of the Pennine Alps – the range between Valais in Switzerland and Piedmont and Aosta Valley in Italy. Includes Chamonix and Zermatt guides.

Tour du Mont Blanc
Jim Manthorpe 1st edn, £11.99
ISBN 978-1-905864-12-6, 208pp, 60 maps, 30 colour photos
At 4810m (15,781ft), Mont Blanc is the highest mountain in western Europe, and one of the most famous mountains in the world. The trail (105 miles, 168km) that circumnavigates it, passing through France, Italy and Switzerland, is the most popular long-distance walk in Europe. Includes Chamonix and Courmayeur guides.

Dolomites Trekking Alta Via 1 & Alta Via 2
Henry Stedman, 2nd edn, £11.99
ISBN 978-1-873756-83-6, 192pp, 59 maps, 38 colour photos
AV1 (9-13 days) & AV2 (10-16 days) are the most popular long-distance hikes in the Dolomites. Numerous shorter walks also included. Places to stay, walking times plus detailed guides to Cortina and six other towns.

Scottish Highlands – The Hillwalking Guide
Jim Manthorpe, 2nd edn, £12.99
ISBN 978-1-905864-21-8, 312pp, 86 maps, 40 photos
This guide covers 60 day-hikes in the following areas: ● Loch Lomond, the Trossachs and Southern Highlands ● Glen Coe and Ben Nevis ● Central Highlands ● Cairngorms & Eastern Highlands ● Western Highlands ● NW Highlands ● The Far North ● The Islands. Plus: 3- to 4-day hikes linking some regions.

Sinai – the trekking guide *Ben Hoffler,* 1st edn, £14.99
ISBN 978-1-905864-41-6, 288pp, 74 maps, 30 colour photos
Trek with the Bedouin and their camels and discover one of the
most exciting new trekking destinations. The best routes in the High
Mountain Region (St Katherine), Wadi Feiran and the Muzeina
deserts. Once you finish on trail there are the nearby coastal resorts
of Sharm el Sheikh, Dahab and Nuweiba to enjoy. **Due Sep 2013.**

Kilimanjaro – the trekking guide to Africa's highest mountain
Henry Stedman, 3rd edn, £12.99
ISBN 978-1-905864-24-9, 368pp, 40 maps, 30 photos
At 19,340ft the world's tallest freestanding mountain, Kilimanjaro
is one of the most popular destinations for hikers visiting Africa.
It's possible to walk up to the summit: no technical skills are nec-
essary. Includes town guides to Nairobi and Dar-Es-Salaam, and a
colour guide to flora and fauna. Includes Mount Meru.

Moroccan Atlas – the trekking guide
Alan Palmer, 1st edn, £12.99
ISBN 978-1-873756-77-5, 268pp, 54 maps, 40 colour photos
The High Atlas in central Morocco is the most dramatic and beautiful section of the entire Atlas range. Towering peaks, deep gorges
and huddled Berber villages enchant all who visit. With 44 detailed
trekking maps, 10 town and village guides including Marrakech.

Corsica Trekking – GR20
David Abram, 1st edn, £11.99
ISBN 978-1-873756-98-0, 208pp, 32 maps, 30 clr photos
Slicing diagonally across Corsica's jagged spine, the legendary
red-and-white waymarks of the GR20 guide trekkers across snow-
streaked passes, Alpine meadows, massive boulder fields and pris-
tine forests. Physically demanding, it's a superlative 170km, two-
week trek. Includes guides to gateway towns: Ajaccio, Bastia,
Calvi, Corte and Porte-Vecchio. *'Indispensible'. The Independent*
'Excellent guide'. The Sunday Times

Nepal Trekking & The Great Himalaya Trail
Robin Boustead, 1st edn, £14.99
ISBN 978-1-905864-31-7, 320pp, 8pp clr maps, 40 photos
This guide includes the most popular routes in Nepal – the
Everest, Annapurna and Langtang regions – as well as the newest
trekking areas for true trailblazers. This is the first guide to chart
The Great Himalaya Trail, the route which crosses Nepal from
east to west. Extensive planning sections.

Trekking in the Everest Region
Jamie McGuinness, 5th edn, £12.99
ISBN 978-1-873756-99-7, 320pp, 80 maps, 30 photos
Fifth edition of this popular guide to the Everest region, the world's
most famous trekking area. Planning, preparation, getting to Nepal;
detailed route guides with 30 route maps and 50 village plans;
Kathmandu city guide: where to stay, where to eat, what to see.

TRAILBLAZER'S LONG-DISTANCE PATH (LDP) WALKING GUIDES

We've applied to destinations which are closer to home Trailblazer's proven formula for publishing definitive practical route guides for adventurous travellers. Britain's network of long-distance trails enables the walker to explore some of the finest landscapes in the country's best walking areas. These are guides that are user-friendly, practical, informative and environmentally sensitive.

● **Unique mapping features** In many walking guidebooks the reader has to read a route description then try to relate it to the map. Our guides are much easier to use because walking directions, tricky junctions, places to stay and eat, points of interest and walking times are all written onto the maps themselves in the places to which they apply. With their uncluttered clarity, these are not general-purpose maps but fully edited maps drawn by walkers for walkers.

● **Largest-scale walking maps** At a scale of just under 1:20,000 (8cm or 3$^1/_8$ inches to one mile) the maps in these guides are bigger than even the most detailed British walking maps currently available in the shops.

● **Not just a trail guide – includes where to stay, where to eat and public transport** Our guidebooks cover the complete walking experience, not just the route. Accommodation options for all budgets are provided (pubs, hotels, B&Bs, campsites, bunkhouses, hostels) as well as places to eat. Detailed public transport information for all access points to each trail means that there are itineraries for all walkers, for hiking the entire route as well as for day or weekend walks.

Coast to Coast *Henry Stedman*, 5th edition, £11.99
ISBN 978-1-905864-47-8, 256pp, 110 maps, 40 colour photos

Cornwall Coast Path (SW Coast Path Pt 2) 4th edition, £11.99
ISBN 978-1-905864-44-7, 352pp, 130 maps, 40 colour photos

Cotswold Way *Tricia & Bob Hayne* 2nd edition, £11.99
ISBN 978-1-905864-48-5, 192pp, 60 maps, 40 colour photos

Dorset & South Devon (SW Coast Path Pt 3) *Stedman & Newton*, £11.99
ISBN 978-1-905864-45-4, 336pp, 88 maps, 40 colour photos

Exmoor & North Devon (SW Coast Path Pt I) *Stedman & Newton*, £11.99
ISBN 978-1-905864-43-0, 192pp, 60 maps, 40 colour photos

Hadrian's Wall Path *Henry Stedman*, 3rd edition, £11.99
ISBN 978-1-905864-37-9, 224pp, 60 maps, 40 colour photos

North Downs Way *John Curtin*, 1st edition, £9.99
ISBN 978-1-873756-96-6, 192pp, 80 maps, 40 colour photos

Offa's Dyke Path *Keith Carter*, 3rd edition, £11.99
ISBN 978-1-905864-35-5, 240pp, 98 maps, 40 colour photos

Peddars Way & Norfolk Coast Path *Alexander Stewart*, £11.99
ISBN 978-1-905864-28-7, 192pp, 54 maps, 40 colour photos

Pembrokeshire Coast Path *Jim Manthorpe*, 4th edition, £11.99
ISBN 978-1-905864-51-5, 224pp, 96 maps, 40 colour photos

Pennine Way *Keith Carter & Chris Scott*, 3rd edition, £11.99
ISBN 978-1-905864-34-8, 272pp, 138 maps, 40 colour photos

The Ridgeway *Nick Hill*, 3rd edition, £11.99
ISBN 978-1-905864-40-9, 192pp, 53 maps, 40 colour photos

South Downs Way *Jim Manthorpe*, 4th edition, £11.99
ISBN 978-1-905864-42-3, 192pp, 60 maps, 40 colour photos

West Highland Way *Charlie Loram*, 5th edition, £11.99
ISBN 978-1-905864-50-8, 208pp, 60 maps, 40 colour photos

'The same attention to detail that distinguishes its other guides has been brought to bear here'.
THE
SUNDAY TIMES

TRAILBLAZER TITLE LIST

For more information about Trailblazer and our
expanding range of guides, for guidebook updates or
for credit card mail order sales visit our website:

www.trailblazer-guides.com

The symbol used at the start of each section of this book is the *Chakana* or Inca Cross, the Inca equivalent of the Tree of Life. The three steps on each side symbolize *Hana Pacha* (the abode of the gods), *Kay Pacha* (the world of men) and *Ucu Pacha* (the underworld or spirit world). The hole through the centre represents the centre of the Inca empire: Cusco; it also stands for the Southern Cross constellation.